Human Resource Management In Canada

Second Edition

THOMAS H. STONE
University of Iowa

NOAH M. MELTZ
University of Toronto

Holt, Rinehart and Winston of Canada, Limited
Toronto

Canadian Cataloguing in Publication Data
Stone, Thomas H.
Human resource management in Canada

2nd ed.
First ed. published under title: Personnel management in Canada.
Includes index.
ISBN 0-03-921991-7

1. Personnel management. 2. Personnel management – Canada. I. Meltz, Noah M. II. Title.
III. Title: Personnel management in Canada.

HF5549.S872 1988 658.3 C87-093741-3

Publisher: Richard Kitowski
Editor: Sheila Cunningham
Publishing Services Manager: Karen Eakin
Editorial Co-ordinator: Edie Franks
Editorial Assistant: Franca Cesario
Copy Editor: Dana Cook
Design: Peter Maher
Typesetting and Assembly: Q Composition Inc.
Printing and Binding: John Deyell Company

Printed in Canada

2 3 4 5 92 91 90 89 88

**This edition is dedicated
to the memory of
Jack H. Meltz,
and to
Casey and Corey Stone
for their patience
and understanding.**

Preface

In the late 1980s and early 1990s, two fundamental factors will affect the practice of human resource management: (1) the need for cost effectiveness in the face of intense worldwide competition; and (2) the increasing role of worker initiative in meeting the challenge of competition. The gradual development of a global economic village, with products made from components produced in different countries, will inevitably intensify competition. At the same time, the shift in employment toward more self-paced, knowledge-based work in both the service and goods-producing sectors will demand greater skill and initiative than was required in the past for more machine-paced, manual work.

Human resource management (HRM) professionals must understand these factors and address their challenges in working to enhance organizational effectiveness. Such understanding requires knowledge of the economic, social, and legal environments, as well as the way in which they affect the human resource management function within an organization. *Human Resource Management In Canada, Second Edition*, was written to assist students of personnel and industrial relations to achieve this goal.

The first edition of this textbook was entitled *Personnel Management in Canada*. In the five years since its publication, the personnel field has moved away from the term "personnel" toward a more encompassing "human resources" concept which recognizes that people are an important organizational resource and asset. While in some quarters the term "human resource management" carries a connotation of active opposition to unions, in our textbook it is a neutral term designed to describe the functions by which employees, whether unionized or nonunionized, are hired and developed to meet the goals of Canadian organziations.

Human Resource Management In Canada, Second Edition, is intended as a sophisticated, but readable, coverage of the essential areas of personnel and human resources. The text has a number of distinguishing features:

1. It presents personnel and human resource management within the context of its contributions to organizational effectiveness. The material was structured in this way to enable students to understand the field vis-à-vis the organization, including economic, legal, and social factors.

2. Discussions of the various personnel/human resource management functions are integrated throughout so students can understand exactly how each function relates to all the others.

3. Terms, concepts, and theories are clearly and completely explained with real-world examples and without excessive jargon.
4. The material is developed in a "lean" style, omitting needless models and pedagogical devices.
5. Each chapter concludes with cases and project ideas so students can apply the theories and concepts they have learned to a "real-world" context.

In preparing this second edition, we have updated and added a great deal of material including recent legislation, research findings, and studies of current practice. In the area of legislation alone, the past five years have seen not only implementation of the Charter of Rights and Freedoms, but also introduction in a Canadian setting of the concepts of employment equity and pay equity.

Throughout this text, efforts have been made to include as much Canadian content as possible. However, examples from the U.S. experience have also been included when deemed particularly instructive or illustrative. Regardless of content source, our goal has always been to provide current, relevant material that will contribute to the student's knowledge of the best human resource management theories and practices.

Plan of the Book

Human Resource Management In Canada, Second Edition, has five parts organized by a functional approach to the material. Part I introduces human resource management: the HRM field itself and the human and legal environments within which it exists. The next three parts correspond to the major areas of human resource management responsibility. Part II describes the planning and staffing functions (human resource planning, job analysis, recruiting, and selection). Part III focusses on functions related to employee development (orientation, training and development, performance appraisal, and career planning). Part IV includes chapters on functions of importance to employee maintenance (compensation, benefits, health and safety, and labour relations). Part V addresses issues and challenges in human resource management.

Throughout, the text emphasizes that human resource management is a dynamic field whose various functions are highly interrelated and interdependent. For the sake of clarity, chapters are arranged in an order analogous to the flow of human resources into and through an organization. (For example, the chapter on recruiting precedes the chapter on selection, which is followed by a chapter on orientation.) The text makes it clear, however, that variations in these arrangements occur in the real world, partly because certain tasks occur simultaneously, and partly because organizations have a wide range of operating procedures.

Human Resource Management In Canada, Second Edition, is accompanied by an instructor's manual which includes a test bank of questions; case answers; additional cases and discussion questions; transparency masters; and other teaching materials.

Thomas H. Stone
University of Iowa

Noah M. Meltz
University of Toronto

Publisher's Note to Instructors and Students

This textbook is a key component of your course. If you are the instructor of this course, you undoubtedly considered a number of texts carefully before choosing this text as the one that would work best for your students and you. The authors and publishers of this book spent considerable time and money to ensure its high quality, and we appreciate your recognition of this effort and accomplishment.

If you are a student, we are confident that this text will help you to meet the objectives of your course. You will also find it helpful after the course is finished as a valuable addition to your personal library, so hold on to it.

As well, please do not forget that photocopying copyright work means the authors lose royalties that are rightfully theirs. This loss will discourage them from writing another edition of this text or other books, because doing so would simply not be worth their time and effort. If this happens, we all lose—students, instructors, authors, and publishers.

Since we want to hear what you think about this book, please be sure to send us the stamped reply card at the end of the text. This will help us to continue publishing high quality books for your courses.

Acknowledgements

We were fortunate when we began work on this second edition to have a set of constructive criticisms and suggestions from adopters of the first edition of the text, *Personnel Management In Canada.* These people were:

Steven Appelbaum, Concordia University
Harish Jain, McMaster University
Alton Craig, University of Ottawa
Ron Crawford, Concordia University
Gene Deszca, Wilfrid Laurier University
Andrew Templer, University of Windsor
Earl Vitalis, Ryerson Polytechnical Institute

Comments from these fine "reviewers" guided our early revisions, and their remarks were especially appreciated.

Another set of reviewers, some of whom were in the first group, read and critiqued the second edition of the manuscript before it went to press. This set of reviewers deserves thanks for their many insightful comments which helped greatly in the fine-tuning of our finished product. The reviewers were:

Alan Anderton, Red Deer College
David Alcock, Memorial University of Newfoundland
Morgan Cooper, Memorial University of Newfoundland
Ron Crawford, Concordia University
Gene Deszca, Wilfrid Laurier University
Vilward Spence, Ryerson Polytechnical Institute
Andrew Templer, University of Windsor
Myron Weber, University of Calgary
Nan Weiner, University of Toronto

Thanks also to Professors Roy Adams and Alton Craig for their additional comments.

Sheila Cunningham and Richard Kitowski of Holt Rinehart and Winston of Canada also deserve thanks for their help on the second edition. We would once again, however, like to acknowledge the contribution of Dennis Bockus and Lenore d'Anjou to the first edition.

Professor Stone wishes to thank the Instructional Support Service of the University of Iowa. Ms. Denise Davis did a fine job of typing all the cases and case answers. Phyllis Irwin also deserves special thanks for her ability to organize and schedule work when it was needed.

Professor Meltz would like to thank the staff of the Jean and Dorothy Newman Industrial Relations Library, Centre for Industrial Relations, University of Toronto. In particular, he would like to thank Bruce Pearce, who provided so much valuable assistance and insight. Elizabeth Perry of the Centre's library was extremely helpful, as were Vicki Darlington and Monica Hypher. The Centre's other staff members, the Director, Professor Morley Gunderson, his assistant, Deborah Campbell, and Carmela Moltisanti and Maria Vareta helped to complete the very supportive role of the Centre.

Special appreciation goes to Professor Meltz's secretary at the School of Graduate Studies, Ms. Katharine Logan, and his assistant, the School's Administrative Officer (Finance and Personnel), Mr. Isaak Siboni, for the constant support they provided during the preparation of the second edition. The life of an assistant dean is subject to innumerable pressures and demands. Were it not for these two outstanding associates, there would have been no time to complete his part of the revisions.

Of course, every major project is a family effort. Professor Meltz's wife Rochelle supported his endeavours, and his children, David, Jonathan, Toba, and Hillel encouraged him.

Lana Stone deserves special thanks for contributing her writing, editing, and typing skills. We thank her for her revisions and additions to the text, including many of the text's cases.

The first edition of this text was dedicated to Jack H. Meltz and Lena Meltz, parents of Noah Meltz, who taught him the quintessence of personnel management: to recognize the dignity of every person and to persevere in a task. In 1985, Noah Meltz's father passed away. This second edition is dedicated to his memory, since Professor Meltz would not have been in this field were it not for the encouragement and example of his father. It is also dedicated to Casey and Corey Stone, who sacrificed much family time so their parents could complete this endeavour.

Contents

PART II Planning and Staffing 89

I The Human Resource Management Context

1

Human Resource Management — A Dynamic Field

The Evolution and Role of Human Resource Management
Four Major Areas of HRM Responsibility
HRM Functions
Assignment of HRM Responsibilities
The HRM Profession
The Context of Change Affecting HRM
Cases

Ann Edwards is a personnel analyst for the government of a small municipality. She reports to the city's human resource director. Edwards describes a typical day in her life as a human resource management (HRM) professional:

> 8:00–9:15 A.M. Changed a position from full- to part-time. Met with city human resource director to discuss cost of living allowance (COLA) in current police contract, city budget problems, and procedure for computer scheduling of performance appraisal dates. Helped head of parks and recreation department with preparation of new performance evaluation forms.
> 9:15–9:30 Recorded dates for future council budget sessions. Discussed job vacancies for senior clerk/typist and keypunch operator with head of finance department.
> 9:30–9:45 Coffee.
> 9:45–11:30 Sidetracked to identify department and division of all employees on CUPE (Canadian Union of Public Employees) seniority list and to prepare list of all city employees by salary range and position title.
> 11:30–12:00 Lunch.
> 12:00–1:00 P.M. Continued list of employees by range and position title.
> 1:00–1:30 Met with chief administrative officer and lawyers to discuss the retirement benefits program.

1:30–2:00 Searched for information to respond to an enquiry from a Canada Employment Centre. (Enquiry related to two former employees. Dates actually worked and dollars actually paid during a specified period had to be verified.)
2:00–2:45 Conducted exit interview with terminating employee.
2:45–3:45 Provided information for the legal department.
3:45–4:45 Attended hearing related to workers' compensation for an injured truck driver.
4:45–5:05 Met with head of road maintenance to discuss transfer of an employee into another position. Question: Is this an appropriate move?
5:05–5:20 Presented to supervisor material compiled by department on range/position title. Decided to work with computer service to develop a program for retrieval of this information.
Comment: Provided interpretation of clause in police contract clause, discussed handling of an outdated payroll cheque with the controller, copied job analysis questionnaire for chief administrative officer, discussed potential layoffs and seniority with two department heads, provided some historical information to enable retrieval of information that is at least eight years old, reviewed a request for educational leave, and on and on it goes. Daily I am interrupted many times to handle such items. I enjoy it. It is a part of the job but does cause delays in bigger projects assigned to me. I am always hopeful that my superiors recognize and understand the nature and impact of this sort of activity. It is a necessary part of human resource management.

During this typical day, Edwards performed activities related to many of the human resource management functions discussed in this book. She dealt with matters ranging from the hiring to the termination of employees. She assisted with forms that evaluate employee performance, compiled a list of municipal employees by salary range and position, discussed retirement benefits, and attended a hearing on whether a former employee was entitled to unemployment insurance. She also interpreted a clause in a police contract and identified departments and divisions of all employees on the union's seniority list. In the course of her day, Edwards helped to design, interpret, and administer human resource policies and practices which contribute significantly to the overall success of her organization.

This book gives the student an understanding of human resource management and of the many diverse functions of HRM professionals in helping organizations manage their most important resource—people. Specifically, the book describes methods and approaches HRM professionals use to acquire, develop, retain, and motivate the human resources needed in today's highly competitive environment. The forces of global competition, increased legislative pressure, and changes in labour force demography demand that HRM professionals anticipate and initiate programs and practices leading to optimal utilization of human resources. This book, therefore, presents the most effective HRM methods and approaches, as well as describing current practices of many of the more progressive organizations. Because excellent human resource management is recognized now, more than ever before, as essential for organizational success, it is suggested that HRM concepts, methods, and issues be studied by all business students, regardless of major or specialty.

The Evolution and Role of Human Resource Management

Every organization strives to meet the goals and objectives set forth by its top management. These goals include survival and growth of the organization and satisfactory levels of profit, production, and service. In attempting to achieve these goals, the resources of an organization must be carefully examined and used. The expeditious use of scarce and valued resources is known as organizational effectiveness.[1]

The role of human resource management, or "personnel management" as it has been traditionally known, is to plan, develop, and administer policies and programs designed to make the best use of an organization's human resources. It is generally acknowledged that the role of HRM professionals is more important today than ever before in the attainment of organizational goals such as survival, growth, and profitability.

From humble beginnings, the personnel management function evolved to embrace HRM positions of strategic and policy-making importance. For example, it is not unusual to find today's HRM executive analyzing and weighing the human resource implications of strategic decisions such as mergers, plant closures, or entry into new product lines. Traditionally, though, personnel management was purely a staff function, with duties delegated by line management. World War I and industrial psychology contributed to the growth and stature of HRM through the development of group-administered, paper-and-pencil intelligence and ability tests. This development enabled personnel professionals to increase organizational effectiveness quickly and inexpensively by screening out less qualified job applicants.

The growth of unions prior to World War II created a need for expertise in bargaining and administering labour contracts. While this need contributed to growth and importance of the HRM field, labour relations represented a reactive and often adversarial function, rather than a proactive, cooperative one. The World War II period saw rapid developments in the training and development area. Larger and more progressive companies saw training and development as an additional means of improving organizational effectiveness. Although the training and development function is often proactive by anticipating and preparing employees for new duties, top management in many companies still views it in a reactive way. This is demonstrated when

[1] R.M. Steers, *Organizational Effectiveness: A Behavioral View* (Santa Monica, Calif.: Goodyear Publishing Co., Inc., 1977), p. 5.

profitability declines and training and development staff are among the first to be cut.

In terms of power and sheer numbers of professionals, HRM received perhaps its biggest boost from human rights legislation of the 1960s on into the 1980s. A 1976 article by Herbert Meyer even referred to personnel directors as "the new corporate heroes" because their new function was to ensure that companies were in compliance with the complex set of human rights and employment standards statutes.[2] Again, the role of personnel management was a reactive one in that top management sought avoidance of costly and embarassing litigation.

While the needs still exist to maintain harmony with organized labour and to avoid damaging litigation, many experts believe HRM is reaching a new status. The hard economic times of the early 1980s and the pressures of global competition, particularly from Japan and the Far East, have contributed to the importance of HRM. Books such as Ouchi's *Theory Z*, Peters and Waterman's *In Search of Excellence*, plus numerous Japanese-managed plants in Canada and the United States, demonstrate the importance of effective HRM to organizational success and profitability.[3,4]

Recognition of the importance of human resource management recently lead Harvard Business School to launch a required course in this area, the first new required course in nearly 20 years. The goal of the course, to make MBAs and managers aware of HRM issues in a dynamic environment, suggests that HRM staff must become more proactive than reactive and must integrate human resource policies and practices with changing business strategies.

Case 1.1 in this chapter provides an example of the efforts of a large, multinational manufacturer, 3M, to both increase line managers' awareness of HRM and to make HRM more proactive. A number of large, progressive organizations have made the move to a more proactive role for HRM. As its value to organizational effectiveness is increasingly recognized, HRM can be expected to take a more proactive place in smaller, less progressive firms as well.

Human resource management can be divided into four major areas of responsibility and a number of specific functions which are performed in both unionized and nonunionized organizations.

Four Major Areas of HRM Responsibility

The major areas of responsibility in human resource management are (1) planning, (2) staffing, (3) employee development, and (4) employee

[2] H.E. Meyer, "Personnel Directors Are the New Corporate Heroes," *Fortune* 93 (1976), pp. 84–88.

[3] W. Ouchi, *Theory Z: How American Business Can Meet the Japanese Challenge* (Reading, Mass.: Addison-Wesley, 1981).

[4] T.J. Peters and R.H. Waterman, Jr., *In Search of Excellence* (New York: Harper & Row, 1982).

maintenance. These four areas and their related HRM functions have the common objective of ensuring that the organization has an adequate number of competent employees with the skills, abilities, knowledge, and experience needed to further its goals. Exhibit 1.1 shows a model of these responsibilities and functions. Although each function has been assigned to a particular area of HRM responsibility, some functions serve a purpose in more than one of the four. For example, performance appraisal measures employees' performance for development purposes as well as for salary administration (a part of the employee maintenance responsibility). The compensation function facilitates retention of employees and also attracts potential employees to the organization (a part of the staffing responsibility). While Exhibit 1.1 is a logical schema for listing HRM functions according to major areas of responsibility, it is only one of a number of ways that they might be organized.

The starting point for the model is the organizational goals and objectives specified by top management. Planning functions, including human resource planning and job analysis, translate these goals and objectives into statements of labour needs (number and type of employees needed). Designing and recommending programs to meet these needs is also part of planning. The second area, staffing, includes the recruiting and selection functions. It requires a strategy for attracting employees with the requisite skills, abilities, knowledge, and experience to do the job.

Employee development is the third major area of HRM responsibility. After workers have been hired (and often after they have been on the job for a fair amount of time), activities in this area seek to ensure that employees possess the knowledge and skills to perform their jobs satisfactorily. It is also concerned with the individuals' career plans and the company's efforts to prepare some employees for positions of more responsibility within the organization. Included in the employee development area are the HRM functions of orientation, training and development, performance appraisal, and career planning.

The maintenance of human resources—retaining an optimal number of competent employees—is the fourth major area of HRM responsibility. Employee maintenance refers to providing employees with adequate pay and benefits for their labour, with good, safe working conditions, and with other desirable aspects of employment, such as a voice in decisions affecting human resource policies. Accordingly, HRM functions of major importance to employee maintenance are compensation, benefits, health and safety, and labour relations.

HRM *Functions*

Individual HRM functions are summarized in Exhibit 1.1 and described briefly in the pages which follow.

Human Resource Planning

In human resource planning (HRP), a determination is made as to the number and type of employees needed to accomplish organizational goals. Research is an important part of this function because planning requires the collection and analysis of information in order to forecast the available supplies of human resources and to predict future needs. Once an organization's employment needs are determined, HRM professionals can plan strategies for obtaining the required human resources. Two basic HRP strategies are staffing and employee development. A staffing strategy involves recruiting and selecting from either external or internal applicants with the required skills and abilities. A development strategy, on the other hand, emphasizes providing current and new employees with required job skills and knowledge through extensive training and development programs. While most employers engage in both staffing and employee development activities, they tend to emphasize one strategy over the other.[5] More recently, HRP has been concerned with handling surplus employees, as many organizations have been forced to "downsize," or reduce the size of their work force.

Job Analysis

Job analysis is the process of describing the nature of a job and specifying the human requirements (skills, experience, training, etc.) needed to perform it. The end product of the process is the job description, which spells out work duties and activities of employees. Job descriptions are a vital source of information to employers, managers, and HRM professionals because job content has a great influence on human resource programs and practices relating to recruiting, selection, training, performance appraisal, career planning, compensation, and labour relations.

Recruiting

Recruiting is the process of attracting qualified applicants to fill job vacancies. This process includes both external recruiting, attracting applicants from outside the organization, and internal recruiting, attracting applicants from among current employees. Recruiting messages list the skills, abilities, knowledge, and experience required for certain jobs. (The requirements are determined through the process of job analysis, while the pay for the positions is based on the organization's compensation policy.)

[5]J.P. Campbell, M.D. Dunnette, E.E. Lawler III, and K.E. Weick, Jr., *Managerial Behavior, Performance, and Effectiveness* (New York: McGraw-Hill, 1970), pp. 68–69.

EXHIBIT 1.1

The role of human resource management

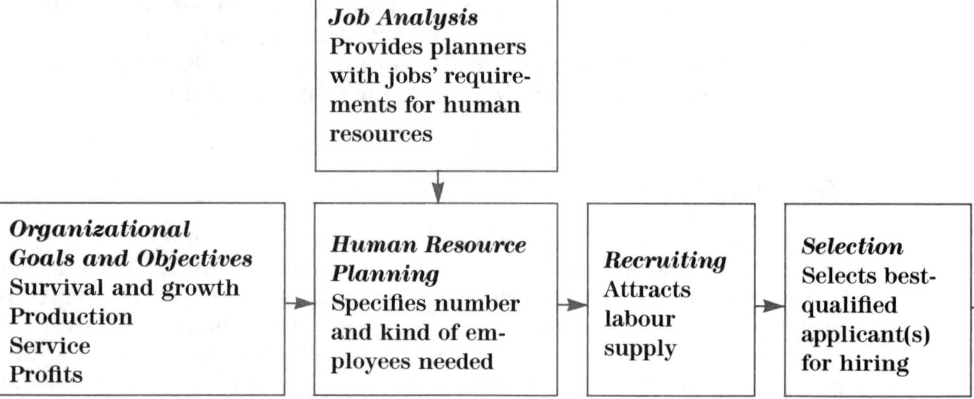

I. Planning
These functions translate organizational goals and objectives into statements of labour needs and design and recommend programs to meet these needs.

II. Staffing
These functions focus on obtaining employees with the skills, abilities, knowledge, and experience required to do the jobs.

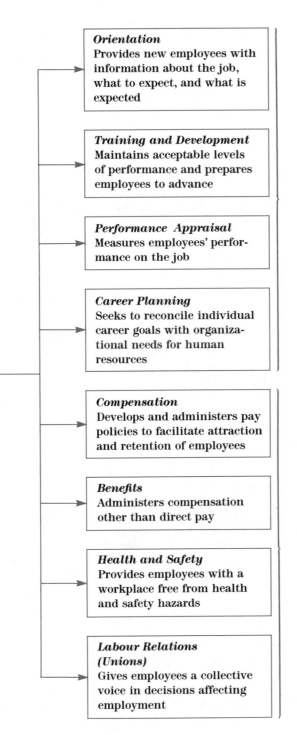

Orientation
Provides new employees with information about the job, what to expect, and what is expected

Training and Development
Maintains acceptable levels of performance and prepares employees to advance

Performance Appraisal
Measures employees' performance on the job

Career Planning
Seeks to reconcile individual career goals with organizational needs for human resources

III. Employee Development
These functions seek to ensure that employees possess the knowledge and skills to perform satisfactorily in their jobs or to advance in the organization.

Adequate number of competent employees with needed skills, abilities, knowledge, and experience to further organizational goals

Compensation
Develops and administers pay policies to facilitate attraction and retention of employees

Benefits
Administers compensation other than direct pay

Health and Safety
Provides employees with a workplace free from health and safety hazards

Labour Relations (Unions)
Gives employees a collective voice in decisions affecting employment

IV. Employee Maintenance
These functions relate to retaining a competent work force by providing employees with satisfactory pay, benefits, and working conditions.

Selection

The most qualified applicant or applicants are selected from among the pool of applicants generated by the recruiting process. With respect to selection, HRM professionals are involved in developing and administering methods that enable the organization to decide which applicants to select and which to reject for given jobs.

Orientation

Orientation is the first step towards helping an employee adjust to the new job and employer. Typically, HRM professionals plan and administer programs to acquaint new employees with particular aspects of their jobs, including pay and benefit programs, work hours, and company rules and expectations.

Training and Development

Training and development gives employees the skills and knowledge to perform effectively in their jobs. In addition to providing training for new or inexperienced employees, organizations often train experienced employees whose jobs are undergoing change or becoming obsolete. Large organizations often have development programs which prepare employees for higher-level responsibilities within the organization. Training and development programs are a way of ensuring that employees are capable of performing their jobs at acceptable levels.

Performance Appraisal

Performance appraisal involves monitoring employees' performance to ensure that it is at acceptable levels. HRM professionals are usually responsible for developing and administering appraisal systems, although the actual appraisal is the responsibility of supervisors and managers. Besides providing a basis for pay, promotion, and disciplinary action, performance appraisal provides information essential for employee development, since knowledge of results (feedback) is necessary to motivate and guide improvements in performance.

Career Planning

A recent HRM function, career planning developed partly as a result of the desire of many employees to grow in their jobs and advance in their careers. HRM professionals engage in such career planning activities as assessing individual employees' potential for growth and advancement in the organization and planning for job experiences and other development opportunities to encourage this growth. In some organizations, HRM professionals chart career paths showing how employees can logically progress from one job to another within the organization.

Compensation

HRM professionals seek to provide a rational method for determining how much employees should be paid for performing certain jobs. Pay is obviously related to the maintenance of human resources; employees must earn a living, and they may seek alternative employment if the organization's pay levels are inadequate. However, the compensation function also affects the planning, staffing, and employee development concerns of HRM professionals. Since compensation is a major cost to many organizations, it is a major consideration in human resource planning. For example, an organization may find it less costly to maintain an employee development strategy than to rely on external staffing for higher-level positions in the organization. Compensation affects staffing in that people are generally attracted to employers who offer relatively high levels of pay in exchange for work provided. Finally, it is related to employee development in that pay can supply an important incentive for motivating employees to higher levels of job performance and to higher-paying jobs in the organization.

Benefits

Benefits are employee compensation other than direct pay for work provided. Thus, the HRM function of administering employee benefits shares many characteristics of the compensation function. Benefits include both legally required items (such as the Canada Pension Plan, workers' compensation, health insurance, and unemployment insurance) and benefits offered at an employer's discretion (including pensions, "sick days," dental and extended health care plans, and employee services, such as cafeteria discounts and parking privileges). The cost of benefits has risen to the point of becoming a major consideration in human resource planning. However, benefits are primarily related to the maintenance area, since they provide for many basic employee needs.

Health and Safety

Before passage of Saskatchewan's Occupational Health and Safety Act of 1972, health and safety programs were usually found only in hazardous industries, such as mining and construction. Now, however, legislation in many provinces requires employers to have labour-management committees to enforce health and safety rules. Compliance with health and safety rules is a major HRM responsibility, as are the development and enforcement of safety rules and regulations and the creation and administration of health and safety programs.

Labour Relations

The term *labour relations* refers to an employer's interactions with employees who are represented by a trade union. The HRM responsibility for labour relations includes negotiating a collective agreement, administering the agreement, and resolving disputes and grievances pertaining to it. Since many aspects of labour relations directly concern employees' welfare, it is a major function of the maintenance area. In fact, the collective agreement affects all major areas of HRM responsibility in unionized organizations.

Employee Records

The oldest and most basic HRM function, one which crosscuts each of the major areas of responsibility, is employee record-keeping. This function involves recording, maintaining, and retrieving employee-related information for a variety of purposes including government compliance. Records that must be maintained include: application forms; health and medical records; employment histories (jobs held, promotions, transfers, layoffs); seniority lists detailing length of time in present jobs, departments, and/or organizations; earnings and hours of work; absences, turnover, and tardiness; and deductions, living allowances, and vacation pay. Complete and up-to-date employee records are essential for most HRM functions. Fortunately for HRM professionals, the recent availability of inexpensive micro- and mini-computers and human resource software has made data storage, manipulation, and retrieval much easier and less time-consuming than ever before.

The above HRM functions are the major ones carried out in most organizations. Depending upon individual organizational needs and stage of growth, HRM staff may engage in other activities. For example, the substantial layoffs of the early 1980s resulted in some HRM staff conducting outplacement programs to help terminated employees find new jobs. In other cases, HRM professionals may be involved in a variety of organizational change programs ranging from improving the quality of working life to assisting with a merger or takeover by another company.

It is likely that the relative importance of various HRM functions changes over the life cycle of an organization. It is likely too that the specific focus of each HRM function changes over time. In a new organization, recruiting, selection, and compensation play key roles in acquiring talented managerial, professional, and technical personnel. At the growth stage, recruiting and selection emphasize obtaining an adequate supply of qualified employees, and internal recruiting becomes more important. Compensation policies become more formalized during this time, and internal equity (perceived fairness of the pay structure) receives greater emphasis than external market competitiveness. Training and development also becomes more important during the growth stage. As the organization matures and declines, recruiting and selection decline in importance, compensation emphasizes cost control, and retraining of older employees becomes an important aspect of training. While labour relations remains important over time, its emphasis changes from one of keeping peace at the growth stage to controlling costs (while also keeping peace) at the maturity stage. During decline, issues of productivity and job security dominate labour relations.[6]

Assignment of HRM Responsibilities

Assignment of responsibility for HRM varies from one organization to another and may be affected by the size, goals, philosophy, and structure of the firm. Even the smallest of organizations engages in the basic HRM functions of hiring, training, providing compensation and benefits, and record-keeping.

Small firms may divide HRM functions among several people, ranging from clerical workers to the head of the organization. A company that expands to several hundred workers usually assigns one employee to HRM on a full-time basis. A major advantage of confining HRM to one individual is that it eases coordination of human resource policies, eliminating the redundancies and inconsistencies that occur when several persons handle the various functions.

With increasing growth and/or profitability of an organization, more people are required to handle the HRM function, and the HRM department must grow. Additionally, such departments tend to branch out into specialized areas. For example, compensation and benefits specialists, training and development specialists, or labour relations specialists may become a part of the HRM department. If health and safety is a major concern, an industrial nurse or safety specialist may be added.

The HRM professional may not handle all of the responsibilities for every group of employees. For example, the recruiting of academic staff in a university is normally handled by professors in the particular departments rather than by HRM professionals. The latter are involved only to assist with orientation of new employees and to ensure that no human rights codes are violated.

Basically, HRM professionals are considered "staff" rather than "line" employees since they provide specialized, technical, and professional advice to production or operations ("line") managers. HRM professionals advise, recommend, develop, and administer policies and programs affecting human resources. Take, for example, the common situation in which HRM professionals are consulted about the problem of absenteeism in an organization. In dealing with such an issue, HRM staffers engage in research to determine the nature and extent of the problem, to examine and evaluate alternative solutions, and to make recommendations to management. If management approves a suggested program, HRM professionals are likely to be assigned responsibility for developing and administering it. In the case of absenteeism, they might develop a program to reward employees with an extra day's pay and

[6] T.A. Kochan and T.A. Barocci, *Human Resource Management and Industrial Relations* (Boston: Little, Brown and Company, 1985), pp. 104–9.

special recognition for each three-month period of perfect attendance. In addition, a policy could be adopted whereby employees who exceed a certain number of absences within a given period may be terminated. In administering absenteeism policies and programs, HRM professionals would keep attendance records, compile lists of employees with perfect records, schedule recognition ceremonies for these employees, publicize the policy on excessive absenteeism, and enforce it by terminating employees whose absences have exceeded the predetermined limit.

Except within their own department, human resource managers have no managerial authority other than that delegated to them by top management, and this may vary from one organization to another. Generally, HRM professionals are likely to exercise greater authority and responsibility when human resources are valued highly in the organization and when HRM staff are respected by top management. However, the trend is for increased responsibilities for all HRM professionals.

According to a recent study, HRM professionals report growth not only in the size of their departments, but also in the extent of their responsibilities.[7] In the United States, HRM executives have considerable responsibility in that (1) nearly two-thirds report to the company's highest official; (2) almost three-fourths need approval of only top management to formulate and administer human resource policies affecting the entire organization; and (3) 86 per cent participate in overall company planning and policy determination.[8]

The HRM *Profession*

Growth of the Profession

In the past decade there has been an enormous growth in the number of HRM professionals. Exhibit 1.2 shows that according to Canadian census data the growth of personnel managers has been absolutely phenomenal: a six-fold increase between 1971 and 1981 (from 4,055 to 25,110). On the other hand, personnel officers grew much more slowly from 25,005 to 30,678. By 1981, the number of personnel managers almost equalled the number of personnel officers. The question arises whether the reported increase in personnel managers includes individuals who would have been identified as officers in 1971. The use of the *Canadian Classification and Dictionary of Occupations* (CCDO) was designed to prevent such inflation in titles, but it is possible that some erosion occurred. Whatever the precise division between managers and officers, the fact remains that a large number of people are employed in various capacities in the HRM field.

[7] J. Ninninger, *Managing Human Resources: A Strategic Perspective* (Ottawa: The Conference Board of Canada, 1982).

[8] Bureau of National Affairs, *Aspects of the Personnel Function*, Personnel Policies Forum, Survey No. 127 (Washington, D.C.: Bureau of National Affairs, October, 1979).

EXHIBIT 1.2

Growth of the HRM profession in Canada

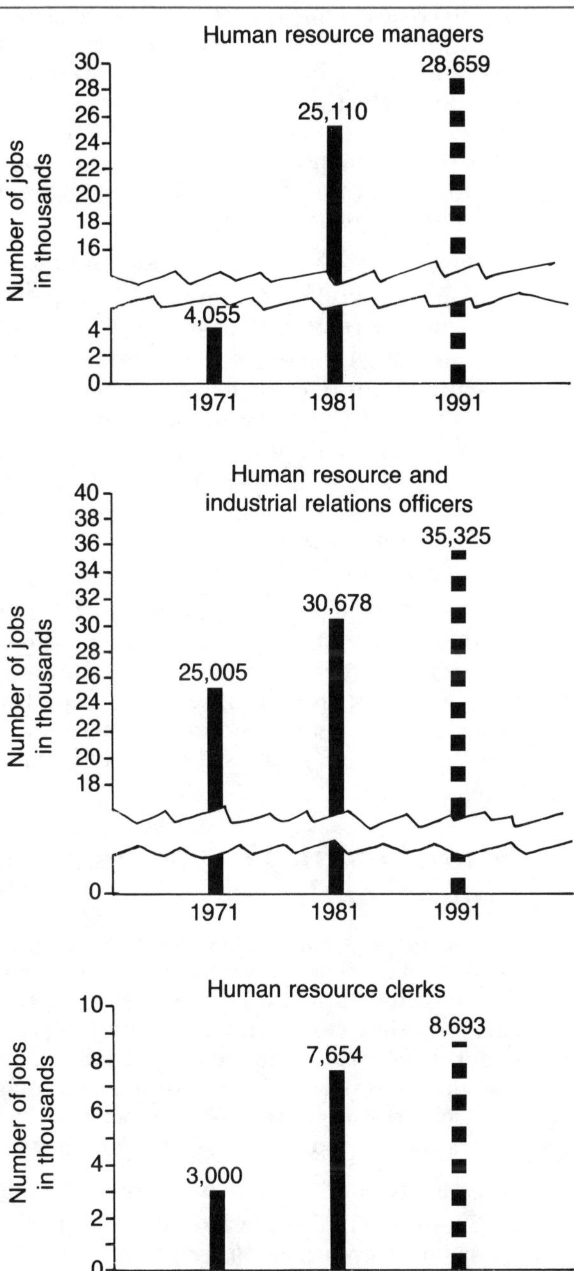

SOURCES: 1971: Census data in P. Kumar, *Personnel Management in Canada: A Manpower Profile* (Kingston, Ont.: Industrial Relations Centre, Queen's University, 1975). 1981 and 1991: *Canadian Occupational Projection System* (COPS). Based on Reference Growth Scenario, July 1986 (Ottawa: Employment and Immigration Canada, 1986).

The Nature of Jobs in the HRM Field

One need only look at classified ads to see the diversity of HRM positions (see Exhibit 1.3). Some of these jobs are very specialized, while others are more generalized and include responsibility for most or all HRM functions. Most HRM jobs are generalist positions simply because most employers in Canada have fewer than 100 employees. Such positions offer the best opportunities to be a jack-of-all-trades in the profession.

HRM jobs range from clerk to vice-president and have been classified into four major types:

1. Support jobs—typists, clerks, and receptionists.
2. Technical and professional jobs—functional specialists in such areas as labour relations, compensation, and training.
3. Operating human resource managers. A person in such a job—often called an HR generalist—handles most or all of the HRM functions in a small organization or in the plant of a larger firm.
4. HRM executives. Persons in these posts are "generalists and administrators who manage larger organizations and HRM departments that include specialists, operating HR managers, and support staff. They provide the linking-pin between top management and the HRM department."[9]

Besides a wide range of jobs in the HRM profession, there are also differences in job responsibilities for the same job title. For example, the training director's job at one company is likely to be somewhat different from the training director's job at another. The precise job description depends upon such factors as the organization's size, its type of business, and its theories of human resource management.

Education and Experience Requirements for HRM Professionals

Education and experience requirements for HRM jobs have increased over the past decade, but many HRM professionals today have had little or no formal education in the field. There are at least two reasons for this situation. One is that many HRM jobs involve clerical tasks or other general activities. The second is that many of today's HRM professionals are former supervisors or functional managers who learned their current jobs through on-the-job experience. Typical educational requirements for the four types of HRM jobs noted above are:

1. Support staff—secondary school or community college diploma.
2. Technical and professional staff—master's degree or Ph.D. in social sciences or industrial relations.

[9] D. Yoder and H.G. Heneman, Jr., "PAIR Jobs, Qualifications, and Careers," in D. Yoder and H.G. Heneman, Jr., eds., *Professional PAIR, ASPA Handbook of Personnel and Industrial Relations*, vol. 8 (Washington, D.C.: Bureau of National Affairs, 1979).

EXHIBIT 1.3

Ads for HRM positions

3. Operating human resource manager—bachelor's or master's degree in business administration or industrial relations, or a diploma in business.
4. HRM executive—master's degree in business administration or industrial relations.[10]

Employers frequently prefer job applicants with experience in their particular industry. For example, HRM professionals with experience in public-sector organizations such as municipal or provincial governments usually do not take jobs in the private sector. Even within the private sector, employers usually prefer applicants with experience in the same industry. Examples of major industry groups include banking, insurance, manufacturing, and retail and finance.

Secretaries and clerks working in the HRM area usually have a secondary school certificate or community college diploma. Most other HRM jobs require a bachelor's degree in commerce, psychology, sociology, or economics. Frequently, students ask how to get a job in HRM when so many ads require experience. There are several ways. One is a co-op program, in which an undergraduate alternately attends university and works for a company. Some organizations offer internships

[10] Terry Hercus, "Professional Education in Industrial Relations and Human Resource Management: A Canadian Perspective," *Proceedings of the 18th Annual Meeting of the Canadian Industrial Relations Association, Dalhousie University, Halifax, May 1981*, vol. 2, pp. 434–54.

in HRM; in Ontario, the Ministry of Labour subsidizes and administers more than 60 of them each summer. Some students also gain experience by working part-time in HRM jobs.

Professional Organizations

Most professions have organizations that promote educational and professional standards among their members. These professional associations also serve as communication channels for information regarding federal and provincial legislation and court decisions affecting the profession.

There are a number of these professional organizations for individuals in HRM occupations. The most common are associations representing general HRM interests (such as the British Columbia Industrial Relations Management Association or the Personnel Association of Ontario). An HRM professional may hold membership in more than one professional association, usually depending on his or her area of specialization and/or professional training. For example, a director of training and development with a graduate degree in psychology might hold membership in the Human Resource Management Association of Manitoba, the Manitoba Society for Training and Development, the Canadian Psychological Association (CPA), and the American Psychological Association (APA).

The largest general professional association in Canada is the Personnel Association of Ontario (PAO), which had 4,800 members in 1986. This association combines 23 local associations, which provide their members many services, including periodic seminars, annual conventions, and sponsorship of a professional education program. The largest of these groups is the 2,700 member Personnel Association of Toronto (PAT).

Other provincial associations cover Quebec, British Columbia, and the Maritimes. Most Prairie cities have local associations. For many years the Canadian Council of Personnel Associations (CCPA) acted as a coordinating group for local associations across the country. In 1982, a variety of factors, including the disaffiliation of several large local associations, led to the decision to disband CCPA.

HRM professionals working for federal, provincial, and local governments may join the 1,389 member Canadian Public Personnel Management Association (CPPMA), which is affiliated with the International Personnel Management Association.

All these organizations play an important role in maintaining high standards among HRM professionals. They keep members abreast of changes and innovations and also serve as a communication network, a source of identity, and a means of influence for many members.

The Context of Change Affecting HRM

Human resource management takes place within a context of change.

Four major areas of change affecting HRM are the business climate, technology, government legislation, and labour force characteristics.

Business Climate

Many industries in the 1980s face increased competition from foreign products. Domestic automakers are a prime example. Despite billions of dollars spent to improve efficiency, domestic manufacturers are still unable to build a small car for what it costs the Japanese. Under the Canada-United States Auto Pact, since many Canadian auto plants produce cars destined for the American market, increased sales of foreign imports in the U.S. results in less business for Canadian manufacturers. One auto industry source says as many as 25,000 jobs in the auto manufacturing and parts industries may be lost over the next decade due to foreign competition.[11]

A related phenomenon affecting the auto industry is construction of new assembly plants in Canada and the U.S. by Japanese and Korean companies. While such plants will provide new jobs, they may create excess production capacity which will lead to shut-down of older, less efficient plants. Thus, the late 1980s may bring as many auto plant closures as the earlier 1980s, but closures will be due to excess capacity rather than decreased demand.

Besides foreign competition, demographic and lifestyle changes also affect demand for certain products. Currently, Canada's major breweries are engaged in a battle to win greater share of a shrinking market for beer. Demand for beer has decreased due to aging of the population (older persons consume less beer). Exacerbating the problem is increased competition from foreign breweries.

Foreign competition and reductions in product demand force many companies to adopt a "lean and mean" approach to management. Operations are streamlined by the introduction of new technologies and jobs are often lost. For the area of human resource management, this may mean layoffs, development of incentives to encourage early retirement, provision of outplacement counselling, and/or retraining of redundant workers whose jobs are lost.

Technology

Advances in technology have changed the way work is done and reduced the need for some workers. More and more jobs are being automated and performed by robots. At Canadian General Electric Co. Ltd. (CGE) of Cobourg, Ont., robots cut out, unload, and spray paint automotive body parts. Because of automation, 110 people can accomplish what it used to take 200 to do. General Motors of Canada Ltd. is also a user of robots. It expects to employ 1,200 of them by the end of 1990. Automation is essential if automakers are to remain competitive.

At INCO Ltd., a mining company, automation has greatly reduced the number of hazardous jobs and those requiring heavy labour. INCO

[11] "The Small Car Invasion," *Maclean's*, December 9, 1985, pp. 30–31.

is switching to an innovative method of mining which increases efficiency and reduces costs, and is also developing a computer-controlled robotic drilling machine that both eliminates driller jobs and requires a skilled computer operator. The streamlining of mining operations has increased the company's productivity and profitability, in part by curtailing the number of workers. At one Sudbury mine, the work force has been cut from 40 to eight. Automation has helped INCO to survive in a time of declining prices for nickel.

While technology has reduced or eliminated the need for some jobs, it has also created a demand for workers with more technical skills. Leading in the area of job creation are the computer services industry, management and business consultants, miscellaneous services to business management, engineering and scientific services, and offices of architects. Examples of new jobs include robotics engineers, optical technologists in the field of fibre optics, computerized X-ray scanner operators, and computer-aided design engineers. Although high-tech industries have grown faster than the industry average over the past decade, high-tech industries still account for only one-fourth of total Canadian employment.[12]

Peter F. Drucker, one of the foremost writers and management consultants of our time, has written that one of the greatest challenges to management and the economy in the 1980s is "redundancy planning," which he defines as "anticipating structural and technological changes in the economy, and preparing to retrain and find new jobs for workers who will have to be laid off."[13] Several industries that are rapidly becoming noncompetitive in world or Canadian markets are shoe manufacturing, textiles, and other manufacturing operations requiring low-level skills. On the other hand, the Canadian economy has a number of very competitive growth industries, such as telecommunication equipment. If future technological changes become even more rapid, the result may be higher levels of unemployment unless there is significant growth in the economy as well as redundancy planning by management and government. Rapidly changing technology creates substantial human resource problems, which must be solved through planning and retraining rather than through unemployment insurance.

For a brief discussion of opposing viewpoints regarding the effect of technological change on employment see Exhibit 1.4.

Government Legislation

Government legislation is another area of change affecting employment and the practice of human resource management. Of continuing importance are provincial and federal laws passed in the 1960s and 1970s relating to human rights, equal pay for work of equal value (especially for women), and occupational health and safety. Such laws

[12] Keith Newton, "Impact of New Technology on Employment," *Canadian Business Review*, Winter 1985, pp. 27–30.

[13] P.F. Drucker, "Planning for 'Redundant' Workers," *Wall Street Journal*, September 25, 1979.

EXHIBIT 1.4

At issue: the effect of technological change on employment

In the twentieth century, technological changes have combined with rising incomes, changing tastes, and shifts in patterns of trade and demographics to produce shifts in the economic centre of gravity. These shifts have had enormous consequences for employment.

Optimists point out that these changes have not caused significant and persistent unemployment. They argue that the additional output stimulated by the new technologies has tended, in the past, to require more than enough labour to offset any inherent labour-saving bias. They see the current wave of technological change as just the latest in a long series of developments that have contributed to higher output, employment and living standards.

Pessimists contend that there is something very different about the current "Information Revolution." They see the potential for massive displacement of human beings throughout the world of work and have little faith in the ability of the output effect to stave off job loss. Nobel Prize winner Wassily Leontief contends that man, as a factor of production, has two dimensions—mental and physical—and that the computer and the robot have already begun to replace both the mental and the physical functions of blue- and white-collar workers. Human workers, says Leontief, will go the way of the horse.

A third group is neutral about the issue of the overall net employment effects of technological change. They contend that, no matter what the outcome, there will certainly be problems of adjustment and adaptation in particular sectors, occupations and skills, and for particular groups of workers. If one accepts this view, it is important to attempt to identify particular problem areas and to frame appropriate policies of mobility, training, education and social security to minimize the pain of transition and adjustment.

A fourth and final group argues that we may be asking the wrong question. They say that, rather than asking, "how many jobs will be lost if we adopt the new technologies?", we should ask, "how many jobs will be lost if we do not?". That is, if other countries advance technologically and we do not, Canada stands to lose international markets along with the industries and jobs that supply them.

SOURCE: From "Impact of New Technology on Employment" by Keith Newton. Copyright Winter 1985 (pp. 27–30) by Keith Newton. Reprinted by permission of *Canadian Business Review*.

and others have a profound effect upon the HRM profession in terms of responsibilities and activities. In a recent survey, human resource managers in Canada identified keeping up with new legislation as the second most important of the emerging demands on the HRM function.[14]

The difficulties of this aspect of the HRM function are enhanced in Canada by the variety of laws affecting employment in the different provinces and in those industries operating under federal government jurisdiction (such as transportation and communication). In the United

[14] P. Kumar, *Professionalism in the Canadian* PAIR Function: Report of a Survey (Kingston, Ont.: Industrial Relations Centre, Queen's University, 1980).

States, an estimated 90 per cent of all employees fall under federal jurisdiction. In Canada, however, the federal government is responsible for less than 10 per cent of all employees. Ten different sets of provincial regulations (plus those of the two territories) cover 90 per cent of all the country's employees. Companies with employees in two or more provinces have to take account of variations in labour relations laws and other legislation.

The various provincial and federal laws are administered by many different boards, commissions, agencies, departments, and ministries. The HRM professional must learn what records have to be maintained or presented to these various bodies. In addition, numerous posters must be displayed in employment areas to acquaint employees with their rights and responsibilities. Again, it is usually HRM officials who are ultimately responsible for informing employees.

The Labour Force

A third area of change affecting organizations and human resource management is the labour force itself. The next chapter is devoted to people both in the context of the labour force and on an individual basis, but some major demographic and value changes must be mentioned here. A well-known demographic fact regarding the Canadian population is that the education level is higher than it has ever been. There is, however, concern that the quality of education has declined. An even more serious concern is the disparity between the skills people learn in school and the jobs available.[15] The resulting situation is ironical—unemployment is high, but many employers have jobs they cannot fill. Some of these jobs require specialized training, such as machining and computer technology, while others are relatively unskilled, such as restaurant help and gardening. Many unemployed people are not trained for specialized jobs, but their education has raised their expectations so much that they will not accept menial jobs. Therefore, some able-bodied workers find themselves standing in unemployment lines.

A second demographic characteristic of the Canadian labour force of the 1980s is that the average age of employees is higher than at any time in recent history. The major cause of this is the "baby bust" which began in the mid-1960s. This period saw the lowest birth rate since the Great Depression. As a result, there are fewer young people entering the labour force today.[16] Along with the reduction of new entrants into the labour force has been the continued exit of older workers (55 years and over). Factors that have decreased the number of older workers

[15] Two federal government task forces recently examined the relationship between skills and jobs: Employment and Immigration Canada, *Labour Market Development in the 1980s* [The Dodge Report] (Hull, Que.: Ministry of Supply and Services Canada, 1981); and *Work for Tomorrow, Employment Opportunities for the '80s* (The Allmand Report) (Ottawa: House of Commons, 1981).

[16] D. Foot, *A Challenge of the 1980s: Unemployment and Labour Force Growth in Canada and the Provinces* (Toronto: Institute for Policy Analysis, University of Toronto, 1981).

include the introduction of the Canada and Quebec pension plans, changes in Unemployment Insurance regulations that reduced benefits available to older workers, and the availability of Workers' Compensation for some persons permanently unable to work. From 1966 to 1978 the participation rate of men 55 years and over fell from 57.5 to 47.1 per cent.[17] By 1985 the participation rate of this group was down to 41.7 per cent.[18] The main groups of older men who continue to work are those who are self-employed and those who are highly-educated: ". . . for the poorly-educated and therefore less well-paid, government transfer income may compare favorably with potential employment income."[19] Workers also tend to withdraw from jobs that are too physically demanding. While workers are leaving the labour force earlier, the effect of changes in technology in eliminating jobs is that today's workers are likely to experience two or more different careers during the span of their work life. The burden of preparing—training and developing—employees for such "second careers" falls upon the business community and government.

Perhaps one of the most significant changes in the past quarter century is the increased proportion of women in the labour force. The road to women's entrance into the work force and into nontraditional jobs has been paved with government legislation, technology, changed attitudes towards the family, and recently, inflation, which has caused more women to seek work. The effects of equality of the sexes in the workplace are far-reaching and have presented many problems for organizations and society as well. While there has been some move toward equality of pay and job opportunities for women, the Abella Commission concluded that there was systemic discrimination in the form of workplace barriers which could only be eliminated through legislation designed to foster employment equity.[20] As our society enters an era of a shortage of properly educated and skilled labour, it is clear that we can no longer waste valuable human resources through human resource practices which are biased according to sex, age, race, ethnic origin, or religion.

Another area of change in the labour force involves values and attitudes. Arnold Deutsch, author of *The Human Resources Revolution: Communicate or Litigate*, describes these elements of change as "new attitudes in the work place adapted from those developed outside; rising expectations for a more rewarding, more human working experience, and a greater 'democratization' of the working world in response to the tides of change."[21] Increasingly, workers want a voice in decisions affecting their jobs and their employment. No longer content to "check their brains at the door," many workers want to contribute ideas for

[17] "The Declining Labour Force Participation Rate of Men Age 55 and Over: An Examination of Possible Causes," Statistics Canada, *The Labour Force October 1980,* cat. no. 71-001, monthly, (Ottawa: Supply and Services Canada, November 1980.)

[18] Statistics Canada, *The Labour Force December 1985.*

[19] *The Labour Force October 1980,* op cit.

[20] Judge Rosalie Silberman Abella, Commissioner, *Report of the Commission on Equality in Employment* (Ottawa: Supply and Services Canada, 1984).

[21] A. Deutsch, *The Human Resources Revolution: Communicate or Litigate* (New York: McGraw-Hill, 1979), p. 56.

improving production, reducing costs, and making the workplace safer. Realizing the potential value of employee inputs, some organizations have introduced quality of working life (QWL) programs which allow workers greater participation in work-related decisions. Kumar's survey of personnel managers identified changing work ethics and employee values as the most significant new demand on the HRM function.[22]

To summarize, in the past quarter century and continuing into the present, changes in business climate, technology, government legislation, and the labour force itself have presented challenges for the business community and society in general. HRM professionals have been actively involved in meeting these challenges, and their role will likely continue to increase in importance.

[22] Kumar, 1980.

Cases

Case 1.1: 3M's Evolving HRM Function

In the 1950s and 1960s, the human resource management function at Minnesota Mining and Manufacturing Company (3M) was called simply "Personnel." Personnel's main focus was labour-management relations, since 3M was more heavily unionized then than it is today. The department's labour relations activities included not only dealing with unionized employees, but also trying to promote a union-free environment. The personnel function was highly compartmentalized at this time; there were four relatively independent units serving staffing, training, compensation, and employee relations needs. Specialists in these areas rarely crossed functional boundaries to work in another area of expertise. Christopher Wheeler, Vice President of Human Resources at 3M since 1983, feels that until the late 1970s, "the role of the personnel function was seen as essentially one of maintenance, as opposed to being proactive as to what should be done or innovative as to how personnel activities were performed."*

In the mid-1970s, 3M decided to align the personnel function more closely with certain segments of the business. This was accomplished by reassigning a number of personnel staffers to various operating divisions in the company. However, a nucleus of personnel staffers remained in the old department and they were reluctant to surrender much authority to their decentralized counterparts. Thus, for several years, 3M had a dual personnel function.

*H.L. Angle, C.C. Manz, and A.H. Van de Ven, "Integrating Human Resource Management and Corporate Strategy: A Preview of the 3M Story," *Human Resource Management*, Spring 1985, vol. 24, no. 1, pp. 51–68.

"Personnel" had a name change in 1979 when its head became known as Vice President of "Human Resources," the position now held by Wheeler.

Wheeler believes that recent social and environmental changes, such as more women in the work force and higher educational levels of workers, mandate changes in the way organizations handle people. For this reason, he has proposed a partnership between line managers and human resource managers at 3M. His strategy is (1) "to get human resource managers to think more like line managers"; and (2) "to get line managers to think more like human resource managers."** In accomplishing this strategy, Wheeler hopes that staffers whose human resource experience has been limited to one specific functional area will develop a better appreciation of the concerns of both the human resource generalist and the line manager. The notion of a partnership between line managers and human resource managers means that new human resource programs and systems will not be imposed, but rather, will be developed and implemented in cooperation with line managers.

Wheeler's strategy requires a substantial management development program. For human resource staff, there are programs to broaden perspectives beyond functional areas. For line managers, there are programs relating to human resource management. These programs will be mandatory, not optional as they have been in the past.

Another tactic to increase line management's sensitivity to human resource problems is the institution of a company-wide employee survey. While many divisions have conducted such surveys in the past, they have never before been required of all divisions.

Finally, Wheeler's program involves moving to a human resource management structure that is between completely decentralized and centralized. While human resource staffers will continue to be assigned to operating divisions, they will remain a part of one large human resource management function. Creating a partnership between line and human resource management will likely result in the hiring of additional human resource staffers. One advantage of this will be the opening of new career paths to human resource professionals.

Questions:

1. What are the advantages and disadvantages of keeping HRM professionals in various functional areas such as compensation and training?
2. Do you think development of the personnel/human resources function at 3M is typical of other companies? Why or why not?
3. What do you think of Wheeler's strategy to make human resource managers and line managers think more like each other? What

**Ibid.

might the advantages be of such a strategy for 3M and its human resources?

Case 1.2: ManuLife: "A Great Place to Work"

It is 9:15 A.M. and Carol Trent has just arrived for work at Manufacturers Life Insurance Company (ManuLife) in Toronto, Ontario. She greets co-worker George Capelli who's been at his desk since 7:30 A.M. George likes to come in early so he can miss rush-hour traffic, but Carol has small children she must drop off at daycare so 9:15 suits her better. ManuLife's flexible hours system, OpTime, allows employees some leeway in scheduling their hours of work.

George hands Carol an issue of *ManuLife World*, the company's uncensored newspaper. "Seen this yet? It's got my editorial in it about electronic performance monitoring—you know, that proposal to keep track of our keystroke rate and down-time. I think it's so degrading."

"I agree," replies Carol, "But I don't think they'll ever do it—at least not after they see the results of the employee opinion survey they sent around yesterday."

Trent has worked as a data processor at ManuLife for the past three years and the company has treated her well. She has been able to take courses of personal interest on company time and work out daily in ManuLife's plush new fitness centre. When she was pregnant last year, the company gave her four months' maternity leave and even supplemented her unemployment insurance payments so she received 60 per cent of her salary.

Regular reviews of her performance show Trent to be a good worker. Like other good workers, she can expect to move up in the company due to ManuLife's commitment to promote from within. Being a woman will not hinder her advancement. (Women make up 30 per cent of all employees at managerial levels and above.) Because ManuLife is a "lateral organization," Trent may "advance" in any number of directions. One former data processor, for example, rose to the position Assistant Vice-President of Individual Insurance. Trent hopes that her career with the company will lead her into accounting and compensation management.

The future of Trent's co-worker, Bertha Gruber, is not as bright. Gruber has been with the company for less than a year and her performance reviews have been consistently poor. Several months ago Gruber was given notice that her work would have to improve or she would be fired. Gruber tried to improve—she even sought help from the Employee Assistance Unit about her drinking—but her efforts proved unsuccessful.

ManuLife sets high performance standards and rewards those who meet them; those who don't are likely to be fired. ManuLife fires a larger percentage of workers than most of its competitors; in fact, firing is responsible for one-third of the company's turnover. To help make firing less painful for managers, ManuLife has a policy of awarding terminated workers up to one and one-half years' severance pay.

Questions:

1. ManuLife is cited by *Canadian Business* magazine as a "great workplace" (September 1984). What human resource policies and practices have helped to make it so? (Consider the areas of planning, staffing, employee development, and maintenance.)
2. What kinds of human and financial resources are required to support the human resource policies in effect at ManuLife?
3. Because ManuLife is such a great place to work, turnover is low —only 9 per cent. Management would prefer a turnover rate of at least 12 per cent in order to increase mobility within its head-office staff of 1,850. What kinds of human resource policies might ManuLife put into effect to encourage more turnover?

NOTE: This fictionalized account is based on D. Stoffman, "Great Workplaces and How They Got That Way," *Canadian Business*, September 1984, pp. 30–38.

2

The Human Asset

In 1981, Ford Motor Company of Canada Ltd. announced it would close its Engine 2 plant at Windsor, Ontario. Closure seemed a logical step since only 83 workers remained at the plant and 1981 losses were projected at $1.6 million. But hold everything. That isn't the end of the story.

Windsor Engine Plant 2, which produced 255-cubic inch, eight-cylinder engines prior to 1982, had instituted an Employee Involvement (EI) program in 1980 with the blessing of both management and the local United Auto Workers (UAW) union. The EI program created a team of seven assembly line workers and supervisors charged with the responsibility of finding better ways to build auto engines. When Ford announced its intention to close the plant, the EI team, headed by machine operator Henry (Hank) Hunt, renamed itself SOS (Save Our Stampings) and swung into action.

Members of SOS invested much of their own time conducting an investigation. They studied records, facts, and figures, and after several months came up with some interesting findings and recommendations. First, they found that steel from their supplier was substandard and insisted it be brought up to par. Second, they discovered a superior lubricant and suggested it be used in preparing steel for the presses. Third, they developed a blow-drying method for reducing moisture and rust on newly-made parts. Management listened and wisely implemented SOS's suggestions. As a result, scrap (waste) was reduced at the plant by 20 per cent (from 23 to 3 per cent), and production was rendered profitable.

Shortly after changes were made, Ford chose Engine Plant 2 as the production site for its 302-cubic-inch engine. Now instead of being closed, Engine Plant 2 supports a work force of 900, including 25 ten-person EI teams. Says Leo Brown, manager of Ford's engine plants: "The worker always knows what's wrong. He wasn't being asked before."[1]

The above example demonstrates the potential of people to be their company's greatest asset. The degree to which that potential is reached depends largely on the way an organization manages and deploys its people. This chapter discusses human resources from both a general and a specific perspective. From a general perspective, we look at the labour force, especially its characteristics, its trends, and common indices used to describe it. From a specific perspective, we examine employee behaviour and performance on an individual level.

Both economic and psychological perspectives are important in planning and administering many human resource policies and practices. For example, research has shown that economic indicators such as the number of people in the labour force and the unemployment rate are related to turnover rates.[2] When the unemployment rate is low and job opportunities exist, it is easier for employees to find alternative employment than when the unemployment rate is high. Thus, employers often find it necessary to adjust pay and benefits upwards and to make other human resource policy changes in order to retain current employees and to attract new ones. A recent model of employee turnover includes economic factors, level of job satisfaction (a psychological factor), and human resource policies and practices.[3] Knowledge of general economic information and specific psychological theory and research is essential if HRM professionals are to help the organization achieve its goals.

The first section of this chapter discusses the labour force, and the second section examines employee behaviour and the psychological aspects of work behaviour.

The Labour Force

Labour Force Statistics

HRM professionals must be able to understand and interpret labour force statistics that reflect demographic changes in the population. Some large employers, such as General Motors, have hired demographers to help HRM professionals plan.[4] Labour force statistics provide

[1] Daniel Stoffman, "Blue-collar Turnaround Artists," *Canadian Business*, February 1984, pp. 38–42.

[2] S.F. Kaliski, *Labour Turnover in Canada: A Survey of Literature and Data* (Ottawa: Labour Canada, 1981).

[3] W.H. Mobley, R.W. Griffeth, H.H. Hand, and B.M. Meglino, "Review and Conceptual Analysis of the Employee Turnover Process," *Psychological Bulletin*, 1979, vol. 86, pp. 493–522.

planners and policy makers with information regarding the number of people employed and unemployed, turnover rates, and the types of industries experiencing growth or decline.

Knowledge of labour force characteristics, trends, and local labour market conditions is particularly useful for the HRM functions of human resource planning, recruiting, and compensation. For example, the fact that the birth rate in Canada has been declining and the mortality rate has been stable for several years means that the demand for an employer's product may not be as great in the future as it has been in the past. It also means that, ten to 15 years hence, the rate of increase of new entrants to the labour force will be much smaller than it was in the early 1970s. This trend may demand a major change in human resource planning programs—perhaps less emphasis on recruiting and selection and more on training and development. Trends and changes in the numbers of people employed in various industries and jobs also affect the planning and administration of many HRM programs. For example, when the unemployment rate is very low, employers have to expend more effort on recruiting; selection standards may have to be lowered in order to fill vacancies, and compensation raised both to attract new employees and to retain current ones. These are only a few examples of the importance to HRM professionals of monitoring various labour statistics and trends so that human resource policies and practices can be modified to meet changes in the supply of and demand for labour.

The major source of labour force data is Statistics Canada, which regularly conducts a number of pertinent surveys and analyzes and publishes the results. *The Labour Force* (catalogue number 71-001), its monthly survey of 52,800 representative households across the country, provides the most complete picture available of the employed and unemployed in Canada. Exhibit 2.1 shows the types of information collected in it, the size and nature of the survey sample, and the definitions it uses. Another Statistics Canada survey, *Employment Earnings and Hours* (catalogue number 72-002) is based on establishment —that is, employer—information; it collects monthly data on the numbers of people employed, hours worked, and average pay or earnings by province and industry.

Some Labour Force Terminology

It is important to use exact definitions in order to permit correct interpretation of statistics and to ensure the consistency of data over time. When changes in definitions are deemed necessary, they almost inevitably affect results. For example, a 1975 revision of Statistics Canada's monthly household survey enlarged the size of the sample and excluded 14-year-olds from its definition of potential members of the labour force; it also substituted a direct form of questioning for an indirect one. (The old survey had asked, "What did this person do mostly last

[4]J.C. Hyatt, "People Watchers: Demographers Finally Come into Their Own in Firms, Government," *Wall Street Journal*, July 19, 1978.

week?" The revised version has, "Last week, did . . . do any work at a job or business?") These changes in themselves made the survey produce a higher unemployment rate for females (8.1 per cent) than for males (6.2 per cent), whereas the old version would have produced the reverse (6.4 per cent versus 7.4 per cent).[5]

Participation rate. An index commonly used to describe the labour force is the *participation rate*, which is broadly defined as the percentage of persons eligible for the labour force who actually are in it. An "eligible" person is any person 15 or older who is not institutionalized. It is important to realize that being "in the labour force" is not a synonym for being employed. A person is considered to be *in the labour force* if he or she is employed or is unemployed but actively seeking employment. When we say the female participation rate reached 54.3 per cent in 1985, we are saying that slightly more than half of the noninstitutionalized women age 15 and older (those "eligible") were actually in the labour force. Some were employed; others were unemployed but seeking work.

Discouraged workers. A related concept is what economists term *discouraged workers*: persons eligible for the labour force who have given up searching for work. They are not counted as among the unemployed but as outside the labour force. There is no single, generally agreed-upon measure of the number of discouraged workers. The labour force household survey makes an estimate based on the number of respondents who indicated that they were not looking for work because they believed none was available. This measure offers many pitfalls: the respondents' belief in the unavailability of work may be erroneous; some may have no real interest in finding work immediately. Nevertheless, the phenomenon of discouraged workers is important, especially in periods of economic slowdown. The labour force survey for March 1986 reported 105,000 persons in this category. If all of them were actually discouraged workers, the "true" unemployment rate for that month was 10.4 per cent rather than the recorded 9.6 per cent.

Projections. As in almost every other aspect of life, nobody can say exactly how the labour force will change in a decade or five years or even six months. Yet many kinds of industrial and government planning require the best possible estimates of how many and what kinds of people will be working—or available for work—at specific times and places in the future. Accordingly, researchers regularly make forecasts about the labour force. Like all economic forecasting, the subject is enormously complicated, but one method is to take trends which occurred in the recent past and *project* them into the future by assuming that the same changes will continue. For example, aside from small numbers of possible immigrants, we know how many people in Canada will be 15 to 24 years of age in 1990. One way to project their rate of participation in the labour force is to assume that the net change from

[5] Statistics Canada, *Comparison of the 1975 Labour Force Survey Estimates Derived from the Former and Revised Surveys* (Ottawa, 1976).

1980 to 1990 will be the same as the net change from 1970 to 1980. This simplifying assumption provides one of a number of alternative ways of coming up with future scenarios for the labour force.

EXHIBIT 2.1

Statistics Canada's definitions of labour force terms

The Labour Force Survey

The statistics contained in this report are based on information obtained through a sample survey of households. Interviews are carried out in about 52,800 representative households across the country, involving some 112,000 respondents.

The Labour Force Survey, started in November 1945, was taken at quarterly intervals until November 1952. Since then it has been carried out monthly. Beginning in January 1976, following more than 3 years of development, substantial revisions to the labour force survey were introduced. Details of these changes are available on request from the Labour Force Survey Sub-Division, Statistics Canada, Ottawa, K1A 0T6.

The sample used in the surveys of the labour force has been designed to represent all persons in the population 15 years of age and over residing in Canada, with the exception of the following: residents of the Yukon and Northwest Territories, persons living on Indian reserves, inmates of institutions and full-time members of the armed forces.

Data collection is carried out during the week following the reference week. Statistics Canada interviewers contact each of the dwellings in the sample through personal and/or telephone interviews to obtain the information needed to produce the labour force data. The questionnaire used in the survey is reproduced at the back of this publication. Each interviewer contacts approximately 50 designated dwellings (the individual assignment size varies by type of area) and conducts a personal interview in all dwellings where interviews are being conducted for the first time. In most areas, provided the respondent agrees, subsequent interviews may be conducted by telephone, an interview technique which has been shown to have no discernable impact on the data and which offers significant savings in time and cost.

Definitions and Explanations

Labour Force

The labour force is composed of that portion of the civilian non-institutional population 15 years of age and over who, during the reference week, were employed or unemployed.

Employed

Employed persons are those who, during the reference week:

(a) did any work at all

(b) had a job but were not at work due to:

- own illness or disability
- personal or family responsibilities
- bad weather
- labour dispute
- vacation

- other reason not specified above (excluding persons on layoff and persons whose job attachment was to a job to start at a definite date in the future).

Unemployed
Unemployed persons are those who, during the reference week:
(a) were without work, had actively looked for work in the past four weeks (ending with reference week), and were available for work;
(b) had not actively looked for work in the past four weeks but had been on layoff and were available for work;
(c) had not actively looked for work in the past four weeks but had a new job to start in four weeks or less from reference week, and were available for work.

Not in the Labour Force
Those persons in the civilian non-institutional population 15 years of age and over who, during the reference week were neither employed nor unemployed.

Unemployment Rate
The unemployment rate represents the number of unemployed persons expressed as a per cent of the labour force. The unemployment rate for a particular group (age, sex, marital status, etc.) is the number unemployed in that group expressed as a per cent of the labour force for that group.

Participation Rate
The participation rate represents the labour force expressed as a percentage of the population 15 years of age and over. The participation rate for a particular group (age, sex, marital status, etc.) is the labour force in that group expressed as a percentage of the population for that group.

SOURCE: Statistics Canada, *The Labour Force*, cat. no. 71-001 (Ottawa, monthly).

General Trends and Characteristics of the Labour Force

General participation rates. The recent overall trend is towards increased participation in the labour force. This means that a higher proportion of the population is entering the labour force today than in the past. As illustrated in Exhibit 2.2, and shown in more detail in Exhibit 2.3, the proportion of the eligible population that was either employed or seeking work remained relatively stable at about 55 per cent in the 1950s and 1960s. Since the early 1970s, however, there has been a small but significant increase in the participation rate, indicating that, as the eligible population has grown, the size of the labour force has grown more than proportionately. In 1980, the Canadian labour force had 11.5 million people. This represented a 64 per cent participation rate, up from almost 58 per cent in 1971 and from approximately 54 per cent in 1951. Projections to 1990 and 1995 suggest that the combined participation rate will continue to increase but at a slower rate than in the 1970s.

Female participation rates. Changes in participation rates among certain groups of the population have been more dramatic. In fact, as

EXHIBIT 2.2

Actual and projected labour force participation rates

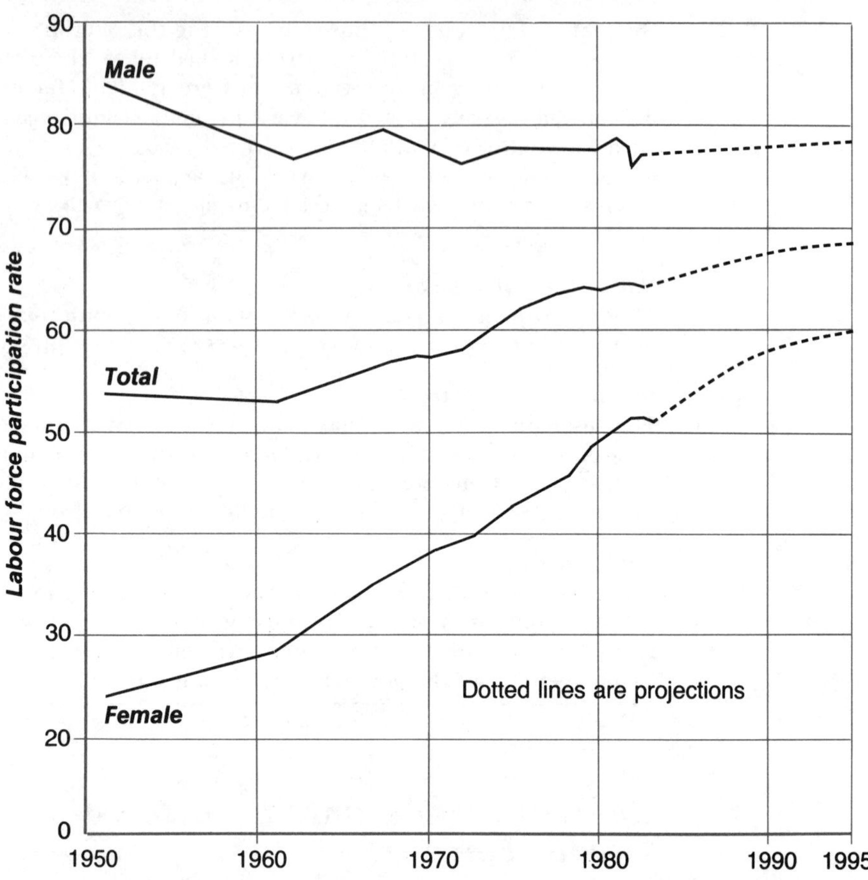

SOURCES: 1951, 1961: Census data; 1966–1980: Department of Finance Canada, *Economic Review, April 1981* (Hull: Supply and Services Canada, 1981); Peter Dungan, Mary MacGregor, André Plourde, *National Projections Through 1995: Base Scenario* (Toronto: Policy and Economic Analysis Program, Policy Study No. 86-5, Institute for Policy Analysis, University of Toronto, June 1986).

illustrated in Exhibit 2.2, the increase in the overall participation rate resulted from a steady surge in the proportion of women who entered the labour force. As shown in Exhibit 2.3, 24.1 per cent of Canadian women were either working or looking for work in 1951, while the figure in 1985 was more than double at 54.4 per cent. By contrast, the participation rate of males in 1985 was lower than that of 1951.

Further examination of the table reveals that the participation rate for women has increased most in the 25 to 44 age group. These have traditionally been regarded as the childbearing years. Now many women in this age group are not having children, and many others are working mothers.

Many factors combine to explain the trend towards women's increased participation in the labour force. These causes include cultural values involving work and the family, changed attitudes towards family size, more labour- and time-saving devices in the home, the rising cost of living, and, most important, the "very considerable expansion in recent decades of jobs that are considered especially 'suitable' for female employment."[6] Women with general educations which qualify them for a variety of lower- and middle-level white-collar positions are often willing to accept lower levels of pay than similarly qualified male applicants.[7]

The trend towards increased female participation has prompted and will continue to prompt changes in human resource policies and practices. In particular, the increasing employment of mothers means that employers must adapt and change some human resource policies, such as working hours and health care programs. For example, the Unemployment Insurance (UI) Act now provides women who are absent from work because of pregnancy a maximum of 15 weeks of benefits that amount to 60 per cent of the average weekly insurable earnings. However, in a trend initiated by the Canadian Union of Postal Workers following a strike in 1981, recent collective agreements have included additions to UI benefits for maternity leave. The CUPW agreement provides for 95 per cent of pay for 17 weeks.

Male participation rates. The trend in male participation rates has been downward, from 83.8 per cent in the civilian labour force in 1951 to 76.7 per cent in 1985. As shown in Exhibit 2.2, this decline was not steady during the 30-year period; rather, the rate rose and fell with economic cycles. The deep recession of the early 1980s again produced a marked decrease.

This downward trend is age-related, concentrated in the younger and older age groups (24 and under and 45 and over). The falloff for male youths, which reversed itself, particularly among teenagers, by 1980, reflected society's increased urbanization and industrialization, which required workers to obtain considerable training. It was a result of the increased accessibility of higher education and a desire by increasingly educated parents to keep their children in school longer.[8] The downward trend for the older group resulted from a number of factors, such as early retirement policies and improved pensions. Thus, we see that economic conditions, social values, and employment policies, such as pensions, all affect the participation rate.

The projections in Exhibit 2.3 indicate a continuation of the decline among older men, an expectation reflecting retirement policies and the growth in real incomes. On the other hand, given the increasing proportion of 45- to 54-year-olds in this group and the effects of high inflation, these rates may be underestimated. Forecasters differ in their projections for the participation rate of male youths; Exhibit 2.3 provides one forecast.

[6] Sylvia Ostry and Mahmood A. Zaidi, *Labour Economics in Canada*, 3rd. ed. (Toronto: Macmillan, 1979), p. 42.

[7] Ibid., p. 43.

[8] Ibid., p. 35.

EXHIBIT 2.3

Labour force participation rates by age group and sex

Year	*M & F combined*	*Total*		*15–19*		*20–24*		*25–44*		*45–64*		*65 & over*	
		M	*F*	*M*	*F*	*M*	*F*	*M*	*F*	*M*	*F*	*M*	*F*
1951	54.2	83.8	24.1	58.6	37.8	92.4	46.9	96.5	23.1	90.7	17.9	38.6	5.1
1961	53.7	77.7	29.5	41.4	34.2	97.2	49.5	94.2	30.3	87.8	29.8	28.4	6.7
1970	57.8	78.2	36.2	43.3	35.0	83.3	58.8	96.7	39.5	90.5	36.0	22.6	5.0
1980	64.1	78.4	50.4	57.8	52.1	86.4	73.0	95.6	62.3	85.2	44.5	14.8	4.4
1985	65.2	76.7	54.3	53.7	52.1	84.0	74.9	94.6	70.4	81.4	47.8	12.3	4.2
1995	68.5	77.1	60.4	55.8	55.0	87.3	81.7	94.4	82.4	81.2	55.9	10.9	3.6

SOURCE: David K. Foot, *A Challenge of the 1980's: Unemployment and Labour Force Growth in Canada and the Provinces* (Toronto: Institute for Policy Analysis, University of Toronto, 1981). Statistics Canada, *Labour Force Annual Averages 1975–1983*, cat. 71-529, occasional, 1984; Statistics Canada, *The Labour Force, December 1985*, cat. 71-001; Peter Dungan, Mary MacGregor and André Plourde, *National Projection Through 1995*, (Toronto: Institute for Policy Analysis, Policy and Economic Analysis Program, June 1986). For 1995 the authors estimated the composition of the participation rates within the age groupings 15–24, 25–54, 55 plus.

Age trends in the labour force. The median age of the working population is increasing and is expected to continue to do so for some decades. The cause is the postwar "baby boomers," who reached working age in the late 1960s and 1970s, plus the recent and continuing fall in the birth rate. Unless the participation rate increases drastically and unexpectedly, the proportion of youths (15 to 24 years) in the labour force will decline from the 1980 level of more than one-quarter to less than one-fifth by 1990, reaching a low point of 16.2 per cent in 2021.[9] The "baby boomers" will be the dominant age group in the labour force until they begin to retire in the early part of the 21st century. The competition for jobs among them is expected to be intense.

Overall growth in the labour force. As a result of a combination of these and other trends, the economy's total supply of labour is expected to grow at about 1.5 per cent per annum between 1985 and 1995, down from 3.2 per cent during the 1970s (which was the fastest growth rate of any of the industrialized countries). Two-thirds of the increase will come from population growth; increased participation will add the rest.[10]

Provincial differences. Interprovincial migration patterns can also affect overall labour force growth since participation rates differ by

[9] David K. Foot, *Canada's Population Outlook, Demographic Futures and Economic Challenges* (Ottawa: Canadian Institute for Economic Policy, 1982).

[10] Ibid., p. v.

province with the highest rates in the West, particularly Alberta, and lowest in the East, particularly Newfoundland, as shown in Exhibit 2.4. The major factors underlying the differences are the age structure of the population and the demand for labour. Provinces with relatively low unemployment rates tend to have relatively high participation rates and vice versa. For example, in 1985, Ontario had the lowest unemployment rate (8.0 per cent) and the second highest participation rate (68 per cent), while Newfoundland had the highest unemployment rate (21.3 per cent) and the lowest participation rate (53.1 per cent). The projected growth rate in Exhibits 2.3 and 2.4 shows low population and labour force growth in Prince Edward Island, Alberta, and Saskatchewan. The latter two are the result of significant net out-migration. For Alberta this represents a reversal of earlier projections which were made before the drop in world oil prices in the mid-1980s, which sharply reduced investment in oil projects and led to a substantial rise in unemployment. Only Ontario stands out as having substantially above average labour force growth.

Part-time workers in the labour force. Another trend in the labour force has been the growth in the number of part-time employees. Statistics Canada defines a part-time employee as one who works less than 30 hours per week. The number of employees working part-time on a voluntary basis has grown steadily in recent years, except during the severe recession of the early 1980s. The rate of increase of part-time workers has been more than twice the rate of increase in full-timers over the past decade.

Involuntary part-time—part-time employment accepted by workers who would prefer full-time work but cannot find it—is also rising. In 1981, 18 per cent of part-timers were involuntary. The figure was 28.5 per cent two years later, when the overall unemployment rate had risen by more than half, and it continued to grow by another per cent in 1985 after unemployment had decreased somewhat.[11]

A variant of part-time work that is in some ways involuntary is also on the rise. Work-sharing involves all employees in a unit agreeing to work part-time rather than have some of them laid off. Between 1977 and 1979, the federal government experimented with using Unemployment Insurance funds to assist work-sharing. Although the experiment resulted in greater-than-expected costs, both unions and companies were enthusiastic about it. In the face of sharp increases in unemployment, the UI-assisted program was reintroduced in fall 1981 and expanded the following spring. By the summer of 1982, an estimated 150,000 Canadian workers were engaged in work-sharing.[12] By the end of 1982, 8,780 firms and over 200,000 employees were participating in work-sharing. A comparison with California (an area with approximately the same population) showed Canadian participation

[11] Statistics Canada, *Labour Force Annual Averages 1975–1983*, cat. no. 71-529, Occasional, February 1984 and *The Labour Force*, cat. no. 71-001, December 1985.

[12] See N.M. Meltz, F. Reid, and G.S. Swartz, *Sharing the Work, An Analysis of the Issues in Worksharing and Job Sharing* (Toronto: University of Toronto Press, 1981); and Carol Goar, "Work-Sharing: A Success No One Really Expected," *Toronto Star*, March 27, 1982.

EXHIBIT 2.4

The labour force by province

	CAN	*Nfld*	*PEI*	*NS*	*NB*	*Que*	*Ont*	*Man*	*Sask*	*Albt*	*BC*
Participation Rate											
1975 (actual)	61.1	49.4	56.5	55.3	53.8	58.5	64.1	60.9	59.2	66.1	61.1
1985 (actual)	65.2	53.0	61.9	58.8	56.8	62.2	68.0	65.8	66.4	71.9	64.3
1995 (projected change)	3.3	2.5	2.1	2.9	2.6	4.6	3.2	2.6	1.9	1.3	2.5
Labour Force (000's)											
1985 (actual)	12,639	224	59	391	304	3,181	4,787	523	491	1,249	1,431
1995 (projected no.)	14,609	259	66	446	347	3,635	5,675	598	542	1,378	1,664
(projected % increase)	15.6	15.6	11.9	14.1	14.1	14.3	18.6	14.6	10.4	10.4	16.3

SOURCE: Peter Dungan, PRISM *Projection Through 1995* (Toronto: Policy and Economic Analysis Program, Institute for Policy Analysis, University of Toronto, July 21, 1986); and Statistics Canada, *Historical Labour Force Statistics 1986* ed., cat. no. 71-201 (Ottawa: Minister of Supply and Services Canada 19, 1987).

being more than twelve times greater in both number of firms and employees. While one factor was Canada's higher rate of unemployment, the costs of participation in work-sharing were also lower in Canada for both employers and workers. In addition, the Canadian program was given enormous public visibility by the then-Minister of Employment and Immigration, Lloyd Axworthy.[13]

Of course, many organizations hire part-time employees not to mitigate the effects of recession but to solve some of their problems, such as scheduling. In the past, part-time employees received no benefits, but now that part-time employment is more common and is accepted by both management and unions, more than half of the permanent part-time employees in the United States receive benefits in proportion to their hours worked. In briefs presented to the Commission of Inquiry into Part-time Work, the majority of employer associations reported that they do not pay fringe benefits to their part-time workers other than the mandatory benefits such as the Canada Pension Plan, Unemployment Insurance and four per cent holiday pay. Employers who do pay benefits tend to be in the public sector, such as health care facilities and municipal governments. Private employers in the insurance industry also reported that they pay benefits to regular part-time workers.[14] Most legislated benefits, such as holiday and vacation pay, are prorated here by the number of hours worked.

In Canada, part-timers are concentrated in retail trade and in service industries.[15] Employers with concentrated periods of activity find it advantageous to use part-timers, especially for relatively low-paying work, because they do not have to pay the full range of benefits for part-time employees. It has been estimated that prorating all fringe benefits for part-time employees would increase straight-time labour costs by an average of 9.1 per cent.[16]

Clearly, the part-time labour force has become an established part of our economy and labour force. Part-time employment will in all likelihood continue to grow for several reasons: (1) the rising proportion of women entering the labour force, many of whom will assume part-time positions; (2) continued growth in the service industries, which employ more than 40 per cent of all part-timers;[17] and (3) the difficulty for single-income families to increase their standard of living.

Minorities in the labour force. While Canada is a country of minorities and ethnic groups, from a labour market perspective the most disadvantaged are the native peoples, particularly Indians. Persons

[13] Frank Reid and Noah Meltz, "Canada's STC: A Comparison with the California Version," in Ramelle MaCoy and Martin J. Morand, *Short-Time Compensation: A Formula for Work Sharing* (New York: Pergamon Press, 1984).

[14] Joan Wallace, *Part-time Work in Canada*, Report of the Commission of Inquiry into Part-time Work, (Ottawa: Minister of Supply and Services Canada, 1983).

[15] Statistics Canada, *The Labour Force,* December 1985, cat. no. 71-001. Part-timers made up 24 per cent of all employees in trade and 25 per cent of all employees in community, business and personal service. These two categories represented over three-quarters of all part-time workers.

[16] Frank Reid and Gerald S. Swartz, *Prorating Fringe Benefits for Part-time Employees in Canada* (Toronto: Centre for Industrial Relations, U. of Toronto, 1982), p. 1.

[17] Gordon Robertson, *Part-Time Work in Ontario: 1966 to 1976* (Toronto: Research Branch, Ontario Ministry of Labour, 1976); and Statistics Canada, *The Labour Force,* cat. no. 71-001, April 1977.

living on the Indian reserves are excluded from labour force statistics, a method of data-gathering that has lowered the measured rate of native unemployment but has not reduced the severity of the problem. A federal government task force report observed that one of the greatest areas of labour force growth in the 1980s could come from the native peoples—accounting for 20 per cent of the growth in the Western provinces. The report called for special training programs, wage subsidies to encourage employment, intensive counselling, and employment support services, such as child care, transportation, and adjustment assistance.[18]

The Abella Commission identified the need for programs of employment equity to remove discrimination against women, native people, disabled persons, and visible minorities. A key element in these programs is government intervention through law to remove what the Commission termed "systemic discrimination" against these groups.[19]

In April 1986 the federal government passed Bill C-62, an act respecting employment equity. Bill C-62 contains two new federal programs: the Legislated Employment Equity Program and the Federal Contractors Program. The Legislated Program applies to Crown corporations and to federally regulated employers with two or more employees, primarily the banking, transportation and communications industries. Employers are required to submit annual reports that show the representation of members of the four designated groups in specific salary ranges, occupational groups, hirings, promotions, and terminations. Employers who fail to report may be fined up to $50,000. The Federal Contractors Programs requires that federal government suppliers of goods and services with 100 or more employees bidding on government contracts worth $200,000 or more, commit themselves to complement employment equity as a condition of their bid. If there is not a satisfactory commitment to employment equity, a bid could be declared invalid. Suppliers who make employment equity commitments and are awarded contracts are subject to on-site reviews.

Industry employment projections. Chapter 1 introduced the concept of redundancy planning, explaining that technological and market changes are causing sizeable changes in the demand for employees in various industries. Some industries are growing and are seeking more qualified employees, while others are declining and laying off workers. Knowing which industries will experience growth and which will experience decline is very useful to human resource planners. This is especially true since the "baby boomers" are now in the labour force, and there will be fewer new workers because of the "baby bust" of the past two decades. The implication is that growth industries must develop programs to recruit, hire, and train experienced employees from declining industries.

[18] Canada Employment and Immigration Commission, *Labour Market Development in the 1980's* [The Dodge Report] (Hull, Que.: Ministry of Supply and Services Canada, 1981).

[19] Judge Rosalie Silberman Abella, *Report of the Commission on Equality in Employment* (Ottawa: Supply and Services Canada, 1984).

All major industry sectors except construction grew during the decade 1975–1985. But some, such as finance, insurance, and real estate, and community, business, and personal service, grew rapidly while manufacturing did not (see Exhibit 2.5). Overall, service-producing industries grew almost six times more than goods-producing industries.

EXHIBIT 2.5

Past and projected employment and employment growth by industry sector

	Employment in thousands			*Percentage change*	
	1975	1985	1995	1975–85	1985–95
Goods-producing industries	3,177	3,348	3,571	5.4	6.7
Manufacturing	1,871	1,981	1,992	5.9	0.5
Construction	603	587	741	−2.7	26.2
Primary (other than agriculture)[1]	199	261	312	31.2	19.5
Agriculture[1]	504	519	526	3.0	1.3
Service-producing industries	6,108	7,964	10,009	30.4	25.7
Finance, insurance, real estate	474	629	758	32.7	20.5
Community, business, personal service	2,520	3,648	4,665	44.8	27.9
Wholesale and retail trade	1,637	2,001	2,637	22.2	31.8
Transportation, utilities, communications	812	884	1,056	8.9	19.5
Public administration	665	802	893	20.6	11.3
Total all industries	9,284	11,311	13,578	21.8	20.0

[1]Classifications have been adjusted for the PREM model.

SOURCES: 1975: Statistics Canada, *Labour Force Annual Averages, 1975–1983*, cat. no. 71-529, Occasional, 1984. 1985: Statistics Canada, *The Labour Force, December 1985*, cat. no. 71-001, 1986. 1995: Peter Dungan, *PRISM Projection Through 1995* (Toronto: Policy and Economic Analysis Program, Institute for Policy Analysis, University of Toronto, July 21, 1986).

The projections to 1995 suggest a continuation of these trends, with the service sector growing faster than the goods-producing sector, though more moderately than in the past. The most significant change expected is fairly strong growth in the construction industry due initially to some pent-up demand for housing following limited construction during the 1981–1983 recession period and its immediate aftermath.[20] In contrast to the 1970s, finance, insurance, and real estate are projected for only moderate employment growth, reflecting the expected impact of increased productivity gains through computerized systems.

Manufacturing as a whole is projected to have almost no growth. Some sectors will, however, show interesting variations. For example, the electrical products and aerospace industries are expected to grow rapidly because of the growth of technologically based output. On the other hand, the automotive industry will be well below average as a result of long-run structural adjustments related to the development of fuel-efficient vehicles and the effects on demand of slower population growth. The major changes in the patterns of employment growth and the severe recession of the early 1980s have focussed attention on job security. A 1982 Gallup poll indicated that for three-quarters of Canadians job security has become the chief work issue.[21] The effect of changes in technology points up the continuing importance of education and training beyond the secondary school level, as well as the need for human resource planning in the economy.

This section has presented labour force statistics and trends, plus the terminology needed to interpret labour force data. Knowledge of labour force data is especially useful to planning and staffing areas of HRM responsibility. We now turn from our more macro focus to a closer inspection of the individual worker and of how behaviour and performance can be explained and directed. This knowledge is especially useful in formulating and administering effective HRM policies for employee development and maintenance.

Individual Behaviour and Job Performance

HRM professionals are required to know a great deal about human behaviour because they are responsible for developing and administering most organizational policies, programs, and rules which impact on employee work behaviour. *Work behaviour* is simply what people do at work. It includes activities directed towards accomplishment of work-related tasks, as well as nonessential activities such as coffee breaks with co-workers and twiddling one's thumbs. Some kinds of behaviour, such as attendance, promptness, compliance with rules, and producing high-quality work are desirable to employers, but others, such as high absenteeism, tardiness, chatting too much, and theft, are undesirable. Most human resource policies and programs are aimed at encouraging desired work behaviour and discouraging undesirable behaviour.

Employers are primarily interested in two major aspects of employee behaviour: job performance and job satisfaction. High levels of performance and satisfaction contribute to the achievement of organizational goals and objectives. This section discusses performance and

[20] Dungan et al., op. cit.

[21] Val Ross, "The Revolution in the Workplace," *Maclean's*, July 4, 1983, vol. 96, page 31.

job satisfaction, as well as ways to encourage appropriate and desired behaviours.

A Model of Performance and Satisfaction

Exhibit 2.6 is adapted only slightly from the Porter and Lawler model of job performance and satisfaction. This model portrays the relationship between two factors, or variables, important to organizational effectiveness—performance and job satisfaction. Though the Porter-Lawler model does not include all the factors related to performance and satisfaction, it does identify some of the major ones. The model can be used as a framework for discussion of factors affecting employee behaviour and how they relate to various HRM functions.

Before examining the model in detail, it is helpful for the student to have a brief overview of its entirety. Performance is the result of an employee's work. It is determined by three factors: (1) abilities, skills, and knowledge; (2) effort; and (3) role perceptions (what an employee is expected to do on the job). Performance leads to both extrinsic rewards, such as pay, promotion, privileges, and recognition, and intrinsic rewards, such as feelings of accomplishment and self-worth. Rewards received for performance result in certain levels of job satisfaction. Level of satisfaction is determined by employee perception of the fairness of those rewards. If, for example, an employee perceives a reward to be quite generous, the level of satisfaction is higher than if the reward is perceived as negligible or is not valued. Job satisfaction, in turn, affects the effort an employee will put into future performance. Generally, more effort is expended by someone who is satisfied with the rewards received for previous performance. Level of effort expended is also influenced by the value an employee attaches to a reward based on performance, and the employee's perception of his or her efforts leading to a given reward (perceived effort → reward probability).

There are many aspects of job performance, including quantity and quality of production, speed of performance, and so on. A basic goal of human resource management is to ensure that employees perform at a level acceptable to the organization.

Abilities, skills, and knowledge. Abilities, skills, and knowledge are work-related physical and mental characteristics of each employee. An *ability* is a person's competence to perform a particular kind of observable behaviour. People have a large number of abilities—verbal ability, mathematical ability, athletic ability, to name a few. Abilities are present in varying amounts in each individual. These differing levels of ability within an individual are referred to as *intra-individual differences*. There are also differences in ability levels *between* individuals, which are referred to as *inter-individual differences*. For example, people differ in their ability to bench-press weight. Exhibit 2.7 shows two hypothetical distributions of the amount of weight bench-pressed by a random sample of 140 men and 140 women. (Amount bench-pressed is a measure of upper body strength.) The average, or

EXHIBIT 2.6

Porter and Lawler's model of job performance and satisfaction

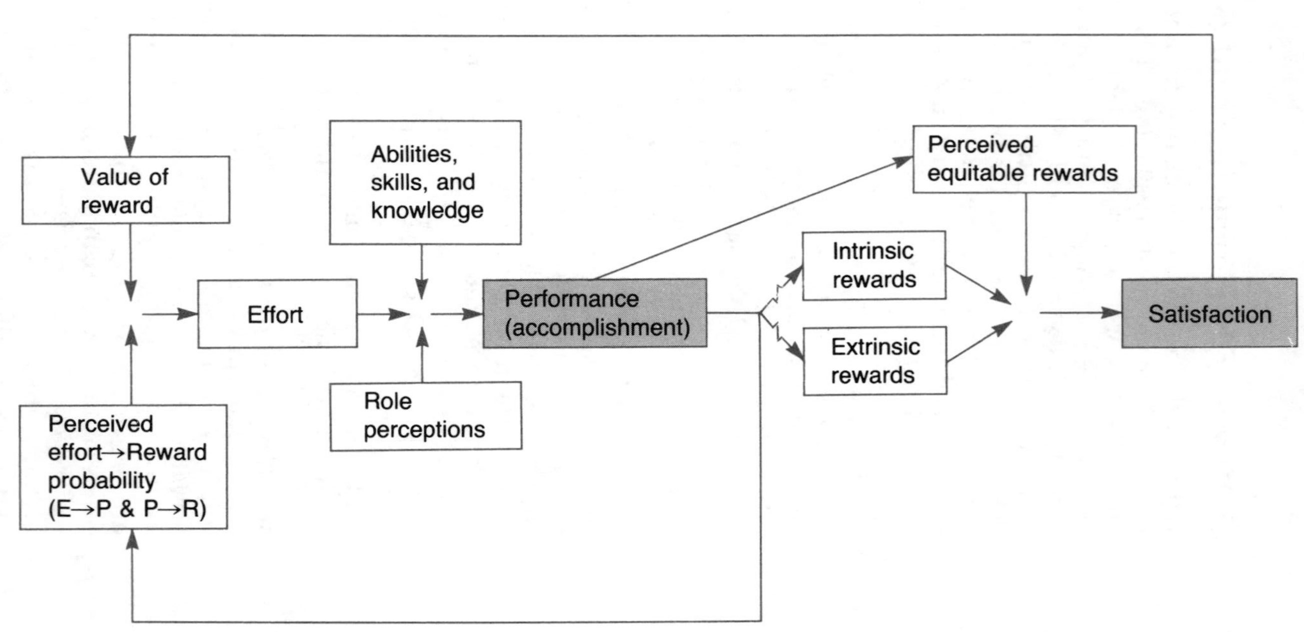

SOURCE: Adapted from Lyman W. Porter and E.E. Lawler III, *Managerial Attitudes and Performance* (Homewood, Ill.: Richard D. Irwin and Dorsey Press, 1968), p. 165.

mean, weight pressed by men in the sample is 264 pounds, compared to approximately 163 pounds for women. The shaded area in the exhibit represents the amount of overlap between men and women in the sample. *Overlap* means simply that a certain number of the members of one group have ability levels equal to or greater than some members of the other group. In this example, 21 per cent of the women can bench-press more weight than 21 per cent of the men (30 women can press 225 pounds or more; 30 men can press less than 200 pounds). It is important for HRM professionals to acknowledge the existence of overlap between groups such as men and women, whites and visible minorities, and so on and not to make categorical decisions about people based on group membership. Because of the phenomenon of overlap, such decisions are discriminatory and wasteful of human resources.

Skills are specific, developed abilities. Skills of interest to organizations include leadership and other interpersonal skills and psychomotor or motor skills, among others. Research has identified 11 types of motor skills, including speed of arm movement, arm-hand steadiness, and wrist-finger speed.[22] Finally, in addition to abilities and skills, employees must have specific knowledge or information to perform their jobs.

Abilities, skills, and knowledge are obviously essential to performance. HRM professionals are responsible for attracting and maintaining employees with the abilities, skills, and knowledge to perform their jobs adequately. The HRM functions of recruiting, selection, and training and development are especially related to the abilities, skills, and knowledge of employees. They are also associated with human resource planning (HRP) and job analysis in that HRM professionals must understand what a job entails in order to specify its human requirements. Further, through HRP and job analysis activities, managers and HRM professionals may decide to design or redesign jobs so that relatively low levels of abilities, skills, and knowledge are necessary for successful performance. Or jobs may be enlarged or enriched, possibly with the addition of new responsibilities, to recruit employees of higher calibre. Though employers may incur lower pay and benefits costs for relatively simple jobs, evidence shows that such jobs lead to employee dissatisfaction, absenteeism, and turnover.[23]

Effort. A second major determinant of performance is the amount of effort employees put into their jobs. In the past, effort at work meant physical exertion and sweat, but, in most jobs today, effort implies mental exertion. *Effort* is the behavioural result of motivation. *Motivation* is the psychological force or energy a person uses to satisfy his or her goals and needs. The level of effort an employee exerts on a job is determined by the satisfaction received from previous performance and rewards, by the value of the reward offered for a given level of performance, and by the perceived effort-reward probability.

[22] E.A. Fleishman, "Human Abilities and the Acquisition of Skill," in E.A. Bilodeau, ed., *Acquisition of Skill* (New York: Academic Press, 1966).

[23] J.R. Hackman, "Work Design," in J.L. Suttle and J.R. Hackman, *Improving Life at Work* (Santa Monica, Calif.: Goodyear, 1977).

EXHIBIT 2.7

Hypothetical distribution of weight bench-pressed by a random sample of 140 men and 140 women

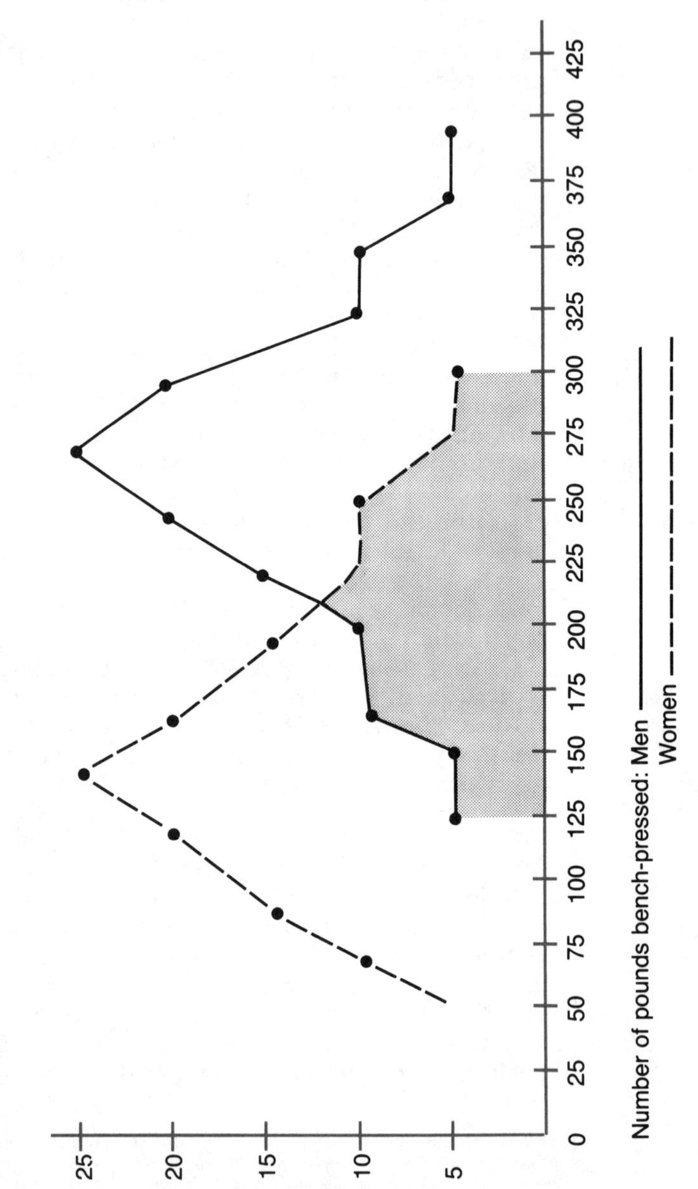

Previous performance and rewards affect level of effort through job satisfaction. For example, if an employee is satisfied with the fairness of rewards such as pay, praise from the boss, and personal feelings of having done a good job, then he or she is likely to exert the same or greater amount of effort again. On the other hand, a dissatisfied employee is likely to exert only enough effort to keep his or her job. One should keep in mind, however, that individuals differ in their responses to dissatisfaction with rewards. Dissatisfaction may motivate some to work harder the next time to achieve the desired rewards.

Employee perceptions of the fairness or unfairness of rewards may be explained by *equity theory*.[24] Equity theory postulates that people compare their inputs (abilities, effort, experience, and education) and their outcomes (pay, promotions, and other rewards) to the inputs and outcomes of other people. The amount of a person's inputs in relation to his or her outcomes is referred to as the *ratio of exchange*. If an employee believes that his or her ratio of exchange is equal to that of another "comparison" employee, the situation is perceived as equitable. A perceived imbalance (say, a person with similar education and experience receives more pay) is likely to produce feelings of inequity and dissatisfaction. Exhibit 2.8 illustrates an equitable and an inequitable ratio of exchange.

Since equity theory involves subjective perceptions, feelings of inequity can be resolved by the subject in a number of ways. Perhaps the simplest way is to choose a different person for comparison. Another is to reduce inputs—most notably, the amount of effort—in order to make the ratio of exchange more equitable. In order to minimize perceived inequities, HRM professionals must try to maintain consistent and fair policies of pay, promotion, discipline, and other actions which affect an employee's pay, benefits, and working conditions.

EXHIBIT 2.8

Equitable and inequitable ratios of exchange

Employee		*Comparison employee*		*Result*
input (abilities, effort) / outcomes (pay, other rewards)	=	input (abilities, effort) / outcomes (pay, other rewards)	→	perceived equity
input (abilities, effort) / outcomes (pay, other rewards)	≠	input (abilities, effort) / outcomes (pay, other rewards)	→	perceived inequity

The second factor determining amount of effort put forth on the job is value of the rewards offered. Rewards serve as incentives when

[24] J.S. Adams, "Inequity in Social Exchange," in L. Berkowitz, ed., *Advances in Experimental Social Psychology*, vol. 2 (New York: Academic Press, 1965).

they are anticipated by employees. Most are willing to work harder to obtain rewards they really want, such as a large pay raise or two weeks' paid vacation in Florida, than for rewards which have little value to them, such as a small raise or a minor promotion. But employers cannot always predict whether an employee will value a particular reward since there is a wide range of individual differences in employees' needs and desires. For a brief look at one company's incentive program, see Exhibit 2.9.

EXHIBIT 2.9

Use of incentives at Mary Kay Cosmetics Inc.

Employee motivation is top priority at Mary Kay Cosmetics, Inc., which is why the company uses a variety of performance incentives and rewards. Mary Kay's program focusses at the outset on simple recognition of new recruits. A recruit might be told by her local company president, for example, that she is a terrific saleswoman, that she has done a great job, and that she will soon be rewarded. Performance incentives for new recruits, among others, include ribbons, certificates, and jewelry. Then there are $5,000 spending sprees, all-expense-paid trips, mink coats, even pink Cadillacs, dangling like carrots to entice Mary Kay's legions to new and greater performance heights. To earn the top prize of a Cadillac, an employee must oversee dozens of other salespeople, and their combined quarterly revenues must reach or exceed $80,000. Large prizes are awarded before thousands of enthusiastic Mary Kay convention-goers, providing still another source of recognition to talented, dedicated workers. Of her business philosophy, Mary Kay, founder of the company says: "I believe you can praise people to success. I'd rather say, 'Gee, wouldn't you like this ribbon, or this car, to prove what you can do?' than to make a lot of demands."

SOURCE: David Olive, "All the Way with Mary Kay," *Canadian Business*, November 1984, pp. 77–81.

The third factor affecting an employee's level of effort is belief or expectancy about the probability of receiving a reward. According to *expectancy theory*, employees exert extra effort when they believe (1) that they can achieve certain performance levels, and (2) that they will receive the rewards attached to certain performance levels. Less effort is expended if employees believe that they do not possess the abilities, skills, or knowledge necessary to perform at certain levels or that performance will not result in desired rewards. An employee's belief that he or she can achieve a certain performance level by exerting some amount of effort is called the *effort → performance*, or *E → P, relationship*. The belief that a certain performance level will earn one an expected reward or rewards is called the *performance → reward*, or *P → R, relationship*. Employers have more control over the P → R relationship because they can choose to administer rewards fairly and consistently, thus raising employees' expectancies that performance will result in certain rewards.

The failure of managers and HRM professionals to maintain consistency between employee performance and rewards can lead to low job satisfaction, low levels of job performance, low levels of trust in management, and high rates of absenteeism and turnover. For example, imagine how frustrated and angry you would be if you worked very hard to meet a deadline on your job, and the $500 bonus your boss promised you was not given. You would be tempted to put forth less effort on a future assignment even if you were again promised a bonus of $500. Your previous experience would have caused you to lower your expectation of receiving the promised reward in exchange for your performance.

Role perceptions. Role perceptions are an employee's understanding of what he or she should do on the job. Even highly motivated employees with all the necessary abilities, skills, and knowledge to perform well may contribute nothing or actually hinder organizational effectiveness if they do not have a clear and correct understanding of what to do on the job. The primary responsibility for clear role perceptions lies with each employee's immediate supervisor. However, several HRM functions also contribute to clear role perceptions. Chapter 8 discusses orientation, in which new employees begin the socialization process and learn what is expected of them. Employees also learn what is expected of them through their job descriptions. Finally, they receive periodic clarification and modification of what their bosses expect from them in performance appraisal interviews, which also provide opportunities to set specific goals for employees.

Goal-setting is a method of providing employees with very specific, measurable roles or job prescriptions. Typical goal-setting methods involve establishing specific, quantitative goals for each employee based upon past performance. Research at the Weyerhaeuser Corporation in the U.S. showed that hundreds of thousands of dollars could be saved through the use of a procedure that assigned specific, quantitative goals to employees.[25] Goal-setting has also proved very useful in improving the effectiveness of training programs.[26]

Summary of job performance. The Porter and Lawler model shows three direct determinants of performance: (1) abilities, skills, and knowledge; (2) effort; and (3) role perceptions. Of these three determinants, abilities are the most basic since employees deficient in them cannot perform at an acceptable level. A major way in which HRM professionals can contribute to organizational effectiveness is by ensuring that employees have the required abilities, skills, and knowledge. This is accomplished through the HRM functions of (1) job analysis, which identifies required abilities, skills, and knowledge; (2) recruiting, selection, and placement, which seek, select, and place people in jobs that match their abilities; and (3) training and development and career planning, which provide programs and job experiences to develop and maintain employee qualifications for current and future jobs.

[25] G.P. Latham and J.J. Baldes, "The 'Practical Significance' of Locke's Theory of Goal Setting," *Journal of Applied Psychology*, February 1975, pp. 122–24.

[26] G.P. Latham and S.B. Kinne III, "Improving Job Performance through Training in Goal Setting," *Journal of Applied Psychology*, April 1974, pp. 187-91.

The second major determinant of performance is the amount of effort exerted on the job. Though jobs vary in the degree to which different levels of effort affect performance, all require some amount of effort (for example, the effort involved in coming to work). Therefore, acceptable job performance requires some minimal level of both abilities and effort, and higher levels of job performance result from additional effort or higher levels of abilities, skills, knowledge, or both. As discussed earlier, level of effort depends upon many factors under the organization's control, including the performance appraisal process, compensation and benefits policies and practices, and supervisors' behaviour towards employees. Though none of these factors is directly controlled by HRM professionals, they have a substantial influence on them through development and administration of appraisal and compensation programs. Further, supervisors' behaviour can be influenced by training and development programs designed by HRM professionals.

Effort can also be affected by the employee's work group at the job. Research has shown that co-workers often have more influence over employee behaviour than do the organization's policies and rewards.[27] Of course, level of effort may also be affected by factors not related to work, such as family problems, illness, and fatigue.

A significant determinant of job performance which is under employer control is role perceptions. Role perceptions are crucial because they guide or direct an employee's work behaviour. Even low-ability employees can perform acceptably in their job if they have a clear understanding of what they should do, while highly talented and motivated employees may contribute little to organizational effectiveness if their role perceptions are ambiguous. Organizations communicate role perceptions to employees through job descriptions, orientation programs, and performance appraisals.

Organization rewards. Exhibit 2.6 identifies two types of rewards: intrinsic and extrinsic. *Intrinsic rewards* are positive outcomes of job performance which employees either receive directly from the job or give themselves. Through work experience, employees learn when they have done a good job, and they reward themselves with feelings of a job well done. *Extrinsic rewards* are those provided by the organization, such as praise from the boss, pay increases, promotions, or some other form of recognition. The relationship between job performance and intrinsic rewards is more reliable and direct than the relationship between performance and extrinsic rewards since the latter depends upon the organization's performance monitoring and appraisal system, which can have a number of shortcomings.

Intrinsic rewards are developed from the extrinsic rewards employees receive from their supervisors and their peers. When an employee first begins a new job, he or she often does not know what constitutes acceptable job performance. Feedback from supervisors and co-workers, along with the employee's past experience, provides this information. From feedback, praise, and other extrinsic rewards, em-

[27] F.J. Roethlisberger and W. Dickson, *Management and the Worker* (Cambridge: Harvard University Press. 1939).

ployees learn what constitutes good and poor performance, and they can then provide intrinsic rewards to themselves. This process is called *internalization*. An employee's experience with extrinsic rewards also provides him or her with expectations about the fairness of rewards for various levels of job performance. These expectations are indicated in the diagram by the dotted arrow from performance to perceived equitable rewards.

Ideally, employers would design performance appraisal and compensation systems which would administer rewards on a contingent basis. That is, the amount of money or other rewards received would depend upon the amount and/or quality of an employee's work. In reality, contingency-type compensation systems are not common except for some salespersons, managers, and manufacturing employees who are paid according to the amount they produce. Some organizations have, however, made innovative uses of extrinsic rewards, such as performance feedback and praise. For example, Emery Air Freight and other companies in the United States have obtained substantial increases in job performance and profits by using behaviour modification programs based upon reinforcement principals.[28] These programs have several major components including specification of standards of performance, careful monitoring of performance by both supervisors and employees, and frequent feedback and rewards based upon level of performance. Thus, in behaviour modification, extrinsic rewards such as praise, performance feedback (knowledge of results), and sometimes money are given only for clearly specified types of job performance. This has the effect of clarifying role perceptions and specifying the performance → reward relationship. This use of extrinsic rewards stands in sharp contrast to typical pay policies, which reward employees who perform at only minimally acceptable levels.

Job satisfaction. Job satisfaction is an attitude of employees regarding aspects of their work. Porter and Lawler's model focusses on satisfaction with rewards that come directly from the job itself—for example, pride in a job well done, feelings of self-worth, praise, recognition, pay, promotions, and so on. In a broader sense, job satisfaction also includes employees' attitudes towards elements in the work environment—for example, satisfaction with company policies, with the boss, with coworkers, and with such physical characteristics of the work environment as lighting, noise, and safety.

Employers have long been interested in job satisfaction. The major reason for their interest has been the long-held, but incorrect, belief that happy workers are productive workers. Years of research have shown that there is a very small relationship between performance and satisfaction and very little evidence that highly satisfied employees are highly productive employees.[29] Currently, a well-accepted relationship between satisfaction and performance is that portrayed in the Porter and Lawler model, namely that satisfaction with rewards is one

[28] W.C. Hamner and E.P. Hamner, "Behavior Modification on the Bottom Line," *Organizational Dynamics*, 1976, no. 4, pp. 3–21.

[29] V.H. Vroom, *Work and Motivation* (New York: Wiley, 1964).

of several factors affecting the amount of effort expended on the job. Employers' interest in job satisfaction is justified, however, for other reasons: research has shown that job satisfaction is negatively related to absenteeism and voluntary turnover (resignation), both of which represent considerable cost to employers.[30]

Job satisfaction is a useful indicator of the condition and effectiveness of many organizational policies and practices. Information about employees' attitudes and feelings can be used to identify problems and to help design changes to resolve sources of discontent. There is evidence that attitude surveys can predict whether employees will engage in and support unionization activities in nonunionized organizations.[31] Specifically, employees who are dissatisfied with various aspects of their jobs are more likely to vote in favour of a union.[32] Other evidence suggests that efforts to increase job satisfaction can be very beneficial to organizations. A study of U.S. bank tellers found that even a moderate increase in job satisfaction resulted in an annual savings to the bank of over $125,000, through reductions in absences, turnover, and tellers' cash shortages.[33]

HRM professionals are frequently responsible for measuring job satisfaction among employees. While it is possible to measure overall job satisfaction, most measurement is of its facets or components. One commonly used tool is the Job Description Index (JDI), which measures five facets of satisfaction: with the work itself, with pay, with co-workers, with promotions, and with supervision.[34] The JDI consists of a list of adjectives or descriptive statements about each of the five components. Items relating to the work itself, for example, include "fascinating," "satisfying," "tiresome," and "endless." The employee responds to each adjective, indicating whether it describes a particular aspect of the job. Research has shown that the five facets of the JDI are independent of each other, and that the results are highly reliable or stable over a moderate length of time.[35] Overall job satisfaction is highest when employees are satisfied with all five components in the JDI. Besides providing an overall measure of job satisfaction, the JDI is useful because it can identify specific areas contributing to satisfaction or dissatisfaction.

In measuring job satisfaction, HRM professionals must consider the advantages and disadvantages of using standard measures versus constructing their own. An advantage of using a standard measure such

[30] R.M. Steers and S.R. Rhodes, "Major Influences on Employee Attendance: A Process Model," *Journal of Applied Psychology*, August 1978, pp. 391–407; Mobley, Griffeth, Hand, and Meglino, pp. 493–522; and G. Robertson and J. Humphreys, *Labour Turnover and Absenteeism in Selected Industries: Northwestern Ontario and Ontario* (Toronto: Ontario Ministry of Labour, 1979).

[31] W.C. Hamner and F.J. Smith, "Work Attitudes as Predictors of Unionization Activity," *Journal of Applied Psychology*, August 1978, pp. 415–21.

[32] J.G. Getman, S.B. Goldberg, and J.B. Herman, *Union Representation Elections: Law and Reality* (New York: Russell Sage Foundation, 1976).

[33] P.H. Mirvis and E.E. Lawler III, "Measuring the Financial Impact of Employee Attitudes," *Journal of Applied Psychology*, 1977, no. 1, pp. 1–8.

[34] P.C. Smith, L.M. Kendall, and C.L. Hulin, *The Measurement of Satisfaction in Work and Retirement* (Chicago: Rand NcNally, 1969).

[35] B. Schneider and H.P. Dachler, "A Note on the Stability of the Job Description Index," *Journal of Applied Psychology*, October 1978, pp. 650–53.

as the JDI is that an employer can compare the satisfaction level of his or her employees with the results gathered by other employers using the same instrument. In some cases, however, employers need to measure employees' attitudes and degree of satisfaction regarding various policies, issues, or problems unique to their organizations. One solution for those who would also like to be able to compare their data with those of other employers is to use both a standardized measure of job satisfaction and a questionnaire covering areas of particular interest.

Employers who use any questionnaires or attitude surveys to measure job satisfaction should be prepared to respond to employees' views. If employers fail to do so, employees are likely to be more dissatisfied than before, since attitude surveys create the expectation that management is responsive to needs and ready to change.

Employers need not rely entirely on attitude surveys or satisfaction questionnaires to measure satisfaction. Various kinds of employee behaviour, including absenteeism and voluntary turnover, also provide indicators of job satisfaction. In unionized organizations, large numbers of grievances and strikes indicate employees' dissatisfaction. Low levels of job satisfaction *may* be reflected in substandard quantity and quality of job performance, and sabotage of equipment or products is a clear indication. A final source of information is exit interviews with employees who are leaving the organization. However, employees who have quit may not be completely candid about why they are leaving, since they may foresee needing a reference from the employer.

Encouraging Appropriate and Desired Behaviours

Organizations seek to encourage appropriate and desired work behaviours in order to facilitate organizational effectiveness. Appropriate and desired behaviours are encouraged by clearly communicating rules and expectations to employees, providing honest and constructive feedback on performance, and offering a variety of rewards and incentives. They are also encouraged by the imposition of disciplinary sanctions on employees who exhibit inappropriate or undesirable behaviours.

Disciplinary sanctions let employees know that certain behaviours will not be tolerated and must be corrected in order to avoid the consequences. Under systems of progressive discipline, consequences of rule violations become more severe as offenses are repeated. For example, a first violation usually brings only an instructive counselling session to ensure that the employee knows the rules and the consequences of failure to comply. A second violation typically results in a written reprimand which becomes part of the employee's personnel file. Penalties for subsequent violations include suspension without pay, final warnings, and ultimately, dismissal. Exhibit 2.10 presents employee behaviours that result in progressive discipline under union contract in one large manufacturing plant. Exhibit 2.11 spells out rule violations that are grounds for immediate dismissal.

EXHIBIT 2.10

Rule violations subject to progressive discipline

1. Smoking in restricted areas.
2. Refusal to comply with a proper request or demand from the employee's supervisor.
3. Ringing, altering, defacing, or tampering with the time card of another employee.
4. Using slugs or tampering with the plant vending machines.
5. Threatening, intimidating, coercing, or interfering with fellow employees on company premises at any time.
6. Disregard of safety rules or practices.
7. Use of profane, vulgar, or threatening language either directed to a fellow employee or supervisor.
8. Leaving the work area or department during working hours or the unauthorized presence in another department's work area without authorization from the employee's supervisor or department manager.
9. Gambling, or the promotion thereof, in any form on the company's premises.
10. Excessive absenteeism or tardiness.
11. Failure to use designated entrance or exits.
12. Failure to report tardiness immediately.
13. Leaving work area to ring out prior to quitting bell or prior to being properly relieved.
14. Stopping work to commence clean-up prior to the sounding of the clean-up bell.
15. Failure to observe parking regulations.
16. Failure to work overtime when required unless such failure is due to circumstances which are substantiated to be beyond the control of the employee; or his failure to work was due to the employee's illness or injury, or the required attendance at a critical illness of a family member.
17. Discarding refuse or litter on the floor or company premises.
18. Failure to maintain job performance and quality standards.
19. Indulging in horseplay, scuffling, water fights, and similar acts on company premises.
20. Fighting on company premises which results in an injury to an employee.
21. Participating in the first 24 hours of any unauthorized strike, slowdown, work stoppage, boycott, picketing or similar interruption or interference with company operations.

HRM professionals often monitor employee behaviour and recommend policies and programs to achieve desired results. For example, HRM professionals are usually responsible for developing progressive discipline systems, and for overseeing such systems to ensure they are administered fairly. Inconsistent administration of discipline threatens job satisfaction and often leads to charges of discrimination.

EXHIBIT 2.11

Rule violations that are grounds for immediate dismissal

1. Possession of firearms or other concealed weapons inside the company building.
2. Theft or appropriation of property of employees; or of outside individuals or organizations servicing the company.
3. The unauthorized taking, removal, or disclosure of company reports, blueprints, records, confidential information, company correspondence or communication of any nature.
4. The unauthorized alteration or falsification of personnel records, payroll records, time cards, or production records.
5. Reporting for work while under the influence of any type of intoxicating beverage and/or narcotics, or either the possession or consumption of intoxicating beverages or narcotics on company premises, other than narcotics being taken under medical prescription.
6. Indecent or immoral conduct on company property.
7. Willful slowdown, work stoppage, or walkout.
8. Flagrant abuse, or destroying of company tools, machines, materials, and equipment or the property of other employees.
9. Sleeping on duty.
10. Carelessness or negligence in performing work duties which results in a substantial monetary loss to the company either in the form of lost production time or for labour and material costs to repair broken machinery, tools, and equipment.
11. Failure to notify the company of pregnancy as soon as the employee knows of this condition.

Two employee behaviours of major concern to employers are absenteeism and voluntary turnover (resignation).

Absenteeism. Absenteeism costs organizations millions of dollars annually in lost production, sick leave, and replacement personnel. One model of absenteeism suggests that two factors explain this behaviour: attendance motivation and ability to attend. Attendance motivation is determined by both level of job satisfaction and external pressures to attend, such as work group norms and financial need. Ability to attend refers to such problems as illness, weather, and transportation difficulties.[36] While organizations have some measure of control over attendance motivation, they have little control over inability to attend.

A recent review of 29 studies confirmed that higher levels of absenteeism are likely when employees are dissatisfied with their jobs or with facets of job satisfaction such as the work itself, pay, co-workers, and supervision.[37] This suggests that absenteeism can be reduced

[36] J. Gandz and A. Mikalachki, "Absenteeism: Costs, Causes, and Cures," *The Business Quarterly*, Spring 1980, pp. 22–30; and "Measuring Absenteeism," *Relations Industrielles/Industrial Relations*, vol. 34, no. 3 (1979), pp. 516–48.

[37] Steven L. McShane, "Job Satisfaction and Absenteeism: A Meta-Analytic Re-examination," *Canadian Journal of Administrative Sciences*, 1984, vol. 1, no. 1, pp. 61–77.

by human resource policies and programs designed to increase job satisfaction, among them quality of working life (QWL) programs such as Ford's described at the beginning of this chapter. Ford's five Windsor plants experienced a marked drop in absenteeism after implementation and continued use of Employee Involvement Programs.[38]

Some organizations have no mechanism for controlling absenteeism, but others have formal absence control programs. Formal programs typically combine careful monitoring of attendance with systems of progressive discipline. Exhibit 2.12 provides excerpts from one manufacturing company's absence control programs for hourly workers. Note that in this particular case, supervisors have primary responsibility for absence control, but that HRM professionals assist by maintaining records and reports and by defining who is excessively absent. Note also that this program emphasizes "day-to-day" attention to absence as a means of avoiding absenteeism and possible disciplinary action.

EXHIBIT 2.12

Excerpts from one company's absence control program

I: Responsibility for absence control

a. The primary responsibility for control of absenteeism must, of necessity, rest with the supervisor. A part of the supervisor's job is to see that everyone in the department is working and that excessive absenteeism is controlled. The individual supervisor is closest to the problem and most affected by it. It is he/she who suffers most when department personnel are absent.

b. Secondary responsibility for attendance lies with the department manager because he/she is responsible for production in the department. If people are absent, schedules cannot be met.

c. Further responsibility lies with the production manager. It is his/her responsibility to see that adequate absence control is maintained and consistent throughout the plant.

d. It is the responsibility of the human resources department to assist the supervisor, department manager, and production manager in maintaining absence records and reports and in determining whether a particular employee has a record of excessive absenteeism.

II: Progressive discipline system for excessive absenteeism

a. First excessive absence interview. You (the supervisor) should interview the employee privately, listen to reasons for absence, and make sure it's known you're trying to help. Never reprimand an employee in front of other people. Never become belligerent or offensive and don't apologize for discipline. Be fair but firm. If, after your discussion, you feel the employee is entitled to discipline, then formally complete a reprimand form. If, after the interview, you feel a reprimand form is not necessary, then fill out a corrective interview report and send a copy to the Human Resources Office. Indicate on either form that further attendance problems may result in further and more serious discipline action up to and including disciplinary layoff or discharge.

[38] Stoffman, p. 41.

b. Second excessive absence interview. The time interval between the first and second offense will, to a certain extent, influence how serious this step should be. The same procedure should be followed in counselling the individual as outlined in step one. Either of the following disciplinary actions may be taken:

1. Another interview and warning of written reprimand;
2. A formal written reprimand. (If this step is chosen, it should be made clear to the employee that if attendance doesn't improve substantially, the next step will be suspension from work (without pay) for periods varying from one to five days.)

c. Third excessive absence interview. The employee should be counselled and a decision made based on the past record of the employee and seriousness of the present offense. Time interval between offenses will be taken into account. Any of the following actions may be taken:

1. Issue another formal written reprimand notice;
2. Issue a one-day suspension from work (without pay);
3. Issue a more lengthy suspension from work for up to five days time off without pay.

d. Fourth excessive absence interview. Time interval will again be a factor. Any of the disciplinary actions taken previously may be repeated for less serious violators, but this step may also include discharge of serious offenders. Before any suspension from work or discharge action is taken, it must be reviewed by the personnel manager.

Note: Many supervisors assume that there's no need to talk to an employee about his/her attendance until the record becomes unsatisfactory. Not so! Supervisors should review an employee's attendance record each time an absence occurs. Without day-to-day attention to absence, a disciplinary problem may mature—one that possibly could have been prevented. This practice not only helps the supervisor clarify the reason for absence, but also lets the employee know that the company is concerned about his/her losing time. The prospect of having to give a face-to-face explanation for each day missed can also discourage not-so-conscientious employees from taking the unnecessary time off.

Another way employers and HRM professionals encourage good attendance is by tying attendance to rewards. For example, attendance can be made a factor in pay and promotion decisions and rewards can be denied to those who are excessively absent. Some companies have special attendance incentive programs. One such program awards employees a full day's extra pay for each quarter of perfect attendance. An employee who has a full year's perfect attendance gets special recognition at the annual company banquet. According to the company's human resources manager, the company hasn't had an absence problem in years.

Turnover. Turnover occurs in organizations when employees exit due to termination of their employment. When employment is terminated by the employee, as in the case of quitting, turnover is said to be ***voluntary***. Turnover is ***involuntary*** when initiated by the employer, as in the case of layoffs or dismissal.

Turnover is both an individual and an organizational phenomenon.

When employees engage in activities associated with leaving organizations, they engage in *turnover behaviour*. At an organizational level, companies sometimes calculate employee turnover rates for use in human resource planning. By measuring rates of exit among various types of workers, planners can project future internal supply and address specific labour needs. Turnover rates may also be calculated in order to assess the degree to which turnover is a problem in the organization. HRM professionals typically conduct exit interviews with departing employees in order to determine causes of turnover in the organization.

Organizations try to control turnover because turnover is expensive. There are costs associated with recruiting, selecting, and training replacement personnel, and costs associated with turnover's disruptive effects on production. High levels of turnover also result in more paperwork for HRM professionals. Turnover requires people processing from entry (recruiting, selecting, orienting, training) to exit (exit interviews, computation and curtailment of benefits).

While turnover is generally thought of in negative terms, it can have a number of benefits, among them performance gains (if poor performers are replaced by better workers); cost savings (if new hires are paid less than departing employees); and increased opportunity for upward mobility (if turnover occurs at higher levels in the organization). Finally, turnover can be used to facilitate organizational change requiring reallocation of human resources. Units and departments of decreasing importance can be allowed to shrink by attrition, while new personnel, if any, are assigned to areas of growing importance.

Voluntary turnover is more likely to occur when levels of employment are high. It is also more likely among young workers, blue-collar workers, workers with short tenure, workers with low job satisfaction, and workers with low organizational commitment. Turnover tends to be higher in low-paying jobs, jobs that are routine and repetitious, and jobs that are low in autonomy and responsibility. It tends to be less likely in organizations with good communication systems, concerned and caring supervisors, employee participation in decision-making, and opportunities for upward mobility.[39]

There are a number of factors that influence individual turnover decisions, but job satisfaction and organizational commitment seem to play key roles. One model of voluntary employee turnover suggests that job expectations interact with organizational characteristics and experiences and job performance level to produce affective responses to the job.[40] Affective responses include both job satisfaction and organizational commitment. Job satisfaction is believed to result when job expectations are met, that is, when actual work experiences and aspects of organizational life conform more closely to held expectations. Organizational commitment is the degree to which an employee identifies with and is involved in a particular organization. It is characterized by a strong belief in and acceptance of the organization's goals

[39] James L. Price, *The Study of Turnover* (Ames, Ia.: Iowa State Press, 1977).

[40] R.M. Steers and R.T. Mowday, "Employee Turnover and Postdecision Accomodation Processes," in L.L. Cummings and B.H. Staw (eds.) *Research in Organizational Behavior* (Greenwich, Ct.: JAI Press, 1981).

and values; a willingness to exert considerable effort on behalf of the organization; and a strong desire to maintain membership in the organization.[41] The implications of this model for turnover management are obvious: turnover can be reduced by efforts to increase job satisfaction and organizational commitment.

Turnover can also be reduced by human resource policies and programs that encourage employee retention. For example, retention is encouraged by competitive pay policies, promote-from-within policies, and policies which give employees a voice in work-related decisions. In some unusual cases, organizations seek to increase turnover. This can be done by withholding rewards and offering incentives to leave, such as early retirement programs.

Summary

This chapter has provided an overview of the "people environment" in which HRM professionals work to further organizational goals and objectives. The human asset was examined from the general perspective of the labour force at large and from a specific perspective focussing on individual behaviour, performance, and job satisfaction.

The labour force section of this chapter defined important terms and discussed major trends occurring in the Canadian labour force. Although a particular employer may not experience exactly the same trends and changes as are occurring at the national level, trends and changes in local labour markets can be analyzed using similar concepts. Knowledge and analysis of labour market conditions and trends are essential to effective recruiting and to retention of an adequate supply of qualified employees.

The second part of this chapter examined determinants of employee job performance and satisfaction, as well as ways to encourage appropriate and desired behaviours. High levels of performance and satisfaction are essential to organizational effectiveness and survival. The Porter and Lawler model of performance and satisfaction was used to explain the relationship of these two variables to each other and to other variables that affect them. Various HRM functions were discussed in terms of components of the Porter and Lawler model. The chapter concluded with a discussion of progressive discipline systems and two employee behaviours of major interest to organizations: absenteeism and turnover.

Project Ideas

1. In 1979, two economists, Butz and Ward, proposed a theory that the fertility rate (number of births per 1,000 women) increases in

[41] Richard T. Mowday, Lyman W. Porter, and Richard M. Steers, *Employee-Organization Linkages: The Psychology of Commitment, Absenteeism, and Turnover* (New York: Academic Press, 1982), p. 27.

recessionary times and decreases in economically good times. The rationale is that "it costs a woman more to take off to have children" in good economic times than in bad.

This theory runs counter to prior experience; the fertility rate declined during the Depression and rose during the prosperous 1960s. Discuss (in class or in a short paper) why this recent theory might be accurate today but inaccurate for earlier years. Also, specify what factors in the economy might affect the link between economic conditions and fertility rates. How does this theory, assuming it has some validity, affect the supply of employees to organizations?

2. Business consultants have often heard a problem employee described in terms of a "personality conflict," or "personality problem." The client often says, "I've tried everything with Jim (or Jane) and nothing seems to work." Such personality problems are usually "resolved" in one of two ways—the organization tolerates a person who is, at least sometimes, an ineffective employee, or the boss finally musters the courage to terminate the employee.

   Try to recall one or two "problem personalities" you have known or worked with. Exactly why were they regarded as problems? What did others do to try to change them? What do you think should have been done?

3. Discuss the Porter and Lawler model of job performance and satisfaction in terms of your personal work experience. Try to recall an example of how each element in the model (abilities, skills, knowledge; effort; role perceptions; and job satisfaction) affected your job performance or work behaviour. How was the level of effort you expended influenced by the value you assigned to the reward and by your perceived probability of receiving that reward? Were you pleased or displeased with the rewards you received for performance? What factors determined whether or not you perceived a reward as equitable or inequitable? Did satisfaction with previous rewards affect your subsequent performance? Be specific in your examples and with respect to the Porter and Lawler model.

Cases

Case 2.1: Excelling at IBM

IBM has been called the world's most profitable industrial company, collecting 40 per cent of the revenue and 70 per cent of the profit from the lucrative business machine industry.* Behind the company's phenomenal success is a simple business philosophy espous-

*D. Kneale, "Working at IBM: Intense Loyalty in a Rigid Culture," *Wall Street Journal*, April 7, 1986.

ing exceptional service, superior performance, and respect for the individual.

Most of IBM's recruits for professional positions come straight from college. A rigorous and informative selection procedure, which does not oversell the company, allows both IBM and job applicant to determine the latter's suitability for a job at IBM. Once hired, nearly all professional recruits start at the same level, go through the same training programs, and work their way up the same step-by-step career path to senior positions. Most choose to spend their entire working lives at IBM.

IBM is a huge corporation (more than 400,000 employees), but work units are generally small, consisting of about nine or ten workers plus a manager who keeps in constant touch. New managers receive 80 hours of training emphasizing the values of service, performance, and individual contribution.

Employees know they must meet performance standards to be successful at IBM. Standards are spelled out in performance plans which specify goals or quotas to be met in the year ahead. Performance plans are given to employees during annual performance reviews. At this time also, the employee is measured and graded according to whether goals for the previous year were met.

Many employees must meet strict sales or production quotas; these are set either for individuals or for entire sales teams. Managers have quotas too and these are met when units under them meet their quotas. The quota system often sparks competition between employees, who may be publicly ranked as to output. On the other hand, a kind of team spirit often develops among those striving to meet team quotas.

Quotas for sales representatives are designed so that approximately 80 per cent of the reps can meet them. Still, it is a proud moment when coveted rewards are received. Depending upon level of performance (output), these may include large amounts of cash, elaborate recognition ceremonies, and generous pats on the back. One sales rep, for example, received a briefcase full of $1 bills (5,000 of them!), plus a check for $5,000 for making 203 per cent of his quota. Another sales rep was not so fortunate; she was fired after 22 years of service for failing to make her quota.

IBM has a 32-page code of business ethics that employees are expected to follow. For example, managers are not to treat their subordinates too harshly or be overly zealous in dealing with the competition. Those who violate these or other corporate norms are likely to find themselves out of a job or assigned to the "penalty box."

According to *Fortune* magazine, "The penalty box (is) typically a fairly meaningless job at the same level, sometimes in a less desirable location . . . To the outsider, penalty box assignments look like just another job rotation, but insiders know that the benched manager is out of the game temporarily. The penalty box provides a place to hold a manager while the mistakes he's made and the hard feelings they've engendered are gradually forgotten. The mechanism lends substance to the belief, widespread among IBM employees, that the company won't fire anyone capriciously (without good reason). The penalty box's existence says, in effect, that in the career of strong, effective managers there are times when one steps on toes. The penalty box lets someone who has stepped too hard contemplate his error and return to play another day.**

Questions:

1. What methods does IBM use to ensure and/or encourage desirable performance from its employees?
2. Discuss IBM's policies in terms of the Porter and Lawler model. How does each contribute to employee performance and satisfaction as portrayed in the model?
3. What do you think of the idea of a penalty box? How do you think employees like the idea? Do you think it is a constructive form of discipline? Why?

**R. Pascale, "Fitting New Employees into the Company Culture," *Fortune*, May 28, 1984, pp. 28–43.

Case 2.2: Turnover and the Turnaround King

In 1974, William Mulholland became Chief Executive Officer (CEO) of an ailing Bank of Montreal (B of M). Seven years later, he'd nursed the patient back to health and come to be known as "the turnaround king." Under Mulholland's hard-nosed leadership, B of M became a leader and innovator in the field of computer operations. B of M also became an important player in the international banking arena, with one-third its 1985 assets of $76.5 billion outside Canada.

Unforturnately, B of M's road to financial success was cluttered with bodies of fallen executives. Dissatisfied, displaced, or otherwise terminated, 36 executive officers exited the bank during a recent two-year period (1983–1984), giving B of M the distinction of having the highest executive turnover rate among Canada's Big Five Banks. (Other banks in the Big Five are Royal, Toronto-Dominion, Nova Scotia, and the Canadian Imperial Bank of Commerce.) Some of those who left were long-time employees of the bank. For example, vice-chairman Hart MacDougall resigned after 30 years' service. Many leavers now hold positions at competing Canadian banks.

Mulholland sees high turnover among his executive ranks as a natural result of his 1983 reorganization scheme, the "Domestic Development Program," which separated commercial and retail banking. The reorganization created 98 commercial banking units for business clientele, while converting 1,164 branch offices into retail banking centres for personal service customers. In the process, as many as 18,000 jobs were redefined. According to Mulholland, the streamlining of bank operations meant there were simply no jobs for some people. And restructuring provided an opportunity to weed out "poor performers." Many of these were offered generous early retirement packages in exchange for leaving the bank.

During restructuring, morale of employees was low and corporate performance suffered. William Harker, an executive vice-president who resigned in late 1984, says anxiety about job loss contributed to low morale. Many were left to wonder where they might fit in, if at all, when restructuring was complete. Some employees even questioned the bank's integrity, suggesting that performance standards had been raised in order to justify firing certain employees who were previously deemed competent.

While most executives who left voluntarily contend their resignations were motivated by "better jobs elsewhere," *Canadian Business* magazine blames high executive turnover at B of M on Mulholland's style and his demands. Mulholland is described as "a tough and demanding boss," one who "will continue to demand high performance even to the point of causing more departures."[†] Quick to criticize, but slow to congratulate, the CEO has been known to explode in anger, calling executives names and subjecting them to public humiliation. Mulholland often chooses not to respond to proposals and suggestions put to him by senior colleagues. He typically keeps people waiting (without apology) and has a tendency in his presentation to confuse employees regarding what is expected of them. Still, Mulholland sees himself as good at handling people.

Despite the bank's high turnover, ex-vice chairman Hart MacDougall states: "I can't think of any (who left) who weren't replaceable—and perhaps by even better people—or that it didn't suit the organization to have them leave.[††] Along the same lines, analyst Gerald Braun notes that sometimes a cleansing of the work force is necessary and desirable. However, even he concedes it would be "ridiculous" for the present high rate of departures to continue.

Questions:

1. This case suggests a variety of reasons for turnover. What are they?
2. What in your opinion is the most likely cause of voluntary turnover among executives at the bank? Support your position.
3. Do you think CEO Mulholland perceives high executive turnover at the bank as a problem? Why or why not?
4. How much control do you think B of M has over turnover? Does it have more control over some types of turnover than others? What kinds of human resource policies might be used to control turnover?
5. What are some negative aspects of turnover suggested by this case? What are some positive aspects? Can you think of any others (either positive or negative)?

[†] R. McQueen, "Yesterday's Savior," *Canadian Business*, February 1985, pp. 49–51; 171–73.

[††] Ibid.

3

The Legal Environment

The environment in which HRM professionals work to acquire, develop, and maintain a qualified work force—the human assets of an organization—is governed by a complete network of laws and regulations. For example:

1. No employer in Canada may discriminate, in hiring or in terms and conditions of employment, on the basis of race, religion, ethnic or national origin, sex, or marital status.
2. Most jurisdictions prohibit discrimination on the basis of age, but the meaning of "age" varies; it is 45 to 65 in British Columbia, 19 and over in New Brunswick, unqualified in Manitoba and the federal jurisdiction, and so on.
3. All jurisdictions have minimum wage provisions, but the rates change frequently and vary among provinces. Some provinces exempt certain types or classes of workers of set lower rates for them.
4. All employers are prohibited from paying different wages to male and female employees who perform the same or similar work. In the federal jurisdiction, Quebec, and Manitoba, however, the requirement is equal pay for work of equal value—a subtle distinction whose legal implications are not yet entirely clear but could have far-reaching consequences.
5. Various aspects of work time—maximum hours per day and per week, rest days, annual vacations and holidays—are legislated. So are the conditions under which minors may be employed. The details vary considerably from jurisdiction to jurisdiction.

6. Employers are required to give notice to individual workers and to groups of workers whose employment is to be terminated. The amount of notice differs not only among jurisdictions but with the number of employees being laid off.
7. A healthy and safe workplace must be provided for employees.
8. Employers must abide by regulations on union-management relations, including the process of unionization and collective bargaining.
9. Employers, as well as employees, are required to make contributions to Unemployment Insurance and to the Canada (or Quebec) Pension Plan.
10. Employers are required to pay into workers' compensation programs; the rates depend on the type of industry.

These laws and regulations represent only a sampling of the legislation that affects administration of HRM functions and activities of HRM professionals.

To a great extent, government regulations shape human resource policies and pose constraints on HRM practices. Compliance with the law requires that certain procedures be performed in certain ways and not in others. For example, human rights acts prohibit recruiting for jobs in such a way as to lead to potential discrimination. Advertisements and application forms cannot refer to such things as race, religion, or sex.

Government regulation also creates considerable paperwork because it requires maintaining specific records. Even if a company's policies and practices are in compliance with the law, the employer must have data available and be ready to invest time and money answering any charges of discrimination or failure to meet required employment standards. And a multitude of forms must be filed relating to the Canada (or Quebec) Pension Plan, unemployment insurance, and so on.

Plaintive remarks about government regulation can probably be heard among HRM professionals in every industrialized country today. Canada, however, has a special problem because its labour-related laws are set by 13 different jurisdictions—all ten provinces, both territories, and the federal government. In fact, Canadian employment law is often called a legal jungle because of the resulting differences in regulations. Firms operating in different provinces are subject to different regulations, and these differences show up whenever an employee is transferred from one province to another. For example, in Ontario an employee must receive two weeks of vacation with pay after one year of employment, but in Saskatchewan it is three weeks. If an employee is transferred after one year of employment in Ontario, does he or she receive two weeks or three weeks of vacation? (The answer is two weeks until a full year has been completed in Saskatchewan.)

Rather than attempt to cover the full range of employment-related legislation in Canada, this chapter concentrates on those laws which guarantee what are termed human rights and on those which establish standards for many aspects of the employment relationship. Both types of laws are subject to almost constant change, both from the enactment of new regulations and from court or board decisions on the interpretation of existing regulations. The wise HRM professional keeps up-to-date on legislation and interpretation pertinent to his or her area. (Other legislation which applies specifically to benefits, health and safety, and labour relations is discussed in Chapters 13, 14, and 15.)

Legislation and Jurisdiction

Canada's present labour laws evolved under the Constitution Act 1867 (formerly known as the British North America Act) under which both the Parliament of Canada and the provincial legislatures have the power to enact labour laws. Judicial interpretation of Sections 91 and 92 have given major jurisdiction to the provinces, with federal authority limited to a narrow field. In practice, federal labour and employment laws now cover less than 10 per cent of the Canadian labour force: those persons who work for interprovincial and international railways; highway transport, telephone, telegraph, and cable systems; pipelines; ferries, tunnels, bridges, and shipping; radio and television broadcasting (including cablevision); air transport and airports; banks; grain elevators; flour and feed mills; and certain Crown corporations.

Each of the ten provinces and two territories has separate human rights and labour standards laws and separate commissions (and courts) to enforce them. An establishment is deemed to be under only one jurisdiction; in cases of uncertainty as to what that jurisdiction is, legal counsels within the pertinent commissions decide the issue. However, a firm with several establishments may operate in a number of different provinces. Exhibit 3.1 presents selected legislation relating to human rights and employment standards in Canada.

Given 13 jurisdictions, the variation in laws is great, not to mention the differences in regulations and interpretations. Keeping informed is important to HRM professionals, particularly those who work for organizations which have plants or offices in several provinces.

Added to this already complex situation is the federal Constitution Act 1982, which contains a Canadian Charter of Rights and Freedoms. The Charter's section on equality rights is designed to provide individuals protection against discrimination. However, section 15(2) permits affirmative action which has as its object " . . . the amelioration of conditions of disadvantaged individuals or groups including those that are disadvantaged because of race, national or ethnic origin, colour, religion, sex, age or mental or physical disability." The provincial legislatures have the right to opt out of some of the equality rights clauses, and some of the laws are being tested in the courts by some provinces and by groups and individuals. Two cases in point are the issues of mandatory retirement and discrimination arising from *bona fide* work rules. Since changes are continually occurring in the interpretation of the Charter as it applies to human rights and employment

EXHIBIT 3.1

Selected legislation relating to human rights and employment standards in Canada, 1986

Jurisdiction	*Human rights*	*Employment standards*
Federal	Canadian Human Rights Act Employment Equity Act	Canada Labour Code. Fair Wages and Hours of Labour Act. Holidays Act. Wages Liability Act.
Alberta	Individual's Rights Protection Act	Employment Standards Act.
British Columbia	Human Rights Act	Employment Standards Act. Public Construction Fair Wages Act.
Manitoba	Human Rights Act Pay Equity Act	Employment Standards Act. Construction Industry Wages Act. Vacations with Pay Act. Wages Recovery Act.
New Brunswick	Human Rights Code	Employment Standards Act.
Newfoundland	Human Rights Code	Labour Standards Act.
Nova Scotia	Human Rights Act	Labour Standards Code.
Ontario	Human Rights Code	Employment Standards Act. One Day's Rest in Seven Act.
Prince Edward Island	Human Rights Act	Labour Act. Minimum Age of Employment Act.
Quebec	Charter of Human Rights and Freedoms	Labour Standards Act. National Holiday Act.
Saskatchewan	Human Rights Code	Labour Standards Act. Wages Recovery Act.
Northwest Territories	Fair Practices Act	Labour Standards Act. Wages Recovery Act.
Yukon Territory	Fair Practices Act	Employment Standards Act.

SOURCES: Labour Canada, *Labour Standards in Canada*, 1986 edition (Hull, Que.: Minister of Supply and Services, 1986); *Canadian Labour Law Reporter* (Don Mills, Ont.: CCH Canadian Limited, 1986); Don Wood and Pradeep Kumar, *The Current Industrial Relations Scene in Canada, 1981* (Kingston, Ont.: Industrial Relations Centre, Queen's University, 1981).

standards, HRM professionals should remain alert to developments![1]

We will first examine the area of human rights, then turn to a discussion of employment standards.

Human Rights: Concepts and Prohibitions

Human rights legislation is intended, in the words of the Canadian Human Rights Act, to give effect to the principle that "every individual should have an equal opportunity with other individuals to make for himself or herself the life that he or she is able and wishes to have, consistent with his or her duties and obligations as a member of society."[2] Insofar as employment is concerned, the purpose of human rights legislation is to prevent people from being treated differently—that is, discriminated against—because of their race, religion, sex, marital status, and so on when it comes to decisions about hiring, pay, and promotion. Rather, these decisions should be made on the basis of individual qualifications.

The Abella Commission identified the fundamental issue of *systemic discrimination.* Systemic discrimination identifies discrimination in the workplace in terms of the impact of employment practices on the employment opportunities of designated group members. The impact, rather than the intention behind behaviour or employment practices is what defines systemic discrimination.[3] Bill C-62, the federal government's Employment Equity Act of 1986, is designed to address systemic discrimination as it affects women, visible minorities, native people, and the handicapped.

A related concept in human rights in employment is *indirect discrimination.* Indirect discrimination occurs in the workplace when an employer has no malice or intention to discriminate but acts in such a way as to deny employment or advancement on grounds that are, in fact, discriminatory. For example, a department store required all employees to work Friday evenings and Saturdays on a rotation basis. Consequently it terminated the employment of an employee who

[1] For ongoing developments in legislation and practice in this field, see *The Current Industrial Relations Scene in Canada* (Kingston, Ont.: Industrial Relations Centre, Queen's University, annual); and *The Employment Law Report* (Toronto: Concord Publishing, monthly). In addition, some aspects of human rights and employment standards are discussed in connection with labour-management grievance arbitration cases. See *Canadian Industrial Relations and Personnel Developments* (Don Mills, Ont.: CCH Canadian Limited, weekly); *Labour Arbitration News* (Toronto: LAN Publications, monthly); CLV Reports (Toronto: Canada Labour Views Company, weekly); D.J.M. Brown and D.M. Beatty, *Canadian Labour Arbitration*, second edition (Agincourt, Ont.: Canada Law Book, 1984); and *The Canadian Labour Law Reporter* (Don Mills, Ont., semimonthly). See also John G. Kelly, *Human Resource Management and the Human Rights Process* (Don Mills, Ont: CCH Canadian Limited, 1985).

[2] Canadian Human Rights Commission, *The Canadian Human Rights Act: A Guide* (Ottawa, March 1984), p. 1.

[3] Judge Rosalie Silberman Abella, Commissioner, *Report of the Commission on Equality in Employment*, (Ottawa: Minister of Supply and Services Canada, 1984), p. 193.

refused to work on Friday evenings and Saturdays because her religion, Seventh-Day Adventist, required strict observance of the Sabbath from sundown Friday to sundown Saturday.

The Supreme Court of Canada, in a unanimous judgement, found that the woman was discriminated against because of creed. The Court held that it is not necessary to prove that discrimination was intentional to find that a violation of human rights legislation has occurred; an employment rule, neutral on its face and honestly made, can have discriminatory effects. Therefore, it is the *result* or the *effect* of an act which is important in determining whether discrimination has occurred.

The Court also held that, where an employment rule has a discriminatory effect, an employer has a duty to take reasonable steps to accommodate the employee unless accommodation creates an undue hardship for the employer. In this case, the employment rule that all employees must work Friday evenings and Saturdays on a rotation basis had a discriminatory effect because of the woman's religion. The employer did not show that accommodating the employee would have created an undue hardship. The Court found that the onus of proving that accommodation will result in undue hardship is on the employer, since the information is in the employer's possession and the employee is not likely to be able to prove that there is no undue hardship. The firm was ordered to pay compensation for wages lost due to discrimination.[4]

The possibility of such "innocent" discrimination means HRM professionals and their employees must be increasingly careful about their advertising, interviewing, and employment practices. To protect themselves from challenge, Harish Jain, an expert at McMaster University, suggests: (1) establishing entry and training requirements that are truly prerequisite to the performance of a job, and (2) conducting structured interviews in which applicants are asked only questions of direct relevance to the job.[5]

An increasingly-recognized type of human rights violation is sexual harassment at work. Sexual harassment includes situations where submission to or rejection of an unsolicited sexual advance is used as a basis for employment or advancement. It also includes situations where physical or verbal conduct that emphasizes the sex or sexual orientation of the individual creates a hostile or offensive working environment. Based on a survey of 2,000 people in 1983, the Canadian Human Rights Commission found that 1.2 million women and 300,000 men believed they had been sexually harassed at work. A study by Professors Harish Jain and P. Andiappan found that unions, like employers, are often guilty of ignoring or resisting action on the issue of sexual harassment.[6] At the same time, many unions, especially those

[4] *Ontario Human Rights Commission and Theresa O'Malley (Vincent) v. Simpsons-Sears Limited*, December 17, 1985. Reported in *Canadian Human Rights Reporter*, vol. 7, May/June, 1986.

[5] Marilyn Goneau, "Discrimination Is Still Part of the Workplace," *The Financial Post*, November 21, 1981.

[6] Harish Jain and P. Andiappan, "Sexual Harassment in Employment in Canada: Issues and Policies," *Industrial Relations/Relations Industrielles*, vol. 41, no. 4 (1986), pp. 758–76

with large numbers of female members, are writing clauses into collective agreements that specifically deal with sexual harassment and commit the employer to a work environment free of this problem. These same unions have undertaken programs to educate their members about the demeaning and offensive nature of sexual harassment and how to deal with it. Human rights commissions and arbitrators have equated sexual harassment with discrimination and the labour codes of Newfoundland, Ontario, Quebec, and the federal government specifically prohibit sexual harassment. In addition, the Quebec Workers' Compensation Board has ruled that sexual harassment that leads to extreme stress, depression, and physical symptoms is an appropriate cause for compensation as a work-related injury.[7]

Prohibitions

Every province, territory, and the federal government has a human rights act or code (see Exhibit 3.1). These acts usually prohibit discrimination in occupancy and property sales, public accommodations, publications, signs, and contracts, as well as in employment and employment-related areas. The discussion here, however, deals only with the aspects that relate to employment practices.

All jurisdictions in Canada have enacted prohibitions against discrimination in employment practices. The wording varies from one jurisdiction to another, but all say that an employer is prohibited from various types of discrimination in hiring, as well as in the terms and conditions of employment and matters relating to promotion and transfer. In most cases, the term "employer" includes not only individual employers but also employers' organizations, employment agencies, and others who act on behalf of employers; the legislation usually also covers unions, employee associations, and professional associations. Labour relations acts, provincial and federal, also forbid discrimination by employers and unions (see Chapter 15).

Each of Canada's 13 jurisdictions forbids a slightly different set of discriminatory acts. Moreover, since enforcement and interpretation are the preserves of commissions and courts within each jurisdiction, there are considerable differences in actual practice.

Exhibit 3.2 summarizes the grounds on which each jurisdiction's human rights act specifically prohibited discrimination in 1986. Some grounds are common to all the acts: race, creed or religion, colour, national or ethnic origin (phrased as "ancestry" by some provinces), marital status, and sex. Several jurisdictions also specify discrimination because of nationality, political belief, or physical handicap. A few add other grounds, varying from having a pardoned criminal conviction to social origin to sexual orientation.

A common prohibition is discrimination because of age, although, as the table shows, there is much variety in the ages to which it applies. Notice that the Manitoba and federal acts leave the prohibition un-

[7] Wilfred List, "Sexual Harassment: It's spreading but is the boss liable?", *The Globe and Mail* (Toronto), March 16, 1987.

qualified, although, in practice, minimum-age-of-employment and school-leaving ages set some bottom limits.

The types of discrimination listed in Exhibit 3.2 should not be regarded as all that is prohibited in any jurisdiction. Human rights laws and their interpretation undergo frequent change, especially with the judicial interpretation of the Charter of Rights. And Manitoba and British Columbia recently added "reasonable cause" clauses, which may be a trend of the future. In essence, *reasonable cause clauses* demand that employers be able to show that their actions in regard to hiring, promotion, and termination are based on reasonable, job-related requirements, not on discriminatory causes.

EXHIBIT 3.2

Prohibited grounds of discrimination in employment

Jurisdiction	*Fed*	*BC*	*Albt*	*Sask*	*Man*	*Ont*	*Que*	*NB*	*PEI*	*NS*	*Nfld*	*NWT*	*Yukon*
Race	●	●	●	●	●	●	●	●	●	●	●	●	●
National or ethnic origin[1]	●				●	●	●	●	●	●	●		●
Ancestry		●	●	●		●		●				●	●
Nationality or citizenship				●	●	●						●	
Place of origin		●	●	●		●		●				●	
Colour	●	●	●	●	●	●	●	●	●	●	●	●	●
Religion	●	●	●	●	●		●	●	●	●	●		●
Creed[2]			●	●		●			●	●	●	●	●
Age	●	● (45-65)	●	● (18-65)	●	● (18-65)	●	● (19+)	●	● (40-65)	● (19-65)	●	
Sex	●	●	●	●	●	●	●	●	●	●	●	●	●
Pregnancy or childbirth	●			●			●						
Marital status[3]	●	●	●	●	●	●	●	●	●	●	●	●	●
Family status[3]	●				●	●	●					●	
Pardoned offence	●						●					●	
Record of criminal conviction		●				●	●						
Physical handicap or disability	●	●	●	●	●	●	●	●	●	●	●	●	
Mental handicap or disability	●	●			●	●	●	●	●	●	●	●	

Dependence on alcohol or drug	●											
Place of residence												●
Political belief		●			●		●		●		●	
Assignment, attachment or seizure of pay[4]											●	
Source of income					●					●		
Social condition[4]							●					
Language							●					
Social origin[4]							●				●	
Sexual orientation[5]							●					●
Harassment[5]	●					●	●				●	

[1] New Brunswick includes only "national origin."
[2] Creed usually means religious beliefs.
[3] Quebec uses the term "civil status."
[4] In Quebec's charter, "social condition" includes assignment, attachment, or seizure of pay and social origin.
[5] The federal, Ontario, and Quebec statutes ban harassment on all proscribed grounds. Ontario and Nova Scotia also ban sexual solicitation.

This chart is for quick reference only. For interpretation or further details, call the appropriate commission.

SOURCES: *Canadian Labour Law Reports* (Don Mills, Ontario: CCH Canadian Ltd., June 1986); *Dossier 85-2* (Ottawa: Canadian Human Rights Commission, March 1985).

Moreover, since the commissions and courts now accept the argument of indirect or systemic discrimination, some common practices and preconceptions have come under scrutiny. For example, commissions have ruled against height and weight requirements for a police constable and for a labourer.

All the jurisdictions' acts provide for some exceptions to the prohibitions, but here, too, there are differences. Most jurisdictions make exceptions where there is a bona fide qualification for employment or for an occupation. A *bona fide qualification* is one which is absolutely necessary to the performance of a job. For example, the Supreme Court of Canada has ruled that wearing a hard hat is a bona fide occupational requirement and that there is therefore no duty to accommodate persons of the Sikh religion who are required to wear a turban and no other head covering. While the Court repeated its finding in *O'Malley v. Simpsons-Sears Ltd.* that it is not necessary to show an intention to discriminate in order for there to be a violation of human rights legislation, the hard hat rule is allowed because it is a bona fide occupational requirement.[8] Another common exception to the prohibitions

[8] *K.S. Bhinder and the Canadian Human Rights Commission v. The Canadian National Railway Company*, December 17, 1985.

relates to age and the operation of a bona fide insurance or pension plan. Some pension plans have a minimum time period for contributions before retirement.

In addition to regulating hiring, promotion, and termination, human rights acts prohibit discrimination in connection with application forms, advertisements, and enquiries about employment. In general, the areas of specific prohibition are the same as those for hiring and advancement. Some provinces do, however, permit information on sex, age, and marital status to be collected on an application form, where the information will be used to combat the effects of past discrimination.

Exhibit 3.3 gives the Canadian Human Rights Commission's guide to screening and selection in employment. The guide's extensiveness is an indication of the care with which employers and HRM professionals must seek job-related information so as not to open themselves to challenges of discrimination.

Enforcement

Each jurisdiction's human rights provisions are enforced through a human rights commission.[9] All the acts use a complaint process whereby any person who believes he or she has been discriminated against files a complaint; the commission then investigates and takes action if it finds the complaint justified. In Alberta, Nova Scotia, Ontario, Manitoba, and the federal jurisdiction, the commission may itself initiate complaints.

Individuals who launch complaints are legally protected against reprisals. For example, the Human Rights Code of British Columbia states:

> No person shall evict, discharge, suspend, expel, intimidate, coerce, impose any pecuniary or other penalty upon, or otherwise discriminate against, any person because that person complains, gives evidence, or otherwise assists in respect of the initiation of a complaint or other proceeding under the act.[10]

In all jurisdictions except Quebec, the commission can make orders requiring compliance which it is an offence to violate. Most provinces also provide for appeal to the provincial supreme court. Orders of a federal human rights tribunal may be made on order of the Federal Court of Canada and are enforceable in the same manner as an order of that court.

Human rights commissions attempt, however, to settle complaints by conciliation and persuasion. Harish Jain explained:

> The bulk of a typical human rights commission's workload consists of cases that do not go before a board of inquiry. The data on conciliation cases and cases under investigation are confidential. A board of inquiry is used only when all efforts at settlement fail.[11]

[9] For details of the enforcement procedure for each jurisdiction, see Labour Canada, *Human Rights*, p. 22.

[10] Ibid., p. 39.

[11] Goneau.

EXHIBIT 3.3

A guide to screening and selection in employment

Subject	*Don't Ask*	*May Ask*	*Comment*
Name	about name change whether it was changed by court order, marriage, or other reason maiden name Christian name		if needed for a reference, to check on previously held jobs or on educational credentials, ask after selection
Address	for addresses outside Canada	ask place and duration of current or recent addresses	
Age	for birth certificates, baptismal records, or about age in general age or birthdate	ask applicants if they have reached age (minimum or maximum) for work as defined by law	if precise age required for benefits plans or other legitimate purposes it can be determined after selection
Sex	Mr/Mrs/Miss/Ms males or females to fill in different or coded applications if male or female on applications about pregnancy, childbirth or child care arrangements includes asking if birth control is used or child bearing plans	can ask applicant if the attendance requirements or minimum service commitment can be met	any applicants can be addressed during interviews or in correspondence without using courtesy titles such as Mr/Mrs/Miss
Marital Status	whether applicant is single, married, divorced, engaged, separated, widowed or living common-law whether an applicant's spouse is subject to transfer about spouse's employment	ask whether there are any known circumstances that might prevent completion of a minimum service commitment, for example	if transfer or travel is part of the job, the applicant can be asked if this would cause a problem information on dependents for benefits can be determined after selection

Subject	*Don't Ask*	*May Ask*	*Comment*
Family Status	number of children or dependents about arrangements for child care	if the employer has a policy against the hiring of close relatives, an applicant can be asked about kinship to other employees	contacts for emergencies and/or details on dependents can be determined after selection
National or Ethnic Origin	about birthplace, nationality of ancestors, spouse or other relatives whether born in Canada if naturalized or landed immigrants for proof of citizenship	since those who are entitled to work in Canada must be citizens, landed immigrants or holders of valid work permits, applicants can be asked if they are legally entitled to work in Canada	documentation of eligibility to work (ie. papers, visas, etc.) can be requested after selection
Military Service	about military service in other countries	inquiry about Canadian military service where employment preference is given to veterans, by law	
Language	mother tongue where language skills obtained	ask if applicant understands, reads, writes or speaks languages which are required for job	testing or scoring applicants for language proficiency is not permitted unless fluency is job-related
Race or Colour	any inquiry which indicates race or colour, including colour of eyes, skin or hair colour		information required for security clearances or similar purposes can be obtained after selection
Photographs	for photo to be attached to applications or sent to interviewer before interview		photos for security passes or company files can be taken after selection
Religion	about religious affiliation, church membership, frequency of church attendance		employers are to reasonably accommodate religious needs of workers
	if applicant will work a specific religious holiday	explain the required work shifts, asking if such a schedule poses problems for applicant	
	for references from clergy or religious leader		

Subject	*Don't Ask*	*May Ask*	*Comment*
Height and Weight			no inquiry unless there is evidence that they are bona fide occupational requirements
Disability	for listing of all disabilities, limitations or health problems whether applicant drinks or uses drugs whether applicant has ever received psychiatric care or been hospitalized for emotional problems	ask if applicant has any condition that could affect ability to do the job ask if the applicant has any condition which should be considered in selection	a disability is only relevant to job ability if it: —threatens the safety or property of others —prevents the applicant from safe and adequate job performance even if reasonable efforts were made to accommodate the disability
Medical Information	if currently under physician's care name of family doctor if receiving counselling or therapy		medical exams should be preferably conducted after selection and only if an employee's condition is related to the job duties. Offers of employment can be made conditional on successful completion of a medical
Affiliations	for list of club or organizational memberships	membership in professional associations or occupational groups can be asked if a job requirement	applicants can decline to list any affiliation that might indicate a prohibited ground
Pardoned Conviction	whether an applicant has ever been convicted if an applicant has ever been arrested does applicant have a criminal record	if bonding is a job requirement ask if applicant is eligible	inquiries about criminal record-virgule convictions—even those which have been pardoned—are discouraged unless related to job duties

Subject	Don't Ask	May Ask	Comment
References			The same restrictions that apply to questions asked of applicants apply when asking for employment references

SOURCE: Canadian Human Rights Commission, November 1984 (Ottawa: Minister of Supply and Services Canada, 1985).

Affirmative Action and Employment Equity

Three closely related concepts dealing with human rights in employment are affirmative action, equal employment opportunity and employment equity. The term affirmative action originated in the United States in 1965, when Executive Order 11246 not only forbade discrimination in employment but required employers with federal contracts to "take affirmative action to ensure that applicants are employed, and that employees are treated during employment, without regard to their race, creed, color or national origin." Subsequent amendments and other legislation extended the categories to include sex and handicaps. The courts and agencies responsible for enforcement have frequently demanded extensive record-keeping, labour market surveys, and performance reviews to prove compliance.

Thus, *affirmative action* has come to mean taking positive action to recruit, hire, and advance women and members of minority groups in jobs in which they were previously under-represented or underutilized in an organization. In essence, affirmative action requires going out of one's way to recruit qualified persons from groups that have previously been discriminated against, even unintentionally. Employers must, however, stop short of providing preferential treatment to women and minority group members since showing preference for such persons is *reverse discrimination*, which obviously subverts human rights legislation. The American courts have begun an attempt to draw the fine line between affirmative action and reverse discrimination.[12]

[12] In the Bakke case, the U.S. Supreme Court held that the University of California could not "reserve" a certain number of places in the freshman class for minorities, when this action resulted in the exclusion of a better-qualified person from the majority group. In *Weber v. Kaiser Aluminum*, however, it held that Kaiser could admit one black for every white to an apprenticeship program, regardless of seniority, because the system was designed to correct past discrimination against blacks in apprenticeship programs and the system resulted from a negotiated agreement between Kaiser and the United Steel Workers. (See Bakke v. Regents of the University of California, *17 Fair Employment Practices Cases*, 1000; and Weber v. Kaiser Aluminum Company, *16 Fair Employment Practices Cases*, 1.

Recently, the U.S. Supreme court ruled that an employer may promote a woman over an arguably more qualified man to help get women into higher-ranking jobs. In this case, the Court upheld an affirmative action plan that was challenged by a man who was denied a promotion by the Santa Clara County Transportation Agency in California. In 1978, the agency had adopted a voluntary affirmative action plan that had a long-term goal of assigning 36 per cent of its jobs to women, minorities and the handicapped. Speaking for the court majority, Justice William Brennan said, "The agency plan requires women to compete with all other qualified applicants. No persons are automatically excluded from consideration; all are able to have their qualifications weighed against those of other applicants." The three dissenting justices said that the male worker was the victim of sex discrimination.[13]

The term *equal employment opportunity* (EEO) indicates fair access to all available jobs for all persons. On occasion, the term is used as a synonym for affirmative action, but in strict usage EEO does not require the establishment of plans to increase the employment of women, members of visible minorities, or the handicapped.

Affirmative action is voluntary in Canada and in recent years, both the public and private sectors have seen a number of voluntary programs, most of them aimed at the employment of women.[14] For example, Bell Canada includes in its human resource department six "equal employment opportunity co-ordinators" whose primary function is to let employees know that they can advance in the company, regardless of sex or ethnic group, if they have job-related qualifications. The Royal Bank has an extensive hiring program aimed at women and ethnic communities and employs an outside consultant to watch for bias in supervisors.[15] Canadian National Rail has also had a long-standing interest in equal employment opportunity for women. CN's experience is described in Exhibit 3.4.

Because programs such as the above have been the exception rather than the rule, the federal government established the Abella Commission in 1983 to examine the situation and make recommendations. The result was the Employment Equity Act of 1986.[16]

The Employment Equity Act is intended to correct the conditions of disadvantage in employment experienced by women, aboriginal peoples, persons with disabilities, and persons who, because of their race or colour, are in a visible minority in Canada. While the Act does not set specific quotas, its reporting procedures are designed to monitor and thereby encourage increased employment among these groups.

An employer under federal jurisdiction with 100 employees or more is required to prepare an annual plan specifying goals to be achieved in implementing equity, along with a timetable for the implementation

[13] "Affirmative action ruling said historic," *The Globe and Mail* (Toronto), March 26, 1987.

[14] Harish C. Jain, "Employment and Pay Discrimination in Canada," in John Anderson and Morley Gunderson, eds., *Union-Management Relations in Canada* (Don Mills, Ont.: Addison-Wesley, 1982), p. 515.

[15] Jain, "Employment and Pay Discrimination," p. 515.

[16] Judge Rosalie Silberman Abella, Commissioner, *Report of the Commission on Equality in Employment* (Ottawa: Minister of Supply and Services Canada, 1984).

EXHIBIT 3.4

Equal opportunity at Canadian National Rail

Equal employment opportunity for women has been a concern of Canadian National Rail (CN) for over a decade. Many of CN's entry-level, blue-collar jobs have traditionally been held by men. In the late 1970s, CN decided to encourage women to apply for some of these positions, including brakeman, yardman, signal helper, and coach cleaner. CN contacted Action Travail des Femmes of Montreal (ATC), an organization that helps place women in non-traditional jobs. Soon ATC began sending referrals to CN.

But CN did not hire many of ATC's clients, leading seven of the women to charge CN with discrimination in hiring. ATC itself charged CN with systematic discrimination against women in non-traditional jobs. Clients' complaints were settled, mostly in their favour, by the Canadian Human Rights Commission. ATC's charge of systematic discrimination was investigated and upheld in 1984 by a tribunal appointed by the Commission.

The tribunal instructed CN to change its discriminatory policies, including one policy that required strength tests for female applicants but not for males. The tribunal also imposed a hiring quota on CN: 25 per cent of its new hires for blue-collar jobs must be women. The quota would stand until CN's blue-collar work force totalled 13 per cent women, the nationwide average for women employed in blue-collar jobs. At the time of the ruling, fewer than 1 per cent of blue-collar jobs in CN's St. Lawrence region were held by women.

In late 1984, CN announced its Employment Equity Program, designed to remove barriers to equal opportunity for women in every division of the company. Each division was to develop a three-to-five year plan, targeting goals and specifying procedures to achieve them. Some divisions found they needed new methods of recruiting; others needed ways to identify qualified candidates for promotion from within. Some divisions saw a need for retraining in order to make women eligible for promotion.

In July 1985, a Federal Court of Appeal struck down the 25 per cent hiring quota imposed on CN, saying it was beyond the authority of the tribunal. According to Judge Hugessen, "The text (of the law) requires that the order look to the avoidance of future evil. It does not allow restitution for past wrongs." Other parts of the tribunal's ruling were allowed to stand.

SOURCE: Louise Piche, "Employment Equity: On Track at CN," *The Canadian Business Review*, Summer 1985, pp. 19–22; "Court Rejects Quota for CN Jobs," *The Globe and Mail* (Toronto), July 19, 1985.

of those goals. And beginning in 1988, every employer has to submit to the Minister of Employment and Immigration, statistics on the number of persons in designated groups by location of employment, occupational distribution, salary ranges, number hired, promoted, and terminated. This information will be available for public inspection and failure to comply will result in a fine not to exceed $50,000.

The federal government also has in place a program to increase the number of Francophones in the civil service, particularly in more senior positions. A record is kept of the number of Anglophones and Francophones in each department and attempts are made to maintain appropriate numbers. In addition, the federal government provides language training to enable unilingual civil servants to become bilingual.

Employment Standards Legislation

Employment standards legislation, also called labour standards legislation, covers a wide and continually changing range of subjects affecting the relationship between employers and employees. From the perspective of the HRM professional, the main provisions of employment are those dealing with statutory school-leaving age; minimum age for employment; minimum wages; equal pay; hours of work; rest days, vacations and holidays; termination of employment; maternity leave; and the recovery of unpaid wages. In employment standards, as in human rights, Canada has 13 jurisdictions. As might be expected, regulations vary widely from one jurisdiction to another, but all are concerned with providing standards of protection for employees. Exhibit 3.1 at the beginning of this chapter lists the pertinent laws in the country's 13 jurisdictions. This section is an overview of their major provisions, as of 1986, unless otherwise indicated. A complete summary of these provisions can be found in the latest issue of Labour Canada's publication *Labour Standards in Canada*.[17] The details are best examined in the various acts themselves or in the publications of CCH (Commerce Clearing House) Canadian Limited.

HRM professionals should remember that the agencies charged with administering employment standards are interested in voluntary compliance. Their staff members are generally helpful when asked about the rules.

Statutory School-Leaving Age

All the provinces and territories forbid the employment of a child of school age during school hours, unless the child is excused for some reason provided in the relevant school attendance act. School-leaving age is 16 in Alberta, Manitoba, Nova Scotia, Ontario, Saskatchewan, and the Yukon, and 15 in the other six jurisdictions. Work exemptions are provided for a variety of circumstances. In five provinces (Manitoba, New Brunswick, Newfoundland, Nova Scotia, Quebec), a child may be exempted temporarily from school attendance on the application of a parent or guardian, if his or her services are required for employment or farm or home duties. Alberta and Saskatchewan have provisions for work experience programs.

Minimum Age for Employment

The desire to establish minimum ages for employment was a goal of trade unions and social reformers in the 19th century. Developments were slow: factory legislation developed cautiously from the 1880s,

[17] Labour Canada, *Labour Standards in Canada* (Ottawa: Minister of Supply and Services, annual).

caught between the more generous impulses of the age and the employers' firm grip on legislatures and party finances. By 1888, children were banned from smaller factories in Ontario, and shopkeepers could not employ boys under 14 or girls under 16 for more than 12 hours a day or 74 hours a week. Quebec and Nova Scotia, then eventually the other provinces, followed this humanitarian lead at a cautious distance. Enforcement in all provinces lagged even more. At the turn of the century, Ontario critics noted that while Toronto employed three inspectors merely to uncover liquor offences, the entire province employed only three inspectors to enforce its Factory Act.[18]

Today the minimum age for employment varies so greatly, by province and by type of work, that employers and HRM professionals are well advised to investigate the regulations for each specific situation they face. For example, in most jurisdictions, a person must be 18 to work below ground in mines, but in Alberta it is 17 and in Nova Scotia it is 16 for metal mines but 18 1/2 for coal mines. Above ground, the standard minimum age is 16, as it is in factories, but a few jurisdictions permit certain kinds of work at 15 and forbid others, particularly heavy kinds, until 18.

Many jurisdictions permit younger youths to work outside school hours or on vacations in shops, hotels and restaurants and in such occupations as messenger, newspaper vendor, and shoe shiner. Many acts prohibit young people's working at night. For example, Alberta forbids the employment of persons under 15 between 9:00 P.M. and 6:00 A.M., while those between 15 and 18 can work from 9:00 P.M to midnight on retail premises selling food or beverages only in the continuous presence of someone 18 years of age or over.

Minimum Wage Rates

All jurisdictions set minimum wage rates, but, in addition to interprovincial differences, there are often special provisions for particular kinds of workers. And the rates are frequently adjusted upwards.

Generally, minimum wage provisions cover almost all workers—excepting only most farm labourers and, in some jurisdictions, domestic workers. A lower minimum rate is usually set for young workers, student trainees, and the handicapped and, in some provinces, for employees who serve alcoholic beverages (Manitoba, Ontario, Quebec) and for domestic workers (British Columbia, Newfoundland, Ontario, Quebec). Ontario provides a higher rate for construction workers.

The interprovincial differences in minimum rates can be sizeable. In June 1986, for example, there was more than a one-dollar difference between the country's highest minimum wage rate (Northwest Territories at $5.00 per hour) and the lowest (British Columbia at $3.65 per hour). Seven of the provinces required $4.00 per hour. Since the minimums change at different intervals in each province, the HRM profes-

[18] Desmond Morton with Terry Copp, *Working People: An Illustrated History of Canadian Labour* (Toronto: Deneau, 1984), p. 84.

sional should keep a table with the relevant rates and the dates of change, which can normally be obtained from the local employment standards branch of the department or ministry of labour.

Equal Pay for Men and Women

All jurisdictions prohibit an employer from paying different wages to male and female employees who perform the *same or similar work* under the same or similar conditions (usually in the same establishment) that requires similar skill, effort, or responsibility.

In the Greenacres Nursing Home case (1970) and the Riverdale Hospital Case (1973), the Ontario Court of Appeal ruled that job comparisons should be based on work actually performed rather than on formal job descriptions. In the latter case, the court also ruled that as long as some men do the same work as women, equal pay is justifiable for the whole occupation.[19]

The Quebec, Manitoba, and federal jurisdictions now require equal pay for *work of equal value*; the criterion applied to assessing the value of work performed by employees in the same establishment is a composite of the skill, effort, and responsibility required for performance and the conditions under which the work is performed.[20] In other words, the requirement is the comparison of dissimilar jobs in terms of their value to the employer.

To determine if employees are performing work of equal value, the skill and effort required in the performance of the work is considered to include any intellectual or physical skill and effort normally required in the performance of the work. The responsibility required is assessed by determining the extent to which the employer relies on the employee to perform the work, having regard for such considerations as the accountability of the employee for machines, finances, and other resources and for the work of other employees.

In 1985, a group of 140 women who were working or had worked for the federal government as home economists and physical therapists were given pay adjustments of up to $30,000 following an interim settlement reached between the federal government and the Professional Institute of the Public Service of Canada involving the principle of equal pay for work of equal value. The settlement, approved by the Canadian Human Rights Commission, held that the home economists and physical therapists, who were mostly women, should have been paid the same as agriculture and forestry employees who were mostly male. The total cost of the settlement was estimated at $2.3 million.[21]

The concept and implications of equal pay provisions are discussed further in Chapter 12.

[19] Jain, "Employment and Pay Discrimination," p. 512.
[20] Ibid., p. 511.
[21] *Canadian Industrial Relations and Personnel Developments*, No. 41 (October 9, 1985), pp. 822–823.

Hours of Work

Hours-of-work provisions relate both to the maximum number of hours of work permitted per day and per week and to the number of hours per day or week after which an overtime rate must be paid. Eight hours of work per day and 40 hours per week are the most common standards (the federal jurisdiction, British Columbia, Manitoba, Newfoundland, Saskatchewan, and the Yukon), but there are other combinations: Alberta, 8 and 44; New Brunswick, 9 and 48; Ontario, 8 and 48; the Northwest Territories, 8 and 44. Nova Scotia and Prince Edward Island have only a standard work week of 48, and Quebec 44 hours.

The accepted rate for overtime is 1.5 times the regular rate, but it comes into effect at different points in different jurisdictions and even after a different number of hours in the same province for different industries. For example, in Alberta overtime generally begins after 8 hours in a day and 44 in a week, but for ambulance drivers and cab drivers it starts after 10 hours in a day or 60 hours in a week. There are so many variations in the different jurisdictions that HRM professionals must consult the relevant employment standards branch.

They are also well advised to peruse the provisions themselves. Every jurisdiction permits exceptions to the general rules to allow for differences in production periods, seasonal variations, and customary standards and also provides for changes to accommodate special problems. (A common feature is the possibility of averaging hours over a number of weeks.) Familiarity with the regulations may suggest grounds on which the regulatory body may grant exemptions. It can also alert HRM officials to any need to obtain a permit beyond a stated maximum.

Weekly Rest Days

All jurisdictions require employers to provide at least one full day of rest each week, on Sunday wherever possible. Exceptions are allowed for farm workers, domestics, and various other categories of workers in different provinces. Special provisions are made for the accumulation of days of rest for workers in highway and railway construction, geophysical exploration, and oil-well drilling in Alberta, for bus operators and truck drivers in B.C., and for watchmen, janitors, and superintendents in Ontario.

Annual Vacations with Pay

Every jurisdiction except Saskatchewan requires two weeks of vacation with pay after one year of employment; in Saskatchewan, the figure is three weeks after one year. Many labour laws increase the amount of vacation after a stated number of years of service with the same employer.

The usual rate for vacation pay begins at 4 per cent of annual earnings (again, Saskatchewan is more generous with three fifty-seconds of annual earnings) and rises as an employee becomes entitled to more vacation. Pay must be given one to fourteen days before the vacation begins, depending on the jurisdiction.

Holidays

Only Prince Edward Island lacks legislation dealing with paid general holidays. The number varies from five in Newfoundland to nine in the federal jurisdiction. British Columbia, Saskatchewan, the Yukon and the Northwest Territories list New Year's Day, Good Friday, Labour Day, and Christmas Day; frequently added are Victoria Day, Dominion Day, Thanksgiving, Remembrance Day, and Boxing Day. Newfoundland has Memorial Day, while Quebec has la fête de Dollard des Ormeaux and la fête de St-Jean Baptiste. Other special provincial days are British Columbia Day, New Brunswick Day, Saskatchewan Day, and Discovery Day (Yukon). In all jurisdictions, employers must provide regular pay for holidays not worked and two to two and one-half times regular pay (or another day off with pay) for holidays worked. Most laws make special provision for work in continuous operation and other selected industries, such as construction.

Termination of Employment

In all jurisdictions except the Northwest Territories, an employer must give notice to most workers whose employment is to be terminated. The length of notice required depends on the number of persons involved and their length of employment, and varies from jurisdiction to jurisdiction. In the case of individual workers, it varies from one or two weeks after one month of employment to eight weeks after ten years. Many jurisdictions require longer notice for the layoff or termination of an entire group of employees; it may be eight, 12, or 16 weeks, depending on the number involved. In Manitoba, 18 weeks notice must be given for groups of more than 300 employees. The Minister of Labour may require the establishment of a joint employer-employee (or trade union) committee to develop an adjustment program.

Federally, severance pay is provided for employees with 12 months' service or more. Ontario has provisions for severance pay in the case of group terminations of 50 or more employees in a six-month period (one week's regular salary for each year of employment for employees with at least five years' service to a maximum of 26 weeks salary).

Maternity Protection

All jurisdictions except the Northwest Territories provide job security for women before and after childbirth. They are protected from dismissal because of pregnancy and are entitled to reinstatement after maternity leave without loss of seniority or benefits. Employers must give mothers leave (without pay), usually 17 to 18 weeks after one year's service. Women who are eligible for unemployment insurance benefits can receive them for up to 15 weeks of maternity leave.

Paternity and adoption leave are provided for in five provinces and the federal jurisdiction. Nova Scotia and Prince Edward Island provide five weeks for adoption leave (for a female employee), and Quebec two days. Saskatchewan provides for six weeks of paternity or adoption leave. In Manitoba a paternity leave of six weeks and adoption leave of 17 weeks are available.

The Recovery of Unpaid Wages

The various Labour Standards Acts provide mechanisms for the prompt recovery of unpaid wages, including salaries, pay, commission, and any compensation for labour or personal services. Inspectors or labour standards officers are usually empowered to inquire or investigate into situations where there is reason to believe that the law has been violated. They first endeavour to arrive at an amicable settlement with the parties. If they cannot, they are empowered to order the transgressors to "cease and desist" and to order that compensation be made to the victims.

Under the Canada Labour Code, an employer who does not provide mimimum standards is liable not only for the arrears of wages and other minimum amounts but also to a fine not exceeding $1,000 or to imprisonment for a term not exceeding one year or both. More severe sanctions exist for failure to observe the required notice of termination provisions.[22]

Summary

This chapter has discussed the concepts of human rights and employment standards. It has presented the major provisions of the laws in Canada's 13 jurisdictions, and suggested the need for the HRM professional to obtain detailed, current information on the areas relevant to his or her work. The impact of these laws will be felt throughout the rest of this book.

[22] Labour Canada, *Labour Standards in Canada*, 1986 edition, (Ottawa: Minister of Supply and Services Canada, 1986).

Project Ideas

1. Contact the nearest provincial and federal human rights commission offices and obtain material on the provincial and federal human rights codes. (The offices are listed in the government section of your telephone book.) Identify any major differences between the two jurisdictions in their approach to prohibiting discrimination on the grounds of sex, ethnic group, and age. What explanations can be offered in support of each?

2. Contact the nearest provincial and federal employment standards offices and obtain material on the provincial and federal employment standards acts. (The offices are listed in the government section of your telephone book, either under employment or labour standards or as a subheading under labour department.) Identify the major differences in the requirements for minimum wages, vacations, and maternity protection. What is the basis for the approaches?

3. Provide examples of sex discrimination, race discrimination, age discrimination, and discrimination against the handicapped based on your own experience, incidents reported in the newspapers, or hypothetical incidents. The examples should demonstrate how these forms of discrimination are similar and how they are different. In each case, be sure to include the criteria on which employment practices and decisions should be based.

Cases

Case 3.1: Is the Cook Guilty of Sexual Harassment?

After being subjected to unwanted kissing, embracing, and fondling by a cook, two waitresses in Manitoba eventually quit when their employer refused to intervene. A tribunal, set up under the province's Human Rights Act, found that the employer had condoned the action of the cook. The tribunal ordered the employer to pay $10,000 to the two waitresses. The employer appealed this decision and the Manitoba Court of Appeal ruled that unless liability is explicitly written into the law, employers are not responsible for acts of discrimination if there was no specific policy to discriminate. The federal Human Rights Act makes employers liable for sexual harassment committed by all employees unless the employer can prove that it exercised "all due diligence" to prevent it. The Ontario code similarly imposes a duty on employers to stop harassment or face liability. The Manitoba code does not contain a provision of employer responsibility.

Human rights advocates were shocked by the Manitoba Court of Appeal decision and by the remarks of Mr. Justice A.K. Twaddle and Mr. Justice C.R. Huband. Justice Huband was quoted as saying: "I am amazed that sexual harassment has been equated with discrimination on the basis of sex. I think they are entirely different concepts." Justice Twaddle agreed: "It is nonsense to say that harassment is discrimination." While some provinces characterize sexual harassment as a prohibited, discriminating act, Justice Twaddle disagreed. "I am conscious, of course, that it is within the power of a legislative body to say that black is white, or that day is night, or that harassment is discrimination." The Manitoba Court of Appeal decision is being appealed to the Supreme Court of Canada.

SOURCE: "Sexual harassment: It's spreading at work but is the boss liable?", *The Globe and Mail* (March 16, 1987). Reprinted by permission of Wilfred List.

Questions:

1. Is it reasonable to hold an employer liable for sexual harassment unless the employer can prove that all due diligence was exercised to prevent it?
2. Do you agree or disagree with Justices Twaddle and Huband? Is sexual harassment discrimination on the basis of sex? Consider the definitions of harassment and discrimination in your answer.
3. Should the Supreme Court, in reviewing the Manitoba Appeal Court decision, take into consideration the fact that several Canadian jurisdictions already hold an employer liable for sexual harassment unless they can prove that they exercised all due diligence to prevent it?

Case 3.2: Getting Ahead at Home Groceries

Hoa Thi Blood isn't smiling today, even though her employer, Home Groceries, advertises "a friendly smile in every aisle." Blood, a 40-year-old Vietnamese woman who works as a cashier at the store, has just been denied a promotion to assistant manager.

Blood has worked at the store for ten years. During that time she has earned a reputation for ringing up purchases quickly and accurately. She has also received commendations for good customer relations and exceptional service. Annual performance reviews document not only her fine performance, but also the fact that she is an honest, reliable, and dependable worker.

Despite her fine qualities, however, the promotion to assistant manager went to Bill Quigley, a co-worker who started out at Home Groceries two years before as a shelf stocker. Quigley's work record is good and he is also very popular with management and co-workers alike. He likes to kid around a lot, go drinking, and pitch for the company's winning softball team.

Blood has never liked softball and she isn't interested in the other social activities that involve so many of the store's employees, from management on down. Instead, when she isn't at work, she keeps herself busy with her family and an occasional course at a nearby university.

When the promotion was denied to her, Blood asked Herb Wolfe, the store manager, "Why?"

"You don't have the necessary experience stocking shelves," he told her.

It was true, she did not. The store had a policy of starting women out as checkers; they never did stock shelves. That work was reserved for men. Blood hadn't even known until now that stocking shelves was required for promotion to assistant manager.

"It just isn't fair," Blood said angrily. "I should have had that promotion. Perhaps the Human Rights Commission will agree with me."

Questions:

1. On what grounds might Blood appeal to the Human Rights Commission?
2. Do you think the Commission will agree with Blood that she should have had the promotion? Why or why not?
3. If Home Groceries was at fault, where did it go wrong?

II Planning and Staffing

4

Human Resource Planning

The Need for Human Resource Planning
Purposes of Human Resource Planning
HRP as a Human Resource Management Function
The Human Resource Planning Process
Projecting Human Resource Supply
Forecasting Future Human Resource Needs
Comparing Forecast Needs with Projections of Supply
Planning Policies and Programs
Evaluating Human Resource Planning Effectiveness
The Personnel Audit
Summary
Project Ideas
Cases

Kanata University is a major Canadian university. Its overall enrolment is stable, but there has been a substantial shift in demand within the university. Specifically, the Faculty of Arts has experienced a 15 per cent decline in enrolment over the past decade, while the Faculty of Business has had a 30 per cent increase. KU's failure to anticipate and accommodate the changing demand has resulted in a stressful situation for university administrators, faculty members, and students. The arts faculty is overstaffed and classes are small. Faculty members of the business school, on the other hand, are overworked and disgruntled: typically, they teach three or four courses per term and their classes are large. Their teaching responsibilities are taking an increasing amount of time, leaving them less time to do research, an activity that is rewarded by the university's pay system. Demand for certain business courses at KU is so great that many business students cannot enrol in the courses they need in order to complete their degrees. This poses particular problems for students who are about to graduate but lack one or more key courses.

Because of its failure to plan for the human resource supply needed to meet demand for its product, KU finds itself in a crisis situation. It is too late to plan to avoid the problem. The only alternative left is to try to adapt to the situation in one of the following ways:

1. Require present business faculty members to teach more courses per term. The research responsibilities of professors could be deemphasized and pay structures changed to provide greater rewards for teaching more courses or handling large numbers of students.
2. Make greater use of graduate students to teach courses, especially at the introductory level.
3. Use some arts faculty members to teach courses included in business degree requirements (for example, math, computer science, statistics).
4. Increase the size of classes, perhaps using TV instruction.

Much of KU's present situation could have been alleviated or avoided by attention to human resource planning. Planners could have examined enrolment patterns at KU and other schools and found signs of a trend away from liberal arts and towards business courses. The shift in demand also could have been foreseen by studying potential job opportunities for arts versus business graduates. Finally, the shift could have been anticipated by studying career-planning data from university-bound secondary school students. Such data show the fields of study students hope to pursue and allow for measures to be taken to meet future demand.

Knowledge of increasing demand for business courses at KU would have allowed planners to forecast the organization's human resource needs. An assessment of the business faculty could have been used to estimate whether the forecast increased demand could be met by the then-available human resource supply. (Of course, planners would have expected the supply to change somewhat by the time the forecast of future demand became a reality.)

Comparing forecasts of future human resource needs with projections of supply, planners at Kanata U could have anticipated the present crisis situation and taken steps to avert it. They would have had several methods available: they could have increased the supply of business faculty members; curtailed demand and limited enrolment in business courses; or shifted some of the demand back to the arts faculty, which has an adequate supply of teaching staff.

In order to increase the supply of Faculty of Business teachers, planners could have suggested the following approaches:

1. Allocation of a larger proportion of university funds for the purpose of hiring additional business professors.
2. Elimination of arts positions as turnover occurred, with reallocation of that funding to new positions in the Faculty of Business.
3. Introduction of aggressive recruiting for both business professors and graduate students, who often teach introductory-level courses.
4. Exploration of the possibility of retraining some arts instructors to enable them to teach business subjects.

Planners could have curtailed demand and limited enrolment in business courses by raising admissions standards to the faculty or by increasing its tuition.

To shift some of the demand back to the arts, KU could have modified the business degree program, making it possible to earn a business minor while remaining in the Faculty of Arts. This would have shifted some of the demand back to the arts school, where demand could have been met more easily.

The Need for Human Resource Planning

Planning for future human resource needs at Kanata University, as at all universities, is particularly difficult because professors take a long time to train (eight to ten years after secondary school). Moreover, those trained in one field cannot be easily retrained to teach in another—the current shortage of finance and accounting professors cannot be readily met by retraining foreign language or classics teachers. In addition, while some information is available on future demand for courses, it cannot be foreseen perfectly.

Nevertheless, Kanata University's experience demonstrates the need for human resource planning (HRP) in organizations. *Human resource planning* is the process of forecasting human resource needs of an organization so that steps can be taken to ensure needed supply. This means avoiding both shortages and surpluses of labour. Until recently, organizational use of HRP was quite limited.[1] A 1980 survey, however, documents the recent emergence of such planning, which is also sometimes called manpower planning. Out of 147 companies studied, 145 had some form of HRP, especially for the short term (one to two years into the future) in relation to operations plans. Larger companies—those with 1,000 employees or more—tended to do more specific and longer term planning.[2]

Undoubtedly, concern over the shortage of certain skills has been a spur to human resource planning in organizations.[3] Factors such as rapid technological change also help explain the increase. Moreover, the process itself can be revealing to an organization that engages in it. Rowland and Summers, who examined HRP in depth in six companies in 1980, observed that what some doubters considered important was:

> not HRP (including forecasting) as a technique, but rather as a process of analysis and revision for the ultimate goal of innovative option generation by top and line management as well as staff.[4]

The process of analysis helps organizations to meet the challenges of rapidly changing technology. The introduction of new equipment,

[1] B.A. Keys and H.H. Wright, *Manpower Planning in Industry: A Case Study* (Ottawa: Economic Council of Canada, 1966), p. 27.

[2] R.J. Clifford and Associates, *Survey of Manpower Planning Practices in Canada* (Ottawa: Employment and Immigration Canada, 1981).

[3] Gordon Betcherman, *Meeting Skill Requirements: Report of the Human Resources Survey* (Ottawa: Economic Council of Canada, 1982).

[4] Kendrith M. Rowland and Scott L. Summers, "Human Resource Planning: A Second Look," *Personnel Administrator*, December 1981, p. 79.

products, and processes invariably results in changes in jobs and in an organization's job structure. Existing jobs may have to change to include new equipment, new tasks, or new ways of doing familiar tasks. Some jobs, such as service station attendants, bank tellers, and draftsmen, may become obsolete with advancing technology. Others may be eliminated due to decreased product demand. Human resource planners foresee such scenarios and recommend strategies for reducing excess supply.

In addition to changing the nature of some jobs and forcing the elimination of others, technological changes create a demand for specialized workers to fill new jobs. The high demand resulting from technological advances usually creates labour shortages because schools and training institutions cannot educate the new labour supply as quickly as it is needed. The time lag involved in training present employees in new skills and/or recruiting new workers with specialized skills means that planning to meet the requirements of future jobs is essential if organizations are to survive and remain competitive. Without effective human resource planning, organizations experiencing the effects of rapid technological change will find themselves with a shortage of skilled employees.

Technological change is not the only kind of change that creates a need for HRP. Legislation can also cause a large, sudden demand for specialized workers. For example, passage of the Environmental Assessment Act of 1975 in Ontario caused an immediate demand for environmental planners. This sudden demand for a new and highly specialized type of labour created shortages which might have been reduced by some advance planning. When it appeared likely that the act would pass, planners could have considered alternative plans of action and chosen a strategy for obtaining the needed specialists.

Purposes of Human Resource Planning

Human resource planning serves many organizational and managerial purposes.[5] Two major ones are: (1) to aid in setting organizational goals and objectives, including consideration of affirmative action; and (2) to examine the effects of alternative human resource policies and programs, and recommend implementation of the alternative that contributes most to organizational effectiveness.

Setting Goals and Objectives

Organizational goals and objectives specify where an organization wants to be at some future point in time. Typically, top management sets

[5] For a series of articles on related subjects, see L. Moore and L. Charach, eds., *Manpower Planning for Canadians: An Anthology*, 2nd ed. (Vancouver: The Institute of Industrial Relations, University of British Columbia, 1979).

goals in terms of profitability, survival and growth, and production and/or service levels. Due to passage of the 1986 Employment Equity Act, many employers under federal jurisdiction are also specifying goals for increasing participation of minorities in their work force. Examples of organizational goals are:

1. To increase company profits by 10 per cent in the next fiscal year (profitability).
2. To open 25 new retail outlets in the Prairies in the next four years (growth).
3. To bottle 20 per cent more diet cola in the next year (production level).
4. To guarantee one-day delivery of all first-class mail within the province by 1990 (service level).
5. To advance more women to management positions (affirmative action).

Human resource planners provide management and business planners with the implications various goals have for human resources. For example, will there be an adequate supply of personnel to staff 25 new retail outlets? How many additional employees must be hired in order to bottle 20 per cent more diet cola in the next year? Human resource planners help management and business planners in evaluating whether given goals can be met.

Consider the case of an electronics firm whose management is exploring the production of a new piece of equipment within the year. By analyzing the human resource requirements for producing this item, human resource planners might provide management with evidence that this goal would be impossible to meet within the next year, very costly within the next two years, but cost-efficient within four years. Given this information, management may want to plan to achieve the goal within a four-year time span.

Examining the Effects of Alternative Human Resource Policies and Programs

Organizational effectiveness was defined earlier as making the most expeditious use of an organization's resources. Human resource planners must consider the long- and short-term costs and benefits of each alternative planning strategy in order to arrive at the one that maximizes organizational effectiveness. For example, if a new piece of equipment is introduced, is it in the best interests of the organization to hire new employees who know how to use the equipment or to invest time and money in training present employees in its use? If an employer faces a decline in demand for a product, will a number of workers have to be laid off, or can the organization retain them, perhaps transferring them to new job assignments?

Alternative HRP policies and programs can be evaluated in several ways. One is computer simulations, which quantify and manipulate practices and human resource movement through an organization, enabling planners to examine the effects of changing or implementing various policies and practices. They are a valuable tool in planning human resource strategies.

Another way is to examine the effects of alternative scenarios such as those suggested in the Kanata U example. Despite the availability of low-cost computers, many employers are likely to consider alternative human resource policies and programs by making forecasts and projections of employees, costs, and benefits. HRP benefits management to the extent that human resource alternatives are considered when strategic decisions are made.

HRP as a Human Resource Management Function

HRP is the most strategic and potentially proactive of all human resource management functions simply because it involves planning. As organizational goals and objectives are developed in the strategic and HRP process, human resource policies and programs are evaluated in terms of how they may contribute to goal attainment. Thus, HRP serves as the coordinating and integrating link to all other HRM functions, and each of the functions is in some way related to HRP. Specific relationships between HRP and other HRM functions are described in Exhibit 4.1.

The HRM functions of job analysis and performance appraisal provide important inputs to the human resource planning process. By analyzing the content of jobs, planners can evaluate the human resource requirements of present and future jobs. Performance appraisal systems provide measures of employee performance. It is important for planners to know performance levels of present employees so that they can make forecasts of the number and kinds of personnel needed to achieve certain goals.

Human resource planning specifies recruiting goals—the number and kinds of employees to attract to positions in an organization. Planning also provides a data base for determining if recruiting goals can be met from within the organization or whether external recruiting will be necessary. If recruiting needs can be met internally, present employees will have to be attracted to the new positions and some retraining and development may be required. HRM professionals can make employees aware of new positions and advancement opportunities through career planning activities. Forecasts of human resource needs also serve as a basis for training and development programs designed to prepare employees to meet future job requirements.

In recruiting needs cannot be met internally, even with training and development, external recruiting is required. Compensation is a key factor here; pay must be competitive in order to attract individuals (who may be happily employed elsewhere). The number and type of labour needed and whether that labour is in short or abundant supply

EXHIBIT 4.1

Human resource planning: an HRM function

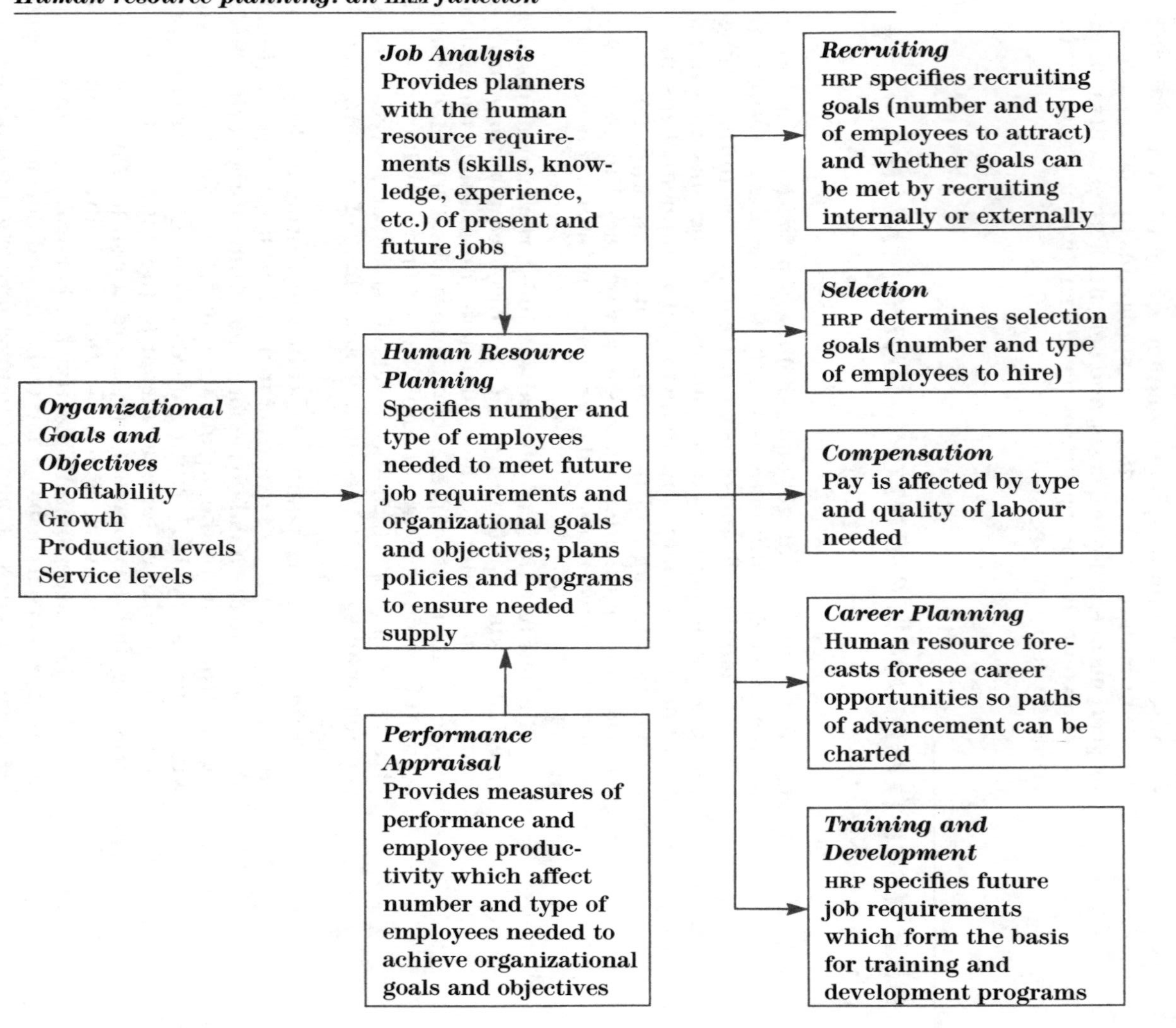
Organizational Goals and Objectives
Profitability
Growth
Production levels
Service levels
Job Analysis
Provides planners with the human resource requirements (skills, knowledge, experience, etc.) of present and future jobs
Human Resource Planning
Specifies number and type of employees needed to meet future job requirements and organizational goals and objectives; plans policies and programs to ensure needed supply
Performance Appraisal
Provides measures of performance and employee productivity which affect number and type of employees needed to achieve organizational goals and objectives
Recruiting
HRP specifies recruiting goals (number and type of employees to attract) and whether goals can be met by recruiting internally or externally
Selection
HRP determines selection goals (number and type of employees to hire)
Compensation
Pay is affected by type and quality of labour needed
Career Planning
Human resource forecasts foresee career opportunities so paths of advancement can be charted
Training and Development
HRP specifies future job requirements which form the basis for training and development programs

affect the dollar amount an organization must pay in order to attract, hire, and retain the required employees. HRP has a direct relation to the selection function in that planning determines selection goals.

Human resource planning sometimes determines that there are too many workers in a certain job category. In this case, steps must be taken to reduce or redistribute supply.

Until recently, human resource planning in organizations was done by HRM generalists or other HRM professionals who had responsibility for training and development or recruitment and staffing. Since the mid-1970s, the rise in importance of human resource planning has caused many organizations to establish full-time positions and support staff to handle the HRP function. The following job description for a manager of human resources planning provides insights into the responsibilities of this HRM specialist.

> **Manager, Human Resources Planning**
>
> Contributes to the corporation by analyzing and recommending policies and procedures and developing systems and models which contribute to the effective hiring, development, and utilization of human resources. Analyzes and recommends revisions to policies, regulations and procedures (e.g., candidate search and selection, performance evaluation, career pathing, promotions, and transfers). Develops and applies systems and models for human resource planning, including forecasting future requirements, defining logical career paths, inventorying human resources and projecting future time periods, identifying future hiring needs by skill type, level, and location, identifying future voids and imbalances, and performing analyses of human resource situations to identify opportunities for improvement.[6]

The Human Resource Planning Process

The human resource planning process has five steps:

1. Project future human resource supply.
2. Forecast future human resource needs.
3. Compare forecast needs with projected supply.
4. Plan policies and programs to meet human resource needs.
5. Evaluate human resource planning effectiveness.

Basically, the process involves comparing projections of available supply with forecasts of human resource needs in order to determine net

[6] J.W. Walker and M.N. Wolfe, "Patterns in Human Resource Planning Practices," *Human Resource Planning*, vol. 1, no. 4, 1978, p. 199.

employee requirements for some future point(s) in time. Net requirements may reflect either shortages or surpluses of certain types of labour. When shortages and surpluses are identified, planners can suggest alternative approaches to ensure that supply conforms to demand.[7]

Exhibit 4.2 diagrams these five steps.

EXHIBIT 4.2

The human resource planning process

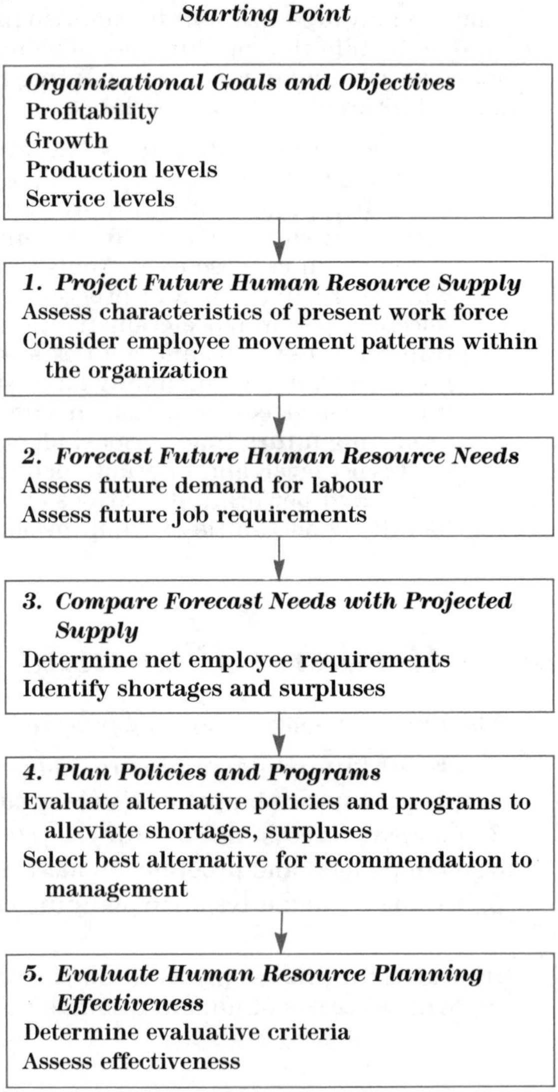

Starting Point

Organizational Goals and Objectives
Profitability
Growth
Production levels
Service levels

↓

1. *Project Future Human Resource Supply*
Assess characteristics of present work force
Consider employee movement patterns within the organization

↓

2. *Forecast Future Human Resource Needs*
Assess future demand for labour
Assess future job requirements

↓

3. *Compare Forecast Needs with Projected Supply*
Determine net employee requirements
Identify shortages and surpluses

↓

4. *Plan Policies and Programs*
Evaluate alternative policies and programs to alleviate shortages, surpluses
Select best alternative for recommendation to management

↓

5. *Evaluate Human Resource Planning Effectiveness*
Determine evaluative criteria
Assess effectiveness

[7] Ontario Manpower Commission, *Human Resource Planning, An Introduction* (Toronto: Ontario Ministry of Labour, 1985).

The first step of the process is projecting an organization's future human resource supply—estimating the number and kinds of employees expected to compose its work force at some future point in time. Projections are based on careful assessment of an organization's current work force and also on patterns of employee movement through the organization over time. These patterns are an important consideration in making projections because the composition of the work force can be expected to change over time through promotions, transfers, and terminations. It is important to note that these projections of supply relate only to the internal supply of human resources.

The second step is to forecast human resource needs based on forecasts of demand for an organization's goods or services. Future needs for human resources—and the kind of employee skills that will be needed—are also determined by the nature of future jobs and their requirements.

Step 3 of the process compares forecast needs for human resources with projections of internal supply to determine net employee requirements. Such comparisons should be made for each job in an organization as well as for the organization as a whole. Once net needs for human resources have been established, planners can evaluate alternative policies and programs for alleviating shortages or reducing surpluses and then select the best strategy for recommendation to management (Step 4).

Finally, an organization's human resource planning effort should be evaluated in order to determine its usefulness to the organization (Step 5). To make this assessment, planners must first determine the criteria for evaluation.

Projecting Human Resource Supply

Projections are estimates of the number and kinds of employees that can be expected to constitute an organization's work force at some future point in time. Projections are based on careful assessment of an organization's *current* supply, plus consideration of employee movement through the organization over time. Exhibit 4.3 displays forms to assist in projecting supply.

Assessing Current Supply

Data on current human resource supply are obtained from inventories of workers' characteristics and skills. These data are collected and stored in a human resource information system (HRIS). Exhibit 4.4 lists some of the kinds of information usually collected and stored in an HRIS. The categories generally include: (1) personal data; (2) work history data; (3) training and development history and career plans;

EXHIBIT 4.3

Forms to assist in projecting supply

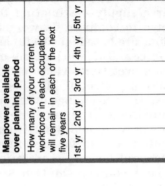

Current workforce		
Which occupations do you currently employ?	You can record current employment and employee movements on Schedule 4. If you have many employees approaching retirement, you can examine current age distribution using Schedule 5.	How many workers do you employ?

Your current workforce will probably change over the planning period as you lose people to retirement, transfers, death, etc.

You can estimate or project these losses using Schedule 6 or project them in greater detail using Schedule 7.

Manpower available over planning period				
How many of your current workforce in each occupation will remain in each of the next five years				
1st yr	2nd yr	3rd yr	4th yr	5th yr

Transfer for matching

SOURCE: Ontario Manpower Commission, *Human Resources Planning Manual* (Toronto: Ontario Ministry of Labour and Ontario Regional Office, Employment and Immigration Canada, 1982).

(4) skills inventory data for current jobs; and (5) aggregate data, such as total number of employees and their age distribution. Most employers already have HRIS's to collect and store some of the information that is necessary for human resource planning. For example, most employers maintain personal and work history data for payroll purposes. However, the data requirements of HRIS's for human resource planning purposes are more comprehensive than for other purposes. Because planners seek to estimate availability of future skills, information on currently available skills is required. But skills change over time because of training and development programs and employee job changes within the organization. Thus, in projecting the nature of future supply, HRIS's must also collect and store information on assessments of employee potential and promotability, employee career objectives, and training programs taken.

The Employment Equity Act of 1986 greatly increases the value of an HRIS to most employers. Whether or not an employer uses an HRIS for HRP purposes, the reporting requirements of this act dictate that employment, pay, and employee mobility data must be available for various race, ethnic, and sex categories of employees.

Affirmative Action regulations in the United States led to the development and growth of computerized HRIS's which were useful both for meeting reporting requirements and for assessing labour supply. In the U.S., employment-related data for categories of employees are used as the basis for determining under-representation of women and other minorities and as the basis for affirmative action goals. The description of the current work force provided by the HRIS may be combined with information about human resource flows to produce the affirmative action goals and timetables required of many U.S. employers.

Skills inventories. A major requirement of an HRIS is information about the skills available among current employees. A job skills inventory includes information about each employee's skills, abilities, knowledge, and experience. This information can be obtained from several sources, including job analysis, performance appraisal data, and educational and training program completion records.

Ideally, a skills inventory would be a major component of a computerized HRIS and would use a standardized coding system for jobs, skills, knowledge, and experience such as that found in the *Canadian Classification and Dictionary of Occupations*. Such a system could be used not only in HRP, but also in deciding employee transfers, promotions, and layoffs.

Analysis of Human Resource Flows

Although projections of future human resource supply are based on assessment of current supply, projections that assume the same employees will be available in one, three, or five years invariably prove incorrect. Methods of projecting human resource supply must take into account patterns of employee movement into, through, and out of organizations. Such movement patterns are referred to as *human resource flows*.

EXHIBIT 4.4

Typical data for a human resource information system

A. *PERSONAL DATA*
1. Name
2. Sex
3. Date of birth
4. Marital status
5. Physical disabilities, if any
6. Education

B. *WORK HISTORY DATA*
1. Date of hire
2. Initial job
3. Starting pay
4. Second job, date of job change, and pay
5. Third and later jobs, if any; dates of job change and pay
6. Current job and organizational unit or department and current pay
7. Performance appraisal data—past and most recent

C. *TRAINING AND DEVELOPMENT HISTORY AND CAREER PLANS*
1. Company-sponsored training programs completed in the last five years
2. Other training, development, or educational programs completed
3. Employee career objectives
4. Assessment of employee potential and promotability

D. *SKILLS INVENTORY DATA* (quantitative description of the skills, abilities, knowledge, and experience necessary to perform the job, as determined by job analysis)

E. *AGGREGATE DATA*
1. Total number of employees
2. Number of employees in each job and class of jobs
3. Sex of employees in each job and class of jobs
4. Age distribution of employees in each job and job class
5. Listing of current vacant positions

Human resource flows logically begin with newly hired employees who flow into the organization at an entry-level job. Entry-level jobs, in most organizations, are the lowest-level jobs in the company. They must, therefore, be filled from the external work force. (Exceptions occur with specializations or in fields such as publishing, where an entry-level editorial position could be filled internally or externally and would be considered a promotion for a clerical or secretarial worker.) From this point, employees can: (1) stay *in* the same job; (2) move *across* to another, but not a higher-level job (transfer); (3) move *up* to a higher-level job (promotion); or (4) move *out* of the organization through voluntary termination (resignation), involuntary termination (layoff, dismissal), or retirement. Downward flows are also available to employees in nonentry-level jobs. Moving from a higher-level to a lower-level job in an organization is known as demotion. Although few would choose it as an alternative, some individuals tolerate demotion, at least temporarily, during recessionary periods or for personal reasons.

There are two general methods for projecting labour supply based on information about human resource flows. The first relies on estimates of supervisors and managers as to the number of employees entering and leaving various positions in their unit, including the number changing jobs within the unit. By adding up these estimates, planners can project the organization's internal labour supply. The second general method involves use of stochastic models.

Stochastic models. The mathematical term "stochastic" is used to describe the process of employee movement, or flow, from one job in an organization to another. An example of a simple stochastic model is the *transition matrix*. Transition matrices are rectangular displays that portray percentages of employees in certain jobs or positions at Time 1 and Time 2. It is important that Time 1 and Time 2 be far enough apart to allow some changes, but not so far apart as to allow multiple changes for individual employees (both demotion and exit, for example). Exhibit 4.5 is a transition matrix for instructors at Kanata U.

EXHIBIT 4.5

Transition matrix for Kanata U, Faculty of Business

Time 1		Time 2						
		A	B	C	D	E	Exit	Total
Full professors	(A)	.80					.20	1.0
Associate professors	(B)	.10	.85				.05	1.0
Assistant professors	(C)		.20	.70			.10	1.0
Visiting professors	(D)			.10	.40		.50	1.0
Teaching assistants	(E)			.10		.60	.30	1.0

As can be seen from the matrix, 80 per cent of full professors (A) at Time 1 remained full professors (A) at Time 2. Twenty per cent of full professors left Kanata U between Time 1 and 2. Among associate professors (B) at Time 1, 85 per cent remained associates (B) at Time 2, while 10 per cent moved up to the rank of professor (A). Only five per cent of associate professors left between Time 1 and 2.

Transition matrices are useful for a variety of analytical purposes, such as tracking career paths and exit rates. In human resource planning, transition matrices are used as the basis for projections of future supply in a process known as *Markov analysis*. Markov analysis bases estimates (probabilities) of future movement on actual flow data described in transition matrices. To see how this is done, let us use the matrix in Exhibit 4.5 to project future supply of instructors at Kanata U's business faculty.

In order to make projections for the forecast period, we begin with the number of instructors currently employed at Kanata U. Let us assume that KU employs 20 full professors, 40 associate professors, 50 assistant professors, 10 visiting professors, and 20 teaching assistants. Using the matrix, we see that 80 per cent of the full professors, or 16, can be expected to remain at KU at the rank of full. They will be joined by 4 new professors from the associate rank (10 per cent of 40) for a total of 20 full professors. Thirty-four associate professors will remain at the associate rank (85 per cent of 40), and 2 associate professors (5 per cent of 40) will exit. Associate professors will total 44 at the end of the forecast period due to 10 assistant professors moving up to the rank of associate (20 per cent of 50).

Stochastic models can be very useful for projecting supply in situations of little change. For example, their projections can be quite accurate if future policies and organizational conditions are similar to what they were when the model was developed. An early example of the use of a stochastic model projected managerial turnover, promotions, and transfers in a large manufacturing firm. The model enabled management to project the availability of managers over a five-year period, thus identifying shortages.[8]

Stochastic models cannot, however, be used as effectively to project future supply if there will be changes that affect supply. For example, if a plant changes location, stochastic models of flow data from the previous location are not a sound base for projecting supply in the new location. Yet even in cases in which stochastic models cannot be used to project supply effectively, they can be helpful in providing planners with an understanding of human resource flows. Stochastic models of flows before and after certain changes can aid in an understanding of the effects of such changes in terms of employee movement through an organization. For example, raising promotion standards (say, requiring that more journal articles be published or that more service be rendered to the university) could have the effect of reducing flow into the ranks of associate and full professors. Stochastic models are often used in computer simulations of human resource systems to examine effects of such changes in human resource policies.

Forecasting Future Human Resource Needs

Organizational goals and objectives serve as a starting point for forecasting future human resource needs. The demand for labour is derived from the demand for an organization's goods and services, as well as from the relationship between labour inputs and the output of goods and services. If the input/output ratio and other factors are held constant, increased demand for goods and services leads to an increased

[8]V.H. Vroom and K.R. MacCrimmon, "Toward a Stochastic Model of Management Careers." *Administrative Science Quarterly*, vol. 13, no. 1, June 1968, pp. 26–46.

demand for labour; inversely, decreased demand for goods and services generally results in a decreased demand for labour.

Exhibit 4.6 is a form designed by federal and Ontario provincial employment agencies to assist employers in the process of planning for human resources. Note that in this early step, human resource requirements are tied to business plans.

Forecasts of the demand for human resources can be short-range, mid-range, or long-range, depending on how far into the future goals are set. Short-range planning looks at the coming year, the main concern being to meet an organization's immediate staffing needs. Emphasis is usually on budgeting and on recruiting programs. Mid-range forecasts focus on goals one to five years away. Long-range planning efforts are usually directed at organizational goals five or more years in the future; they reflect organizational philosophy concerning the direction of the firm and its responses to environmental change. Obviously, of the three, long-range forecasts for human resource needs are the most difficult to make because they are based on predictions of conditions in the distant future. J.W. Walker, a leading authority on human resource planning, has drawn an analogy between forecasting human resource needs and weather forecasting:

> Somewhat like weather forecasting, the assessment of changing environmental conditions is a difficult and uncertain task in human resource planning. We may survey the clouds, the winds, and weather conditions prevailing elsewhere as we develop forecasts of conditions to come. But we cannot always predict the future weather accurately and we certainly cannot change it. Nevertheless, the information is vital in our efforts to anticipate and prepare for it.[9]

Six different methods, or approaches, can be used to forecast future human resource needs. Some are more appropriate to short-range forecasting, while others are designed for long-range planning. The methods include (1) planning for the status quo, (2) rules of thumb, (3) unit forecasting, (4) the Delphi method, (5) scenarios, and (6) computer simulation.

Planning for the Status Quo

The simplest approach to forecasting human resource needs is to assume that the current supply and mix of employees will be adequate for the forecast period and that staff ratios will remain constant. In this case, planning simply involves taking steps to replace any employees who either are promoted or leave the firm.

An example of planning for the status quo is *management succession planning*, which seeks to ensure that there is at least one qualified manager to replace any higher-level manager in the organization. Management succession planning is quite common. An in-depth survey of

[9] J.W. Walker, *Human Resource Planning* (New York: McGraw-Hill, 1980), p. 24.

EXHIBIT 4.6

Tying human resource requirements to business plans

Your future requirements for production/customer service personnel will be influenced by such business planning factors as change in output volume, change in product/service mix, and introduction of new processes and equipment. So, you will need to set down your business plans before you look at your human resource requirements. The forms below will help you.

Production/customer: service: present

What products or customer services do you currently sell?	What are your sales of each? ($ 000s or units)	▶ You can examine the relationship between individual products/customer services and their current employment requirements using Schedule 1.	Summarize the types of occupations of workers you need for your production service	How many workers in each are needed?

▶

Planned/projected

What products or customer services do you plan to sell in the next 5 years?	What sales levels do you plan to reach ($ 000s or units)					▶ You can project manpower requirements by occupation for individual products/customer services using Schedule 2 For multi-year planning, complete a separate schedule for each year of the planning period.	Summarize the types of occupations you will require for the planned/production service	How many workers in each occupation will you require?				
	1st yr	2nd yr	3rd yr	4th yr	5th yr			1st yr	2nd yr	3rd yr	4th yr	5th yr

Transfer requirements for each occupation for matching against available internal supply.

SOURCE: Ontario Manpower Commission, *Human Resources Planning Manual* (Toronto: Ontario Ministry of Labour and Ontario Regional Office, Employment and Immigration Canada, 1982).

six corporations' planning and staffing activities in 1980 found it was the only type of human resource planning being undertaken extensively by the organizations studied.[10]

Planning for the status quo is often adequate in the short run for organizations that experience little change in demand for their products and whose technologies remain relatively stable. An example of an organization that could use this approach successfully is a retail business in an area experiencing little population growth. Even this simple approach to forecasting of future needs should, however, begin with a complete description and analysis of current staffing requirements, to ensure that present needs are being adequately met by the current number and mix of employees.

Rules of Thumb

Some organizations use rules of thumb as a basis for forecasting changing human resource needs. For example, one firm has successfully used one production supervisor for every 12 production employees in the past and firmly believes this 1:12 staffing ratio is optimal. Thus, if it forecasts demand for 144 additional production employees, it plans to create positions for 12 new production supervisors.

Another rule of thumb based on previous experience is that one person can produce 2,000 units of output per day. Using this guideline, an organization that wants to produce an additional 10,000 units per day will need an additional five employees to accomplish its goal.

Because rules of thumb assume that past relationships between number of employees and outputs can be applied to future conditions, they are most useful in work environments that remain relatively stable. If conditions change, past formulas for success may not apply.

Rules of thumb can also be based on various indicators, or *predictor variables*, which have proved in the past to bear a relationship to what is being forecast. For example, a manufacturer may have a rule of thumb that annual sales of a product will reach $1 million if sales in the first two months equal $100,000 or more. In this case "the first two months of sales" is a predictor of a certain level of forecast product demand. Using this rule of thumb for forecast demand, production can be scheduled and human resource needs determined.

A more formal, quantitative version of rules of thumb combines several predictor variables into a multiple regression equation. This equation assigns weights to the different predictor variables. One large firm successfully used multiple regression equations, based on quarterly data, to forecast human resource requirements in different departments.[11]

[10] Rowland and Summers, p. 78.

[11] Albert B. Drui, "The Use of Regression Equations to Predict Manpower Requirements," in L. Moore and L. Charach, *Manpower Planning for Canadians* (2nd ed.) (University of British Columbia: Institute of Industrial Relations, 1979), pp. 393–403.

Unit Forecasting

The unit forecasting approach simply requires supervisors and managers to estimate their human resource needs for the next year or forecast period. The unit forecasts are then added for a total forecast. This approach is often referred to as a "bottom-up" approach to forecasting, because judgements are made by lower-level management and simply added together at a higher organizational level. This method is usually used for making short-range forecasts.

The unit forecasting approach can be highly structured or very informal. An informal method has each supervisor or manager submit a statement of the number of new employees needed to fill all jobs in which vacancies are expected or additional employees needed. A more structured version requires managers to respond to a questionnaire about the nature of future jobs and their requirements, the number of expected vacancies in each job category, and their expectations as to whether job vacancies can be filled internally via training, promotion, or transfer or whether additional personnel must be recruited externally. A sample questionnaire for unit forecasting is given in Exhibit 4.7. This sample questionnaire is not detailed, but it does provide examples of the types of questions that supervisors and managers could be asked in order to forecast human resource needs. Note that many of the questions emphasize information about future job requirements. This is because changes in job requirements often entail corresponding changes in employee skills, knowledge, and interests. (For example, if a restaurant introduces Caesar salad prepared at tableside, the job requirements for waiter and waitress must change to include the skill of and interest in preparing Caesar salad at tableside.) Questionnaire results can be analyzed by top management or human resource planners and used as a basis for forecasting the needs of divisions and the organization as a whole.

The Delphi Method

The unit forecasting method seeks opinions from lower-level management regarding short-range staffing needs. The Delphi method, on the other hand, relies on expert opinion in making long-range forecasts.

"Where is the organization going?" is a key question in long-range planning. Top management must address this question periodically in deciding whether the organization should continue producing the same goods or services it has in the past or should add, delete, or modify them. Decisions of this type require expert judgement based upon analysis of forecast changes in technology, the economy, and the legal and social environment.

The Delphi method provides one method of obtaining consensus regarding factors affecting an organization's future directions and human resource needs. It involves obtaining independent judgements from a panel of experts, usually through a questionnaire or interview, on a particular issue or question affecting the nature and magnitude

EXHIBIT 4.7

Unit forecasting questionnaire

1. List any jobs that have changed since the last forecasting period and any that will change in the next forecasting period.
2. List any jobs that have been added or eliminated in the last forecasting period and any that will be added or eliminated in the next forecasting period.
3. List the job requirements (skills, knowledge, etc.) for each job listed in numbers 1 and 2 above.
4. List expected vacancies for each job category for the next forecasting period.
5. For each job vacancy, note whether the vacancy can be filled with present employees or whether additional employees will have to be hired.
6. If vacancy can be filled with present employees, note whether training will be required. Specify nature of training needs.
7. What percentage of employees are performing their jobs up to standard?
8. How many employees in the next forecasting period will require training to perform their jobs satisfactorily?
9. How many employees will be absent in the next forecasting period due to disability, educational, or other leaves?
10. How much overtime was needed in the last forecasting period, and how much will be needed in the next forecasting period?

of demand for an organization's products or services. The five steps in the Delphi method are:

1. An issue, question, or problem is identified.
2. A small group or panel of ten or fewer experts is identified.
3. Independent judgements about the issue are obtained from each expert through a questionnaire or structured interview.
4. An intermediary or facilitator collects, analyzes, and feeds back information from the first questionnaire or interview to each expert.
5. Steps 3 and 4 are repeated until there is a consensus on the issue or problem.

The Delphi method avoids face-to-face encounters between the experts so as to prevent such factors as social interaction, personality, and other psychological biases from affecting the judgement process. Because the panel members never interact, the role of intermediary or facilitator is very important in summarizing and feeding back information to each member. One study of the Delphi method found it to be more accurate and useful than a regression model for forecasting human resource needs.[12]

[12] G. Milkovich, A.J. Annoni, and T.A. Mahoney. "The Use of Delphi Procedures in Manpower Forecasting," *Management Science*, vol. 19, no. 4, 1972, pp. 381–88.

Scenarios

Scenarios are descriptive scenes that allow planners to consider combinations of several factors in order to forecast human resource needs for each set of circumstances. For example, one scenario might assume environmental conditions in the next three years will include a recession, the entrance of a new competitor into the company's major market, and technological advances requiring some modifications in the production process. An alternative scenario for the same three-year period might include the entrance of a new competing firm and technological changes requiring some modifications, but no recession. A third scenario for the same time span might describe a situation in which there is no recession, no competing firm, and only minor technological advances. Using this method, forecasts can be made for meeting the human resource needs of each set of circumstances portrayed.

The scenario approach is useful in making mid- to long-range forecasts of needs. At some point, however, top management must choose one scenario as the one most likely to occur so that human resource policies and programs can be implemented to ensure needs are being met. An advantage of the scenario method is that it compels planners to consider and plan specifically for more than one contingency. Thus, an alternative is available if the chosen scenario does not prove to be a true representation of conditions as they unfold over time.

Computer Simulation

Use of computer simulation models is one of the most sophisticated methods of forecasting human resource needs. A computer simulation is a mathematical representation of major organizational processes, policies, and human resource movement through an organization. Computer simulations usually include the kinds of assumptions found in scenarios. Additional factors included might be minimum and maximum number of employees in each job, minimum lengths of time in jobs before promotion can occur, average rates of hiring for new employees, turnover and termination data, and data concerning costs and productivity rates. Many of the factors represented in a computer simulation of an organization are particularly useful for projecting the future supply of labour, but such models can also be very useful for both forecasting future human resource needs and evaluating alternative human resource policies.

Computer simulations are useful in forecasting human resource needs because they can provide infinitely detailed scenarios. Thus, needs for human resources can be pinpointed for any combination of organizational and environmental variables. In the example that opened this chapter, planners or administrators at Kanata University could have used computer simulation to examine the impact of varying amounts of shift in demand from arts to business, engineering, or any other major area. The *rate* of shift in demand could also have been analyzed. The impact of a three-year shift from, say, 30 to 40 to 60 per cent of incoming students' selecting business is very different from a shift pattern of 30 to 35 to 42 per cent. Differences in this rate have implications for planners. The more rapid the shift, the less time and fewer options KU administrators have for making adjustments in faculty.

Use of Forecasting in Organizations

Little is known about use of forecasting in organizations, but one recent survey of planners found infrequent use of both long-range planning (beyond five years) and sophisticated needs forecasting procedures.[13] A recent review of the literature on forecasting reported greater use of sophisticated techniques in organizations in stable and somewhat complex environments. Large organizations also tended to use more sophisticated techniques.[14] While little is known about differential use of forecasting techniques, a model by Stone and Fiorito suggests that technique use can be explained by decision-maker perceptions of environmental uncertainty. When uncertainty is moderately low, as in the case of stable and somewhat complex environments, forecasting is both necessary and feasible, resulting in greater use of sophisticated techniques. Less use is made of sophisticated techniques in more dynamic, uncertain environments because forecasting is less feasible in situations of greater change. Techniques are used least frequently in simple and stable environments where there is simply less need for forecasting.[15]

While this section has presented a number of different methods of forecasting, it is important to note that even the careful use of excellent methods cannot guarantee an accurate forecast of the future. However, even an inaccurate forecast can prove useful to an organization. If a forecast of environmental and demand changes results in anticipation and planning for human resource shortages and surpluses, it has served a purpose.

Comparing Forecast Needs with Projections of Supply

The third major step in the process of human resource planning is comparing forecast needs with projections of internal supply. By subtracting projected supply from forecast needs, planners can determine an organization's net employee requirements for a future point in time. Exhibit 4.8 is a form to help planners determine surpluses and shortages in each occupation for years one through five.

[13] Robert H. Schwartz, "Practitioners' Perceptions of Factors Associated with Human Resource Planning Program Success," *Human Resource Planning*, vol. 8, no. 2, 1985, pp. 55–66.

[14] Thomas H. Stone and Jack Fiorito, "A Perceived Uncertainty Model of Human Resource Forecasting Technique Use," *Academy of Management Review*, vol. 11, no. 3, July 1986, pp. 635–42.

[15] Ibid.

EXHIBIT 4.8

Form to determine surpluses and shortages

matching and action planning															
List occupations required and employed	Human resources available internally over the next five years					Human resources required over the next five years					Will you have a surplus or a shortage in each occupation? (subtract requirements from supply)				
	1st yr	2nd yr	3rd yr	4th yr	5th yr	1st yr	2nd yr	3rd yr	4th yr	5th yr	1st yr	2nd yr	3rd yr	4th yr	5th yr

SOURCE: Ontario Manpower Commission, *Human Resources Planning Manual* (Toronto: Ontario Ministry of Labour and Ontario Regional Office, Employment and Immigration Canada, 1982).

Exhibit 4.9 gives net employee requirements for instructors in KU's Faculty of Business for the maximum change-in-demand situation. Planners forecast a need for 152 instructors, and they project a supply of 118; thus, net employee requirements are 34 additional instructors. Net employee requirements are expressed as positive or negative numbers. Negative numbers indicate shortages in supply and positive numbers indicate surpluses. Kanata U projects a surplus of only one type of instructor, associate professors.

EXHIBIT 4.9

Net employee requirements, Kanata University Faculty of Business

Type of instructor	*Number of instructors*		
	Forecast need	*Projected supply*	*Net employee requirements*
Full professors	20	20	0
Associate professors	42	44	+2
Assistant professors	46	38	−8
Visiting professors	12	4	−8
Teaching assistants	32	12	−20
Total	152	118	−34

Net employee requirements should be determined for each job in an organization as well as for the organization as a whole. The reason is that overall supply may be adequate, while shortages exist in some areas and surpluses in others. For example, KU may have enough instructors to meet students' educational demands, but a closer look reveals that instructors are not distributed in such a way as to meet demand. There is a surplus of instructors in an area where demand is declining (arts) and a shortage in an area where demand is increasing (business).

The process should also include a comparison of the skills required in jobs with forecast shortages against the skill requirements of jobs having forecast surpluses. These data are useful to planners in the next step of human resource planning: determining policies and programs to handle predicted shortages or surpluses in supply of labour. If job skills in areas in which there are surpluses are similar to those in areas in which there are job shortages, one alternative is to transfer employees to jobs where shortages exist.

Planning Policies and Programs

After determining net employee requirements, planners generate and evaluate alternative human resource policies and programs designed to handle the anticipated shortages and surpluses. They present their considerations to management, along with their recommendations on policies and programs. Exhibit 4.10 is a form to help planners perform this step.

EXHIBIT 4.10

Form for planning alternative solutions

If you project mismatches in any occupation, you can start planning training and development activities.

How many people each year will you train or upgrade for each occupation?					How many people each year will you hire externally for each occupation?					How many people each year will you promote or transfer into each occupation?				
1st yr	2nd yr	3rd yr	4th yr	5th yr	1st yr	2nd yr	3rd yr	4th yr	5th yr	1st yr	2nd yr	3rd yr	4th yr	5th yr

SOURCE: Ontario Manpower Commission, *Human Resources Planning Manual* (Toronto: Ontario Ministry of Labour and Ontario Regional Office, Employment and Immigration Canada, 1982).

Planning for Anticipated Shortages

Anticipated labour shortages can be met in several ways. The organization can:

1. Transfer employees to jobs in which shortages exist.
2. Train employees to move up to jobs in which shortages exist.
3. Have employees work overtime.
4. Increase employee productivity.
5. Hire part-time employees.
6. Hire temporary full-time employees.
7. Hire permanent full-time employees.
8. Subcontract work to other firms.
9. Forego increases in production.
10. Install equipment to perform some of the tasks that would have been done by workers (capital substitution).

Basically, these options represent variations on three approaches: the organization can try to use its present employees better (Options 1 to 4); it can hire additional workers (Options 5 to 7); or it can seek to lower its requirements for labour (Options 8 to 10).

Utilizing present employees. Making better use of present employees is a very common response to a labour shortage. Simply transferring employees within the organization is, of course, not always possible. The firm may not have a surplus of workers in other jobs, or the individuals who could be transferred may not have the job skills required for the area of shortage. Overtime or training may be the more appropriate response, with the choice depending on the lead time available and the amount of training involved. In 1979, the Economic Council of Canada conducted the Human Resources Survey, a broad-based survey of employers' human resource problems and practices. Approximately half the respondents had experienced "hiring difficulties" during the previous two years; as shown in Exhibit 4.11, 58.1 per cent responded with vocational training and 37.1 with the use of overtime.[16] Similarly, a detailed study of the shortage of tool and die makers, who are highly skilled workers, found that overtime was employers' most common response; some firms also increased the number of apprentices they were training.[17]

Another way of countering a labour shortage with existing employees is to increase productivity. *Productivity* refers simply to the amount of product or service provided by a specific number of employees in a given unit of time. The higher the level of productivity, the fewer employees are needed to produce a given level of output. For example, ten highly productive computer programmers may be able to

[16] Betcherman, p. 33.

[17] Noah M. Meltz, *Economic Analysis of Labour Shortages: The Case of Tool and Die Makers in Ontario* (Toronto: Ontario Economic Council, 1982), pp. 32–5.

EXHIBIT 4.11

Specific responses to shortage situations 1977–79 (n = 1,573)

	Percentage of all situations
Training personnel	58.1
Overtime	37.1
Searching outside region	35.2
Lowering qualifications	26.9
Improving wages and benefits	23.4
Curtailing production	17.2
Subcontracting	15.7
Searching outside Canada	10.6
Capital substitution	2.5

NOTE: Total exceeds 100 per cent because of multiple responses.

SOURCE: Gordon Betcherman, *Meeting Skill Requirements: Report of the Human Resources Survey* (Ottawa: Economic Council of Canada, 1982), p. 33.

do the job of 15 less productive ones. Employee productivity can be increased in a number of ways, including:

1. Offering monetary incentives, such as pay increases or bonuses, for higher productivity or performance levels.
2. Improving employees' job skills so that they can produce more or produce the same amount in less time or at a lower cost to the organization.
3. Redesigning work processes and methods so that greater outputs are achieved. (Workers often have valuable contributions to make in this regard. See Ford Engine Plant 2 example at the beginning of Chapter 2.)
4. Using more efficient equipment so that greater outputs are achieved.

Hiring outside the organization. Organizations can also plan to meet anticipated labour shortages by hiring new employees. Whether the strategy is to take on part-timers or full-timers, whether to hire temporary or permanent employees, it is at this point that the state of the external labour market becomes important to the HRP process. The extent to which an organization can rely on external sources of supply depends in large part on the general state of the labour market and on the state of the market for that particular kind of labour in that particular locality.

There is a complex relationship between human resource planning at the firm level and national manpower projections. National, or macro, projections attempt to project overall demand-supply situations, while an individual firm may anticipate a shortage of workers with a particular skill. The degree of success the employer can expect in recruiting persons with that skill will depend on the composite developments in the relevant labour market. If there is a general excess supply, then the firm should have no trouble recruiting in the external (outside of the firm) labour market. If everyone else is looking for the same skill at the same time, then individual employers will have difficulty recruiting the people they need. Because national projections deal with the whole economy, their occupational categories may sometimes be broader than the categories an individual firm would use. Nevertheless, the Canada Employment and Immigration Commission's (CEIC's) Canadian Occupational Projection Systems (COPS) model, which is used to project demand and supply, contains approximately 500 occupations based on the four-digit *Canadian Classification and Dictionary of Occupations* (CCDO).[18]

These projections include estimates of changes in requirements based on projections of output and attrition through retirements and deaths, along with projections of sources of supply from training and educational institutions and immigration. An attempt is also made to estimate interoccupational transfers. The result is a system which provides projections of the general demand-supply situation in a range of occupations for Canada and the provinces. The larger the geographic area and employment base, the more specific the details. Regional offices of CEIC are the appropriate points of contact for details on the availability of specific data and the costs of providing the data.

Even with access to macro human resources projections, the individual firm has to do some analysis in order to understand how the particular organization's recruiting could be affected by macro labour market developments. For example, even in a shortage situation, a high paying firm or one with many opportunities for promotion, will have much less difficulty recruiting workers than a low paying or limited opportunity firm.[19] By the same token, even in a time of high unemployment (surplus of workers), a firm with very poor wages and working conditions may have trouble finding people who are prepared to work there. HRM professionals, therefore, have to interpret broad labour market developments and projections in the light of the specific wage, working condition and size of the firm. A small, high paying, good working condition firm in a large labour market should have little trouble recruiting high quality workers, whatever the situation in the labour market. And vice versa for poor paying organizations. Any quantitative analysis by HRM professionals should be strongly supplemented by qualitative supply outlooks from provincial labour and manpower

[18] Canadian Occupational Projection System (COPS) Employment and Immigration Canada. See: *Job Futures: An Occupational Outlook to 1992,* 1986–1987 edition. (Ottawa: Minister of Supply and Services Canada, 1986).

[19] Noah M. Meltz and John H. Blakely, *Linking Firms' and Macro Human Resource Planning.* (Toronto: Ontario Manpower Commission, Ontario Ministry of Labour, 1984.)

departments or the regional offices of the Canada Employment and Immigration Commission.[20]

A study of the accuracy of Canadian macro human resource projections in the 1960s and 1970s concluded that, in general, the estimates were reasonably close to what actually occurred.[21] The results of three national occupational projections were examined.[22] In all three cases a majority of the major occupation groups were within ± 10 per cent of the actual employment, while for detailed occupations a third were within ± 10 per cent of the actual and almost one-half were within ± 20 per cent. A study of American projections also found that results were fairly close to the actual.[23] The conclusion is that these models can provide useful information for assessing future labour market developments.

When planners are able to foresee shortages for certain types of labour, they must develop strategies to obtain the necessary human resources. In general, when labour is scarce, organizations must recruit aggressively and offer potential employees attractive inducements. Aggressive recruitment often consists of looking for candidates in another locality, even outside the country, where the shortage may not exist. For example, the Human Resources Survey found that 35.2 per cent of firms that encountered shortages searched for workers in other regions and 10.6 per cent looked to import labour (see Exhibit 4.11).[24]

Inducements can be in the form of high levels of pay, generous benefits packages, or good opportunities for career advancement. Such inducements can be highly effective in recruiting. For example, in the early 1970s, Canada had a shortage of nurses. In 1974–75, the salaries of nurses increased by 50 per cent and the shortage disappeared.[25]

Alternative recruiting policies and programs are discussed in Chapter 6.

[20] The Ontario Manpower Commission also has a demand-supply occupational projection model. See: *Labour Market Outlook for Ontario, 1984–1988* (Toronto: Ontario Manpower Commission, Ontario Ministry of Labour, 1984). Various labour market projection models are examined in David K. Foot, *Labour Market Analysis with Canadian Macroeconomic Models: A Review* (Toronto: Centre for Industrial Relations, University of Toronto, 1980.)

[21] David K. Foot and Noah M. Meltz, *Canadian Occupational Projections: An Analysis of the Economic Determinants 1961–1981* (Hull, Quebec: Employment and Immigration Canada, 1985.)

[22] The three projections which were examined are: N.M. Meltz and G.P. Penz. *Canada's Manpower Requirements in 1970*, Department of Manpower and Immigration, (Ottawa: Queen's Printer, 1968); B. Ahamad, *A Projection of Manpower Requirements by Occupation in 1975, Canada and Its Regions*, Department of Manpower and Immigration, (Ottawa: Queen's Printer, 1969); and Canadian Occupational Forecasting Program, *Forecasts of Occupational Demand to 1982*, Department of Manpower and Immigration, (Ottawa: Information Canada, 1975).

[23] R.B. Freeman, "An Empirical Analysis of the Fixed Coefficient, 'Manpower Requirements' Model, 1960–1970," *The Journal of Human Resources*, vol. XV, no. 2, (Winter 1980), pp. 176–99.

[24] Betcherman, p. 33.

[25] David Stager and Noah M. Meltz, "Manpower Planning in the Professions," *The Canadian Journal of Higher Education*, vol. 7, no. 3 (1977), p. 79.

Other responses. As we have seen, organizations can respond to labour shortages by adjusting their labour supplies from within or without. Three other approaches are possible: subcontracting work to other firms; foregoing increases in production; and substituting capital for labour by mechanizing jobs that have been performed by hand. Subcontracting may be a viable alternative if the labour shortage is expected to be of short duration, if the firm believes it is more important to fill orders than to delay them, or if specialized skills are available outside at cheaper cost. If the costs of recruiting are too high, or the shortage is too severe, it may be necessary to forego increasing production. For example, in the late 1970s some tool and die firms simply closed their order books since they were already booked several years in advance. Capital substitution is usually expensive and can be justified as an answer to a labour shortage only if the shortage looks to be of long duration. However, many organizations are turning to capital substitution in order to streamline operations and become more competitive.

Planning for Anticipated Surpluses

In the 1960s and 1970s, planners focussed mainly on avoiding costly shortages of scarce and valued labour. Today, due to introduction of new technologies and reduced demand for products, many organizations are forced to "downsize," or reduce the size of their work force. Thus, excess supply has emerged as a growing concern of human resource planners. Nearly one-fourth of employers surveyed in one study reported using human resource forecasting in order to avoid layoffs.[26]

There are a number of strategies for dealing with labour surpluses; among them:

1. plant closures.
2. permanent layoffs.
3. incentives to early retirement.
4. shrinkage via attrition.
5. retraining and transfer.
6. temporary shutdowns.
7. temporary layoffs.
8. reduced work week.
9. work-sharing.
10. cutting or freezing pay and/or benefits.

Surpluses are dealt with in three basic ways by the above strategies. Strategies 1–4 require permanent work force reductions; strategy 5 redistributes supply to areas of demand; and strategies 6–10 favour retention of surplus workers with accompanying cost-saving measures.

[26] C.R. Greer and D. Armstrong, "Human resource forecasting and planning: A state-of-the-art investigation," *Human Resource Planning*, 1980, vol. 3, no. 2, pp. 67–78.

Permanent reductions. Drastic measures, such as plant closures and permanent layoffs, are rarely chosen lightly, yet they affect tens of thousands of Canadian workers annually. Such measures are usually taken in response to reductions in product demand which make continued operation impractical or impossible. While planning seeks to avoid drastic solutions, sometimes they cannot be helped. Planning does make it possible, however, for management to give workers advance notice of closure or layoffs. Research has shown that advance notice reduces the negative impact of layoffs on employees.[27]

Two more attractive alternatives are letting the work force shrink by attrition and offering incentives to early retirement. Letting the work force shrink by attrition is a gradual process, requiring advance planning. This is not an emergency response, but rather a method of avoiding problems of oversupply, especially in certain areas, by curtailing hiring, promotion, and transfer into jobs in which surpluses are expected.

Offering incentives to early retirement is a fairly recent solution to labour surplus problems. Early retirement programs offer incentives such as bonuses and full retirement benefits "for a limited time only" to those nearing retirement who chose to exit at the company's convenience. One problem with early retirement programs is that they are offered across-the-board to all employees who have reached a certain predetermined age, length of service, or combination of the two. This sometimes results in the loss of employees the company would like to retain. Early retirement programs may also be quite costly. However, they are viewed by many as a humane alternative to layoffs. International Business Machines (IBM), Air Canada, and Sears are examples of companies who have at one time or another offered incentives to early retirement.

Redistribution of workers. Redistribution of workers is a possibility if surpluses exist in some areas but not others. This option requires advance planning since displaced workers often must acquire new skills in order to be useful in areas of increased demand. Unfortunately, programs of retraining and transfer are rare. One company that has used this approach successfully is IBM, which uses a combination of human resource planning, training, and transfer to achieve a balance among units in its work force. Where surpluses exist, qualified and interested employees are trained in new capacities and equipped for second careers in the company. Successful program participants include obsolete assemblers who are now clerical workers, engineers who work as computer programmers, and technicians who transferred to customer service.[28]

Cost-saving measures. Cost-saving measures include temporary shutdown, temporary layoffs, reduced work weeks, work-sharing programs,

[27] J.P. Gordus, P. Jarley, and L.A. Ferman, *Plant Closings and Economic Dislocation* (Kalamazoo, MI: W.E. Upjohn Institute, 1981), pp. 124–26.

[28] Beverly Jacobson, *Young Programs for Older Workers* (New York: Van Nostrand Reinhold, 1980), p. 12.

and cuts or freezes in pay. Under a reduced work week, employees work fewer hours and receive reduced pay. Under work-sharing programs, employees work reduced hours and receive Unemployment Insurance benefits for hours not worked. Canada experimented with a program of work-sharing between 1977 and 1979, then reintroduced the program in 1981 in the face of a substantial increase in unemployment. The program permits workers to draw Unemployment Insurance benefits for part of the week without losing entitlement to future UI benefits. For example, instead of laying off, say, one-fifth of its staff, a firm reduces the work week for all employees in a unit from five to four days, and the workers receive UI benefits for the fifth day.[29]

The last alternative, cutting or freezing pay in order to avoid layoffs, debuted in U.S. auto and airline industries. Since then it has been used in a number of Canadian companies, including MacMillan Bloedel, which cut pay to managerial employees and withheld salaries of other personnel. This method has also been used by the governments of Quebec and Manitoba.

Evaluating the Alternatives

After generating alternative approaches to solving anticipated labour shortages or surpluses, planners must evaluate the alternatives and select the best for recommendation to management. Many considerations affect choice of a planning strategy; three basic ones are: (1) size of the anticipated shortages or surpluses; (2) expected duration of the change in demand for human resources; and (3) amount of lead time before shortages or surpluses occur.

The size of a shortage or surplus affects choice of a planning strategy. Small shortages can usually be handled by transferring employees in from other jobs, by attention to methods of improving employee productivity (including introduction of more efficient equipment and use of short training programs), by making heavy use of overtime, and by hiring temporary employees. Large shortages, on the other hand, usually require employers to use external sources of permanent labour, since internal supplies are usually inadequate to meet the demand. Small surpluses can usually be managed by transferring employees, by reducing work hours, and by curtailing hiring or promotion in that area. In the case of large surpluses in one area and shortages in another, it may be cost effective for an organization to train surplus employees to assume the responsibilities of jobs in which there are shortages. Temporary and permanent layoffs are more appropriate when surpluses are great than when they are small.

Another factor affecting choice of a planning strategy is expected duration of the change in demand. If the change is only temporary, temporary solutions often suffice. Many seasonal businesses, for example, must plan for wide variation in both duration and magnitude of demand. Toy manufacturers, seed companies, and gift-wrap manufacturers,

[29] N.M. Meltz, F. Reid, and G.S. Swartz, *Sharing the Work: An Analysis of the Issues in Worksharing and Job Sharing* (Toronto: University of Toronto Press, 1981).

for example, experience such variation regularly. In fact, its very predictability aids HRP.

Labour shortages of short duration can be handled by hiring additional, usually temporary, employees. Forecasts of long shortages, on the other hand, require consideration and implementation of many human resource policies and programs, including recruiting, hiring, and training. The costs associated with these programs can be large, especially if they involve skilled or professional workers. Short-duration surpluses are usually met with temporary layoffs or plant shutdowns, but in cases that involve skilled and professional workers, the potential cost of eventual replacement may be greater than the cost of maintaining surplus people. Employers may thus retain skilled workers during short-duration surpluses, rather than risk their finding other employment while they are laid off. Medium-duration surpluses are sometimes handled by temporary adoption of a three- or four-day work week. Long-duration surpluses invariably require the termination of employees.

Regardless of the magnitude or duration of shortages and surpluses, they can almost certainly be handled more effectively if an organization has sufficient lead time to prepare for them. Surprise changes in the supply-demand equation for labour are costly to both employer and employee. Without ample lead time, an organization has a limited number of responses available. For example, KU lost the option of hiring additional business faculty to meet its needs because it did not have the necessary lead time to budget for and recruit them. Surprises can usually be avoided by constant, careful monitoring of the economic, legislative, technological, and cultural environments.

Human resource planners can make a major contribution to organizational effectiveness and profitability by providing managers with alternative strategies for solving labour-supply problems. Planners should provide management with information on each alternative concerning: (1) its financial and human costs and benefits; (2) its effects on other organizational components, such as units not directly affected by the labour problem; (3) the length of time required to execute it; and (4) its probable effectiveness in reducing the shortage or surplus. There are three mathematically sophisticated methods useful in evaluating alternative human resource programs and in determining optimal combinations of human resources, money, and time. These methods are *linear programming, goal programming*, and *computer simulation*.

Linear programming. Linear programming is a mathematical technique that provides an optimal solution for reaching a quantitative goal, such as minimizing total labour costs within a number of conditions or constraints. Linear programming begins with the selection of a goal or variable, such as labour costs, training time, or some other quantifiable factor. Next, planners select the major factors or constraints which determine and affect the goal to be optimized. For example, administrators at Kanata University could have used linear programming to determine the minimum cost of handling an undergraduate enrolment of 1,500 within the constraints of certain maximum class sizes and numbers of instructors in various ranks. A linear programming solution would have specified the values of each constraint necessary to handle the given enrolment at minimal (optimal) cost. Linear programming also provides planners with information on which constraints have some slack and which don't.

This method eliminates unfeasible solutions. If, for example, constraints of a maximum class size of 30 and a maximum faculty of 50 result in an unfeasible solution, additional linear programs could be run using different constraints to reach a feasible solution. The use of linear programming is limited by the necessity of specifying the goal and all constraints in quantitative terms.

Goal programming. Goal programming is a more sophisticated and realistic version of linear programming. It is more realistic than linear programming because it includes stochastic models and multiple goals can be specified. Multiple goals such as increasing profits by 10 per cent, maintaining current quality levels, *and* hiring bilingual salespeople are typical of the realities managers face.

Goal programming is a method of finding optimal solutions for a number of goals in combination. For example, Kanata University would probably like to solve its problems while achieving several other objectives, such as:

1. Keeping the Faculty of Business' salary budget within 15 per cent of the previous year's.
2. Increasing new faculty positions by no more than 5 per cent beyond the previous year's level.
3. Retaining all tenured faculty members in the Faculty of Arts.

Of course, any one of these goals may be more important than another. Goal programming can provide a solution that takes such priorities into account.

Goal programming was developed by the Office of Civilian Personnel in the U.S. Navy. Because of its complexity and associated costs, its use has been limited to large organizations, primarily the military and other government organizations.

Computer simulation. Computer simulation was discussed earlier as a method of forecasting human resource needs. It can also be used to examine the effects of alternative policies and programs to reduce forecast shortages and surpluses. By considering each alternative in relation to the simulated human resource system, it provides an assessment of the probable effects of a policy or program on various components of the system or the system as a whole. These data form the basis for comparing one alternative with another in order to determine which can best serve an organization's purposes. An example of a computer simulation is the Minnesota Manpower Management Simulation developed by Mahoney and Milkovich.[30] A realistic model of a hypothetical casualty insurance company, this simulation permits examination of

[30] T.H. Mahoney and G.T. Milkovich, "Computer Simulation: A Training Tool for Manpower Managers," *Personnel Journal*, December 1975, pp. 609–12, 637.

the effects of personnel decisions on human resource flows and organizational performance.

Evaluating Human Resource Planning Effectiveness

Organizations should evaluate their human resource planning efforts to determine their effectiveness in helping to achieve organizational goals and objectives. Evaluating in terms of costs and benefits is difficult. The costs are fairly clear, but the benefits are more intangible and difficult to measure.

For this reason, the benefits of human resource planning are often expressed not in positive terms but as the avoidance of costly problems, such as labour shortages, which can result in lost sales or other lost business opportunities. There are also benefits associated with avoiding oversupply. Surpluses can result in an organization's paying excessive wages and benefits and in boredom and low morale among employees who have little opportunity to be productive.

Evaluating effectiveness of HRP is sometimes difficult since what is in the best interests of an employer may not be in the best interests of employees or the community. For example, a strategy of downsizing through layoffs and early retirement may benefit the company, but demoralize many employees. While laid off workers may argue that HRP has been ineffective in their organizations, the layoff strategy may have resulted in greater profitability and higher prices of the company's stock. The HRP process may be regarded as successful if HRM staff have been able to alert and work with top management regarding likely labour shortages and surpluses. The fact that forecasting occurs, that potential shortages and surpluses are identified, and that alternative approaches are examined—these are all signs of an effective HRM function.

Since HRP seeks to forecast human resource needs, an obvious measure of its effectiveness is how well human resource needs are anticipated and met. One measure of the effective anticipation of human resource needs is the number of job vacancies in an organization and how long they remain vacant. Large numbers of jobs standing vacant for long periods of time indicate an organization's failure to plan effectively for its human resource needs.

The effectiveness of human resource planning can also be evaluated according to the purposes stated at the beginning of this chapter. Pertinent questions include: (1) How useful is human resource planning in setting organizational goals and objectives? (2) Does the planning process provide management with the information it needs to make sound decisions affecting policies and programs? and (3) Is management willing to consider inputs from the planning process in setting organizational goals and in making policy and planning decisions?

It is difficult for any planning process to achieve its aims without the cooperation and blessing of management.

The Personnel Audit

The personnel audit is a comprehensive examination of the effectiveness of all aspects of personnel and industrial relations in an organization.[31] It serves as a control function evaluating effectiveness of the human resources area. Though HRM staff may separately evaluate effectiveness of various functions such as HRP, recruiting, selection and compensation, a personnel audit includes all HRM programs and policies. However, an evaluation of HRP which included the HRM programs and policies used in pursuit of HR goals could be called a personnel audit. In general, evaluation of any specific HRM functions may be a part of a personnel audit.

There are several reasons why organizations may conduct periodic personnel audits. First, since labour costs are a large if not the largest component of total product or service costs, it is logical that management should utilize some control over the human resource area. Secondly, HRM staff may use personnel audit data to justify the existence and budgets of their staff and programs.[32] A third valuable function of the audit is that it provides, like other control mechanisms, valuable feedback from employees and line managers. This feedback may be used to modify and improve various HRM programs and policies to make more efficient use of human resources. Personnel audits may also discover problems such as unqualified HRM staff, lack of understanding of or compliance with human resource policies by line managers, and low levels of employee satisfaction with various policies and programs. Excessive absenteeism, turnover, or difficulty hiring adequate numbers of qualified employees may, for example, indicate needed changes in compensation, recruiting methods, and perhaps supervisor training. Thus, the personnel audit serves as an information gathering process and as the basis for changes in policy and practice.

Personnel audits may collect and utilize many types of data. Some of the more common data used are: the ratio of HRM staff to employees, changes in number of employees over several time periods, turnover, absenteeism, compensation and benefit costs, number of grievances filed, and number of workplace injuries. Additional sources of audit data which are sometimes used include surveys of employee attitudes toward various HRM programs and policies and managerial perceptions of HRM programs and their results. Some types of data such as absences

[31] W.R. Mahler, "Auditing PAIR," in D. Yoder and H.G. Heneman, Jr. (eds.) *Handbook of Personnel and Industrial Relations* (Washington, D.C.: Bureau of National Affairs, 1979), pp. 2.91–2.103.

[32] D.E. Dimick and V.V. Murray, "Correlates of Substantive Policy Decisions in Organizations: The Case of Human Resource Management," *Academy of Management Journal*, 1978, vol. 21, pp. 611–23.

must be continually collected while others such as surveys are done only periodically. There are, of course, many other sources of data which may be useful for personnel audit purposes. Some audit procedures include a descriptive component in which the major activities of the HRM unit are identified and compared with policies and procedures for internal consistency.

A study of an insurance company and a hospital provide insights into typical audit findings.[33] The presence of an acting manager of human resources instead of a permanent one at the insurance company caused the HR staff to feel a lack of power and direction; operating managers also felt that the situation reduced the effectiveness of the HR unit. Additionally, operating managers felt, among other things, that the lack of an in-house training program hindered performance and that the performance rating form was ineffective and needed updating. Managers in the hospital, on the other hand, felt their HR department was too authoritarian and controlling and should serve in an advisory role. The audit of the hospital also revealed that recruiting and hiring policies needed to be centrally coordinated rather than left to individual departments, and job descriptions, career counselling, exit interviews, and turnover statistics needed to be improved.

A recent study examined the relationship between 37 personnel audit measures, executive perceptions, and magnitude of personnel budget on a per capita basis.[34] This study of 26 independent plants of a large electronics manufacturer found that the 37 audit measures resulted in nine factors. These nine factors represented the major HRM functions plus one factor related to managerial behaviour and a second to policies and procedures. High levels of employee satisfaction with personnel units were associated with high scores on the staffing and compensation aspects of the audit. The importance of staffing and compensation in this company is apparent from this finding. Results indicated that magnitude of personnel budget per capita is positively related to three factors: (1) net profits per capita, (2) employee satisfaction with personnel and (3) executives' perception of the overall contribution of personnel to achievement of organizational goals. This finding suggests a relationship between effectiveness of the HRM area and profitability. There is, therefore, some evidence that the personnel audit is useful to describe and evaluate HRM functions, as well as being related to executive perceptions of personnel.

Though the benefits of conducting periodic personnel audits appear to outweigh their costs, it is likely that few employers conduct thorough audits on a regular basis. Some employers may evaluate various programs and policies only when there are indications of problems such as high turnover, high labour costs or low quality or quantity of output. The more systematic personnel audit offers benefits to both HRM and operating managers.

[33] T. Hercus and D. Oades, "The Human Resource Audit: An Instrument for Change," *Human Resource Planning*, 1982, vol. 5, no. 1, pp. 43–9.

[34] L.R. Gomez-Mejia, "Dimensions and Correlates of the Personnel Audit as an Organizational Assessment Tool," *Personnel Psychology*, vol. 38, no. 2, pp. 293–308.

Summary

This chapter deals with one of the newest and most significant HRM functions, human resource planning. Though relatively few organizations currently employ human resource planners, economic, technological, and legislative changes will lead more employers to seek professionals with human resource planning skills. The growing importance of skilled labour will further increase the use of human resource planning in top management decisions. As human resource planning grows in importance and usage, current methods of forecasting, projection, and simulation will be refined.

Human resource planning is an important development for the HRM profession since it requires a systematic and goal-oriented approach to all major HRM functions, from recruiting to training and development to compensation. It links human resources to organizational goals and leads to a systematic evaluation of the effectiveness of all human resource programs. Finally, it requires managers and HRM professionals to consider human resource programs as interrelated, rather than as separate and distinct programs. Considering the relative costs and benefits of a policy of hiring experienced, trained employees, as opposed to hiring inexperienced employees and training them, is an example of an approach to a planning problem that recognizes the interrelatedness of the separate HRM functions.

Project Ideas

1. Locate a manager or a HRM professional in an organization engaged in human resource planning. Interview the individual on the nature of the planning effort, and relate the details in a written report. Find out what type of human resource planning is done (short-, medium-, or long-range), and how often. Do forecasts make subjective estimates, or are quantitative models used? What kind of human resource information system does the organization have and how is it used in making forecasts? Also find out who in the organization is involved in human resource planning and how the planning efforts affect other human resource functions in the organization. If a number of students in the class conduct such interviews, oral reports can be given, demonstrating a range of real-world planning activities.

2. Construct a hypothetical city and forecast its need for parking meter readers. (In other words, create a hypothetical situation on which to base forecasts of the need for parking meter readers.) Give such descriptive details as population, proportion of the population that drives to work, number of parking meters, and so on. Be specific and include in your description of the city as many pieces of information as you can think of that could affect your forecast of the

need for meter readers. After describing your hypothetical city forecast its need for parking meter readers. Describe the rationale(s) behind your forecast. Did you use any rules of thumb or other forecasting methods?

3. Develop a simple transition matrix for your faculty or another small group or organization. Categorize people according to their position in the organization (for example, "first year," "second year," "alumnus," and so on). Record each person's position at the present point in time, and then, several months later, record each person's position again. Record, in a table such as the one below, how many people have remained in the same position or category and how many have moved to each of the other possible categories. If there is much movement between categories, suggest possible causes. The purpose of this exercise is to give the student a better understanding of the operation of flow factors.

Transition matrix

Number of persons in position or category for time 1	***Number of persons in position or category for time 2***				
	Pos. 1	Pos. 2	Pos. 3	Pos. 4	Pos. 5
Pos. 1					
Pos. 2					
Pos. 3					
Pos. 4					
Pos. 5					

Cases

Case 4.1: Ontario Hydro's Corporate Planning Process

Ontario Hydro, with its 81 power plants and 30,000 employees, is one of the world's largest publicly-owned utilities, providing electricity to nearly 3 million customers. Yet only recently has the company established a formalized, integrated corporate planning process.

Prior to the 1970s, corporate planning at Ontario Hydro was characterized by fragmentation, and planning centred mainly around the design, development, and construction of facilities. Rarely was a thought given to a plan's human resource implications; rather, it was assumed that the necessary human support systems would be available, and they were, for the most part, in the predictable environment of the 1950s and 1960s. These were times when growth was steady and demand for the company's product could easily be forecast.

In the 1970s, the company's environment became less predictable, increasing its need for planning. The demand for energy decreased and it became more difficult to find capital for purposes of expansion. Certain types of labour were also harder to find; for example, engineers were in short supply due to growth in the energy industry. This situation reversed itself, however, after the recession of the early 1980s when engineers were once again plentiful. Other forces contributing to the uncertain environment of the 1970s were increased government intervention, and changing employee attitudes toward work.

In the mid-1970s, Ontario Hydro separated its planning and administrative functions from operations in order to consolidate the planning function, which is coordinated by the Planning and Administration Group. Three planning processes evolved and are now in use:

1. Corporate strategic planning, which is intended to provide a corporate vision to guide the next 20 years;
2. Corporate reference planning, a medium-term, 10-year time frame which translates the strategic plan into a committed facilities plan; and
3. Work program planning and budgeting, which covers the short-term (1–3 years) and provides specific work plans and resource approvals for the next 12 months.*

Human resource planning (HRP) is an integral part of each planning process; in fact, policy dictates that human resource requirements be forecast as a part of other forecasts. Policy also dictates that "managers at all levels shall engage in human resource planning as an integrated and supporting part of work program planning."**

During strategic planning, the human resource implications of alternative strategies are considered, and long-range forecasts of human resource requirements are prepared. In corporate reference planning, alternative plans are assessed as to whether their human resource implications are manageable. Such assessment requires close monitoring of the internal work force, as well as external monitoring

*J.C. Rush and L.C. Borne, "Human Resources Planning Contributions to Corporate Planning at Ontario Hydro," *Human Resource Planning*, 1983, vol. 6, no. 4, pp. 193–205.

**Ibid.

of labour market trends. To monitor the internal work force, Ontario Hydro has developed a variety of analytical tools and systems which allow it to monitor work force demographics, staff flows, and employee capabilities.

The role of HRP in short-term work program planning and budgeting is illustrated in the following example provided by Rush and Borne, who studied Ontario Hydro's corporate planning process:

> In guidelines for the 1982 budget, branch executives were warned of a scarcity of skilled human resources and a relatively large proportion of retirements during the budget period. The human resource strategy to be undertaken was (a) to develop the resource from graduates of Canada's educational system; (b) to reduce dependency on those with scarce skills; and (c) to consider the option of buying services. It was suggested that for (a) this might involve redesigning jobs to meet entry-level skills and developing necessary skill in these younger people. For (b) this might involve freeing those scarce resources from tasks easily done by others and using these people to develop skills in others.***

Ontario Hydro's scenario for the 1980s, and perhaps the 1990s, is one of slow growth and environmental uncertainty. In order to adapt, the company must increase productivity while decreasing the size of its work force. According to Rush and Borne, "The primary key to success will be effective management of the corporation's internal labour market, supplemented by efficient and highly targeted external recruitment."****

Questions:

1. What factors contributed to the need for corporate planning at Ontario Hydro? Discuss how each may affect the need for planning.
2. Ontario Hydro saw little need for human resource planning prior to 1970. Why? What benefits, if any, are to be gained by using human resource planning in a fairly predictable environment?
3. What do you think of Ontario Hydro's policy requiring strategic planners to consider the human resource requirements of plans? What are some advantages and disadvantages of such a policy?
4. Based on the scenario for the 1980s, human resource planners at Ontario Hydro will be considering strategies to shrink the size of the work force. Discuss the pros and cons of some possible strategies for meeting this objective.

*** Ibid.
**** Ibid.

Case 4.2: Use of a Markov-Type Model at Weyerhaeuser Company

In 1972, executives at Weyerhaeuser Company, a leading lumber firm, announced plans for company expansion. This raised the question of whether existing human resources could meet manpower needs. The Manpower Planning Department, a unit of Human Resource Planning, was instructed to look into the matter. Shortly thereafter, a person with operations research (OR) expertise was hired to help the company develop a corporate manpower plan.

By developing such a plan, Weyerhaeuser was moving away from replacement charts based on yearly trend analyses to a more "macro," longer-range view of its manpower needs. Consistent with this view, a Markov-type model was developed by the OR expert to facilitate analysis of human resource flows throughout the organization.

According to researchers who studied it, the model basically "analyzed the flow of personnel from the source of supply (internal or external) to the point of demand (requirements for particular jobs). In addition, the model allowed planners to use transition rates (the rate at which people moved from one level to the next in the hierarchy) as constraints or variables in balancing supply and demand. For example, by assuming constant transition rates the company could forecast (project) what manpower supply for certain position levels would be for particular time periods. By varying transition rates, planners could analyze the impact of alternative policies governing the movement of personnel in the organization. Manpower flows within the company could then be modified (through promotion policies, for example) so that deficits or surpluses could be corrected."†

The Markov-type model became an integral part of Weyerhaeuser's seven-step Human Resource Planning System in 1972 and was used consistently until mid-1974. At first, it addressed manpower needs for a scenario of growth and expansion, projecting manpower supply at each of seven position levels over time. One early use of the model resulted in a replacement planning program that identified back-ups for employees targeted for promotion. This program facilitated staffing by ensuring that vacancies would be filled readily.

Later, during the 1973–1974 recession, the model focussed on human resource implications of the slowdown. It was during this time that the company realized it had to reduce the size of its work force. A number of alternatives, including general layoffs, were considered before the decision was made to shrink the work force via attrition. Analyses provided by the Markov-type model were instrumental in the choice of this particular reduction strategy. One important analysis revealed that total manpower requirements at

† P.F. Buller and W.R. Maki, "A Case History of a Manpower Planning Model," *Human Resource Planning*, 1981, vol. 4, no. 3, pp. 129–37.

Weyerhaeuser were dictated largely and consistently by turnover rather than growth. Another key analysis was a cash flow analysis, which compared the costs of a general layoff with the costs of an attrition strategy.

During the two years of its greatest use, the Markov-type model yielded highly similar forecasts of Weyerhaeuser's manpower requirements. Even changes in company growth did not significantly alter the demand for human resources. Manpower flows were remarkably stable. Thus, planners became less concerned with monitoring employee flows and more concerned with efficient utilization of people in their present positions.

By 1975, the model was being used only occasionally for the study of manpower flows in certain segments of the company. However, the number of employees included was often too small to yield meaningful statistical results. In 1976, its use ceased entirely and its developer, who was also head of Manpower Planning, was promoted and left the department.

Questions:

1. What factors explain the initial development and use of the Markov-type model at Weyerhaeuser? In your opinion, which factor was most influential? Why?
2. What factors explain discontinuance of the model? In your opinion, which factor was most influential? Why?
3. Do you think Weyerhaeuser would have developed the Markov-type model to facilitate downsizing rather than expansion? Why or why not?
4. Weyerhaeuser's experience was one of using a particular planning technique for a while and then discontinuing it. How typical do you think this is of other organizations' experience with human resource planning? Why?

5

Job Analysis

Harold Muldridge was recently appointed human resources director of Waterford, a municipality with a population of 250,000. When Muldridge took the job, the chief executive officer told him to examine employee selection and performance appraisal procedures, which did not seem to be as effective as they should be. Muldridge was given the authority to hire several assistants to help with this endeavour, but the nature of their jobs was left largely up to him. Before Muldridge could make any progress on the selection and appraisal systems, several other problems were brought to his attention. An aspiring clerk in the records department wanted to know about opportunities for advancement, and Muldridge had little information to provide. The municipal vehicle-repair mechanics complained that they were underpaid for their work, and Muldridge could not say otherwise. Funds were obtained for a program to train drivers in the transport of handicapped persons in special vans, but the content of the training program remained unspecified. By this time, it was obvious to Muldridge that Waterford needed job analysis, which is basic to addressing all of the problems he was encountering and others in an organization.

This chapter deals with job analysis and how organizations use it. It discusses job analysis responsibilities, methods, problems, and issues.

Job Analysis: A Definition

While job analysis may seem a new and unfamiliar topic, its results are seen every day in Help Wanted columns of most newspapers. Job descriptions are an end product of job analysis; want ads represent miniature job descriptions.

Job analysis is the process of determining the nature or content of a job by collecting and organizing relevant information. A complete job analysis contains information about the following five factors, plus anything else deemed appropriate to describe fully the nature of the job: (1) work products—what the job seeks to accomplish; (2) necessary worker activities or behaviour required by the job; (3) equipment used; (4) factors in the work environment; and (5) personal characteristics required to do the job, such as typing speed, physical strength, or interest in working with children. The personal requirements of a job are referred to as job specifications. *Job specifications* are the human requirements deemed necessary for minimally acceptable performance on the job. They can include skills, abilities, level of education, experience, interests, personality traits, or physical characteristics. The ad in Exhibit 5.1 contains all of these factors except (3) equipment used.

Job analysis also includes organizing and summarizing information into job descriptions. A complete job description contains job title plus information relating to each factor already mentioned. Exhibit 5.2 is an example of a job description for a clerk/typist job in a municipal government. Note that it includes an overall description of the job, a listing of specific duties associated with the job, and a section on job specifications, including the requirements for education, experience, and specific, task-related knowledge and abilities. Note also that the overall description states the conditions under which work will be performed ("close supervision") and the level of performance expected ("an acceptable level"). "Other duties as assigned" is a catch-all phrase designed to give the employer some flexibility in the kinds of work that may be assigned to the clerk/typist.

Job-Related Definitions

The work of an organization is divided into individual responsibilities that are structured in the form of jobs. A *job* is a set of duties or responsibilities whose completion serves to further organizational objectives. Jobs that are similar in their duties, activities, and personal requirements and which can be found in different organizations at different times are classified into *occupations*. Employment and Immigration Canada's *Canadian Classification and Dictionary of Occupations* (CCDO) lists 30,000 job titles.[1] It groups almost 7,000 occupations (many have more than one job title) into progressively

[1] Manpower and Immigration Canada, *Canadian Classification and Dictionary of Occupations*, 1971 (Ottawa: Information Canada, 1971). New definitions and recent changes in the CCDO are in Employment and Immigration Canada, 1980 Guide. *Canadian Classification and Dictionary of Occupations* (Hull, Quebec: Ministry of Supply and Services Canada, 1980).

EXHIBIT 5.1

A familiar result of job analysis

Industrial Hygienist

4 Factors in work environments

Due to Suncor's rigorous safety standards and the existence of stringent petroleum industry occupational Health and Safety regulations, we are seeking a qualified and experienced industrial Hygienist. This position reports directly to the Loss Prevention Superintendent and will be based at our Oil Sands Operation in Fort McMurray, Alberta, however, approximately twenty percent of the incumbent's time will be spent at other Resource Group sites throughout Western Canada.

1 Work product

The incumbent will develop, monitor and recommend methods and procedures designed to ensure that the quality of the working environment, as experienced by Suncor employees, customers and members of the general public, is maintained at the highest possible level at all times. Other responsibilities include testing and recommending personal protective equipment and the training of employees in health hazard recognition techniques and ways of avoiding undue exposure.

2 Worker activities

5 Personal characteristics: Job specifications

Candidates should possess a post graduate degree in industrial Hygiene and have three to five years field, or equivalent work experience in the area of industrial Hygiene. A good knowledge of current legislation as it applies to the exposure, treatment, transportation and safe handling of hazardous material is also required, preferably within the petroleum industry.

Suncor offers an extremely competitive remuneration package that includes a savings plan with company contributions. Please forward your resume, quoting file #1032, in confidence, to: **Suncor Inc. Resources Group, Oil Sands Division, P.O. Bag 4014, Fort McMurray, Alberta T9H 3E2.**

No Agencies Please

broader categories, using a seven-digit code rather like a library's book-classification system. At the top of the inverted pyramid are 23 major groups, such as social sciences and related fields, medicine and health, and sales.

EXHIBIT 5.2

A typical job description

Clerk/typist in a municipal government

Under close supervision, to perform a variety of clerical duties at an acceptable level of performance, and other duties as assigned.

Typical duties

1. Types letters and other material from rough drafts or dictation devices; posts and updates information on various types of records and maintains files.
2. Answers enquiries from employees and the public about routine and established procedures and policies or refers to the appropriate individual or office.
3. Assists in preparing and checking forms, records, applications, and other materials for completeness and conformity with established procedures; makes routine follow-up to secure additional required information.
4. Composes routine correspondence; prepares departmental payroll records; orders departmental or divisional supplies.
5. Computes and extends figures that may involve several arithmetical processes.
6. Collects fees, prepares invoices, and verifies unusual entries.
7. Operates standard office equipment, including adding machines and calculators.

Job specifications

Education and experience: any combination equivalent to completion of secondary school and one year clerical and typing experience.

Knowledge and abilities: knowledge of office procedures and practices; ability to meet the public effectively; ability to type from clear copy at the rate of 45 words per minute; ability to do clerical work involving a limited use of independent judgement requiring speed and accuracy; ability to make arithmetical computations.

There is a difference between a job and a position, although the two terms are often used interchangeably. The major distinction is that jobs are performed by people, but people occupy positions. Most jobs in an organization usually have more than one position. For example, banks have several positions for the job of bank teller, and most grocery stores have a number of positions for the job of grocery checker. Workers in similar positions in an organization have very similar or the same duties and responsibilities because they are performing the same job. Thus, an organization may have 70 positions filled by 70 employees, but only 12 different jobs.

A job, or a position for a job, consists of a set of *duties*, or work-related responsibilities. Completion of duties requires certain behaviour specific to the task at hand. For example, the duties of a university professor usually include teaching courses, counselling students, conducting research, and rendering service to the university.

In order to complete one's duties, a number of tasks must be accomplished. A *task* is a specific work activity carried out to achieve a specific purpose. Tasks related to the duty of teaching courses include writing course outlines, preparing and giving lectures, and grading papers and examinations. The smallest unit used in most job analyses is an *element*, defined as a particular aspect of a particular task. Removing paper from one's desk drawer is an element related to the task of preparing a lecture or writing a course outline. Most job-analysis methods and job descriptions do not specify job elements. Such detail is necessary only for describing jobs that are highly repetitive and manual, such as assembly-line jobs, and jobs in which pay is determined by the number of units produced (piecework). Elements are also used in engineering methods of job analysis, such as time-and-motion studies and micro-motion analysis.

Organizational Uses of Job Analysis

Job analysis serves a variety of purposes in organizations. These can best be understood by examining job analysis in relation to other HRM functions. Relationships are summarized in Exhibit 5.3.

Human Resource Planning

As discussed in the previous chapter, job analysis plays a crucial role in human resource planning by providing information on the nature of a job and the skills required to do it. In assessing the needs of an organization, human resource planners use job analysis data to compare the skills required for particular jobs with the actual skills of employees in the organization (as determined by skills inventories). If employees' actual skills do not match the required skills of present jobs, organizations can take several actions to reduce the discrepancy. First, they can recruit, select, and hire persons with those skills that have been determined to be lacking or in short supply. Second, current employees can be trained to increase their present skill levels or to acquire new skills. Third, jobs can be redesigned, with or without the addition of more automated equipment, so that the skills required more closely match those available to the organization. A fourth alternative, useful in some cases, is to contract the work to groups or individuals outside the organization.

Human resource planners and management rely heavily on job analysis in carrying out organizational change and development programs. For example, the quality of working life (QWL) movement and, more recently downsizing, have led to enlargement and enrichment of jobs. In this case, job analysis information is used to redesign jobs so that they contain a greater variety of tasks (enlargement) and/or require higher levels of autonomy and responsibility (enrichment). Redesign

EXHIBIT 5.3

Organizational uses of job analysis

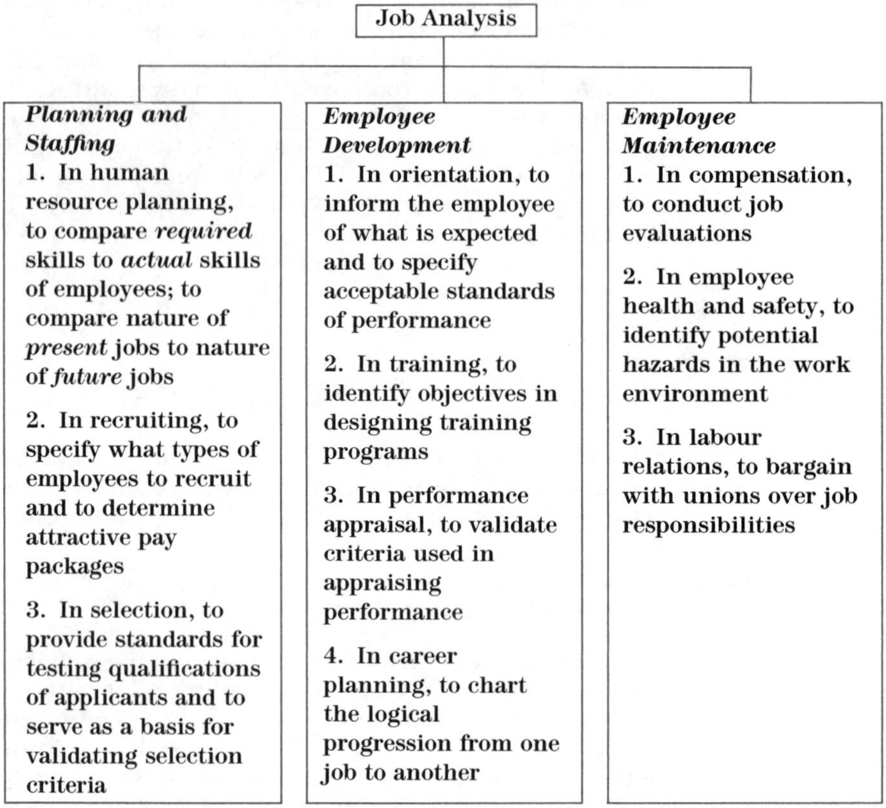

Job Analysis

Planning and Staffing

1. In human resource planning, to compare *required* skills to *actual* skills of employees; to compare nature of *present* jobs to nature of *future* jobs
2. In recruiting, to specify what types of employees to recruit and to determine attractive pay packages
3. In selection, to provide standards for testing qualifications of applicants and to serve as a basis for validating selection criteria

Employee Development

1. In orientation, to inform the employee of what is expected and to specify acceptable standards of performance
2. In training, to identify objectives in designing training programs
3. In performance appraisal, to validate criteria used in appraising performance
4. In career planning, to chart the logical progression from one job to another

Employee Maintenance

1. In compensation, to conduct job evaluations
2. In employee health and safety, to identify potential hazards in the work environment
3. In labour relations, to bargain with unions over job responsibilities

is, therefore, a major part of management's strategic plan for restructuring the organization. As such, it often creates a need for training, development of new career paths, adjustments in pay, and changes in labour agreements.

In any case, analyzing the nature of present jobs is an initial step in planning how jobs must change to meet future needs of the organization. Human resource planning requires a job analysis method that collects comparable data on a wide variety of jobs. These data are necessary to compare similarities and differences among jobs.

Recruiting

Analyzing jobs helps define what types of employees to recruit—what skills, abilities, knowledge, and experience are needed to do the job. In the example at the beginning of the chapter, if Harold Muldridge had had job descriptions for the assistants he was authorized to hire, he would have had a much clearer idea of what job-related characteristics to look for in the persons recruited to fill these positions.

In order to recruit employees successfully, an organization must offer pay that is equitable and competitive with that of other organizations. One can determine the range of pay (the "going rate") for a particular job by comparing its description with those of similar jobs in the labour market. This type of information would have been useful to Muldridge in demonstrating to the vehicle-repair mechanics that they were not being underpaid in relation to similar mechanics working for other organizations. Another use of job descriptions in recruiting is in composing advertisements for job vacancies. For recruiting purposes, a job analysis method must provide information on the personal qualifications necessary to perform a job's tasks.

Selection

In selection, job specifications provide standards for testing the qualifications of applicants to perform successfully in a given position. For example, if job specifications require that a clerk/typist type 45 words per minute, then 45 words per minute serves as one standard of performance against which an applicant will be measured. Different job specifications require that different selection methods be used for testing applicants' qualifications.

The criteria used for selection must be job-related; that is, they must test the applicant on behaviour and skills necessary to the job and not on characteristics irrelevant to acceptable performance. It is important to note, however, that a job analysis method for selection purposes must provide detailed and complete information on the personal qualifications for jobs.

Orientation

In orientation, the job description is used to convey to employees information regarding required duties and acceptable standards of performance. The job description tells the new employee what is expected. For example, the clerk/typist described in Exhibit 5.2 knows that he or she is expected to perform the duties listed in the job description and also to exhibit "knowledge of office procedures and practices; ability to meet the public effectively; ability to type from clear copy at the rate of 45 words per minute; ability to do clerical work involving a limited use of independent judgement requiring speed and accuracy; and ability to make arithmetical computations." Any one (or all) of these job specifications could serve as a criterion against which to measure an employee's performance once the job has been undertaken.

Training and Development

Job specifications serve as training objectives in training and development programs. As an example, consider again the case of human resource director Harold Muldridge. He had received funds for a program to train bus drivers in the transport of elderly and handicapped persons, but the content of the training program was unspecified. A clear job description for bus drivers transporting these special populations would have enabled Muldridge to identify objectives for his training program. For example, the job specifications might have read:

> Interest in helping handicapped persons; ability to operate specially equipped vans; a knowledge of disabling conditions and how each affects transport; familiarity with special devices used by the handicapped, such as wheelchairs, walkers, seeing-eye dogs.

Based on these job specifications, the objectives of the human resource director's training program would be to impart the necessary knowledge and training to drivers so that they could demonstrate mastery of the required job behaviours. Such activities would include (1) training drivers in the operation of specially equipped vans; (2) informing drivers of disabling conditions and how each affects transport; and (3) familiarizing drivers with special devices used by the handicapped. The effectiveness of the training program could then be assessed by determining how successfully drivers were able to meet the stated job specifications after training. For training purposes, job analysis methods must specify necessary job behaviours and the standards of performance employees must achieve.

Performance Appraisal

It has already been pointed out that job specifications can serve as criteria against which to appraise an employee's performance. The criteria used to appraise performance must be related to job content and not to extraneous factors. For example, driving ability would be a valid criterion for appraising the performance of van drivers transporting the handicapped. Job analysis is a mechanism by which to choose appraisal criteria.

Career Planning

Many of today's employees expect to pursue interesting and challenging careers. A *career* is a sequence of positions or jobs held by one person over a relatively long time, usually ten or more years. Comparison of job descriptions for different-level jobs in an organization can be used to chart the logical progression of an employee from one job to another. If Muldridge had had access to data of this type, he could have told the aspiring clerk in the records department that he or she could expect to be promoted to Clerk II after two years of service and eventually to Supervisor of Records when the position became vacant. To be useful for career planning, a job analysis method must provide comparable data on jobs so that the similarities and differences between jobs at different levels are evident.

Compensation

Job analysis is undertaken most often for purposes of job evaluation. *Job evaluation* is the process of assigning relative value to jobs within an organization. Job evaluation provides a rationale for paying a Secretary II $125 more per month than a Secretary I, and a Computer Programmer $160 more per month than a Secretary II. It is difficult to conduct a good job evaluation without access to recent and complete job descriptions. Over a span of time, jobs may change so that one job's pay relative to another's becomes inequitable. This fact, plus employee and/or union complaints of unfair pay, can indicate the need for re-evaluation of certain jobs.

Job analysis methods for purposes of job evaluation must enable comparison of jobs on certain compensable factors. *Compensable factors* are those which an organization chooses to use as a basis for differentiating between pay levels—for example, various educational, experience, and skill levels.

Employee Health and Safety

In some jobs, the nature of the tasks, working conditions, or equipment used can be hazardous to an employee's health and safety. Complete and accurate job descriptions document potential hazards so that steps can be taken to protect the employee. Identification of potential hazards allows safety engineers to design protective equipment. HRM professionals and safety specialists can enact and enforce safety rules for employees' protection, and safety programs can be developed.

Labour Relations—Unions

In labour relations, job descriptions are used in bargaining with trade unions over pay, working conditions, and the ways in which certain jobs are done.[2] In order to gain control over the working environment of their members, unions normally prefer job descriptions to be very narrow and closely defined, whereas management usually wants them to be more flexible. When job descriptions are narrow, management must renegotiate collective agreements even when very small changes occur. For example, with a closely defined job description, the addition of a new piece of equipment could force renegotiation of an agreement if use of the equipment became an employee's responsibility. Human resource officers frequently retain reasonable flexibility and control over job content even with a collective agreement by including the clause, "and other assigned duties," at the end of a job description.

[2] In the Scarborough Firefighters Case (1979), the Ontario Supreme Court held that job descriptions can be the subject of negotiation (*Labour Law News*, September 1979, vol. 5, no. 9).

Responsibilities for Job Analysis

Responsibilities of HRM professionals for job analysis can be divided into two major categories: conducting analyses and using job analysis information. Responsibility for conducting a job analysis includes: (1) choosing an appropriate method; (2) conducting the analysis; and (3) preparing job descriptions.

Choosing an appropriate method of job analysis involves consideration of how data will be used. As we have seen, various uses of job analysis data require collection of different kinds of information. For example, information required for the purpose of job evaluation (assigning relative value to jobs in an organization) are quite different from those required by safety staff and engineers. The former require only enough information about working conditions to be able to categorize them according to a number of factors, while the latter require enough detail about working conditions and work-related hazards to design equipment and methods to alleviate unhealthy or unsafe conditions. Determining how data will be used is an important consideration in choosing a job analysis method, because certain methods are more appropriate for some purposes than for others.

In implementing a method of job analysis, it is important that HRM professionals gain the cooperation of managers, supervisors, and, often, employees. These groups can provide valuable inputs into the process of job analysis, or they can provide unwelcome resistance. In many cases, the HRM professional serves as trainer, advisor, and coordinator for job analyses carried out by supervisors and employees. This is particularly true when a questionnaire is used and data are collected from many employees of large organizations. In this case, the HRM professional is involved in development of the questionnaire as well as all planning, training, and administrative activities associated with the analysis. For example, supervisors must be trained to review their subordinates' questionnaires for omissions, exaggerations of duties, responsibilities, or required skills, and other errors. If disputes arise between supervisor and subordinates, the HRM professional must resolve them equitably while pursuing descriptions that are accurate and complete.

After job analysis data have been collected, job descriptions must be prepared. This involves classifying and summarizing data according to specific duties, task-related behaviour, personal requirements, and other descriptive characteristics of jobs.

The HRM specialist responsible for conducting job analysis is the *occupational analyst*, also called the *job analyst*. Large organizations often employ full-time occupational analysts; smaller organizations may hire them as consultants. *The Canadian Classification and Dictionary of Occupations* provides the following description of an occupational analyst, which demonstrates the range and variety of activities required in the process of job analysis.

1174–122 OCCUPATIONAL ANALYST

Analyzes and synthesizes job data to provide occupational information for personnel, administrative, information and other ser-

vices of private, public or governmental organizations:
Consults with management to determine type, scope and purpose of analysis required. Searches for background information on nature of organization and its activities, and studies relevant data. Initiates job study by touring establishment, obtains or prepares charts showing broad functions of each department, and lists job titles used within establishment. Observes and studies jobs performed, and interviews workers, supervisors and managerial personnel to ascertain nature of work performed, worker characteristics required and other relevant factors. Writes detailed job definitions to describe work performed and other significant data, such as educational requirements, training time, environmental conditions, physical activities, and skills and abilities required for satisfactory job performance. Makes comparative analyses of job descriptions and specifications to determine employment activities that are common to a number of similar jobs. Writes occupational descriptions by combining and synthesizing groups of similar jobs. Prepares, from documentation services, drafts of occupational descriptions for validation by experts in the field of work or for verification through visits, observation and interview, and writes finished manuscript.
May prepare occupational classification systems, career information booklets, interviewing aids for employment officers and manpower counsellors, job evaluation reports and other aids to industrial, governmental and other organizations in activities; such as, personnel administration, manpower research and planning, training, placement, occupational information and vocational guidance.
May specialize in a particular activity and be designated accordingly; for example,
Job Analyst
Job Evaluator
Occupational Analyst, Classification System
Occupational Monograph Specialist
Position Classifier
Salary Analyst[3]

Not all job analyses, however, are conducted by occupational analysts. In fact, the responsibility for conducting job analysis is often assumed by other HRM professionals or supervisors trained in the use of job analysis methods.

Methods of Job Analysis

Job analysis methods can be classified into four basic types: (1) observation methods; (2) interview techniques; (3) combined observation/interview approaches; and (4) questionnaires, including job inventories or checklists. This section describes and discusses these methods.

[3] CCDO 1971, vol. 1, p. 36. Reprinted by permission of Occupational and Career Information Branch, Employment and Immigration Canada.

Exhibit 5.4 compares the methods on a number of dimensions and can be used as a reference throughout this discussion.

Observation Methods

Observation of work activities and worker behaviour is a type of job analysis which can be used independently or in combination with other types. Three methods of job analysis based on observation are: (1) direct observation; (2) work methods analysis, including time-and-motion study and micro-motion analysis; and (3) the critical incident technique. Though they employ the same basic technique, these methods differ in terms of who does the observing, what is observed, and how it is observed.

Direct observation. This method makes use of recorded observations of employees in the performance of their duties. The observer either takes general notes or works from a form which has structured categories for comment. Everything is observed: what the worker accomplishes, what equipment is used, what the work environment is like, and any other factors relevant to the job. For simple, repetitive jobs, one or two hours of direct observation may suffice to describe the job adequately. More complex and diverse jobs require multiple and often extended observations to achieve the same result. This is why direct observation is used primarily to describe manual, short-cycle jobs (such as that of a machine operator) or in combination with other methods of job analysis. It is especially useful for identifying the health and safety hazards of particular jobs.

Direct observation is typically part of most job analyses because it is of value for the analyst to have some understanding of both the basic nature of the work and the context in which it is performed. However, direct observation methods have certain natural limitations. First, they cannot capture the mental aspects of jobs, such as decision-making or planning, since mental processes are not observable. Second, observation methods can provide little information relating to personal requirements for various jobs because this kind of information is also not readily observable. Thus, observation methods provide little information on which to base job specifications.

Work methods analysis. A sophisticated observation method, work methods analysis is used by industrial engineers to describe manual and repetitive production jobs, such as factory or assembly-line jobs. Two types of work methods analysis are time-and-motion study and micro-motion analysis. In time-and-motion studies, an industrial engineer observes and records each activity of a worker, using a stopwatch to note the time it takes to perform separate elements of the job. Micro-motion analysis uses video equipment to record workers' activities; the tapes are analyzed to discover acceptable ways of accomplishing tasks and to set standards on how long certain tasks should take. Such data are especially useful for developing training programs and setting pay rates.

EXHIBIT 5.4

Comparing job analysis methods

Job analysis method	*Major user of method*	*What method involves*	*Major human resource uses*	*Major advantage(s)*	*Major disadvantage(s)*
Direct observation	Job analyst	Observation; recording	Health and safety; part of other methods	Can provide reasonably complete picture of manual, repetitive jobs	Limited to manual, repetitive jobs; mental process or worker qualifications cannot be observed
Work methods analysis	Industrial engineer	Observation; recording (stopwatch or movie camera)	Compensation; health and safety; training	Serves as data base for setting performance standards	Limited to manual, repetitive jobs; same as above
Critical incident technique	Supervisor or manager	Judgement; observation; recording	Performance appraisal	Captures nonroutine, unusual behaviour	Lengthy data collection process; translation into job descriptions is difficult
Interviewing	Job analyst	Interviewing; recording	Job descriptions; training; with other methods	Can provide in-depth information	Time-consuming process
Functional job analysis (FJA)	Job analyst	Observation; interviewing; judgement; recording	Job descriptions; recruiting; selection; HRP	Widely applicable; useful job classification system	Requires analyst trained in FJA
VERJAS	Manager; HRM professional	Observation; interviewing; recording; judgement	Job descriptions; performance appraisal; compensation; recruiting; selection	Multi-purpose method	Time-consuming
Job inventories and checklists	Job occupant	Judgement (rating)	HRP; selection; training	Data collection is fast; data for different jobs are easily compared	Time-consuming to construct the inventory
PAQ and PMPQ	Job analyst; supervisor; job occupant	Judgement (rating)	HRP; compensation; selection; training	Rapid results; ease of job comparisons	Does not provide a written description of job or duties

Critical incident technique. The critical incident technique involves observing and recording examples of particularly effective or ineffective behaviour.[4] It can be used for all jobs, but is most advantageous for more complex, less routine jobs. Behaviour is judged "effective" or "ineffective" in terms of the results it produces. For example, if a shoe salesperson comments on the size of a customer's feet and the customer leaves the store in a huff, the salesperson's behaviour could be judged ineffective. The critical incident method requires a supervisor or other person familiar with a job to record, in an ongoing log, information relating to behaviour observed to be either particularly effective or ineffective. Over time, this process results in a growing description of a job.

The following information should be recorded for each critical incident: (1) what led up to the incident and the situation in which it occurred; (2) exactly what the employee did that was particularly effective or ineffective; (3) the perceived consequences or results of the behaviour; and (4) a judgement as to the degree of control the employee had over the results his or her behaviour produced (to what degree should the employee be held responsible for what resulted?).

The critical incident method differs from direct observation and work methods analysis in that observations are not recorded as behaviour occurs, but only *after* it has been judged particularly effective or ineffective in terms of results produced. This means that a person using the critical incident method must describe behaviour in retrospect, rather than as the activity unfolds. Accurate recording of past observations is more difficult than recording behaviour as it occurs.

This method has the advantage of being able to capture both routine and nonroutine aspects of behaviour. However, describing a job adequately requires a very lengthy process of incident collection. Further, since incidents can be quite dissimilar, classifying the data into usable job descriptions can be difficult. The fact that this method of job analysis focusses on employee behaviour and is able to capture dynamic aspects of jobs which other methods might miss makes it especially useful for the development of performance-appraisal instruments that seek to evaluate employees according to acceptable or unacceptable job behaviours.

Interview Techniques

Interview techniques involve discussions between job analysts (or other interviewers) and job occupants or experts. Employees may be interviewed singly or in groups. Job analysis data from individual and group interviews with employees are often supplemented by information from supervisors of employees whose jobs are analyzed. Job analysis interviews can also be held with a small panel of experts, such as supervisors or long-time employees who are very familiar with the job. Interviews of this type are called *technical conferences*. The end product of a

[4] J.C. Flanagan, "The Critical Incident Technique," *Psychological Bulletin*, 1954, vol. 51, pp. 28–35.

technical conference is a job description that reflects a consensus of the experts' thinking.[5]

Interviews can be unstructured, with questions and areas of discussion unspecified, or they can be more highly structured, with each point for discussion spelled out. Using a structured format increases the likelihood that all aspects of a job will be covered in an interview; it also enables the collection of comparable data from all persons interviewed, making information classification easier.

One problem with this technique is that it can be very time-consuming if many employees must be interviewed. Another problem is that interviews—like some methods of observation—may create suspicion among workers. This is especially true of job analysis conducted to assign relative monetary values to jobs (as in job evaluation). Workers who feel that the analysis may affect their pay or status are often motivated to distort information about the job, most likely inflating their importance. For this reason, gaining the cooperation of workers can be important in achieving accurate job analysis results. In short, interview techniques can be time-consuming and therefore costly, but when properly used they can provide reasonably complete data for use in preparing job descriptions. They can also be used effectively to identify training needs of employees.

Interviews are a basic part of most job analyses, particularly in smaller organizations. When information must be gathered from many employees fairly quickly, interviews of a few employees and supervisors are often used to supplement information gathered from questionnaires.

Combined Observation/Interview Approaches

Observation and interview techniques are often used in combination as components of more sophisticated job analysis methods. Two methods that combine both techniques are functional job analysis and VERJAS (Versatile Job Analysis System).

Functional job analysis. Functional job analysis (FJA) is a comprehensive method developed by the Training and Employment Service of the U.S. Department of Labor. An analyst using this method observes, interviews, and records information on a structured job analysis "schedule" that uses very precise terminology. The analyst provides a job summary and a description of tasks for each job analyzed. He or she also assigns "work performed ratings" and ratings of "worker traits."

Work performed ratings specify the nature of the relationship a worker has to data, people, and things (DPT). Three separate eight-point scales are used in assigning a DPT rating. Scale items are descriptive terms, indicating increased levels of complexity, with higher numbers indicating less complex relationships to data, people, and things. Worker trait ratings are assessments of personal characteristics needed for satisfactory performance of the job.

[5] Ernest J. McCormick, *Job Analysis: Methods and Applications* (New York: AMACOM, 1979).

Analysts using FJA must be well-trained in order to write precise job descriptions and make accurate ratings. Analysts should also be trained in observation and interview techniques.

Because of its descriptive summary and listing of job duties, FJA is especially useful to the recruiting and selection functions. It is also very useful in human resource planning and career planning because it is applicable to a variety of jobs and provides a quantitative way to compare job similarities and differences.

The Canadian Classification and Dictionary of Occupations (CCDO) uses a variation of FJA to classify and describe jobs. For each specific occupation, or job, CCDO provides an occupational code number, occupational title, industry designation, coded job characteristics, a statement of job duties, and related occupational titles. CCDO's statement of job duties for an Occupational Analyst was presented earlier in this chapter.

CCDO's coded job characteristics refer to educational and training requirements, physical demands, and worker functions in relation to data, people, and things (DPT). Educational requirements are measured by the General Educational Development scale (GED), a six-point scale which focusses on levels of reasoning and mathematical and language development. CCDO assigns Occupational Analyst a GED rating of 5, the second highest level, representing the need to apply principles of logical and scientific thinking, to interpret an extensive variety of technical instructions, and to deal with abstract and concrete variables. Training requirements are indicated by a Specific Vocational Preparation (SVP) rating from 1 (short demonstration only) to 9 (over 10 years). Occupational Analyst has an SVP rating of 7 (over 2 years up to and including 4 years).

Physical demands of the job are coded according to environmental conditions (EC) and physical activities (PA). Physical activities include both physical requirements (how heavy the work is) and worker capacities (kind of physical activity required). According to EC and PA codes, the work of an Occupational Analyst is located inside (EC I) and is sedentary, involving talking and hearing (PA S56).

Worker functions are coded, as in FJA, by assessing relationships of job activities to data, people, and things. Occupational Analyst has a DPT rating of 068, indicating that the occupation requires a high level of synthesizing (0), some speaking to people (6), and no significant relationship to things (8). CCDO's assessment of the job's required worker traits and career possibilities is shown in Exhibit 5.5.

EXHIBIT 5.5

Occupational qualification requirements for Occupational Analysts (CCDO Code 1174–122)

Aptitudes and capacities

Personnel and Related Officers require:

—learning ability to understand and apply the principles of personnel administration in such fields as employment, counselling, occupational and salary analysis, labour relations and student financial-aid programs;

—verbal ability to communicate effectively with people at all levels of education and training and from a wide variety of occupational backgrounds, and to present information lucidly, both orally and in writing;
—numerical ability to prepare financial and material estimates and reports;
—clerical perception to review reports, collective-bargaining agreements, contracts, personnel records and other written material.

Training and entry requirements

Personnel and Related Officers usually require:
—a bachelor's degree with a major in psychology, sociology or business administration;
—a minimum of two years on-the-job experience; and
—completion of specialized courses provided by universities, community colleges or employers in personnel administration, labour relations, or job and occupational analysis.

Advancement and transfer possibilities

Advancement

Advancement for individuals with sufficient experience and managerial potential may be to 1136-110 INDUSTRIAL-RELATIONS MANAGER or 1136-114 PERSONNEL MANAGER, while others with leadership qualities and supervisory potential may advance to the supervisory occupations in this chapter.

Transfer

Transfers may occur to other occupations in this chapter. Those who have a bachelor's degree in the social sciences or business administration may transfer to occupations in psychology, sociology or business administration, and those with appropriate qualifications and certification may transfer to occupations in teaching, occupational guidance or counselling.

Clues for relating persons to occupational requirements

Personnel and Related Officers require significant interests in, and dispositions for work involving the following:

Interests

—activities involving business contact with people;
—activities concerned with people and communication of ideas;
—activities resulting in prestige or esteem of others by acting as an arbiter in labour-management disputes, or as a counsellor assisting job seekers or employees to solve their problems.

Temperaments

—dealing with people in actual job duties beyond giving and receiving instructions;
—the evaluation of information against sensory or judgmental criteria by resolving staff problems, such as employee performance, absenteeism and grievances by interviewing employees and supervisors and recommending or initiating remedial action based on experience or precedent;
—the evaluation of information against measurable or verifiable criteria;
—influencing people in their opinions, attitudes or judgments about ideas or things;

—the direction, control and planning of an entire activity or the activities of others;
—a variety of duties often characterized by frequent change.

Other clues
—tact, discretion, integrity with others, and the ability to establish rapport.

SOURCE: Manpower and Immigration Canada, *Canadian Classification and Dictionary of Occupations*, 1971, vol. 2, pp. 15–16. Reprinted by permission of Occupational and Career Information Branch, Employment and Immigration Canada.

Both the FJA and the CCDO method offer organizations a systematic approach to analyzing and classifying jobs and job characteristics. The generality of the methods means that they may be used for most jobs. However, since both methods require trained analysts, they are most likely to benefit large employers.

VERJAS. Versatile Job Analysis System is a new method of job analysis that combines observation and interview techniques, as well as other job analysis procedures. Authors of the system describe it as "a job analysis melting pot in both origin and use."[6]

VERJAS is administered by managers or human resource staff assigned to study jobs. The method includes five basic steps, which are set out as follows by the authors of the method:

1. Write an overview of the job describing the purpose for which the job exists and the primary duties involved in accomplishing that purpose. This step provides job description information.
2. Describe the action, purpose, and result of each task involved in carrying out job duties, and then identify the training mode and rate its relative importance. This step provides a description of specific expected job behaviour, which is useful in identifying worker competencies, developing performance standards, and defending personnel practices as job related.
3. Describe the context of the job; its scope, effect, and environment. This step assures documentation of information needed to determine the value of a job.
4. Identify basic worker competencies needed for minimum acceptable performance of job tasks. This step is essential for determining employee specifications that are used in recruiting.
5. Identify the special worker competencies that make for successful job performance. This step is useful in developing selection criteria and identifying training needs.[7]

The VERJAS system provides job analysts with forms and instructions for completing each of the above steps. Exhibit 5.6 is a task worksheet for performing step 2.

[6] Stephen E. Bemis, Ann Holt Belenky, and Dee Ann Soder, *Job Analysis: An Effective Management Tool* (Washington, D.C.: Bureau of National Affairs, 1983), p. 11.
[7] Ibid., pp. 62–3.

EXHIBIT 5.6.

Worksheet for step 2 of the VERJAS method

Task Worksheet

Job Title: Clerk Typist/Receptionist Position No.: 327 Duty No.: 1 Task No.: 1

Part I. As the first step in preparing the task statement, respond to the following four questions.

1. What action(s) is (are) performed? Types
2. What is acted on? Letters, memos, and reports
3. What is (are) the purpose(s) or expected output? IN ORDER TO produce first copy
4. What machines, tools, equipment, manuals, laws, rules, or other work aids are used? USING Electric typewriter, Organization style manual

Write a task statement in this space, using the above responses.

Types letters, memos, and reports from handwritten material according to standard formats in order to produce final copy using an electric typewriter and organization style manual.

Part II. Task Evaluation

Perf. at Entry?	Training Mode						Importance Level			Reason for Important/Critical Ratings				
	Brief Orient	How Long?	O-J-T	How Long?	Class Trng.	How Long?	Not Imp.	Imp.	Crit.	Prep. Time	Lev. Diff.	Cons. Err.	Freq.	Other
Yes	Yes	1 Day	No		No				✓	✓				

Division W, XYZ Corp.
Organization

Joanne Margolis
Signature

6-11-83
Date

SOURCE: Stephen E. Bemis, Ann Holt Belenky, and Dee Ann Soder, *Job Analysis: An Effective Management Tool* (Washington, D.C.: Bureau of National Affairs, 1983), p. 68.

VERJAS provides information pertinent to most organizational uses of job analysis, though it does little to facilitate comparison of job similarities and differences. The system is also limited to description and analysis of existing jobs, since these are the starting point for VERJAS' analysis. Though the VERJAS method is fairly new and little research has examined it, the method is simple and basic enough to be carried out in most organizations.

Questionnaires

Questionnaires can be filled out by employees individually or by job analysts for a group of employees. Questionnaires vary in the degree to which they are structured. Some ask open-ended questions that seek unspecified answers; for example:

1. Describe the duties of your job.
2. Describe your daily routine.
3. What skills do you feel are essential to the performance of your duties?

A questionnaire gains structure by specifying response alternatives. For example, if Item 1 were structured, it might read:

Check whether or not your duties include the following:

typing letters	___ Yes	___ No
taking dictation	___ Yes	___ No
filing correspondence	___ Yes	___ No
answering telephone	___ Yes	___ No

Questionnaires are often used to gather job analysis information when input from a large number of employees is desired and when speed and cost are major considerations. Questionnaires are relatively inexpensive to administer and they permit data to be collected in a very short time. However, developing a questionnaire takes time and some degree of familiarity with the job in question. Time, effort, and expertise are also required to code and analyze information after it has been collected, although structured response categories make coding and analyzing easier.

Questionnaires can be used by most organizations for most kinds of jobs, assuming employees can read and understand the instruments. Generally, however, questionnaires are most commonly used for white-collar, professional, and managerial jobs. If an organization chooses to use a questionnaire for job analysis purposes, an HRM professional must either develop a questionnaire for use in his or her particular organization or use one of the professionally-developed, structured questionnaires discussed below.

A problem with questionnaires is that they assume a certain level of reading competence. For example, the Position Analysis Questionnaire requires university-level reading ability.[8]

[8] R.A. Ash and S.L. Edgell, "A Note on the Readability of the Position Analysis Questionnaire (PAQ)," *Journal of Applied Psychology*, 1975, vol. 60, pp. 765–66.

Job inventories or checklists. Job inventories or checklists are structured questionnaires that require a respondent to check or rate behaviour and/or worker characteristics necessary to a particular job or occupation. Job inventories can be either task-oriented (job-oriented) or qualifications-oriented (worker-oriented), but most include both task and qualifications components. Exhibit 5.7 is an example of a task-oriented job checklist. Qualifications-oriented checklists ask respondents to check or rate knowledge, skills, abilities, or other worker characteristics presumed to be relevant to the performance of a particular job.

The U.S. Air Force developed the job inventory method of job analysis in the 1960s, and it was first applied to military operative, semi-skilled and skilled jobs, and some officers' jobs. In recent years, the job inventory approach has been used successfully to describe a broad range of jobs, from clerical, sales, and engineering occupations to managerial positions and professional jobs.[9] Because job inventories provide detailed information about particular worker behaviour and required qualifications, they are especially useful in selection and training, which require specific information in these areas. Comparison of detailed information from job inventories is also very useful to human resource planners who need to know the content of and specific qualifications for jobs.

Job inventories, by definition, tend to be specific to particular jobs or occupations, since they rate specific task behaviour or job qualifications. One disadvantage of this fact is that a specific inventory must be constructed for each job or occupation. The construction process involves the collection of job-related information and development of a preliminary job inventory. The preliminary version is given to a sample of job occupants to determine the appropriateness of items to be included in the final inventory. Any task-related behaviour that has been omitted can be added at this time. An analysis of results is used in constructing the final task inventory. Job inventories have all the advantages of highly structured questionnaires, including comparability of collected data and ease of administration.

Position Analysis Questionnaire (PAQ). PAQ is a highly structured questionnaire, similar in design to job inventories, but different in scope. It was designed by Ernest J. McCormick and associates of Purdue University for analyzing blue-collar and nonmanagerial jobs in terms of a number of job elements. Earlier in this chapter we defined an element as a particular aspect of a particular task. McCormick uses the term more broadly to describe "some general work activity, work condition, or job characteristic."[10] PAQ has 194 items, and 187 of them

[9] S. Gael, "Development of Job Task Inventories and Their Use in Job Analysis Research," *JSAS Catalog of Selected Documents in Psychology*, 1977, vol. 7, no. 1, Ms. 1445; W.W. Tornow and P.R. Pinto, "The Development of a Managerial Job Taxonomy: A System for Describing, Classifying, and Evaluating Executive Positions," *Journal of Applied Psychology*, 1976, vol. 61, pp. 410–18; and L.H. Hough, *Professional Activities Description Questionnaire* (Minneapolis, Minn.: Personnel Decisions Research Institute, 1979).

EXHIBIT 5.7

A task-oriented job checklist

		TIME SPENT					IMPORTANCE					LEARNING TIME					
	THIS IS A PART OF MY JOB	MUCH LESS TIME Than Other Activities	LESS TIME Than Other Activities	ABOUT THE SAME Amount of Time as Other Activities	MORE TIME Than Other Activities	MUCH MORE TIME Than Other Activities	UNIMPORTANT	Minor Importance	IMPORTANT	Very Important	CRUCIAL	1 Day or Less	2 or 3 Days	4 or 5 Days	Up to a Month	1-3 Months	More than 3 Months
		1	2	3	4	5	1	2	3	4	5	1	2	3	4	5	6
153. Plan special sales promotions and see that they are carried out according to plan.																	
154. Keep track of and follow up on the activities of subordinates.																	
155. Transcribe from dictating machine records or tapes.																	
156. Schedule dates or times for appointments, meetings, etc. or delivery, pick-up, and repair of merchandise by checking with those involved for time and place.																	
157. Perform routine preventive mechanical maintenance on machines or equipment.																	
158. Look up, search for, or locate information in readily available sources such as files, parts lists, records, manuals, tables, catalogs, etc.																	
159. Set objectives for a department or unit of the company.																	
		1	2	3	4	5	1	2	3	4	5	1	2	3	4	5	6

SOURCE: M.D. Dunnette, L.H. Hough, and R.L. Rosse, "Task and Job Taxonomies as a Basis for Identifying Labor Supply Sources and Evaluating Employment Qualifications," *Human Resource Planning*, 1979, vol. 2, no. 1.

represent job elements related to six major divisions: (1) information input; (2) mental processes; (3) work output; (4) relationships with other persons; (5) job context; and (6) other characteristics. Exhibit 5.8 presents these major divisions along with examples of job elements relating to each. The first three divisions are analogous to running a computer program. In order to perform a job, a computer must receive information from one or more sources (information input). It must then process this information in order to produce work outputs. Similarly, an employee must receive information (information input), process it (mental processes), and act upon it in order to achieve certain results (work output). The fourth division, "Relationships with other persons," focusses on the kinds of interpersonal relationships required by the job. The work situation or environment is measured by items in the fifth division, "Job context." The sixth division, "Other job characteristics," includes a variety of items related to work schedules, apparel worn on the job, job responsibilities, and job demands. Additionally, seven items at the end of PAQ relate to the method of pay and the amount of pay employees receive. To analyze a job using PAQ, a job analyst, supervisor, or the employee determines whether each item applies to the job being analyzed and, if so, the degree to which it applies.

An analyst familiar with PAQ can complete the questionnaire in less than an hour. Though supervisors and employees can also use PAQ, they should be trained to use it properly. A PAQ manual is available for instructional purposes, and a technical manual provides information on the questionnaire's development, procedures for use, and potential applications.[11]

PAQ has many advantages. It can be applied to a wide range of jobs; its results can be obtained rapidly and compared to substantial existing data and research findings. Such data are especially useful to the career planning function in which different level jobs are compared in terms of job specifications. Such comparison allows planners to chart logical paths of progression between jobs. A further advantage is the many computerized data analysis packages available to PAQ users, including use of PAQ for wage survey and job evaluation, performance appraisal, and training and selection.[12]

One disadvantage of PAQ is that it does not result in a descriptive summary of a job or a listing of duties and tasks related to it. Rather, this questionnaire profiles a job in terms of the degree to which certain job elements are present. Another disadvantage of PAQ is that it may not distinguish between very similar jobs since it is designed to be generally applicable across jobs.

***Professional and Managerial Position Questionnaire* (PMPQ).** PMPQ was developed in the late 1970s in order to analyze professional and

[10] Ernest J. McCormick, P.R. Jeanneret, and R.C. Mecham, *Position Analysis Questionnaire* (West Lafayette, Ind.: Purdue University, 1969).

[11] Ernest J. McCormick, P.R. Jeanneret, and R.C. Mecham, *PAQ: Job Analysis Manual* © (Logan, Utah: PAQ Services, Inc., 1977).

[12] Ibid.

EXHIBIT 5.8

Job elements from the Position Analysis Questionnaire*

1. Information input (where and how the worker gets the information used in performing the job)
   a. written materials
   b. behaviours
   c. touch
   d. estimating speed of moving objects
2. Mental processes (reasoning, decision making, planning, and information processing activities involved in performing the job)
   a. reasoning in problem solving
   b. analyzing information or data
   c. using mathematics
3. Work output (physical activities the worker performs and the tools or devices used)
   a. precision tools
   b. foot-operated controls
   c. assembling/disassembling
   d. finger manipulation
4. Relationships with other persons (relationships with other persons required in performing the job)
   a. entertaining
   b. coordinates activities
   c. supervision received
5. Job context (physical and social contexts in which the work is performed)
   a. indoor temperature
   b. noise intensity
   c. frustrating situations
6. Other job characteristics (activities, conditions, or characteristics, other than those described above, relevant to the job)
   a. specific uniform/apparel
   b. irregular hours
   c. working under distractions
   d. travel

*PAQ further specifies job elements into questionnaire items.

SOURCE: Ernest J. McCormick, P. R. Jeanneret, and R. C. Mecham, *Position Analysis Questionnaire*, © 1969 Purdue Research Foundation.

managerial jobs, which were not adequately described by PAQ. PMPQ is a highly structured questionnaire which may be completed by the job incumbent or other person familiar with the job.

PMPQ is divided into three sections: job functions, personal requirements, and other information. Regarding job functions, items relate to the major categories of planning and scheduling work activities; processing of information and ideas; exercising judgement; communicating; interpersonal activities and relationships; and technical activities. After specific job activities are rated, the six major categories are rated along several dimensions such as complexity and degree of responsibility held by the incumbent. Personal requirements items relate to education, training, experience, and personal characteristics.

While PMPQ is relatively new, it appears to be a promising tool for analyzing professional and managerial jobs. It has many of PAQ's advantages, including rapid generation of results and ease of comparison with existing data. One disadvantage of PMPQ is that it results in more of a job profile than a typical job description.

Job Analysis Problems and Issues

Job analysis methods, like other business or scientific tools, should be evaluated according to certain standards or criteria. The most important criterion is *completeness*. Information must be collected on all aspects of the job. Any method that fails to do this is deficient. Of course, job analysis methods must also be evaluated in terms of the degree of detail they provide about the job, costs, and the amount of time needed to obtain results. As suggested earlier, it is important to consider the intended uses of job analysis information before selecting one or more methods of analysis.

As with all data collection instruments, care must be taken to ensure that job analysis instruments are used in a consistent manner. The reliability of job analysis information is maximized when persons conducting job analyses are thoroughly trained in use of the method. More reliable results are also more likely to be obtained when the analysis methods used are more structured, rather than less structured.

There are a number of reasons why a method of job analysis may fail to provide a complete or representative picture of a job. First, the same job may be described differently by different people. The following analogy between a picture and job analysis is illustrative:

> Pictures differ in degree of clarity, the "trueness" of their representation of reality. They also differ in point of view. A picture taken from one angle may present quite a different view than one taken at a different angle. So it is with job analysis. One can interview two or three incumbents (i.e., job occupants) and their supervisor and find substantial differences in their descriptions of the job. Perhaps the discovery of differing viewpoints about the nature of a job is more the exception than the rule. However, their existence serves as a warning to the analyst to seek out more than one viewpoint for "photographing" the job. With enough pictures one can finally figure out what one is looking at.[13]

M. D. Dunnette has identified three other factors that make it difficult to obtain a complete job description. He refers to them as

[13] G.M. Drauden and N.G. Peterson, *A Domain Sampling Approach to Job Analysis* (St. Paul, Minn.: Test Validation Center, 1974).

(1) "time-determined changes"; (2) "employee-determined changes"; and (3) "situation-determined changes."[14]

Time-determined changes are of two types. The first involves job-related duties or tasks that are performed only occasionally or at widely spaced times. A deficient analysis may be descriptive of a job at one point in time, but not at another. To be complete and representative, a job analysis method should lead to a description of a job at all points in time. This can be accomplished by sampling job behaviour across time using methods such as critical incidents or observation.

The second type of time-determined change relates to the effect of employees' varying experience levels. The same job may look quite different when performed by an inexperienced employee and by an experienced one. Experienced employees may also have additional tasks and responsibilities, but even if they do not, their greater competence may alter one's impression of a job. Therefore, a job analysis method must include questioning job occupants at different levels of experience in order to obtain a true picture of a job's duties and task-related activities.

The second factor identified by Dunnette is employee-determined changes. A job may be difficult to describe because different employees in it may perform somewhat different tasks depending on their individual skills, experience, and interests. Thus, the same job may *appear* different by virtue of the person in the position. A complete description can be obtained by sampling an adequate number of employees.

The third factor that Dunnette cites is situation-determined changes, meaning that job content may change as a result of physical or human forces operating in the work environment. These changes can be caused by emergencies, noise levels, job pressures, or actions of the boss, the work group, or previous job occupants. An example of a situation-determined change is that brought about in a manufacturing plant that experienced a series of bomb threats. When the threats first began, the plant had no formal plan for handling them. Several times, the manager evacuated most of the employees and asked supervisors to search the plant for a bomb. Finally, someone from outside the plant facetiously suggested to the human resource manager that he include as a part of the supervisors' job description: "periodically searches for bombs in the plant." Situation-determined changes are, by their nature, very difficult to anticipate, but Dunnette suggests that various "aspects in the job setting that could potentially alter job content" be identified and described.[15]

Another factor resulting in job description differences is human judgement. Human judgement is needed to reach conclusions based on observation, to assign ratings required by FJA, PAQ, and PMPQ, and to determine job specifications. Even when job-related behaviour and tasks are completely described, judgement is required to assign minimal levels of education, experience, skills, and ability. Consequently, job descriptions vary according to different judgements concerning

[14] M.D. Dunnette, *Personnel Selection and Placement* (Belmont, Calif.: Wadsworth, 1966).

[15] Ibid.

specifications. One study of 58 pairs of managers and subordinates from three organizations found that 85 per cent of the pairs agreed on half or more of the job duties of the subordinate, but only 64 per cent agreed on half or more of the job specifications.[16] This study may suggest that job specifications should reflect a consensus rather than an individual judgement.

In this chapter, we have pointed out the usefulness of job analysis to many human resource functions. On the other hand, we must caution that detailed and precise job descriptions can be a major source of inflexibility in organizations. Jobs must be allowed to grow and change so organizations can adapt to an increasingly competitive environment.

One of the adaptations that is currently occurring is a trend toward a reduction in the number of job classifications within organizations. Unions have been conceding such reductions in return for greater job security or higher wage increases.[17] In a few cases, job classes have been almost completely eliminated in favour of payment based on the acquisition of skills. An example of payment for skill is the collective agreement between the Energy and Chemical Workers Union and Shell Canada's chemical plant in Sarnia, Ontario.

A likely issue for job analysis in the future relates to pay equity legislation. Ontario's Pay Equity Act (Bill 154) requires employers to use a gender-neutral job classification system to compare female job classes. The pay equity bill was passed in the spring of 1987. More attention will therefore be focussed on job classification systems elsewhere to eliminate or at least reduce any gender bias.

Summary

Job analysis serves a variety of purposes in an organization. HRM responsibilities for job analysis range from conducting job analyses to using job analysis information in most of the other human resource functions. For purposes of discussion, job analysis methods have been divided into four basic types: (1) observation methods, including direct observation, work methods analysis, and the critical incident technique; (2) interview techniques; (3) combined observation and interview approaches, such as functional job analysis and VERJAS; and (4) questionnaires, including job inventories or checklists, the PAQ and

[16] N.R.F. Maier, L.R. Hoffman, J.J. Hoover, and W.H. Read, *Superior-Subordinate Communication in Management*, Research Study 52 (New York: American Management Association, 1961).

[17] Wilfred List, "Making Work Rules Flexible-New Pressure Facing Unions," *The Globe and Mail* (Toronto), December 30, 1985; and Casey French, "Unions at Port Waler agree to be flexible," *The Globe and Mail*, December 24, 1986.

[18] Patricia Owen, "How Pay Equity Proposal Might Work: Three Examples Show Ways Companies Compute Work Values," *The Toronto Star*, March 21, 1987.

PMPQ. Care must be taken in selecting a method of job analysis because some methods are more suitable for some job analysis purposes than for others. Problems arise in job analysis because employees may have differing perspectives of their jobs, may perform at different levels, and may emphasize different aspects of the job. Problems may also arise if job content changes over time or in certain situations. Human judgement may also account for variable job analysis results.

Project Ideas

1. Obtain several job descriptions from local businesses, hospitals, or service organizations. Discuss them in terms of completeness. To what extent do they provide information regarding work products, worker activities, equipment used, job context, and job specifications or personal requirements? Try to find out what job analysis methods were used to collect the information in the descriptions and how long ago it was collected. Prepare a brief written or oral report discussing the descriptions, the job analysis process(es) employed, and any ideas you have for improving the descriptions.

2. Pick a common job, such as waiter, bus driver, sales clerk, or bank teller, and gather job analysis information in three different ways from three different employees in the same position. Use observation to gather information from one employee; interview a second; and give a simple questionnaire to a third. Compare the information obtained from each method. Which method provided the most complete information and why? What factors besides the nature of the method used might explain any differences in the resulting job descriptions?

3. Pick a common job, such as waitress, bus driver, sales clerk, or bank teller, and use any one of the job analysis methods to describe it. After preparing your job description, look up the job in the *Canadian Classification and Dictionary of Occupations* and find its description. Compare the two descriptions. Discuss any discrepancies and why they exist.

4. Prepare job specifications (personal requirements) for the occupational analyst position described in this chapter. Try to relate each personal requirement to one or more of the necessary activities described for the job. If the entire class does this project, resulting specifications can be compared.

5. Obtain several job descriptions *without* job specifications (or use any of those from the CCDO provided below). Give them to several friends and ask each independently to write job specifications for each job. Prepare job specifications yourself. Discuss similarities and differences in the resulting specifications.

PERSONNEL-SELECTION OFFICER (military)
Interviews and assesses suitability and potential of individuals in Canadian Forces for specific trades, assignments or training or educational programs, and makes appropriate recommendations: Performs duties as described under master title, 01-320 OFFICER (military). Interviews and tests personnel to assess their suitability for training plans, for transfers from one trade to another, and for specific trades or assignments. Interprets results of cognitive and non-cognitive tests and provides counsel based on test results. Conducts psychological and sociological research for selection and evaluation purposes. Provides counselling to individuals who are leaving Canadian Forces to help them secure suitable civilian employment. Advises and trains personnel engaged in recruiting functions for Canadian Forces. Teaches university level courses at Canadian Military Colleges.

LIBRARY CLERK (educ.)
library attendant.
Compiles records, sorts and shelves books, and issues and receives library materials; such as, books, films, and phonograph records, performing any combination of the following duties:
Issues books to patrons, writes identification data and due-in date on cards, or uses photographic record-keeping device. Inspects returned books for damage, verifies due-date, and computes and receives overdue fines. Reviews records to compile list of overdue books and sends overdue notices to borrowers. Sorts books, publications, and other items; such as, phonograph records and films, according to classification code. Returns them to shelves, files, or other designated storage areas. Examines material on shelves to verify accuracy of placement. Locates books and publications for patrons. Issues borrower's identification card according to established procedures. Files cards in catalogue drawers according to system. Answers telephone inquiries and queries from patrons in library, referring persons requiring professional assistance to 2351-114 LIBRARIAN (educ.). Types material cards or issue cards and duty schedules. Makes minor repairs to books, using mending tape, paste and brush.
May be designated according to type of library or department, or task performed; for example,
Bookmobile Clerk
Branch-Library Clerk
Library Clerk, Art Department
Library Clerk, Book Return
Library Clerk, Braille and Talking Books

INSURANCE INSPECTOR, LOSS-PREVENTION
Inspects insured properties to evaluate conditions affecting underwriting standards, and develops and promotes safety programs: Inspects buildings, vehicles and operations of commercial and industrial establishments, to determine physical conditions or un-

safe practices. Compiles data affecting premiums by measuring area or frontage or making scale drawings of properties. Prepares reports with recommendations for corrective action. Analyzes claims and accident-history data or inspects scene of accident, to determine causes and effects, and to develop safety program compatible with needs and resources of insured. Conducts meetings to promote safety programs among educational, civic and industrial groups, by informing them of government and company safety standards and regulations, using motion pictures and other visual aids to supplement discussion.

STOREMAN (clerical)
stock checker; stock clerk.
Receives, stores, orders and issues supplies and merchandise and keeps records:
Counts and sorts incoming articles to verify receipt of items on requisitions or invoices, and examines them for conformance to specifications. Stores articles in containers or bins or on shelves, according to identifying information such as style, size or type. Fills orders or issues supplies from stock. Prepares inventories and requisitions material to fill incoming orders. Compiles reports of use of stock-handling equipment, adjustment of inventory counts and stock records, spoilage or damage to stock, location changes and refusal of shipments.
May be designated according to type of stock handled or location; for example,
Stock Clerk, Narcotics
Storeman, Ship
Stores Clerk, Machine Shop
Warehouseman

TRAFFIC CHECKER (gov. serv.; motor trans.)
Secures information for use in highway planning by interviewing motor vehicle drivers at specified road intersection or highway:
Places equipment, such as barriers, signs and automatic vehicle counting devices on roads or highways. Signals driver to stop, presents identification credentials, and explains reason for stopping vehicle. Questions automobile, bus or truck driver to obtain data, such as itinerary and purpose of trip. Records results of interview and permits driver to continue journey. Secures information on load carried, whether passenger or cargo, and type and weight of vehicle.
May obtain information by observing traffic along bus, streetcar or subway routes and record information for analysis and planning of transit services. May count traffic only at a specified spot and be designated accordingly,
Traffic Counter

TOOL GRINDER (any ind.)
Sharpens tools, such as chisels, drills, knives and cleavers:
Starts bench or pedestal grinder, and holds tool to be sharpened

against machine rest so that cutting edge of tool bears against grinding wheel at correct angle. Dips tool in water repeatedly to prevent overheating of cutting edge. Inspects cutting edge and continues grinding process until required sharpness is attained. May finish cutting edges by using a finer abrasive wheel or whetstone. May tend semi-automatic machine by clamping tool to be sharpened in holder of machine carriage, and turning handles to feed carriage across grinding wheel, so that cutting edge of tool is ground at correct angle.

Cases

Case 5.1: What Shall We Do with the Displaced Sawyer?

Bob Hanks is Director of Human Resources at Alburnett Mills, a sawmill in a small town near Vancouver, British Columbia. Alburnett used to employ 500 workers, but automation has reduced the work force to less than 400. Today Hanks is concerned about long-time employee Bud Wilkes, whose job will become redundant in about six weeks due to the introduction of a computer-controlled saw.

Wilkes has worked as a sawyer at Alburnett Mills for half of his 43 years. One of his primary responsibilities has been to determine where cuts should be made in order to yield the most lumber. Wilkes has performed this job well, meeting or exceeding all job requirements.

Alburnett has laid off workers before, but Hanks feels especially bad about letting Wilkes go. Wilkes has no other work experience to help him find a new job. Besides, he is a good worker whom Hanks would prefer to retain, even though it might mean retraining. A search of job vacancies at the Alburnett mill yields the following possibilities for Wilkes: hydraulic-barker operator; tie and timber inspector; and sawmill foreman. Descriptions and worker requirements for each of these jobs, including the job of sawyer, are given on the following pages. These are adapted from the *Canadian Classification and Dictionary of Occupations* (CCDO).

Questions:

1. Study the job description and specifications for Wilke's present job. Then study specifications and descriptions for the jobs of hydraulic-barker operator, tie and timber inspector, and sawmill foreman. Which, if any of the jobs are demotions? promotions? lateral transfers?

2. Assume you are Bob Hanks and want to place Wilkes in the job he is best suited for. Which job will that be? Defend your choice in terms of similarities between the chosen job (and its requirements) and the job of sawyer.
3. Will Hanks need to perform any selection tests to see if Wilkes is qualified for the job you think he's best suited for? If so, what tests might be necessary? (You may assume that Wilkes possesses all of the aptitudes and capacities necessary for the job of sawyer.)
4. Assuming that Wilkes possesses only those aptitudes and capacities necessary for the job of sawyer, what training will be necessary for each of the new positions?
5. What methods of job analysis described in this chapter facilitate comparison of jobs according to their job specifications?

Sawmill Sawyer

Work Performed

This occupation is concerned with processing logs into rough lumber and sawing, splitting and plaining rough lumber into stock of various sizes. Worker functions include: operating, tending or feeding circular saws, band saws or other lumber-mill equipment to cut logs or lumber to specified dimensions; compiling data through observation of logs to determine cuts that will produce optimum grade and amount of lumber; and comparing size and appearance of cut stock to specified standards. Work activities include: adjusting machine blades or cutters for depth and width of cut required; moving hand and foot controls to start, stop and regulate speed of equipment; and cutting out defective sections in wood stock.

Aptitudes and Capacities

Workers require:

- learning ability to understand lumber-milling methods and techniques and to follow instructions;
- spatial perception to operate, adjust and repair machines and to align logs and lumber on feeding mechanisms;
- eye-hand coordination to synchronize controls of log carriages, saws, conveyers and other lumber-mill machines;
- manual dexterity to work with the hands easily and skillfully when moving controls and adjusting machines or when using work aids to clear jammed equipment;
- finger dexterity to use tools and other work aids when adjusting or maintaining machines;
- eye-hand-foot coordination, to move hand and foot controls simultaneously, and occasionally to climb or balance on or around equipment;
- visual acuity, near and far, to perform activities such as adjusting machines and guiding and positioning materials on machines;

- capacity to work and remain alert in the presence of loud noises and vibrations from machines, with occasional exposure to hazards such as moving parts, flying particles and dust.

Interests and Temperaments

Workers also require significant interests in and dispositions for work involving the following: Interests: (1) activities that are basically non-social in nature and are carried on in relation to processes, machines and techniques; (2) dealing with things and objects; and (3) routine, concrete and organized activities. Temperaments: (1) the evaluation of information against sensory or judgmental criteria, such as observing characteristics of logs or lumber to determine optimum usage; (2) the precise attainment of set limits, tolerances or standards; and (3) repetitive or short cycle operations carried out according to set procedures or sequences.

Training and Entry Requirements

Workers normally require ten years of general education and three months to two years of on-the-job training.

Hydraulic-Barker Operator

Work Performed

This occupation is concerned with removing bark from logs, trimming pressed board or plywood panels and reducing logs to chips, excelsior or wood flour. Worker functions include: operating or tending barking machines, sizing saws, pulverizers or chipping machines; and comparing appearance and dimensions of processed wood-products to specified standards. Work activities include: pushing buttons or moving levers to start and stop machines; adjusting guides and cutting knives; regulating conveyor speeds; clearing blockages; and cleaning equipment and work areas.

Aptitudes and Capacities

Workers require:

- learning ability to understand written or oral instructions and apply them when operating or tending log or wood-processing equipment;
- eye-hand coordination to adjust controls, operate overhead hoists or clear conveyor blockages;
- manual dexterity when using hand tools to replace or repair cutting tools, screens or conveyor belts;
- physical capacity to perform light to heavy work, lifting one hundred pounds with frequent lifting or carrying of objects weighing up to fifty pounds, depending on the occupation involved; such as lifting sacks of wood flour, rolling logs or shovelling spilled scrap;

- visual acuity, both near and far, to inspect wood flour and to observe wood-processing operation from varying distances;
- spatial perception to correctly set cutting heads, rotating knives or water-jet nozzles to bark logs;
- eye-hand-foot coordination to simultaneously operate hand and foot controls that regulate wash water and log rotation;
- adaptability to both inside and outside work conditions, and to loud noises from saws, pulverizers or barking machines.

Interests and Temperaments

Workers also require significant interests in and dispositions for work involving the following: Interests: (1) activities that are non-social in nature and are carried on in relation to sawmill processes, machines and techniques; (2) dealing with things and objects; and (3) activities of a routine, concrete and organized nature. Temperaments: (1) repetitive or short cycle operations carried out according to set procedure or sequences; (2) the precise attainment of set limits, tolerances or standards; and (3) the evaluation of information against measurable or verifiable criteria, such as setting guides and saws to required dimensions of panels, using rule and hand tools.

Training and Entry Requirements

Workers normally require eight to ten years of general education and one to six months of on-the-job training and related experience.

Tie and Timber Inspector

Work Performed

This occupation is concerned with quality control activities in the processing of lumber and other wood products, except paper pulp. Worker functions include: comparing characteristics of lumber, telephone poles, shingles, plywood panels and other processed items to specified standards; compiling data from specifications to determine appropriate inspection procedures and standards of quality; handling lumber and wood products; manipulating marking tools and measuring instruments; and recording inspection, grading or test results. Work activities include: determining moisture content of treated poles; examining products for knots, splits and other defects; measuring dimensions; and grading products according to texture, size, color and other specifications.

Aptitudes and Capacities

Workers require:

- learning ability to understand and follow quality control proce-

dures and techniques in the processing of lumber and other wood products;
- numerical ability to make measurements and calculations quickly and accurately;
- form perception to inspect lumber for defects such as knots, stains, faulty edges and worm holes, to perform routine tests and to grade lumber;
- clerical ability to take measurements, record test results or write reports;
- eye-hand coordination and manual dexterity to handle measuring and testing instruments and products;
- physical capacity to perform light to medium work involving reaching for and handling lumber or wood products, with frequent stooping and bending to inspect and mark grade or identification;
- adaptability to work either inside or outside while exposed to loud continuous noises from woodworking machinery.

Interests and Temperaments

Workers also require significant interests in and dispositions for work involving the following: Interests: (1) work of a non-social nature, carried on in relation to processes, machines and techniques; (2) dealing with things and objects; and (3) routine and organized work. Temperaments: (1) the evaluation of information against measurable or verifiable criteria, such as in the examination and testing of wood products to ensure adherence to specifications; (2) the precise attainment of set standards; and (3) repetitive or short cycle operations carried out according to set procedure or sequences.

Training and Entry Requirements

Workers normally require eight to ten years of general education and three to twelve months experience in a related occupation.

Sawmill Foreman

Work Performed

This occupation is concerned with supervising and coordinating activities or workers engaged in forestry and logging. Worker functions include: determining assignments, manpower requirements, work methods, materials and schedules required; and assigning duties to workers, interpreting work procedures and ensuring tasks are satisfactorily completed. Work activities include: requisitioning materials and supplies; hiring and training workers; setting up machines and equipment; inspecting materials received; enforcing safety regulations; preparing production reports; recommending measures to improve work methods, equipment performance, quality of product or service, and working conditions; and conferring with workers to resolve complaints and grievances.

Aptitudes and Capacities

Foremen require:

- learning ability to understand and effectively apply supervisory principles and practices and the techniques appropriate to the field of work supervised;
- verbal ability to communicate effectively with superiors and subordinates and to understand work orders;
- spatial perception to understand the functional nature of machines and equipment and to interpret technical drawings;
- form perception to discern pertinent detail in things and objects such as drawings and finished products;
- eye-hand coordination, and finger and manual dexterity to operate machines and equipment and to use tools;
- capacity to perform medium to heavy work, requiring the lifting of one hundred pounds maximum and carrying objects weighing up to fifty pounds.

Interests and Temperaments

Foremen require the significant interests in and disposition for work involving the following: Interests: (1) work resulting in prestige or the esteem of others; and (2) work which is basically nonsocial in nature and is carried on in relation to processes, machines and techniques. Temperaments: (1) the direction, control and planning of an entire activity or the activities of others; (2) dealing with people in actual job duties beyond giving and receiving instructions; the evaluation of information against measurable or verifiable criteria such as ascertaining and ensuring that the quality of work meets established standards; (3) a variety of duties often characterized by frequent change; and (4) the precise attainment of set limits, tolerances or standards.

Other Requirements:

- ability to maintain harmony in working relationships among workers and to motivate others;
- ability to demonstrate a sound, technical knowledge and to inspire confidence;
- initiative and drive;
- good physical condition;
- evidence of leadership and demonstrated success in a nonsupervisory job.

Training and Entry Requirements

Foremen normally require ten to fourteen years of general or technical education with varying amounts of successful lower level job experience in similar fields. Some companies may accept less than three years of formal education where the employee has demonstrated initiative, work ability and leadership qualities in lower-level jobs.

Working foremen usually enter into supervisory work from the worker ranks, since demonstrated skill in a particular field of work is very important. Training as a foreman may be given by the employer, either on the job or in formalized courses. The employer may also require training on his own initiative in technical or other schools.

SOURCE: (Preceding four job specifications) Manpower and Immigration Canada, *Canadian Classification and Dictionary of Occupations*, 1971 (Ottawa: Information Canada, 1971). New definitions and recent changes in the CCDO are in Employment and Immigration Canada, *CCDO Guide* and a series of five update booklets which are obtainable from Canadian Government Publishing Centre, Supply and Services Canada, Hull, Quebec, K1A 0S9.

Case 5.2: Differing Descriptions for Two Secretary IVs

Doreen Murella is paying a rare visit to John Oaks, Director of Human Resources at Parker & Hobbs' Pharmaceuticals, where she has worked for the past eight years. Murella, currently secretary to Sol Friedman, Director of Public Relations, wonders why her job classification (and hence, her pay grade) is the same as Sarah Higgins, who is secretary to the manager of the research and development lab. Both she and Higgins, who recently joined the firm, are classified "Secretary IV," the highest level for secretaries, but Murella feels her job is far more demanding than Higgins'. Murella has never complained about her job responsibilities before; in fact, she seems to enjoy the relative autonomy and responsibility of her position.

Murella only recently discovered differences in job duties for the two secretarial positions. She and Higgins had become better acquainted at a company-sponsored weight-loss support group. When Parker & Hobbs asked employees to fill out a position description questionnaire as part of a comprehensive pay plan review, Murella and Higgins compared notes revealing similarities and differences in their job responsibilities.

Job descriptions for the two secretaries appear below, along with percentages of time spent yearly on each of the varied job duties. Also provided is a description of the Secretary IV classification, which Oaks may find useful in his discussion with Murella.

Job Description: Secretary to the Director, Public Relations Department (Murella)

Duties:

1. Transcribe and type letters, reports, and public relations materials for Director; schedule appointments; make travel arrangements and prepare travel expense vouchers; perform all other related duties as assigned by Director (35%);

2. Serve as liaison for general public on questions, complaints and problems regarding the company and its products. Answer all enquiries according to company procedure, or route them to proper person for attention (20%);
3. Monitor expenditures from all public relations accounts; report on development of possible problems and suggest corrective action (15%);
4. Review and approve expenditures in general areas of printing, office supplies, and postage, etc. (10%);
5. Maintain personnel records for public relations staff (10%);
6. Handle all arrangements for company tours including scheduling and arranging for guide (10%).

Job Description: Secretary to the Manager, Research and Development Lab (Higgins)

Duties:

1. Enter correspondence, presentations, and manuscripts into word processor from dictation and hand-written source materials (40%);
2. File correspondence, reports, and other materials in a timely and orderly fashion (12%);
3. Answer telephone as secretary to the Manager; in his absence, provide information or refer caller to other appropriate staff (10%);
4. Arrange for meetings, conferences and travel for the Manager, including submittal of required travel forms (10%);
5. Schedule appointments for Manager (5%);
6. Answer telephone as backup to Secretary IIs (5%);
7. Review payroll and personnel work when submitted for signature (5%);
8. Obtain information from various sources as instructed by Manager for use in correspondence and reports (3%);
9. Scan daily newspapers for laboratory-related materials (2%);
10. Update reference materials as new items are received (2%);
11. Make copies of correspondence on copy machine (2%);
12. Give advice pertaining to office procedure or problem solving to other secretarial staff (1%);
13. Develop and initiate new office forms or procedures (1%);
14. Schedule use of automobiles assigned to the lab (1%);
15. Assign use of the lab's conference room (1%).

Class Description: Secretary IV

General class description:

Under general supervision, performs secretarial work involving recurring contact with directors, department heads, staff, and the general public. Contacts require exercising discretion in obtaining and providing factual and confidential information requiring a knowledge of both the assigned and related work areas and company operations. Duties may involve use of electronic word/data processing equipment and/or conventional office equipment. Provides administrative supervision to secretary, clerical personnel as required.

Characteristic duties and responsibilities:

1. Reviews enquiries and otherwise represents assigned and related work areas, exercising discretion in obtaining and providing factual and confidential information related to company operations;
2. Arranges for meetings and conferences including preparing an agenda, assembling and distributing data required for coverage of the agenda items, and other information in follow-up;
3. Reviews and develops office procedures and policies and makes recommendations for revision and implementation in both the assigned and related work areas;
4. Participates in budget preparation including calculation of projected costs and expenses necessary for grant proposals or other related financial accounts.

Related duties:

1. Coordinates intra-unit operations, procedures and activities with other secretarys and/or clerical personnel in order to maintain consistency in the application of policies and procedures as related to assigned work area;
2. Collects and compiles data for specialized reports requiring some informational search and a knowledge of the operations of both the assigned and related work areas;
3. Composes correspondence requiring judgement in the application of policies and procedures in both the assigned and related work areas;
4. Interviews, recommends hiring, and supervises the training of secretary/clerical personnel; makes recommendations with respect to merit salary increases, promotions, and other status changes;
5. Initiates standard forms and documents such as personnel action sheets, purchase orders and invoices, and verifies departmental statements;
6. Maintains records on personnel budgetary and purchasing transactions;
7. Assigns, coordinates, and reviews the work of other/clerical personnel for conformance to established guidelines;
8. Types and proofs minutes of meetings, correspondence, tabular data, reports, medical records, examinations, etc., articles and other material from rough draft, dictating machines, various other source data and instructions;
9. Makes travel arrangements and prepares expense vouchers.

Questions:

1. What is it about this situation that bothers Murella?
2. Assume you are John Oaks. How will you deal with Murella's complaint?
3. Based upon the two women's job descriptions and the class description for Secretary IV, do you feel both women are accurately classified as Secretary IV? Why or why not?
4. Speculate on why Murella and Higgins are in the same job class. Might there be reasons other than those captured in their job descriptions?

6

Recruiting

DRILLCO is a drilling supply and rig maintenance company in Alberta. At the peak of the oil boom, DRILLCO had a work force of 400. But when oil prices dropped drastically in 1986, top management realized recovery would not come quickly. They adopted a strategy of downsizing to reduce DRILLCO's work force by 25 per cent.

The plan was to avoid layoffs by encouraging workers to take early retirement. Human Resources Director Henry Jackson and Benefits Specialist Sylvia Ketelman developed an attractive early retirement package, consistent with DRILLCO's policy of generous pay and benefits for all. The early retirement package was available for a limited time to any employee aged 50+ who had been with the company at least 15 years. DRILLCO, a well-established company founded in 1955, had many employees in the eligible category, including sales and supply personnel, office and warehouse workers, and rig repair and maintenance people.

Response to the voluntary exit package was slow at first, with only those in their 60s taking the retirement option. Jackson and Ketelman were worried until a few days before the deadline when 70 employees departed. This left DRILLCO with 300 employees, about the right number according to top management, given expected reductions in business. Jackson and Ketelman received a congratulatory letter for achieving the work force reduction to the satisfaction of both management and those who left.

All went well until several months later when management noted a growing number of complaints from clients regarding quality and speed of service for oil rig repair and maintenance. This was very distressing since DRILLCO had always enjoyed an excellent reputation for quality service. Upon checking, management discovered that the repair and maintenance unit was very busy; in fact, it was understaffed and had too few experienced employees, especially to service older drilling equipment.

Jackson was asked to look into the matter. His investigation revealed that a disproportionate number of repair and maintenance people had elected to take early retirement. Due to the plan's eligibility requirement, the unit had lost a large number of experienced employees, leaving only a small number of less experienced workers to do all maintenance and repair work. The problem was compounded by the fact that, while sales had dropped to the expected level, demand for maintenance and repair had slackened only slightly. It was now apparent to Jackson tht he had not adequately planned for the reduction in force—the across-the-board exit package had caused many needed workers to quit.

A rather embarassed Jackson told management that he would now need to recruit a number of experienced repair and maintenance people to replace some of those lost to early retirement. He didn't think this would be difficult, however, with unemployment at double digit levels in Calgary. He placed a recruitment ad in the local newspaper and wasn't at all surprised to receive over 100 applications for the 20 positions.

Closer inspection revealed, however, that very few of the applicants had the expertise, skills, and experience necessary to meet DRILLCO's high job performance standards. After a month of advertising, Jackson had hired only five job applicants.

Jackson was concerned because there was a growing backlog of maintenance and repair work to be done. The company was falling further and further behind in its commitments and now two large clients were threatening to switch to a competitor. Jackson decided it was time to broaden his recruiting effort, perhaps even look to new sources. He considered advertising in Houston, Texas, but rejected the idea because of time and paperwork associated with immigration regulations. He decided instead to place recruitment ads in several regional and Atlantic-province newspapers, being careful to specify level of skills and experience required. In addition, he contacted all recently retired DRILLCO maintenance personnel and offered them the opportunity to work part-time for the company. The combination of these two approaches eventually yielded the necessary personnel.

This chapter discusses *recruiting*, the process of attracting applicants with certain skills, abilities, and other personal characteristics to job vacancies in an organization. While the need for recruiting in times of expansion and low unemployment is obvious, the above situation demonstrates the usefulness of recruiting even in periods of downsizing and high unemployment.

The chapter begins with a discussion of the role of recruiting, recruiting responsibilities, and 6 factors affecting recruiting. It then turns to an examination of 13 different recruiting methods and sources. A final section describes some of the ways recruiting efforts are evaluated.

The Role of Recruiting

Recruiting has been defined as the process of attracting applicants with certain skills, abilities and other personal characteristics to job vacancies in an organization. Applicants may be recruited either *internally*, from inside the organization's work force, or *externally*, from outside the organization, via recruiting messages such as job postings (internal) or newspaper advertisements (external). Recruiting messages seek a *qualified* response rather than a general one. This means that recruiters want only those persons with certain job-related qualifications to apply. The fact that recruiting messages seek and are able to obtain a qualified response means that applicants are to some degree "self-selected" for the jobs for which they apply. One can therefore assume that those who apply have some interest in the job and believe they possess the required qualifications. The recruiting process ends and selection begins once an applicant has contacted an employer regarding a job opening. However, recruiting efforts to "sell" the organization sometimes continue until an applicant accepts a job offer.

Recruiting attracts the necessary work force to further organizational objectives, such as survival, growth, service, production, or profit. Of course, not all organizational needs for labour are anticipated by planners. Recruiting also serves to attract workers to unexpected job vacancies caused by turnover and to new positions created by sudden demands for a company's goods and services. Recruiting is always an important function because it affects the quality of people an organization has available for hiring and promotion.

The role of recruiting in an organization and its relationship to other HRM functions is given in Exhibit 6.1. Briefly, the human resource planning function specifies recruiting goals in terms of number and type of workers the organization needs to attract. Specific worker requirements are determined via job analysis, which also provides recruiters with job descriptions for use in recruiting messages. Recruiting is facilitated by competitive pay and attractive benefits and these are determined in compensation and benefits functions. The recruiting function is closely tied to selection, as both are parts of the employment process. Those recruited form a selection pool from which to choose and hire the best qualified applicant(s).

Recruiting Responsibilities

HRM professionals have three major responsibilities related to recruiting: (1) develop a recruiting plan, including a budget; (2) prepare recruiting messages and implement the plan; and (3) evaluate the effort. They are also responsible for analyzing recruiting needs of the organization, but this responsibility is part of the human resource planning

EXHIBIT 6.1

Recruiting: An HRM function

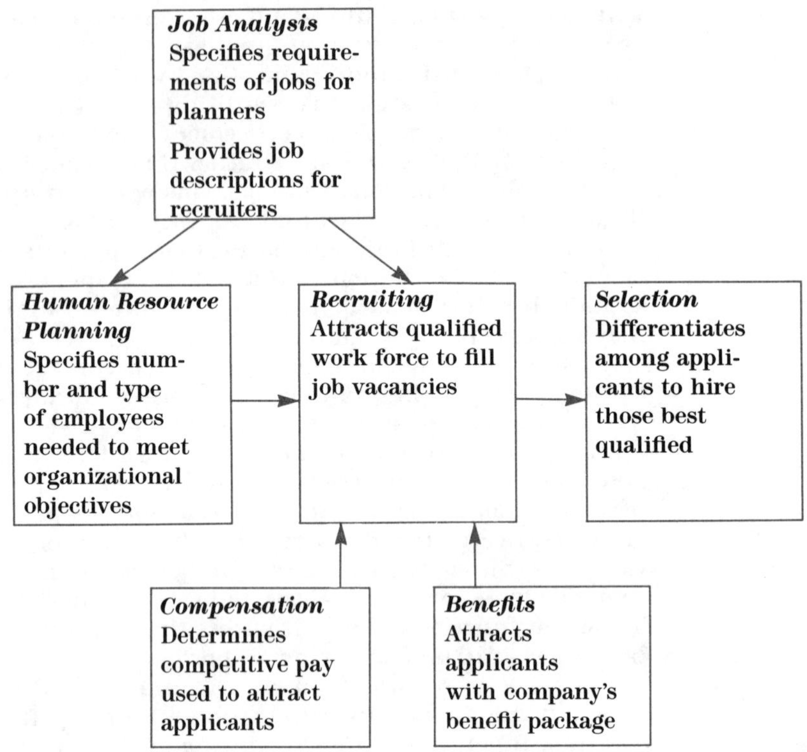

function. In the DRILLCO example, Jackson failed to recognize the implications for recruiting of his downsizing strategy.

Only very large organizations employ full-time recruiters. The majority of organizations use other HRM professionals to perform responsibilities of the recruiting function.

Recruiting Plans

A recruiting plan is a plan of attack for achieving recruiting goals. Developing the plan is essentially a process of choosing an appropriate method and source from which to recruit. Possible sources of external recruiting include schools, colleges, employment agencies, and various segments of the population, among others. The source for internal recruiting is an organization's present work force. A number of factors affect recruiting plans and strategies, and these are discussed in a following section.

A recruiting budget is a necessary part of the plan. This budget is prepared by HRM professionals, subject to management approval or prior consideration. Preparing a budget requires actual cost information plus estimates of running time for advertisements, required travel, long-distance telephone calls, and length of the recruiting effort, among others. Because of the difficulty of making such estimates, many budget-preparers base expected costs on information from previous recruiting efforts.

Recruiting Messages

Implementing a recruiting plan involves preparation of recruiting materials including recruiting messages. As noted above, recruiting messages are designed to encourage applications from only those with the required skills, abilities, and interest to perform a certain job. Recruiting messages are not limited to ads; they also include internal job postings, recruiting brochures and letters, or personal and videotaped presentations by company representatives.

Effective recruiting messages contain the following:

1. Job or position title.
2. A brief, but clear description of job duties.
3. A statement of skills, abilities, knowledge and experience required to do the job.
4. Working conditions (e.g., location, hours, days, level of supervision, level of pay, nature of benefits).
5. When and where to apply.
6. How to apply (e.g., send resume, come in and fill out an application, phone for an interview, apply at a Canada Employment Centre).

In developing recruiting messages, care must be taken not to portray the job or the employer too favourably. Overselling the job or employer can lead to dissatisfaction and turnover in the long run if the reality of the job fails to meet initial expectations. Overselling is often a temptation since recruiters are competing against one another for talented and sometimes scarce labour. Further, recruiters are often judged by the number and quality of applicants they recruit, and not by how long their recruits stay with the organization.

Evaluating the Effort

After the recruiting effort is completed, it should be evaluated. This involves collecting information on the costs and effectiveness of various recruiting methods and sources used. This information should be stored for use in developing future plans.

It is also advisable to monitor the effectiveness of recruiting sources and methods while recruiting is underway. This enables new methods and sources to be tried in case of poor results from earlier approaches. For example, Jackson of DRILLCO found he had to broaden the scope of his recruiting effort when local newspaper ads failed to provide a well-qualified pool of applicants.

Factors Affecting Recruiting

A number of factors influence recruiting plans and strategies. These include: (1) organizational stage of development; (2) organizational recruiting policies; (3) type of labour to be recruited; (4) conditions of the labour market; (5) legal requirements; and (6) cost and time constraints.

Organizational Stage of Development

In Chapter 1, we suggested that the relative importance of HRM functions and their specific activities vary according to an organization's stage of development. Obviously, more effort will go toward recruiting when an organization is in a growth stage than when it is in maturity or decline. At the maturity stage, recruiting is typically more internal than external. Even when an organization is downsizing, both internal and external recruiting may be necessary as illustrated by the DRILLCO example. In addition to changes in the magnitude and focus of recruiting, it is likely that stage of development will cause recruiting messages and methods to change. For example, recruiting messages for a rapidly expanding employer might emphasize growth and promotion opportunities, while messages for a mature employer might point to job security and excellent salary and benefits.

Organizational Recruiting Policies

Organizations tap different sources and use different methods depending on whether they favour internal or external recruiting for higher-level jobs (those above entry-level). Currently, the preferred policy in most organizations is internal recruiting. Policies of internal recruiting afford employees desired opportunities for growth and advancement. Large organizations are more likely than small ones to have internal recruiting policies, because large organizations have greater pools of employees from which to choose in filling job vacancies. Organizations that choose policies of internal recruiting also tend to spend relatively large amounts on training and development programs to help employees move up. Of course, organizations with internal policies still must rely on external recruiting to fill entry-level positions. External recruiting may also be necessary if a sudden unexpected demand for a company's product or service creates a need for more labour at all levels of ability and experience.

Type of Labour to Be Recruited

Recruiting goals are specified in terms of number and type of labour needed. Type of labour needed affects choice of a recruitment source and method, scope of the applicant search, and the ultimate costs of recruiting. Each type of labour has its own market which must be tapped in order to gain recruits. Some sources are better than others for tapping certain markets. For example, vocational schools are a good source for skilled entry-level workers; colleges are a better source for professional and managerial employees. Generally, markets are smaller for labour types that are highly specialized or that require higher levels of education and experience. Jobs requiring these skills are more difficult and costly to fill; hence, the search for qualified applicants must be broader in scope. Since certain methods are better suited to extensive search than others, the type of labour to be recruited affects choice of a recruiting method. For example, a recruiting effort to attract female executives must be broad in scope and may even require the services of a costly executive search firm because of the scarcity of women executives. On the other hand, a recruiting goal of attracting 50 persons to stuff envelopes could probably be met by simply placing an inexpensive advertisement in a local newspaper.

Recruiting efforts also seek applicants who match the organization's culture. In addition to skills, abilities, and experience, management seeks the "right kind of people," those whose values are congruent with those of the organization. Harmon and Jacobs, authors of *The Vital Difference*, argue that successful companies have a distinct personality and "look for people with personalities like their own."[1]

Conditions of the Labour Market

Labour market conditions exert a strong influence on recruiting. Labour markets are local, regional, national, or international, depending on the geographical area in which the forces of supply and demand operate for a particular labour type. Recruiting for jobs that require less highly skilled labour (such as clerical, sales, and service occupations) can usually be done in local labour markets, while regional markets function for jobs requiring more highly skilled labour (for example, water pollution specialists, computer programmers, and registered nurses). Professionals and executives are generally recruited from national markets, while engineers and various scientific specialists, such as astronomers, physicists, and chemists, enjoy international markets.

The boundaries of a local labour market are defined by the distance workers are willing to commute to work. If they are willing to commute 30 miles to work, the local labour market has a 30-mile radius, and communities outside this 30-mile radius are not within an employer's local labour market. For example, although Toronto and Oshawa are less than 30 miles apart, most people in the area are not willing to commute from one city to the other to work. Therefore, Toronto's local labour market does not include Oshawa, and vice versa.

One difference between recruiting in local versus regional, national, or international markets is that, in the latter, recruiting efforts must induce workers to relocate. An organization's location seems to

[1] F.G. Harmon and G. Jacobs, *The Vital Difference* (New York: AMACOM, 1985), p. 137.

be an important factor for many people considering a job change. One reason which has been cited for firms' moving part or all of their head offices from Montreal to Toronto has been the inability to recruit professionals due to Quebec's language, education, and taxation policies. Relocation costs can also be a factor. To increase labour mobility, some organizations pay moving expenses and even subsidize the purchase of homes. In the late 1970s, firms in Alberta and British Columbia often resorted to these practices to attract labour.

When supply of a certain type of labour cannot meet the demand, shortages result and the labour market is called *tight*. A labour market is *loose* if labour supply is abundant. When unemployment is relatively high, external recruiting for many types of labour will be faster and less expensive than when unemployment is low. Of course, the general level of employment may have little effect on the specific type of labour an organization needs to recruit. For example, high unemployment in the Western provinces caused by low oil and grain prices will likely have little effect on the ease with which hospitals are able to recruit surgeons and radiologists. A shortage in a certain type of labour drives up the price of that labour and forces organizations to broaden their geographical areas of search for applicants. Exhibit 6.2 shows the effect of various market conditions on the scope of a recruiting effort, the type of effort, and the cost of labour. Tight markets require broader search efforts. In the late 1970s, the shortage of skilled workers in Canada led 35 per cent of employers with shortages to search for workers outside their region and 11 per cent to search outside the country.[2] During the same period, the province of Alberta was so short of skilled workers that it set up an office in Toronto to recruit labour from Ontario. In addition, Alberta megaprojects were given priority in overseas recruiting by Employment and Immigration Canada.

EXHIBIT 6.2

Effect of labour market conditions on recruiting efforts for a keypunch operator

Condition of labour market	*Scope of effort*	*Type of effort*	*Cost of labour*
Tight (shortages exist)	regional	Use private employment agency	high
Intermediate (supply not abundant, but no shortages exist)	local-regional	Visit vocational schools with keypunch programs	average
Loose (abundant supply)	local	Place ads in local newspaper and list vacancies with Canada (Quebec) Employment Centres	low

[2] Gordon Betcherman, *Meeting Skill Requirements, Report of the Human Resources Survey* (Ottawa: Economic Council of Canada, 1982), p. 33.

When organizations experience difficulty recruiting particular types of labour, they often tap new sources such as the secondary labour force, moonlighters, and temporary workers. Members of the *secondary labour force* are usually people who have elected not to seek conventional employment. They are typically mothers of young children, students, handicapped persons or retired persons. Lee Iacocca tapped the secondary labour force when he recruited retired Ford executives at Chrysler Corporation (see Case 6.1).

Since members of the secondary labour force usually do not seek out employment, organizations must use somewhat unusual recruiting methods to reach them. One grocery store chain sends recruiters from store to store in a van which has become a mobile recruitment centre. Other stores use public address systems to inform customers of vacancies. Some McDonald's restaurants of Canada recently used place mats to advertise job openings. Each place mat featured the slogan "Come and Join the Crew," a sales pitch about working for McDonald's, and an employment application. McDonald's recruiting place mat appears in Exhibit 6.3. To attract workers in the secondary labour force, employers may need to offer special inducements such as part-time employment, higher pay, subsidized day care, flexible working hours, or the opportunity to work at home. According to one study, members of the secondary labour force make excellent part-time employees.[3]

Another source of labour that is tapped when shortages exist is *moonlighters*—persons who hold more than one full- or part-time job. According to Statistics Canada's labour force survey of 1982, 3.3 per cent of all employees held two or more jobs.[4] Periods of inflation seem to cause more moonlighting as people try to keep up with increased costs.

Temporary workers are being used increasingly to meet employee shortages, especially when demand for labour is forecast to be short-term. Temporary workers tend to be clerical or lower-level blue-collar workers, although some sales and professional positions may also be filled by temporaries. Temporary employees may serve an important role in recruiting in two ways. First, a temporary worker may fill in while the process continues to find a permanent employee. Second, in some situations, excellent permanent employees may be recruited from temporary help. Organizations benefit from the use of temporaries because their total labour costs are lower. Temporaries only work when needed, they typically require no training, and their benefits are paid by the temporary agency that leases them.

This section has discussed how market conditions can affect recruiting plans. Labour market conditions affect the scope of a recruiting effort, the source and method used, and the going rate of pay necessary to attract applicants to a job. Information regarding supply of particular types of labour in local markets can be obtained through Canada and Quebec Employment Centres and through personnel officers' associations, such as the Personnel Association of Ontario, the Inter-

[3] M.J. Gannon, "A Profile of the Temporary Help Industry and Its Workers," *Monthly Labor Review*, 1974, vol. 97, pp. 44–49.

[4] Statistics Canada, *The Labour Force*, cat. no. 71-001 (Ottawa, July 1982).

EXHIBIT 6.3

McDonald's recruiting place mat

Come and Join the Crew

We're **McDONALD'S**, a company that understands people and their working needs. We understand how difficult it is to hold down a job and still keep up with your busy schedule.

At **McDONALD'S**, our flexible scheduling will give the free time you need to accommodate school or any other interests.

But flexible scheduling isn't the only reason to take a look at **McDONALD'S**. Consider our complete training, competitive wages with regular merit raises and advancement potential as well as the opportunity to meet new people, make new friends and participate in the outings, social activities and recognition programs available for all our restaurant staff. All the right reasons are here. Come and take a look!

Apply in person, (no phone calls please).

McDONALD'S RESTAURANTS

EMPLOYMENT APPLICATION

Date ______ Social insurance number ______

PERSONAL INFORMATION

Name ______ last ______ first ______ middle ______ Phone ______

Present address ______ no. & street ______ city ______ province ______ postal code ______ How long there ______

Previous address in Canada ______ no. & street ______ city ______ province ______ postal code ______ How long there ______

Are you presently employed? ______ Date of availability ______ Referred by ______

Have you ever worked for McDonald's before? ______ If so, where? ______

Are you presently attending school? ______ If so, at what level? ______

If you are under 15, please state your age* ______ Position applied for ______

*Please Note: You may be required to provide proof of age prior to hire.

Have you ever been convicted of a criminal offense related to the position applied for and for which you have not been pardoned? ______ Are you legally entitled to work in Canada? ______

AVAILABILITY

HOURS AVAILABLE	MONDAY	TUESDAY	WEDNESDAY	THURSDAY	FRIDAY	SATURDAY	SUNDAY
FROM							
TO							

EMPLOYMENT BACKGROUND

List your PRESENT OR LAST position FIRST.

DATE MONTH & YEAR	COMPANY NAME AND ADDRESS	TELEPHONE NUMBER INCLUDING AREA CODE	NAME AND POSITION OF SUPERVISOR	YOUR POSITION	SALARY/WAGE START	SALARY/WAGE END	REASON FOR LEAVING
FROM							
TO							
FROM							
TO							
FROM							
TO							

As a condition of my application/employment, I authorize investigation of all statements contained in this application. I understand that McDonald's decision will be based solely on non-discriminatory considerations and that misrepresentation or omission of facts called for is just cause for the rejection of my application or dismissal. If hired, I agree that, due to labour shortages, promotions or training I may be required to transfer from one restaurant to another. I also agree that, at all times, I will follow the rules and regulations of McDonald's restaurants in Canada.

Signature

This application expires at the end of 30 days

McDonald's

national Personnel Management Association, and other local affiliates and personnel groups. Information on regional and national labour market conditions is available through regional offices of the Canada Employment and Immigration Commission, industry associations, and newsletters and journals of union and professional associations. Information about labour force characteristics, unemployment, and turnover can be found in Statistics Canada publications, such as *Employment Earnings and Hours* (catalogue number 72-002) and *The Labour Force* (catalogue number 71-001). *The Financial Post* is also a good source of information on labour market changes.

Legal Requirements

Recruiting plans and messages are also affected by legal prohibitions and requirements. For example, human rights legislation requires that recruiting messages express no preference for a particular sex, race, age, ethnic or religious group. Such references are prohibited unless membership in one of these groups is a bona fide occupational qualification for the job. This is discussed further under "Recruitment advertising" in the Methods Section, below.

Legislation especially affects the recruiting plans and goals of employers under federal jurisdiction with 100 or more employees. These employers must structure their recruiting plans and methods to attract qualified applicants of a special target population: women, native people, Francophones or Anglophones, the handicapped, and so forth. There is no one method of affirmative action recruiting, but reaching a special population requires getting a recruiting message to the "right place," one of maximum exposure to the target group. This often requires the use of nontraditional methods of recruiting, such as notices on bulletin boards of ethnic community centres or posters in shopping malls.

Cost and Time Constraints

Cost and time constraints pose obvious limitations on recruiting efforts. For example, an organization with very little money budgeted for recruiting does not even consider hiring a graphic artist to design attractive recruiting materials. Rather than spend money to advertise openings, an organization with few cash resources for external recruiting often uses a system in which potential applicants are referred to the organization by present employees. Such organizations may also make use of Canada Employment Centres, which refer applicants at no cost.

More recruiting options are open to organizations with larger recruiting budgets. Such organizations can afford to advertise more widely, perhaps in a newspaper with national circulation, and to recruit actively by visiting universities and colleges, even in other parts of the country. Exhibit 6.4 compares recruiting methods according to cost and time factors. The most expensive methods are school recruiting and the use of executive search firms, which charge a fee for recruiting executives and managerial-level employees. Advertising can also be very expensive, depending upon the type of media used (radio, television, or newspaper), where it appears (in a publication with limited versus national circulation), and the length of time it runs.

Cost constraints can cause problems for organizations if relatively inexpensive methods prove unsuccessful. An example of the problems that can result is given by a manager of a medium-sized company that had several executive positions to fill. Management ruled out an executive search firm as too costly and decided instead to place advertisements in several newspapers across the country. Three months of advertising attracted no qualified applicants for the positions. The company finally contacted an executive search firm that was able to supply qualified applicants within a few weeks. In this case, the recruiting method deemed less costly turned out to be a waste of money, and the "costly" method turned out to be very cost-effective.

EXHIBIT 6.4

Cost and time variations of recruiting methods

Method	*Approximate cost relative to other methods*	*Approximate time involved relative to other methods*
Posting and bidding	low	short
Skill inventories	low	short
Employee referral	low	short-medium
Walk-ins	low	short
Union hiring halls	low	varies with market conditions
Recruitment advertising	varies with type of ad and market conditions	varies with market conditions
Special events	average	short
Vocational, technical, and trade school recruiting	average-high	medium-long
University and college recruiting	high	long
Professional meetings	average-high	medium-long
Canada (and Quebec) Employment Centres	low	varies with market conditions
Private employment agencies	average-high	medium
Executive search firms	high	medium

Time constraints can also limit choice of a recruiting method. Organizations experiencing a sudden increased demand for goods and services have little time to engage in efforts such as school recruiting. Rather, they must meet the demand for new labour as quickly as possible. Exhibit 6.4 shows that time involved for many recruiting methods varies according to market conditions. When labour markets are tight, it generally takes longer for recruiting efforts to be successful.

An example of the effect of time constraints on a recruiting effort was provided by a human resource manager of an auto parts manufacturing firm. Faced with a sudden demand for the company's product, the company manager informed the human resource manager on Friday afternoon that he needed 50 new employees by Monday! Since it was too late to advertise in the local newspaper, the human resource manager searched through a number of applications on file and also requested that the local Canada Employment Centre refer any suitable applicants in a hurry.

Generally, the recruiting function is rendered less costly and more efficient by human resource forecasting. Advance knowledge of needs for certain labour types allows organizations to plan less costly and more efficient strategies for obtaining needed personnel, particularly when the labour market is tight.

Recruiting Methods and Sources

There are two basic categories of recruiting methods and sources—those used for internal recruiting and those used for external recruiting.

Internal Methods

Many nonentry-level vacancies are filled by employees who have been identified as next-in-line for promotion. Other vacancies require that promotable candidates be identified. Two methods used to attract and identify current workers for higher-level positions are posting and bidding and skill inventories.

Posting and bidding. Posting and bidding is a common method of recruiting from within an organization's work force. It involves posting a notice of a job vacancy on company bulletin boards; employees have a specified length of time (usually a week) to "bid" for the vacancy. When employees bid for posted job vacancies, they fill out vacancy bid request forms. Bidding is analogous to making formal application for a job.

Several guidelines can be suggested for the posting and bidding method. First, all permanent job openings and transfers should be posted for at least one week prior to external recruiting. Second, both job descriptions and specifications should be clearly defined. Third, all applicants should receive feedback on the status of their applications and any actions that result.

The system of posting job vacancies and allowing employees to bid for them has traditionally been used for blue-collar union jobs. In fact, posting and bidding is usually required for jobs covered by collective agreements with trade unions. Under these agreements, a posted job is awarded to the qualified bidder who has the most seniority.

The posting and bidding method has recently increased in popularity. Common now in government, its use in private industry is also increasing. Posting and bidding is a good way of stimulating employee career development. It provides a vehicle for enabling women, members of ethnic groups, and bilingual employees to move up in an organization. Another advantage is that it is not costly or time consuming.

Use of skill inventories. Another approach to internal recruiting is the use of skill inventory information on the present work force. An employer using this method searches through skill inventories to identify employees who are qualified for vacant jobs. They are then contacted and asked whether they want to apply. This method can be used in conjunction with posting and bidding to ensure that job vacancies come to the attention of all qualified employees.

An advantage of this method is that it affords a thorough search of possible applicants from within an organization. If skill inventory information is readily available, the method is not costly or time-consuming. Skill inventory data are often a part of human resource information systems (HRIS) that were discussed in Chapter 4.

External Methods

External recruiting goes outside the organization to attract applicants. It can take many forms; the most common are discussed in this section.

Employee referral. The employee referral method involves informing present employees of job vacancies and asking them to recommend or refer applicants to the organization. Some organizations offer small cash rewards to employees as incentives for referring qualified applicants. This is most often done when the market for certain labour is very tight.

The employee referral method is a popular one in many industries because it is neither costly nor time-consuming and it often yields good results. For example, research has shown that employees recruited by this method tend to have lower turnover than workers recruited by other methods.[5]

One disadvantage of employee referral is that it can serve to perpetuate existing sex and ethnic distributions in organizations. This is because people tend to know, associate with, and refer others like them-

[5] Donald P. Schwab, "Organizational Recruiting and the Decision to Participate," in K. Rowland and G. Ferris (eds.) *Personnel Management: New Perspectives* (Boston: Allyn and Bacon, 1982).

selves. In the United States, courts have several times ruled as discriminatory specific recruiting efforts based on employee referrals. On the other hand, the employee referral method can be used constructively to achieve objectives such as affirmative action by asking for referrals from women and members of specific language groups or visible ethnic minorities.

Walk-ins. People who come to organizations seeking employment without referral and without organizational encouragement are called *walk-ins.* Though they have not actually been recruited, walk-ins do provide a very inexpensive source of job applicants for an organization. They are a common source of lower-skilled, blue-collar, and clerical labour in a local labour market.

Walk-ins are most prevalent when unemployment in a local area is high and when demand for labour is low. In times of high unemployment, employers may wish to discourage walk-ins with signs saying "Not accepting applications at this time."

Union hiring halls. Union hiring halls are very specialized placement agencies restricted to members of a particular union and to employers of a particular industry. Longshoremen and some construction unions, for example, commonly require employers to recruit first from their hiring halls. Employers submit their requisitions for new employees to the halls, which then forward job applicants to the employer. Under this method, unions become the primary recruiters for certain types of labour.

Recruitment advertising. Recruitment advertising includes newspaper advertising, advertising or announcements in university and college placement bulletins and professional newsletters and journals, and ads on radio, television, and billboards. Some large companies have job lines with taped messages concerning job vacancies. A job seeker simply phones in to see what is available.

All the methods of advertising share a common purpose: to convey information to potential job applicants. Besides providing information on the nature of the job and employee qualifications, recruitment ads often seek to "sell" potential applicants on the advantages of the organization or the attractiveness of the job. Ads directed to applicants in national markets may mention location as a selling point. For instance, a company in a small community might stress the freedom from smog and rush hour traffic jams.

It is important that recruiting messages convey honest information to applicants about the job and what it is like to work for the organization. Honest messages facilitate good matches between employees and organizations by allowing applicants to self-select out if they feel poorly suited to the job or work environment. Mismatches based on faulty information can be costly to employers, as they lead more often than not to employee dissatisfaction and turnover. An example of a newspaper recruitment ad is given in Exhibit 6.5.

EXHIBIT 6.5

Newspaper recruitment ad

We are looking for a
results-oriented, goal-driven

Chief Financial Officer

You are knowledgeable in finance, accounting and information processing and will create and command teams responsible for treasury, controllership and information processing. You will need sophisticated asset-liability technique experience including matching, product pricing and rate-setting. Profit centre and financial product cost accounting are a must.

We have full-function, on-line, real-time banking computer systems presently in use but it demands expansion for more effective management exception reporting.

As the successful candidate, you will work extremely hard with your colleagues on the senior management team, reporting to the Managing Director. Your first priority will be the consolidation of operations and investigation of new opportunities. You will quickly learn the uniqueness and the challenges of credit union operations.

Capital City Savings has recently been created by amalgamating the eight community credit unions of Edmonton into one super sized financial institution with $660 million in assets.

This position provides for a $70,000 - $80,000 salary range plus benefits. Only candidates qualified by academic training and senior financial experience (preferably banking) will be considered.

Capital City Savings & Credit Union Ltd.

Forward your resume in confidence by April 15, 1987 to:

Mrs. Donna Leggett
Manager of Human Resources Department
Capital City Savings & Credit Union Ltd.
10568 - 104th Street
Edmonton, Alberta
T5H 2W1

SOURCE: From Report on Business: Advertisement for a Chief Financial Officer, *The Globe and Mail* (March 31, 1987). Reprinted with permission of Capital City Savings & Credit Union Limited.

V. M. Evans has provided a number of suggestions about recruitment advertising.[6] Arguing that good ads should "reward the reader" and that information is the key ingredient, he points to four market segments that recruitment ads should influence. The first and major segment is the group of potential applicants which constitutes the "qualified response" the ad seeks to attract. A second segment is the 70 to 75 per cent of readers who are already employed, even if only a small percentage of them are actively seeking other employment. Evans provides data showing that ads help build organizational images which determine where people seek jobs when they are actively searching. The third segment is the organization's own employees, who view advertising as a source of information about their company. Ads also provide a source of information for the fourth segment: customers, potential customers, investors, investment analysts, government officials, and others. Evans's article places the role of recruitment advertising in a very important position, not only for recruiting but for the creation and maintenance of an organization's image for virtually all interested parties. This means that ads must be carefully prepared with all relevant segments or audiences in mind, remembering that their major function is to generate applications from qualified applicants.

Recruitment ads should be carefully prepared for another reason: they must not indicate a preference for persons of a particular sex, marital status, religion, or ethnic group. Recruitment ads that do indicate a preference are discriminatory under human rights legislation. Even recruitment ads which seek to increase the number of women, minorities, and handicapped in an organization must not indicate any worker preference.

As we saw in Chapter 3, an ad *can* indicate a preference for a member of a particular sex, religion, or ethnic group if the preferred worker characteristic is a bona fide occupational qualification for the job. This situation exists when only a person of a particular sex, religion, or ethnic group can perform the job. For example, advertising for a nun could indicate a preference for a Catholic woman, since being a Catholic woman is essential for the sisterhood. Accordingly, a sex preference could be indicated for the jobs of sperm donor and wet nurse.[7] Bona fide occupational qualifications are very narrowly defined, and very few jobs have them. Recruitment ads must also not discriminate against people on the basis of age, although, as we saw in Chapter 3, "age" for the purposes of nondiscrimination varies among the provinces.

Recruitment advertising has the advantage of being able to reach any type of labour in any labour market both easily and quickly. Large organizations can use company and/or union publications to advertise job vacancies in internal recruiting efforts. Local, regional, and national markets can be reached by placing ads in appropriate publications. Ads for professional and managerial employees can be placed

[6] V.M. Evans, "Recruitment Advertising in the '80's," *The Personnel Administrator*, 1978, vol. 23, pp. 21–5, 30.

[7] R.D. Arvey, *Fairness in Selecting Employees* (Reading, Mass.: Addison-Wesley, 1979).

in professional journals, newsletters, and similar publications. The key to effective recruitment advertising is to place the right ad in the right place at the right time. This requires a knowledge of labour market conditions and what audience an ad will reach. A Florida hospital used this kind of knowledge to recruit nurses in Montreal in 1978. When the province of Quebec first required all nurses to pass French-language examinations in order to be licensed, 40 per cent failed. Capitalizing on the situation, the hospital ran recruiting ads on one of Montreal's English-language television stations and received a "torrent of applications."

Costs of advertising vary. Local newspaper and radio ads are relatively inexpensive, but ads in larger newspapers and national publications can be quite costly. Television advertising is most expensive, but one ad can reach a large number of people.

Special recruiting events. Special recruiting events, such as job fairs and open houses, are another external recruiting method. Job fairs are events in which many different employers gather at one location to interview applicants for jobs. Open houses are another kind of special event in which one employer hosts a get-together for job seekers. For example, Scotiabank has been one of the many employers of data processors using the latter method recently. Ads in a Toronto newspaper urged "DP professionals . . . to discover new career dimensions" with a management team; "there's no need to book ahead; just turn up" at one of the all-day sessions.[8]

Special recruiting events are best suited to recruiting in the local labour market. They have the advantage of being able to get in-depth information to large numbers of potential applicants in a short time.

Vocational, technical, and trade school recruiting. Vocational, technical, and trade schools are major sources of semiskilled and skilled labour in various fields including mechanics, refrigeration, electronics, and data processing. To recruit recent graduates of these schools, recruiters usually send leaflets and brochures and other information about the company to the school, encouraging interested students to apply. Recruiters may also visit the school to talk with potential applicants.

Some Canadian jurisdictions offer a considerable number of training programs for the skilled trades and low-level management at the community colleges. These highly trained graduates are often particularly valuable workers, and recruiting for them may reach the extent described in the next section for university and college students in academic and professional programs. Recruiting at vocational, technical, and trade schools usually takes place in the local labour market; but for highly skilled labour, especially in the community colleges, it may extend to the regional market.

University and college recruiting. Universities and colleges provide a major source of highly educated labour, including most professionals

[8] *The Globe and Mail*, September 21, 1982.

and managerial trainees. One way of recruiting on campuses is to have managers or other company representatives visit classrooms and lecture the students. Another way is to seek out promising students and visit the campuses to talk with them and other interested students. Large companies and the federal government hire recruiters for the sole purpose of recruiting on campuses.

The selection of schools to visit depends on several factors, the first of which is the type of job to be filled. If, for example, an organization needs water pollution control specialists, recruiters must visit schools with programs in environmental studies. Very few schools have such programs, so this will narrow the search. The size of the firm is another factor. A large organization is likely to send recruiters to many good schools throughout Canada, while a small one usually recruits mainly from schools in its region.

A third factor affecting the choice of schools is information from past recruiting efforts. An organization will probably cease its recruiting efforts at a university or college that has never provided a satisfactory recruit. (Of course, sometimes a firm recruits at a university simply because a member of upper management is an alumnus.)

University and college recruiting is a very specialized method with four steps: (1) attract students so they will submit résumés and sign up for an interview; (2) interview students; (3) invite selected students for site visits; and (4) hold site visits.

Step 1: Attracting students. A firm must attract students so that they will submit their résumés and sign up for interviews with the organization's recruiter. University and college placement offices can play a supportive role by distributing a company's recruiting materials and publicizing recruiter visits. Recruiting, however, involves more than simply visiting a campus and waiting to see who shows up for an interview. Often before the scheduled visit, recruiters scour student résumé books (available through placement offices) searching for particularly promising candidates. Students identified in this manner are contacted by letter or telephone and actively encouraged to meet with the recruiter when he or she is on campus. Says one prominent recruiter: "You can only talk to 12 or 14 people a day, so you want to get the right people on your schedule."[9] University and college recruiters also seek to establish and maintain contacts with faculty members who can alert them to qualified applicants or channel a student's interest to a particular company.

One study found that two reasons for students' signing up for an interview with a company were the company's type of work and its reputation.[10] Though little can be done to change an organization's type of work, it may be possible to redesign entry-level jobs for university and college graduates. Companies can also work to improve their reputations or images among students. One way to do this is to improve the information students have about an organization. Attractive brochures and pamphlets can be developed. Representatives can

[9] B. Wysocki, Jr., "Chasing Collegians," *Wall Street Journal*, March 27, 1979.

[10] O. Behling and H. Rodkin, "How College Students Find Jobs," *Personnel Administration*, September-October 1969, pp. 35–42.

participate in career days programs, increasing a company's exposure through informal contacts with students. Organizations can sponsor campus activities or even fund buildings or parts of buildings. Finally, "image-creating" organizations can be hired to suggest changes to improve an organization's reputation. Sometimes simply changing the organization's name is beneficial. For example, AID Insurance recently changed its name to The Allied Group.

Step 2: Interviewing students. An effective recruiting interview serves as an information exchange between recruiter and student. The student wants to learn more about the organization, and the recruiter wants to learn more about the student. The recruiter generally seeks information about the student's background and career goals. The student's appearance (neat? attentive? interested? personable?) is also important to a recruiter's decision about pursuing the student further.

Trained interviewers are very important in university and college recruiting. A poor interviewer can damage an organization's image and discourage applicants. A student who has had a bad interview experience is likely to discuss it with other students, and future recruiting efforts at the school may be affected. Even if an organization is not interested in a particular student, a good recruiter must be courteous and attempt to give a favourable image of the organization. In addition, recruiters need training on the types of questions they can and cannot ask in an interview because of human rights legislation.

Step 3: Inviting students for site visits. Using information from student résumés and recruiting interviews, a recruiter pre-screens potential applicants and decides which to invite to the organization for a site visit. This decision is sometimes made by the recruiter independently, sometimes in consultation with other managers.

Step 4: Site visits. Site visits are almost always paid for by the organization and serve partly to "sell" the candidate and partly to further assess his or her abilities and usefulness to the organization. The latter purpose is really part of the selection process. Candidates who meet an organization's selection criteria will receive job offers.

The University and College Placement Association offers a number of useful services to organizations that frequently recruit at universities and community colleges in Canada. The association's *Career Planning Annual* provides information on UCPA member employers who do recruiting. In addition, advice is provided to students who are seeking jobs. Members of the association receive the *UCPA Journal*, which covers trends in career counselling, placement, and recruitment. The association also publishes a number of useful guidelines and handbooks.

University and college recruiting is a lengthy process that requires human resource planning. Requests for interview time and space must be made well in advance of actual recruiting visits, often six to twelve months in advance for schools whose graduates are in great demand. Thus, an organization must have some estimates or forecasts of the number and kinds of positions it will need to fill a year or more later.

Recruiting costs are high because of paying for travel, food, and lodging costs, both for recruiters on campuses and candidates invited for site visits. Large firms may have the additional expense of salaries for full- or part-time recruiters. Other expenses associated with university and college recruiting are materials and advertising costs.

Recruiting at professional meetings. Professional associations, such as the Association of Professional Engineers of the Province of Ontario and the Personnel Association of Toronto, are major sources of experienced or recently graduated professionals. Recruiting highly educated professionals is similar to university recruiting, but it is usually more informal and often done by professionals themselves rather than by recruiters from human resource departments. This is especially true for Ph.D.s.

Most professional associations have national, regional, and sometimes international meetings at which recruiting or placement centres function. The placement centres at professional meetings provide a mechanism for potential applicants and representatives of an organization to contact one another. Résumés of potential applicants are available in one area of the placement centre, and job openings are listed in books in another area. Thus, an organization can use the placement centre to locate potential applicants, and would-be applicants can use it to locate potential employers. Job seekers and organization representatives can contact one another by leaving messages at the centre. Tables are provided for informal discussions, and contacts are made which sometimes result in individuals being invited for site visits to certain organizations. Besides providing a meeting place for job seekers and employers, professional associations publish job openings in professional journals and placement bulletins.

Professional association meetings provide recruiters with a large pool of qualified applicants, by virtue of membership in the group. That is, because they belong to the professional association, applicants are to some degree pre-selected according to professional qualifications. Professional meetings are an inexpensive way of making contact with potential applicants if organization representatives already plan to attend the meeting for other reasons. However, completing the recruiting process requires site visits to the organization, and this can be costly.

Public employment agencies. An organization can choose to delegate the responsibility for searching for applicants to an employment agency. The most extensive public system in Canada is that of the Canada Employment and Immigration Commission, which operates 460 regular Canada Employment Centres (CECs), along with itinerant services to 187 remote or isolated communities. It also provides services through more than 100 CECs on university and community college campuses.[11] The province of Quebec has its own provincially run employment centres, as well as CECs.

CECs provide employers with a selection and job referral service. Job seekers are instructed in the development of personal job-search plans and are provided with leads to employment opportunities that have not been listed by employers. Employment counsellors may also

[11] Employment and Immigration Canada, *Annual Report 1985–1986* (Hull, Que.: Ministry of Supply and Services Canada, 1986), p. 8.

attempt to interest prospective employers in job-seeking clients. In addition, CECs process unemployment insurance applications and administer employment programs subsidized by the federal government.

Canada (and Quebec) Employment Centres are virtually no-cost and can be of great service to an organization in both the recruiting and selection functions. Increasing use of automated equipment in selected CECs is increasing their efficiency. Most CECs have Job Information Centres where workers can make occupational and job choices from available lists, get assistance from a referring officer, and get information about job vacancies and employment conditions. In addition, there is a computerized, country-wide, national job bank. Local CECs can list job vacancies on behalf of employer clients and can also look for vacancies in the job bank on behalf of workers' clients. At any one time in 1986, the bank contained approximately 3,500 job vacancies. The job bank system helped to place 4,000 workers in 1986.[12]

Some people unjustly assume that only applicants of low quality are available through the government agencies. Actually, many employers today recruit exclusively through CECs for certain types of labour. Because of the full range of services they offer at no cost, CECs (or Quebec centres) can be a most economical recruiting method for organizations, especially those too small to employ a personnel staff or recruiting specialist. In times of high unemployment, the Centres are especially useful to help employers screen very large numbers of job applicants.

Private employment agencies. Private employment agencies often flourish in labour markets where CECs are ineffective and in other markets as well. In total, commercial agency placements amounted to 4.5 per cent of Canada Manpower (Employment) Centre placements in 1973. Private employment agencies usually handle all types of labour except for lower-skilled labour such as factory workers. In 1973, 83.3 per cent of private agencies' placements involved clerical workers.[13]

The primary difference between public and private employment agencies is that most private agencies are profit-oriented businesses that require a fee for services rendered. In most cases, these fees are paid by employers. Most provinces have legislation regulating these fees. Alberta, British Columbia, Manitoba, and Nova Scotia prohibit their being charged to job seekers, and Ontario does the same for most classes of agencies.

Some private employment agencies are nonprofit organizations. An example is the Technical Service Council, an industry-sponsored employment service specializing in professional and technical personnel.

Many agencies serve the local market, but some are nationwide, offering computerized job and applicant information. Since many firms specialize in one or two types of labour (for example, temporary clerical, computer operators, supervisory personnel), it may be necessary for an employer to use several different private employment agencies.

[12] Ibid.

[13] Lawrence Fric, *Commercial Employment Agencies: Their Role in the Canadian Labour Market* (Ottawa: Department of Manpower and Immigration, 1975).

Private employment agencies are a good source of professional, technical, and managerial employees and of all kinds of experienced employees. Fees charged by private employment agencies vary, but if an organization does not have the time or human resources to conduct an extensive search, even an expensive private employment agency can be cost beneficial.

Executive search firms. Executive search firms, frequently called "headhunters," are a type of private employment agency specializing in experienced managerial and executive-level labour. Many specialize in recruiting certain types of executive talent.

In the late 1970s, with experienced managers and executives in short supply, there was a growth in executive search firms. The recession of the early 1980s reduced the demand and forced many search firms to resort to layoffs and other cost-cutting techniques. Other firms began to specialize in finding jobs for executives who had been terminated. This service is called *outplacement*.

Executive search firms operate in various ways. Some simply maintain files of résumés sent in by executives who are seeking other employment. When contacted by a client organization, such a firm searches its store of résumés to provide names of potential applicants. Other search firms recruit more aggressively, discreetly contacting executives and encouraging them to consider changing their organizational affiliations.

All fees for executive search efforts are paid by the client organization, and they are high, usually amounting to 25 to 30 per cent of an executive's first year's pay.[14] Some executive search firms, especially those in accounting, charge on a time-plus-expenses basis. Some firms charge a fee whether or not a candidate is hired through their efforts. Others charge on a contingency basis; if the client organization hires a candidate found by the search firm, the client must pay the fee.

Selecting an executive search firm can be difficult. Choosing the wrong firm for an organization's needs can be costly in terms of money and time spent. The better executive search firms belong to the Canadian Association of Management Consultants. As in any industry, there are some very good firms and some rather poor ones. An employer should require a search firm to provide references and a list of client organizations.

Summary of Methods and Sources

The recruiting methods and sources described above represent a wide variety of choices for HRM professionals. As we have seen, different methods have different advantages and, depending on recruiting goals, some methods are preferable to others. Key considerations in choosing a method are the type of labour and type of market a method usually reaches. Depending upon the recruiting method or source chosen,

[14] J.A. Thompson, "The MBA Guide to Executive Recruiters: Who They Are, How They Work," *MBA*, May 1976, vol. 10, pp. 25–7, 30–1, 40. See also Fric, pp. 64–5.

EXHIBIT 6.6

Summary of recruiting methods and sources

Method	*Type of labour*	*Labour market*	*Recruiter activity*	*Advantage*	*Disadvantage*
Posting and bidding	Any level above entry level but below professional and managerial level	Internal	Post notice of vacancy and accept bid	Employee development	Cannot reach external market
Skill inventories	Any level above entry level	Internal	Search files	Employee development	None
Employee referral	Any type	External, mostly local	Inform employees of vacancies and request referrals	Access to women and linguistic and ethnic minorities	Can perpetuate existing characteristics of the work force
Walk-ins	Lesser-skilled labour	Local	Take applications	Free	Greatest supply when demand is lowest
Union hiring halls	Members of certain unions	Local	Send requisition to union hiring hall	Compliance with collective agreement	Limits choice of employer
Recruitment advertising	Any type	Any market	Prepare and run ad	Can easily and quickly reach all markets	Can be costly
Special events	Any, except professional and managerial level	Local	Plan, advertise, and hold function	Can get in-depth information to large groups in a short time	None

Exhibit 6.6 continued

Method	*Type of labour*	*Labour market*	*Recruiter activity*	*Advantage*	*Disadvantage*
Vocational, technical, and trade school recruiting	Semi-skilled and skilled labour	Local, perhaps regional	Send information and visit schools; sometimes interview students	Large pool of types of labour which are often much needed	Sometimes time-consuming for higher-level recruits
University and college recruiting	Professional and managerial trainees	Regional and national	Seek out promising candidates; interview students	Large pool of qualified applicants	Costly, time-consuming
Professional meetings	Professionals	Regional, national, international	Informal discussions with job seekers	Large pool of pre-selected applicants	Can be costly
Canada Employment Centres	Lesser-skilled labour	Local, access to regional, national and international	Contact agency to refer applicants	Free; on-line computer system	Limited access to skilled and professional labour
Private employment agencies	Any, except lesser-skilled labour	Local, with regional and national networks	Contact agency to refer applicants	Delegation of search responsibility	Costly for higher-level recruits
Executive-search firms	Experienced executives	National	Contact agency to refer applicants	Access to executives	Expensive

recruiters are engaged in different activities ranging from simply taking applications from walk-ins, to soliciting applicants by visiting community agencies and appropriate schools. Exhibit 6.6 summarizes and compares recruiting methods and sources discussed in this section.

Evaluating the Recruiting Effort

Developing a recruiting plan and preparing a budget require some knowledge of the costs and relative effectiveness of the various recruiting methods. One of the best sources of this knowledge is data collected by an organization from past recruiting efforts. HRM professionals have a responsibility to collect information on the recruiting methods they use so methods can be evaluated and compared in terms of their cost effectiveness. This data should be maintained and used in making future recruiting decisions.

A measure of a method's cost effectiveness takes into account how much a method costs *and* how effective it is in meeting recruiting goals. Considering the effectiveness of methods is important because there is no cost advantage in using an inexpensive method if it fails to produce the desired results. Ideally, one should identify the least expensive method that can be effective.

Data from previous recruiting efforts, though useful, cannot present a completely accurate picture of present recruiting costs and effectiveness. Costs change with time, and methods that prove effective at one time may not prove effective at others because of changed market conditions. A method that was successful when market conditions were loose should not be presumed to be effective when they are tight.

Many indices can be used to evaluate effectiveness of a recruiting method. Some of these are given in Exhibit 6.7. Methods can be evaluated and compared according to the number of applicants attracted, the number of applicants attracted in a certain time period, and/or the cost of recruiting per applicant attracted. For example, if a newspaper ad costs $50 and attracts 25 applicants, the cost per applicant is $2. This can be compared with the cost per applicant for another method, perhaps an open house that costs $200 and attracts 50 applicants at a cost of $4 apiece. Another way to evaluate a method is to calculate the ratio of qualified to unqualified applicants attracted. If two methods draw the same number of applicants, but one method draws mostly unqualified applicants, the method that attracts the larger proportion of qualified applicants is the more effective method. Other indices include time from start to hiring of an applicant, total recruiting cost per applicant hired, and job performance and tenure of applicants attracted by a method.

Certain methods, such as university and college recruiting and professional meetings, can be evaluated according to the number of applicants interviewed, the proportion of those interviewed who get invitations for site visits, and the proportion of those who accept invitations when offered. For example, a firm could stop recruiting efforts at a university if very few persons signed up for interviews, if few

EXHIBIT 6.7

Indices for evaluating recruiting efforts

1. Number of applicants attracted per method
2. Number of applicants attracted by length of time
3. Costs per applicant attracted
4. Ratio of qualified to unqualified applicants attracted
5. Time from start to hiring of applicant
6. Total recruiting cost per employee hired
7. Job performance and tenure of employee(s) attracted by method
8. Number of candidates interviewed
9. Proportion of those interviewed who receive invitations to visit
10. Proportion of those invited who accept offers to visit

invitations for site visits were extended to those who did sign up, or if very few persons accepted invitations for site visits.

Janz has developed an approach to evaluating the cost effectiveness of recruiting methods using a utility equation containing selection-related factors, recruiting factors (such as the cost of generating an applicant pool), and job performance information (including tenure and value of the job to the organization). This method also demonstrates the important relationship between the recruiting and selection functions.[15]

Because of the wide availability of indices for evaluative purposes, an initial step in evaluating a recruiting effort is determining the criteria to be used. The choice of criteria depends to a large extent on whether an organization places more emphasis on cost reduction or on minimizing recruiting time.

While research examining the effectiveness of various methods is important for effective recruiting, Schwab has identified several issues regarding interpretation of such research.[16] A major question is why some methods are more effective than others. One possibility is that some methods, such as employee referral, provide better and more realistic information about jobs. An alternative possibility is that there are qualitative differences in applicant pools tapped by the different methods. If differences in effectiveness are due to differences in information conveyed, attempts could be made to put more complete and accurate information into the least costly methods. If, on the other hand, differences in methods are due to qualitative differences in applicant populations, the most qualified population should be identified and used as the major recruiting source. Schwab also suggests that research into method effectiveness should take into account the interaction between recruiting methods and the labour market. It may be that the quality of applicants reached by different methods changes as the state of the labour market varies.

[15] J.T. Janz, "Exploring the Implications of the Utility Equation for Selection, Recruitment, and Turnover Reduction Programs," *Proceedings of the 1982 Administrative Sciences Association of Canada*, University of Ottawa, 1982, pp. 18–28.

[16] Donald P. Schwab, pp. 113–14.

Summary

This chapter has discussed the role of recruiting in an organization and its relationship to other human resource functions. Recruiting attracts qualified applicants to an organization to supply the human resources necessary to achieve the organizational objectives of survival and growth. Recruiting is an important function because, in addition to attracting future members of an organization, it also helps create and maintain an organization's public image.

Responsibilities for recruiting include developing a recruiting plan and preparing a recruiting budget; preparing recruiting messages and implementing the plan; and evaluating the recruiting effort. As we saw in the DRILLCO example at the outset of the chapter, achieving recruiting goals may be somewhat of a challenge. HRM professionals have a wide variety of methods to choose from and sources to tap, and as many as six diverse factors may influence the process.

Project Ideas

1. Discuss a recruitment experience you have had. Describe what methods were used to recruit you and whether or not they were successful. For example, what recruiting methods attracted your interest to certain jobs? Describe the application procedures you encountered and the results. If you have ever used the services of a Canada Employment Centre or a private employment agency, discuss what was involved. What kinds of information did you have to supply? Were you interviewed? What kinds of questions did you have to answer? Were you successfully placed in a job? If you have ever used the services of a university or college placement office, describe your experiences with it.

2. Visit a Canada Employment Centre. Call in advance for an interview with the director of placement. Prepare a list of questions to ask and summarize your findings in a short report. Examples of questions: (1) How many employers use the centre to recruit applicants each year (or month)? (2) Does the number of employers using the CEC vary over time? If so, why? (3) How does the agency place applicants? (4) Does the agency place all levels of labour skill and experience or only certain types? (5) Is a computer used to help match applicants to jobs? and (6) What percentage of job applicants who register with the office are placed through the office?

3. Examine several newspapers with local, regional, or national circulations. Prepare a short report on the different kinds of recruitment ads. How do the ads differ? How are the job ads organized? Try to classify a number of ads according to various criteria, such as: (1) company-placed ads versus those placed by employment agen-

cies; (2) good descriptions of job activities versus vague descriptions; (3) very clear statements of education and experience required versus no or ambiguous statements; and (4) attractiveness and appeal. Include examples in your report.

4. Interview an employer regarding his or her company's recruiting program. Who is responsible for recruiting? What do the recruiters do? Are they trained? If so, how? What recruiting methods and sources are used? Is the effectiveness of recruiting methods evaluated? On what criteria? How are recruiting budgets determined? How far in advance of actual need is recruiting done? Answers to these and similar questions should form the basis of a short report. If several students conduct interviews with a number of employers, the recruiting efforts can be compared.

5. Have the class role-play recruiting interviews. Divide the students into three sections: job applicants, interviewers, and observers. The group of job applicants should be students nearing graduation. They should prepare résumés. (The UCPA's *Career Planning Annual* can be used as a source of information about preparing a résumé.) The second group—the interviewers—should meet, perhaps with the instructor, to generate a list of questions to ask applicants. Depending on the availability of time, applicants can be interviewed by one or more interviewers. Interviewers should always have a copy of the applicant's résumé at least 10 to 15 minutes before the interview in order to have some background information on the person being interviewed. The group of observers should observe and take notes on how the interviewer and the applicant respond to one another's questions. After the role-playing, the observers should comment about how the interview was handled and how the applicant presented himself or herself. Role-playing may take place simultaneously by arranging chairs in groups of three in the classroom (each group would have an interviewer, an applicant, and an observer). Since recruiting interviews should be a vehicle for the exchange of information, it would be advantageous for interviewers to pretend to represent a specific company or organization. This would enable applicants to ask questions about the company and encourage two-way communication.

Cases

Case 6.1: Building the Team at Chrysler

One of Lee Iacocca's first tasks as Chief Executive Officer of Chrysler Corporation was building a management team. He especially needed first-rate financial people and he knew where to find them. Shortly before leaving the presidency of Ford Motor Company, he had asked J. Edward Lundy, Ford's top finance man, to compile a list of the company's best financial talent. Lundy not only compiled the list, he ranked people A, B, or C. Iacocca brought the list with him (with Ford's permission) when he came to Chrysler. Now it would prove invaluable.

Iacocca looked over the "A" list; it contained the names of about 20 "first-rate bean counters." But Iacocca wanted more than just a bean counter. He wanted someone with real business savvy, someone like Gerald Greenwald, whose name appeared on list "B".

Iacocca had met the 44-year old Greenwald several times and liked him. Currently an aggressive manager with the highly successful Ford subsidiary in Venezuela, Greenwald was always anxious to move out of finance and up in the company. This would be a good move for him if he were willing to leave Ford.

A meeting between the two men was arranged and Greenwald agreed to come to Chrysler to set up its financial controls. But Greenwald never let Iacocca forget that he wanted to be more than just a controller, so Iacocca made him this offer: "If you can find somebody else as good as you are, I'll free you to do other things."* "Somebody else" turned out to be Steve Miller, who Greenwald promptly recruited from Ford of Venezuela.

Besides new financial talent, Iacocca found he had to replace almost all of the company's officers. Fortunately, the same careful scrutiny of the work force that revealed incompetencies also revealed dynamic young talent, overlooked by previous management. Regarding discovery of these hidden resources, Iacocca comments, "To this day, I can't believe that the former management didn't notice them. I'm talking about people with fire in their eyes: you can practically tell they're good just by looking at them."** Many of the "hidden talents" were given new job responsibilities. Steve Sharf, for example, is now head of all manufacturing at Chrysler.

Iacocca still needed several additions to his management team, so he turned to a pool of people whose experience and proven ability he felt were going to waste: retired Ford executives. From this pool he hired Gar Laux, who had been one of his general managers at Ford, as head of sales and marketing. Laux's personality would be a definite plus in helping to build better relations with Chrysler dealers. Iacocca also hired Hans Matthias, who used to be his chief engineer at Ford, as a consultant on quality.

Also important to quality was Dick Dauch, who worked at General Motors and Volkswagen before moving to Chrysler. Dauch was responsible for the addition to Chrysler's team of 15 top people from his two former employers.

* L. Iacocca with W. Novak, *Iacocca: An Autobiography* (Toronto: Bantam Books, 1984), p. 170.

** Ibid., p. 171.

Iacocca summarizes his successful recruiting strategy as follows: "I took all the guys from Ford that I knew in marketing, finance, and purchasing, but when it came to quality car building I went for the best GM and Volkswagen people. So I had the old and the new, the line and the staff, and the retirees—and they all got along. It was that unique melting pot that turned our quality around so quickly."***

Questions:

1. Describe the different recruiting sources and methods used at Chrysler.
2. What were the reasons for using these sources and methods?
3. Do you see any potential problems or disadvantages to Chrysler's use of these methods and sources?

***Ibid., p. 176.

Case 6.2: Expansion at Quinan Stores

Business has been good at Quinan Stores in St. Johns, Newfoundland, and management has decided to expand its downtown store to include a bakery and deli, a cosmetics department, and a sporting goods department. No Quinan store has ever had a bakery and deli, but several suburban outlets have very small cosmetics and sporting goods departments. Quinan stores have a reputation for high quality merchandise and personal attention to customers. Employees in the new departments will be expected to meet Quinan's high standards of performance.

Management has estimated that the expansion, scheduled to open in nine months, will require 21 new employees. The bakery and deli will require two bakers, two butchers, two sales clerks, and one manager. The cosmetics department will need seven sales clerks and one manager; the sporting goods department, five sales clerks and one manager. Estimates were based on expected levels of customer demand for the new products and services and level of service the store wants to maintain (clerk-to-customer ratio).

While Quinan tries to promote from within whenever possible for supervisory and managerial-level positions, the uniqueness of the new departments makes it unlikely that qualified applicants can be found internally for these positions.

Michael Robbins has worked as a human resource specialist for Quinan Stores for the past two years. His responsibilities have included recruiting, but never on such a grand scale. Robbins has his work cut out for him now; his boss, Vice President of Human Resources Hilda Tjoveld, has asked him to prepare a recruiting plan and budget for staffing the expansion.

Robbins begins by gathering data on Quinan's previous recruiting efforts. Data are available on methods used to recruit sales clerks, supervisors and managers, but not bakers and butchers. Data pertain to average cost per applicant, average cost per hire, average time to hire, and average employee tenure. Cost per hire include costs associated with processing applications, interviewing applicants, and selecting candidates for hire. Data are provided in Tables 1 and 2.

Table 1 Recruiting Data for Sales Clerks, 1985-1986

Recruiting method	*Average cost per applicant*	*Average cost per hire*	*Average time to hire*	*Average tenure (mos.)*
Morning Star newspaper ad	$20	$840	3 weeks	20
Evening News newspaper ad	$15	$900	3 weeks	22
Canada Employment Centre	0	$500*	4 weeks	14

Table 2 Recruiting Data for Supervisors and Department Managers, 1985-1986

Recruiting method	*Average cost per applicant*	*Average cost per hire*	*Average time to hire*	*Average tenure (mos.)*
Canada Employment Centre	0	$900*	8 weeks	18
Acme Employment Agency (private)	0	1,500 (10% of annual salary for position filled)	5 weeks	23
Kilgore Manpower (private)	0	$1,500 (10% of annual salary for position filled)	3 weeks	19

* While CEC will pre-screen applicants, Quinan expects to interview four to six candidates for each position.

Questions:

1. Assume you are Robbins and prepare a recruiting plan and budget for the needed personnel at Quinan's. What method or methods will you use for recruiting each type of labour? What are your cost and time estimates? In developing your plan, feel free to suggest methods other than those used in the past, but be sure to justify your plan in terms of effectiveness criteria or other concerns.
2. After you have prepared your plan, assume a scenario in which labour market conditions are tighter than in the years for which recruiting data are available. How might tighter market conditions alter your recruiting plan?

7

Selection

Kristine Lavelle, human resource officer for Expo Airlines, a young, regional airline, is considering the merits of adding a cognitive ability test to the procedures currently used to select customer service representatives. These employees typically handle reservations, ticketing, and boarding of passengers. Current procedures include the use of application forms and interviews to screen job applicants. The cognitive ability test Lavelle is considering is similar to an intelligence test; it measures verbal and quantitative abilities. The company selling the test claims that it has a validity of .30 for a variety of jobs and that it has been successfully used to screen applicants in many companies. Lavelle is not sure how to interpret a validity of .30, but she does know that the test will cost about $20 per applicant.

Until now, Expo Air has had a policy of hiring the first job applicants to meet a set of minimum job requirements. Nearly 100 customer service representatives have been selected in this fashion, and 60 per cent have successfully completed training at a cost of $2,500 per trainee. (The remaining 40 per cent either dropped out of training voluntarily or failed to pass and were dismissed.) Ralph Abrams, the airline's training director, has suggested it would save the company money if trainees were better qualified. He cites performance gains and reduced turnover as benefits of selecting better qualified applicants.

Lavelle wishes she knew how much improvement in training and job performance would result from adding the cognitive ability test to current selection methods. She also wonders if this test would be useful for selecting any other types of employees, such as flight attendants, supervisors, or office personnel.

Lavelle's questions and concerns are typical of many managers and HRM professionals who strive for improvements in work force quality and overall organizational effectiveness. In this chapter, we discuss both selection theory and instruments and address some of Lavelle's questions and concerns.

Selection: Definition and Process

Selection is the process of differentiating among applicants in order to identify (and hire) those with a greater likelihood of success in a job. Although some selection devices are also useful within an organization for promotion or transfer, this chapter focusses on selecting applicants from outside the organization.

The most accurate differentiations would result if an employer could try each applicant in a job for a given length of time and observe the results. Since time and costs make this approach unfeasible, organizations do the next best thing: they collect information about an applicant which can be used to predict the likelihood of his or her success in a particular job. This information is collected by a sequential selection process that serves to narrow the pool of applicants by eliminating less desirable ones at each stage along the way.

The selection process employs a variety of instruments and screening devices in order to narrow the selection pool. Each applicant must successfully negotiate a number of hurdles in order to stay in the running for a particular job vacancy. Or, an applicant may self-select out at any stage in the process. Typical hurdles include the preliminary interview, the application form, the employment interview, tests, reference and background checks, a physical examination, a final interview with the boss, and a hiring decision. The selection process is portrayed in Exhibit 7.1.

The selection process proceeds sequentially from collecting relatively general information about an applicant to collecting more specific in-depth information. For example, application blanks solicit a broad range of information; the employment interview offers an opportunity to probe more deeply. Employment tests provide even more detailed information about an applicant's skills, knowledge, and abilities. Generally, later steps in the selection process tend to be more expensive than the earlier ones.

As we have seen, the selection process actually begins with recruiting. Because recruiting messages seek a qualified response, applicants are to some extent pre-selected by the time they become a part of the selection pool.

Screening by the organization often begins with a preliminary interview—a brief exchange of information between a receptionist or secretary and the job applicant. The receptionist usually answers basic

EXHIBIT 7.1

The selection process

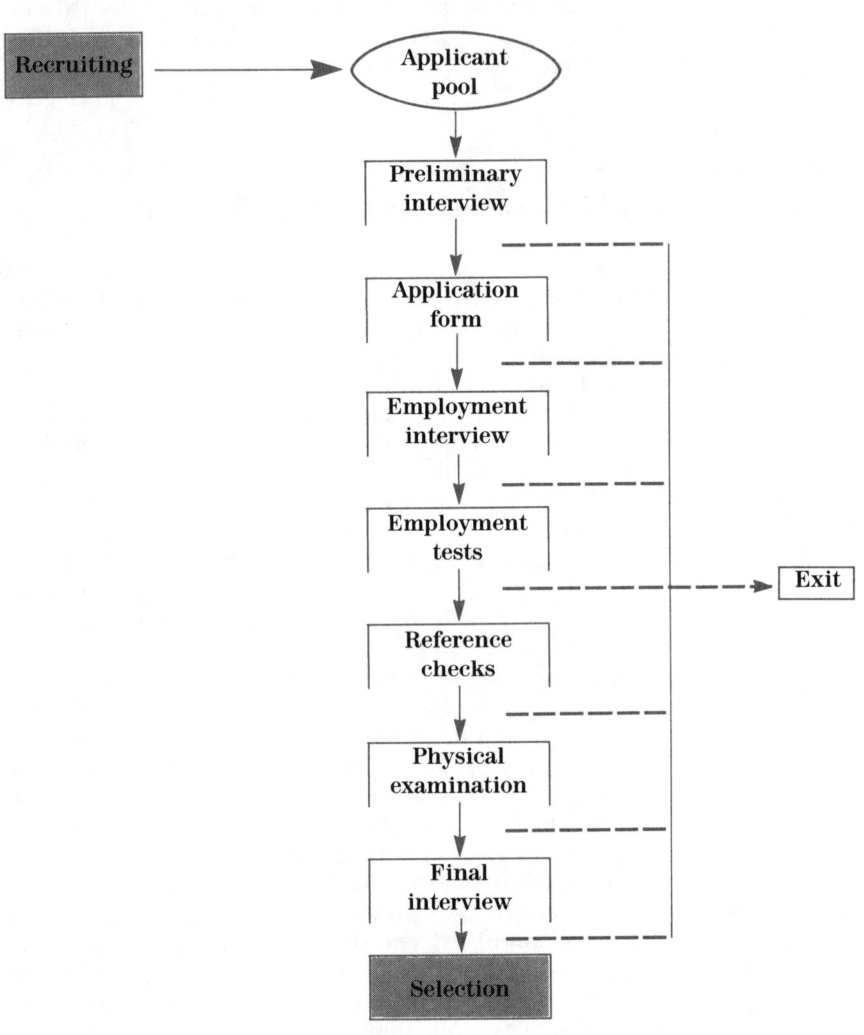

questions about job details, such as work hours, pay, and so on. The applicant is usually given an application form to complete.

Completing an application form is the second step in the selection process. Typical application forms request information on the applicant's home address, last employer, prior work experience, names and addresses of references, and so on. When this step has been completed, an HRM professional examines the application form. Less qualified applicants are eliminated at this point, while the more qualified continue to the next hurdle: the employment interview.

The employment interview is a face-to-face meeting between an applicant and an interviewer, usually an HRM professional from the organization. It provides an opportunity to pursue information from the application form and to obtain any other information relevant to the applicant's ability to do the job. Assessments of the applicant's appearance, ability to use the language of work, and interpersonal skills may be made during the interview. Applicants who are not eliminated at this stage may be required to take certain tests, depending on the nature of the job.

HRM professionals use a variety of tests for selection purposes. Ability tests measure an applicant's "current competence to perform an observable behavior or a behavior resulting in an observable product."[1] Aptitude tests measure potential or undeveloped abilities. Personality tests and interest inventories seek to determine whether an applicant's personality and/or interests are compatible with job requirements. Language tests may be appropriate for bilingual positions.

If an applicant is still in the running after testing, reference and background checks may be made. Such checks ensure that an applicant has not been misrepresented and that the information he or she has provided is true.

Following this, an applicant may be asked to submit to a physical examination. Applicants who survive the screening process to this point are referred to management for final interviews.

In the final interview, an applicant meets with the person who will be his or her boss. The supervisor usually interviews several applicants. In this interview, both applicant and interviewer explore compatibility and mutual interests. At this stage of the selection process, only the best qualified applicants remain, and the "chemistry" between superior and subordinate may well determine whether an applicant receives a job offer.

In actuality, many organizations do not use all the possible steps of the selection process. Most use an application form and an employment interview, but tests and physical examinations are usually used only for certain types of jobs. Testing is generally not required for relatively simple jobs that are easily learned, such as manufacturing jobs, or for higher-level professional jobs, such as lawyer, professor, and engineer. Physical exams tend to be required for relatively strenuous jobs, such as police officer and firefighter, and for jobs involving public safety, such as bus driver and pilot. Reference checks are more likely to be used for jobs requiring a reasonable amount of responsibility for money, equipment, or the public safety. Organizations that use the entire process tend to be large companies and federal, provincial, and municipal governments. Specific instruments used in the selection process are discussed later in the chapter.

[1] U.S. Equal Employment Opportunity Commission, *Uniform Guidelines on Employment Selection Procedures*, F. R. 42, no. 251, Dec. 30, 1977, 65542-52.

Relation to Other HRM Functions

Selection is related most closely to the HRM functions of recruiting, human resource planning, job analysis, performance appraisal, orientation, and training and development. These relationships are described below and in Exhibit 7.2.

EXHIBIT 7.2

Selection: relation to other HRM functions

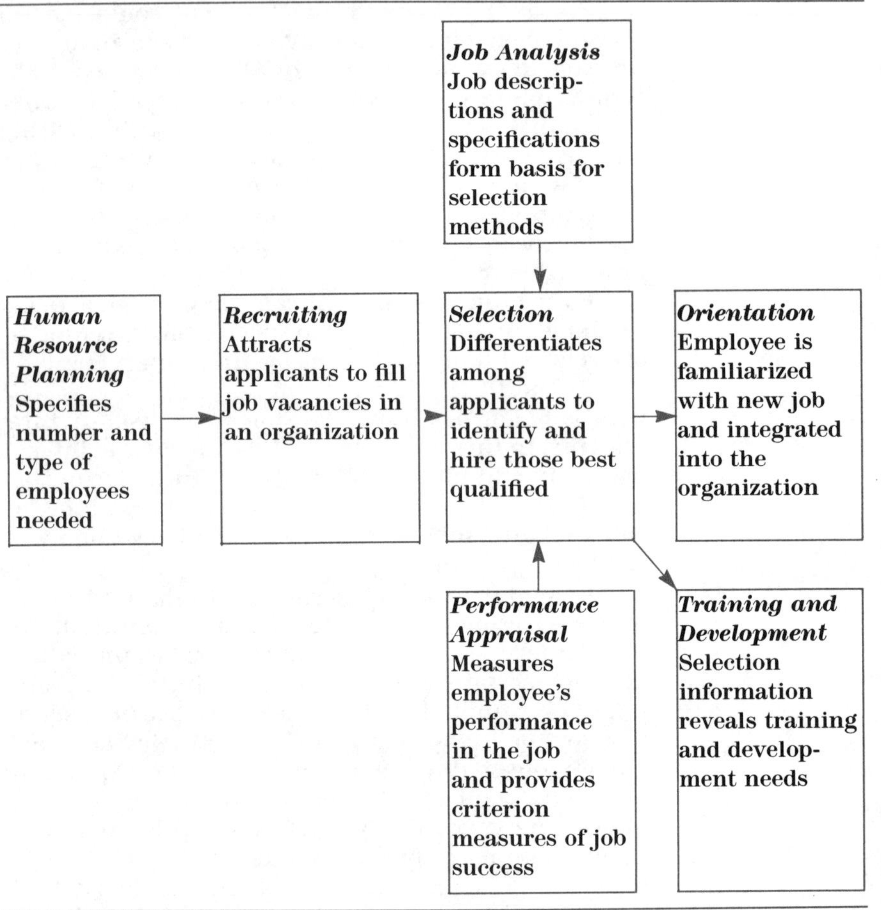

Recruiting

Recruiting can be viewed as a preliminary part of the selection process, and its effectiveness has implications for the selection function. If recruiting does not attract more applicants than an organization needs to hire, the selection function has a limited usefulness. As more applicants are recruited and participate in the selection process, the probability of hiring a successful applicant increases.

Human Resource Planning

Recruiting and selection together represent a major human resource planning strategy for acquiring the qualified labour necessary to achieve organizational goals and objectives. The HRP function specifies the number and type of employees needed. Recruiting and selection are hampered if time constraints reduce the chances of attracting a sufficiently large selection pool. Since recruitment and selection can take several days to several months to complete, advance forecasting of specific employment needs is essential. If the planned numbers and types of employees are not available, adjustments may have to be made in the mix of occupations or in the amount and types of production.

Job Analysis

Job analysis is basic to the selection function. Job descriptions and specifications dictate the kinds of predictors of success appropriate for each job. For example, predictors for a clerk/typist job might include the results of a job-sample typing and/or filing test or a clerical ability test.

Performance Appraisal

Performance appraisal data provide the selection function with criterion measures of success on the job. Such measures can be used to establish the validity of predictors.

Orientation

For newly hired employees, orientation follows selection. Orientation familiarizes the new employee with the job and with the company's expectations. Orientation also helps integrate the employee into the organization.

Training and Development

Selection also has inputs to the training and development function. Specifically, information collected through use of selection instruments reveals training needs of both newly hired and current employees.

The Role of Selection in Organizational Effectiveness

Recruiting attracts to an organization a pool of applicants who have the basic qualifications to fill job vacancies. If all applicants performed all jobs equally well, an organization could fill its vacancies on a first come-first served basis. The fact that individual differences do exist means that employers can benefit by selecting applicants with higher levels of job-related abilities, skills, and knowledge, and those whose interests and needs are better suited to the job.

Selection is part of a staffing strategy to build and maintain a productive and profitable organization. Rather than increase productivity of the organization's existing labour force, selection, for the most part, regulates quantity and quality of incoming human resources. Selection contributes to organizational effectiveness by helping to ensure high base rates of success for jobs.

The *base rate of success* for a job is the percentage of individuals who reach an acceptable level of performance in the job within a reasonable length of time. The base rate of success for Expo Air's training program for customer service representatives was 60 per cent, or .6. While definitions of "success" vary, generally, a successful employee is one who consistently performs the duties and tasks required by the job at or above a minimally acceptable level. An employee is judged unsuccessful if he or she repeatedly fails to perform important elements of the job at a minimally acceptable level. The organization retains successful employees, if possible. Less successful workers are candidates for training, transfer, demotion, or termination.

HRM professionals continually strive to improve base rates of success for jobs. One way they do this is by devising, testing, and using new and better predictors of actual work behaviour and on-the-job success. Another way is to apply existing selection procedures more vigorously, for example, by raising hiring standards to employ more highly qualified workers. Successful efforts to "beat the base rate" (to improve the percentage of successful employees in jobs) contribute to organizational effectiveness in two ways. First, they result in a higher quality work force. Second, they reduce the costs associated with errors in selection.

Improving Quality of the Work Force

Improvements in base rates of success for jobs reflect improvements in quality of the work force, since a greater proportion of employees are performing successfully. Recall from Chapter 2 that a substantial range of individual differences in abilities exists between people. A selection policy such as Expo Air's, which hires people meeting only minimum qualifications, typically results in hiring employees from the lower part of the distribution of abilities. Research shows that use of minimum qualifications hiring procedures can result in productivity declines that are almost as great as those from abandoning selection procedures.[2] One reason for this is that, in most cases, there is a linear relationship between ability test scores and job performance.[3] Therefore, no true dichotomy exists between qualified and unqualified applicants. Thus, optimal use of selection procedures requires rank ordering candidates from highest to lowest and hiring from the top down.

There are great financial advantages to hiring employees with higher levels of ability since they can increase levels of performance and productivity in an organization. As suggested in the Expo Air case, they can also help reduce training costs and the cost of turnover due to unacceptable performance.

High-ability employees are most beneficial to an organization when placed in jobs in which they can make maximum use of their special skills. Talents are wasted if employees are placed in positions that do not require their use. Deciding which job an employee should be assigned to in an organization is referred to as *placement*. Placement is a part of the selection function but does not always occur because organizations usually consider applicants only for the specific job they are applying for. Thus, applicants are to a great extent pre-placed by virtue of making application for a specific job. However, both employer and applicant benefit if an applicant is considered for a number of jobs in the organization and, if hired, placed in a job best suited to his or her abilities and the organization's needs. For example, an employee with a high degree of manual dexterity could be more useful to an organization in an assembly-line job in which workers perform at their own pace, rather than on an assembly line with a controlled speed.

Of course, even high-ability employees may not produce more than co-workers of lesser ability unless they are motivated to do so. For this reason, many employers offer monetary incentives for superior performance by paying employees on the basis of the quantity and/or quality of their output. Even if employers must pay more for high output, high-performing employees are a better investment for an organization. Because their productivity levels are higher than those of low or average performers, fewer high-performing employees are needed to complete the work. Through the selection process, high-performing employees can be identified and hired, thus saving an employer money.

Reducing the Costs of Errors in Selection

Exhibit 7.3 shows the four possible outcomes of a selection decision. Two of these—the true positive ("high hit") and the true negative ("low hit")—are correct decisions. The other two outcomes represent errors. In the "false positive error," the selector predicts success for the applicant in the job and makes the decision to hire, but failure results.

[2] M.J. Mack, F.L. Schmidt, and J.E. Hunter, *Estimating the Productivity Costs in Dollars of Minimum Selection Test Cutoff Scores* (Washington, D.C.: U.S. Office of Personnel Management, 1981).

[3] American Psychological Association, Division of Industrial and Organizational Psychology. *Principles for the Validation and Use of Personnel Selection Procedures*, 2nd ed., (Berkeley, Calif., 1980).

In the "false negative error," an applicant who would have succeeded is rejected because the selection process predicts failure. Each of these selection errors is costly to an organization. But the costs of hiring an employee who fails to perform at a minimally acceptable level are usually greater than the costs of failing to hire an individual who would have succeeded. One should recognize that while the decision to hire or not hire an applicant is a dichotomous choice, the line between failure and success is not actually dichotomous. That is, some false positives may be less costly to an employer than others, and there will be a range of performance among high hits.

The false positive error. A false positive error incurs three types of costs for the organization. The first are those incurred while the person is employed—the results of production or profit losses, damaged public relations or company reputation, accidents due to ineptitude or negligence, absenteeism, and so on. More costs are associated with training, transferring, or terminating the employee; they can include severance pay and the costs of any grievance proceedings resulting from a decision to terminate. The costs of replacing the unsuccessful employee include costs of recruiting, selecting, and training a replacement. Generally, the more important the job, the greater the costs of a selection error. For example, the failure of a human relations director is potentially more detrimental (and therefore more costly) to an organization than is the failure of a janitor. Furthermore, replacement costs for the human relations director would be greater.

EXHIBIT 7.3

Outcomes of the selection decision

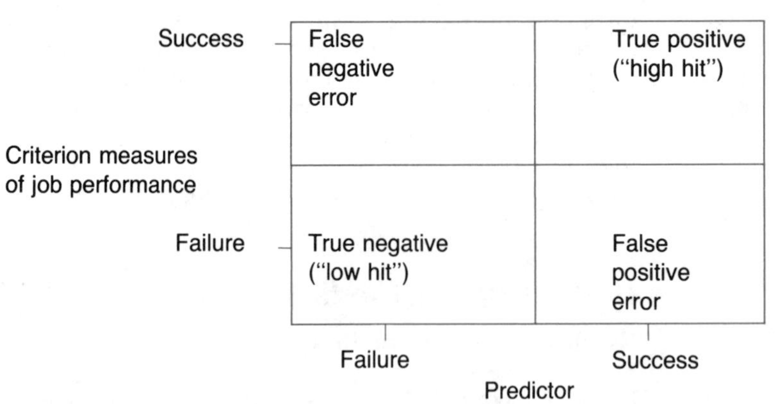

The false negative error. In a false negative error, an applicant who would have succeeded is rejected because failure was predicted. Most false negative selection errors go unnoticed, unless the applicant happens to complain to the human rights commission or be hired after all for some other reason. Costs associated with this type of error are difficult to estimate. One situation in which the impact of both false positive and false negative selection errors can be detected and measured, however, is professional sports, such as football and hockey. Coaches and scouts analyze game films, statistics, scouting reports, and other data and decide whether they wish to draft a particular player. If they do draft him and his performance fails to meet expectations, a false positive selection error has occurred. Suppose, however, a team decides against drafting a player and another team chooses him. If he subsequently turns out to be a star, the first team's rejection may represent a false negative selection error.

Although most organizations are unable to spot such errors, much less assess their costs, they do exist but can be minimized by using valid selection methods and procedures.

The selection function is an important one—and a difficult one—for HRM professionals. In addition to making selection decisions about people based on certain predictors of actual work behaviour, HRM professionals must determine those predictors, define "job success," and demonstrate, through a complex process known as validation, that predictors are usually related to measures of work behaviour for each job.

Validating Predictors

If predictors are invalid, decisions based on them are no more accurate than decisions based on a toss of a coin. *Validity* is the degree to which a measure accurately predicts job performance. Selection instruments are valid to the extent that predictors measure or are significantly related to work behaviour, job products, or outcomes. The process of demonstrating that a predictor is significantly related to a measure of work behaviour, job products, or outcomes is *validation.*

Validation is required to ensure that predictors are, in fact, able to make useful discriminations among applicants on the basis of their likely success in a job. Through the validation process, relatively accurate predictors can be found. Valid predictors enable employers to hire employees who have a relatively high likelihood of success and to avoid hiring those who would in all probability fail. Validation must also be done to ensure that predictors are job-related—that they measure characteristics directly related to job behaviour and/or job outcomes—and do not break human rights laws.

The Validation Process

The validation process examines the nature of the relationship between a predictor and a criterion measure of successful performance on a job. A *predictor* is any piece of information that can be used to screen applicants. Predictors include information from application blanks (education level, experience, and so on) and reference checks; scores on tests of skill, ability, or aptitude; data from interest and personality inventories; and interviewer ratings of an applicant.

Criterion measures are any measures of work behaviour, job products, or outcomes that have value to an employer. "Job success" is an abstract concept that means different things to different employers. Even for the same job, two employers may define success differently. For example, one manufacturer of valve springs defines it as production of 8,500 valve springs per day, no more than two days absent per month, and a scrap rate of less than 5 per cent. Another manufacturer defines success as production of 7,500 valve springs per day and no more than one day absent per month. Note that the second employer does not include scrap rate as a criterion of successful job performance.

Since success is a concept which can include countless aspects of work behaviour and job products, employers must decide which aspects are most crucial to success for a particular job. These aspects may then serve as criterion measures of success for a job.

HRM professionals validate predictors of success using some of the following criteria: quantity of output (number of letters typed, forms filed, valve springs produced); quality of output (number of errors, amount of scrap); supervisors' ratings of job performance; length of time on the job (tenure); number of absences (absenteeism); and degree of success in training programs. In order for a predictor to be useful, the validation process must demonstrate that a significant statistical relationship exists between it and a criterion measure of successful job performance.

Correlation coefficients. The most common index of the degree of relationship between two measures or variables, such as a predictor and a criterion measure, is the *correlation coefficient*, symbolized by r. Correlation coefficients vary from -1.0 to $+1.0$. (In practice, the plus sign is usually omitted from positive correlation coefficients.) A negative correlation coefficient indicates an inverse relationship between the variables: when the value of one goes up, the value of the other goes down. An example of an inverse relationship is that between labour costs and labour supply. Generally, as the supply of a particular type of labour decreases, the hiring wage for that labour goes up. A positive correlation coefficient indicates a relationship in which the values of both variables go up or down together. An example of a positive relationship is that between labour costs and the skill levels of employees. Generally, increased labour costs are associated with increased skill levels since wage rates are higher for more skilled workers. Stronger statistical relationships are indicated by larger values of r. Regardless of the size of a correlation coefficient, one may not infer a causal relationship between the two variables.

The significance of a statistical relationship refers to the degree of confidence one can place in it. That is, what are the chances that a correlation coefficient or some other index of the strength of a relationship could have occurred by chance or luck? The statistical significance of a statistical relationship depends on two factors: the magnitude of the relationship and the sample size from which the relationship was calculated. A correlation of small magnitude (such as .15) may be statistically significant if it is obtained from a very large sample. On the other hand, a correlation of .40 may be statistically irrelevant if it is obtained from a small sample.

The significance of a statistical relationship is indicated by a small letter *p* and a two- or three-digit number. *Uniform Guidelines on Employee Selection Procedures* specifies that predictor-criterion relationships should be $p = .05$ or less.[4] A *p* value of .05 means that the statistical relationship between two variables would occur by chance only 5 out of 100 times. The smaller the *p* value, the more confident one can be that a correlation does not occur by chance.

Correlation coefficients can be used for two different purposes in the validation process. The first is to establish a relationship between the predictor and the criterion, which is expressed in terms of a correlation coefficient known as a *validity coefficient.* The second use of correlation coefficients is to demonstrate the consistency or reliability of the predictor and/or the criterion. This type of correlation coefficient is called a *reliability coefficient.* Keep in mind that while correlation coefficients may be commonly referred to as validity or reliability coefficients, this merely expresses a particular use of the correlation coefficient. In reality, the validity or reliability of a test or any other measure cannot be reduced to a single number. The measurement validity of a particular test, for example, typically requires examination of the relationship between scores on that test and a variety of other non-test behaviours.

Validity coefficients. A validity coefficient expresses the degree of relationship between a predictor and a criterion measure. For example, the validity coefficient between scores on a perceptual speed and accuracy test (predictor) and the average number of beer bottles packed per day (criterion measure) is .60 ($r = .60$).[5] Thus, the validity of the test for predicting the average number of beer bottles packed is .60. This positive relationship is shown in a scatter diagram or plot in Exhibit 7.4. Each dot in the diagram represents one employee's test scores in relation to number of bottles packed. As shown by the scatter plot, employees with high test scores tend to have higher levels of output, while employees with lower scores tend to have lower levels. But the relationship is not perfect. Some employees have high test scores but low levels of output (see the lower right corner of diagram). If there were a perfect correlation between test scores and work outputs, the dots would fall in a straight line.

Data show that validity coefficients usually vary between .30 and .60.[6] Therefore, the speed and accuracy test used in this example is a very good predictor. However, even a predictor with a validity of .30 is more useful in making a selection decision than a simple toss of a coin.

It is difficult to use either a correlation coefficient or a scatter diagram for making selection decisions. For this reason, predictor-criterion relationships are often described in expectancy tables. Exhibit 7.5 shows an expectancy table constructed from the data in the scatter diagram in Exhibit 7.4. A minimum criterion of 6,500 bottles

[4] U.S. Equal Employment Opportunity Commission.

[5] M.D. Dunnette, *Personnel Selection and Placement* (Belmont, Calif.: Wadsworth Publishing Co. 1966).

[6] Edwin E. Ghiselli, *The Validity of Occupational Aptitude Tests* (New York: Wiley, 1966).

EXHIBIT 7.4

Relationship between tests scores and job behaviour (r = .60)

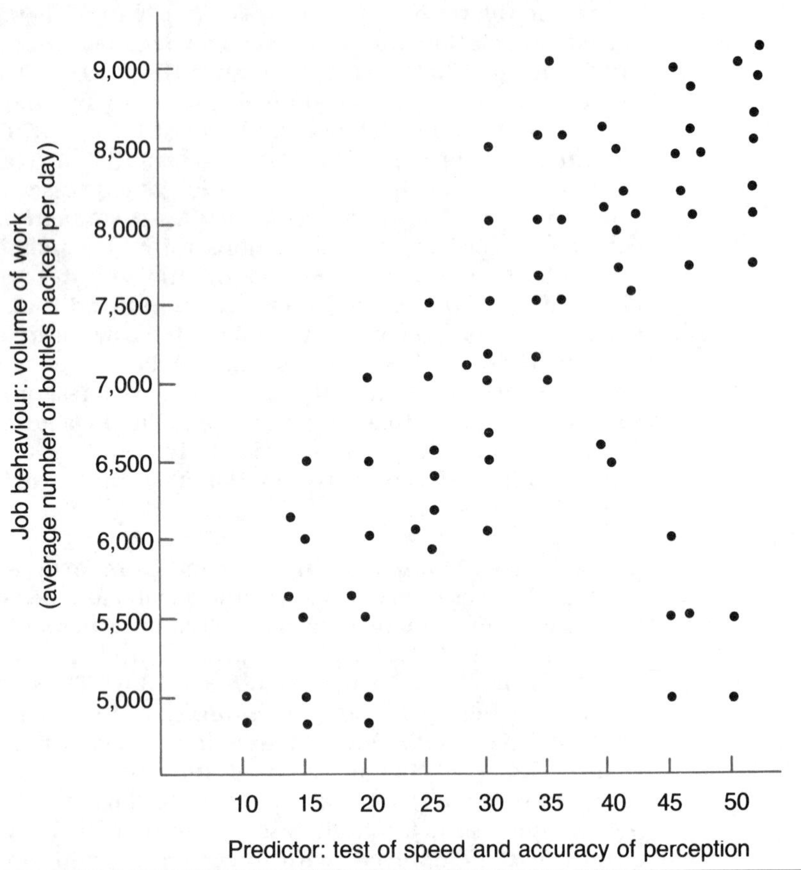

SOURCE: Adapted from M.D. Dunnette, *Personnel Selection and Placement.* Copyright © 1966 by Wadsworth Publishing Company, Inc. Reprinted by permission of Brooks/Cole Publishing Company, Monterey, CA.

per day was chosen. The expectancy table simply shows the probability, or odds, of individuals with particular test scores packing 6,500 or more bottles per day. These probabilities were obtained by calculating the percentage of employees at each test score who packed an average of 6,500 or more bottles per day. For example, a test score of 26 to 30 predicts an 89 per cent probability—eight out of nine persons, on average, will pack 6,500 or more bottles per day. Expectancy tables should be developed using large samples of applicants and employees to ensure reliability of the probabilities.

Expectancy tables provide an easy and understandable way to describe statistical relationships between a predictor and a criterion measure. They also easily portray nonlinear and curvilinear relations. For example, note that Exhibit 7.4 has a slight tendency towards a curvilinear relationship as some employees with very high test scores do not pack bottles at the "standard rate" of 6,500 per day. Relationships

EXHIBIT 7.5

Probability of applicants' packing 6,500 or more bottles per day for various speed and perceptual accuracy test scores

Test scores	*Probability and odds of packing 6,500 or more bottles per day*
10 or less	0
11–15	.14 or 1 in 7
16–20	.29 or 2 in 7
21–25	.57 or 4 in 7
26–30	.89 or 8 in 9
31–35	1.0 or 10 in 10
36–40	1.0 or 10 in 10
41–45	.67 or 8 in 12
46–50	.80 or 8 in 10

SOURCE: Data in the scatter diagram in Exhibit 7.4.

of this type can occur when people with very high levels of ability are not motivated to perform well on the job.

Reliability coefficients. A measure cannot be valid unless it is also reliable. *Reliability* is the consistency of a measure over time or between different measures of the same concept or behaviour. A metre stick is a reliable measure of height because it yields the same result for a person at two or more points in time (assuming that the person has not grown in the interim). It is also reliable because it yields the same result as another measure of height, such as a tape measure or a yardstick. The reliability of predictors and criterion measures is expressed in terms of reliability coefficients. Typical reliability coefficients fall between .70 and .90, with .80 indicating very high reliability for a predictor.

There are several ways to obtain a reliability coefficient for a test or other predictor. Each method of estimating reliability measures sources of unreliability: stability across time, internal consistency at one point in time, or both. The test-retest, or stability, estimate measures sources of unreliability due to changes in the person and in the measurement situation over time. In this case, a high reliability coefficient indicates that people's responses to a predictor at one time are very similar to their responses to the same predictor at another time. This method usually uses relatively short time intervals of several weeks.

A second type of reliability estimate is the internal comparison. Of the many types of internal comparison or consistency estimates in use, one of the better ones is the odd-even method. To obtain a reliability coefficient using the odd-even method, one correlates the odd- and the even-numbered items of a single predictor (test) given to a group at *one point in time.* A high internal consistency estimate means that responses to the odd-numbered items are very similar to those of the even-numbered items. Thus, the items are highly consistent with one another, and the reliability is high. This method of reliability estimation is commonly used since it is easily and quickly done. However, it provides no information about stability across time.

The best reliability estimate is the equivalent-form method. This method requires two separate tests or predictors designed to measure the same ability, skill, or other characteristic. These two predictors are given to the same group of people at two different times. If they have a high reliability coefficient, people respond very similarly to them despite the time lapse and the use of different tests. For example, suppose your instructor wants to estimate the reliability of the mid-term examination. Using the equivalent-form method, he or she could prepare two exams covering exactly the same material and give them to the class several weeks apart. A high correlation between the two sets of scores would indicate both stability and internal consistency reliability; a low coefficient could indicate either low internal consistency or low stability over time. To determine the source of unreliability in this case would require an internal consistency estimate treating both mid-terms as one test.

Major Types of Validation

Three major types of validation are used to validate predictors. According to *Uniform Guidelines on Employee Selection Procedures*, these types:

> reflect different approaches to investigating the job-relatedness of selection procedures and may be interrelated in practice. They are (1) criterion-related validity; (2) construct validity; and (3) content validity. In criterion-related validity, a selection procedure is justified by a statistical relationship between scores on the test or other selection procedure and measures of job performance. Construct validity involves identifying the psychological trait (the construct) which underlies successful performance on the job and then devising a selection procedure to measure the presence and degree of the construct. An example would be a test of leadership ability. In content validity, a selection procedure is justified by showing that it representatively samples significant parts of the job, such as a typing test for a typist.[7]

Criterion-related validity. A predictor has *criterion-related validity* if a statistically significant relationship can be demonstrated between it and some measure of work behaviour or performance. Examples of performance measures are production rates, error rates, tardiness, absences, length of service, and supervisors' ratings. Suppose a department store uses one year of sales experience as a predictor for its sales personnel. To validate this predictor, the employer would have to demonstrate that a statistically significant relationship exists between one year of sales experience and some measure of work behaviour or job

[7] U.S. Equal Employment Opportunity Commission.

products, perhaps number of sales and/or a low percentage of errors in ringing up purchases.

Exhibit 7.6 illustrates how the three types of validity are demonstrated for a clerk/typist job. In each case, the process begins with job analysis, which determines major job activities and critical work behaviour on which to base selection procedures and to determine criterion measures. The criterion measures chosen are the number of letters and forms typed per day and the number of letters and forms correctly filed per day—measures of quantity and quality of job outputs. In criterion-related validity, typing and filing tests are used as predictors. A statistically significant relationship must be demonstrated between the scores on these tests and the criterion measures of job performance.

There are two general types of criterion-related validity: concurrent and predictive. They are similar in that both involve the same basic steps: (1) job analysis; (2) selecting potentially useful predictors; (3) administering predictors; (4) examining the statistical relationships between predictors and criterion measures; and (5) cross-validating using a different sample. These two validation strategies differ within the third step: administering the predictors. In *concurrent* validity, potential predictors are administered to current employees; in *predictive* validity, they are given to job applicants. The concurrent method produces results faster than the predictive method since measures of job performance are already available for current employees. Though concurrent validity is used more often than predictive validity, examining for it can easily yield relationships between predictors and performance criteria that are biased and difficult to interpret; differences between job applicants and experienced employees (for example, age, experience) often make it difficult to generalize from the predictor-criterion relationships observed for current employees to those of job applicants.

Criterion-related validity has been very popular in the past, but recent research has shown that the sample size necessary to demonstrate it is larger than had previously been thought, from approximately 200 to 300.[8] Another problem is that criterion measures of performance must themselves be validated to ensure that they accurately measure aspects of work behaviour rather than factors unrelated to the job.

Construct validity. Instead of direct testing or using other information to predict job success, some selection methods seek to measure the degree to which an applicant possesses psychological traits called *constructs*, including intelligence, leadership ability, verbal ability, mechanical ability, manual dexterity, and so on. Constructs deemed necessary for the successful performance of jobs are *inferred* from job behaviour and activities as summarized in job descriptions. They are the job specifications part of job descriptions. Exhibit 7.6 shows the construct validation process for the clerk/typist job already discussed. From the major activities of typing and filing letters and forms, three

[8] F.L. Schmidt and J.E. Hunter, "The Future of Criterion-Related Validity," *Personnel Psychology*, 1980, vol. 33, no. 1, pp. 41–60.

EXHIBIT 7.6

Three kinds of validity

Criterion-related validity

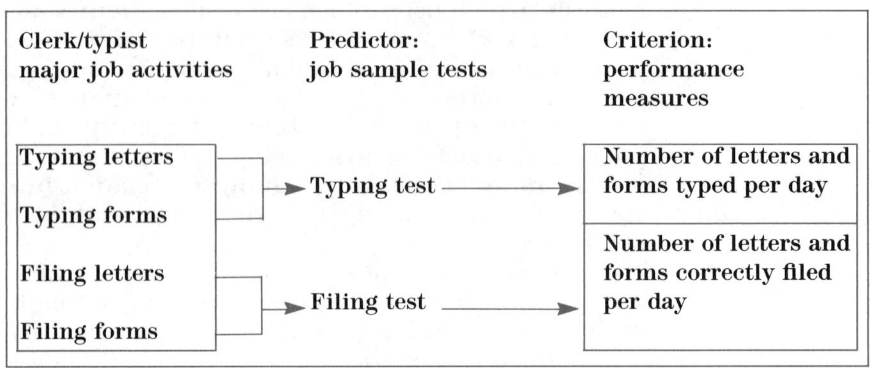

Construct validity

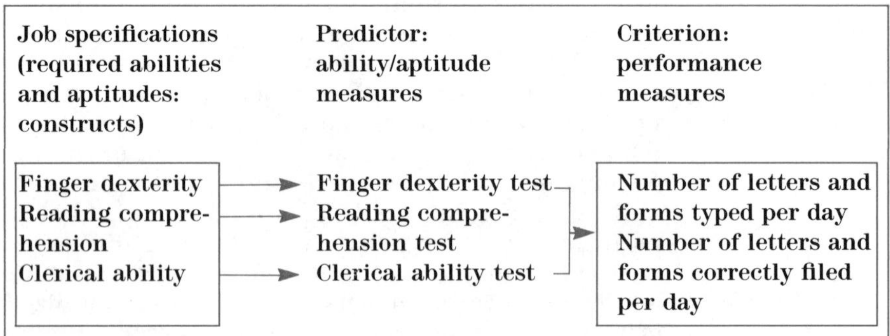

Content validity

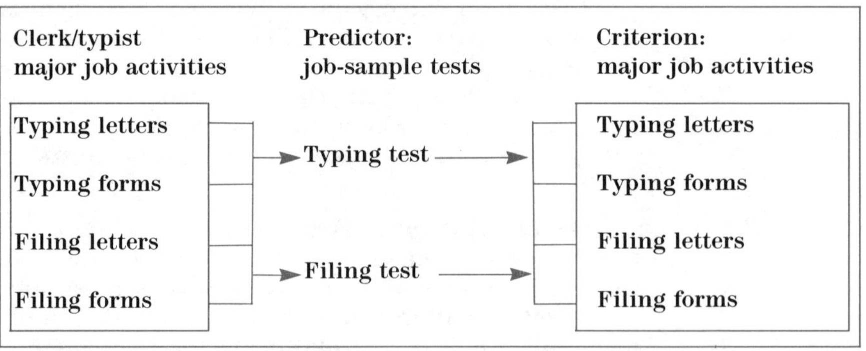

constructs have been inferred to be necessary: finger dexterity, reading comprehension, and clerical ability. These constructs can be tested by a finger dexterity test, a reading comprehension test, and a clerical ability test. When properly validated, the scores on these tests can be used to predict actual work behaviour or performance, measured in this case by the number of letters and forms typed per day and the number of letters and forms correctly filed per day.

Construct validity requires demonstrating that a statistically significant relationship exists between a selection procedure or test and the job construct it seeks to measure. For example, does a reading comprehension test reliably measure how well people can read and understand what they read? In order to demonstrate construct validity here, one needs data showing that high scorers on the test actually read and understand more difficult material than do low scorers on the test. The same type of relationship between test scores and actual nontest behaviour is necessary to demonstrate construct validity for any psychological construct. Fortunately for HRM managers, construct validation is usually done by research psychologists working for test development companies or for large companies or universities.

Besides demonstrating statistically significant relationships between constructs and tests to measure them, construct validity requires that there be (1) a demonstrated relationship between a predictor and a criterion measure, and (2) a demonstrated relationship between criterion measures and work behaviour or job products.

Content validity. A selection procedure has *content validity* if it representatively samples significant parts of a job, such as a filing test for a file clerk or a test of cash register operation for a grocery checker. Selection tests that approximate significant aspects of a job are called *job-sample* tests. Job-sample tests require applicants to perform certain aspects of a job's major activities, thus demonstrating competence at tasks which are an actual and important part of the job. Significant aspects of a job are determined through job analysis and set forth in job descriptions. To increase content validity, job-sample tests should approximate aspects of the job as closely as possible.

Content validity is limited in usefulness to relatively simple jobs that have few significant aspects of work behaviour to represent. It is most appropriate when applicants are expected to know how to perform jobs and when very little training is provided.

Selection Instruments and Procedures

HRM professionals are responsible for choosing, using, and sometimes developing selection instruments and procedures. It is important that these be administered in a standardized way. This means that selection instruments must be administered to every applicant in the same way and under the same conditions. Results must also be interpreted in the same way for all applicants. Without standardization of selection procedures, decisions are unreliable and reduce the validity of the selection process. HRM professionals should keep records of the selection process, since proof of standardization can become useful if the organization's hiring practices are challenged on human rights grounds. This section discusses a number of selection instruments including application blanks, employment interviews, tests, background and reference checks, physical examinations, and polygraph tests.

Application Forms

Application forms are a means of collecting written information about an applicant's education, work, and other experiences, both past and present. Almost all organizations ask applicants to complete an application form of some type. Typical application forms request information about an applicant's home address, last employer, previous work experience, education, and other information pertinent to employment, such as the names and addresses of references. Skill in the other official language may be requested if the job is a bilingual one. As pointed out in Chapter 3, employers are somewhat limited by law as to the kinds of information they may seek through application forms (see Exhibit 3.3).

Application forms are used in a variety of ways. One common use is to screen out applicants who do not meet minimum hiring standards. Some individuals who do not meet these standards can be spotted before receiving an application, but those who are not can be identified and eliminated by the information on their forms.

The application form also serves as a guide for the employment interview. Since it usually provides much general information about an applicant but not much in-depth detail, it may suggest the need for an interviewer to question or for the applicant to enlarge upon some areas. For example, an employer may want to investigate more fully the reasons for leaving a previous job.

Application forms may also serve to collect information on predictors of work behaviour and/or work performance. When used in this way, they are usually called weighted application blanks.

Weighted application blank. A ***weighted application blank*** (WAB) is an application form in which weights or scores are assigned to different answers to each question. For example, two years of secondary school receives a certain score and four years another. Scores are determined by analyzing the relationship between the responses to items and measures of job performance (such as absences, productivity, and turnover).

One scoring method for WABS and for biographical inventory blanks (discussed in the next subsection) is the ***horizontal per cent method.*** This method weighs items according to the percentage of people who are successful on the job for each response category. For example, suppose 60 people answer yes to Item 1 in Exhibit 7.7. Forty-five of the 60 are high-performing workers and 15 are low performers. Thus, a yes response receives a weight of 75, since 45 is 75 per cent of 60.

By adding up an applicant's score on a WAB, some measure of job performance can be predicted. Since WAB development requires a large number of workers (at least several hundred), this method is limited to large employers or smaller ones with high rates of turnover.

WABS have been used successfully to screen applicants according to their propensity for quitting. A WAB for this purpose is developed by comparing biographical data for a group of quitters against biographical data for a matched group of remainers. Items which discriminate between stayers and quitters are then weighted according to how well

EXHIBIT 7.7

Sample items for a biographical inventory blank

1. Have you found your life to date to be pleasant and satisfying?

2. Check each of the following from which you have ever suffered.
   a. allergies
   b. asthma
   c. high blood pressure
   d. ulcers
   e. headaches
   f. gastrointestinal upsets
   g. arthritis

3. What was your length of service in your most recent full-time job?
   a. less than 6 months
   b. 6 months to 1 year
   c. 1 to 2 years
   d. 2 to 5 years
   e. more than 5 years
   f. no previous full-time job

4. When are you most likely to have a headache?
   a. when I strain my eyes
   b. when I don't eat on schedule
   c. when I am under tension
   d. January first
   e. never have headaches

5. Over the past five years, *how much* have you enjoyed each of the following? (Use continuum 1 to 4 below.)
   a. loafing or watching TV
   b. reading
   c. constructive hobbies
   d. home improvement
   e. outdoor recreation
   f. music, art, or dramatics, etc.
      1. very much
      2. some
      3. very little
      4. not at all

SOURCE: W.A. Owens, "Background Data," in M.D. Dunnette, ed., *Handbook of Industrial and Organizationl Psychology* (Chicago, Rand McNally, 1976).

they differentiate between the two groups. Once developed, the WAB is administered to applicants, scored, and used to predict each applicant's quit or stay propensity. One organization's WAB used the following biographical data to predict turnover among a group of female garment workers: home ownership; age between 30 and 39 years; youngest child beyond six years of age; and nine years or less of formal education.[9]

[9] Gordon C. Inskeep, "Statistically Guided Employee Selection: An Approach to the Labour Turnover Problem," *Personnel Journal 49*, January 1970, pp. 15–24.

Research has shown that WABS are very useful for predicting length of tenure in an organization, job performance, and work interests. Personal data of the type collected in WABS are also useful for predicting managerial success.[10] Further, a survey comparing the validity of predictors from application-blank data versus test scores found that the former had stronger relationships with measures of job performance than did the latter.[11]

Biographical inventory blank. A ***biographical inventory blank*** (BIB) is an application form very much like a WAB, but its format is more structured. BIBS often use a multiple-choice or true-false format; unlike WABS, they sometimes include questions about present behaviour. Sample items from a BIB are shown in Exhibit 7.7.

Like WABS, BIB items can be used as predictors of job performance. However, relationships between items and measures of job performance must be re-examined frequently because changes in the job, supervisors, organizational policies, and the type of applicants recruited can dramatically affect the usefulness of particular items as predictors.

Employment Interviews

The sequential selection process contains three types of interviews: the initial interview, the employment interview, and the final interview with the person who will be the employee's immediate superior. The most comprehensive of the three and the one of most concern to HRM professionals is the employment interview.

The employment interview is a face-to-face conversation between an applicant and an employer's representative, usually an HRM professional for the organization or an interviewer for an agency, public or private, which refers suitable applicants to an employer. On occasion, a representative of the operating department concerned may also be present. The interview is a vehicle for the exchange of information between the applicant and the interviewer regarding the former's suitability for and interest in a job the employer seeks to fill. Information provided in the application for employment can be probed more deeply in the interview, and other information relevant to an applicant's qualifications can be elicited. Since interviews can be rather flexible, any missing pieces of information about an applicant can be collected at this time. The employment interview also provides an interviewer with a sample of an applicant's behaviour in a one-to-one interaction situation. Following an interview, the interviewer usually formalizes his or her judgement of an applicant into an overall assessment of suitability for the job.

Management's main concern in the employment interview, as in selection generally, is to find a good match between candidate abilities

[10] W.A. Owens, "Background Data," in M.D. Dunnette, ed., *Handbook of Industrial and Organizational Psychology* (Chicago: Rand McNally College Publishing Co., 1976).

[11] Ghiselli.

and demands of the job. However, there is another type of match to consider, that between a candidate's needs and what the organization has to offer in the way of need fulfillment. It has been suggested that a mismatch between needs and job reinforcers (rewards) leads to low satisfaction and quits, while a mismatch between abilities and job demands leads to low performance and dismissal.[12] HRM professionals should consider both types of match in assessing job applicants. Honest information conveyed in employment interviews serves to reduce turnover by allowing applicants to self-select out if they think their needs won't be met.

A number of factors are believed to affect both the interview itself and interview outcomes. Exhibit 7.8 categorizes these factors into those associated with the interviewer, the applicant, and the situation. While most of the variables listed in Exhibit 7.8 have been investigated, there is little evidence of how these factors are related.

EXHIBIT 7.8

Factors affecting employment interviews and their outcomes

Applicant
1. Age, race, sex, etc.
2. Physical appearance
3. Educational and work background
4. Job interests and career plans
5. Psychological characteristics: Attitude, intelligence, motivation, etc.
6. Experience and training as interviewee
7. Perceptions regarding interviewer, job, company, etc.
8. Verbal and nonverbal behavior

Situation
1. Political, legal, and economic forces in marketplace and organization
2. Role of interview in selection system
3. Selection ratio
4. Physical setting: Comfort, privacy, number of interviewers
5. Interview structure

Interviewer
1. Age, race, sex, etc.
2. Physical appearance
3. Psychological characteristics: Attitude, intelligence, motivation, etc.
4. Experience and training as interviewer
5. Perceptions of job requirements
6. Prior knowledge of applicant
7. Goals for interview
8. Verbal and nonverbal behavior

Applicant, Situation, Interviewer → *Employment interview* → *Interview outcome*

SOURCE: R.D. Arvey and J.E. Campion, "The Employment Interview: A Summary and Review of Recent Research." Copyright © 1982, vol. 35, pp. 281–322. Reprinted by permission of *Personnel Psychology*.

[12] John P. Wanous, *Organization Entry: Recruitment, Selection, and Socialization of Newcomers* (Reading, Mass.: Addison-Wesley, 1980), pp. 10–16.

Interview problems and rater errors. The value of the interview as a selection method is problematic. Research shows that they have good reliability for internal consistency and test-retest (same interviewer twice), but low inter-rater reliability (between different raters).[13] The reason for low inter-rater reliability is that interviews are apt to be unstructured and subjective. Recent research suggests that panel interviews with multiple interviewers show promise for increasing the reliability and validity of the interview.[14] Another technique which shows promise is behaviour description interviewing. This technique involves asking specific job-related questions about an applicant's prior work experience.[15]

The unstructured nature of employment interviews can result in a number of problems, including: (1) rater error; (2) talkative interviewers hampering the collection of job-related information; (3) variance in the questions asked of applicants; (4) interviewers asking "trick" questions; and (5) interviewers asking inappropriate questions relating to an applicant's sex, religion, or national origin.[16] Rater errors include hasty judgements, central tendency errors, leniency and strictness errors, the halo error, contrast effects, stereotyping, and personal bias. Evidence shows that decisions about applicants are made early in the employment interview and that interviewer attitudes bias these decisions. For example, one study disclosed that interviewers' ratings are influenced positively when applicants hold attitudes similar to their own.[17]

Many common rating errors can be considered deviations from a normal or bell-shaped distribution. For example, the *error of central tendency* occurs when most applicants are rated as average, when one would expect many to be rated as above or below average. In *leniency and strictness errors*, most applicants are given either uniformly high or uniformly low ratings, rather than being more widely dispersed. This type of dispersion error creates problems because the small difference between applicants renders discrimination between them nearly impossible. Additionally, strictness can lead to rejection of acceptable applicants (false negatives), while leniency may result in hiring poor performers (false positives).

With *halo error*, an applicant is seen as generally good or bad because one rated characteristic overshadows all others in the interviewer's mind. *Contrast errors* occur when an average applicant is rated higher than deserved because he or she is interviewed after several poor applicants, or lower than deserved following several good ones. *Stereotyping* is the tendency to compare applicants with a stereotype of the ideal applicant; stereotypes of ideal applicants vary

[13] L. Ulrich and D. Trumbo, "The Selection Interview Since 1949," *Psychological Bulletin*, 1965, vol. 63, pp. 100–16.

[14] Richard D. Arvey and James E. Campion, "The Employment Interview: A Summary and Review of Recent Research," *Personnel Psychology*, vol. 35, 1982, pp. 281–322.

[15] Tom Janz, Lowell Hellervik, and David C. Gilmore, *Behavior Description Interviewing* (Boston, Allyn and Bacon, Inc., 1986).

[16] T.W. Mullins and R.H. Davis, "A Strategy for Managing the Selection Interview Process," *Personnel Administrator*, March 1981, pp. 65–7, 71–4.

[17] G.D. Baskett, "Interview Decisions as Determined by Competency and Attitude Similarity," *Journal of Applied Psychology*, 1973, vol. 57, pp. 343–45.

from one interviewer to another and may be unrelated to actual job requirements. These errors may be avoided or at least minimized by the methods and approaches discussed below.

Improving employment interviews. The value of the employment interview as a selection instrument can be increased by following commonsense guidelines. One expert suggests:

1. A structured interview guide containing questions for applicants should be used to increase reliability.
2. An interviewer should be given complete job descriptions and job specifications for each job being interviewed for. This tends to reduce interviewer bias because actual requirements are spelled out in detail.
3. An interviewer should be trained in interviewing and know how to avoid errors such as talking too much and making hasty judgements.
4. An interviewer should be trained to deal with all applicants, regardless of their level of qualifications, since the interview is also a public relations vehicle.
5. An interviewer should receive special instructions on how to avoid discrimination and complaints of discrimination.[18]

A suggested interview plan is given in Exhibit 7.9.

Interviewers should receive feedback regarding the validity of their decisions on each applicant. While it is not possible to provide performance feedback on applicants who were not hired, interviewers should be told which of the applicants they referred to management were hired and how well these people perform on the job. If interviewers use an interview guide and keep records of their decisions, they should be able to learn from their past decisions. Edwin Ghiselli, a famous industrial psychologist, used this approach while acting as a consultant to a brokerage firm. From data collected over a long period of time, he was able to predict with a high degree of accuracy whether a stockbroker would remain with the firm for a period of at least three years.[19] Since the interview is more valid for behaviours which are observable in the interview, such as verbal and interpersonal skills, it should be used to predict these things rather than job performance as a whole.

A relatively new interviewing technique called the *behaviour description interview* has potential for significantly improving the employment interview. Using a structured interview format, questions are asked concerning certain aspects of an applicant's past behaviour. These aspects are selected because of their relevance to effective and ineffective on-the-job performance.[20]

[18] N. Schmitt, "Social and Situational Determinants of Interview Decisions: Implications for the Employment Interview," *Personnel Psychology*, 1976, vol. 29, pp. 79–101.

[19] Edwin E. Ghiselli, "The Validity of a Personnel Interview," *Personnel Psychology*, 1966, vol. 19, pp. 389–95.

[20] Janz, et al., 1986.

EXHIBIT 7.9

Interview Plan

1. Greeting and statement of the purpose of the interview; tell applicant you will be taking notes during the interview
2. Yes-no questions about unchangeable aspects of the job; if the applicant cannot meet these requirements (i.e., can't do shift work if required), then terminate the interview at this point
3. Questions designed to fill in the gaps in an application blank
4. Interviewer describes the organization and the job, using organization chart, job description, etc.
5. Structured oral questions (ask and record answers); do not make judgements at this time, just gather information
    a. Work history (What special aspects of your work experience have prepared you for this job? Why are you leaving your present job? etc.)
    b. Education and training (How does your education prepare you for this job? What additional training would you like if you get this job? etc.)
    c. Career goals (What kind of a job do you see yourself holding five years from now? How does this job fit into your own career plan? etc.)
    d. Performance on your last job (Everyone has strengths and weaknesses; what are your strengths? What are your weaknesses? How did your last superior evaluate your performance? etc.)
    e. Absenteeism, sick leave, tardiness record
    f. Convictions and credit rating (if appropriate and permissible under jurisdiction's human rights legislation)
    g. Salary and benefits (What kind of benefits do you think are important? What salary would you like to make? etc.)
6. Ask applicant if he or she has any questions, comments, or additions
7. Tell applicant what happens next (We have two more interviewees, then we'll decide and let you know within a week. Can we call you at home? etc.)
8. Close interview; never offer the job at this point
9. Review notes, make ratings on scales provided, and document your scale ratings; beware of bias (halo error, contrast and similarity error, etc.) when rating

SOURCE: Adapted from E.L. Levine, *The Joy of Interviewing* (Tempe, Ariz.: Personnel Services Organization, 1976).

As an example of how the method works, let us consider the job of a bank teller. Empirical research has uncovered five behaviour dimensions that distinguish between good and poor performance for this job. These dimensions relate to pleasantness versus rudeness to customers; cooperativeness versus dissension with peers; making good use of time versus wasting time; checking for errors versus making mistakes; and reporting problems versus hiding problems from the supervisor. Interview questions relate to each of these five dimensions.

For example, with respect to the customer relations dimension an applicant would be asked: "Tell me about the nicest compliment you received when serving a customer. What did the customer want? Do you remember what you said at the time?" Another question on this same dimension asks the applicant: "Tell me about the most irritating customer you have had to deal with. When did this happen? What did the person do that was irritating? What did you say in response?"[21] Note that the behaviour dimensions have both positive and negative aspects and that questions probe in a very detailed manner into specific instances of previous work behaviour.

Recent research has shown that behaviour description interviewing produces inter-rater reliabilities and validities significantly higher than other interview methods.[22] In fact, Janz, a professor at the University of Calgary, believes that behaviour description interviewing can be as reliable and valid as testing if interviewers are properly trained. He also reports that applicants are more satisfied with the interview because they feel it is fair and very relevant to the job.

Interviewing and human rights concerns. HRM professionals must be careful in interviewing to avoid questions which may breach the jurisdiction's human rights provisions against discrimination on the grounds of race, creed, colour, age, sex, marital status, nationality, ancestry, or place of origin. For example, the Ontario Human Rights Commission's guidelines for questions on application forms and during interviews include:

1. An interviewee cannot be asked for a birth or baptismal certificate, place of birth, place of birth of parents, grandparents, or spouse, or any enquiry into national origin. After hiring, a person may be asked for a birth certificate.
2. A photograph cannot be requested during interviews but may be requested after hiring.
3. Elementary school name and location cannot be asked, nor can the nationality, racial, or religious affiliation of a school.
4. Interviewees cannot be asked about their willingness to work on any particular religious holiday. After hiring, a person may be asked when leave of absence might be required for the observance of religious holidays.
5. Employers can ask whether a person is legally entitled to work in Canada. After hiring, an employer may ask for documentary proof of eligibility to work in Canada. Eligibility means being a Canadian citizen, a landed immigrant, or a holder of a valid work permit.[23]

[21] Janz et al., 1986, pp. 122–23.

[22] G.P. Latham, L.M. Saari, E.D. Purcell, and M.A. Campion, "The Situational Interview," *Journal of Applied Psychology*, 65, 1980, pp. 422–27; and J.T. Janz, "Initial Comparisons of Patterned Behaviour Description Interviews vs. Unstructured Interviews," *Journal of Applied Psychology*, 67, 1982, pp. 577–80.

[23] Ontario Human Rights Commission, *Human Rights in Employment: A Guide for Employers, Employees and Employment Agencies* (Toronto, 1981).

Existing research evidence suggests that interviews have often worked against hiring of the elderly, the handicapped, and especially women.[24] For this reason, interviewers should be particularly careful in interviewing persons from these groups. For example, a female applicant should be addressed by her name, rather than as "girl" or "dear." The don'ts include flirting, patronizing, and joking. Some jurisdictions, including Ontario, permit enquiries about marital status; others do not, but none allow it to be used to discriminate.

Other details of what human rights laws permit and forbid in the selection process vary among Canada's 13 jurisdictions. HRM professionals must know the regulations in the jurisdictions in which they work and keep up-to-date on changes and new interpretations.

Tests

Tests are a useful selection device for many jobs. Many organizations commonly use ability tests and aptitude tests; personality and interest measures are used less frequently because they are often not clearly related to the job and because results can be faked. Interest inventories and personality tests are most often used in selecting managerial candidates.

There are many different types of tests, but all share several features. All psychological tests have a set of standardized stimuli (test items), are administered in a standardized way, and are evaluated in a standardized manner.

Tests of abilities, aptitudes, and skills. Three types of employment test are commonly used for assessing abilities, aptitudes, and skills. These are cognitive ability tests, psychomotor tests, and job sample tests. All three have minimum scores, called cut-off scores, for the purpose of screening applicants. Cut-off scores can be raised or lowered depending on the number of applicants. If there are a lot of applicants for only a few positions, the cut-off score can be raised, thereby increasing the odds of hiring well-qualified employees.

Cognitive ability tests are used to measure a wide variety of abilities, aptitudes, and skills, including verbal and quantitative ability, mechanical comprehension, spatial ability, inductive and deductive reasoning, memory, and others. General intelligence tests and most university entrance examinations are cognitive ability tests. Most cognitive ability tests are paper-and-pencil tests. Two cognitive ability tests that might be used for assessing mechanical aptitude of an applicant for the job of auto mechanic are the Revised Minnesota Paper Form Board Test and the Bennett Test of Mechanical Comprehension.[25] The former measures the ability to perceive geometric shapes

[24] R.D. Arvey, *Fairness in Selecting Employees* (Reading, Mass.: Addison-Wesley Publishing Co., 1979).

[25] R. Likert and W.H. Quasha, *Revised Minnesota Paper Form Board Test* (Psychological Corporation, New York, 1941–1948); G. K. Bennett, *Test of Mechanical Comprehension* (Psychological Corporation, New York, 1940).

in relation to one another; the latter uses pictures to examine knowledge of mechanical facts and principles.

At the outset of this chapter, Lavelle of Expo Airlines was considering use of a cognitive ability test in order to identify higher quality applicants. Lavelle was told that the test had a validity of .30, but she was not sure if it would be a useful predictor at Expo Air.

As it turns out, Lavelle can use the cognitive ability test with confidence; it will be just as valid at Expo Air as it has been in other organizations. Not only can she use the test for customer service representative jobs, she can also use it for most other jobs at the company. Up until the late 1970s, psychologists contended that validity for a test was both job-specific and organization-specific. This was because research had shown tests to be valid for some jobs, but not others in the same organization. But in the late 1970s, Schmidt, Hunter, and others conducted a series of validation studies using samples much larger than those used in previous studies. In one such study, validities for seven cognitive abilities tests were examined for five clerical job families using data from 370,000 clerical workers. All seven tests were found to be highly valid for all five job families.[26] Other studies have confirmed that the most frequently used cognitive ability tests are valid for all jobs and job families.[27] The term *validity generalization* is used to describe the fact that a test has validity across jobs and organizations.

Recent research has also shown that cognitive ability tests which are valid for predicting success in training programs are also valid for predicting job performance.[28] Thus, when Expo Air properly uses a cognitive ability test to select people for their training program, they are also selecting people who will do well on the job.

Psychomotor tests are another common type of employment test. These tests measure how accurately or rapidly a person can move his or her hands, fingers, feet, or entire body. They also measure coordination between body parts, such as eye-hand coordination or eye-hand-foot coordination. Psychomotor tests are most useful for jobs requiring skilled physical activities. Cognitive ability tests and psychomotor tests may be used to select both experienced and inexperienced persons into jobs or training programs.

Job sample tests are another type of employment test. Job sample tests require applicants to demonstrate specific job duties or constructs such as mechanical ability. For example, applicants for a mechanic's job could be asked to locate and fix a number of things wrong with a car or truck. Applicants for the job of interviewer might be asked to interview a client. Organizations can develop their own job sample tests with the assistance of a qualified HRM professional.

[26] F.L. Schmidt, J.E. Hunter, and K. Pearlman, "Task Differences and Validity of Aptitude Tests in Selection: A Red Herring," *Journal of Applied Psychology*, 66, 1981, pp. 166–85.

[27] F.L. Schmidt and J.E. Hunter, "Employment Testing: Old Theories and New Research Findings," *American Psychologist*, 36, no. 10, October 1981, pp. 1128–37.

[28] K. Pearlman, F.L. Schmidt, and J.E. Hunter, "Validity Generalization Results for Tests Used to Predict Training Success and Job Proficiency in Clerical Occupations," *Journal of Applied Psychology*, 65, 1980, pp. 373–406.

Job sample tests have recently received considerable support from various sources. A review of research using them found they generally had higher validities than paper-and-pencil tests.[29] One researcher found job sample tests superior to the paper-and-pencil Mechanical Comprehension Test in a sample of maintenance mechanics.[30] Job sample tests, if properly constructed, have high levels of content validity. They are also less likely to cause difficulties for members of some minority groups than are paper-and-pencil tests, which usually require a certain level of reading ability. Job sample tests are most useful for hiring experienced, trained applicants, rather than low-skill or trainee positions.

Closely related to job sample tests are *job simulation exercises* that place an applicant in a simulated but realistic situation to see how well he or she can cope. An example is Merrill Lynch's account-executive simulation exercise, in which a *Wall Street Journal* reporter participated. Below he recreates the simulated situation for readers:

> My "in" basket is brimming with memos and unanswered letters. My desk calendar shows that conflicting appointments haven't been taken care of, and a client may pop in at any moment. Ignoring it all, I call a local industrialist who, I have been told, may be willing to buy some stock.
>
> "You've got to be kidding," he screams when I make my pitch. "Based on your recommendation, my brother lost $97,000 on a $100,000 investment, and now he is going to sue you."
>
> Who me?
>
> Well, sort of. Welcome to the Merrill Lynch account-executive simulation exercise, or, as dubbed by some, the Merrill Lynch stress test. It's a nail-biting three hours filled with alternating despair and satisfaction that leaves many longing for the good old days of calculus finals. Still, whether you leave in frustration or imbued with self-confidence, this exercise can't help but get you keyed up.[31]

Job simulations such as this are proving useful as selection instruments for professional and managerial jobs. If properly developed, they are high in both content and criterion-related validity. Applicants are also more likely to accept such tests than they are paper-and-pencil tests because job simulation tests, like job sample tests, have face validity. A test is said to have *face validity* when it appears to applicants to be a good, fair test of a required ability or skill.

Language tests. Language tests may be appropriate for bilingual jobs or other jobs that involve verbal skills in a language that is not the applicant's mother tongue—import-export work, tour guiding, order-

[29] J.J. Asher and J.A. Sciarrino, "Realistic Work Sample Tests: A Review," *Personnel Psychology*, 1974, vol. 27, pp. 519–34; J.E. Hunter and R.F. Hunter, "Validity and Utility of Alternative Predictors of Job Performance," *Psychological Bulletin*, 1984, vol. 96, no. 1, pp. 72–98.

[30] J.E. Campion, "Work Sampling for Personnel Selection," *Journal of Applied Psychology*, 1972, vol. 56, pp. 40–44.

[31] L. Rout, "Going for Broker: Our Man Takes Part in Stock-Selling Test," *Wall Street Journal*, April 4, 1979.

taking, sales, some government jobs, bilingual secretary, and so on. Language tests are a form of skills and ability test and, like other such tests, may be of the pencil-and-paper or job sample variety. In deciding which sort to administer, HRM professionals should consider whether the job requires mostly written or spoken communication.

Personality tests. People often believe that certain jobs require particular personalities or temperaments. For example, an accountant may be thought of as conservative, meticulous, and quiet, while a used-car salesman may be pictured as aggressive, flashy, and smooth-talking. While it is probably true that some kinds of people often occupy certain jobs, there is little evidence that people must have a specific personality type to be successful at a particular type of job. It is more common that the job itself shapes the job holder's behaviour, and people create stereotypes of others according to their job behaviour.

Nonetheless, two general types of personality test are sometimes used in selection decisions. These are self-report personality tests and projective techniques. These personality measures have been used most often in the selection of candidates for managerial positions; they are also common in assessment centres, which are a popular method of identifying potential managerial talent.

Self-report personality tests have sets of questions or statements designed to describe and measure aspects of a person's personality. Examples of self-report personality measures frequently used in managerial selection are the Guilford-Zimmerman Temperament Survey and the California Personality Inventory. One problem with such tests is that applicants frequently view them as an invasion of privacy. They also require a trained psychologist for proper interpretation.

Projective techniques require those taking the test to respond to ambiguous stimuli rather than to questions or statements as in self-report measures. Examples of projective techniques are the Thematic Apperception Test (TAT), the Rorschach Inkblot Test, and the Miner Sentence Completion Scale. The TAT consists of a set of pictures to which the applicant responds by writing a brief story. Presumably, the story reveals something about the respondent's needs or motives. The Rorschach is a series of inkblots which the person being tested must identify as objects. The objects a person sees in the inkblots supposedly reveal something about his or her personality. There is little evidence that either the TAT or Rorschach Inkblot Test is useful for selection purposes. The Miner Sentence Completion Scale is one of the very few tests specifically designed for managerial selection. Miner has presented data supporting the usefulness of his scale in predicting various criteria such as promotion rate, managerial level, and performance ratings.[32]

One study supporting the usefulness of personality measures, particularly projective ones, is a part of the assessment centres used by American Telephone and Telegraph (AT&T). Results of this study show

[32] J.B. Miner, *Motivation to Manage* (Atlanta: Organizational Measurement Systems Press, 1977).

that the projective assessment of motivational variables such as achievement motivation, self-confidence, and willingness to assume leadership showed low but positive correlations (.11 to .30) with seven- to nine-year salary progress for a group of 200 AT&T managers.[33] This study suggests that if projective personality measures are used by trained psychologists to assess factors clearly relevant to management, they can make modest contributions to the selection process. The cost of this approach, however, is relatively high compared with alternative predictors, such as biographical data from application blanks and interviews.

Personality measures are not likely to be useful selection instruments for a number of reasons. First, it is difficult to demonstrate that personality characteristics are job relevant. Job specifications usually focus on the skills and abilities needed for a job rather than on personality traits. Personality measures are designed to measure specific personality constructs, not the typical behaviour patterns associated with a job. Second, personality tests are generally less reliable than ability tests. A demonstration of low ability may allow an interviewer to conclude with certainty that the applicant could not perform a job, but one can almost never reach such a conclusion from a low score on a personality measure.

Interest inventories. Interest inventories are not truly tests, since they have no correct or incorrect answers. Rather, they consist of a series of questions or statements designed to elicit indications of interests and preferences. For example, they may ask the respondent to agree or disagree with a statement such as "I really enjoy taking things apart to see how they work."

When scored, such inventories provide information about how similar the respondent's interests are to those of successful people in various occupations. Examples of interest inventories are the Strong-Campbell Vocational Interest Blank and the Kuder Preference Record. These interest inventories, especially the former, have demonstrated the ability to predict tenure in an occupation over periods of 20 or more years. One review of the validities of selection methods found a mean validity of .10 for interest measures.[34]

One problem with interest inventories is that they are easy for the respondent to fake. For example, a person applying for the job of summer camp director would be sure to indicate an interest in working outdoors with young people and in administering activities. For this reason, interest inventories are rarely used in selection, but they are often used for job placement and career counselling. As organizations increase their commitment to placement, counselling, and development, rather than selection, there will be an increased use of interest inventories.

[33] D.L. Grant, W. Katkovsky, and D.W. Bray, "Contributions of Projective Techniques to Assessment of Management Potential," *Journal of Applied Psychology*, 1967, vol. 51, pp. 226–31.

[34] J.E. Hunter and R.F. Hunter, 1984.

Selecting and evaluating tests. Examination of job descriptions and specifications serves to direct HRM professionals' choice of tests to those most appropriate for certain job types. Once test possibilities have been identified, each test's manual should be examined and validation information sought in the *Mental Measurements Yearbook.*[35]

The major source of information for a new test is the test manual. It should be well-documented and cover: (1) the purpose of the test, (2) how the test was developed, (3) test reliability, (4) validation evidence, (5) normative data, (6) specific information on scoring the test, and (7) guidelines for interpreting test scores. A test that does not supply this information in its manual is not likely to be a good predictor. Tests with an excellent manual that are favourably reviewed in the *Mental Measurements Yearbook* are excellent candidates as predictors. Finally, better tests are likely to be those which have had the most validation studies done with large samples and those with relatively high validities.

New Canadian HRM professionals are often surprised to discover that virtually all tests used in this country come from the United States. Even Canadians who develop tests tend to publish them for the larger American market. For example, James Battle's Culture-Free Self-Esteem Inventory was originally developed in Alberta as the Canadian Self-Esteem Inventory. This situation troubles some Canadian experts because it means that the measures have been validated in the U.S. for a somewhat different population.

The idea that validities of tests differ significantly from one group to another is referred to as *differential validity*. Research in the U.S. in the late 1970s examined this hypothesis with regard to race (black vs. white) and culture (Hispanic vs. U.S.). These studies found that cognitive ability tests were equally valid across races and cultures and that differences found in earlier studies were due to small sample sizes.[36] Thus, when large samples are used or when adjustments are made for sampling error, it is quite likely that a test valid in the U.S. is equally valid for similar jobs in Canada.

Background and Reference Checks

Many employers request the names, addresses, and telephone numbers of references for the purpose of verifying information and, perhaps, gaining additional background information on an applicant. Although references are requested on the application form, they are usually not checked until an applicant has successfully reached the fourth or fifth stage of a sequential selection process. When the labour market is very tight, organizations sometimes hire applicants before checking references.

Reference checks are a good idea judging by several recent U.S. studies documenting use of phony credentials. "Operation Dipscam,"

[35] O.K. Buros, *The Eighth Mental Measurements Yearbook*, vol. 2 (Highland Park, N.J.: Gryphon Press, 1979).

[36] F.L. Schmidt and J.E. Hunter, 1981.

an investigation by the Federal Bureau of Investigations (FBI), reports that one out of every 200 Americans possesses fraudulent credentials that often are used for gaining employment. Among federal employees, about 200 hold phony academic or medical degrees. The report continues that one third of employed Americans were hired on the basis of credentials that were altered in some way.[37] A second study found that one in ten applicants for executive positions lied about their academic degrees. This study also found that only 32 per cent of surveyed employers always checked out academic claims. Claims were checked "hardly ever" by 27 per cent of employers; "occasionally" by 24 per cent; and "frequently" by 17 per cent.[38]

Most employers who request references either request written letters of reference or make telephone reference checks. Many organizations require several letters of reference, even though such letters may have no real selection function. Some research has shown that individually typed letters produce a better response than do form letters.[39] Many authors suggest that telephone reference checks provide the best combination of accuracy and low cost. The telephone reference has the advantage of soliciting immediate, relatively candid comments, and attitudes can sometimes be inferred from hesitancies and inflections in speech. An employer is often reluctant to put into writing negative information about a previous employee. Also, letters of reference may be written by a secretary or assistant rather than by the person requested. The field investigation—requesting a reference in a personal visit—is perhaps better than the telephone reference, but it is far more expensive.

Validities between letters of reference and job performance are typically very low (.08 to .14).[40] Low validities are likely due to the lack of standardization of letters and the fact that the applicant often selects the letter writer. References from previous supervisors are more useful for predicting job success of applicants than are letters from friends, neighbours, or co-workers. A previous supervisor has observed the work of a subordinate and usually knows why the employee left the job. Of course, a previous supervisor may not be objective about the applicant or may not have known the applicant well. Therefore, it is a very good practice to request information about the relationship between an applicant and a previous supervisor or any other reference. A study by Knouse found that human resource directors had a more positive impression of an applicant when letters of reference were well-written with specific examples and when the letter writer was well-acquainted with the applicant.[41]

[37] "Phony Academic Degrees Held by Federal Workers," *Iowa City (Iowa) Press Citizen*, March 10, 1986.

[38] "False Credentials," *Wall Street Journal*, July 3, 1985.

[39] A.N. Nash and S.J. Carrol, Jr., "A Hard Look at the Reference Check: Its Modest Worth Can Be Improved," *Business Horizons*, October 1970, pp. 43–9.

[40] R.R. Reilly and G.T. Chao, "Validity and Fairness of Some Alternative Employee Selection Procedures," *Personnel Psychology*, 1982, vol. 35, pp. 1–62.

[41] S.B. Knouse, "The Letter of Recommendation: Specificity and Favourability of Information," *Personnel Psychology*, 1983, vol. 36, pp. 331–41.

Physical Examinations and Health Questionnaires

Many organizations gather information about an applicant's health and physical abilities through physical examinations. For some jobs, physical exams are required by law. Because of their expense, physical exams are usually given near the end of a sequential selection process. Thus, organizations require physical exams only for those applicants who have not been rejected by prior, less expensive selection procedures.

One of the primary purposes of a physical examination is to ensure that an applicant is physically able or fit to perform the job for which he or she is applying. For example, police and firefighters are often required to carry heavy objects, run, and perform other strenuous activities. While job sample tests can be used to determine if an applicant can do the necessary physical activities, medical personnel should record heart rate and blood pressure to measure the effects of the activity on the person.

Organizations can also use physical exams to place employees in jobs most appropriate to their physical abilities and in which they are least likely to be injured. Based on physical characteristics, such as height, weight,and musculature, employees can be classified according to the type of work they are able to do (light work only, heavy work, and so on). By such classification, organizations reduce the odds of injury or accident.

A more recent use of physical exams is to screen applicants for drug use. Drug use among workers contributes to accidents, absenteeism, low productivity, and costly employee errors. Surveys show that use of marijuana and cocaine occurs on the job as well as outside the workplace.[42] It is no wonder, then, that a growing number of employers in Canada include drug testing as part of their selection procedures. A recent survey found that 25 per cent of Fortune 500 companies screened applicants for drug use in 1985. An additional 20 per cent were expected to begin testing in 1986.[43] The test most often used for drug screening is a urinanalysis test called EMIT (Enzyme Multiplied Immunoassay Test). This test is 97 per cent accurate under the best of conditions, but unfortunately, errors in a number of laboratories have rendered test results suspect. For this reason, any positive test results should be confirmed by a second urinanalysis test.

There is relatively little evidence on the reliability or validity of physical exams for predicting job performance. One publication presenting a number of studies on American pilots found that different doctors did not always agree on physical problems, and the validity of physical exams for predicting accident reduction and other criteria was low.[44]

J. B. Miner and M. G. Miner have suggested that having applicants fill out a health questionnaire is a viable substitute for giving them

[42] "More Firms Require Employee Drug Tests," *Wall Street Journal*, August 8, 1985.

[43] "Battling the Enemy Within," TIME, March 17, 1986, pp. 52–61.

[44] R.A. McFarland, *Human Factors in Air Transportation* (New York: McGraw-Hill, 1953).

physical examinations.[45] Specifically, the authors recommend the Cornell Medical Index—Health Questionnaire, which contains 195 yes/no items covering present physical conditions and medical history. While there is some evidence that people tend to hide some health problems, the questionnaire results correlate highly with actual physical examination acceptances and rejections. Health questionnaires can also be used in conjunction with physical exams to shorten them and direct an examining physician's attention towards specific problem areas.

Physical exams and fitness programs are a good idea for employees who have been on the job for a number of years. A U.S. Department of Justice survey suggested that physical exams and fitness programs may be more important for experienced officers than for officer applicants. The report cited back trouble and heart conditions as major causes of early retirement and limited-duty assignments. Unfortunately, periodic physical exams and fitness programs for current employees are quite uncommon. Of 302 police departments in the survey, for example, only 43 had any form of fitness program and only 30 had a weight-control program.[46]

Polygraph Test

The polygraph, sometimes called the lie detector, is a device related to both psychological tests and physical examinations. Its purpose is to determine if subjects are telling the truth about their past and present behaviour. The polygraph measures three physiological responses: (1) cardiovascular response (heart rate); (2) galvanic skin response (sweating); and (3) respiratory response (breathing). In a polygraph examination, the operator asks questions and the subject, who is wired to the machine, responds to each; the polygraph then records the three physiological responses.

The polygraph was originally developed for police investigations, but its use has become increasingly popular in industry, especially in financial and security-related organizations and jobs. Many employers view the polygraph as a method of reducing employee crime and theft. Another frequent use is to speed up the reference-checking process and perhaps reduce its costs. Whether a good reference check would be less expensive than a polygraph examination depends on the type of reference check and the quality of the polygraph examiner.

Many problems and objections are associated with the use of polygraph examinations as a selection device, and applicants and employees are easily offended by an employer who treats them as possible criminals. One might overlook some of these objections if polygraph examinations always revealed the truth. Unfortunately, this is not the case. There is very little evidence that they are either reliable or valid. One study found a high degree of reliability among ten experienced

[45] J.B. Miner and M.G. Miner, *Personnel and Industrial Relations*, 3rd ed. (New York: Macmillan, 1977).

[46] M. Diamond and C.S. Feldman, "Not All the Finest Are the Fittest," *Austin American-Statesman*, Parade section, April 15, 1979.

examiners in identifying the presence or absence of specific physiological reactions.[47] This study, however, did not investigate the important question of the consistency in interpretations of polygraph data. Also, even if the method itself were relatively reliable and valid, most polygraph operators are not adequately trained to interpret the results of the tests. Despite such problems, the use of polygraph examinations seems to be increasing in private industry.

Recently, a number of paper-and-pencil honesty tests have been developed as an alternative to polygraph tests. However, one review of ten honesty tests found little evidence of their validity for predicting honesty.[48]

Selection of Managerial Personnel

Selecting managers is almost always more complex, difficult, and expensive than selecting nonsupervisory employees. Most managerial jobs have greater variety and complexity than lower-level jobs, and very few are identical. These facts make prediction of managerial success difficult and important. Managerial jobs often have low base rates of success, and the potential costs of failure are high. Fortunately, managerial positions usually have many applicants, permitting an organization to benefit from a large applicant pool.

More than other jobs, managerial positions tend to be filled from within an organization via promotion. However, external recruiting and selection is also very common.

A number of predictors have been used to select managers, including cognitive ability tests, self-report and projective personality measures, biographical data, interviews, job sample tests and simulations, and assessment centres. Cognitive ability tests have been found to predict success to some degree for higher levels of management.[49] Evidence from several studies also shows that personality measures alone (the Guilford-Zimmerman Temperament Survey) and in combination with cognitive abilities tests have successfully predicted managerial success.[50] Projective personality measures, including the Miner Sentence Completion Scale and the Thematic Apperception Test, have also proved useful. Personality measures can add to the ability to

[47] E.C. Edel and J. Jacoby, "Examiner Reliability in Polygraph Chart Analysis: Identification of Physiological Responses," *Journal of Applied Psychology*, 1975, vol. 60, pp. 632–34.

[48] P.R. Sackett and M.M. Harris, "Honesty Testing for Personnel Selection: A Review and Critique," *Personnel Psychology*, 1984, vol. 37, pp. 221–43.

[49] G. Grimsley and H.F. Jarret, "The Relation of Past Managerial Achievement to Test Measures Obtained in the Employment Situation: Methodology and Results — II," *Personnel Psychology*, 1975, vol. 28, pp. 215–31.

[50] G. Grimsley and H.F. Jarret, "The Relation of Managerial Achievement to Test Measures Obtained in the Employment Situation: Methodology and Results," *Personnel Psychology*, 1973, vol. 26, pp. 31–48; Grimsley and Jarret, 1975; and V.J. Bentz, "The Sears Experience in the Investigation, Description, and Prediction of Executive Behavior," in F.R. Wickert and D.E. McFarland, eds., *Measuring Executive Effectiveness* (New York: Appleton-Century-Crofts, 1967).

predict managerial success, especially when candidates have already been screened in terms of cognitive abilities. Biographical data, especially work history information, can be useful in selecting managers and first-line supervisors, because past behaviour is a good predictor of future behaviour when the managerial job is similar to past jobs or experiences.[51]

A popular approach to managerial selection in recent years has been the assessment centre. An *assessment centre* is a collection of methods for the purpose of assessing the managerial potential of applicants or current employees. These methods include interviews, job samples or simulations, business games and exercises, and sometimes projective and self-report personality measures. Assessment centres are usually held for one to three days and are run by experienced managers. Candidates at assessment centres are often already employed by the sponsoring organization. They are usually supervisors or members of lower management. Managers serving as assessors are usually trained by the industrial-personnel psychologists who organize and supervise the centres.

Assessment centres are popular in both Canada and the United States. Perhaps one of the major reasons for its success is that it uses multiple methods with multiple assessors who are managers themselves in jobs similar to those for which the candidates are applying. It is not surprising that assessment centres are often better at predicting managerial success than are other methods; they include a number of different methods, and a group judgement is made by managers. The concept of the assessment centre is discussed further in Chapter 11.

The Utility of Selection

Selection procedures must be examined periodically to determine their usefulness to an organization. From an employer's perspective, the utility, or overall usefulness, of a selection procedure is the "bottom line." Management's primary goal is to minimize labour costs while maximizing productivity. The concept of utility permits examination of the role of selection in achieving this goal.

One definition of *utility* calls it

> the overall usefulness of a personnel selection or placement procedure. The concept encompasses both the accuracy and the importance of personnel decisions. Moreover, utility implies a concern with costs — costs related to setting up and implementing personnel selection procedures and costs associated with errors in the decisions made.[52]

51 A.K. Korman, "The Prediction of Managerial Performance: A Review," *Personnel Psychology*, 1968, vol. 21, pp. 295–322; and H. Laurent, *The Validation of Aids for the Identification of Management Potential* (Standard Oil of New Jersey, 1962).

52 Dunnette, p. 174.

The utility of a predictor or selection instrument depends on four factors: (1) the accuracy or validity of the predictor; (2) the selection ratio; (3) the base rate of success; and (4) the costs and benefits of selection decisions.

Generally, the utility of a selection method is higher when it results in a higher base rate of success for a job. Base rates of success increase when higher validity predictors and lower selection ratios are used. *Selection ratio* is the proportion of applicants hired to the number of applicants for a job:

$$\text{Selection ratio} = \frac{\text{Number of applicants hired}}{\text{Number of job applicants}}$$

If an organization hires five sales representatives from a pool of 25 applicants, the selection ratio for the job is 0.2 (20 per cent). If, on the other hand, the organization attracts only seven applicants for its five positions, the selection ratio is much higher—0.7 (70 per cent). When selection ratios are high, selection methods have limited usefulness because most of those who apply will have to be hired, regardless of predictions of success or failure. If selection ratios are very high, hiring standards may have to be lowered to meet human resource needs. For example, if only five applicants are attracted to the sales representative positions, all five may have to be hired, even though some are only minimally qualified. In this case, selection information could be used to place the new employees in training programs to increase their competencies for certain work behaviour. *The selection function increases in importance when the selection ratio is low enough for meaningful differentiations to be made among job applicants. However, since there are costs associated with processing applicants, very low selection ratios may not be cost-effective for an organization in some situations.*

If a base rate is already quite high, it is difficult to find a predictor that can increase it. In this case the utility of a predictor is low since there is little room for improvement. Base rates of success for jobs tend to be high for jobs that are easy and low for those that are complex. Selection is less useful for easy jobs because there is less need to differentiate among applicants if almost any of them can perform the job. When job requirements are more complex, a smaller proportion of applicants will be able to perform the job successfully, and selection becomes more important. Because defining success is more difficult for complex jobs, it is also more difficult to develop effective selection procedures for them.

Besides validity, selection ratios, and base rates, the concept of utility includes cost considerations, particularly those relating to selection decisions. Both actual and potential costs and benefits of such decisions may be examined. Actual costs include those for all applicants, such as recruiting and selection process costs, and costs for newly hired employees, such as orientation and training costs, wages, and benefits. Potential costs are those associated with selection errors. Potential benefits come primarily from hiring applicants who exhibit high levels of job performance. *The more important a job is to organizational effectiveness, the greater the importance of selection.*

Selection errors are far more costly for important jobs than for jobs of lesser importance. One measure of a job's value to an organization is the standard deviation of job performance in dollars (SD_y).

The SD_y of job performance is a measure of the potential range, or variation, of the dollar value of job performance. For some jobs, differences in performance extremes (excellent to incompetent) have little effect in terms of dollar value to an organization. For example, variability in performance for a clerk/typist is relatively insignificant compared to the effects of performance variability for a marketing manager. The utility of a predictor rises with the SD_y of a job because the potential costs of placing an unsuccessful person in a high SD_y job are much higher than the costs of placing an unsuccessful person in a low SD_y job. Of course, the potential benefits of a successful placement in a high SD_y job are higher than those in a low SD_y job.

Recently, Schmidt and others developed a method for estimating SD_y using supervisory estimates of employee output.[53] This method required supervisors to estimate the value to the organization of a poor, average, and high performer in a given job. Based on 29 studies using this method of estimating SD_y, the authors concluded that SD_y is equal to approximately 40 per cent of annual pay for a job.[54] For example, SD_y for a job with an annual salary of \$50,000 is \$20,000. Another method of estimating SD_y is the Cascio-Ramos method.[55] This method is more complex than Schmidt's and typically yields lower estimates.

Because of the difference in SD_ys for jobs, low validity predictors often have greater utility to an organization than high validity predictors. For example, an informed employer might gladly pay \$5,000 to have each managerial candidate evaluated in an assessment centre whose results have a .25 correlation with managerial success. The organization could compensate for the low validity by using a low selection ratio (for example, assessing ten or more candidates and accepting the top person). On the other hand, the same employer might be reluctant to pay even \$250 per applicant for a test whose results correlated .51 with success at a clerk/typist job. In this case, utility of the selection method is considerably lower since the job is less important to the organization and qualified applicants can easily be found.

The four factors affecting utility interact and must be considered together. Generally, utility is higher for jobs with a low base rate of success and a high SD_y. However, if recruiting provides very few applicants and a very high percentage of them must be hired, the utility of even a high validity predictor is low. On the other hand, the utility of a relatively low validity predictor is high if the base rate is low and the SD_y is high. In the latter case the utility of the low validity predictor could be increased by using a low selection ratio. The validity of the

[53] F.L. Schmidt, J.E. Hunter, R.C. McKenzie, and T.W. Muldrow, "Impact of Valid Selection Procedures on Work-Force Productivity," *Journal of Applied Psychology*, 1979, vol. 64, pp. 609–26.

[54] F.L. Schmidt, J.E. Hunter, and K. Pearlman, "Assessing the Economic Impact of Personnel Programs on Workforce Productivity," *Personnel Psychology*, 1982, vol. 35, pp. 333–47.

[55] W.F. Cascio, *Costing Human Resources: The Financial Impact of Behavior in Organizations* (Boston: Kent Publishing, 1982).

predictor is, of course, important, since the higher the validity, the more accurate the selection decisions.

Recall that Lavelle of Expo Airlines was interested in knowing how much performance improvement in dollars would result from adding the cognitive ability test to the interview and application form. Until the late 1970s, there were no methods available to estimate utility of a selection method, though the concept of utility had been available for some time. In the late 1970s, Schmidt, Hunter, and others developed a formula for estimating the increase in dollar value of job performance resulting from use of a new or additional predictor.[56] The formula is a decision aid to HRM professionals like Lavelle who must choose and evaluate alternative selection instruments. For a discussion of the Schmidt et al. formula and its application at Expo Airlines, see Appendix 7A at the end of this chapter.

A recent Canadian study investigated the utility of testing for clerical/administrative groups in the Canadian Forces.[57] This study included all the previously-discussed factors affecting utility, as well as the time value of money (net present value) and other financial factors related to testing and its benefits. Results of this study revealed an average annual utility of over $51 million for clerical/administrative personnel. This very large sum is based upon an average tenure of 18 years, an SD_y of $10,680, a validity of .52, a selection ratio of .33, and a testing and implementation cost of $608.60 per selectee. Among other things, this study illustrates that the utility of cognitive ability tests can be surprisingly large even for somewhat lower-level jobs.

Summary

Selection is one of management's most valuable means of increasing organizational effectiveness. Recent research estimating the utility to organizations of using predictors with good validity and hiring from the top down show large financial gains. The principle of validity generalization suggests that, at least for cognitive ability tests, employers can confidently use these predictors for most jobs without the expense of conducting their own validity studies. Even with these recent selection advances, HRM professionals must still play an important role in developing and implementing an effective selection system.

The key to selection is the use of valid predictors of job success. Criterion-related validity, construct validity, and content validity are three approaches to ensuring a significant relationship between a predictor of job success used in selection and job performance.

The selection process itself is a progressive screening of applicants, usually by some combination of application blanks, employment interviews, tests, and background and reference checks. Physical

[56] F.L. Schmidt, et al., 1979.

[57] Steven F. Cronshaw, "The Utility of Employment Testing for Clerical/Administrative Trades in the Canadian Military," *Canadian Journal of Administrative Sciences*, 3 (December 1986), pp. 376–85.

examinations and language tests may also be used when appropriate. Polygraph tests are sometimes used although they present many problems.

Application blanks are used for coarse screening and for guides to employment interviews; weighted application blanks and biographical inventory blanks also gather information for prediction. The employment interview presents opportunities for exchange of honest information, but also leaves room for several kinds of rater errors. It can be improved by training interviewers and using structured guides that focus on job requirements.

Many kinds of tests exist. Pencil-and-paper tests and job sample tests, which screen for skills, abilities, and aptitudes, are generally more clearly related to job content than are personality tests or interest inventories. All selection methods must be used in a way that avoids discrimination on any grounds prohibited within the jurisdiction. The selection of managers requires special care; cognitive ability tests, personality tests, and biographical data are often used, and assessment centres are increasingly common.

Project Ideas

1. One source of discrimination and waste of human resources comes from job specifications (minimum ability, experience, and/or education standards) that are higher than necessary for adequate job performance. One way of studying this situation is to examine job descriptions and compare them with job specifications. Specifications are often stated in recruiting advertising. Talk with a human resource officer of a local organization and ask how the organization arrives at the job specifications used for various jobs. Approach the interview in an unbiased way and you will learn. Perhaps you could ask the human resource officer to show you several job descriptions and explain how job specifications were derived. Write a short report of your interview.

2. Developing employment tests is a thriving industry. Obtain, through the library or with the help of your instructor, sales brochures from several test publishers. Also obtain a copy of an employment test and its manual. Compare the brochure's description with the test and the manual. What type of information does the manual provide? Are detailed instructions for both administration and scoring of the test given? Are there test norms? Are reliability and validity studies reported? Were any of the studies done by researchers not associated with the test publisher? Personnel officers must be careful consumers in terms of purchasing tests and other selection-related methods.

3. Obtain job descriptions for several jobs, preferably a simple, common job, such as bus driver, and a more complex one, such as bank

teller or personnel assistant. Develop job specifications and a selection procedure for each. Discuss why you chose each selection method and what specific information you will get from it. What cut-off scores or standards would you recommend for each method? What changes in the selection process would you make if the labour market became tighter?

Cases

Case 7.1: Disputed Selection at Sunnybrook

Marty Souchek, head of Personnel at Sunnybrook Hospital, is not at all pleased with a recent labour arbitration ruling requiring him to initiate a new selection procedure for the position of charge nurse in one of the hospital's operating theatres. The charge nurse position had been filled several months before with the promotion of operating room (OR) nurse Jodi Jacobsen. However, another applicant for the position, OR nurse Grace Chacko, promptly filed a grievance. Chacko, who had seniority, contended that Sunnybrook improperly applied the provisions of article 10.07 of the collective agreement between the hospital and the Ontario Nurses' Association. This article states:

> 10.07 In cases of promotion or transfer (other than appointments to positions outside the bargaining unit), the following factors shall be considered by the hospital:
> a. skill, ability, experience, and qualifications;
> b. seniority.
> Where the factors in (a) are equal, seniority shall govern.

Chacko's grievance lead to an arbitration hearing in which the nurses' union representing Chacko argued that she should have been awarded the promotion since she had seniority and was equal to Jacobsen in skill, ability, experience and qualifications. The hospital, on the other hand, argued that article 10.07 had been properly applied and that the union had failed to show that Chacko was Jacobsen's equal.

After hearing evidence in the case, arbitrators concluded that there was a defect in Sunnybrook's selection procedure that could have affected its outcome. They ordered a new selection procedure to determine who rightfully deserved the position.

Souchek studied his notes. Before initiating any new selection procedure, he wanted to know what went wrong with the hospital's first attempt to fill the charge nurse position.

Notice of the opening had been posted with the following stated job specifications: "Demonstrated administrative ability, excellent interpersonal relationships, and above average technical skills."

Four persons applied for the position, including Ms. Jacobsen and Ms. Chacko. Each filed a standard Sunnybrook Hospital application form and supporting statements with the personnel office. Each applicant received a brief preliminary interview with the personnel assistant and then each was interviewed by the head nurse, Grace Miller.

Grace Miller testified at the hearing that she judged Ms. Jacobsen superior to Ms. Chacko in all categories of administrative skill, including ability to articulate and communicate, ability to judge situations, ability to problem-solve, ability to make decisions, and capacity to self-initiate. However, evidence presented by the union revealed little factual base for many of Miller's conclusions. For example, Miller had reached her assessment of Chacko's ability to articulate and communicate, at least in part, by comparing cover letters submitted with application forms. In fact, cover letters were not even required, and Miller had never suggested to Chacko that her letter would be used in evaluating her candidacy.

Miller also based her opinion of Chacko's ability to articulate and communicate on Chacko's responses to interview questions. However, evidence presented by the union showed that Miller never asked Chacko to elaborate or expand upon her answers beyond a simple "I think I can do it." There was also evidence presented that the atmosphere of the interview might have been affected by a negative relationship which had existed for some time between Chacko and the head nurse. On the other hand, Miller and Jacobsen enjoyed a positive relationship.

Finally, evidence was presented that cast doubt on Jacobsen's technical ability in the operating theatre in question, namely ophthalmology. Specifically, Jacobsen was observed on several occasions using the wrong instruments or equipment for the task at hand.

Questions:

1. Put yourself in Souchek's shoes and identify deficiencies in the first selection procedure for the charge nurse position.
2. How could the selection procedure have been improved?
3. What ingredients would you include in a new selection procedure in order to determine which candidate to promote?
4. Using this case as an example, discuss the benefits of a careful application of selection criteria in the case of promotions. Are there also any costs?

SOURCE: C. G. Simmons, K. P. Swan, and D. D. Carter, eds., *Labour Arbitration Cases* (Third Series), vol. 2 (Aurora, Ont.: Canada Law Book, 1982).

Case 7.2: Flyer Industries: Building a Better Bus

When Kenneth Clark took over as Chief Executive Officer (CEO) of Flyer Industries Ltd. in late 1983, he inherited a $32.5 million deficit and a busload of problems. It seems Clark's predecessor was more interested in selling the company's product, buses, than he was in quality control. In fact, the 53-year-old company had never had a research and development lab or an emphasis on quality control. Buses simply rolled off the assembly line with no prior testing of their structure or design. Because production often began with incomplete drawings and untested designs, problems surfaced on the assembly line causing delays and last-minute modifications. It was common practice to order spare parts on short notice at a cost far exceeding what it would have cost Flyer to manufacture the part itself. The company employed no industrial engineers to help streamline production and no cost-accounting procedures to determine the cost of building a bus. (When a cost was later determined, it was discovered that Flyer lost $17,500 on every bus it sold in 1983.)

Flyer's engineers and assembly-line workers informed management of problems on the line, but management turned a deaf ear. The company's board of directors never got wind of problems at the plant because they relied on optimistic verbal reports given to them by management.

Despite the rosy picture painted by management, it was difficult to ignore complaints from buyers of the buses. Vancouver, which purchased 245 Flyer trolleys in 1983, complained of doors that slammed shut on passengers, poorly positioned hand grips, and door frames that impeded driver visibility. Further, the buses' electrical systems produced sparks and short circuited during the winter months. Another city complained of problems with the buses' cooling system. The trolleys overheated and stalled at temperatures above 26°C. Other purchasers noted problems with rust, structural cracks, breaking windshield wipers, and faulty axle bolts.

Low morale and discontent characterized Flyer's work force of 450 manufacturing personnel and several hundred others. Absenteeism averaged 7 per cent in 1983 and was as high as 32 per cent in some departments. Labour-management relations were unhealthy evidenced by company losses of $100,000 in arbitration rulings between 1973 and 1983. Turnover was also high. In 1983 alone, 40 employees either resigned or were forced out of their jobs. Many of those who left were experienced employees, some in middle management positions. In the 12 years before Clark was appointed CEO, workers operated under several management teams and six different CEOs. According to Clark, "Different CEOs came in with specific skills in such areas as manufacturing, engineering, or marketing. They attacked the company with similarly single-minded devotion, leaving the rest of the company to flounder."†

While Flyer claimed to have a promotion ladder, workers saw little chance of moving up. For one thing, the company offered no formal training to upgrade their skills. For another, the few promotions that did occur seemed to defy logic. One employee appointed to vice-president of engineering, for example, had no engineering degree. And a purchasing agent moved up to an executive vice-presidency after only two years with the company. There were no

†A. Nikiforuk, "Winging It," *Canadian Business*, November, 1984, pp. 85–94.

job descriptions to guide or constrain Flyer's hiring and promotion practices and as many as ten different evaluation systems existed to assess employee performance.

Questions:

1. What do you believe to be management's most serious mistakes or errors in judgement? How could these mistakes have been avoided?
2. Clark and others have blamed Flyer's problems on unqualified personnel (including management) and lack of technical expertise. What evidence do you find that such might be the case? Do you agree with Clark's assessment? Why or why not?
3. If you were serving as Clark's human resources consultant, what strategies would you suggest to ensure Flyer a better qualified work force now and in the future?
4. CEO Clark devised a three-step salvage operation for Flyer. Decide on a salvage plan of your own and justify each step.

Appendix 7A: Estimating Utility Gains of a Predictor

The Schmidt et al. utility formula is analogous to capital budgeting models in finance, which are used to choose among alternative capital investments.

The formula is as follows:

$$\Delta\overline{u} = (\Delta r_{xy})\ SD_y\overline{Z}_x$$

$\Delta\overline{u}$ is the increase in dollar value of output per person hired per year. Δr_{xy} is the difference in validity between the original predictor(s) and the new predictor. SD_y represents performance variability in dollars and is estimated at 40 per cent of annual pay for the job. $\overline{Z}_x$ is the average test score of employees hired expressed in standard score form. Selection procedure scores are standardized by transforming them to a mean of 0 and a standard deviation of one. This allows test scores to be interpreted as points on a normal distribution. The value of $\overline{Z}_x$ is determined from the percentage of applicants hired (selection ratio) assuming a top down hiring procedure. Exhibit 7A.1 is a conversion table for estimating $\overline{Z}_x$ from the selection ratio.

Note that in this formula for estimating utility, SD_y replaces the base rate of success concept. The reason for this is that the formula estimates value to the organization of employees hired, and SD_y reflects job performance gains due to higher ability employees. The base rate

EXHIBIT 7A.1

Table for estimating value of $\overline{Z}_x$

Test scores are typically normally distributed in job applicant populations. In a normal distribution, the test cutoff score (minimum acceptable score) and the average (standardized) score of those selected can be computed from the selection ratio. Here are some representative values:

Selection ratios	*Cutoff score*	*Average test score of those selected ($\overline{Z}_x$)*
100%	No lower bound	.00
90	−1.28	.20
80	− .84	.35
70	− .51	.50
60	− .25	.64
50	.00	.80
40	.25	.97
30	.51	1.17
20	.84	1.40
10	1.28	1.76
5%	1.64	2.08

SOURCE: F.L. Schmidt and J.E. Hunter, "Employment Testing: Old Theories and New Research Findings," *American Psychologist*, October 1981, vol. 36, no. 10, pp. 1128–37.

concept, while conceptually useful, makes no differentiations among successful employees. Thus, utility is higher when validity of the new predictor is greater than that for the previous predictor (reflected in a high Δr_{xy}), when the dollar variability of job performance (SD_y) is large, and when higher-scoring applicants are hired (higher $\overline{Z}_x$ values). This method of estimating utility assumes only that all applicants who are offered jobs are hired, that applicants are hired from the top down, and that the pool of applicants is a random sample from the population of applicants. Other versions of Schmidt's utility formula subtract the cost of selection methods, but these are usually negligible compared to performance gains.

Using this formula, let us estimate utility of the cognitive ability test Expo Air is considering for its customer service representative jobs. Remember that the cognitive ability test has a validity of .30 and assume that validity of existing methods at Expo Air (the interview and application form) together is .15. The difference between predictors is .15, which is Δr_{xy} in the formula. Assume also that average salary for service representatives is $30,000. Forty per cent of this is $12,000, or SD_y. Finally, assume the selection ratio for these jobs is 70 per cent. According to the table in Exhibit 7A.1, $\overline{Z}_x$ can be estimated at .50.

Inserting these values in the utility formula we find that

$$\Delta\overline{u} = (.15)(12{,}000)(.5) \text{ or } \$6{,}000.$$

Recall that this $6,000 is the gain in utility for only one employee per year. To obtain utility of the cognitive ability test at Expo Air, this $6,000 figure must be multiplied by the number of service representatives hired each year (50) and by their average length of tenure (4.0 years). Thus, the airline will save $300,000 per year, minus the cost of testing, or approximately $1.2 million over four years. Further gains could be realized by lowering the selection ratio, though this would probably require additional recruiting and testing costs to obtain applicants meeting the higher test cutoff score. If a selection ratio of 30 per cent were used, for example, the value of $\overline{Z}_x$ would increase to 1.17 and the gain per hire per year would become $14,040.

Gains from the addition of even a moderately valid predictor are substantial, particularly when a lower selection ratio is used. While we have not subtracted the cost of testing, it is typically a very small proportion of the gain in utility, particularly when low selection ratios are used.

III Employee Development

8

Orientation

Jane Simpson is a new shipping clerk at CanTèque Electronics. When she accepted the job last Thursday, she was given a map and instructed to report to the company meeting room Monday at 7:30 A.M. She was also told that the meeting would be a half-day orientation session for new employees.

On Monday morning, Simpson found about 25 other new employees in the meeting room. Someone from the human resources department checked her name on a list, gave her a name tag, and offered her a cup of coffee and a doughnut. At 7:45, the manager of human resources asked everyone to take a seat. He introduced himself, welcomed the new employees to CanTèque, and briefly explained the morning's activities. They included:

1. A 25-minute movie about CanTèque.
2. Completion of employee information forms: a TD-1 income tax withholding form, a Canada Pension Plan form, a form for the provincial health plan, other necessary payroll information, and family-related information.
3. Distribution of an information packet for new employees containing descriptions of the supplementary medical insurance program, pension plans, other benefits packages and company services, and an employee handbook.
4. A slide-show presentation detailing employee benefits.
5. A 20-minute coffee break.
6. A plant tour.

7. Instructions on policy matters: how to report absence, where to park, etc.
8. A question and answer period.
9. Completion of a form evaluating the orientation program.

By lunch time Simpson was enthusiastic about her employer, but she also felt that she had been given a tremendous amount of information to digest in a very short time. She wondered which parts of it she needed to know right away. She was also somewhat anxious about her new job responsibilities.

After lunch, Simpson was introduced to her supervisor and several of her new co-workers. After some small talk, the supervisor began telling Simpson about her job. Orientation was over and job training had begun.

CanTèque's orientation program is typical of many organizational orientations. While it gave Jane Simpson and other new employees a great deal of information about their new employer, it provided few insights about actually working for CanTèque and succeeding in the organization. This chapter concerns orientation as an HRM function—what it is and what it can and should be.

Orientation: A Definition

Orientation is the process of introducing new employees to the organization, its philosophy, policies, rules, and procedures. It marks the beginning of *socialization*, the process by which an employee is indoctrinated to the organization's culture—its norms, values, and ways of doing things.

Socialization is a period of adjustment in which new employees learn what is expected in terms of appropriate behaviour and acceptable performance. They also come to know what they can expect from the organization in return for their efforts. These things are learned not only through formal orientation programs, but also via informal exchanges with co-workers and observation of supervisors and others who may serve as role models for the employee. Pascale and others argue that the socialization process continues well beyond orientation and is affected by other HRM functions such as training, performance appraisal, and compensation.[1] It has even been suggested that socialization may begin in some organizations as early as the recruiting stage, when people are attracted who fit the "corporate image."

While the formal orientation period is only a part of the socialization process, it is an important period since instilling values and norms to new hires is vital to managing an organization's culture. Many recent management books argue that an organization's culture is crucial to its level of effectiveness and profitability.

[1] R. Pascale, "Fitting New Employees into the Company Culture," *Fortune*, May 28, 1984, pp. 28–43.

Relation to Other HRM Functions

The relationship of orientation to other HRM functions is shown in Exhibit 8.1. In most organizations, some form of orientation follows the selection and hiring of new employees. Orientation provides new hires with basic information about working conditions, policies, procedures, pay and benefits and introduces management and co-workers. Information conveyed during orientation may also correct false impressions created by recruiting messages and selection interviews.

Note that performance appraisal provides inputs to the orientation function in that new employees are informed of acceptable levels of performance and, over time, with assessments of job performance. This is an important aspect of socialization, for most employees want to know what is required for successful job performance.

For most jobs, some degree of training follows orientation. While orientation provides new employees with general information about the job and organization, training provides them with the specific knowledge and skills necessary to perform the job.

How Orientation Contributes to Organizational Effectiveness

Orientation contributes to organizational effectiveness by facilitating the socialization process so that new hires become integrated into the organization as soon as possible. The sooner new hires feel comfortable in the organization, the sooner they can be productive workers. In order to make new hires feel comfortable, it is often necessary to reduce their anxieties, clarify their role expectations, and provide a sense of where they fit into the organization as a whole.

The ease with which new hires adjust to the job and work environment is often a function of the expectations they bring to the job. If expectations are realistic, adjustment is relatively simple. If, however, expectations are unrealistic or unreasonable, adjustment is more difficult and quitting may result. In the latter case, orientation can facilitate retention by bringing employee expectations more into line with reality. IBM, Procter & Gamble, and other companies known for their strong, achievement-oriented cultures purposely give new hires trying experiences in order to promote more realistic expectations.[2]

Even when expectations are not unrealistic or unreasonable, orientation can prepare new hires for the almost inevitable ambiguities and frustrations they will face, including uncertainties about the boss's expectations, about acceptable performance, about getting along with

[2] Pascale, 1984.

EXHIBIT 8.1

Orientation: relation to other functions

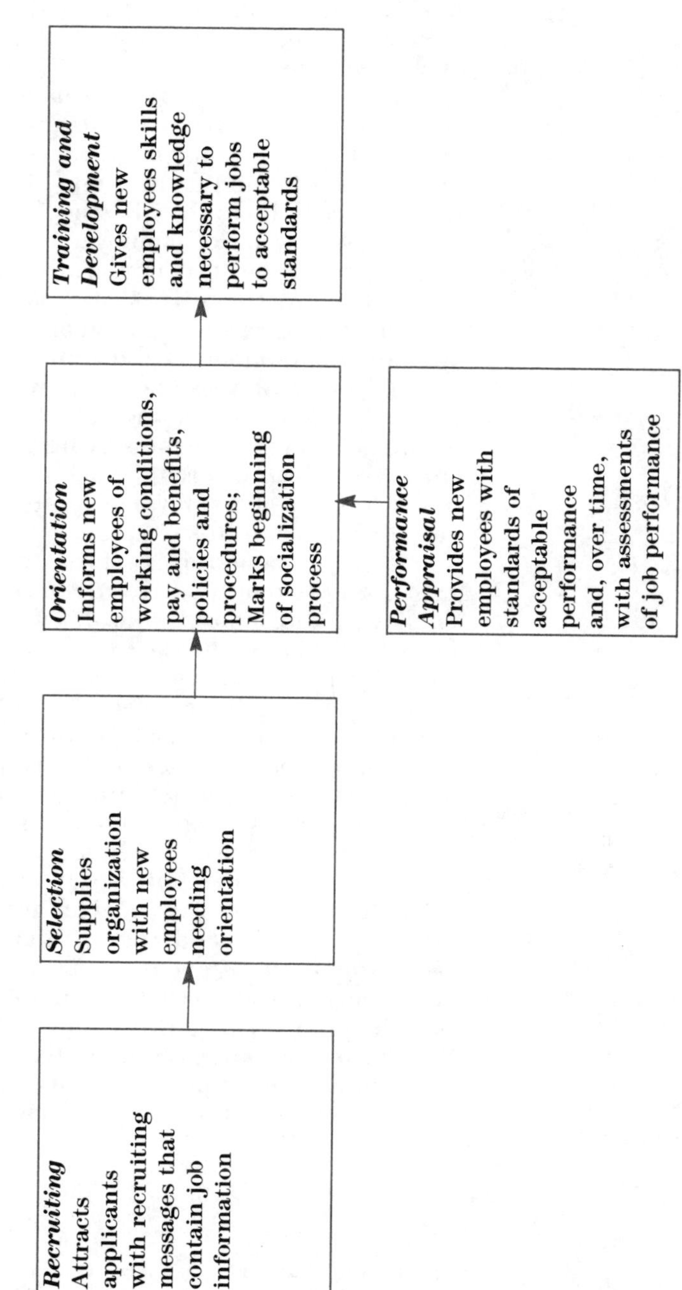
Recruiting
Attracts applicants with recruiting messages that contain job information
Selection
Supplies organization with new employees needing orientation
Orientation
Informs new employees of working conditions, pay and benefits, policies and procedures; Marks beginning of socialization process
Training and Development
Gives new employees skills and knowledge necessary to perform jobs to acceptable standards
Performance Appraisal
Provides new employees with standards of acceptable performance and, over time, with assessments of job performance

co-workers, and about dealing with the fact that the job may not be as interesting or autonomous as they had hoped. Research has shown that orientation programs that reduce anxiety of new employees can reduce training time and costs, waste and production costs, and rates of absenteeism.[3]

Many studies of turnover have found a large number of quits occurring in the very early stages of an employee's career with an organization. One study of 1,736 new hires placed by a public employment agency found that over one-third (632) had quit by the end of six months.[4] New hires in this study were in low-wage, blue-collar jobs for a cross section of employers. Early termination is costly to employers, given the costs of recruiting, selecting, and training replacements. Corning Glass Works estimates that it costs $30,000 to $40,000 per person to hire and train an optical designer, a CAD/CAM engineer, a systems programmer, or a technical sales person.[5] Early termination of high SD_y employees and those with skills that are in short supply can cost employers even more. Orientation programs can contribute to organizational effectiveness by helping to reduce turnover among new employees. Corning credits a 69 per cent reduction in turnover in the first two years of employment to its new orientation system, which is described later in this chapter.[6]

Even if orientation is successful in smoothing the way for new hires, some turnover will result due to mismatches or poor "fit" between employees and organizations. If a mismatch has occurred, it is to everyone's benefit that this fact be discovered at the earliest opportunity. Organizations can save substantial training costs and individuals can avoid "spinning their wheels" at jobs for which they are unsuited. Orientations that provide realistic previews of the job and the employer contribute to organizational effectiveness by permitting early detection of mismatches. Information on mismatches, as well as on successful matches, should be communicated to those responsible for selection so that it may be used to reduce the possibility of future mismatches.

Finally, documentation of information given to new hires during orientation sessions can provide the organization with protection from later legal action and costly litigation. New hires often sign lists recording their attendance at orientation sessions and they may sign forms indicating that they understand company rules and various benefit options. Thus, if an employee is later disciplined for a rule violation, he or she cannot claim to have never been informed of the rule. Likewise, if an employee claims that he or she was not informed of a certain benefit option, the company can show otherwise.

[3] E.R. Gommersall and M.S. Myers, "Breakthrough in On-the-Job Training," *Harvard Business Review*, vol. 44, July–August 1966, pp. 62–71.

[4] J.P. Wanous, S.A. Stumpf, and H. Bedrosian, "Job Survival of New Employees," *Personnel Psychology*, 1979, vol. 32, pp. 651–62.

[5] E.J. McGarrell, Jr., "An Orientation System That Builds Productivity," *Personnel*, November–December 1983 pp. 32–41.

[6] McGarrell, 1983.

Orientation and the Socialization Process

Orientation marks the beginning of socialization and may be used to prepare employees for some of the ambiguities and frustrations they are likely to experience. The following descriptive model of the socialization process views such ambiguities and frustrations as tasks, or learning experiences, which a new employee must master in order to become an accepted member of the organization.

Schein's Socialization Model

Schein's three-stage socialization model describes the steps in preparing for a job and entering an organization. The three stages are: (1) entry, (2) socialization, and (3) mutual acceptance.[7] The model is illustrated in Exhibit 8.2.

Entry stage. An individual selects an occupation and prepares to enter it by obtaining appropriate education and training. During this period, Schein states, people develop an idealistic image of what it is like to work in a particular occupation. Such images are usually unrealistic, emphasizing the positive aspects of the work and ignoring its negative features. Also during this period, the individual develops attitudes and values which he or she regards as appropriate for succeeding in the chosen occupation. This process is called *anticipatory socialization.*

The final part of the entry stage is looking for the first job. At this point, the potential employee begins to make contact with various employers through the recruiting process. This part of the entry stage often presents problems for both employer and applicant. Schein argues that both tend to emphasize their most favourable aspects and hide their negative elements, resulting in the development of unrealistic expectations. These distortions of reality prevent both interviewer and applicant from determining if a good fit exists between the worker and the organization. Recruiting materials often oversell the organization; the result is disillusioned and dissatisfied employees. Many problems of this sort can be avoided by realistic analyses of an organization's jobs and promotion and compensation policies and practices, and by making appropriate changes in recruiting and selection methods. Once new employees report to work, orientation can serve to align their expectations with the actualities of working for the particular employer.

Socialization Stage. Organizational socialization begins when the new employee begins work. From the employee's point of view, socialization is a process of "breaking in and joining up, of learning the ropes, of

[7] E.H. Schein, *Career Dynamics: Matching Individual and Organizational Needs* (Reading, Mass.: Addison-Wesley Publishing Co., 1978).

figuring out how to get along and how to make it."[8] From the organization's point of view, it is a process of "induction, basic training, and socialization of the individual to the major norms and values of the organization."[9] If the organization conducts an orientation program, it takes place at this point and helps to further the employee's socialization.

EXHIBIT 8.2

Schein's socialization model

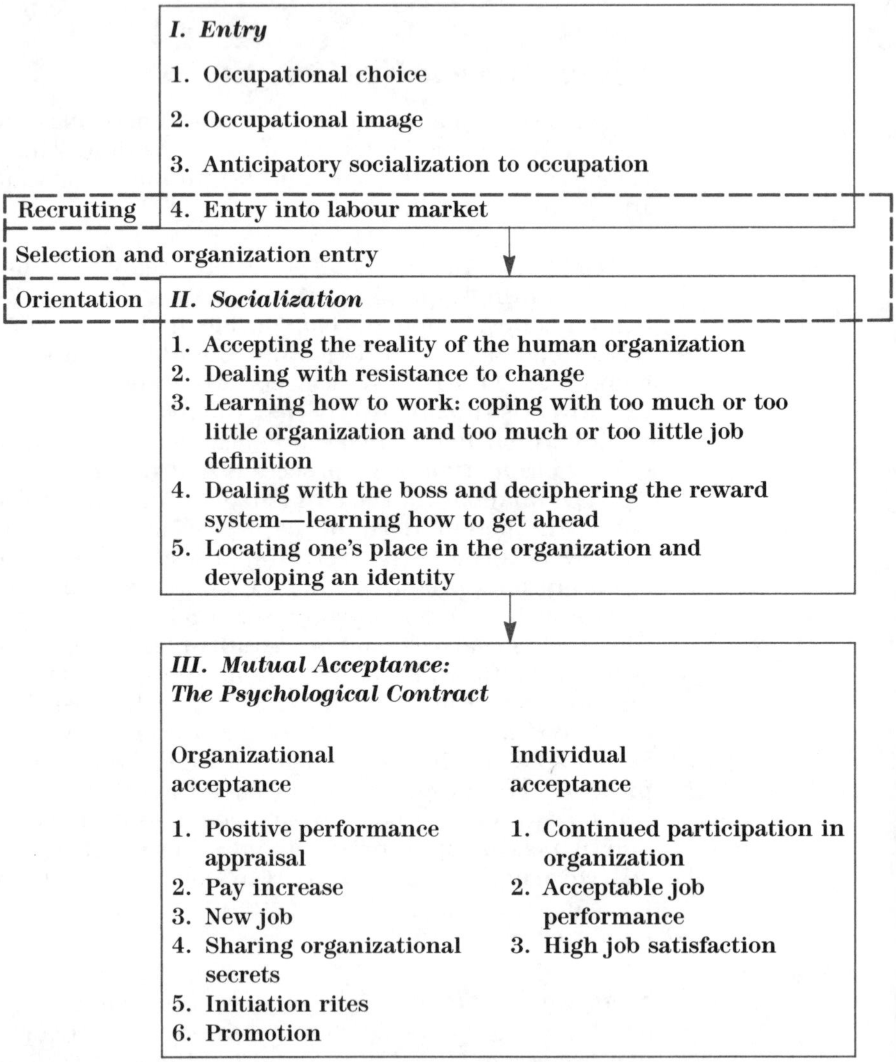

I. Entry

1. Occupational choice
2. Occupational image
3. Anticipatory socialization to occupation
4. Entry into labour market

Recruiting

Selection and organization entry

Orientation

II. Socialization

1. Accepting the reality of the human organization
2. Dealing with resistance to change
3. Learning how to work: coping with too much or too little organization and too much or too little job definition
4. Dealing with the boss and deciphering the reward system—learning how to get ahead
5. Locating one's place in the organization and developing an identity

III. Mutual Acceptance: The Psychological Contract

Organizational acceptance	Individual acceptance
1. Positive performance appraisal	1. Continued participation in organization
2. Pay increase	2. Acceptable job performance
3. New job	3. High job satisfaction
4. Sharing organizational secrets	
5. Initiation rites	
6. Promotion	

[8] J. Van Maanen, "Breaking In: A Consideration of Organizational Socialization," in R. Dubin, ed., *Handbook of Work, Organization, and Society* (Chicago: Rand-McNally, 1975).

[9] Schein, p. 81.

As an individual begins his or her first "real" job, there is invariably the experience of reality shock: discovering that it is very different from expectations.[10] Orientation can reduce this gap by better preparing new employees for what they will experience in their first months of employment. For an example of reality shock on Wall Street see Exhibit 8.3.

EXHIBIT 8.3

Reality Shock on Wall Street

When Elaine Ide Wood was hired into the mergers and acquisitions department at Morgan Stanley & Co., Inc. a few years back, she was on top of the world. "I felt tremendous," says Ms. Wood, a Harvard Business School graduate. "It was the ultimate in a high-powered, fast-learning job on Wall Street, and to me, Wall Street was the heartbeat of business."

But after less than two months of analyzing takeover deals, she quit, distressed by the seemingly endless workload. "I want to work 50 hours a week. Sixty hours is fine, and 70 or 80 is okay when there's a project. But working 90 or 100 hours a week just isn't the way I wanted to live my life," she says. Today she's marketing manager for an industrial-robot company.

The appeal of life in Wall Street's fast lane is strong. Lured by the expectations of high salaries, prestige and excitement, top business and law school graduates queue up for jobs at big investment banking and law firms.

The attractions are obvious. Salaries at big Wall Street law firms start at about $50,000. At big securities firms it isn't unusual to find people in their early 30s making $100,000 or more. The rash of mergers and acquisitions, with tales of "poison pills," "white knights" and "shark repellant," adds an aura of glamour to the field.

But chasing just a piece of that glamour can be tiresome. One 32-year-old lawyer says that working on a famous and controversial securities default case means plowing through "hundreds of thousands of documents" to piece together events "in a given department in a given period of time. It's monotonous."

Even the excitement of handling big sums can wear off with time. One 27-year-old was proud to be helping manage a $7 billion money market fund. But after a while he tired of checking rates, making phone calls and reinvesting maturing securities. "Whether it was $1 million or $100 million, the procedure was still the same," he says. He quit when he decided that "except for the tension, a baboon could do what I was doing."

The pressure rarely lets up. "The attitude is 'it's fine you made a million dollars yesterday, but what have you done for me today,' " says a vice president at Salomon Brothers Inc. "It can be fatiguing. If you haven't booked your business for the day, you can't relax." People become preoccupied with their work to the exclusion of all else, he adds. "It's hard to measure yourself in any but the starkest terms: How many millions of dollars have you raised?" he says. "It's a very narrow world."

SOURCE: From "Some Business Grads Learn to Hate Their Glamorous Wall Street Jobs," by Amanda Bennett. Reprinted by permission of the *Wall Street Journal*.

[10] E.C. Hughes, *Men and Their Work* (Giencoe, Ill.: Free Press, 1958).

Schein presents five tasks to be mastered in this stage: (1) accepting the reality of the human organization; (2) dealing with resistance to change; (3) learning how to work: coping with too much or too little organization and too much or too little job definition; (4) dealing with the boss and deciphering the reward system; and (5) locating one's place in the organization and developing an identity.

The first task of Schein's socialization stage is accepting *the reality of the human organization*. Schein's research revealed that a large part of the reality shock of organizational entry came from the fact that new employees expected near-perfection on the part of organizations and the people in them. The reality to be accepted in this early stage of the socialization process is that organizations are not perfect and that a major source of this imperfection is, in fact, the people in the organization. Schein quotes new employees saying, after their first year of employment:

> People are a nuisance . . . .
>
> The number of unproductive people there are in corporations is astounding.
>
> All the problems I encounter boil down to communication and human relations.[11]

The second task of the socialization process is *dealing with resistance to change*. New employees, especially recent graduates of education or training programs, enter their first jobs filled with ideas and knowledge that they are eager to use in solving organizational problems. They expect their employers to be equally eager to have them use their newly acquired knowledge and skills. More often, however, new employees are given relatively routine, unchallenging jobs and told that their ideas and solutions to problems are impractical. Such experiences prove frustrating to many new employees.

The third experience in organizational socialization is *learning how to work: coping with too much or too little organization and too much or too little job definition*. New employees generally expect a reasonable amount of definition and clarity about what they should do in their jobs, as well as a certain amount of feedback on their performance. Schein's research shows that these expectations often go unmet. Frequently, new employees must carve out their own jobs and learn both what to do and how to do it largely on their own. One new employee expressed this frustration as:

> Not knowing whom to ask or what to ask; not knowing what the ball park is . . . the problem of not knowing what it is you need to know.[12]

[11] Schein, pp. 94–95.
[12] Ibid., p. 97.

Of course, some new employees experience the opposite problem: a very tightly defined job with no flexibility for individual abilities and needs. New employees must often learn how to judge their own performance, since feedback from the boss is often inadequate. Again, these organizational realities are particularly frustrating because they are not what the new employee expected.

A fourth task in the socialization process is *dealing with the boss*. Research has shown that the first boss is the most important person in determining a new employee's degree of career success.[13] The boss usually has control over many work opportunities and provides many of the rewards and punishments a new employee receives. A related need of new employees is *deciphering the reward system*. In many organizations, written criteria for promotion or advancement do not provide a realistic description of what it actually takes to get ahead in the organization. Schein found considerable ambiguity among new employees on this point. Some felt "it's whom you know that counts," while others believed "it's who knows you." Some felt advancement depends upon "high visibility, getting along well, being important to the boss," while others said that "you get ahead by having the ability and working hard."[14] Very few orientation programs provide information of this type, but it is clear that new employees want and need it in order to direct their energies accordingly.

The final task in the socialization process is *locating one's place in the organization and developing an identity*. An organization, like any other group, has a status hierarchy in which some people have more power, influence, or prestige than others. Although newcomers invariably lack the status associated with experience in the organization, both old and new employees must learn how much influence and status should be afforded new members. Some organizations, such as Procter & Gamble, give newly hired college graduates kindergarten-like tasks of colouring a map of sales territories. Other organizations may demand 12- to 14-hour workdays. Such bootcamp-like experiences are designed to generate feelings of humility and induce doubt about one's own values and beliefs, therefore increasing receptivity to the organization's values and norms.[15]

Mutual acceptance stage. The third major stage of Schein's socialization model is mutual acceptance. From the time an applicant first makes contact with a prospective employer to the end of the socialization process, some ambiguity, caution, and lack of trust exist between the individual and the organization. The major reason is that neither has complete information about the other's abilities or resources, motives, values, and needs. When the mutual acceptance stage is complete, the new employee and the organization have negotiated a psychological contract indicating their mutual acceptance and trust.

[13] D.W. Bray, R.J. Campbell, and D.L. Grant, *Formative Years in Business* (New York: Wiley, 1974); and D. Berlew and D.T. Hall, "The Socialization of Managers," *Administrative Science Quarterly*, 1966, vol. 11, pp. 207–23.
[14] Schein, p. 99.
[15] Pascale, 1984.

Schein describes this *psychological contract* as a set of expectations held by the employee and the employer regarding pay, rights, privileges, and obligations of the employee to the organization.[16] Certain work behaviour and levels of input into the job and the organization are expected from the employee, and certain outcomes (pay, benefits, rewards, privileges) are expected by the employee for his or her efforts. During the entire socialization process, the new employee, even when still an applicant, is negotiating a psychological contract with the organization. The process is rarely as formal as negotiations between labour and management when a collective agreement is being worked out. Rather, a psychological contract is negotiated over time through interactions between the new employee and other organization members, particularly the boss and co-workers. Organization members communicate to newcomers the behaviour that is expected of all organization members. Underlying this expected behaviour, or *norms*, are *values*, defined as general attitudes and concepts regarding appropriate behaviour which organization members feel are important. An organization has rules, regulations, and procedures designed to ensure that members behave in ways consistent with its norms and values. For example, it may uphold a value of fairness. A corresponding norm of employee behaviour is "a fair day's work for a fair day's pay." The organization could enforce this norm through formal rules specifying standards of production and by informal work-group standards. Values and norms such as this are often major components of an employee's psychological contract.

New employees are eager to learn how hard they must work to satisfy their boss, get a raise, and perhaps earn a promotion. In some cases, co-workers communicate different—usually lower—levels of work norms from those of the boss. In these cases, separate psychological contracts are negotiated with the boss and with co-workers. For example, a psychological contract with the boss might include a higher-than-average level of production in exchange for a good pay raise and his or her approval. The contract with co-workers, on the other hand, might include an average level of production in exchange for their acceptance. Clearly, the two psychological contracts may conflict. If they do, which one the new employee chooses as pre-eminent depends on his or her needs and values.

The psychological contract requires a sense of fairness or equity in the relationship between employer and employee in terms of what each gives and receives. An employee may or may not feel that the amount or quality of work expected by the boss is fair in terms of what the organization is willing to provide in pay, benefits, and other rewards. However, to achieve mutual acceptance, both employer and employee must feel that the ratio of exchange is fair. The psychological contract for this exchange, negotiated during the socialization process, defines what employer and employee expect of each other in the future. Violation of the contract by either party is likely to lead to voluntary or involuntary termination.

[16] Ibid.

New employees are also eager to receive from their boss or other organization members signs of their acceptance into the organization. Schein lists six events as signs of an organization's acceptance of a new employee:

1. A positive first performance appraisal.
2. A pay increase.
3. A new job assignment.
4. Sharing of organizational secrets, such as how others evaluate the new employee and how the organization "really" works.
5. "Initiation rites," such as a party.
6. A promotion.[17]

Although each of these events signals organizational acceptance, promotion carries the most weight.

Socialization is a gradual process that can require several years' work in an organization. Therefore, even the most ambitious and effective orientation program cannot be expected to socialize the new employee completely.

"Social Orientation": The Texas Instruments Experiment

It has been suggested that orientation should help reduce employees' anxieties about a new job and a new organization. A study on orientation conducted at Texas Instruments in the mid-1960s has become a classic because there have been very few, if any, other experiments on the subject.[18] Texas Instruments felt that its new female assemblers were anxious about whether they could be successful on the job. Experienced employees did not make the situation any easier; they subjected the newcomers to hazing, which made them even more anxious. Texas Instruments decided to try a different type of orientation, a social orientation designed to reduce anxiety, increase new employees' performance, and reduce turnover, which was high in the first few months of employment.

A control group of new employees was given the traditional two-hour orientation; a test group received that program plus an additional six hours of social orientation. The latter focussed on four major areas.

1. Employees were assured that their chances of succeeding on the job were good. Data were presented demonstrating that 99 per cent of employees reached production standards. The point was made many times during the orientation period that everyone in the group would be successful.
2. New employees were warned about the hazing they would receive; they were told to take it in good humour and not let it bother them.

[17] Ibid.

[18] Gommersall and Myers.

3. Employees were told to take the initiative in communicating with their supervisors. It was stressed that they should raise problems or questions even if they appeared stupid or silly and even if the supervisor was busy.
4. New employees were encouraged to get to know the boss. Just as students ask other students about what type of person a professor is, employees like to know something about their boss. The Texas Instruments experiment provided new employees with a short personality sketch of each supervior, including hobbies, interests, and managerial style.

Texas Instruments reported very positive results from the social orientation. Training time in the experimental group was reduced by 50 per cent, training costs by 66 per cent, waste by 80 per cent, product costs by 15 to 30 per cent, and tardiness and absenteeism by 50 per cent.[19] More recent reports indicate that management at Texas Instruments credits social orientation for a 40 per cent drop in early career turnover since the program began.[20] Texas Instruments' orientation seminars are now distributed worldwide in seven different languages. They also served as a model for Corning Glass Works' orientation system that is described later in the chapter.

Realistic Job Previews: Their Application to Orientation

One technique for reducing reality shock is *realistic job previews* (RJPS), which communicate to an applicant or new employee what it will actually be like to work for a company and perform a certain job. The idea of providing job applicants or new hires with information about what their jobs will *really* be like has existed since the mid-1950s, when a researcher mailed booklets describing actual job experiences of insurance agents to agent applicants.[21] However, not until the 1970s did J. P. Wanous popularize the concept of realistic job previews.[22]

RJPS can be developed in a number of ways. The most common is to interview current employees, asking them to relate actual experiences (good and bad) and state their attitudes towards the job. Another is to film or videotape employees at work and ask them for comments. The information provided in a well-done RJP is not all positive; employees are encouraged to describe some of their problems and frustrations. This information is presented to applicants or new employees verbally or in films, videotapes, or booklets.

[19] Ibid.

[20] McGarrell, 1983.

[21] J. Weitz, "Job Expectancy and Survival," *Journal of Applied Psychology*, 1956, vol. 40, pp. 245–47.

[22] J.P. Wanous, "Effects of a Realistic Job Preview on Job Acceptance, Job Attitudes, and Job Survival," *Journal of Applied Psychology*, 1973, vol. 58, pp. 327–32; and "Organizational Entry: Newcomers Moving from Outside to Inside," *Psychological Bulletin*, 1977, vol, 84, pp. 601–18.

Research shows that RJPS lower job expectations without completely "turning off" applicants to jobs. Additionally, RJP advocates argue that previews create more positive job attitudes and reduce turnover. Wanous's review of a number of studies found some support for this position.[23]

McShane and Baal relate the following RJP experience which was described to them by a machinery distribution company in British Columbia:

> Recruits from the Lower Mainland and other areas of British Columbia had for some time been shown a film of the company's operations on the north coast. Since the film was shot on one of the few sunny days in the northern raintown community, the new hires looked forward to the beautiful scenery, recreation, and work—all in sunny weather. When they were stationed in raintown, however, the chilling and unexpected realities of the dreary weather was too much for many with the result that turnover was very high. This, in turn, cost the firm dearly in lower productivity and high recruiting/selection expenses.
>
> Following the literature on realistic job previews (Wanous, 1980) the company replaced the unrealistic film on raintown with a more realistic one which was taken on a rainy day. The result has been a dramatic reduction in turnover with corresponding higher productivity and lower personnel costs. In fact, employees who have been shown the new film claim that the weather is not nearly so bad as they had originally expected because there is the occasional sunny day.[24]

From a cost/benefit standpoint, it is advantageous for employers to provide applicants with realistic job previews as early in the employment process as possible. If applicants have a realistic perception of the jobs they are applying for, they are in a better position to determine if they would be a good match. An organization can save selection, hiring, and start-up costs if an applicant discovers early in the process that a poor match exists. RJPS need not be used exclusively *before* hiring, however; using them afterwards, as part of the orientation process, provides benefits as well.

Orientation Programs and Procedures

Most organizations have some type of orientation procedure. One survey of 196 North American organizations found that 86 per cent offered

[23] Wanous, "Organizational Entry"; and J.P. Wanous, *Organization Entry: Recruitment, Selection, and Socialization of Newcomers* (Reading, Mass.: Addison-Wesley, 1980).

[24] S.L. McShane and T. Baal, *Employee Socialization Practices on Canada's West Coast: A Management Report* (Burnaby, B.C.: Simon Fraser University, December 1984.)

some type of orientation. In over half the organizations, these included formal orientation sessions.[25]

Formal Orientation Sessions

Formal orientation sessions are developed and conducted by HRM departments and tend to last one to four hours. Like CanTèque's program, they generally include presentations by HRM professionals, audio visual presentations, distribution of written materials, and company tours. Almost all formal orientation sessions cover the following topics:

1. Employee benefits
2. Services for employees
3. Company products or services
4. Company rules and regulations
5. Company organization
6. Training and promotion
7. Company history

It is interesting that most organizations have the same formal orientation session for all employees, regardless of job level.[26]

There is considerable variation among employers regarding the frequency of formal orientation sessions. According to the above survey, almost equal numbers conduct sessions "as needed," "weekly," and "bimonthly or monthly." More than half hold orientation on an employee's first day at work. Typically, fewer than 30 new employees attend a formal orientation session, with more than half the surveyed organizations reporting attendance in groups of no more than 15.[27]

Informal Orientation Procedures

Informal orientation procedures are used by organizations that do not have formal sessions. Responsibility for orientation in this case is shared by the HRM department and an employee's immediate supervisor. New employees are often instructed to report to the HRM department for an explanation of company policies before being referred to the supervisor for an on-the-job briefing about specific work procedures. HRM professionals generally provide the new hire with written materials such as insurance and benefit brochures, employee handbooks, copies of rules and regulations, company newspapers and magazines. These sessions tend to be brief, according to the above survey—one hour or less in nearly half the surveyed organizations.

[25] Bureau of National Affairs, "ASPA-BNA Survey No. 32 Employee Orientation Programs," *Bulletin to Management*, August 25, 1977.

[26] Ibid.; and McShane and Baal, 1984.

[27] Bureau of National Affairs.

Organizations with informal orientation procedures often rely on checklists of topics to be discussed with the new employee. Checklists are used by the HRM department, the supervisor, or both, and serve to document the new employee's having been informed of company policies, rules, and benefit options. One small manufacturing company provides its supervisors with the following instructions for using a detailed checklist: "All supervisors will review with each new employee the general guidelines of performance, expected duties, and the supervisor's own personal philosophy during the first few days of employment. Preferably, the checklist should be completed the first day, and under no circumstances more than five days from the date of hire. The employee will sign the form after it has been discussed and give it to the supervisor for inclusion in his/her personnel folder."[28]

Other informal orientation procedures include giving special orientation instruction to supervisors, briefing present employees before the arrival of a new employee, and choosing present employees as "buddies" for the new employee.

Combining Formal and Informal Procedures

Many organizations combine formal and informal procedures in their orientation programs. Typically, such programs provide a formal orientation session in conjunction with more informal, on-the-job orientation by supervisors. A sophisticated combined approach is used at Corning Glass Works.[29] Corning's orientation system is a long-term, nine-stage program which combines formal sessions and seminars with on-the-job orientation by supervisors. Corning's system is unlike many combined approaches in that on-the-job orientation is highly formalized. The system is described in Exhibit 8.4.

Orientation at Corning begins prior to employment with distribution of orientation materials and pre-arrival contacts. The first day's orientation activities are not unlike those of other organizations, including reading of an employee workbook, taking a tour of the building, and meeting co-workers. But unlike many organizations, including CanTèque, orientation at Corning does not end after Day 1. In fact, the entire first week of a new hire's employment at Corning is spent getting to know the supervisor, co-workers, the job, and the organization. Workbook questions guide the employee's learning. During this time also, employee and supervisor work together to set performance goals for the coming six months. Regular assignments begin in the second week of employment, and in the third and fourth weeks, the new hire attends a community seminar and an employee benefits seminar. During the second through fifth month of employment, the new hire attends six more seminars on a variety of work-related topics, again answering questions in the workbook. Answers to workbook questions are reviewed with the supervisor. During this period, biweekly progress

[28] Ibid.
[29] McGarrell, 1983.

reviews are held with the supervisor. In the sixth month, workbook answers are completed and performance goals are reviewed with the supervisor. Phase I orientation is over and the new hire is awarded a certification of completion. Phase II orientation begins and continues through the fifteenth month of employment.

EXHIBIT 8.4

Corning's orientation system

Timetable Events in Corning's Orientation System

Material distribution. As soon as possible after a hiring decision is made, orientation material is distributed:

- The new person's supervisor gets a pamphlet titled *A Guide for Supervisors*.
- The new person gets an orientation plan.

The pre-arrival period. During this period the supervisor maintains contact with the new person, helps with housing problems, designs the job and makes a preliminary MBO (management by objectives) list after discussing this with the new person, gets the office ready, notifies the organization that this has been done, and sets the interview schedule.

The first day. On this important day, the new employee has breakfast with his or her supervisor, goes through processing in the personnel department, attends a *Corning and You* seminar, has lunch with the seminar leader, reads the workbook for new employees, is given a tour of the building, and is introduced to co-workers.

The first week. During this week, the new employee (1) has one-to-one interviews with the supervisor, co-workers, and specialists; (2) learns the how-tos, wheres, and whys connected with the job; (3) answers questions in the workbook: (4) gets settled in the community; and (5) participates with the supervisor in firming up the MBO plan.

The second week. The new person begins regular assignments.

The third and fourth weeks. The new person attends a community seminar and an employee benefits seminar (a spouse or guest may be invited).

The second through the fifth month. During this period, assignments are intensified and the new person has biweekly progress reviews with his or her supervisor, attends six two-hour seminars at intervals (on quality and productivity, technology, performance management and salaried compensation plans, financial and strategic management, employee relations, and EEO and social change), answers workbook questions about each seminar, and reviews answers with the supervisor.

The sixth month. The new employee completes the workbook questions, reviews the MBO list with the supervisor, participates in a performance review with the supervisor, receives a certification of completion for Phase I orientation, and makes plans for Phase II orientation.

The seventh through the 15th months. This period features Phase II orientation: division orientation, function orientation, education programs, MBO reviews, performance reviews, and salary reviews.

SOURCE: "An Orientation System That Builds Productivity," by E. J. McGarrell, Jr. Reprinted by permission of the publisher, from *Personnel* (Issue: Nov.–Dec./83, pp. 32–41), American Management Association, New York.

Corning's program uses many techniques to help socialize new employees, including interviews, seminars, and workbooks. Information is provided intermittently, rather than in one big chunk, facilitating learning by reducing information overload. New hires at Corning receive frequent periodic feedback from supervisors so they can measure their progress and learn what is valued in the organization. Because ultimate responsibility for orienting employees lies with the supervisor, all supervisors attend a three-hour training workshop on orientation.

Orientation in Practice

Research on orientation practices in organizations is extremely limited, but a recent study by McShane and Baal documents socialization practices on Canada's West Coast.[30] The study focussed on 85 of British Columbia's largest public and private corporations, employing a total of 200,000 employees in B.C. and 600,000 across Canada. Thirty of the organizations had no orientation program; new hires simply reported for work, were documented by the personnel or HRM department, and started their jobs immediately. Twenty-three of the companies had what the authors described as a "basic" orientation program, though 12 of these were "marginal." Basic orientation programs included components such as company brochures, information about wages and benefits, an explanation of the job, an overview of the company and the new hire's place, assignment of a buddy to smooth the way, a formal performance review and the practice of ongoing feedback. Thirty-two companies had "advanced" orientation programs. These included basic ingredients plus others, such as use of various media, tours, representation of top management, continuation into the work week, program evaluation by new hires, among others.

Orientation programs were more likely in firms with large numbers of employees and high corporate sales. They were least likely in manufacturing, processing, product transportation, mining, forestry, and energy industries. Advanced programs were most prevalent in the wholesale-retail sector of the economy and in both public and private service sectors, including government, hospitals, educational institutions, finance, insurance, communications, and people transportation.

Of the 55 companies in the study with formal programs, 87 per cent offered orientation to all employees. Most began orientation on the first day of employment or within the first two weeks. Sixty per cent said they conduct orientation "all at once," in one big session ranging from one hour (10 per cent) to 4 hours (39 per cent) to one day (16 per cent). Slightly over one-third said orientation lasts two to five days (14 per cent) or one week or more (22 per cent). Two-thirds of the programs included follow-up sessions a month or more later to demonstrate interest in the new employee and to elicit concerns and opinions.

[30] McShane and Baal, 1984.

It is not clear how many of these programs served to reduce anxieties of new employees. Only a few of the companies used any type of realistic job preview or tried to clarify expectations in some form of psychological contract. It is clear, however, that much information was conveyed to new hires regarding the organization and their place in it. As Corning and others have found, orientation is an excellent vehicle for communicating corporate culture.[31] Several common corporate themes emerged during orientation in the B.C. companies. These included the values of teamwork, a pioneering spirit, an emphasis on people, and an emphasis on the customer.[32]

Most orientation programs in the B.C. companies were established by HRM professionals who also had responsibility for conducting orientation programs. While HRM professionals coordinated programs and provided information about the company, supervisors tended to be responsible for introducing new employees to the job and new department. Current employees played a role in orientation too, though this was found to vary with the job and with whether the company had a formal orientation program. Where no formal program existed, current employees often showed new hires around. Buddy systems, which team a new hire with an experienced employee, were often used to orient employees in the retail sector.

Evaluation of Orientation Programs

We have seen that HRM professionals are responsible for developing and conducting orientation programs, including preparing and presenting orientation materials. HRM professionals may also train or instruct supervisors for their role in orientation, but this is considered a training function. Orientation programs should be evaluated to determine whether they are accomplishing their stated objectives, and this is also a responsibility of HRM professionals. In order to evaluate their programs, many organizations solicit feedback from new hires at the end of orientation sessions. Seventy per cent of B.C. organizations with formal orientation programs do this either informally or via a questionnaire.[33] Follow-up sessions may offer a better opportunity to elicit feedback from new hires about program effectiveness. By this time they have been on the job for a month or more and have a better perspective from which to judge a program's strengths and weaknesses. Opinions can also be elicited in exit interviews. This source is especially useful in cases of early termination.

[31] McGarrell, 1983.
[32] McShane and Baal, 1984.
[33] Ibid.

Program effectiveness can also be measured against such criteria as training time and turnover rates. For example, Corning measures results of its orientation system by comparing quit rates of two groups of 1981–82 hires: those who attended the orientation seminars and those who did not.[34]

Summary

This chapter has focussed on orientation and how it can serve organizational effectiveness by helping to facilitate socialization of new employees. Effective orientation programs help to reduce anxieties, clarify expectations, and give new employees a sense of the overall organization and where they fit in. While most organizations use some type of orientation procedures, including formal orientation sessions, it is likely that many organizations scratch only the tip of the socialization iceberg. The experiences of Texas Instruments and Corning Glass Works demonstrate the impact orientation can have on organizational effectiveness.

Project Ideas

1. Recall when you became a new member of an organization or group. What type of orientation did you receive? How long did it last? What types of experiences did you have during this time? How did you feel about them? How did you know when you were an "accepted member"? Could your orientation and socialization period have been improved? How? Be prepared to discuss your experiences with other class members.

2. Contact two or three organizations and obtain copies of their employee handbooks. (If handbooks are not available, obtain copies of company rules and policies.) What kinds of information are conveyed in the handbooks? What types of employee behaviour are regulated by company rules and policies? Discuss these questions in a written report, and compare the organizations in terms of their philosophies, policies, rules, and procedures.

3. Interview an employer about his or her organization's orientation program. Obtain a description of its nature and goals. Does the employer regard the program as successful? Do formal procedures exist for evaluating it? Include with your report any written materials available about the program.

[34] McGarrell, 1983.

Cases

Case 8.1: White-Collar Shock for a Blue-Collar Worker

It is 5 P.M. and Frank LaRue is in his small office cubicle (no window, no door) working feverishly on his first computer programming project for Development Tech, a management and human resources consulting firm of 46 employees. LaRue is in the third week of a three-month internship with Development Tech. LaRue hasn't slept in three nights. He is a driven man—a man with something to prove. His boss said so himself on LaRue's first day at work.

"You're going to have to prove yourself, son," he said. "I'd prefer to hire a college grad for this job."

LaRue was determined to prove himself, but unsure how to do it. If there were rules for getting ahead at Development Tech, they certainly weren't well-publicized. Even his job description was less than explicit. The lack of job definition made LaRue uneasy. He was used to having every detail of the employment relationship spelled out under union contract.

LaRue, age 25, would probably still be working as a steelworker if Neptune Steel hadn't had to lay him off. For LaRue, working in the steel mills was a family tradition. His father, his uncle, and his cousins before him had all worked for Neptune Steel. LaRue enjoyed being a part of a team that produced such an important commodity as steel. He didn't even mind the work, though it was hot and hazardous in "the hole" where he and three others banded hot strips of steel onto a hot-strip rolling machine. The atmosphere at Neptune was relaxed despite the job's hazards and a guy could say almost anything and get away with it. At the end of his eight-hour shift, LaRue typically forgot about work and went drinking with his buddies.

But that was yesterday. Today, after completing a 14-month course in computer programming (and graduating at the top of his class), LaRue sits hunched at his desk trying to "make it" in a white-collar world of deadlines and headaches. The work is challenging, intense, anything but relaxing, and the workplace is different from any he's ever known.

LaRue admits he sometimes feels "like a refugee trying to adjust to a new country." He seldom knows what to expect and rarely knows what is expected. Consequently, he does what he's told and says as little as possible. Relationships with co-workers are strained. LaRue fears some colleagues will never accept him because he's been labelled a "labourer," and "once a labourer, always a labourer." Even if his colleagues did accept him, LaRue isn't sure they could ever be "buddies" because of the competitive climate at Development Tech. LaRue used to work on a cooperative team, but here he's on his own competing against "the other guy" for limited rewards and promotions. LaRue isn't sure he likes such a system. Seniority was easier to live with. You just waited your turn like everybody else and eventually you moved up in the organization. In the meantime, you could all go out for a beer.

LaRue sighs and packs up his briefcase. He knows he has a long night ahead of him if he's going to finish his program by tomorrow, a week ahead of schedule. Like the boss said, he's got a lot to prove.

Questions:

1. How does the work environment at Development Tech differ from Neptune Steel? Consider the reasons behind differences between the two employers.
2. In your opinion, how good are LaRue's chances of "making it" at Development Tech (i.e., of being retained after his internship)? Do you think LaRue will choose to stay if given the chance? Cite evidence to support your opinions.
3. What economic, labour market, and personal factors might influence the above retention decisions? How might a good orientation program help to facilitate retention in this case?
4. Design an orientation program for computer programmers at Development Tech. Include special features to help socialize new hires like LaRue who come from a "blue-collar" background.

NOTE: This fictionalized account is based on C. Hymowitz, "Culture Shock Affects Steelworker Who Switched to White-Collar Job," *Wall Street Journal*, June 1, 1983.

Case 8.2: Firefighting Drop-Outs

One hundred firefighters are employed by the fire department of River Falls, which has three stations in the city of nearly 70,000. The department's record is good: its inspection and prevention program has reduced fire hazards substantially and it has received commendation from the mayor for promptness of response to emergencies and for firefighting effectiveness. Morale and esprit de corps run high among River Falls' firefighters; they are a proud, cohesive bunch who often socialize with one another in their "off" hours.

Applicants for the fire department's few annual openings must score well on a battery of firefighting knowledge tests, rigorous physical and agility tests, and an interview by a board of city officials including the fire chief and one experienced firefighter. Applicants are hired on a six-month probationary basis; their performance is rated after one, three, and six months by the lieutenant and captain of their station. New firefighters undergo rigorous training, but receive only a short orientation including a tour of fire department facilities and a discussion of daily schedules.

The human resources director of River Falls, Roger Cameron, has noticed that between 15 and 20 per cent of newly hired firefighters do not survive the probationary period. Cameron, who has been at River Falls just over two years, first noticed this phenomenon six months ago when he interviewed Georgio Candino, a firefighter who quit after two and half months. As a job applicant, Candino had performed well on both ability and physical tests and had good interview ratings. Candino didn't have much to say at the time of his exit interview, except to suggest that he had not been well accepted by the other firefighters.

This incident made Cameron curious. He checked personnel records for the five years previous and found six additional quits and two dismissals of firefighters within the probationary period. Records also showed a number of complaints regarding tricks played on new firefighters, such as salted orange juice, boots lined with sludge, and fake assignments. For example, it was common practice to tell recruits they were being sent to fight a fire, when actually they were being sent to help a cat out of a tree. The department generally ignored such complaints, viewing the pranks as a natural part of the initiation process.

Cameron noticed that most such complaints were filed by firefighters who quit or were dismissed during the probationary period. While many of the tricks were harmless attempts to humiliate or "test" new recruits, some were potentially hazardous to a firefighter's safety. For example, Candino had once had the middle finger cut off one of his safety gloves. Another time, a firefighter reached for his hat only to find it had been used as a bedpan.

Where matters of safety were concerned, the department generally took notice; more than once in the past it had posted a cautionary warning that, where safety was concerned, disciplinary action would be taken against the offender. This was never done, however, because the department was unable to identify the responsible party; no one would admit to pulling the pranks and group norms made "squealing" unthinkable.

Cameron realizes that hazing is a common part of initiating new members to organizations and groups, but he wonders if something should be done about it in the fire department.

Questions:

1. What key questions might Cameron seek answers to in order to determine whether something should be done about hazing in the fire department?
2. Assume you are Cameron and weigh the pros and cons of hazing new firefighters. Why might experienced firefighters want to haze recruits?
3. What actions might Cameron take to control hazing or minimize its effect on new firefighters?
4. What effects might rules regulating hazing have on new firefighters, experienced firefighters, and the fire department as a whole?

9

Training and Development

Chapter 8 introduced Jane Simpson, a new shipping clerk at CanTèque Electronics. Simpson has no experience. What information she has about her job was conveyed in the classified ad she responded to and in a subsequent employment interview with CanTèque. Simpson will have a better idea of what her job entails after talking with her supervisor and receiving some on-the-job training.

Training is defined as any organizationally planned effort to change the behaviour or attitudes of employees so that they can perform to acceptable standards on the job. In Jane Simpson's case, training consists of a four-step process known as *job instruction training.* For each task that Simpson must learn, she is: (1) told how to do it; (2) shown how to do it; (3) asked to perform it herself; and (4) given a review of her performance. If Simpson makes an error, the four steps are repeated until she learns the correct behaviour.

On-the-job training is very common for new employees in many organizations. However, training is not limited to on-the-job situations. New police officers often attend police training academies before being assigned to duty. Management trainees usually receive a combination of classroom and on-the-job training.

In addition, current employees often require training when jobs are changed to include new equipment, procedures, responsibilities, or performance standards; when employees are promoted or transferred within the organization; and when performance appraisals or other quality control measures indicate the existence of a problem caused by lack of knowledge or by skill deficiency. Training can also prepare employees for future positions in the organization. For example, assistant managers are often groomed for the position of manager. This type of training is known as *development*. Because many employees value growth, some development opportunities are provided more as an employee benefit than to meet organizational needs for qualified workers.

Training and Development: An Area of Growth

Training has always been vital to organizations since it is one means of maintaining acceptable levels of employee and organizational performance. HRM's responsibility for training and development has grown over the past ten or 20 years and will probably become increasingly important. A survey by Statistics Canada estimated that 7.9 per cent of all paid workers in Canada in 1973 had received employer-sponsored training.[1] By 1978, a study of 12,041 establishments found that 15.1 per cent of their employees had received such training; it was most common for executive, managerial, and professional workers (23.7 per cent), followed by office workers (14.8 per cent).[2] Another demonstration of growth in the amount and importance of training was the 1979 founding of the Canadian Society for Training and Development, whose sustaining members are earlier-established provincial societies in British Columbia, Alberta, Manitoba, Ontario, and Atlantic Canada. Most recently, training in "people skills," including communicating and getting along with others, has come into vogue. In 1980, only a few firms in Canada specialized in teaching these skills; now there are hundreds, generating annual revenues of $150 million (up from $38 million in 1978).[3]

Clearly, training is a booming business. Five factors help to explain its rise in importance:

1. The creation of new jobs and the obsolescence of existing ones caused by the rapid rate of technological change.

[1] Statistics Canada, *The Labour Force*, cat. no. 71–001 (Ottawa, January 1975).
[2] R.J. Adams, *Education and Working Canadians*, Report of the Commission of Inquiry on Educational Leave and Productivity, Labour Canada (Ottawa: Minister of Supply and Services Canada, 1979), p. 149.
[3] G. Allen, "Politics in the Office," *Maclean's*, July 15, 1985, pp. 32–6.

2. Management attitudes towards maximizing available human resources.
3. Employees' expectations of challenge and growth opportunities on the job.
4. Human rights legislation and a growing awareness of the need to provide opportunities for women, native people, and immigrants.
5. The existence of government-funded training programs.

First, the rapid rate of technological change from the early 1960s to the early 1980s has created many new jobs and rendered many old ones obsolete. The 1971 *Canadian Classification and Dictionary of Occupations* contained 25,000 job titles, a net increase of 9,000 over the occupations classified in 1961.[4] New jobs often create a need for acquisition of new knowledge and skills, and training can meet this need. Further, as technological advances make jobs obsolete, displaced workers often need to be trained or retrained so they can remain in the work force. Planning for the retraining and employment needs of workers displaced because of job obsolescence is called *redundancy planning*.

The second factor explaining the growth of training and development is management attitudes towards human resources. In the past, when labour was abundant and relatively inexpensive, it was possible to hire and fire employees to meet changes in the quantity and types of labour needed. Today, however, shortages of some types of labour and the rising costs of the employment process encourage management to maximize available human resources. The result is a new human resource strategy that emphasizes training and development programs to provide current employees with the skills and knowledge necessary to meet the organization's changing job requirements.

A training and development strategy was adopted recently by Xerox Corporation. Faced with the need to be innovative, Xerox implemented an intense, nine-month program to prepare 29 carefully-selected redundant technical support people for jobs in either electronic or computer engineering, or computer science. This approach not only helped solve redundancy problems at Xerox, it also helped meet critical labour shortages and provided growth and advancement opportunities for certain valued workers.[5] Training and development will continue to grow in importance as the "baby bust" of the 1960s reduces the supply of new labour force entrants in the 1980s and 1990s and as immigration becomes a less likely source of skilled workers.

Also contributing to the growth of training and development is the attitude of employees, who have come to expect more than a well-paying, secure job. Partly because of increased education and the influence of mass media, today's workers expect challenging jobs with

[4] Canada Employment and Immigration Commission, *Canadian Classification and Dictionary of Occupations*, vol. 1 (Ottawa: Information Canada, 1971).

[5] R.A. Morano and N. Deets, "Professional Retraining: Meeting the Technological Challenge," *Training and Development Journal*, May 1985, pp. 99–101.

opportunities for upward mobility and growth. Thus, jobs tend to be viewed as a first step of a career, rather than as an end in themselves. In this sense, training and development become employee benefits, preparing individuals for better jobs in the organization.

The increasing attention paid to various special groups in society has added to the growth of training programs. Human rights legislation forbids discrimination against women, members of ethnic minorities, and other groups in providing training and development. The need to accommodate various kinds of people enlarges the demand for training programs. So does the relatively high proportion of recent immigrants in many local labour markets. The National Training Act of 1982 contains a wide range of provisions to expand skill training for the unemployed, youth, women, native people, and persons with physical disabilities.

Finally, training has grown with the increasing availability of federal government funding for it. In 1960, Ottawa introduced new federal-provincial cost-sharing programs; the amount spent on technical training through them between 1960 and 1965 was six times what had been spent in the previous 40 years.[6] Since then, legislation and programs have come and gone, but the direction has always been towards more training; in 1979–80, the federal government spent $669.7 million on various training programs involving 309,463 persons, more than half of whom were in full-time programs.[7] In 1980, the existence of skills shortages at a time of high unemployment prompted the establishment of two federal task forces; their reports made somewhat different recommendations, but they agreed on the need for increased training opportunities.[8]

Contribution to Organizational Effectiveness

Training and development provide employees with the knowledge and skills they need to remain qualified for their jobs. Periodic training is often necessary because the nature of a job may change to include new responsibilities, performance standards, equipment, or work methods. For many jobs, training and development are essential simply to keep abreast of current developments in the field. A case in point is HRM professionals' continuing need to be informed of changing legal

[6] N.M. Meltz, "Manpower and Immigration Policy," in Lawrence H. Officer and Laurence B. Smith, eds., *Issues in Canadian Economies* (Toronto: McGraw-Hill Ryerson, 1974).

[7] Employment and Immigration Canada, *Annual Statistical Bulletin 1979–80, Canada Manpower Training Program*, cat. no. WH-7-088E (Ottawa, December 1980).

[8] D. Dodge, *Labour Market Development in the 1980's*, Report of the Task Force on Labour Market Development, Employment and Immigration Canada (Ottawa: Minister of Supply and Services Canada, 1981); and W. Allmand, *Work for Tomorrow*, Report of the Parliamentary Task Force on Employment Opportunities in the '80's (Ottawa: Minister of Supply and Services Canada, 1981).

requirements and of new techniques and methods for dealing with the various HRM functions. Training is also often necessary in order to remain qualified because integral skills may be rarely used on the job. For example, a police officer must periodically take target practice to maintain skill in using a gun.

Besides assuring a qualified work force, training and development can increase organizational effectiveness by helping to raise many employees' performance capabilities beyond merely acceptable levels. A more skilled labour force allows an emloyer to adopt advanced technologies and higher production standards. Depending on an organization's philosophy, type of business, and size, an emphasis on training and development can be more cost-effective than alternative approaches, such as simplifying jobs or recruiting quality employees from other employers. Xerox's Critical Skills Retraining Program, described above, resulted in substantial savings, compared to the alternatives of reductions in force, relocation, redeployment, and recruitment.[9]

The availability of training and development opportunities can facilitate recruiting. Training and development can also be an important employee benefit for the retention of workers who value opportunities for growth and advancement. To the extent training is effective at raising performance levels, there should also be less need to dismiss employees for unacceptable performance.

Management may also seek to improve effectiveness of their organization via a program of organization development (OD), which makes use of various types of training methods. *Organization development* is a long-term process of changing employees' attitudes and behaviour so that members of the organization can interact better. By improving interpersonal relations within the organization, OD seeks to improve the effectiveness of an organization's operation and its ability to cope with change. Organization development programs are usually part of a larger program to create major changes in an organization. In such organization change programs, outside consultants and top management work with HRM managers to develop and implement training and OD programs. Some employers have instituted OD programs to improve employee relations, deter unionization, and reduce turnover.

One successful OD program used a variety of training methods and devices to reduce excessive turnover among blue-collar workers.[10] As part of an initial diagnosis of the company's ills, an investigation by outside consultants revealed that workers were troubled by poor pay and unsympathetic management. A first step, then, was for consultants to give managers feedback on worker attitudes in these areas. Based on this discussion, managers decided they should participate in a two-day team building workshop to gain a more accurate picture of themselves and how they were seen by others. This workshop made use of a number of exercises, as well as the modelling of pertinent behaviours. After the team building workshop, a supervisory skills workshop was

[9] Morano and Deets, 1985.

[10] J.E. Hautaluoma and J.F. Gavin, "Effects of Organizational Diagnosis and Intervention on Blue-Collar Blues," *Journal of Applied Behavioral Science*, 1975, vol. 11, pp. 475–98.

held for production managers who were very high in the unpopular "Theory X" (autocratic) management style. These managers explored different supervisory styles via lecture-discussions and films, then role-played critical incidents at the plant. A number of blue-collar workers attended the workshop (but did not participate), and it was helpful for them to see their supervisors making honest attempts to improve. The authors who reported on this program noted a marked reduction in turnover among employees with a tenure of one month or more. They also noted much more positive job attitudes as a result of the intervention. However, some of the increased satisfaction may have resulted from pay raises that were approved during the time of intervention.

Relation to Other HRM *Functions*

Exhibit 9.1 demonstrates the relationship of training and development to other HRM functions. For new employees, training follows orientation and precedes performance review. For current employees, performance appraisals often precede training by serving to identify those with performance deficiencies who could benefit from training and those whose potential makes them candidates for development.

Four HRM functions are directly related to training and development: job analysis, performance appraisal, selection, and career planning. Job analysis describes the activities and behaviours necessary to perform a job. The objective of the training program is to master these activities and behaviours. For example, according to the job description of a shipping clerk, Jane Simpson must pack parts for shipment. Thus, one objective of Simpson's training program is to master part-packing. The performance appraisal function, by specifying acceptable standards of performance, prescribes the level of performance necessary to master the required behaviour or activity. If a performance criterion were attached to Simpson's training objective, it might read: employee must be able to pack parts for shipment *at the rate of six per minute without causing any breakage*. The italicized portion of this objective indicates the level of performance necessary to master the required activity.

After training and some time on the job, an employee's performance is usually evaluated. Such appraisals can serve as criteria for measuring the success of training programs. If, for example, after three months' employment Simpson is having difficulty performing her duties, this may indicate that her training program was not altogether successful. Of course, her poor performance may be caused by factors unrelated to the training program. For example, she may be poorly motivated, or perhaps her job is too difficult and should be simplified.

Selection information can be used to identify and place employees in appropriate training programs. For example, test scores or interviews often reveal strengths and weaknesses of newly hired employees.

EXHIBIT 9.1

Training and development: relation to other functions

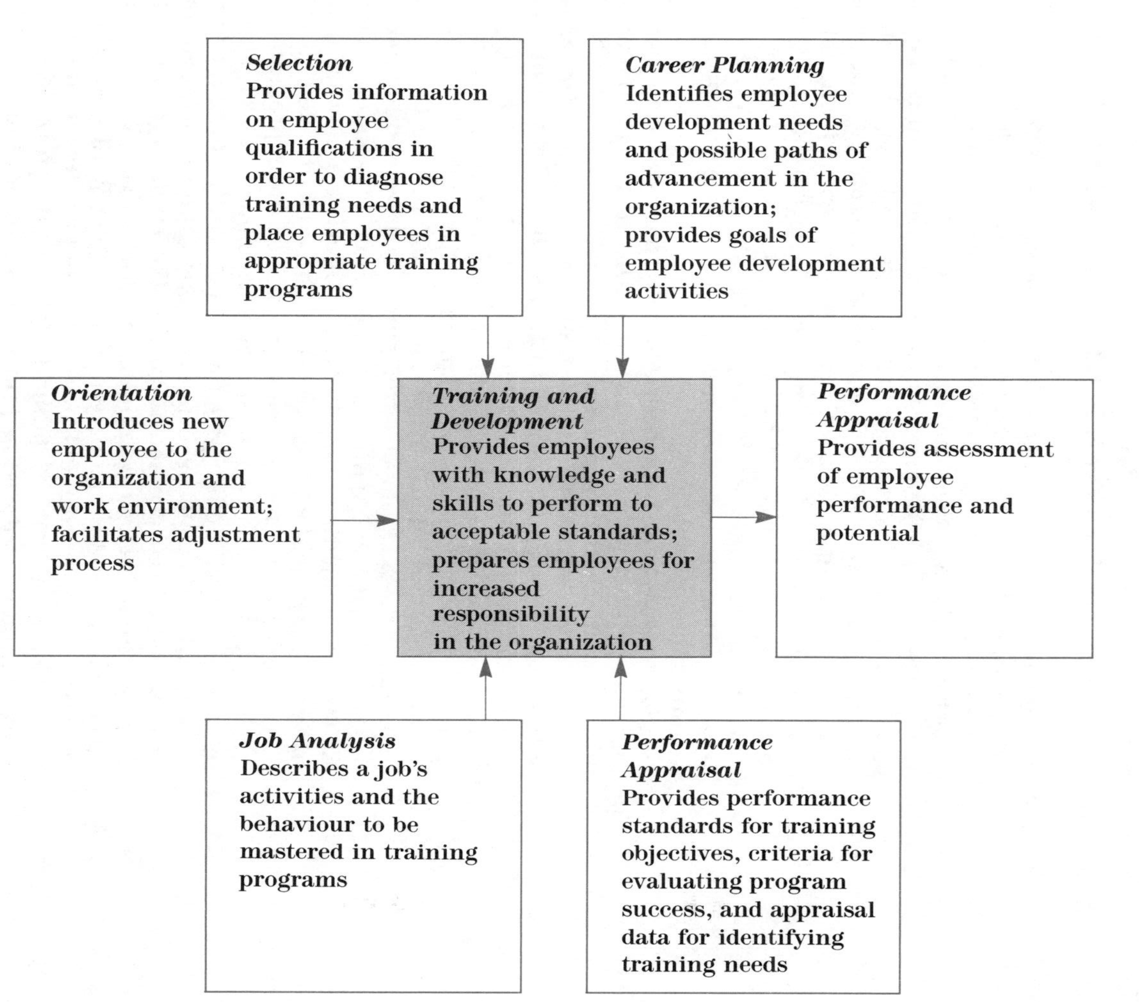

Selection
Provides information on employee qualifications in order to diagnose training needs and place employees in appropriate training programs
Career Planning
Identifies employee development needs and possible paths of advancement in the organization; provides goals of employee development activities
Orientation
Introduces new employee to the organization and work environment; facilitates adjustment process
Training and Development
Provides employees with knowledge and skills to perform to acceptable standards; prepares employees for increased responsibility in the organization
Performance Appraisal
Provides assessment of employee performance and potential
Job Analysis
Describes a job's activities and the behaviour to be mastered in training programs
Performance Appraisal
Provides performance standards for training objectives, criteria for evaluating program success, and appraisal data for identifying training needs

With regard to development, the career planning function identifies employee development needs and possible paths of advancement through the organization.

Responsibilities for Training and Development

Responsibilities for training and development are typically shared between HRM professionals and supervisory and management personnel. While supervisors and managers are responsible for making sure that employees in their departments are properly trained and developed, HRM professionals have major responsibility for training programs. A point to remember is that conflict can arise between the HRM department, which wants to assist employee development and promotion, and the operating department, which is concerned with production and the continuity of its employees. Some operating departments resent "intrusion" by the HRM department. To avoid such a conflict, HRM staff must demonstrate to operating departments the benefits of development programs. They must also introduce such programs with a minimum of disruption.

Supervisors and managers generally participate in the training function by identifying training needs in their departments and by providing informal training and development for their subordinates. The supervisor's role is an important one. Long after formal training is over, the supervisor remains to communicate and reinforce appropriate work behaviours. Serving as a role model, the boss conveys verbal and nonverbal messages about organizational norms and values. He or she also assigns tasks and provides feedback on the adequacy of performance and what can be done to improve it. The supervisor's important role in employee development is discussed further in Chapter 10: Performance Appraisal and Chapter 11: Career Planning. Of 4,200 establishments responding to an Ontario Manpower Commission survey, 88 per cent of the largest establishments (200 or more employees) indicated they sponsored formal training programs in 1984, while for the smallest establishments the figure was 24 per cent. The incidence of training programs was 9 per cent in primary industries, 51 per cent in durable goods manufacturing and 60 per cent in public administration (government). White collar employees participate to a greater extent in formal training programs (27.5 per cent) than do service and production employees (20 per cent). Within the white-collar category, the greatest incidence of training occurs among managerial and professional workers (almost 30 per cent). In the case of service workers, those employed in protective service and food and beverage services received the most training (27.4 per cent). The lowest amount of employer-sponsored training was for the construction trades and transport and equipment operators."[11]

[11] Ontario Manpower Commission, *Training in Industry: A Survey of Employer-Sponsored Programs in Ontario* (Toronto: Ontario Ministry of Labour, April 1986).

A recent Bureau of National Affairs (BNA) survey of 159 large and small organizations in different industries found that nine out of ten firms have some type of formalized training program for management and nonmanagement employees.[12] In nearly three-fourths of the firms, the HRM department had some responsibilities for training and development. The person in charge of training was typically the head of HRM or a training and development (T&D) specialist within the department. Nearly a third of the firms had separate training and development departments, which, in most cases, reported to the head of human resources management or industrial relations. Separate departments occurred more often in large organizations (those with a work force of 1,000 or more) and in nonbusiness establishments, such as health care organizations, educational institutions, and government agencies. The BNA survey also discovered that it is very common for departments other than T&D and HRM to design and implement formal training programs, either for members of their own department or for employees in other departments. In the latter case, for example, a safety and health unit might develop a safety awareness program or a stress management clinic to benefit all employees.

Five major responsibilities for training and development form the framework for this chapter. They are: (1) determining training and development needs; (2) specifying training objectives; (3) choosing a training program; (4) implementing the program; and (5) evaluating the program.

Determining Training and Development Needs

Although more than 70 organizations in Canada market various training programs and materials,[13] many companies have unmet training and development needs, especially at the supervisory level. It is not uncommon for an employee with no supervisory experience to be promoted to supervise a number of employees. Though many prepackaged training programs exist for supervisors and managers in areas such as decision-making, problem-solving, motivating employees, setting goals and so on, new supervisors often do not receive any supervisory skills training until after they have been in their jobs for some time.

On the other hand, a considerable amount of needless training takes place. It occurs for several reasons: (1) management identifies a performance deficiency and incorrectly labels it as a problem that can be remedied through a training program; (2) employees are taught

[12] Bureau of National Affairs, *Training and Development Programs PPF Survey No. 140* (Washington, D.C.: BNA, September 1985).

[13] *Short Courses and Seminars: Business and Management Training Programmes*, Development Publications 10, no. 1 (Willowdale, Ont.: Development Publications, 1982).

material or skills they already know; (3) an existing, popular training program is purchased by an organization and used, whether or not it satisfies an identified training or development need.

Unmet training and development needs can be identified and needless, inappropriate training eliminated if a thorough training-needs assessment is conducted. The purpose of any such assessment is to discover and describe any individual, unit, or organizational performance problem for which training is an appropriate solution. Such a problem may be anticipated, as in the case of employees whose career goals indicate the desire to move up in the organization. A training need exists whenever existing or expected performance problems are caused by employees' deficiencies in knowledge or skills.

Identifying Needs

HRM professionals identify training and development needs by: (1) monitoring organizational information, such as human resource flows and policy and procedural changes that affect the nature of jobs; (2) asking supervisors and managers about the training and development needs of their subordinates; and (3) accepting and analyzing training requests from managers and others.

Many training needs can be anticipated and identified by monitoring organizational information. For example, by monitoring flow of employees into and through the organization, HRM professionals can identify the training needs of employees who are new, newly transferred, promoted or bumped to lower-level jobs. Bumping to lower-level jobs sometimes occurs in unionized firms when layoffs are necessary. Because workers with less seniority are laid off first, vacancies sometimes occur in their typically lower-level positions. These vacancies must be filled by workers with greater seniority, many of whom formerly occupied higher-level positions. The need to train even "bumped down" workers is illustrated by an employee demoted to a job of machining burrs off of connecting rods at a tractor manufacturing company. The employee did $25,000 worth of product damage his first day on the new job.[14]

Monitoring career planning information is helpful in determining development needs of individual employees. Career planning identifies possible paths of advancement in the organization and also employee career goals. Performance appraisal information and selection data can also be used to identify likely candidates for promotion. When training needs are identified in advance of new assignments, development programs can be initiated to prepare employees for assuming new job responsibilities. The BNA survey, above, found that of 135 firms conducting in-house training for management-level employees, one-third had formal programs to prepare nonmanagement workers for supervisory or management positions.[15]

[14] A. Kotlowitz, "Caterpillar Faces a Showdown with UAW," *Wall Street Journal*, March 5, 1986.
[15] BNA, 1985.

Training needs that come from changes in jobs can be identified and anticipated by monitoring policy and procedural changes which affect jobs. Changes such as the introduction of higher quality standards or new or additional work procedures and equipment require accommodation by employees and often some training.

Finally, organizational operations can be monitored for signs of actual performance problems. When records indicate poor performance, a possible cause is employees' deficiencies in knowledge or skills.

A second way to identify training needs is simply to ask supervisors, managers, or others about their present or anticipated requirements. Questionnaires, interviews, or both are ways of gathering this kind of information.

Performance problems are also often brought to the attention of T&D professionals by supervisors, managers, and others. Whether such problems actually represent training needs is the next question for T&D professionals to consider.

Analyzing Performance Problems

Jane Simpson has been identified by her supervisor as having a performance problem with one aspect of her job: packing parts. She is required to pack six parts per minute with no breakage. Unfortunately, after three months on the job, she is still able to pack only four parts per minute, and she breaks an average of two per day. Simpson has a performance problem, but does it require a training solution? R.F. Mager and P. Pipe, consultants and authors of several books on training, suggest a method for analyzing performance problems.[16] It consists of a series of questions representing key determinations. These are summarized in the flow diagram in Exhibit 9.2.

The first determination is whether the performance problem is important enough to merit attention. If it is, the next step is to determine whether the problem is caused by a deficiency in either skill or knowledge. A key question in this determination is "Could the employee do it (perform the required behaviour) if his or her life depended on it?" If not, the problem is caused by a true knowledge or skill deficiency for which training may be an appropriate solution. If Simpson has been trying very hard but still is unable to master part-packing without breakage, her problem falls in this category.

The next determination is whether the employee has ever performed the task adequately. Simpson has not, so she falls in this category. If performance has never been adequate, a formal training program is an appropriate solution, assuming that the employee is trainable. If other shipping clerks are having the same problem as Simpson, another appropriate solution is to simplify the task so that employees' existing knowledge or skills are adequate. For example, using a different kind

[16] R.F. Mager and P. Pipe, *Analyzing Performance Problems or 'You Really Oughta Wanna'* (Belmont, Calif.: Fearon-Pitman Publishers, Inc., 1970).

EXHIBIT 9.2

Mager and Pipe's flow diagram for determining solutions to performance problems

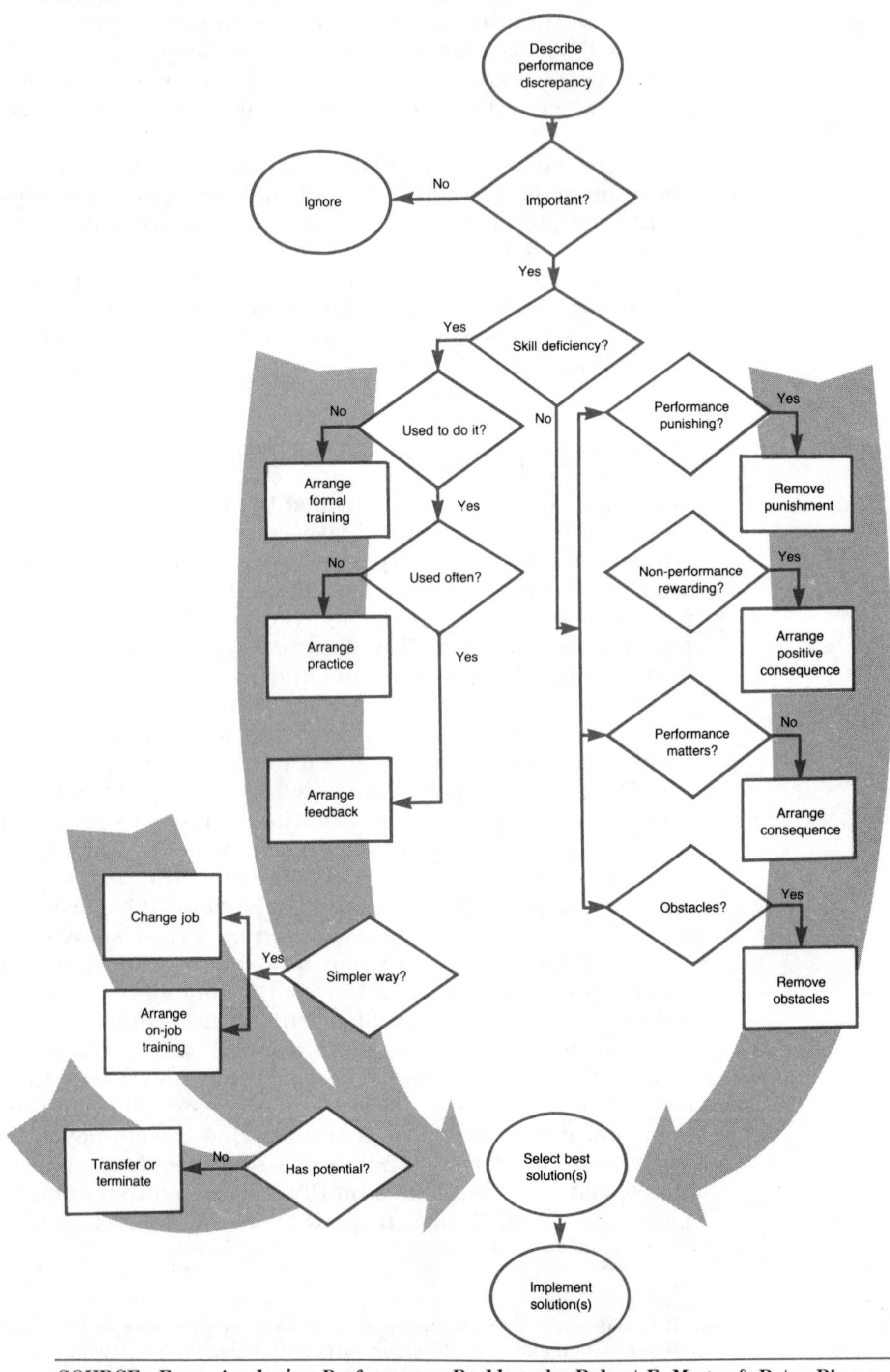

SOURCE: From *Analyzing Performance Problems* by Robert F. Mager & Peter Pipe. Copyright © 1984 by David S. Lake Publishers, Belmont, CA 94002.

of packing material might increase packing speed while also reducing breakage. Or the company might consider lowering performance standards to allow for some breakage and fewer parts packed per minute.

If, on the other hand, performance has been adequate in the past, the cause of a present deficiency may simply be lack of practice opportunities or inadequate performance feedback. Formal training programs are inappropriate in such cases. Appropriate solutions include providing opportunities for practice or more frequent feedback. Of course, if unpractised skills have been forgotten almost entirely, some amount of relearning has to take place before practice can be beneficial.

If the problem is not caused by a deficiency in skill or knowledge, what *is* the cause? Perhaps the employee lacks the necessary motivation to perform well. Or obstacles such as stress or personal problems may impede satisfactory performance. In cases like these, training is obviously not the solution. Performance problems that are not caused by deficiencies of knowledge or skills demand nontraining solutions, such as attaching positive consequences to desirable performance or removing obstacles to acceptable performance. Obstacles can often be removed by improving working conditions, sponsoring wellness programs, and/or referring troubled employees for counselling. Or, it may be necessary to impose discipline, even the threat of termination, in order to motivate correction of performance deficiencies.

Specifying Training Objectives

After determining training needs, T&D professionals specify training objectives, which describe what trainees will be able to do upon completion of training. Mager lists three characteristics of a useful instructional objective: (1) it should define the behaviour that will be accepted as evidence that the trainee has mastered the objective; (2) it should specify the important conditions under which the performance is expected to occur; and (3) it should specify a level of performance that will be considered acceptable.[17]

Since one kind of behaviour required for the job of shipping clerk is "assuring proper weight on all shipments handled," an objective for Jane Simpson's training program might be:

> *Given a standard mailing scale, the employee will be able to weigh packages accurately, i.e., within a gram of their actual weight 100 per cent of the time.*

In this instructional objective, the behaviour described is weighing packages. "Using a standard mailing scale" is the condition under which performance occurs. The level of performance considered necessary for mastery of the objective is "within a gram of their actual weight 100 per cent of the time."

[17] R.F. Mager, *Preparing Instructional Objectives*, 2nd ed. (Belmont, Calif.: Fearon-Pitman Publishers, Inc., 1975).

It is important to specify training objectives. Well-specified objectives define the content of training programs by providing clear statements of exactly what is to be learned. The success of training programs can be measured in terms of the extent to which training objectives are accomplished. And specifying training objectives provides trainees with a clear understanding of exactly what they will be expected to do after participation in the training effort.

Choosing a Training Program

Many choices confront the person charged with training responsibilities. One major decision is whether necessary training will be provided "in-house" (within the organization) or by outside organizations. Xerox Corporation decided that its redundant technicians should be schooled at a nearby technical institute which customized classes to meet Xerox's needs. Participants were relieved of their work assignments for nine months in order to take a full class load (16 hours of courses each quarter). While attending classes, employees received full pay and were given computer terminals for use in their homes.[18]

If in-house programs are used, T&D professionals can assemble the materials and plan the methods of presentation themselves, or they can order and implement prepackaged training programs. Prepackaged programs and outside training sessions must be selected carefully to ensure that their goals are consistent with training objectives of the organization. Unfortunately, many companies choose programs without first conducting a needs analysis or formulating training objectives. With so many companies marketing books, cassettes, films, and programs on training, HRM professionals are constantly deluged with brochures and advertising for these products. While the majority have much to offer, managers who do not properly assess their training and development needs may be unwise consumers. Of course, nontraining benefits may accrue to some popular programs being offered simply because employees appreciate and enjoy them. Given the expense of most training and development programs, however, a prudent organization will exercise restraint in the number and type of programs selected.

Choice of a training program is determined by: (1) type of training content; (2) extent to which the program incorporates key learning principles; (3) trainee characteristics; and (4) cost factors. These considerations are summarized in Exhibit 9.3.

Type of Training Content

Training program content is determined by nature of the training need and specified training objectives. Content can be divided into four basic

[18] Morano and Deets.

EXHIBIT 9.3

Choosing a training program: considerations

1. Area of training content (What type of behaviour or material is to be learned?)
   a. Information acquisition
   b. Motor skills
   c. Interpersonal skills and attitude change
   d. Decision-making and problem-solving skills
2. Extent to which the training program incorporates key learning principles
   a. Does program provide knowledge of results?
   b. Does program reinforce desired behaviour?
   c. Does method provide practice opportunities?
   d. Does method motivate the employee to learn and apply the new knowledge and skills to the job?
   e. Does the program facilitate transfer of new behaviour to on-the-job situations?
3. Trainee characteristics
   a. How many employees need training now? In the future?
   b. What level(s) of ability do trainees possess?
   c. What individual differences exist in employees who will be receiving training?
4. Cost of the program
   a. What is the size of the training and development budget?
   b. What does the program cost?

areas, each representing a type of behaviour or material to be learned: (1) information acquisition; (2) motor skills; (3) interpersonal skills and attitude change; and (4) decision-making and problem-solving skills. In practice, many programs incorporate more than one content area. For example, a program to help supervisors appraise performance might convey information about new appraisal techniques, develop interpersonal skills, and sharpen decision-making powers. A safety training program might combine information acquisition with motor skills by requiring that employees practice new safety behaviours.

Information acquisition. One of the most common training needs is to provide employees with information relevant to their jobs. Such information frequently concerns new company policies, programs, or benefits, new laws and regulations affecting jobs, or new job performance standards. An underlying assumption of providing employees with information is that acquiring it will result in changes in behaviour. For example, a training program that provides HRM professionals with information about human rights legislation will, one hopes, result in compliance with the law. It may also result in changes in company policy and practices regarding the employment of members of various ethnic groups. Methods that seek to convey information must do so in such a way that the information is retained for some time. Information must also be presented efficiently.

Motor skills. Motor skills (or psychomotor skills, as they are sometimes called) are related to the performance of specific physical activities. Learning these skills involves learning to move various parts of the body in response to specific external and internal stimuli. Common motor skills are walking, riding a bicycle, tying a shoelace, throwing a ball, and driving a car.

To learn a motor skill, one must first acquire information so that one knows *what* one should do, then *how* to perform that action. Practice and performance feedback are necessary. For example, one cannot learn to drive a bus from simply reading a book or watching a film; one must actually perform the activity in order to master it. In the performance, one practises the necessary motor movements while receiving feedback and reinforcement from an instructor. Through practice and reinforcement, one learns to make certain motor responses at specific times in response to external stimuli, such as traffic flow and road signs, and to the internal stimuli from one's own muscles and nerves. Feedback provided by internal stimuli of this type is called *proprioceptive feedback.* It is very important for skilled motor movements, such as those required in equipment operation and use of tools.

Interpersonal skills and attitude change. Interpersonal skills constitute the behaviour necessary for interaction with others in work and nonwork situations. Examples of interpersonal skills include listening, communicating, persuading, and showing understanding of others' feelings. Since interpersonal skills are frequently used to influence others, changing others' attitudes is included in this area of training content. Acquiring interpersonal skills is also useful in developing leadership and bargaining skills.

Learning interpersonal skills is similar to learning motor skills in that both require opportunities to practise and to receive feedback on performance. Specifically, training in interpersonal skills involves learning to understand the behaviour of others and learning what to say and do in various situations. This is a common training content area for supervisors and managers.

Decision-making and problem-solving. Decision-making and problem-solving focus on methods and techniques for making organizational decisions and solving work-related problems. This kind of learning improves trainees' abilities to define and structure problems, collect and analyze information, generate alternative solutions, and make an optimal decision from among alternatives. Training of this type is often provided to potential managers, supervisors, and professionals.

Incorporating Key Learning Principles

Since learning is the goal of any training effort, a second consideration in training program choice is extent to which a program incorporates the key learning principles of feedback, reinforcement, practice, motivation, and transfer. Some programs and methods, such as job instruction training, incorporate all five principles, while other methods, such as lectures and films, are limited in this regard. The extent to which a program or method incorporates a certain learning principle is important because, depending on the area of training content, certain learning principles may be more important than others.

Since one cannot actually observe learning taking place, its occurrence must be inferred. *Learning* is inferred to have taken place when a relatively permanent change in behaviour or behaviour potential occurs between two points in time as a result of reinforced practice or experience. The term *behaviour potential* recalls the fact that learning can take place even though a person has not had the opportunity to demonstrate that learning via performance. For example, individuals with cardiopulmonary resuscitation (CPR) training may never need to use it to aid a heart attack victim. However, the potential to use it exists as evidence of learning. The definition of learning as a "relatively permanent change in behaviour" calls attention to the fact that some forgetting of learned material is inevitable.

Feedback. The most basic learning principle is *feedback*, or knowledge about one's performance. It is difficult to imagine learning occurring without feedback. For example, imagine learning archery without being permitted to see if you hit the target. Feedback serves two major functions in the learning process: it lets learners know whether they are performing correctly, and it reinforces desired behaviour.

Feedback informs trainees of the correctness or incorrectness of their responses to certain stimuli. If a student chose alternative "d" to a multiple-choice question, feedback informs him or her if "d" is correct or incorrect. Ideally, feedback also informs the student of the correct response; one can learn from mistakes only if one knows what is wrong and how it can be corrected. Thus, the student who incorrectly answers "d" should be provided with feedback that "d" is incorrect and that "b" is the correct alternative. Though learning is facilitated when such feedback is provided, relatively few training methods provide it. Feedback is also more informative and useful to the learner when it is given soon after responses are made and when it refers to specific responses to be learned rather than to factors of lesser importance in the learning situation. One training method that includes excellent informational feedback is programmed instruction. This method requires learners to answer questions based on small blocks of information. Each answer is followed immediately by feedback in the form of correct answers to the questions.

Reinforcement. Reinforcement has a greater impact on learning and performance than any other learning principle. The principle of reinforcement was stated nearly a century ago by E.L. Thorndike in his Law of Effect: responses that are closely followed by a "reinforcing state of affairs" tend to be strengthened and to occur more frequently in the future in response to the same stimuli.[19] In other words, the occurrence of desired behaviour can be increased by attaching desirable

[19] B.M. Bass and J.A. Vaughan, *Training in Industry: The Management of Learning* (Monterey, Calif.: Brooks/Cole, 1966).

consequences (positive reinforcers) to it. A classic example of a reinforcer is the gold star a teacher affixes to a pupil's paper. Another example is a hockey coach's rewarding players for outstanding plays by placing visual symbols of accomplishment on their helmets. Gold stars and visual symbols provide recognition for desired behaviour. Such reinforcers gradually increase its occurrence.

Organizations use reinforcers such as recognition, praise, and bonuses to encourage desirable behaviour, but their primary use in training and development is to teach new behaviours. The process often used for this purpose is shaping, a systematic reinforcement of successively higher levels of performance. Suppose a teacher is teaching a child to read. The teacher shapes the behaviour (reading) first by reinforcing the student's recognition of the simplest words in the reader. As the child becomes more proficient, reinforcement is given for progressively more difficult words. Thus, the learner's new behaviour is shaped until an acceptable level of performance is reached.

The frequency of reinforcement is also important. Learning theory generally argues that a *continuous reinforcement schedule* (in which each correct response is reinforced) is most useful in learning new tasks. However, such an approach is impossible to maintain in the work environment because a supervisor is not always available to provide the necessary reinforcers. For this reason, many training programs begin partial, or intermittent, reinforcement schedules before an employee returns to the work environment to use newly learned behaviour on the job. An *intermittent reinforcement schedule* provides reinforcers for some correct responses but not for all. This approach is easier to maintain in the work environment and results in more consistent employee behaviour in the absence of reinforcers.

Perhaps one of the most useful forms of intermittent reinforcement is called variable ratio. A *variable ratio reinforcement schedule* is one in which employees are rewarded for desired behaviours on a random basis. For example, attendance may be improved by a program which gives employees a playing card for each day they arrive at work on time. At the end of each week, the employee with the best poker hand receives cash or some other form of reward. Employees perform the desired behaviour of coming to work on time, but they have only a random chance of being rewarded.

While organizations find partial reinforcement useful in maintaining desirable behaviour, even this type of reinforcement is extrinsic. That is, trainees are dependent upon someone or something outside themselves for reinforcement. Ideally, learners provide themselves with reinforcement for correct behaviour. When people reinforce their own behaviour, reinforcers are intrinsic. Trainees can be taught to use intrinsic reinforcement by first learning the standards of correct behaviour from external reinforcement and feedback from the trainer. They also learn to obtain satisfaction from correct behaviour itself. For example, after one has learned to read, reading becomes reinforcing in itself. Similarly, employees can find satisfaction in doing their jobs well.

Reinforcers are highly personalized; what one person finds reinforcing may not be reinforcing to another. For example, one person may find simple recognition to be a desirable consequence of good work, while another may need a more tangible reinforcer, such as an increase in pay. An employee who values autonomy may be reinforced by less supervision, while another finds close supervision more reinforcing. Thus, it is important to determine in advance what reinforcers will best suit one's purposes.

Feedback can be intrinsically rewarding. Most learners would prefer to have feedback on their performances (even when it is negative) rather than no knowledge of results. The reinforcement value of feedback is obvious from the importance most people place on game scores: how often do people play a game without keeping score?

A recent newspaper article reveals what one city refuse collector finds reinforcing about his work. The number and variety of reinforcers is rather surprising, given the nature of the job. The article is excerpted in Exhibit 9.4.

EXHIBIT 9.4

What one refuse collector finds reinforcing about his job

It is 7 A.M., and while most of the city is asleep, Babcock and his eight co-workers are getting ready to hit the streets to pick up what the rest of us have no use for—garbage.

"If anyone thinks my job is easy, I invite them to come on my truck," Babcock said during the dawn interview. "We're doing a hard job. I never thought I'd look down a street and feel satisfied by seeing empty garbage cans. We take a lot of pride in the department. We're like a family."

City officials are so pleased with the work of the sanitation department employees, that three years ago city officials gave them a certificate of appreciation. Babcock and his co-workers proudly display the certificate if the occasion arises.

"I can see progress in my work and feel satisfied," said Babcock, adding that his line of work protects residents, particularly children, from disease and other troubles brought on by poor sanitation conditions.

Babcock, who previously worked in a factory, said he prefers collecting garbage. "You never knew where the product went," he said, adding that he enjoys contact with people and appreciates favourable comments from them.

"All it takes is one 'thank you' from the public to make your day," he said. "Sometimes one 'thank you' is better than a whole pay check. This doesn't mean we need a pat on the back everyday."

Collecting refuse isn't easy, and this is one reason Babcock said he finds it rewarding. "It's good, hard, physical labour."

SOURCE: From "Collecting Trash Is a Dirty Job," by G. Norman. Copyright March 31, 1986. Reprinted by permission of the *Daily Iowan* (Iowa City, Iowa).

Practice. The learning of specific behaviour is the result of reinforced practice or experience. *Practice* is defined as repetition or rehearsal in order to remember or improve a response, a behaviour, or material. Feedback must reinforce practice so that the learner knows whether it is leading to the intended results. Without feedback, certain responses or behaviour may be practised and learned incorrectly. For example, a beginning piano student who has no feedback may learn a piece of music incorrectly because she has no way of knowing that she is making errors when playing a particular measure.

Explaining practice is difficult because even psychologists who study human learning disagree about what constitutes it. For some people, practice requires physically performing an action, writing out material, or reading it aloud. For others, practice may be purely a mental activity. For example, a salesman might mentally rehearse a sales presentation.

Though continuous reinforcement is important for learning new behaviour, practice is more instrumental in ensuring proper retention and performance. Generally, active practice is believed to be superior to the less active variety in facilitating the learning and retention of material. Retention of newly learned behaviour and material is also greater when practice is distributed rather than massed. *Distributed practice* means that practice sessions are interspersed with rest or other activities. Recent cognitive learning research suggests that the spacing between practice sessions be gradually increased. Also, old material should be reviewed as new material is introduced.[20] *Massed practice* is practice with virtually no rest periods. Of course, massed practice is more time-efficient than distributed practice, a fact that probably explains why business training programs often violate the distributed-practice principle. (Massed practice is also popular with students who put off studying until the night before an exam.)

One question about practice is the "whole versus the part": material and behaviour can be rehearsed as a whole or divided into parts and practised separately. Generally, the "whole" method is superior, unless a task is complex and has a low degree of organization, in which case the "part" method may be more efficient. For example, a simple, repetitive piano piece can easily be learned as a whole, practising both right and left hands together from the start. A more difficult piece with greater variety may, however, be learned more effectively by practising first the right hand part, then the left hand part, and finally, playing both hands together. Depending upon the response to be learned, the "whole" method is sometimes not appropriate for learners of lesser ability.

A recent review of theory and research regarding recommendations for design of practice found a fairly high degree of commonality. For example, recommendations from behavioural theory were similar to those from the most recent cognitive-based learning theory. The concept of automaticity is an example of a new concept from cognitive theory that is applicable to practice. *Automaticity* refers to practising a skill to the point at which it requires very little attention capacity of the brain. For example, typing is a skill that has been automatized by good typists, but not by those who "hunt and peck." Automaticity is important because recent research suggests that performance of complex tasks, such as computer programming and even reading, requires

[20] D.F. Salisbury, B.F. Richards, and J.D. Klein, "Designing Practice: A Review of Prescriptions and Recommendations from Instructional Design Theories," *Journal of Instructional Development*, vol. 8, no. 4, 1985, pp. 9–19.

learning of some sub-tasks to this level.[21] The implication for practice is that it must proceed through three stages—speed, accuracy, and automaticity. For example, in distinguishing letters from numbers, practice sessions would initially emphasize error-free performance, then speed, and finally, automaticity, i.e., the ability to make these distinctions while performing a second task simultaneously.[22]

Any training method or program that does not permit trainees to control the pace at which material is presented is low on opportunities for practice. For example, the lecture method does not allow for practice opportunities. The learner in a lecture usually does not have time to repeat, even mentally, material he or she has just learned because new material is continually being presented. Of course, opportunity to practice is more important for learning motor skills than for learning the kind of material usually presented in a lecture.

Motivation. Training programs should help motivate trainees to learn. Most learning processes have both intrinsic and extrinsic motivators. For example, learning to perform a new task may prove satisfying in itself because of pride in accomplishment, and this pride intrinsically motivates the trainee to continue learning and performing the newly learned task. On the other hand, the trainee may be extrinsically motivated to learn the new task because mastery will result in a desirable new job assignment.

An ideal training method would be very intrinsically motivating throughout the entire learning process. When trainees are intrinsically motivated, they are not dependent upon trainers or others to provide motivation for learning. Often, however, extrinsic motivators must be relied upon in the initial stages of learning. For example, praise and criticism used in the early stages of training are extrinsic motivators. Trainees are generally motivated to seek praise and avoid criticism. In time, they may come to internalize the standards necessary to receive praise; then, good performance becomes intrinsically motivating and reinforcing. Such a process is most likely to occur in training methods and programs in which trainers provide close attention to and reinforce appropriate trainee behaviour. On-the-job training programs and well-run apprenticeship programs facilitate the transition from extrinsic to intrinsic motivation.

Several methods have been suggested for increasing trainees' intrinsic motivation to learn. These include stressing the future value of the material, providing feedback on progress towards the learning goals, and relating the material to "interesting, meaningful materials already studied outside the training program."[23]

A substantial body of research supports setting specific, hard goals to obtain the best effort and performance from people.[24] Training

[21] J.R. Anderson, *Cognitive Psychology and Its Implications*, (San Francisco: Freeman, 1980).

[22] Salisbury, et al., 1985.

[23] Ibid.

[24] G.P. Latham and G.A. Yuki, "A Review of Research on the Application of Goal Setting in Organizations," *Academy of Management Journal*, 1975, vol. 18, pp. 824–45.

programs can and should make use of the goal-setting process to maximize performance gains.

Transfer of learning. The "bottom line" in any training program or method is whether acquired learning is properly transferred to the job. When learning from one situation (such as a training program) is successfully applied to a different situation (such as the job), *positive transfer* is said to occur. Transfer can also be neutral or negative. *Neutral transfer* means that what has been learned is not applied to another situation. In *negative transfer*, learned behaviour or material has an adverse effect on performance. For example, a bicyclist may attempt to stop her new hand braked bike with her foot because her old bike had coaster brakes. The driver of a new car may turn on his windshield wipers instead of his turn signal if the knobs' positions are the reverse of what they were in his old car. In each case, learned behaviour appropriate to an old situation results in poor performance in a new situation.

Assuring positive transfer is one of the most important aspects of a training program. A number of factors have been suggested as necessary for producing the transfer of learning to new situations, including:

1. Maximize similarity between the learning and performance situation.
2. Practise the new task extensively (overlearning).
3. Provide a range of learning experiences so the trainee can generalize.
4. Identify key elements of the material or behaviour so that the learner is able to determine the appropriateness of transfer.
5. Emphasize knowledge of general principles.
6. Provide feedback on job performance and otherwise reinforce proper transfer of new materials and behaviour to the job.[25]

Overlearning, or practising a new task extensively, is particularly necessary when knowledge is critical but rarely used. For example, the individual who receives CPR training should probably overlearn the techniques; the chances of encountering a heart attack victim are rather remote, but if the need does arise, it is critical to remember the correct behaviour.

Another situation in which overlearning is helpful is in learning a new response to an old or familiar stimulus. For example, imagine learning to drive in a country in which a red light means go and a green light means stop. In an emergency situation, a driver familiar with our red-stop, green-go associations would probably revert to the old responses (negative transfer), possibly causing an accident. Overlearning is one way to avoid such problems.

An organization should provide on-the-job performance feedback and other reinforcers for the proper transfer of newly learned materials and behaviour to the job. Newly learned behaviour and responses must

[25] I.I. Goldstein, *Training: Program Development and Evaluation* (Monterey, Calif.: Brooks/Cole, 1974); and A.P. Goldstein and M. Sorcher, *Changing Supervisor Behavior* (New York: Pergamon Press, 1974).

be reinforced in the work environment or they will quickly be forgotten. A classic study illustrates this point. A training program for foremen designed to increase their consideration towards their subordinates was successful according to initial post-training measures. However, within several months, the foremen had reverted to their pretraining behaviour. They did so simply because the newly learned behaviour had not been reinforced by the work environment and upper management. This study demonstrated that behaviour which is changed through training will not transfer or persist in the job situation unless the job and the organizational environment reinforce it.[26]

Since transfer is an important factor, T&D professionals must consider how to achieve it in the training methods they choose, in the training program, and especially in the work environment itself. Planning for transfer can begin immediately after specification of the training objectives. Transfer should be regarded as the appropriate generalization of learned material to nontraining, on-the-job situations.

Trainee Characteristics

Also affecting choice of a training program is trainee characteristics —specifically, the number of employees who need training, their ability levels, and individual differences in training needs.

Number of employees who need training. Some training methods, such as lectures, films, videotapes, and programmed instruction, are easily adapted to large numbers of trainees. However, other methods, such as behaviour modelling, role play, job instruction training, and coaching, require low trainee-trainer ratios, in most cases fewer than ten trainees for every trainer. The coaching method, in which a supervisor coach provides guidance and feedback to subordinates, usually has only two to four trainees to every trainer. While most training methods can be used for small numbers of employees, more costly methods, such as programmed and computer-assisted instruction, require a large number of trainees over time in order to justify their initial expense.

If only a small number of employees need a certain kind of training or development, T&D professionals commonly use methods and programs that already exist within the organization or programs sponsored by other organizations. For example, trainees may enrol in workshops given by a university or community college or attend professional meetings. This approach avoids the costs associated with developing or purchasing a new program. If, on the other hand, large numbers of employees require training and the need is expected to recur, development costs can be justified more easily.

Trainee ability levels. Ability levels of trainees is another factor to consider in selecting a training method. For example, if reading ability

[26] E.A. Fleishman, E.F. Harris, and H.S. Burtt, *Leadership and Supervision in Industry* (Bureau of Educational Research, Report No. 33, The Ohio State University, 1955).

is low, the level of written materials must be adjusted accordingly. A recent estimate placed Canada's illiteracy rate at 20 per cent and its teenage dropout rate from high school at 30 per cent.[27] Employees who cannot read and write pose problems for training programs, while also increasing the risk of costly errors and accidents. The Canadian Business Task Force on Literacy, composed of 32 major corporations, is working to make employers aware of this problem. For employees with limited reading abilities, training materials may be modified and greater reliance placed on audio and video presentations. Because of low reading levels of recruits, the U.S. Army rewrote its field manuals to the fifth-grade level and increased its use of videotaped material. Job instruction training is also appropriate for low-level readers, since it relies on demonstrating behaviour to be learned.

In many organizations, a related problem is variation in ability levels within a group of trainees. Imagine trying to design a training program for employees whose IQs range from 80 to 150. Some aspects of a company—such as company policies, performance standards, or income-tax information—must be communicated to just such a diverse population. If the program is geared to a high intelligence level, employees of lesser intelligence will not understand much of the information presented. But if it is geared to a low level, employees of higher intelligence will likely be bored and perhaps insulted. Thus, training programs must take trainee ability levels into account and make an effort to gear program material appropriately.

Individual differences in training needs. Trainees do not enter the training situation with identical needs, even if all are to learn the same behaviour or material. Differences in work experience and in levels of ability and motivation affect the amount and type of training an employee requires. For example, an employee with two years' experience as a telephone operator can master a new switchboard with less training than an employee who has never worked a switchboard.

To accommodate individual differences in needs, training can take a *criterion-referenced approach*, which assesses individual trainees before they enter the program. Trainees can start at slightly different points in the program, depending on how much they already know. Many North American organizations, including American Airlines, Xerox, and the U.S. Army, have successfully used this approach with substantial savings in training costs and time. American Telephone and Telegraph reported savings of $37,800,000 from 1968 to 1973 as a result of switching to a criterion-referenced approach for telephone linesmen.[28]

Self-paced training programs recognize differences in levels of ability and motivation and enable trainees to work at their own speed. Programmed and computer-assisted instruction allow trainees to work at their own pace. These methods can also be easily adapted to a criterion-referenced approach.

[27] M. Ritts, "What If Johnny Still Can't Read?" *Canadian Business*, vol. 58, no. 5, May 1986, pp. 54–7.

[28] R.F. Mager, "The Winds of Change," *Training and Development Journal*, October 1977, pp. 12–20.

Cost Factors

Budgetary considerations play a major role in choice of a training program. Budget size is likely to increase as a function of the number of trainees, their organizational level (more dollars per trainee for higher-level trainees), and the extent of training needs. Training budgets are likely to be higher in highly profitable organizations, in organizations that have had successful training programs in the past, and in organizations that emphasize training and development as a human resource planning strategy. Larger budgets permit smaller class sizes, more and better training materials and equipment, and more and better trainers. A generous training budget should be used to maximize learning and the transfer of learning to the job situation. For example, a large budget could be used to divide a long, two-day session into five four-hour sessions. A large budget could also permit hiring an excellent lecturer in place of showing a film or videotape. Of course, companies occasionally waste money on unnecessary items or purchase training programs that are more complicated than they need to be. If possible, increased expenditures for training programs should be evaluated to determine their effects on learning and performance. In some cases, the cheaper method may prove the better method.

Training and Development Methods and Aids

This section describes major methods and aids used in training and development programs. Although each is presented under the heading of its primary use, many are appropriate for more than one content area. For a comparison of T&D methods according to several important criteria see Exhibit 9.5.

Information Acquisition

Methods and aids used primarily for the acquisition of information include lectures, seminars, films and videotapes, programmed instruction, computer-assisted instruction and interactive videodisc instruction.

Lectures. In the lecture method, a trainer verbally presents information to a group, which can range from very small to very large. Visual aids, such as a chalkboard or slides, are often used in conjunction with lectures. With the availability of cable and satellite television, companies can now broadcast live lectures to many remote locations simultaneously. Furthermore, technology has made it possible for lecturers to receive questions and comments from viewers in the hinterlands. Technological capabilities such as these make it possible to train many people more rapidly than ever before, while also substantially reducing travel costs for trainers, trainees, and their sponsoring organizations.

EXHIBIT 9.5

A comparison of T&D methods

Training method	*Content area of primary use*	*Degree to which method facilitates learning*					*Accommodation of individual differences*	*Initial costs*
		Feedback	*Reinforcement*	*Practice*	*Motivation*	*Transfer*		
Lecture	Information acquisition	Limited	Limited	Limited	Limited	Limited	Limited	Low
Seminars	Information acquisition	Limited	Limited	Limited	Limited	Limited	Moderate	Moderate-Low
Films and videotapes	Information acquisition	Limited	Limited	Limited	Limited	Limited	Limited	Moderate
Programmed instruction	Information acquisition	Excellent	Moderate	Good	Good	Limited	Moderate-Good	High
Computer-assisted instruction	Information acquisition	Excellent	Excellent	Excellent	Excellent	Limited	Good	High
Interactive videodisc instruction	Information acquisition, decision-making skills	Excellent	Excellent	Excellent	Excellent	Good	Excellent	High
Job instruction training	Motor skills	Good	Good	Good	Good	Excellent	Good	Low
Vestibule training	Motor skills	Good	Good	Good	Good	Good	Moderate-Good	High
Apprenticeship training	Motor skills	Good	Good	Good	Good	Excellent	Good	Moderate

EXHIBIT 9.5

A comparison of T&D methods

Training method	*Content area of primary use*	*Degree to which method facilitates learning*					*Accommodation of individual differences*	*Initial costs*
		Feedback	*Reinforcement*	*Practice*	*Motivation*	*Transfer*		
Coaching	Motor skills, interpersonal skills, decision-making skills	Moderate	Moderate	Limited	Good	Excellent	Excellent	Low
Video systems	Motor skills, interpersonal skills	Excellent	Good	Good	Excellent	Good	Good	Moderate
Conference/ discussion	Interpersonal skills, information acquisition	Limited	Moderate	Limited	Good	Limited	Moderate	Moderate-Low
Role Play	Interpersonal skills	Good	Good	Good	Moderate	Good	Moderate	Moderate-Low
Behaviour modelling	Interpersonal skills	Excellent	Good	Good	Moderate	Excellent	Moderate	High
T-groups	Interpersonal skills	Moderate	Moderate	Good	Moderate	Moderate	Moderate	Moderate-High
Case method	Decision-making skills	Moderate	Moderate	Good	Moderate	Moderate	Limited	Low
In-basket technique	Decision-making skills	Good	Moderate	Good	Good	Good	Limited	Low
Business games	Decision-making skills	Good	Moderate	Limited	Good	Moderate	Limited	Moderate-High
Internships	All content areas	Moderate	Moderate	Moderate	Good	Excellent	Limited	Low
Job rotation	All content areas	Moderate	Moderate	Limited	Good	Excellent	Moderate	Low

The lecture method has its shortcomings even when the trainer is excellent. Except for questions from students, communication is one-way. For the most part, trainees sit passively listening or taking notes with little if any immediate feedback or reinforcement for learning or opportunities to practise the material being presented. Transfer of learning from lecture to the job depends on overlearning, verbal or pictorial identification of key features of the task, and emphasis on general principles. A lecture does not allow for varying ability levels of trainees, and the learning pace is structured by the instructor for the group as a whole. Despite its shortcomings, the lecture remains a common training method because of its low cost per trainee and the fact that trainees are familiar with and generally accept the method.

Seminars. Many agencies, firms, and universities offer seminars on topics of interest to employers. Seminars usually feature lectures, handouts, and some discussion among participants. While some seminars limit group size, others are open to large groups. Seminars are typically held in hotels, convention centres, or other locations outside the company. Increasingly, however, companies are bringing human resources consultants into the organization to conduct training sessions and seminars. One firm that offers such seminars is MICA Management Centre. With a staff of 17, plus guest speakers, MICA offers seminars on 66 topics in the cities of Toronto, Calgary, Ottawa, and Montreal. The most popular seminar topics relate to stress management and assertive management, according to the company's executive vice president.[29]

In-house seminars can be expensive. One Ottawa-based speaker and seminar leader charges $2,400 per day for presentations relating to "people skills."[30] Some charge less, but others charge more.

Seminars are similar to lectures in terms of incorporating key learning principles. The value of a seminar depends upon expertise of the speaker and relevance of the topic to actual needs of the company.

Films and videotapes. Films and videotapes are pre-recorded audio and visual presentations of material to be learned. They can be shown on either movie screens or television sets and are well-suited for use with any number of trainees. They can be purchased or rented ready-made at affordable prices or prepared specifically for one firm. An advantage of films and videotapes over lectures is that they can show objects and processes in detail and in motion, facilitating transfer because visual images tend to be remembered longer than verbal ones and visual presentations can have greater similarity to the job situation.

Films and videotapes suffer some of the same disadvantages as the lecture method; namely, the audience is passive and has no opportunity for feedback, reinforcement, or practice. In addition, they are even more impersonal than lectures because there is no live instructor. Of course, videotapes or films are often used as only one part of a program that also includes live presentations; in such a case, the audio-visual and the lecture method are complementary.

[29] G. Allen, "Politics in the Office," *Maclean's*, July 15, 1985.
[30] Ibid.

Programmed instruction. Programmed instruction presents information in small blocks through either printed pages or a computer screen. After reading each block of material, the learner must answer a question about it. Feedback in the form of correct answers is provided after each response. A major advantage of programmed instruction is that it is self-paced; each trainee can progress through the program at his or her own speed. It provides a high degree of reinforcement and knowledge of results and motivates most trainees in that they are actively engaged in the learning experience. Also, the material is structured, giving much opportunity for practice. However, transfer of learning can be a problem since the learning situation is so unlike the job situation. The development costs of programmed instruction are high but may be justified because the method is very flexible and can accommodate a number of employees at different times and in different locations. Research has shown that programmed instruction results in faster learning, but not in learning superior to that achieved with other methods.[31]

Computer-assisted instruction. Computer-assisted instruction (CAI) is similar to programmed instruction in that it uses a computer's storage and memory capabilities to individualize instruction. Thus, learners can begin at a level appropriate to their abilities (a criterion-referenced approach) and proceed at their own pace. The computer analyzes the learner's responses and determines what material is to be presented next. In terms of the learning principles, computer-assisted instruction is much like programmed instruction except CAI's feedback can be as rich and colourful as modern electronic games, complete with audio and visual displays. Computer costs are high (an estimated $2,000 to $20,000 per hour of instruction[32]), but repeated use of a program may justify the costs. Research shows that computer-assisted instruction leads to faster, but not necessarily superior learning. One recent study of CAI use for training in electronics found that it resulted in shorter learning times than conventional classroom training, with the same level of learning achievement. Learning times for CAI users were even shorter when two trainees teamed up to use the same computer.[33]

Interactive videodisc instruction (IVI). Interactive videodisc instruction is similar to computer-assisted instruction, but it includes the graphic capabilities of television or film as well as the interactive capabilities of the computer. Interactive capabilities make criterion-referenced, self-paced learning possible since the content, level, pace, and sequencing of material all depend upon trainee responses. Through the use of branching, software can be designed to allow trainees to skip material they already know, review material not yet mastered,

[31] Goldstein, *Training.*
[32] J. Main, "New Ways to Teach Workers What's New," *Fortune*, October 1, 1984, pp. 85–94.
[33] D.L. Dossett and P. Hulvershorn, "Increasing Technical Training Efficiency: Peer Training via Computer-Assisted Instruction," *Journal of Applied Psychology*, 1983, vol. 68, no. 4, pp. 552–58.

and cover material according to their own pace and style. Using this method, learners are presented with video displays of work situations such as an engine that needs adjustment or a fire in a chemical warehouse. After choosing from a set of alternative responses to the situation, the trainee is shown the consequences, right or wrong, of the chosen alternative. These are vividly displayed in the form of audios and videos of actual situations.

Videodisc technology has been combined with computer graphics and simulators to approximate highly realistic work settings such as airplane cockpits and ship bridges. The simulators duplicate controls and instruments and provide sensations a person would feel while actually operating the equipment. With the addition of videodiscs, trainees can also see and hear what they would actually experience as a result of their responses. Thus, pilot trainees can be taught how to land at major international airports, under all types of weather conditions without ever leaving the ground.

Though one hour of videodisc material may cost from $35,000 to $100,000, companies such as International Business Machines (IBM), Ford, J.C. Penney, Hewlett-Packard, America Telephone and Telegraph (AT&T), and General Electric are making use of the method.[34] As yet, little research has been done on IVI, but it appears to reduce learning time and should improve learning due to the intrinsically motivating nature of the method.

Motor Skills

Learning motor skills requires practising demonstrated behaviours and receiving performance feedback. Methods and aids frequently used to teach motor skills include job instruction training, vestibule training, apprenticeship training, coaching, and video systems.

Job instruction training. Job instruction training is one of the older methods of on-the-job training, especially for manual jobs. This was the method used to train Jane Simpson for the job of shipping clerk. Job instruction training is sometimes referred to as "Tell, Show, Do, and Review," because of its steps: (1) "Tell" (the trainee is told how to do the activity); (2) "Show" (the trainee is shown how to do it); (3) "Do" (the trainee has an opportunity to practise the activity); and (4) "Review" (the trainee receives feedback and correction on practice attempts). The person in charge of training is usually the immediate supervisor or an experienced co-worker. Job instruction training implements all the learning principles. It is an excellent method, though it may be somewhat costly in terms of a trainer's time since it requires close monitoring of trainees.

Vestibule training. Vestibule training is very much like job instruction training except that it occurs off the job, away from the production

[34] Main.

area. It is usually employed to teach trainees how to use the machinery and tools that they will be using on the job. Although vestibule training uses the learning principles, it may present some problem for transfer of learning unless its machinery and tools are identical to those used on the job. Also, vestibule training cannot simulate work environment conditions such as noise, distractions from co-workers, and job pressures. Rather, it allows the employee to develop necessary skills in a pressure-free environment. And the absence of noise and other distractions may contribute to more rapid mastery of skills.

Apprenticeship training. Apprenticeship training combines job instruction and vestibule training in that it provides instruction both on and off the job. This method is used in various skilled trades—industrial, construction, and others. The training includes work under the supervision of certified workers in the trade and time spent in school, usually a community college. Training periods vary from three to five years in length and normally end with an examination that must be passed for certification. Provincial governments regulate the type and amount of instruction required for apprenticeship and pay rates in relation to those of certified workers. When training is provided in a unionized plant, the collective agreement sets out a schedule for it as well as the rates of pay for apprentices. It may also stipulate who is to be given preference when apprenticeship positions become available.

While the apprenticeship method tends to develop well-qualified workers in the skilled trades, it has been criticized because the numbers trained have generally been less than the demand for these workers in Canada. Moreover, since apprentices have to be employed to receive instruction, their numbers fluctuate with the general level of employment. And because apprenticeship is time-consuming, it requires a very long lead time for human resource planning. Proposals have been made to integrate apprenticeship training more fully with community college programs in order to ensure a greater number of apprentices in Canada.[35]

Coaching. Coaching is a method of on-the-job training commonly used for all kinds of trainees, from unskilled to managerial. In this method, a trainer or boss (the "coach") works with one or a few trainees, assigning tasks, monitoring performance, and providing reinforcement and feedback. Coaching is a continuous process of shaping a trainee's behaviour. The method is critically dependent upon quality of the coach—his or her ability to communicate, to motivate, and to provide supportive, noncritical, realistic performance feedback. It is important that coaches convey to trainees a clear statement of their job responsibilities. Though seemingly an obvious point, one expert recently estimated, based on a major 1982 survey, that salaries totalling $300 million had been paid to federal employees "confused about their job responsibilities."[36] Coaches must also convey information about performance expectations and standards by which work will be judged.

[35] Adams, Dodge, and Allmand.
[36] Allen.

Coaching as a method incorporates all five learning principles, but practice opportunities may be limited since it is often difficult to learn and practise material in an organized way when one's employer is "running a business not a training centre." This method can also be costly if one person serves as a full-time coach for only a few trainees.

Video systems. Companies with video systems, which include cameras and recorders, can videotape groups of trainees at practice or simulated sessions, then play back their actions for discussion. The playback segments of this method are often preceded, and perhaps followed, by pre-recorded taped demonstrations by experts. These can be purchased or developed using the organization's own equipment. The demonstration segments of this method are like other film and videotape training materials, while playback of the practice sessions provides immediate performance feedback which is very reinforcing. The opportunity to see one's performance on screen can also be a motivating factor. This method is frequently used to demonstrate and play back motor and interpersonal skills.

Interpersonal Skills and Attitude Change

The teaching of interpersonal skills, such as effective communication, listening, and techniques of persuasion, usually occurs in a small-group format. Feedback and practice opportunities are especially important. Methods for this training include conference/discussion, role play, behaviour modelling, and T-groups (sensitivity training).

Conference/discussion. The conference/discussion method is a directed discussion on a specific topic conducted with a relatively small group of trainees. Trainees participate in a great deal of verbal interaction with the discussion leader and with one another. As a result, conference/discussion is useful for teaching and exploring difficult conceptual material and for changing attitudes and opinions. It provides much opportunity for feedback, reinforcement, practice, motivation, and transfer, largely through the active interchanges between participants.[37] Conference/discussion is a popular managerial training method, but it is more expensive than the lecture method since group size is limited to 20 or less.

Role play. Role play teaches interpersonal skills by having two or more trainees interact within the context of a realistic situation. The situation is defined in a case format so that each trainee receives the same information. Each trainee plays the role of a specific person in the situation, such as the boss or one of several subordinates.

Role play is a very useful method for learning interpersonal skills since trainees are actively engaged in a situation in which new behaviour

[37] Bass and Vaughan.

can be practised. The trainer is very important to success of this method since he or she provides feedback and reinforcement, although videotaping the role plays can also facilitate feedback. The success of learning transfer depends on how well role play approximates interpersonal situations on the job. The cost of the method is moderately high since a trainer cannot handle more than one or two small groups of role players.

Behaviour modelling. Behaviour modelling, a relatively new method for teaching interpersonal skills and attitude change, is based on Albert Bandura's social learning theory.[38] The method is very specific in its training objectives. It teaches specific supervisory skills by: (1) presenting a model or good example of the behaviour to be learned; (2) allowing trainees to practise the modelled behaviour; and (3) providing feedback and reinforcement on practice attempts. To the degree that interpersonal skills learned prove useful on the job, some attitude change occurs. This method requires the development of specific behavioural models, which are then filmed or videotaped. Trainees view these films and receive opportunities to role-play the modelled behaviour. Feedback and reinforcement are provided by the trainer, other trainees, and videotaped playbacks of practice attempts. Because trainees are actively involved in the learning process and can easily see the value of the modelled behaviour in the simulated situations, they are easily motivated. Behaviour modelling has, in principle, the greatest number of transfer mechanisms of any method in Exhibit 9.5. Behaviour modelling situations are designed to approximate on-the-job situations as closely as possible; ample opportunities for overlearning exist; and a variety of situations can be portrayed. Instructors and written materials provide the key elements of the skills to be learned, and general principles useful for transfer can also be acquired.To some degree this training method accommodates individual differences: it is sufficiently flexible to permit giving more time to slower learners, and trainees at different levels can be grouped. Behaviour modelling tends to be a relatively expensive training method because group size must be limited to ten or 12 trainees.

Most studies on behaviour modelling have shown that trainees have positive reactions to this method and acquire new knowledge and skills as a result. However, only a few studies have demonstrated positive transfer of newly learned skills to the job. Of four behaviour modelling studies using objective measures of behaviour change on the job after training, only two found behavioural changes on the job and these were attributed to supervisors' motivation to change.[39] In one of the studies, supervisors were directed and encouraged by their

[38] A. Bandura, *Principles of Behavior Modification* (New York: Holt Rinehart and Winston, 1969).

[39] G.P. Latham and L.M. Saari, "The Application of Social Learning Theory to Training Supervisors through Behaviour Modeling," *Journal of Applied Psychology*, 1979, vol. 64, pp. 239–46; M. Sorcher and R. Spence, "The Interface Project: Behavior Modeling and Social Technology in South Africa," *Personnel Psychology*, Autumn 1982, vol. 35, no. 3, pp. 557–82.

bosses to use their newly acquired skills; in the other, subordinates of the supervisors received identical training at the same time, although in separate groups.

T-groups. The T-group method—also known as *sensitivity training* —uses a small number of trainees, usually fewer than 12 in a group, who meet with a passive trainer to gain insight into their own and others' behaviour. Meetings have no agenda, and questions deal with the "here and now" of the group process. Discussion focusses on "why participants behave as they do, how they perceive one another, and the feelings and emotions generated in the interaction process."[40]

T-groups exemplify the faddishness of some training methods. They became very popular in the early 1960s but are now seldom used. Although research shows that they often produce desired changes in interpersonal behaviour and are useful for individual growth and development, they rarely have positive effects on organizational performance.[41]

T-groups are highly involving and give participants some opportunity to practise new behaviour, but the material to be learned is very unstructured; feedback and reinforcement are primarily in the hands of other group members, and transfer is difficult unless everyone on the job has also been in a T-group.

Decision-Making and Problem-Solving Skills

Training methods to improve decision-making and problem-solving skills generally attempt to structure situations in which trainees can put these skills to work. The methods include the case method, the in-basket technique, business games, internships, and job rotation.

Case method. One of the oldest methods of teaching decision-making and problem-solving skills is the case method. It presents trainees with a long and detailed written description of a business or organizational problem and asks them to propose a solution. The object of the case method is to teach trainees how to analyze information, generate decision alternatives, and evaluate the alternatives. Cases can be analyzed by individuals or small groups. Feedback and reinforcement are provided through oral discussion in class or written comments from the instructor or class members. Through case analysis, trainees learn to transfer the appropriate principles to examples of "real" problems. Though there is little conclusive research evidence about effectiveness of the case method, it is widely used in business schools and industry. It is one of the least expensive methods of teaching decision-making and problem-solving skills.

[40] J.R. Hinrichs, "Personnel Training," in M.D. Dunnette, ed., *Handbook of Industrial/Organizational Psychology* (Chicago: Rand McNally, 1976), p. 856.

[41] Ibid.

A four-week business management course for managers at General Electric used an uncommon method called the "living case" method. This method presents decision makers with data and materials about unresolved *present-day* challenges facing a company.[42]

In-basket technique. The in-basket technique is a simulation training method that puts the trainee in the role of a person who must suddenly replace a manager. The trainee receives background information about the organization and the person he or she is replacing, as well as letters, memos, and phone messages. He or she must organize the information, make decisions, and prepare memos and letters to handle the problems presented. In-baskets can be developed for almost any type of job involving managerial or professional decision-making. The method is highly involved and covers major features of managerial jobs. Thus, it has good motivational properties and provides opportunities for transfer. Its value as a training technique depends on the amount of feedback and reinforcement provided, which varies among trainers. The in-basket technique is also a common component of assessment centres used to identify managerial talent.

Business games. The most famous business game in existence is probably Parker Brothers' *Monopoly*. The business game technique requires trainees to make sequential decisions. It is a more dynamic method than case studies since the decisions made early in the game affect not only the outcome but the alternatives available later during play. Trainees work by themselves or in teams in which each member takes the role of manager of a functional area such as human resource management, finance, and marketing. Trainees usually regard business games as highly involving and motivating since, as in any game, they keep score and compete with each other. Modern business games commonly use a computer to analyze the trainees' decisions and provide their organizational consequences. A game can simulate an organization's entire operations over several years, or it may be restricted to one or two functions, such as marketing or manufacturing.

With the assistance of a grant from the Burrough's Corporation (now UNISYS), researchers at the University of Iowa are developing interactive business games in which trainees use computers to compete against each other or the computer. In one game, trainees play the part of a boot manufacturer who can advertise in various magazines displayed on their terminals. Trainees choose how they want to advertise the product, then wait for consumer reaction and respond to it. Problems with the product, such as short sole life, are introduced so that decisions must be made regarding remedial actions to take. This computer business game and others like it can be expanded to include multiple companies. In this case, each trainee takes the role of a

[42] E.S. Andrews and J.L. Noel, "Adding Life to the Case-Study Method," *Training and Development Journal*, February 1986, pp. 28–9.

different company, and decisions of one trainee affect the market environment of all the other companies. Other games being developed at U of I simulate collective bargaining. In these games trainees sharpen their bargaining or negotiating skills.

Because of the nature of business games, trainees do not know the decision-making and problem-solving principles to be learned until after completing the game. They also do not get feedback or reinforcement from the instructor until afterwards, though many games do provide quarterly feedback on company performance. Though business games are relatively expensive to develop, if they are properly designed and well-run, they provide a unique method of teaching trainees how to analyze information, make decisions, and work within the context of those decisions.

Internships and job rotation. In addition to off-the-job methods for improving decision-making and problem-solving skills, two on-the-job methods are commonly used for acquiring these skills: internship and job rotation. They are usually used after trainees have completed all or part of their formal off-the-job training.

Internships are designed to teach professionals or managers the skills and knowledge to do their new jobs. In principle, they are similar to apprenticeships in the skilled trades, although they are not regulated by the provinces. Trainees learn by observing experienced professionals performing their jobs, by questioning these experienced workers, and by performing some tasks under supervision.

Job rotation programs move managers or managerial trainees from one job to another in the organization with the goal of familiarizing the trainees with each job or organizational unit. The length of time in each unit is usually three to 12 months.

Although transfer of learning is no problem for either of these methods, both may lack opportunities for the practice of critical but rare behaviour. Also, feedback and reinforcement depend on the supervisor. Learning on the job through internships and job rotation may place learners in pressure situations in which mistakes are very costly. However, since trainees help produce goods or services, these on-the-job methods are relatively inexpensive.

Implementing the Training Program

Once a training program has been chosen, HRM professionals are responsible for its implementation. This responsibility includes planning and executing training sessions and building a corps of competent trainers. As we have already noted, government assistance is often available for training programs, frequently through federal-provincial cost-sharing programs. An employer who wants to explore the possibility of obtaining assistance for establishing or expanding a training program first contacts a Canada Employment Centre (CEC). The CEC assigns a T&D specialist to consider the request. CECs are also ready to supply advice and information on training content and methods. Provincial authorities have responsibility for the registration and certification of apprentices.

Training Sessions

Training sessions must be well planned. A poorly planned and executed program can create negative impressions for trainers and trainees alike. Trainers should know well in advance the general purpose of training and the dates, duration, and location of the program. Materials must be readied and any equipment put in operational order. Whether the training program lasts one hour or a year, each part should be coordinated with trainees' regular work activities to minimize disruption of their work and of the organization's operations and to maximize learning, practice, and transfer opportunities. This requires careful planning and coordination of trainees, trainers, their bosses, and material and equipment suppliers.

Trainers

Unless an organization employs enough trainers to meet training needs (and most do not), the implementation of training programs involves building a corps of competent trainers. Consulting organizations can provide trainers as needed. More often, however, managers, supervisors, and HRM staff within the organization serve as trainers.

A trainer is basically a teacher, and a teacher's primary goal is to influence students' attitudes and behaviour. Organizations too often assume that an experienced employee, supervisor, or manager is a good teacher, especially in the case of on-the-job training. Like any other interpersonal skill, training or teaching can and should be taught to those with training responsibilities. Generally, trainers should be taught how to organize and present their material, motivate and reinforce trainees, and prepare them to apply new material to the job. Training the trainers is an important responsibility of HRM professionals and T&D specialists.

Training Rooms

Training rooms should have certain characteristics. Specifically, they should be flexible, isolated, properly lit and ventilated, and able to accommodate computer equipment and a variety of training activities, such as videotape viewing, role plays, group discussions, and computer use. Furniture, including tables and chairs, should be easily moved to facilitate different training activities. Most management conferences, for example, use a U-shaped seating arrangement, while team tasks or small-group exercises cluster only a few chairs around each of a number of tables. Isolation, both physical and psychological, is necessary to ensure that trainees are able to concentrate on learning, rather than worrying about work problems. Lighting control is necessary, particularly for film and video displays. And anyone who has fallen asleep in an over-heated, stuffy classroom realizes the value of maintaining a comfortable temperature (between 22.5° and 24°C), humidity level (about 50 per cent), and airflow (12 to 15 feet per minute).[43]

Training Programs in Practice

BNA's survey of 159 organizations provided insights into training program content and methods used by the firms. We look first at training programs for nonmanagement employees. Findings are based on 138 firms that conduct formal in-house training for such employees.

Training Programs for Nonmanagement Employees

The most common training topics for nonmanagement employees are shown in Exhibit 9.6. New employee training, safety/security, com-

EXHIBIT 9.6

Training topics for nonmanagement employees

Training topic	*Per cent of companies covering topic (n = 138)*
New employee training	59%
Safety/security	53
Communication skills	49
Skills reinforcement/upgrading	49
Human relations skills	48
Company orientation	46
New technology/procedures	46
Information management	42
Time management	32
Career/personal development	24
No details provided	22

SOURCE: Derived from the Bureau of National Affairs, *Training and Development Programs PPF Survey No. 140* (Washington, D.C.: BNA, Sept. 1985, p. 6.

[43] D. Laird, "What Should Training Rooms be Like?" in D. Laird, *Approaches to Training and Development* (Reading, Mass.: Addison-Wesley, 1985), pp. 185–202.

munication skills, skills reinforcement/upgrading, and human relations skills top the list, followed closely by company orientation, new technology/procedures, and information management. Time management and career/personal development are also offered by some firms. Although not shown in the table, type of training offered varies among employee groups. For example, safety/security training is more common for production/service workers than for office/clerical workers, professional/technical workers, and sales personnel. On the other hand, the latter groups more often receive training related to communication skills.

Methods used for training nonmanagement employees are given in Exhibit 9.7. Lecture/demonstration and films/slide programs/videotapes are by far the most common in-house methods used to train nonmanagement workers. Computer-assisted instruction is used by 22 per cent of the firms, and 36 per cent use other kinds of programmed (self-paced) instruction. Less common are vestibule training and other training methods.

Besides in-house training, most firms also make available opportunities for outside training by offering tuition aid or sending workers to seminars and workshops.

EXHIBIT 9.7

Methods used for training nonmanagement employees

Method	*Per cent of companies using method (n = 138)*
In-house methods:	
Lecture/demonstration	76%
Films/slides/videotapes	64
Computer-assisted instruction	22
Other programmed (self-paced) instruction	36
Vestibule training	12
Other	7
Outside training:	
Tuition aid	77
Seminars/workshops	72

SOURCE: Derived from the Bureau of National Affairs, *Training and Development Programs PPF Survey No. 140* (Washington D.C.: BNA, Sept. 1985), pp. 10–11.

Training Programs for Supervisors and Managers

Surveyed firms offering formal in-house training and development programs for supervisors and managers number 135. As seen in Exhibit 9.8, at least half the firms report covering the following topics: coaching/counselling/discipline; leadership skills; performance appraisal; Equal Employment Opportunity/affirmative action; selection/interviewing techniques; safety/security; and work planning/scheduling/time management.

EXHIBIT 9.8

Common T&D topics for supervisors and managers

	Per cent of companies covering topic (n = 135)	
Training topic	*First-level supervisors*	*Middle managers*
Coaching/counselling/discipline	69%	59%
Leadership skills	65	58
Performance appraisal	64	66
EEO/affirmative action	60	56
Selection/interviewing techniques	53	49
Safety/security	63	41
Work planning/scheduling/time management	50	46
Communication techniques/business writing	47	43
Decision-making/problem-solving	45	49
Labour relations/grievances/contract administration	45	33
Wage and salary administration	40	41
Employee benefits programs	40	36
Company orientation	33	28
Productivity measurement/improvement/control	29	30

SOURCE: Derived from the Bureau of National Affairs, *Training and Development Programs PPF Survey No. 140* (Washington D.C.: BNA, Sept. 1985), pp. 14–15.

Also frequently offered to supervisors and managers (by 40 per cent or more of the firms) are programs relating to communication techniques/business writing; decision making/problem solving; labour relations/grievances/contract administration; wage and salary administration; and employee benefits.

Common T&D methods for supervisors and managers are shown in Exhibit 9.9. The most common in-house methods are lecture/discussion, films/slide programs/videotapes, and on-the-job coaching, used by approximately three-fourths of the firms. At least half report using role plays and case studies, and about one-third report using programmed (self-paced) instruction, committee assignments, and management/business games.

Outside opportunities are also frequently used for training and developing supervisors and managers. Organizations often send supervisors and managers to seminars and professional or trade association meetings and provide tuition aid.

EXHIBIT 9.9

Common T&D methods for supervisors and managers

Method	*Per cent of companies using method (n = 135)*	
	First-level supervisors	*Middle managers*
In-house methods:		
Lecture/discussion	78%	73%
Films/slides/videotapes	76	70
On-the-job coaching	73	61
Role playing	63	55
Case study	51	52
Programmed (self-paced instruction)	43	37
Committee assignments	35	43
Management/business games	28	30
Outside training:		
Tuition aid	74	73
Seminars	67	74
Professional and trade association meetings	56	69

SOURCE: Derived from the Bureau of National Affairs, *Training and Development Programs PPF Survey No. 140* (Washington D.C.: BNA, Sept. 1985), pp. 17, 20.

Evaluating the Training Program

For years, psychologists and personnel researchers bemoaned the fact that many employers took on faith the effectiveness of their training and development programs.[44] If results from the BNA survey are representative, researchers may finally have made their point. The BNA

[44] See, for example, J.P. Campbell, "Personnel Training and Development," *Annual Review of Psychology*, 1971, vol. 22, pp. 565–602, and Hinrichs, "Personnel Training."

survey found that 70 per cent of the surveyed companies conduct formal evaluations of their management and nonmanagement training programs. Of this 70 per cent, over 96 per cent obtain trainee feedback; approximately 65 per cent measure on-the-job performance changes; one fourth examine changes in company performance, such as production volume, profits, sales, absenteeism, and turnover; and about 15 per cent conduct before and after testing of trainees.[45] Thus, it appears that many of today's organizations are evaluating their training programs. The reasons for doing so are presented below.

Why Evaluate?

The major reason for evaluating training programs is to determine if they are accomplishing specific training objectives. For example, the success of a program to teach T&D specialists to write training objectives can be measured in terms of how well the specialists can write objectives after completing the program. A training program that does not change employees' knowledge, skills, or attitudes in the desired direction should be modified or replaced. Economists have attempted to measure the impact of training by comparing the before and after earnings of persons who undertook training with those who did not. A 1972 study estimated that adult occupational training in Canada produced \$2.00 to \$3.00 in benefits to the employee for each \$1.00 invested.[46] (This calculation was, however, viewed with some reservation because, among other things, no control group was used.)

A second reason for evaluation is to ascertain whether changes in trainees' capabilities come from the training program. This is particularly important when a training program is first begun, since good results may lead to its adoption for other employees. To determine that a training program is responsible for changes in trainees, it is necessary to compare the trainees' performance, both before and after the program, with the performance of a control group. For example, a training program on managerial decision-making can be given to one group of management trainees, but not to another. If, after training, *both* groups demonstrate similar increases in decision-making skills, improvement is not attributable to the training program. If, on the other hand, only those who participated in the training program demonstrate increases in their decision-making skills, then the program has probably had some degree of success.

Another reason to evaluate training programs is to explain failure if it occurs. A basically sound program may fail to meet its objectives for many reasons. Perhaps training objectives were too ambitious, and although trainees may have made substantial progress towards their mastery, the program seems to have failed because it fell short of its objectives. A sound program may also fail because of circumstances

[45] BNA.

[46] Economic Council of Canada, *Eighth Annual Review: Design for Decision-Making* (Ottawa: Information Canada, 1971).

beyond its planners' control. Perhaps the program was not implemented properly because of equipment breakdown or human failure. Depending upon the reasons for a program's lack of success, the program may either be retained or discontinued.

Training programs should also be evaluated to determine their cost effectiveness. Like any other human resource or business programs, training programs must demonstrate cost effectiveness in order to justify their continuation. Basically, to be cost effective, a training program must result in gains in employee performance or job-related behaviour that outweigh the costs of training. When training programs are evaluated for cost effectiveness, programs can be compared to determine the least costly way of achieving desired results. For example, if both on-the-job training and a formal safety instruction program result in increased use of protective devices on the job, an organization would want to retain the less costly program for meeting these training needs in the future.

Conducting the Evaluation

The evaluation of training programs has four parts: (1) setting training objectives; (2) gathering pre-training data, sometimes called ***baseline data*** because they show the level, or base, of a trainee's performance before training; (3) gathering data during and after training; and (4) comparing the pre- and post-training data. If possible, the results of this comparison should then be compared with those of a control group of similar employees who were not trained.

The process of evaluating training programs begins in the planning stages of training with the specification of training objectives. Training objectives, which are obtained from a needs analysis, provide standards for the evaluation of program effectiveness.

Baseline data are of three general types: (1) measures of knowledge or skill obtained through tests or other standardized measures; (2) on-the-job behaviour and performance measures (such as individual production rates, error rates, customer complaints); and (3) organizational results measures (such as profitability, production costs, and scrap rate). These three types differ in their relationship to individuals: knowledge and skill measures accurately reflect an individual's pre-training performance, while organizational results data may be affected by many factors unrelated to the individual or how much was learned in training.

The third part of evaluation requires gathering data during and after training. By monitoring the progress of trainees during training, "bugs" can be worked out of the program. Post-training data, which can be gathered immediately after training and at various times thereafter, are usually of two types. The most commonly gathered are trainee reactions to the program, which are usually solicited by questionnaire. Unfortunately, information of this type is of little value in evaluating the effectiveness of training. It can, however, provide some guidelines for modifying the program in order to increase its organization, motivating effect, and use of materials. A generally negative reaction from trainees, especially regarding how much they feel they learned in the program, can indicate a need for major program changes.

The second type of post-training data demonstrates whether learning has taken place by comparing the pre-training and post-training test scores of trainees. Ideally, the same tests have also been given to a control group at the same times. When employees are randomly assigned to either a control or experimental group and a true experiment is conducted, effectiveness of training can be scientifically examined. Even if pre-measures cannot be obtained, comparison of post-training results between experimental and control groups provides excellent information on program effectiveness. This is because random assignment assures that experimental and control groups are equivalent and any differences are due to the training program.

Since training objectives usually specify mastery of material or results to be used on the job, it is necessary to collect on-the-job performance data to determine whether learning has successfully been transferred to the job. In many cases, learning may be short-lived or may transfer unsuccessfully. Job performance and organizational results data must therefore be collected and analyzed for some time after training. Few organizations examine the effects of training programs beyond one year, but if performance returns to pre-training levels in a little more than a year, it may be difficult to justify the costs of training. (Such results may also indicate that training was not an appropriate solution to a performance problem.)

It is possible to estimate the utility of a training program in much the same way as we estimated the utility of an additional predictor in the selection chapter (see Appendix 7A, p. 250). For a discussion of estimating the utility of a training program, see Appendix 9A, p. 328.

Summary

The training and development area has experienced recent growth, and this trend can be expected to continue. The major contribution of training and development to organizational effectiveness is to help maintain a qualified work force. Training and development responsibilities are handled by HRM professionals, including T&D specialists, and supervisors and managers.

Training programs should begin with a training needs assessment in which organizational information is monitored and performance problems are analyzed. While many organizations omit or short-cut this assessment phase, it is necessary in order to develop specific behavioural training objectives, to select proper training methods and programs, and to formulate evaluation methods and measures. After training needs are determined and translated into objectives, programs or methods must be developed or selected. Choice of a training program is affected by four major considerations: (1) nature of the material to be learned (information, motor skills, interpersonal skills and attitude change, decision-making and problem-solving skills); (2) extent to which the program incorporates the key learning principles of feedback, reinforcement, practice, motivation, and transfer of learning; (3) characteristics of trainees, their numbers and abilities; and (4) budgetary constraints. Considerable care must be given to the actual operation or running of a training program. Sessions must be planned in advance for smooth execution, trainers may need to be trained, and programs should be coordinated with trainees' regular work activities to minimize disruption. Finally, evaluation of training programs should be well planned before training begins. A good evaluation procedure involves a control group and pre- and post-training measures of trainees' abilities, job behaviour, and/or organizational performance outcomes. The evaluation process should be regarded as an integral part of any training program. Information from evaluation is necessary to revise, improve, or completely change the content or methods of training programs used.

Project Ideas

1. Describe from your personal experience a learning situation in which you had to improve or master a certain skill or behaviour. Explain the learning process or the training situation involved. How did the process facilitate the key learning principles of feedback, reinforcement, practice, motivation, and transfer of learning? Were any of the learning principles more or less important to you or to the mastery of the task at hand? Why?

2. Read R.F. Mager's short, amusing paperback *Preparing Instructional Objectives*, 2nd ed. (Belmont, Calif.: Fearon-Pitman, 1975). Choose four jobs that you are familiar with and generate two useful training objectives for each (according to Mager's definition of "useful"). Write a brief paper relating how your training objectives demonstrate the key principles in Mager's book.

3. Consider each activity and behaviour required for the job of public-opinion collector as described below in the Department of Manpower and Immigration's *Canadian Classification and Dictionary of Occupations* (Ottawa: Information Canada, 1971). What methods could be used to train an inexperienced person in each kind of required behaviour? Choose an optimal method for training in each and explain why you chose it over other possible methods. Assemble the optimal methods into a training package.

4199–214 PUBLIC-OPINION COLLECTOR (clerical) DPT:368
public interviewer.
GED: 3 SVP: 3 EC: B PA: L 4 5 6

Interviews public and compiles statistical information on topics, such as public issues or consumer buying habits:

Contacts people at their homes or places of business, approaches them at random on street, or contacts them by telephone following specified sampling procedures. Asks questions following outline on questionnaire, and records answers. Reviews, classifies and sorts questionnaires following specified procedures and criteria.

May tally and prepare statistical reports on answers to questions. May participate in federal, provincial or local population surveys and be designated accordingly, Census Taker (gov. serv.)

4. Examine training and/or business journals to find an article describing an organization's training program. Describe this program in a short report. What methods does it use? What are some of its advantages? Can you think of any disadvantages? Are there any situations in which it would not be appropriate? (Students can learn about a variety of real-world training efforts if a number of oral reports are given on this topic.)

Cases

Case 9.1: Training and Development at Deli-Delite

Anne Dotsworth has recently joined the staff of Deli-Delite Industries, a Toronto-based food processing plant. As human resource specialist, she serves in an advisory capacity to General Manager Harry Walsh. One of Dotsworth's first assignments is to recommend training and development programs for key personnel under Walsh. She has a budget of $3,000 to work with.

Since Dotsworth is new to Deli-Delite, she begins by familiarizing herself with Walsh's immediate subordinates. They are Anton, National Sales Manager; Benson, Traffic Manager; Carmella, National Brand Manager; Dixon, Product Manager; and Ellwood, Controller. Reading through personnel files of the five, Dotsworth gives special attention to information regarding performance reviews, promotions, past training and development activities, and career aspirations. The most pertinent data are summarized into short composites for each employee. Dotsworth refers to the composites as she surveys a list of training and development opportunities prepared by her predecessor. She is now ready to make some recommendations.

Questions:

1. Assume you are Dotsworth. Which of the listed training or development program(s), if any, do you feel might benefit Anton? Benson? Carmella? Dixon? and Ellwood? Why?

2. Given your $3,000 budget, which of the listed programs will you recommend and for which employees? Will some employees receive no training or development? Provide a brief rationale for your recommendations to Walsh.

NOTE: This case is based on an exercise developed by E. Hill, H. Lichtman, and C. MacMillan.

Composites of Managerial Staff

ANTON (age 35) Anton is the Division's rising star. Starting in the sales force eight years ago, his exemplary performance quickly accelerated him through a Regional Sales Manager position to his current National Sales Manager position. Anton has responsibility for all key accounts, i.e., high volume accounts, and supervises a sales staff of 15. There has been a rumour that the company's closest competitor has approached Anton with an attractive job offer.

BENSON (age 63) Benson has been Traffic Manager for the Division for ten years now, having joined the company at its inception at Walsh's request. Benson appears to enjoy the autonomy of his one-man operation and has no aspirations for advancement. Since no major breakthroughs have occurred in the transportation industry over the past five years, and since his work has been satisfactory, Benson has been allowed to choose a personal development-type training course to attend each year. Since his in-laws moved to Winnipeg in 1980, Benson has chosen to attend courses offered in Winnipeg, scheduling them to coincide with his wife's vacation.

CARMELA (age 38) As National Brand Manager, Carmela has six product managers reporting directly to her. Although hers is primarily a strategic planning and supervisory function, she has been unable to fully relinquish the day-to-day "fire-fighting" responsibilities to her subordinates. Hence, there are never enough hours in the day for Carmela and she is often short with her subordinates. A recent exit interview with a product manager indicated that Carmela didn't give him a chance to run his own product line.

DIXON (age 55) Dixon is the Division's Production Manager. His latest performance appraisal indicates that his analytical skills need sharpening. This became apparent when Dixon failed to grasp the significance of capital budgeting calculations which pointed out the infeasibility of a proposed equipment purchase. Dixon admitted never being particularly good with numbers and appeared reluctant to spend the time necessary to fully understand the financial ramifications of his proposal.

ELLWOOD (age 53) Ellwood, a certified accountant, is the Divisional Controller. He is an extremely self-motivated, outgoing individual who has a thorough grasp of his job duties. His department runs smoothly and efficiently. Ellwood is working part-time on his MBA at a local university and Deli-Delite is paying his tuition. (This need

EXHIBIT 9.10

Training and Development Opportunities

Title	*Location*	*Duration*	*Cost*	*Course Outline*	*Special Features*
Fundamentals of traffic	Toronto, Harbour Castle	2½ Days	$810	How to manage traffic so it makes a real contribution to company profits How to best organize the traffic function What you should know about the rates and routing cycle How to translate transportation documents into valuable sources of information How to prevent claims and proceed when you do get hit Modes of transportation and how each affects your costs and time records Motor carrier regulation—what you must know	
Management Course for Controllers	Toronto, Holiday Inn	3 Days	$906	Managing yourself, your career and your staff How to make time work for you How to recognize and avoid barriers to effective communications How to set realistic standards of performance for greater success How to eliminate the obstacles to problem-solving and decision-making Successful coaching and counselling techniques How to deal successfully with change	
Action Tools for the Middle Manager	Winnipeg, Holiday Inn	4½ Days	$1,140	Managing your job and your career How to manage your time How to work with the people side of your job	

				How to use delegation effectively to get things done How to make sure your message is understood How to develop and administer a departmental standards of performance program How to measure performance and review results The positive approach to problem-solving and decision-making How to use coaching and counselling to develop staff	
Making Effective Presentations	Toronto, Sutton Place	2 Days	$468	Obstacles to effective communications Organising speeches, proposals and presentations Speaking and thinking on your feet Overcoming anxiety and developing stage confidence Using visual aids to enhance your message	Closed circuit television sessions Small group work
Effective Speed Reading	Toronto, Chelsea Inn	1 Day	$186	Evaluation of your present reading speed Why a rapid reader has better comprehension and retention Techniques for increasing reading speed and concentration Practical session to apply speed reading techniques	Activity-oriented workshop
Improving Managerial Skills	Toronto, Holiday Inn	3 Days	$756	Your role as a manager How to motivate employees (Theory X and Y) Interpersonal relationships Communicating with employees Appraising performance Managing your time	

Title	*Location*	*Duration*	*Cost*	*Course Outline*	*Special Features*
				Delegating your work Decision-making Planning and organising	
Fundamentals of Finance and Accounting for Non-Financial Managers	Toronto, Westbury Hotel	3 Days	$960	The financial community—stock markets, banks, government, financial counsellors, internal financing Financial planning and control—profit planning and budgeting, evaluation of investment performance Nature and organization of business firms—promotion, organization, finance, management Financial statement analysis—understanding accounting language, reading annual reports	Presentations Case Studies Informal Discussions Role playing
Executive Course in Sales Management	Toronto, Warwick Hotel	4½ Days	$1,044	Scope of the General Sales Manager's function and responsibilities Elements of effective sales planning Communicating within the sales organization The General Sales Manager and the management to the sales function Financial aspects of the General Sales Manager's function Pricing strategies and profit concepts Sales compensation as a tool to gain management objectives	
Wilderness Seminar on Stress Management	Banff National Park	10 Days	$1,800	Learning to handle stress more effectively Entrants must pass a stiff physical examination	Mountaineering Canoeing River rafting

not be included in the current T&D budget.) Even so, Ellwood is always anxious to attend further courses so he can meet with other members of his profession or industry. Ellwood has specifically mentioned a forthcoming seminar for controllers offered by the York Executive Development program. According to Ellwood, all his "buddies" will be in attendance.

Case 9.2: Banking on Training at York Bank and Trust

Byron Dennison, Vice-President of Training and Development for York Bank and Trust, is puzzled. He has just been handed the results of a six-month study which bank officials thought would help determine a strategy for training supervisors on the subject of performance appraisal. Now he's not so sure.

Six months earlier, the bank had decided to try performance appraisal training for supervisors as one way to increase employee productivity and improve communication. Before it implemented a large-scale program, however, it wanted to be sure that performance appraisal training for supervisors would have the intended effect on teller satisfaction and performance. It if did, what kind of training program would be most cost-effective?

To answer these questions, Dennison and his staff developed two performance appraisal training programs. One program, called "content-only training," was a four-hour lecture-discussion session on the content of performance reviews. It dealt with defining the teller's job, establishing performance standards, setting performance goals, developing a goal-oriented action plan, and discussing a follow-up to the plan. The second program, called "content-plus-procedure training," included the four-hour content segment plus two weekly three-hour sessions on planning and conducting reviews and follow-ups. This program also used a lecture-discussion format, but in between the two three-hour sessions, supervisors had a chance to conduct a practice performance review. These were analyzed and discussed at the second three-hour session.

To test the effectiveness of both programs, Dennison decided that some supervisors would receive no training, a second group would receive content-only training, and a third group would receive content-plus-procedure training. Consequently, 20 supervisors were randomly assigned to the three groups: seven received no training, seven received content-only training; and six received content-plus-procedure training. Dennison conducted the sessions, which lasted three weeks.

Within three months of the training program, supervisors conducted one of their quarterly reviews of teller performance. Supervisors with no training conducted reviews with 21 tellers, those with content-only training had reviews with 18, and those with content-plus-procedure training evaluated 13. After participating in the performance reviews, tellers were asked to fill out a questionnaire indicating their degree of usefulness. These data would be compared with teller reaction to the same questionnaire administered prior to training. As a before-and-after measure of teller performance, the bank used severity of offages, a measure of accuracy in balancing that reflects severity of imbalances at the end of each workday.

Now Dennison pondered results of the study and wondered what to make of them. The study, which held constant premeasured differences between tellers, found no statistically significant differences in satisfaction and performance between tellers under the untrained supervisors and those under the highly trained supervisors, although the latter group showed somewhat higher satisfaction and performance after the training intervention. What the study did show was that tellers evaluated by the content-only group rated the appraisal process significantly lower in usefulness that did the content-plus-procedure group. Performance of the tellers in the content-only group was also significantly lower than either of the other two groups, although their satisfaction with appraisal was about the same.

Questions:

1. Assume you are Dennison and suggest some alternative explanations for the surprising results of the study. For example, what might explain the similarity in performance and satisfaction between tellers reporting to untrained vs. highly trained supervisors? What might account for the lower performance of tellers reporting to the content-only training group?
2. What recommendations, if any, regarding implementation of a performance appraisal training program would you make on the basis of the York Bank study?
3. Given the results of the study, what do you think Dennison's next step(s) should be regarding performance appraisal training for supervisors at the bank?

SOURCE: Based on a study by N.K. Napier and J. Deller, "Train Right or Don't Train at All," *Training and Development Journal* (February 1985), pp. 90–93.

APPENDIX 9A: Estimating Utility of a Training Program

It is possible to estimate the utility of a training program in much the same way as we estimated the utility of an additional predictor in the selection chapter (see Appendix 7A, pp. 250). In estimating the utility of a good training program, however, the statistic "d" replaces Δr_{xy} in the formula. The statistic "d" is the difference between the means, in standard deviations units, of a trained (experimental) group and an untrained (control) group. A "d" value of 1.00 indicates that the mean of a trained group is one standard deviation higher than the untrained control group. Assuming normal distribution of performance scores or measures, this means that training raised the performance level of the trained group to the 85th percentile of the control group. Exhibit 9A.1 from the *American Psychologist* describes how to calculate the dollar effectiveness of a training program for computer programmers.

EXHIBIT 9A.1

Calculating utility of a training program

Schmidt, Hunter, and Pearlman (1982) show that the utility of an intervention is given in dollar terms by $U = NTSD_y d_1 - NC$, where: N = the number of workers in the intervention; T = the average duration of the intervention effect; SD_y = the standard deviation of job performance in dollars; d_1 = the difference in job performance in true score standard deviation units; and C = the average cost of the intervention per worker. If the intervention has a permanent effect on job performance, then the duration of the effect T would be the tenure of the worker. However, some interventions probably have only a temporary effect, and this fact must be taken into account in estimating T. The value d_1 can be taken directly from an evaluation study only if performance is perfectly measured; otherwise the observed value must be corrected for error of measurement (i.e., divided by the square root of the reliability of the performance measure).

Let us illustrate this formula with a hypothetical training program for computer programmers. Based on the review by Asher and Sciarrino (1981), the *d* value for a typical training program can be very conservatively estimated as .40. If we assume an average reliability for the performance variable of .90, our estimate of d_1 is only slightly larger than *d*. That is, $d_1 = .40/\sqrt{.90} = .42$. Assume that the cost of the training program is $30 per day for teaching expenses and $100 per day in lost work time. For a 10-day program, the cost per programmer would be $300 + $1000 = $1300. Next, assume that 100 programmers will be trained. The standard deviation of job performance could be estimated either at the figure found in a study on computer programmers using the judgment method (Schmidt, Hunter, McKenzie, & Muldrow, 1979) or by 40% of annual wage; that is, $10,413 or .40 ($25,000) = $10,000. We will use our local figure of 40% of wage or $10,000.

We now have all the information we need to compute the dollar value of the computer programmer training course except for one item: *T*, the duration in years of the training effect. Where they are not permanent, the effects of organizational interventions probably decline gradually with time rather than disappearing abruptly. For example, the effects of programmer training might decline to zero over a period of 4 years. Taking this into account, the best estimate of *T* might be the duration of the period of decline divided by 2. This leads to an estimated duration of 2 years for effect of the programmer course. The increase in productivity would then be $NTSD_y d_1$ = (100)(2)($10,000)(.42) = $840,000, while the cost of the program would be NC = (100)($1,300) = $130,000, for a net utility of $710,000. Larger values for *d* would produce correspondingly larger net utility figures. The percentage increase in output resulting from the training program is $d_t(20\%) = .42\,(20\%) = 8.4\%$.

REFERENCES:

Asher, J.J. & Sciarrino, J.A. *A Statistical Power Analysis for Research Designs in Training.* Unpublished manuscript, San Jose State University, 1981.

Schmidt, F.L., Hunter, J.E., McKenzie, R., & Muldrow, T. "The Impact of Valid Selection Procedures on Workforce Productivity," *Journal of Applied Psychology*, 1979, *64*, 609–26.

Schmidt, F.L., Hunter, J.E., & Pearlman, K. "Assessing the Economic Impact of Personnel Programs on Workforce Productivity." *Personnel Psychology*, 1982, *35*, 333–47.

10

Performance Appraisal

Terry Waters, Station Manager of CJAM Radio, arrives at work Friday morning troubled and apprehensive. The source of his anxiety is a 10:00 A.M. performance review session scheduled with disk jockey Rex Hart, who has been with the station six months. Waters likes Hart, who is basically a fine person, but many listeners are offended by Hart's "far-out" brand of humour. Already, more than a dozen people have telephoned to express their displeasure over various comments Hart has made. Furthermore, analysts note that CJAM's share of the listening audience has declined over the past few months. And several major advertisers have threatened to withdraw their support from the station unless Hart changes his tune.

Waters knows he must discuss the negative aspects of Hart's performance in the performance review session and he is certain Hart won't like what he has to say. The disk jockey will probably be surprised and upset at first, then defensive and angry. Waters hates to be the one to tell him he will either have to shape up or ship out. It is the most difficult and unpleasant part of Waters' job.

Many supervisors and managers would agree that giving a negative appraisal is one of the hardest parts of their job. Still, honest feedback is essential if employees are to improve certain aspects of their performance. Negative feedback need not be given in a brutal, uncaring manner; it can and should be presented in a constructive, supportive way, which minimizes defensiveness and allows learning to take place. In this chapter we discuss the many organizational purposes of appraisal, appraisal methods and instruments, and the appraisal interview itself.

Performance Appraisal: A Definition

Performance appraisal is the process of collecting, analyzing, evaluating and communicating information relative to individuals' job behaviour and results. The performance of organizational units and organizations as a whole can also be assessed, but this chapter focusses on the appraisal of individuals.

Performance appraisal can be formal or informal. Users of formal systems schedule regular sessions in which to discuss an employee's performance. Informal appraisals are unplanned, often chance statements made in passing about an employee's performance. Most organizations use a formal appraisal system, while also providing varying degrees of day-to-day feedback on performance.

Some organizations use more than one appraisal system, applying a different method to different types of employees or for different purposes. Formal procedures are most prevalent for evaluating office workers and lower-level managers; top managers and production employees are evaluated less frequently.[1] In organizations without a formal appraisal system, employees must guess the employer's attitude towards them and their work from subtle or indirect indicators (for example, how their boss relates personally to them versus other employees or how large a raise is received in relation to others). In such a situation, employees are likely to be ineffective on the job and feel anxious and insecure simply because they are unsure of what is expected of them and how they are doing.

An example of a high-performing company that recently improved its performance appraisal system is PepsiCo. In the early 1980s, average tenure in PepsiCo's top 470 jobs was just 18 months; managers weren't being told how they were doing in their jobs and bonus cheques were given with very little explanation of what behaviours led to the dollar amount received. Believing they could reduce turnover and burnout of valued people, top management modified the appraisal process so appraisals focussed more on what managers were doing daily, how they were planning for the long-term, and what they were doing to develop their subordinates, as well as themselves.[2]

[1] U.S. Bureau of National Affairs, "Employee Performance: Evaluation and Control," *Personnel Policies Forum*, no. 108, February 1975; and R.I. Lazer and W.S. Wikstrom, *Appraising Managerial Performance: Current Practices and Future Directions* (New York: The Conference Board, 1977).

[2] T. Hall, "Demanding PepsiCo Is Attempting to Make Work Nicer for Managers," *Wall Street Journal*, October 23, 1984.

The Purposes of Performance Appraisal

Although performance appraisal occurs on an individual level, it is a major component of the organizational control process. As such, it serves to link performance of lower-level units with that of higher-level units. Boards of directors or other planning groups begin the process by developing plans that include goals and objectives. These goals and objectives become the standards by which the performance of top management is evaluated. Similarly, top management develops goals for various strategic business units (SBU's) that affect the performance standards of their subordinate managers. Theoretically, this process continues down to the specific performance goals and standards of the lowest-level employee. Therefore, when lowest-level employees meet their performance standards, this enables higher levels in the organization to attain their goals.

The performance appraisal system is an important mechanism for communication and control of organizational goals, objectives, and values. This means that, to be effective, a performance appraisal system must have the full support of the highest level of management. For example, W. Edwards Deming, a founder of the quality control movement, argues that higher quality products may be produced at lower cost through commitment to quality from top management, rather than from more automation and mass inspections.[3]

The organizational purposes served by performance appraisal are many and varied. They can be classified into three major areas: administrative, employee development, and monitoring/assessment purposes.

Administrative Purposes

Performance appraisals for administrative purposes provide employers with a rationale or basis for making many HRM decisions, such as those relating to pay, promotions, demotions, terminations, and transfers. For administrative purposes, a global, or overall, rating for each employee is usually desired in order to facilitate employee comparisons. Since most appraisal methods provide ratings of employees on a number of different factors of job performance, in order to be useful for administrative purposes, multiple ratings must be combined into a composite rating for each employee. Composite ratings can be obtained in several ways. One is to add the ratings for each performance factor and use the total as a composite; another is to average the factors to obtain a mean. A more sophisticated composite weights each performance factor according to its contribution to job effectiveness. (Of course, job effectiveness itself is usually a composite measure.) Administrative

[3] "An Interview with W. Edwards Deming", *Pacific Basic Quarterly*, Spring/Summer, 1985.

decisions based on performance appraisal data, such as salary increases, are often conveyed to employees during regularly scheduled performance appraisal interviews.

Employee Development Purposes

When communicated to individual employees, appraisal data serve development purposes by providing employees with performance feedback. Such feedback reinforces desirable behaviours, while seeking to guide and motivate employees to improved performance where needed. Feedback also helps employees, especially new ones, clarify role expectations, performance expectations, and standards. For example, if employees find themselves rewarded for tasks that are not specified in their job descriptions, they will probably continue to do them since they have resulted in positive feedback. Similarly, tasks that are specified but go unnoticed or unrewarded may come to be ignored. Over time, employees' role perceptions change to include performance of unspecified but rewarded tasks and nonperformance of the tasks that have gone unnoticed. While appraisal interviews provide needed performance feedback, they do not occur often enough to meet employee needs for feedback. For this reason, it is good practice for managers and supervisors to provide their subordinates with frequent, informal feedback as well.

In contrast to administrative purposes, employee development purposes require evaluations of employee effectiveness on a number of job-related performance dimensions so that areas needing improvement can be readily identified. In this type of appraisal, performance is more often measured against absolute standards, rather than other employees.

Because administrative and development appraisals differ so widely in their intent, it is suggested that they be conducted separately and use different methods. Unfortunately, many organizations attempt to use the same appraisal method for both administrative and development purposes, and difficulties often result. Several researchers have noted the problem of conflicting objectives in appraisal interviews intended to serve the two purposes.[4] In such an interview, the evaluator must assume the role of both judge (administrative purpose) and helper (development purpose). Research at General Electric showed that when this conflict occurs, administrative issues, such as the amount of a pay increase, tend to dominate the interview.[5] This does little to further employee development. Some organizations have solved this problem by scheduling separate appraisals for each of the appraisal purposes.[6]

Ontario Hydro has taken an innovative approach to the problem of rating for both administrative and development purposes. Depart-

[4] D. McGregor, "An Uneasy Look at Performance Appraisal," *Harvard Business Review*, 1957, vol. 35, no. 3, pp. 89–94; and N.R.F. Maier, *The Appraisal Interview: Objectives, Methods, and Skills* (New York: John Wiley, 1958).

[5] H.H. Meyer, E. Kay, and J.R.P. French, Jr., "Split Roles in Performance Appraisal," *Harvard Business Review*, January-February 1965.

[6] Lazer and Wikstrom.

ment-level managers of salaried employees are permitted to use any number of performance factors and attach as much importance to them as they wish as long as they arrive at a rating for each employee on a single, five-point scale, which determines merit pay. This system provides maximum freedom for the purposes of employee development, while yielding the single, overall rating for each employee that is needed for administrative purposes.

Monitoring/Assessment Purposes

Performance appraisal is one way organizations monitor quality of the work force. (Other more indirect ways include costs of providing a service or product and customer satisfaction.) Organizations need to monitor work force quality to ensure that acceptable standards of performance are being maintained. If they are not, steps can be taken to simplify jobs, train workers, motivate workers, help them solve personal problems, or dismiss them, depending upon the reasons for poor performance.

Performance appraisal data are also collected, stored, and analyzed for program assessment purposes, such as validating selection procedures and determining success of training and development programs. Records of employee performance can also show how effective recruiting, selection, and placement have been in supplying a qualified work force.

Appraisals for monitoring/assessment purposes should incorporate a number of reliable and representative measures of job behaviour and job results. This is to ensure that appraisal data are valid measures for use as criteria in studies of program effectiveness and in validation of the instruments and methods used in HRM decisions.

Relation of Performance Appraisal to Other HRM Functions

The relation of performance appraisal to other HRM functions is shown in Exhibit 10.1. One's first formal performance appraisal usually occurs after training and six months or a year on the job. Standards against which performance is evaluated are derived from job descriptions, which are developed through job analysis. As revealed in the previous section, performance appraisal data are used to determine training and development needs, validate predictors, assign pay, and evaluate program success. In human resource planning, they can be used to indicate likely human resource flows, pointing up future needs for human resources. For example, if an organization has 20 middle-managers capable of moving up, it will have little need to recruit externally to fill six executive positions.

EXHIBIT 10.1

Performance appraisal: relation to other functions

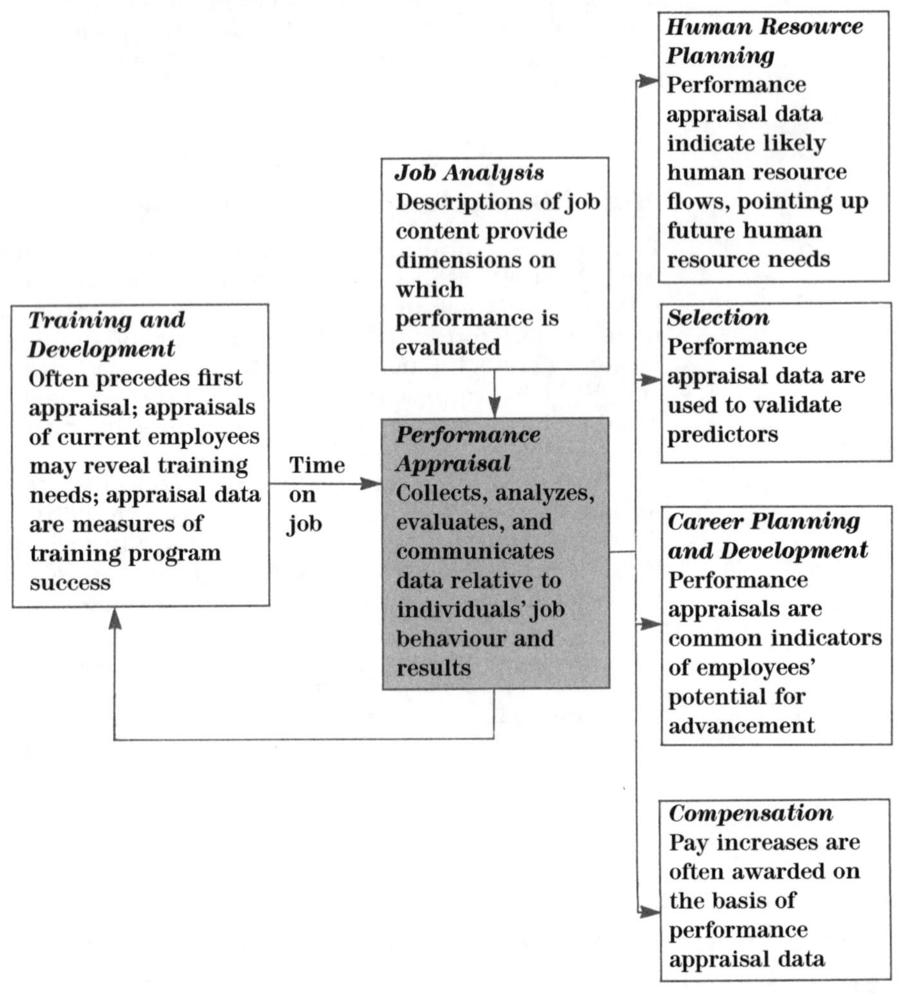

Responsibilities for Performance Appraisal

With respect to performance appraisal, HRM professionals engage in activities related to three major areas of responsibility: (1) designing an appraisal system; (2) implementing the system; and (3) collecting, storing, and analyzing appraisal data for a variety of purposes. Designing an appraisal system requires determining organizational needs for appraisal and deciding which method(s) best suit those needs. Implementation activities include readying materials, training raters so that appraisal purposes and procedures are understood, and scheduling appraisal interviews.

Designing an Appraisal System

Designing an appraisal system is not a simple matter: there are many possibilities, including adopting an existing system from another organization, purchasing one from a consulting firm, developing one's own system or hiring a consultant to develop one. Because of the number of options, some HRM professionals may be tempted to seek advice from neighbouring organizations about procedures they use or recommend. This is not a good approach because organizations differ in their needs and intended uses for performance appraisal data. In designing an appraisal system, HRM professionals should consider needs of their own organization. Key considerations are (1) who should be evaluated; (2) what criteria should be used; and (3) how will appraisals be used.

Determining Needs for a System

Who should be evaluated? First, the organization must determine what types of employees it wants to evaluate. This decision has implications for the type of system chosen. For example, a system that effectively appraises managerial performance is quite different from one for evaluating the performance of clerical workers. Different jobs place different demands on appraisal systems. Jobs that are difficult to describe or that vary substantially in terms of activities and tasks create difficulties for appraising performance. Managerial jobs, for example, are difficult because they involve a great deal of variety, brevity, and fragmentation. One study found that half of a manager's activities lasted nine minutes or less, and that *ad hoc* contacts were much more common than planned encounters.[7] These facts suggest great difficulty in constructing adequate appraisal instruments. At the opposite extreme, some jobs have very little variation in performance. Many manufacturing, production-line, and continuous-process operations fall into this category. It simply does not make sense to install a formal appraisal system for employees whose performance is constrained by the equipment and processes used on the job. When interdependence among workers is high, as in the case of employees on a tractor assembly line or a refuse collection team, individuals do not have complete control over their own performance. Obviously, an appraisal system should

[7] H. Mintzberg, *The Nature of Managerial Work* (New York: Harper & Row, 1973).

not judge people on results that are beyond their control. In such cases, it makes more sense to consider other means of evaluation.

What criteria should be used? Next, an organization must decide what criteria to use for evaluation. Does it want a system based on evaluating individual traits, behaviour, or job results? This decision depends in part on who is being evaluated and how the organization intends to use performance appraisals.

Early rating scales evaluated workers on individual traits or personal characteristics that were presumably related to job performance. Initiative, aggressiveness, reliability and personality are examples of traits on which employees have been rated. One problem with such criteria is that traits themselves are difficult to define and may be subject to varying interpretations by evaluators. For example, what one evaluator perceives as desirable aggressiveness, another may perceive as undesirable hostility. Another problem is that organizations have often used trait rating forms for a wide variety of jobs, so some employees were rated on traits with little relevance to their jobs. The recent trend is away from trait rating towards evaluation of employees on their behaviour or in terms of results achieved.

Rating employees according to job behaviour is based on the assumption that effective and ineffective behaviours exist and have been identified for each job or type of job. A behaviour is judged effective or ineffective in terms of the results it produces (either desirable or undesirable). For example, a customer service representative could be judged on the way he or she calms irate customers. Evaluating employees on their behaviour is especially important for purposes of employee development.

Most managers would probably prefer to base appraisals on some form of results indices, such as dollar volume of sales, amount of scrap, and quantity and quality of work produced, since these appear to be more objective measures of performance than standard rating scales. Thanks to the advent of computer surveillance and monitoring, many organizations are now able to collect highly detailed job results data for certain types of employees, including telephone operators, video display terminal and keypunch operators, reservations agents, grocery store cashiers, and others. One of the most sophisticated computer monitoring systems in use is Bell Canada's, which measures 76 aspects of an operator's performance.[8] Bell's system is described in Case 10.2 at the end of this chapter.

Sometimes appraisals may, of necessity, focus on results rather than behaviour. For example, the content of managerial jobs is highly variable, making it difficult to specify appropriate behaviours for evaluation purposes. Thus many managers are measured according to results indices such as turnover, absenteeism, grievances, profitability, and production rates in their departments. These indices can also be used

[8] L. Archer, "I Saw What You Did and I Know Who You Are," *Canadian Business*, November 1985, pp. 76–83.

to evaluate the performance of organizational units. When results indices are used for appraisal purposes, appraisal instruments, such as rating scales, are rarely used.

How will appraisals be used? A third question to consider in determining needs for a system is: how will appraisals be used? Will they be used to decide pay increases, to provide performance feedback to employees, to assess training needs, or to validate selection procedures? As we have seen, different purposes necessitate collection of different kinds of appraisal data and, therefore, affect choice of an appraisal instrument or system.

General Requirements of Performance Appraisal Systems

Regardless of an organization's specific needs for performance appraisal, if a system is to accomplish its objectives, it must meet five general requirements: reliability, validity, practicality, fairness, and impact.

Reliability

Reliability is the consistency of a measure over time and between raters. Consistency over time means that the passage of time should not affect the findings or results of an instrument. This form of reliability is not very crucial for performance appraisal since one expects to see changes in performance over time. Consistency between raters is a more important requirement of performance appraisal measures. It means that different raters using the method should have a reasonable amount of agreement on their evaluation of the same employee. Generally, research shows that well-trained raters become quite consistent in their ratings. Highest degrees of consistency should occur when raters observe a given employee from the same organizational position. Lower degrees of consistency are inevitable when evaluators differ in their perspectives and opportunities to observe. To handle differences in perspective, many appraisal forms record the nature of the relationship between evaluator and evaluatee and give greater weight to evaluators who have better knowledge. It is generally believed that an immediate superior is in the best position to evaluate the performance of a subordinate, though this is not always the case in practice. Reasonably high reliability is necessary for validity.

Validity

An appraisal method or index is *valid* if it accurately measures job performance. The validity of appraisal measures must be established by demonstrating various relationships between appraisal scores or results and other job- and performance-related behaviour and/or results. Establishing the validity of an appraisal system is not a "one-shot" project. It is, or should be, a continuing attempt to understand how scores or ratings relate to other personnel and organizational performance indices. Depending on their purpose, performance ratings should correlate positively with promotion rate, pay increases, and, to a lesser degree, with objective indices of performance, such as productivity and profitability.

The major aspect of validity in performance appraisal is content validity. An appraisal instrument has *content validity* to the extent that it includes most of the important job behaviours and/or results of the job. Many appraisal instruments attempt to cover too many different jobs. It is naive, for example, to expect an accounting department, a shipping and receiving department, and a production department to have common jobs, common job behaviours, and common performance goals. The only way the same instrument could be used in a variety of departments would be to include only the most general factors or those based on personal traits. And ratings of such factors are likely to be very unrelated to actual job behaviour and/or performance.

Using appraisal instruments that attempt to cover too many jobs can result in some employees' being evaluated on criteria not related to their jobs, while other essential criteria are overlooked. Measures that evaluate employees on aspects of performance that are not job-related are said to be *contaminated.* Measures are called *deficient* if they fail to evaluate employees on certain criteria which are job-related. Content validity suffers when measures prove either contaminated or deficient.

Another threat to validity is rater errors such as the halo effect, central tendency, severity, and leniency. The *halo effect* occurs when a rating on one dimension of an appraisal instrument substantially influences the ratings on other dimensions for the same employee; as a result, the evaluation is about the same across all performance dimensions. Errors of central tendency, severity, and leniency are said to be "constant" errors because a rater tends to make them in evaluating all subordinates. *Central tendency* is a lack of variation among ratings of different subordinates; most employees end up being rated as average. *Leniency* refers to an evaluator's tendency to rate most employees very highly across performance dimensions, whereas *severity* is the tendency to rate most quite harshly. All these errors result in an inability to identify differences in performance among employees.

Practicality

To meet the requirements of practicality, an appraisal system must be acceptable to both evaluators and those being evaluated. If an appraisal system is unacceptable, its use will be resisted, and resulting appraisals and decisions will be suspect. Practicality dictates that an appraisal system must measure something significant to individuals and the organization. If it does not, it will have little utility for employees or the organization.

Fairness

Employees must feel that appraisals are conducted fairly and that their consequences (raises, promotions, and so on) are fair. A system perceived as unfair will likely prove unacceptable to employees. For this reason, many unions give considerable attention to performance appraisal systems. Collective agreements may specify that any changes require consultation with the union and/or that the union has the right to review results. Grievances involving appraisals are not uncommon.

Results of a study by Meyer suggest that achieving perceived fairness in an appraisal system may be difficult because employees tend to rate their performance highly.[9] Meyer's study showed that 95 per cent of employees in occupations ranging from accountants and engineers to blue-collar workers from several companies rated their own performance as "above average," and nearly 70 per cent felt they were in the top 25 per cent of their co-workers.

Impact

If, after spending valuable time conducting appraisals, supervisors and managers discover that employees with low ratings get the same rewards as those with high ratings, then the system loses its impact. Without impact, the system loses credibility, and practicality is likely to suffer.

Performance Appraisal Methods

Performance appraisal methods are numerous and varied. Methods are grouped below, somewhat arbitrarily, into those best suited to administrative purposes versus employee development purposes. Methods geared to administrative purposes include job results indices, the essay method, graphic rating scales, mixed standard scales, ranking, forced distribution, peer evaluation, and field review. Methods more suited to employee development include behavioural checklists, behaviourally anchored rating scales (BARS), and management by objectives (MBO). Exhibit 10.2 compares appraisal methods on a number of characteristics.

Methods for Administrative Purposes

The intent of methods for administrative purposes is to generate a global or composite rating for each employee in order to allocate pay

[9] H. Meyer, "The Pay for Performance Dilemma," *Organizational Dynamics*, Winter 1975, pp. 22–38.

EXHIBIT 10.2

Performance appraisal methods

	Method	*Characteristic*					
		Major purpose: Adminis-tration (A); Develop-ment (D)	Typical content	Frequency of use	Develop-ment costs	Usage costs	Acceptance of raters and ratees
	Results indices	A	Results	Very common	Variable	Variable	Fair to low
	Essay	A	Variable	Common	Low	High	Fair
Rating scales	Graphic rating scale	A, D	Traits & behaviour	Very common	Average	Low	Fair
Rating scales	Mixed standard scales	A	Traits & behaviour	Rare	High	Average	Low
Rating scales	BARS	A, D	Behaviour	Uncommon but growing	High	Low	Good
	Straight ranking	A	Overall assessments	Fairly common	Low	Low	Low
Ranking methods	Alternative ranking	A	Overall assessments	Fairly common	Low	Low	Low
Ranking methods	Paired comparisons	A	Overall assessments	Uncommon	Low	Average	Low
Ranking methods	Forced distribution	A	Overall assessments	Uncommon	Low	Low	Low
	Field review	A	Behaviour, results, traits	Uncommon	Average	High	Fair to good
	Peer nomination	A	Overall assessments	Uncommon	Low	Low	Good
	Behavioural checklist	A, D	Behaviour & traits	Common	Average	Low	Fair
	MBO	A, D	Results	Common in management	High	High	Good

and other organizational rewards. Methods for administrative purposes typically do not focus on individual strengths, but rather, seek to compare employees based on their performance levels.

Job results indices. Job results were discussed briefly as one of three possible criteria on which to base appraisals. Though not an appraisal method per se, job results are a source of data which can be used to appraise performance, either singly or in conjunction with other methods. Typically, an employee's job results are compared against some objective standard of performance. This standard can be absolute or relative to the performance of others.

Job results are especially useful for appraising the performance of higher-level workers, such as managers and professionals. However, their use in appraising lower-level employees, such as clerical workers, is growing due to increased use of computer surveillance and monitoring systems. One-fifth of the 834 delegates attending the 1983 Ontario Federation of Labour convention reported working under some form of electronic monitoring.[10] Case 10.2 describes Bell Canada's computerized performance monitoring system, TOPS, and some of the controversy surrounding its use.

One might think that, because job results are quantifiable, using them would circumvent the problems of validity and reliability. However, results indices are frequently subject to contamination and deficiency. For example, evaluating an insurance salesperson's performance on the basis of the face value of policies sold may be a deficient measure since it does not reflect the many other useful and profitable activities the individual undertakes for the company. The index may also be contaminated if it does not take into account differences in sales territories that result in the salesperson being evaluated on results that are outside his or her control.

In most organizations it is very difficult to find objective indices that are not somewhat deficient or contaminated. Even those that are neither may have unacceptably low reliability over time, caused by unpredictable fluctuations in the characteristics being measured.[11] Other problems occur when numerous job results indices are combined to yield an overall rating for a person. For example, imagine having to weigh the importance of Bell's 76 performance measures in order to determine an overall assessment for each operator. This does not mean that job results indices are useless, only that their reliability and validity must be examined closely.

Essay method. The essay method involves an evaluator's written report appraising an employee's performance, usually in terms of job behaviour and/or results. Essay appraisals are often justifications of pay, promotion, or termination decisions, but they can be used for development purposes as well. Since essay appraisals are to a large extent

[10] D. Swift, "The Electronic Supervisor," *Maclean's*, June 17, 1985, pp. 32–3.

[11] P.C. Wright, "Performance Appraisal, A Double Edged Sword," *Industrial Management*, June 1982.

unstructured and open-ended, lack of standardization is a major problem; by nature, they are highly susceptible to evaluator bias, which may in some cases be discriminatory. Since the evaluator does not have to report on all job-related behaviour or results, he or she may simply comment on those that reflect favourably or unfavourably on an employee. This does not usually represent a true picture of the employee or the job, and content validity suffers. Though widely used, the essay method is unacceptable to most unions and does not form a sound data base for justifying decisions about pay, promotion, and dismissal. Its development costs are very low, but its usage costs can be high because of the time supervisors and managers must spend writing and reviewing the essays.

Graphic rating scales. Graphic rating scales are one of the most common methods of performance appraisal. They require an evaluator to indicate the degree to which an employee demonstrates a particular trait, behaviour, or performance result. Rating forms are composed of a number of scales, each pertaining to a particular performance-related aspect, such as job knowledge, responsibility, or quality of work. Each scale is a continuum of scale points, or *anchors*, which range from high to low, good to poor, most to least effective, and so forth. The scales usually have five to seven points, though they can have more or fewer. Graphic rating scales may or may not define their scale points. For example, scale points are not defined in the following five-point scale, which asks students to rate their professor on overall teaching effectiveness:

	Very poor				*Very good*
Teaching effectiveness:	*1*	*2*	*3*	*4*	*5*

This is an example of a poor graphic rating scale; not only are scale points undefined, but so is the concept of "teaching effectiveness." An evaluator must use his or her own definition of what is being measured and determine what constitutes very poor to very good performance. This results in a vague and subjective measure. Undefined measures and scale points leave room for broad interpretation by evaluators and more often than not result in low reliability.

There are better graphic rating scales; one example is given in Exhibit 10.3. This graphic rating scale, which is used to evaluate office employees in a western city, includes as performance dimensions traits or characteristics (appearance, personality, job knowledge), behaviour (responsibility, service awareness), and results (quality of work, quantity of work). Note that the form calls for an overall assessment of each ratee's promotion potential.

Rating scales should have the following characteristics:

1. Performance dimensions should be clearly defined.
2. Scales should be behaviourally based so that a rater is able to support all ratings with objective, observable evidence.
3. Abstract trait names such as "loyalty," "honesty," and "integrity" should be avoided unless they can be defined in terms of observable behaviour.

4. Points, or anchors, on each scaled dimension should be brief, unambiguous, and relevant to what is being rated. For example, in rating a person's flow of words, it is preferable to use anchors such as "fluent," "easy," "unimpeded," "hesitant," and "laboured," rather than "excellent," "very good," "average," "below average," and "poor."[12]

Carefully constructed graphic rating scales have a number of advantages:

1. Standardization of content, permitting comparison of employees.
2. Ease of development, and relatively low development and usage cost.
3. Reasonably high rater and ratee acceptance.

A disadvantage of most rating scales is that they are susceptible to several rating errors, including the halo effect, central tendency, severity, and leniency.

Mixed standard scales. In a mixed standard scale, each performance dimension has three statements relating to it: one illustrating good performance, one average performance, and one poor performance. Statements represent behavioural examples obtained from knowledgeable persons, usually supervisors. The evaluator's task is to indicate whether an employee fits the statement, is better than the statement, or is worse than the statement. Statements are randomly mixed, which tends to reduce rater errors by making it less obvious which statements reflect effective or ineffective performance.

Mixed standard scales are a relatively recent development; they have been applied in only a few settings. Research on mixed standard scales shows that while this method is not superior to other methods, it can result in less leniency in administrative decisions.[13] However, mixed standard scales may prove unpopular with evaluators because the rating process is time-consuming and the relative effectiveness of statements is hidden.

A mixed standard scale is shown in Exhibit 10.4. The nine statements in this scale relate to the three performance dimensions of efficiency, carefulness, and relations with other people.

Ranking. Ranking methods compare one individual to another, resulting in an ordering of employees in relation to one another. Rankings often result in overall assessments of employees, rather than in specific judgements about a number of job components. *Straight ranking* requires an evaluator to order a group of employees from best to worst overall or from most effective to least effective in terms of a particular criterion. *Alternative ranking* makes the same demand, but

[12] W.F. Cascio, *Applied Psychology in Personnel Management* (Reston, Va.: Reston Publishing Co., Inc., 1978).

[13] H.J. Bernardin, L. Elliot, and J.J. Carlyle, "A Critical Assessment of Mixed Standard Scales," *Proceedings of the Academy of Management*, 1980, pp. 308–12; and T.L. Dickinson and P.M. Zellinger, "A Comparison of the Behaviorally Anchored Rating and Mixed Standard Scale Formats," *Journal of Applied Psychology*, 1980, vol. 65, no. 2, pp. 147–54.

EXHIBIT 10.3

Personal evaluation report for office workers

Instructions to the evaluator:
This report should be an honest and objective evaluation of the employee's performance. The factors should be rated on the basis of current performance and not on future expectations. Avoid letting your appraisal of one quality influence your judgment on another. Do not give disproportionate weight to single, isolated deviations from the normal.

Name	Department	Date
Job title	Length of time on this job	

Quality of work (disregard quantity)

5	4	3	2	1
__Extremely neat and accurate.	__Good accurate worker. Makes few mistakes.	__Adequate, some improvement desirable.	__Barely up to minimum standards. Often inaccurate.	__Below minimum standards. Much room for improvement.

Quantity of work (disregard quality)

5	4	3	2	1
__Outstanding volume.	__Well above average volume.	__Adequate volume.	__Barely up to minimum standards.	__Below minimum standards. Much room for improvement.

Job knowledge (technical)

5	4	3	2	1
__Expert. Has superior knowledge.	__Well-rounded knowledge. Seldom needs assistance.	__Possesses acceptable knowledge.	__Knowledge is adequate to perform minimum job requirements.	__Very limited knowledge. Needs frequent assistance.

Responsibility (ability to plan and direct work)

5	4	3	2	1
__Plans and carries out own work in a superior manner. Self-sustaining.	__Plans and carries out work well. Requires little supervision.	__Requires occasional work direction.	__Carries out only the most obvious tasks without follow-up.	__Always waits to be directed.

Appearance (personal grooming habits)

5	4	3	2	1
__Outstanding. Makes excellent impression.	__Neat. Better than average impression.	__ Presentable by average standards. Good impression.	__Fair appearance. Could use some improvement.	__Careless, unkempt.

Personality (ability to get along with others)

5	4	3	2	1
__Exceptionally pleasing. Very highly regarded.	__Favorable impression. Well-liked and accepted.	__Usually well-liked. Usually makes a favorable impression.	__Some difficulty gaining acceptance.	__Negative. Antagonistic. Arouses resentment.

Service awareness (ability to please public)

5	4	3	2	1
__Always pleases public. Goes out of way to serve them.	__Gets along with public. Seems to please them.	__Does an adequate job in public relations.	__Seldom goes out of way to please public.	__Does not try to satisfy. Appears disinterested.

Promotional potential (Check the appropriate statement below and explain reason for choice)

__Now ready for promotion or transfer (indicate job duties that you believe employee is capable of performing)
__Of maximum value to the company and of greatest personal effectiveness in present assignment
__Adequate in present job but not yet qualified for promotion
__Not adequate in present job - no potential for promotion

the ranking process must be done in a specified manner (for example, by first selecting the best employee in a group, then the worst, then the second-best, then the second-worst, and so on). In *paired comparison*, a more sophisticated ranking method, each employee in a group is compared to every other member in the group through a series of comparing pairs.

EXHIBIT 10.4

A mixed standard scale

Instructions: If the employee fits the statement, put a 0 in the space opposite the statement; if the employee is better than the statement, put a + in the space; if the employee is worse than the statement, put a − in the space.

____ Is on good terms with everyone. Can get along with people even in disagreement.

____ Employee's work is spotty, sometimes all right and sometimes not. Could be more accurate and careful.

____ Has a tendency to get into unnecessary conflicts with people.

____ Is quick and efficient, able to keep work on schedule. Really gets going on a new task.

____ The accuracy of employee's work is satisfactory. It is not often that you find clear evidence of carelessness.

____ Gets along with most people. Only very occasionally has conflicts with others on the job, and these are likely to be minor.

____ Is efficient enough, usually getting through assignments and work in reasonable time.

____ Work is striking in its accuracy. Never any evidence of carelessness in it.

____ Some lack of efficiency on employee's part. Employee may take too much time to complete assignments and sometimes does not really finish them.

SOURCE: Adapted from F. Blanz and E.E. Ghiselli, "The Mixed Standard Scale: A New Rating System," *Personnel Psychology*, 1972, vol. 25, pp. 185–99.

An example can illustrate the three methods of ranking. Assume that an office manager has been asked to rank the office's five secretaries in terms of overall performance. Using straight ranking, the manager judges Karen best, Lee second-best, Holly third-best, Frank fourth, and Heather fifth. The same rank-ordering might or might not result using alternative ranking, but in either case evaluative judgements would have been made in a specified way. Assuming that the same rank-ordering results, the office manager first judges Karen best, then Heather worst, then Lee second-best, then Frank next-to-worst, and finally Holly third-best. Using paired comparison, any one of the secretaries, say, Karen, is first compared to any one of the others, say, Frank, and determined to be better or worse. Then Karen is compared to Lee or Holly or Heather, and the process continues until she has been compared to each of the others. The office manager then turns to one of the other secretaries and compares him or her to every other secretary in a similar manner. To determine rankings using the paired-comparison method, an evaluator simply adds the number of times each person was judged superior (for example, Karen was judged superior four times and, therefore, is ranked first among the five secretaries).

The paired-comparison method can be quite time-consuming and laborious if there are a number of employees to be evaluated. The number of comparisons necessary can be found by the formula $N(N-1)/2$, where N is the number of employees. Paired comparison of ten employees, for example, requires 45 comparative judgements to be made.

Alternative-ranking and paired-comparison methods attempt to increase the reliability of rankings by structuring the way in which rank-orders are determined. While reasonably successful, these methods are still subject to bias and error, which may be seen by comparing different raters' rankings of the same employee. Even when raters are equally familiar with the employees, they may vary in what they see as important components of job performance. Ranking methods usually do not specify the job components on which an evaluator should judge overall performance.

Comparative evaluation systems such as ranking are rarely popular. No matter how close a group of employees in level of performance and no matter how well they perform on the job, some will rank high and some will end up at the bottom. Evaluators are often reluctant to make such comparisons. Also, rankings do not permit much comparison of employees across groups. For example, it is difficult to say whether the second-ranked employee in Unit A is as good as or better than the second-ranked employee in Unit B. One researcher has, however, suggested a method by which raters familiar with employees in different units can establish their relative rankings.[14] Despite the problems of ranking methods, they can be very useful in differentiating among employees if an organization has a very limited number of promotions or dollars to allocate.

Forced distribution. Forced distribution is a form of comparative evaluation in which an evaluator rates subordinates according to a specified distribution. Unlike ranking methods, forced distribution is frequently applied to several components of job performance, rather than only one. Students who are graded on a curve are already familiar with this method of appraisal. For example, a manager may be told that he or she must rate subordinates according to the following distribution: 10 per cent low; 20 per cent below average; 40 per cent average; 20 per cent above average; and 10 per cent high. In a group of 20 employees, two would have to be placed in the low category, four in the below-average category, eight in average, four in above average, and two in the highest category. The proportions can vary; for example, a supervisor could be required to place employees into the top, middle, and bottom thirds of a distribution. Forced distribution is primarily used to eliminate rating errors, such as leniency and central tendency, but the method itself can cause rating errors because it forces differ-

[14] P.F. Ross, "Reference Groups in Man-to-Man Job Performance Ratings," *Personnel Psychology*, 1966, vol. 19, pp. 115–42.

entiation among employees even when performance is quite similar. Even if all employees in a unit are doing a good job, a certain number must be placed at the bottom of the continuum. For this reason, raters and ratees do not readily accept this method, especially in small groups or when group members are all of high ability.

Peer evaluation. In peer evaluation methods, employees judge the performance of their co-workers. Three methods of peer evaluation are peer rating, peer ranking, and peer nomination. *Peer ratings* are simply ratings of peers done by group members, rather than by a superior; any type of rating instrument can be used. Similarly, *peer ranking* is any ranking method in which group members assign rankings to one another. In *peer nomination*, each member of a well-defined group designates a number of group members as highest (and sometimes lowest) on a particular performance dimension. This frequently researched method has been shown to distinguish with a high degree of reliability and validity group members who are very high (or very low) on a performance dimension.[15] It has had a relatively long record of success in identifying successful officers in the armed services. Its use in nonmilitary situations has been limited, but evidence suggests its usefulness in making decisions about promotions. Of the other peer evaluation methods, peer ratings are most useful for performance feedback purposes, while peer rankings hold some promise for pay decisions since they compare co-workers with one another.

Field review. Field review is an appraisal by someone outside the employee's own department, usually someone from the corporate office or the HRM department. The process involves a review of the employee's records and interviews with the employee and sometimes with his or her superior. Field review is used primarily in making promotion decisions at the managerial level. It is also useful when comparable information is needed about employees in different units or locations. The method has two disadvantages.

1. An outsider is usually not very familiar with conditions in the particular work environment which may affect the employee's ability or motivation to perform.
2. An outside reviewer does not have the opportunity to observe the employee's behaviour or performance over time and in a variety of situations, but only in a very short, artifically structured interview situation.

Methods for Employee Development Purposes

Performance appraisals conducted for purposes of employee development should be very different from those conducted for administrative

[15] J.S. Kane and E.E. Lawler III, "Methods of Peer Assessment," *Psychological Bulletin*, 1978, vol. 85, pp. 555–86.

purposes. Because of their intent to guide and to motivate improved performance, appraisal methods for employee development should:

1. Focus on a number of elements of job behaviour or results.
2. Have explicit or implicit standards of performance.
3. Be specific to a particular job or type of job.

Appraisal methods used for employee development include: the behavioural checklist; behaviourally anchored rating scales (BARS); and management by objectives (MBO). Though these methods meet the criteria of a development purpose, they can also be used for administrative purposes.

Behavioural checklist. A behavioural checklist is a rating form containing statements that describe both effective and ineffective job behaviours which relate to a number of dimensions determined to be relevant to the job. A rater is asked to check those statements that are descriptive of the employee's behaviour. To develop a behavioural checklist, a panel of experts rates a large number of behavioural statements relevant to a job or set of jobs. Statements which are reliably rated and represent the entire range of performance effectiveness are selected for inclusion in the checklist. Exhibit 10.5 presents a number of items which are part of a behavioural checklist for a salesperson.

EXHIBIT 10.5

Items from a behavioural checklist for a salesperson

Instructions: Please check those statements descriptive of the employee's behaviour.

____Calls on customers immediately after hearing of any complaints
____Discusses complaints with customer
____Gathers facts relevant to customers' complaints
____Transmits information about complaints back to customers and resolves problems to their satisfaction
____Plans each day's activities ahead of time
____Lays out broad sales plans for one month ahead
____Gathers sales information from customers, other salesmen, trade journals, and other relevant sources
____Transmits sales information to manager
____Is truthful in dealing with customers
____Is truthful in dealing with superiors
____Suggests new approaches to selling
____Systematically calls on all customer accounts

SOURCE: Adapted from M.D. Dunnette, *Personnel Selection and Placement* (Belmont, Calif.: Wadsworth, 1966).

If an appraisal is for administrative purposes, the rater is not told which types of behaviour are effective or ineffective; an HRM professional can tabulate any required overall assessment. If, however, the behavioural checklist is intended for development purposes, the rater must know which behaviours are effective and which are not, so he or she can make suggestions for the employee's improvement.

One of the first behavioural checklists was developed for salespersons of the Minnesota Mining and Manufacturing Company (3M).[16] More than 100 critical incidents of effective and ineffective behaviour were collected from sales managers and categorized into 13 categories.

Behavioural checklists are well suited to use in employee development because they focus on behaviour and results, are specific to the job for which performance is being rated, and use absolute rather than comparative standards. However, they can also be used for administrative purposes. An advantage of this method is that raters are asked to describe rather than evaluate a subordinate's behaviour; for this reason, behavioural checklists may meet with less resistance than some other methods. There may be some objection, however, to the lack of information about which types of behaviour are considered effective and ineffective. And if scale values are assigned to various kinds of behaviour in determining an overall evaluation for an employee, an evaluator may not like the fact that these values are kept hidden. To the extent that behaviours are not identified as either effective or ineffective rater errors, such as leniency, severity, central tendency, and the halo effect, are minimized. An obvious disadvantage of behavioural checklists is that constructing the instrument demands an investment of much time and money.

Behaviourally anchored rating scales. Behaviourally anchored rating scales (BARS), sometimes called behavioural expectation scales, are rating scales whose scale points are defined by statements of effective and ineffective behaviour.[17]. They are said to be behaviourally anchored because statements describe a continuum of behaviour ranging from least to most effective. In the most common form of BARS, an evaluator must indicate which behaviour on each scale best describes an employee's performance. Exhibit 10.6 is a BARS scale for the knowledge and judgement dimension of a grocery checker's job.

In another form of BARS, evaluators record observations of each employee's behaviour throughout the year or appraisal period. When it comes time to actually evaluate the employee, the evaluator refers to his or her written record and gives each observed behaviour its assigned BARS value. Thus, documentation in the form of a diary or written record is available both to justify administrative actions and feedback to employees.

[16] W.L. Kirchner and M.D. Dunnette, "Identifying the Critical Factors in Successful Salesmanship," *Personnel*, 1957, vol. 34, pp. 54–9.

[17] See P.C. Smith and L.M. Kendall, "Retranslation of Expectations: An Approach to the Construction of Unambiguous Anchors for Rating Scales," *Journal of Applied Psychology*, 1963, vol. 47, pp. 149–55.

EXHIBIT 10.6

A BARS scale for the knowledge and judgement dimension of a grocery checker's job

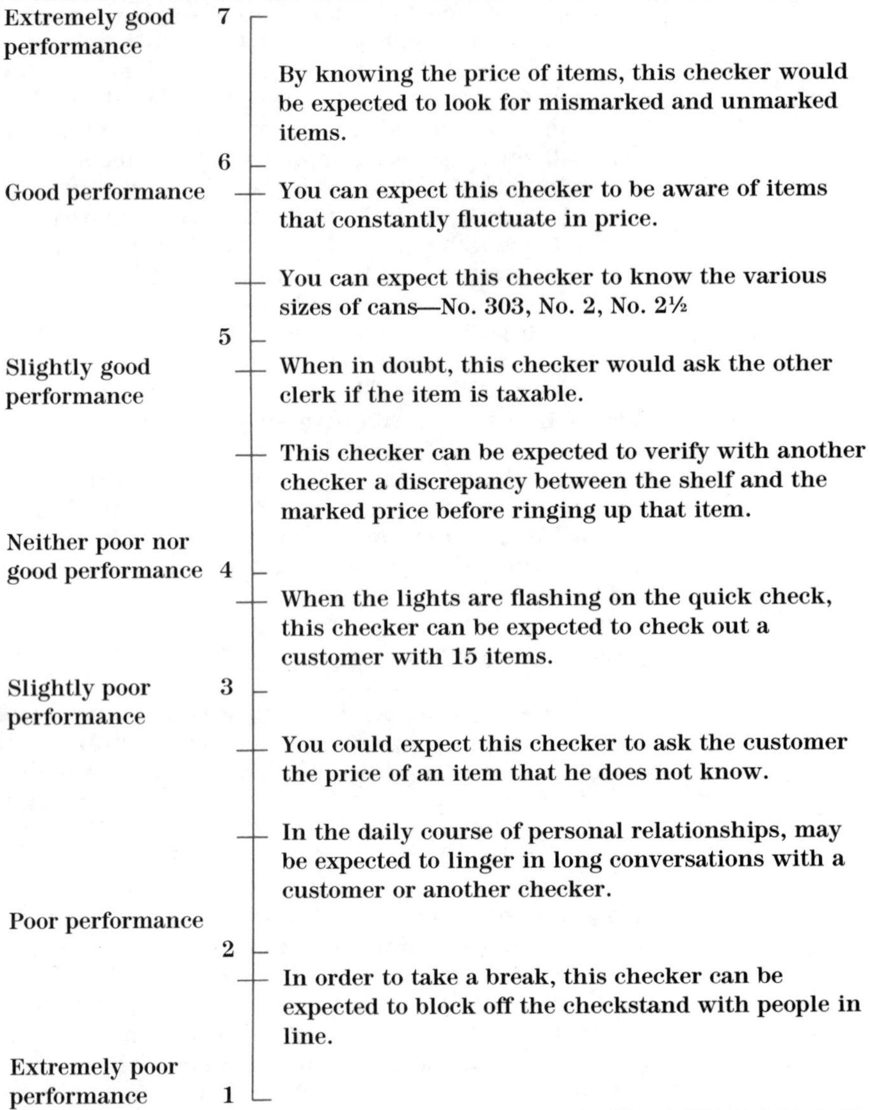

Extremely good performance 7
By knowing the price of items, this checker would be expected to look for mismarked and unmarked items.
6
Good performance
You can expect this checker to be aware of items that constantly fluctuate in price.
You can expect this checker to know the various sizes of cans—No. 303, No. 2, No. 2½
5
Slightly good performance
When in doubt, this checker would ask the other clerk if the item is taxable.
This checker can be expected to verify with another checker a discrepancy between the shelf and the marked price before ringing up that item.
Neither poor nor good performance 4
When the lights are flashing on the quick check, this checker can be expected to check out a customer with 15 items.
Slightly poor performance 3
You could expect this checker to ask the customer the price of an item that he does not know.
In the daily course of personal relationships, may be expected to linger in long conversations with a customer or another checker.
Poor performance
2
In order to take a break, this checker can be expected to block off the checkstand with people in line.
Extremely poor performance 1

SOURCE: L. Fogli, C. Hulin, and M.R. Blood, "Development of First-Level Behavioral Job Criteria," *Journal of Applied Psychology*, 1971, vol. 55, no. 1, pp. 3–8.

BARS differ from other rating scales in that scale points are specifically defined kinds of behaviour. Also, BARS are originally constructed by the evaluators who will use them. There are four steps in the BARS construction process:

1. Listing all the important dimensions of performance for a job or jobs.
2. Collecting critical incidents of effective and ineffective behaviour.
3. Classifying effective and ineffective behaviours to appropriate performance dimensions.
4. Assigning numerical value to each behaviour within each dimension (i.e., scaling of behavioural anchors).

The process begins with evaluators (and sometimes their subordinates) discussing and listing all the important dimensions of performance for a job or jobs. For example, other performance dimensions for the grocery checker's job include conscientiousness, skill in human relations, skill in operation of the cash register, skill in bagging, organization of the check-out work, and skill in monetary transactions.[18] The construction process continues with a second group of evaluators, who observe, record, and collect examples of effective and ineffective job behaviour, which are called critical incidents. They make up the body of behavioural checklists and BARS form. For some time, psychologists argued that these critical incidents must be very job-specific; however, recent studies have demonstrated that the BARS procedure can be applied to a reasonably broad group of jobs by making the descriptions of job behaviour less specific.[19]

When a large number of instances of effective and ineffective behaviour has been collected, a third group of evaluators is given the first group's list of job performance dimensions and the set of critical incidents. Their task is to match, or classify, specific behaviour to appropriate performance dimensions. Consider the following behaviour from Exhibit 10.6: "In the daily course of personal relationships, [the employee] may be expected to linger in long conversations with a customer or another checker." The third group of evaluators must decide to which performance dimension this behaviour belongs. Does it relate to the knowledge and judgement dimension or to skill in human relations? Behaviour must be classified into a given dimension by 60 to 80 per cent of the evaluators in order to be included in the scale for that dimension. New dimensions may be added if there are a number of uncategorized critical incidents. Separate groups of evaluators are involved in this retranslation process to ensure that the words and terms used in the performance dimensions and the descriptions of behaviour have the same meaning for different people. Therefore, the third group of evaluators, those classifying the behaviour, are not biased by involvement in the earlier steps. The result is a set of behaviour/performance dimensions with each represented by a number of behavioural descriptions.

[18] L. Fogli, C. Hulin, and M.R. Blood, "Development of First-Level Behavioral Job Criteria," *Journal of Applied Psychology*, 1971, vol. 55, no. 1, pp. 3–8.

[19] J.G. Goodale and R.J. Burke, "Behaviourally Based Rating Scales Need Not Be Job Specific," *Journal of Applied Psychology*, 1975, vol. 60, pp. 389–91; and M. Beer, R. Ruh, J.A. Dawson, B.B. McCaa, and M.J. Kavanagh, "A Performance Management System: Research, Design, Introduction and Evaluation," *Personnel Psychology*, 1978, vol. 31, pp. 505–35.

A final step in the BARS construction process is assigning scale values to each behaviour within each dimension. The critical incidents must represent the full range of performance in any one dimension: they cannot be clustered at one or both ends of the continuum but must be distributed evenly along it. High degrees of agreement among evaluators are required in this scaling procedure. Ideally, a fourth group of evaluators performs this step, but it could be done by either of the first two groups. (Actually, there is no evidence that one group of conscientious evaluators could not effectively handle all four steps.)

In the United States, a Conference Board survey reported that about 9 per cent of the 293 companies it surveyed used behaviourally anchored rating scales.[20] The authors suggested, however, that this may be an overestimate of BARS use. Of the sample appraisal forms they received, fully one-third did not correspond to the way in which they were classified on the respondents' surveys. Further, the most typical discrepancy involved appraisal forms that met the definition of a conventional rating scale but were mistakenly identified as BARS.

As with most new rating formats, the purpose of BARS was to eliminate or reduce rating errors such as leniency and halo, while increasing the accuracy of ratings. A substantial amount of research has compared BARS to other appraisal methods. This research shows that BARS do not outperform other simpler, less costly methods, such as graphic rating scales, when it comes to reducing rating errors and increasing accuracy.[21] There is some evidence, however, that BARS improves evaluator attitudes toward performance appraisal.[22]

Management by objectives. Management by objectives is a method of appraising individuals on the basis of objective results indices, such as sales, letters typed, units constructed, number of customer complaints, errors in filing, amount of downtime, days sick, days tardy, etc. MBO combines a goal-setting phase and a performance review phase. In the goal-setting phase, a superior and subordinate discuss the subordinate's job responsibilities and mutually agree on one or more results-oriented goals. Goals frequently focus on problem areas or special projects, rather than routine aspects of the job. Ways of measuring progress toward goals are also specified at this time so the subordinate can assess how well he or she is doing.

An MBO form of an industrial firm is shown in Exhibit 10.7. This form is used in the goal-setting phase to record mutually-agreed upon target results and deadlines for each of six results measures. Actual results and deadlines will be noted and assessed in subsequent performance review sessions.

[20] Lazer and Wikstrom.

[21] H.J. Bernardin and R.W. Beatty, *Performance Appraisal: Assessing Human Behavior at Work* (Boston: Kent Publishing Company, 1984).

[22] R.W. Beatty, C.E. Schneier, and J.R. Beatty, "An Empirical Investigation of Perceptions of Ratee Behavior Frequency and Ratee Behavior Change Using Behaviorally Anchored Rating Scales (BARS)," *Personnel Psychology*, 1977, vol. 31, pp 647–58; and J.M. Ivanevich, "A Longitudinal Study of Behavioral Expectation Scales: Attitudes and Performance," *Journal of Applied Psychology*, 1980, vol. 65, pp. 139–46.

EXHIBIT 10.7

MBO form for an industrial firm

Key Responsibility Area	*Weight*	*Measures of Results*	*Perf. Std.*	*Results*		*Deadlines*	
				Target	*Actual*	*Target*	*Actual*
1. Product delivery	30%	Per cent of deliveries on schedule	95%				
		Per cent of customer complaints	3%				
2. Product quality	25%	Per cent of rejects	5%				
		Amount of rework	2%				
3. Operating efficiency	20%	Cost per unit per month	$37				
		Equipment utilization	90%				

SOURCE: From *Performance Appraisal and Review Systems* by S.J. Carroll and C.E. Schneier. Copyright © 1982 by Scott, Foresman and Company. Reprinted by permission.

Phase two is the performance review session, a regularly scheduled get-together between superior and subordinate for the purpose of assessing progress toward goals, revising goals, and/or setting new ones. For most managers, this interview is probably the most difficult part of the appraisal process because of the interpersonal skills required to make it a productive and motivating session. Skills appropriate for effective development interviews include active listening, acceptance of the subordinate's disagreement, openness to communication, and the ability to create a climate of trust. Basically, MBO casts the superior in the role of helper, rather than judge, and this may conflict with the superior's day-to-day management style.[23]

There are, however, several aspects of MBO that make the performance review session somewhat easier and more acceptable to evaluators than appraisal interviews associated with other methods. First, since the subordinate clearly understands the goals or results on which the evaluation is based, and since he or she also knows how progress is being measured, the review session often becomes something of a self-review or self-appraisal. Furthermore, many managers find it easier to evaluate a person on results or progress toward goals than to make judgements about personal attributes or the degree to which an employee exhibits particular job-related behaviours.

When a subordinate accomplishes MBO goals, he or she often expects some sort of tangible reward. Indeed, at the managerial and professional level, MBO is commonly tied to salary increases and bonuses, which are administrative concerns. However, problems can result if a raise or even a one-time bonus is attached to goal accomplishment. Many employees may achieve their goals and deserve a reward, but, at the same time, the goals achieved may have very different value to the organization. Should the lowest-performing employee in a department receive a large financial bonus for improving more than any other employee? Should the top-performing employee receive no award because of failure to accomplish a very difficult goal? Attaching financial rewards to MBO goals can create such problems, but proper planning and allocation of compensation funds can help to solve them.

MBO is a very popular method of performance appraisal, especially for evaluating managerial performance. The Conference Board survey of managerial appraisal systems in the United States found MBO the most frequently used method of performance appraisal for all 293 surveyed companies.[24] MBO is commonly used for both administrative and development purposes. Although some managers resent the excessive paperwork sometimes associated with MBO, they generally accept it as an appraisal method.[25]

[23] R.J. Burke and D.S. Wilcox, "Characteristics of Effective Employee Performance Review and Development Interviews," *Personnel Psychology*, 1969, vol. 22, pp. 291–305.

[24] Lazer and Wikstrom.

[25] Wright.

A comprehensive review of 185 MBO studies, most of them case studies, found that MBO programs had generally positive effects on employee productivity and/or job satisfaction.[26] MBO appeared to be more effective in the short-term (less than two years) and in private-sector organizations. Other research on MBO has suggested that the key factor in performance improvement and employee satisfaction is the setting of moderately difficult goals, rather than the subordinate's participation in the goal-setting process.[27]

Latham and Wexley have identified three reasons why goal-setting affects performance.[28] First, goal-setting has a *directive* effect, channeling energy in one particular direction. Second, attaining goals requires putting forth *effort*. Effort is a major determinant of performance, according to Porter and Lawler's model of performance and satisfaction (see Chapter 2). Third, attaining difficult goals requires *persistence*, which may be viewed as "directed effort over time." In short, these authors conclude that "goal-setting is effective because it clarifies exactly what is expected of an individual."[29]

Based on their review of the literature on MBO, Carroll and Schneier have suggested nine factors contributing to MBO program failure.[30] These are given in Exhibit 10.8 and include lack of support from top management, lack of training for evaluators, and the setting of easy goals, among others.

A Performance Appraisal System: Corning Glass Works

Because of differences in intended use, most appraisals for administrative and for development purposes should use different methods and be conducted at different times. However, this section describes an appraisal system that takes an alternative approach, one that was designed to include components specific to both administrative and development purposes.

Corning Glass Works' Performance Management System (PMS) measures and develops the performance and potential of 3,000 managers and professional employees.[31] The system includes three major components:

[26] J.N. Kondrasuk, "Studies in MBO Effectiveness," *Academy of Management Review*," 1981, vol. 6, no. 3, pp. 419–30.

[27] D.L. Dossett, G.P. Latham, and T.R. Mitchell, "The Effects of Assigned versus Participatively Set Goals, KR, and Individual Differences When Goal Difficulty Is Held Constant," *Journal of Applied Psychology,* 1979, vol. 64, pp. 291–98; and T.I. Chacko, "An Attributional Analysis of Participation and Knowledge of Result in a Goal-Setting Context," Ph.D. dissertation, University of Iowa, 1977.

[28] G.P. Latham and K.N. Wexley, *Increasing Productivity Through Performance Appraisal* (Reading, Mass.: Addison-Wesley Publishing Company, 1981).

[29] Ibid., p. 126.

[30] S.J. Carroll and C.E. Schneier, *Performance Appraisal and Review Systems* (Glenview, Ill.: Scott, Foresman and Company, 1982).

[31] Beer et al.

EXHIBIT 10.8

Factors contributing to MBO program failure

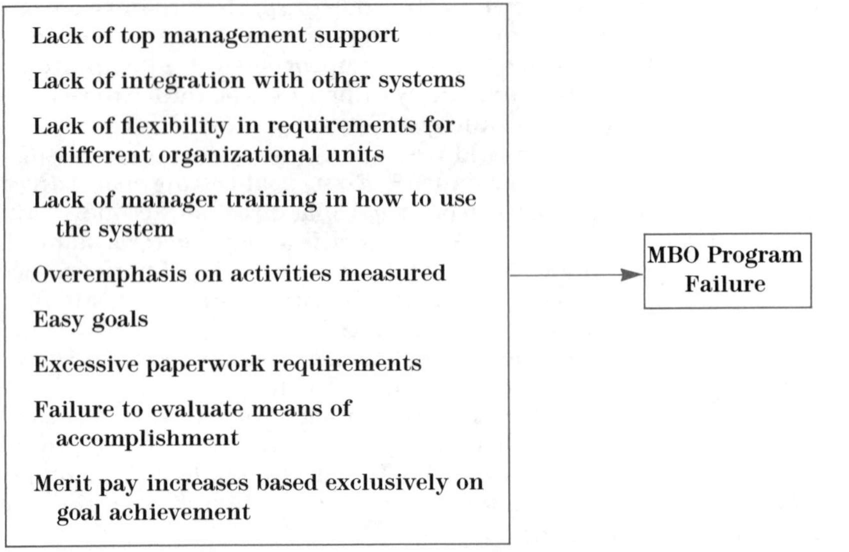

Lack of top management support
Lack of integration with other systems
Lack of flexibility in requirements for different organizational units
Lack of manager training in how to use the system
Overemphasis on activities measured
Easy goals
Excessive paperwork requirements
Failure to evaluate means of accomplishment
Merit pay increases based exclusively on goal achievement
MBO Program Failure

SOURCE: From *Performance Appraisal and Review Systems* by S.J. Carroll and C.E. Schneier. Copyright © 1982 by Foresman and Company. Reprinted by permission.

1. Performance development and review (PD&R), to appraise performance and profile individual employees' strong and weak areas.
2. Management by objectives (MBO), to guide the efforts of employees and provide data on results to complement PD&R ratings.
3. Salary and placement review, to take administrative action based on PD&R and MBO data.

The system took several years to develop and represents a substantial step beyond the situation at Corning in 1968, when even appraisals for administrative purposes were based on casual exchanges between managers over the phone or in a bar. An initial step was development of the PD&R component, which involved construction of rating scales using a BARS-like procedure. Items in the rating scales were constructed to apply to a number of jobs rather than to be job-specific. Some of the dimensions and behavioural items identified for supervisory performance are listed in Exhibit 10.9. Note that the dimensions of Corning's PD&R scales reflect the type of linking of organizational goals to employee performance discussed early in the chapter. Specifically, managers are responsible for productivity of their unit and for communicating company objectives in the course of conflict resolution. Other scales such as control and supportiveness capture important individual aspects of the manager's performance.

EXHIBIT 10.9

Items from Corning Glass Works' performance development and review behavioural rating scales

Subordinate participation—delegates authority and involves subordinates in decisions and in setting objectives

Involves subordinates in decision-making process
Permits subordinates to participate in decision-making process when appropriate
Consults with subordinates in setting their performance objectives
Delegates authority to his subordinates

Control—maintains necessary discipline among subordinates and follows up on work assignments, taking corrective action if necessary

Fails to follow up on work assignments given others
Fails to take action when errors or faulty work are observed in subordinates
Permits subordinates to make poor presentations before other organizational units of higher level management
Maintains necessary discipline

Supportiveness—supports subordinates through appropriate utilization and development of their capacities

Builds confidence in subordinates by supporting their actions
Understands the capabilities and limitations of subordinates
Selects and places qualified personnel
Gives adequate instructions to subordinates when new methods are initiated or new work assigned

Unit's productivity—his subordinates maintain a high level of quality in their work and accomplish large amounts of work

Subordinates accomplish a large amount of work
Maintains a high level of quality in the work of subordinates
Subordinates tend to be lax in their work, even to the point of poor quality results

Conflict resolution—maintains cooperative and cohesive work group by effectively communicating company objectives and helping to resolve conflict

Takes action to settle conflicts among subordinates
Communicates objectives of company and organizational unit to subordinates
Helps subordinates settle their differences
Communicates with subordinates by providing vital information affecting organizational unit and its members

SOURCE: M. Beer, R. Ruh, J.A. Dawson, B.B. McCaa, and M.J. Kavanagh, "A Performance Management System: Research, Design, Introduction, and Evaluation," *Personnel Psychology*, 1978, vol. 31, pp. 505–35.

PD&R was used for both administrative and development purposes. For the former, the end of the rating form asked for a global evaluation of the person being rated. This was sent to the personnel department for use in salary and placement decisions. When used for development purposes, the behavioural rating scales were scored ipsatively. *Ipsative scoring* results in profiles of employees' strengths and weaknesses, as opposed to comparisons of one subordinate with another. These profiles proved useful as a basis for discussions between superiors and subordinates in developmental appraisal interviews. However, some managers had difficulty understanding the ipsative scale scores at first and misused them by attempting comparison of one employee with another. Now many employees are familiar enough with PD&R to rate their own performances before the appraisal interview and to discuss discrepancies between their own ratings and those of their superior.

The second component of the Performance Management System is MBO, which Corning regards as most useful for guiding the efforts of employees and for focussing on results. MBO, therefore, complements PD&R by appraisal of results.

The third component is the salary and placement review. Though there is no prescribed method for this review, both PD&R and MBO data should feed into salary, promotion, and other HRM decisions. A recent Corning policy requires a PD&R before a salary increase can be processed.

Corning implemented this program with an extensive two-day training session. Much of this time was spent training managers to conduct appraisal feedback interviews effectively. Behaviour modelling training was used in which managers saw films of effective and ineffective interviews (role-played by Corning managers). The trainees then role-played a developmental interview using PD&R scale scores as a guide. An unusual strategy for creating acceptance of the system was to include both managers and their subordinate managers in the same training sessions.

At this point one might conclude that Corning has developed the perfect method of performance appraisal. Yet, no matter how perfect a method seems to be from its description or from unsystematic information regarding its use, a vigorous evaluation of its effectiveness should be done. A study of four Corning divisions that used the system for one year was conducted, using a lengthy questionnaire survey. While the survey results were generally very positive, they revealed some problems. One was confusion regarding how to use part of an interview guide concerning career development planning and training objectives; a committee was appointed to revise it. A somewhat more serious problem occurred in the use of PD&R for both developmental and administrative purposes. Using the same instrument for two such dissimilar purposes resulted in some resistance to appraisal by both evaluators and those being evaluated. Finally, the system was not being used universally throughout the organization; some managers neglected it because it had not received as much formal endorsement from higher management as they had expected.

Now, however, the system is in use throughout Corning. The PD&R component is widely accepted and used as an aid to two-way communication between superiors and subordinates. Efforts are being made to tie PD&R to career planning by developing lists of the types of behaviour important for various jobs. Such lists would permit employees to work on behaviour needing improvement in order to qualify for different jobs within the organization. Despite a few problems, Corning's Performance Management System is an uncommon example of the development, implementation, and evaluation of a performance appraisal system to serve both administrative and developmental purposes.

Implementing an Appraisal System

HRM professionals have considerable responsibility for implementing appraisal systems. They must prepare necessary materials, schedule appraisals, see that they are conducted, and make sure that appraisal purposes are understood. One problem that often stands in the way of implementation and proper use of a system is resistance, especially on the part of evaluators.

The Problem of Evaluator Resistance

This chapter began with an example of a radio station manager who was anxious about an upcoming performance review session with one of his DJs. Actually, many managers dread face-to-face appraisal interviews, especially when they must give negative feedback to a subordinate.[32] One executive recalls the manner in which his first performance appraisal was given: "My boss had the appraisal on his desk and he said: 'I'm not supposed to show you this. But I have to go to the bathroom now and I'll be back in about fifteen minutes.' With that, he opened the file on his desk and left."[33]

As a result of their attitudes toward appraisal, many evaluators choose leniency over accuracy when faced with performance problems. This solves the short-run problem of having to confront subordinates with negative information, but may, in the long run, damage trust in the system's fairness and its ability to allocate rewards based on performance criteria. Withholding negative information also denies employees feedback that may be instrumental to their improvement. And, if instances of poor job performance are overlooked during performance review, employees will surely come to believe that poor performance is acceptable. Imagine the chagrin of these same employees if they are subsequently dismissed. They may file a grievance or lawsuit against the company, believing that dismissal was "without cause." If it was, the organization is required to provide either reasonable notice of termination or compensatory pay.

[32] T.H. Stone, "An Examination of Six Prevalent Assumptions Concerning Performance Appraisal," *Public Personnel Management*, October 1973, pp. 166–70.
[33] J. Terry, "In Praise of Appraisals," *Canadian Business*, December 1984, pp. 81–5.

One human resource manager relates the experience of being asked by a supervisor to dismiss an employee for unacceptable job performance. In preparation for the chore, the manager examined the same supervisor's earlier performance evaluations of the subordinate. To his surprise, there was nothing in the record to indicate less than adequate performance! Neither the human resource manager nor the terminated employee was happy with the supervisor's earlier decisions to "spare the unpleasantness of a negative evaluation."

Why do so many supervisors and managers dislike performance appraisal? There are a number of possible reasons. Many may simply dislike "playing God," passing judgement on others.[34] Some may doubt their skills in handling the appraisal interview, especially their ability to deal with defensive and angry reactions of subordinates to negative information. Others may not understand the system being used. For example, managers at Corning had difficulty at first interpreting ipsative scale scores. Evaluators may also distrust the appraisal process and fear that appraisal data will not be used fairly and objectively for pertinent HRM decisions.[35]

Occasionally, raters resist giving an accurate appraisal because it may have negative implications or consequences for them.[36] For example, armed service officers have been known to be reluctant to rate poorly performing subordinates accurately because an individual with a low evaluation may be very difficult to transfer to another unit. Raters may also have the fear of making future rater-ratee interactions unpleasant. Many managers and supervisors carefully consider the consequences of their appraisals, frequently taking the approach that is most rewarding, or less punishing, for themselves in the short run.

Because of evaluator resistance to performance appraisal, HRM professionals often find it necessary to build support for an appraisal system. There is some evidence that commitment of evaluators to an appraisal method or system is more important to success of the system than is sophistication of the system itself.[37] Commitment can be increased and resistance overcome by involving managers in the development of a system, providing training geared to an increased understanding and acceptance of the system, and making performance appraisal an important and rewarded part of every manager's job.

Involving Raters in the Development of a System

There is no reason why an appraisal system cannot be designed with the same careful, analytical approach used in the design of most products. For example, it is quite possible (and also beneficial) to solicit

[34] McGregor.

[35] H.J. Bernardin and R.W. Beatty, *Performance Appraisal: Assessing Human Behavior at Work* (Boston: Kent Publishing Company, 1984), p. 268.

[36] A.L. Patz, "Performance Appraisal: Useful but Still Resisted," *Harvard Business Review*, May-June 1975, pp. 74–80.

[37] E.E. Lawler III, *Pay and Organizational Effectiveness* (New York: McGraw-Hill, 1971).

ideas from people who will use the product. Inclusion of users in the process generates a set of very practical design criteria and also lets product users know that their input is valued. By involving supervisors and managers who will be using an appraisal system in its design and construction, understanding of the system and commitment to it are greatly improved. Involvement at this stage also reduces the amount of training necessary for evaluators. Yet the only appraisal method which typically uses this approach is BARS.

Training Raters

Substantial research supports the value of rater training as a means of improving the reliability and validity of appraisals.[38] Training can also be an important tool in gaining evaluator acceptance and understanding of the appraisal system. Evaluator training must accomplish two purposes. First, it must convince evaluators of the value of making accurate appraisals. This can be done by providing them with an understanding of the system and its importance to the organization. Training programs should explain how appraisals will be used and provide information on why accurate appraisals are essential for these purposes. Though beyond the scope of the training program, reinforcers and rewards should be provided and used as incentives for making fair, objective appraisals. The second training goal—one which is especially important to increasing acceptance of the system—is to teach evaluators about the appraisal process and about handling the appraisal interview. Unless the first training goal is accomplished, time and effort will probably be wasted pursuing the second.

HRM profesionals must train evaluators to handle the appraisal process, which has two components: (1) observing and collecting data on what is measured; and (2) making evaluative judgements. Evaluators should be instructed in the use of appraisal instruments and made aware of the types of rater error.

By definition, the evaluative process means comparing people to one another or to some absolute standard. If a promotion decision is to be made, the evaluative process involves comparisons of one candidate to another (assuming there are competing candidates). When appraisal data are used for development purposes, judgements are often more absolute than comparative.

The evaluative process is often more involved than making straightforward comparative or absolute judgements about people and their performance. Evaluators also make judgements about the reasons behind individual success and failure. These judgements affect organizational outcomes, such as rewards and punishments, for the employee. Stone and Slusher first suggested the applicability of attribution

[38] H.J. Bernardin and C.S. Walter, "Effects of Rater Training and Diary Keeping on Psychometric Error in Ratings," *Journal of Applied Psychology*, 1977, vol. 62, pp. 64–9; G.P. Latham, K.N. Wexley, and E.D. Pursell, "Training Managers to Minimize Rating Errors in the Observation of Behavior," *Journal of Applied Psychology*, 1975, vol. 60, pp. 550–55; and Smith and Kendall.

theory to the performance appraisal process.[39] *Attribution theory* describes how people explain their own and others' successes and failures. According to Weiner's classification scheme, people explain success or failure in terms of ability, effort, task difficulty, and luck.[40] Ability and effort are internal, "person" factors, while task difficulty and luck are external, "environment" factors. Attribution theory seeks to explain the circumstances under which behavioural consequences are attributed to one factor as opposed to another. For example, a ward supervisor sees a registered nurse fail in trying to give an elderly patient an intravenous injection. In order to form a judgement about the nurse, the supervisor explains the failure in terms of lack of ability, lack of effort, task difficulty, or bad luck. Whichever the supervisor decides is the reason for failure will affect outcomes for the employee (whether he or she will be punished, encouraged, or unaffected when it comes to performance review).

Evidence suggests that attributions of ability are made early in an employee's career.[41] These early attributions are important because a supervisor will assign tasks on the basis of perceived ability, and because the employee may set his or her level of aspiration accordingly.[42]

Variations in performance which correspond to high and low incentives are likely to be explained as the results of effort rather than ability, task difficulty, or luck. For example, if the reward for achieving a certain objective is a large bonus, the reason for success is more likely to be perceived in terms of expenditure of effort. There is some evidence that effort is judged as greater following success than failure.[43] Other research suggests that if failure is attributed to lack of effort, rather than to lack of ability, more punitive action is taken.[44] If almost everyone fails at a given task, a supervisor will probably explain this by regarding the task as very difficult, though some supervisors might say that all their subordinates are incompetent and lazy. Finally, unexplainable and unexpected failures and successes are usually attributed to luck. Although task difficulty and luck may have been causative

[39] T.H. Stone and E.A. Slusher, "Attributional Insights into Performance Appraisal," *JSAS Catalog of Selected Documents in Psychology*, ms. no. 964, vol. 5, 1975.

[40] B. Weiner, I. Frieze, A. Kukla, L. Reed, S. Rest, and R.M. Rosenbaum, "Perceiving the Causes of Success and Failure," in E.E. Jones, D.E. Kanouse, H.H. Kelley, R.E. Nisbett, S. Valins, and B. Weiner, eds., *Attribution: Perceiving the Causes of Behavior* (Morristown, N.J.: General Learning Press, 1971).

[41] H.H. Kelley, "The Process of Causal Attribution," *American Psychologist*, 1973, vol. 28, pp. 107–28; and E.E. Jones, L. Rock, K.G. Shaver, G.R. Goethals, and L.M. Ward, "Pattern Performance and Ability Attribution: An Unexpected Primacy Effect," *Journal of Personality and Social Psychology*, 1968, vol. 10, pp. 317–40.

[42] A.K. Korman, "Expectancies as Determinants of Performance," *Journal of Applied Psychology*, 1971, vol. 55, pp. 218–22.

[43] H.M. Jenkins and W.C. Ward, "Judgment of Contingency between Responses and Outcome," *Psychological Monographs*, 1965, vol. 70 (1, whole no. 594); and B. Weiner and A. Kukla, "An Attributional Analysis of Achievement Motivation," *Journal of Personality and Social Psychology*, 1970, vol. 15, pp. 1–20.

[44] B. Weiner, H. Heckhausen, W.U. Meyer, and R.E. Cook, "Causal Attributions and Achievement Motivation: A Conceptual Analysis of Effort and Re-Analysis of Locus of Control," *Journal of Personality and Social Psychology*, 1972, vol. 21, pp. 239–48.

factors in a person's performance, evaluators tend to attribute most behavioural consequences to ability and effort.[45]

Many inaccurate appraisals are due to poor judgement or inappropriate use of available information about an employee's performance. A training program incorporating attribution theory could make evaluators aware of some of the factors influencing their judgements.

Most supervisors and managers could also benefit from training in effective handling of the appraisal interview. One survey of 227 Canadian manufacturers, however, found that very few organizations provide training for raters.[46] Fortunately, because of the current popularity of "people skills" training, it is likely that more of today's managers are learning skills that will help them to conduct effective interviews. "People skills" training, as well as specific appraisal interview training, should help managers feel more comfortable in the appraisal interview situation.

The Appraisal Interview

Appraisal interviews are scheduled with employees to communicate outcomes of the performance appraisal process, such as salary adjustments, promotion and termination decisions (administrative purpose). They are also held to review performance, reinforce desirable behaviours, point out performance deficiencies, and develop plans for improvement (development purpose). While many organizations use one interview for both administrative and development purposes, it is best to conduct separate interviews for these very distinct purposes.

Preparing for the Interview

Before the appraisal interview, a supervisor or manager should prepare by collecting, organizing, and reviewing data related to the subordinate's performance. There is also evidence that it is helpful for the subordinate to prepare for the meeting. Greater preparation by subordinates has been linked to higher levels of participation in the interview and to positive interview outcomes.[47] To allow adequate time

[45] R.E. Nisbett, C. Caputa, P. Legant, and J. Maracek, "Behavior as Seen by the Actor and as Seen by the Observer," *Journal of Personality and Social Psychology*, 1973, vol. 27, pp. 154–64.

[46] John F. Duffy and Andrew C. Peacock, "Contingency Factors in the Effects of Rater Training on Interrater Agreement: Some Lint in the Bellybutton," *Canadian Journal of Administrative Sciences*, vol. 3, no. 2, December 1986, pp. 317–28.

[47] R.J. Burke, W. Weitzel, and T. Weir, "Characteristics of Effective Employee Performance Review and Development Interviews: Replication and Extension," *Personnel Psychology*, 1978, vol. 3, pp. 903–19.

for preparation, subordinates should be notified of appraisal interviews at least several days in advance. The interview should be held in a private place, free from interruptions, and adequate time should be reserved—at least half an hour for administrative interviews and more for development interviews.

The supervisor should also decide on the format of the meeting, which will vary according to an employee's performance level and job type. Cummings and Schwab suggest three different appraisal interview formats, or programs: DAP, MAP, and RAP.[48]

A *developmental action program* (DAP) approach is used in interviews with high performers who show potential for advancement. The focus here is on planning work, not evaluating performance. Subordinate and superior work together to set goals, determine performance standards, and decide on development needs. MBO is a form of DAP.

MAP, a *maintenance action program*, is appropriate for employees who perform acceptably but show little potential for advancement. The focus here is on maintaining acceptable performance. Under this approach, an employee is informed that his or her performance is acceptable, but that there is little evidence of development potential.

A *remedial action program* (RAP) approach is taken with employees who have demonstrated consistently poor performance. This type of interview focusses on performance improvement, with the supervisor providing feedback on performance deficiencies and giving examples of acceptable and unacceptable performance. A RAP approach extends beyond the appraisal interview situation, since progressive discipline may be required if performance does not improve. General procedures to follow in a RAP approach are given in Exhibit 10.10.

Approaches to the Appraisal Interview

Maier describes three approaches to appraisal interviews: "tell and sell," "tell and listen," and "problem-solving."[49] These are described in Exhibit 10.11.

Most managers take a "tell and sell" approach, which involves communicating appraisal results to employees and, through salesmanship, encouraging them to begin a plan of improvement. A superior using this approach sits as a judge, assuming that subordinates need only be informed of their deficiencies in order to want to correct them.

In the "tell and listen" approach, a superior once again serves as a judge, but encourages feedback from the subordinate. The superior uses listening skills and reflects, or restates, feelings and reactions of the subordinate. This serves to reduce defensiveness because the subordinate feels he is understood and accepted.

[48] L.L. Cummings and D.P. Schwab, *Performance in Organizations: Determinants and Appraisal* (Glenview, Ill.: Scott, Foresman and Company, 1973), pp. 118–26.

[49] N.R.F. Maier, "Three Types of Appraisal Interview," *Personnel*, March–April 1958, vol. 34, pp. 27–39.

EXHIBIT 10.10

Procedures to follow in a RAP approach

1. Clear feedback to the individual about why the superior feels the performer has performance problems.
2. Frequent use of behavioural critical incidents to point out examples of poor and acceptable performance.
3. A highly specified, imposed program for corrective action, with performance measures and time perspectives clearly and formally established.
4. Monthly review sessions, more frequent if performance is continuing to deteriorate, with the focus of these sessions on the superior communicating to the employee how the superior feels the employee is doing against the program established in the previous step.
5. If performance increases, then go to longer time intervals of performance specifications and measurement; if continual improvements over a sustained period occurs, then transfer the individual to a MAP.
6. If performance does not improve or decreases even further, then establish a highly specified sequence of events in terms of activities, measurements, and short-time perspectives, with the explicit conclusion being termination if no performance improvements are shown; this frequently results in voluntary self-termination. A key element here is the employee's understanding that he has moved into this phase; therefore, explicit communications to this effect are crucial.

SOURCE: L.L. Cummings and D.P. Schwab, *Performance in Organizations: Determinants & Appraisal* (Glenview, Ill.: Scott, Foresman and Company, 1973), p. 123.

EXHIBIT 10.11

Three approaches to appraisal interviews

METHOD	*TELL AND SELL*	*TELL AND LISTEN*	*PROBLEM-SOLVING*
Role of Interviewer	*Judge*	*Judge*	*Helper*
Objective	To communicate evaluation and get employee to change.	To communicate evaluation and encourage discussion.	To stimulate growth and development in employee.
Assumptions	Employee desires to correct weaknesses if he/she knows them. Any person can improve if he/she so chooses. A superior is qualified to evaluate a subordinate.	People will change if defensive feelings are removed.	Growth can occur without correcting faults. Discussion of job problems leads to improved performance.

METHOD *Role of Interviewer*	*TELL AND SELL* *Judge*	*TELL AND LISTEN* *Judge*	*PROBLEM-SOLVING* *Helper*
Reactions	Defensive behavior suppressed. Attempts to cover hostility.	Defensive behavior expressed. Employee feels accepted.	Problem-solving behavior.
Skills	Salesmanship. Patience.	Listening and reflecting feelings. Summarizing.	Listening and reflecting feelings. Reflecting ideas. Using exploratory questions. Summarizing.
Attitude	People profit from criticism and appreciate help.	One can respect the feelings of others if one understands them.	Discussion develops new ideas and mutual interests.
Motivation	Use of positive or negative incentives or both (extrinsic in that motivation is not related to task content).	Resistance to change reduced.	Increased freedom. Increased responsibility (intrinsic motivation in that interest is inherent in the task).
Gains	Success most probable when employee respects interviewer.	Develops favorable attitude to superior, which increases probability of success.	Almost assured of improvement in some respect.
Risks	Loss of loyalty. Inhibition of independent judgment.	Need for change may not be developed.	Employee may lack ideas. Change may be other than what superior had in mind.
Values	Perpetuates existing practices and values.	Permits interviewer to change views in the light of employee's responses. Some upward communication.	Both learn since experience and views pooled. Change is facilitated.

SOURCE: "Three Types of Appraisal Interview," by N.R.F. Maier. Reprinted by permission of the publisher, from *Personnel*, (Issue: March-April 1958, vol. 34, p. 29) American Management Association, New York.

The objective of a problem-solving approach is to stimulate employee growth and development through discussion of job problems. Instead of eliciting defensiveness from subordinates, this approach prompts problem-solving behaviour. A superior using this approach listens, reflects feelings and ideas, and serves as a helper, rather than judge. Several studies show that subordinate reactions to performance review are more positive when a problem-solving approach is used.[50]

Characteristics of Effective Appraisal Interviews

Exhibit 10.12 presents factors contributing to the effectiveness of performance appraisal interviews. We have already discussed some of these factors, such as skills acquired by training and adequate preparation. Other factors of importance are participation of the subordinate, supportiveness of the superior, and a goal-setting, problem-oriented approach.

Appraisal interviews are most effective when subordinates have high levels of participation and are allowed to voice their opinions.[51] Participation has been found to increase satisfaction with both the appraisal process and with the supervisor conducting the appraisal. One expert suggests that a subordinate should talk eight or nine times more than the person conducting the interview. The supervisor should, of course, control and guide the interview through directive techniques, including proper use of questions.[52]

Appraisal interviews are also more effective when superiors are supportive and noncritical.[53] Supportiveness facilitates acceptance of appraisals, while criticism makes acceptance more difficult. Beyond a certain point, criticism may have a negative effect on performance. A classic study of 92 managers at General Electric found that an above-average number of criticisms from the boss resulted in both increased defensiveness and subsequent reductions in performance.[54]

Other key ingredients of effective appraisal interviews include setting specific goals and working toward solutions for problems that interfere with performance.[55]

The important role of the supervisor or manager is obvious at this point. Through their handling of the appraisal interview, supervisors and managers not only affect levels of employee motivation and job performance, they also influence attitudes toward appraisals, manage-

[50] N.R.F. Maier, *The Appraisal Interview* (New York: Wiley, 1958); and H.H. Meyer and E.A. Kay, *Comparison of a Work Planning Program with the Annual Performance Appraisal Interview Approach.* Behavioral Research Report No. ESR17, General Electric Company, 1964.

[51] Burke, Weitzel, and Weir.

[52] R.G. Johnson, *The Appraisal Interview Guide* (New York: AMACOM, 1979), pp. 72, 113.

[53] Burke, Weitzel, and Weir.

[54] H. Meyer, E. Kay, and J.R.P. French, "Split Roles in Performance Appraisal," *Harvard Business Review*, 1965, vol. 43, pp. 123–29.

[55] Burke, Weitzel, and Weir.

EXHIBIT 10.12

Factors contributing to the effectiveness of performance appraisal interviews

Stage			
SKILLS		**Skill Building** Training in communication, counseling and/or consulting skills	
PREP-ARATION	**Superior's Preparation** Think about organization and job goals of subordinate Review criteria/standards Review anecdotal records of subordinate performance and typical days Select major area of contribution	**Subordinate's Preparation** Review job/task goals Review criteria/standards Identify own strengths and weaknesses Plan for own development task assignments and career needs	
PROCESS	Participation of subordinate in session	Constructive/helping attitude/behavior of superior	Perception that organization rewards are contingent on outcomes of performance appraisal
SUBSTANCE	Develop action plan to alleviate job problems deterring desired performance	Set future performance targets	Determine indicators of results expected
FOLLOW-UP	**Follow-Up** Prepare draft of action plan and what was agreed upon Present to subordinate for approval		

SOURCE: "Combining BARS and MBO: Using an appraisal system to diagnose performance problems" by C.E. Schneier and R.W. Beatty. Reprinted from the *Personnel Administrator*, copyright © 1979, The American Society for Personnel Administration, 606 North Washington Street, Alexandria, VA 22314, $40 per year.

ment and the organization. Exhibit 10.13 presents seven dimensions of behaviour which have been identified as important for the success of managerial appraisal interviews, including structuring and controlling the interview; establishing and maintaining rapport; reacting to stress; obtaining information; resolving conflict; developing the interviewee; and motivating the interviewee. These dimensions were identified by Borman, Hough, and Dunnette in their development of behaviourally anchored rating scales for interviewer behaviour.[56] Effective and ineffective behaviours relating to each dimension are given in the Exhibit.

EXHIBIT 10.13

Seven dimensions of interviewer behaviour

1. ***Structuring and controlling the interview:*** Clearly stating the purpose of the interview, maintaining control over the interview, and displaying an organized and prepared approach to the interview *versus* not discussing the purpose of the interview, displaying a confused approach, and allowing the interviewee to control the interview when inappropriate.
2. ***Establishing and maintaining rapport:*** Setting an appropriate climate for the interview, opening the interview in a warm and nonthreatening manner, and being sensitive to the interviewee *versus* setting a hostile or belligerent climate, being overly friendly or familiar during the interview, and displaying insensitivity towards the interviewee.
3. ***Reacting to stress:*** Remaining calm and cool even during an interviewee's outbursts, apologizing when appropriate but not backing down or retreating unnecessarily, and maintaining composure and perspective under fire *versus* reacting inappropriately to stress, becoming irate or defensive in reaction to complaints, and backing down inappropriately when confronted.
4. ***Obtaining information:*** Asking appropriate questions, probing effectively to ensure that meaningful topics and important issues are raised, and seeking solid information *versus* glossing over problems and issues, asking inappropriate questions, and failing to probe into the interviewee's perception of problems.
5. ***Resolving conflict:*** Moving effectively to reduce any conflict between the interviewee and other employees, making appropriate commitments and setting realistic goals to ensure conflict resolution, and providing good advice to the interviewee about his or her relationships with other employees *versus* discussing problems too bluntly or lecturing the interviewee ineffectively regarding the resolution of conflict, failing to set goals or to make commitments appropriate to effective conflict resolution, and providing poor advice to the interviewee about his or her relationships with other employees.
6. ***Developing the interviewee:*** Offering to help the interviewee develop professionally, displaying interest in the interviewee's professional growth,

[56] W.C. Borman, L.M. Hough, and M.D. Dunnette, *Performance Ratings: An Investigation of Reliability, Accuracy and Relationships Between Individual Differences and Rater Error.* Final Report to the Army Research Institute for the Behavioral and Social Sciences, Alexandria, Va., 1978.

specifying developmental needs, and recommending sound developmental actions *versus* not offering to aid in the interviewee's professional development, displaying little or no interest in the interviewee's professional growth, failing to make developmental suggestions, and providing poor advice regarding the interviewee's professional development.

7. ***Motivating the interviewee:*** Providing incentives for the interviewee to stay with the organization and to perform effectively, making commitments to encourage the interviewee to perform his or her job well and to help the organization accomplish its objectives, and supporting the interviewee's excellent performance *versus* providing little or no incentive for the interviewee to stay with the organization and to perform effectively, failing to make commitments to encourage the interviewee's continued top performance, and neglecting to express support of the interviewee's excellent performance record.

SOURCE: From Bernardin and Beatty, *Performance Appraisal: Assessing Human Behavior at Work* (Boston: Kent Publishing Company, 1984), pp. 279–80.

Collecting and Storing Appraisal Data

Besides developing and implementing appraisal systems, HRM professionals collect and store appraisal data in order to monitor quality of the work force and assess the effectiveness of various HRM programs. Records of appraisal data are also essential to protect against charges of discrimination and unjust dismissal.

Appraisal Data for Program Assessment

Program assessment purposes were discussed earlier; they include using performance appraisal data to assess the effectiveness of recruiting, selection, and placement procedures and to evaluate training and development programs. Studies of program effectiveness require "before" and "after" measurements. For recruiting, selection, and placement procedures, performance appraisal data may be used to help determine whether organizational predictors of success are, in fact, predictive of success. One study found that 72 per cent of all the selection studies published in the *Journal of Applied Psychology* between 1955 and 1975 used some type of rating scale as a criterion measure.[57] The effectiveness of training and development programs can be ascertained by controlled studies comparing employees' performance before and after participation in such programs.

The ideal appraisal system would yield numerous reliable and representative measures of job behaviour and job results. Numerous measures are necessary for several reasons. First, any single measure may be deficient in itself or contaminated by situational factors. Second,

[57] F.J. Landy and D.A. Trumbo, *The Psychology of Work Behavior* (Homewood, Ill.: Dorsey Press, 1976).

most jobs are sufficiently complex that one measure cannot completely cover their required behaviour or their results. Finally, different measures may be required for different organizational purposes, and these purposes may change over time. For example, the quantity of production may now be of major importance, but at a future time the firm may wish to select employees who perform very high quality work.

The responsibility for data collection and storage is a vital one for appraisal systems because data collected and retained in appraisal forms are very often the only record of an employee's job performance.

Appraisal Data to Protect Against Charges of Discrimination and Unjust Dismissal

Appraisal data provide crucial documentation should personnel actions be contested on human rights grounds or on charges of unjust dismissal. For example, if an employee charges sex discrimination because she was denied a promotion, an employer can produce appraisal records that indicate the employee was less qualified than male candidates for the position.

Increasingly, Canadian courts and arbitrators are requiring employers to prove "just cause" for dismissing employees without notice. Without cause for dismissal, an employer must provide "reasonable" notice or compensatory pay.[58] "Reasonable" is a subjective term: its definition varies from one situation to another. For example, "reasonable" may mean a year in the case of a high-level executive or an older employee who has little chance of re-employment; or it may be only a few months, as in the case of a more employable person. In order to prove "just cause" for dismissal, employers need sound performance data, usually evidence of fraud or gross misconduct.

In order for appraisal data to be useful for this purpose and for defending against charges of human rights violations, appraisal systems themselves must be "defensible." Based on their review of significant U.S. court cases involving performance appraisal, Lubben, Thompson, and Klasson offer a number of generalizations as to "what appears to constitute a defensible performance appraisal system." Among them are:

1. The overall appraisal process should be formalized, standardized, and, as much as possible, objective in nature.
2. The performance appraisal system should be as job-related as possible.
3. A thorough, formal job analysis for all employment positions being rated should be completed.
4. Evaluators should be adequately trained in the use of appraisal techniques that employ written qualification criteria for promotion or transfer decisions.
5. An evaluator should have substantial daily contact with the employee being evaluated.

[58] W. Trueman, "When Workers Take Root," *Canadian Business*, April 1984, pp. 82–5.

6. The administration and scoring of the performance appraisals should be standardized and controlled.[59]

Summary

This chapter has examined the performance appraisal function and the use of appraisals in administrative decision-making, employee development, work force monitoring and program assessment. With respect to performance appraisal, HRM professionals have responsibility for designing appraisal systems, implementing them, and collecting and storing appraisal data for a variety of purposes. In designing an appraisal system, HRM professionals must determine the organization's particular needs for appraisal and whether the system or method meets the general requirements of reliability, validity, practicality, fairness, and impact. Implementing a system involves preparation of materials, scheduling, and taking steps to ensure that raters accept and understand the appraisal system. Evaluators often resist appraising performance, but much of this resistance can be overcome through rater training in appraisal methods and handling of the appraisal interview.

Project Ideas

1. Describe an incident in which your performance was evaluated. Describe the appraisal itself (positive-negative, how determined, how conveyed to you) and the resulting outcomes in terms of extrinsic rewards. Did you perceive the appraisal as fair? Why or why not? How did the actual outcomes compare to the desired or expected outcomes? Was your level of job satisfaction affected in any way as a result of the appraisal and its outcomes? How? Was there any effect on your subsequent performance? The sharing of student experiences should demonstrate a variety of consequences associated with different types of appraisals. The role of individual differences in reactions to performance appraisals and their outcomes should also be evident.

2. Choose a job description from Chapter 5 to generate dimensions for a graphic rating scale. Try to establish at least five identifiable points for each dimension and, if possible, provide behavioural definitions for each dimension or scale. Examine each scale and classify it according to whether it applies to a personal characteristic, a type of behaviour, or a job performance result. This project can

[59] G.L. Lubben, D.E. Thompson, and C.R. Klasson, "Performance Appraisal: Legal Implications," *Personnel*, May–June 1980.

be done individually or in small groups. If students or groups work independently, different rating scales for the same job can be compared and discussed.

3. Divide the class into three groups to develop behaviour/performance dimensions for use in BARS construction for a familiar occupation, such as maid, waiter, or drivers' training instructor. Group 1 should generate a list of performance dimensions, while Group 2 works to specify agreed-on effective and ineffective behaviour relating to the job. When Groups 1 and 2 have completed their tasks, Group 3 should try to match the kinds of behaviour to the dimensions. When the process is complete, each group should discuss its experience in its assigned task. Though any scales which might result from this class project will have no validity, students will gain an understanding of the BARS construction process.

4. Role-play a performance appraisal interview between a superior and a subordinate. Maier's *The Role-Play Technique: A Handbook for Management and Leadership Practice* (LaJolla, Calif.: University Associates, 1975) is a good source for role-playing cases. After the role play, carefully examine the interview process and outcomes. Does the "boss" feel that his or her purposes were accomplished in the interview? Compare the subordinate's perception of the interview with the boss's. Were they the same? If not, explore why. In your discussion focus on behaviour that makes open communication and understanding between boss and subordinate easier. Development of good interview skills requires a knowledge of appropriate behaviour, opportunities for practice, and feedback and reinforcement. The role-playing setting is one method of developing interview skills.

5. Search relatively recent issues of *Journal of Applied Psychology, Personnel Psychology, Canadian Journal of Administrative Sciences, The Personnel Administrator*, and other personnel or human resource management-related journals for articles on performance appraisal. Read, briefly summarize, and criticize several articles. This is an excellent way to get some ideas on recent theories, research, and practices in performance appraisal.

Cases

Case 10.1: Performance Review at Berghoff's

Raj Chandra, manager of men's clothing at Berghoff's Department Store, checks his watch as he paces nervously outside his boss's office. Marcus Berghoff, son of the owner, is late for the 11 A.M. appointment he made with Chandra yesterday. Chandra wasn't told the purpose of the meeting, only that the boss wanted to see him. He wonders if it has anything to do with the customer who came in last week demanding that he credit her account for a defective pair of jeans. He had told the woman, Lucy Wilson, that it was against store policy to take back the jeans, since she had already washed them. He suggested instead that the store's seamstress could fix the jeans. But Wilson was insistent and Chandra finally gave in. Wilson was, after all, a very good customer. Only last month she had purchased six of Berghoff's finest silk ties.

The clock reads 11:15 when Chandra is finally called into Berghoff's office. He's never had the pleasure before and he isn't sure he wants it now. Berghoff, an imposing man in his late 40s, sits at a large desk facing an uncomfortable-looking, straight-backed chair which is obviously meant for Chandra.

"Would you like a cup of coffee?" Berghoff asks amiably, motioning for Chandra to make himself comfortable.

"Why, yes, thank you." Chandra sits down.

Berghoff asks his secretary to bring Chandra a cup of coffee. "Nice weather we're having, isn't it?" he continues. "How are your wife and kids . . . you do have a wife and kids, don't you?"

"Yes, I do, Mr. Berghoff. They are very well, thank you."

"Well, Mr. Chandra, you've been with us for about a year now and I uh, I guess it's about time we had our little talk."

"Fine, sir," says Chandra, "I guess it is about time." He wonders why he feels so nervous; sales are up in his department and he is confident of his ability to manage his eight subordinates.

"What I want to talk to you about . . ." Berghoff is interrupted by the ringing of his office phone.

Chandra sips his coffee while Berghoff makes a date to play tennis at the racquet club later that afternoon with someone named Frank.

"Now, as I was saying," he continues, "I want to talk to you about, uh . . . , about the fine job you've been doing. I see that you've exceeded your department's sales goals, profit is up, and theft is down. The two new clerks you hired and trained are working out well."

Chandra, feeling pleased relaxes somewhat in his chair. "Thank you, I appreciate . . ."

"That doesn't excuse the fact, however," Berghoff interrupts, "that you flagrantly broke the rules. You know as well as I do we have a company policy against accepting returns that have been washed or worn. Rules . . ."

"I can explain . . ." Chandra begins.

"Rules," continues Berghoff, "aren't made to be broken. We didn't get where we are today by letting people return things they've already . . ."

"But I can explain!" Chandra interrupts in frustration.

"No explanations, no excuses!" says Berghoff, raising his voice and stamping his fist on the desk to punctuate his point. "We go by the book around here, in case you haven't noticed."

"I did notice, sir, but you see, she said . . ."

"I don't care what she said. You went against company policy.

The next time you do something like this I'm going to have to dock your pay."

"Yes sssir," Chandra stammers. "Will there be anything else?"

Bergoff pushes his chair back from his desk, stands up, smiles, and walks around to Chandra. In a calmer mood, he places a hand on Chandra's shoulder and says, "I think you're going to work out just fine, son. Just don't break any more rules."

Chandra leaves the office, feeling both stunned and frustrated. Despite his accomplishments, the boss picked up on a little rule violation that could easily have been explained if only Berghoff had listened. As he returns to his department, Chandra wonders how long he can work for a boss who won't listen—one who values rules more than a manager's good judgement.

Back in his office, Berghoff heaves a sigh of relief, glad the encounter is over. "It's never easy to give a negative appraisal," he thinks, "but sometimes it has to be done."

Questions:

1. Analyze Berghoff's handling of the review session. What were his mistakes and how might they be corrected?
2. Based on your analysis, restructure the review session and rewrite its dialogue to demonstrate how the interview could have been handled more effectively by Mr. Berghoff.

Case 10.2: Performance Monitoring at Bell Canada

The 20 operators on shift this morning are all women, although Bell does employ some men, and they make anywhere from $293 to $431 weekly. On her VDT screen a young operator is checking out her own performance. The computer tells her that she has taken 119 calls since starting work a little more than an hour ago, and that her average work time (AWT) per call of 25 seconds is two seconds better than the average so far today.

Behind the operator stands her supervisor, Judy Wenman, who says the system is a big change from when she joined Bell as an operator 13 years ago. Wenman, at the time manager of operator services, says that AWT wasn't recorded then because it could take as long as five minutes to place a call from Toronto to Montreal. Just prior to the introduction of Bell's Traffic Operator Position System (TOPS) in 1977 AWT was 85 seconds; it's now 25.

If an operator's TOPS statistics start to fluctuate, it's a signal to Wenman that something is wrong—usually in the operator's phone manner. That's where monitoring calls, a practice Bell has used for decades, comes in handy. Upon being hired, Bell operators are warned that their calls will be listened to periodically. The company says it gives advance notice of the approximately 200 calls it monitors annually on each operator, and that it is done to improve service. "There are ways to speed up and still be polite. An operator doesn't have to hear about the customer's children or what's for dinner," says Mel James, director of information for Bell Canada, Ontario region. He defends eavesdropping because the company uses it as a teaching tool, "not a club."

The Communication Workers of Canada (CWC) disagrees. George Larter, president of CWC's Local 50 in Toronto, says Bell targets operators it thinks are performing poorly. "Some aren't listened to at all; others are monitored without warning hundreds of times a year." Larter, an operator since 1976, refutes James's assertion that the dual monitoring system is not used to discipline employees: "At least three operators have been recently suspended without pay for as long as three days because of their AWT figures, or for what Bell calls 'improper operator practices.' "

James doesn't deny that "in the wrong hands" the system is a weapon, but argues that TOPS and eavesdropping are just one part of Bell's employee evaluation and promotion process. "Anyone who lets the machine obsess them will naturally perform poorly, and maybe they are in the wrong job," he suggests. As for misuse, he says that any supervisor "cracking the whip needlessly" would quickly attract union attention. "We'd say to them, 'Hey cool it down there.' " Will the supervisor comply? Larter doesn't think so. "Supervisors are nervous. They're surplus and they have to look good. Mr. James may say 'cool it,' but does he really expect them to?" At any rate, James says that because Bell is entirely computerized, no other way exists to measure employee performance. "There's no paper around anymore, so the machine keeps score. That's what makes them fearful."

Still, in the paper era, Bell couldn't gather the information it now does on its operators. With the touch of a key, managers can examine 76 measurements of an operator's performance, including the average number of seconds between the customer coming on the line and the operator depressing the first key; the average number of keystrokes required to get the requested listing; the average number of screenings pulled to find a listing; and the average time between the pushing of the last key and the customer dropping out of the system. With operators answering between 700 and 1,000 calls per shift, it's remarkable that most operators' statistics hardly fluctuate. But for those riding out personal or financial troubles—or just a hangover—the computer is the first to know. Management is the second.

It is this type of record keeping that particularly concerns Larter and his fellow unionists. While the computer pinpoints an operator's down days, it of course has no way of recognizing the reasons why someone's performance is off. As Larter says: "By the time a performance review occurs, the circumstances that led to poor TOPS scores can be forgotten. The operator stands condemned."

Questions:

1. What are the major reasons behind Bell Canada's use of computer performance monitoring? Do you think Bell uses the system mainly for administrative or development purposes? Which do you feel the system is better suited to and why?
2. Large numbers of employees and their unions oppose computer performance monitoring. What are some of the reasons for their opposition?
3. Compare computer performance monitoring systems to performance appraisal processes that do not have computer monitoring. How are they alike and how are they different? How do computer monitoring systems measure up in terms of the requirements for all appraisal systems?
4. Identify the problems you see in using computer performance monitoring. How might these problems be alleviated?

FROM: L. Archer, "I Saw What You Did and I Know Who You Are," *Canadian Business*, November 1985, pp. 76–83.

11

Career Planning

Reasons for Career Planning
Career Planning: Relation to Other Functions
What People Want from Their Careers
Elements of Career Planning Programs
Career Planning Programs
CEIC Aids for Career Planning
Facilitating Career Planning and Development
Career Planning Issues
Summary
Project Ideas
Cases

Ted Maxwell has been employed as a medical records clerk at a large hospital, City General, for 12 months. He has adjusted well to his job and to the work environment. Maxwell is happy with his decision to join the hospital staff, and an annual appraisal of his work indicated that he is doing a good job. Because Maxwell is happy with his job choice and with City General, he is beginning to wonder what kind of future he might have with the organization. Like many workers of the 1980s, Maxwell welcomes a challenge and the opportunity to grow and develop to his full potential. Too, Maxwell's superiors may be wondering how they can develop and utilize Maxwell to the best of his abilities in order to meet future staffing needs. The HRM function that seeks to reconcile individual career plans and needs with organizational needs is known as career planning, or career management.

Career planning includes: (1) assessment of employee abilities and potential; (2) determination of logical paths of movement between jobs; and (3) efforts to channel individual career interests in directions compatible with the organization's future human resource needs.

Although the term "career development" is sometimes confused with "career planning," the two are not synonymous. Career development, discussed in Chapter 9, refers to the process and activities involved in preparing an employee for future positions in the organization.

Reasons for Career Planning

Career planning is a relatively new HRM function, and established programs are rare except in very large or progressive organizations. Organizational involvement in career planning is increasing, however. Many job candidates—especially, but not only, those who are highly educated—want a career, not "just a job," and many employees have high expectations about gaining satisfaction from their work, now and in the future.

There are a number of reasons for career planning; the following are cited as influential by 225 companies who engage in career planning activities:[1]

1. Desire to develop and promote employees from within.
2. Shortage of promotable talent.
3. Desire to aid individual career planning.
4. Strong expression of interest by employees.
5. Desire to improve productivity.
6. Affirmative action program commitments.
7. Concern about turnover.
8. Personal interest of unit managers.
9. Desire for a positive recruiting image.

From this list, we see that the impetus behind career planning may come from either of two sources or both: (1) from employees who desire satisfying work and personal growth; or (2) from employers who strive to retain and effectively utilize their human resources.

Employee Desires for Satisfying Work

In North America, the decades since World War II have seen a general increase in concern for the quality of life and work, in good times and in bad. Workers expect more than paycheques from their jobs. Work is often viewed as a medium for satisfying personal needs, as an experience in which the employee grows to meet increasing challenges. This broad view of the role of work is evidenced by the federal and Ontario governments' establishment of Quality of Working Life programs. QWL centres, whose boards include representatives of management and organized labour, provide information and research data on ways in which unions and management can work together to redesign their organizations to offer more satisfying work experiences.

[1] J.W. Walker and T.G. Gutteridge, *Career Planning Practices* (New York: AMACOM, 1979).

In part, the phenomenon of seeking satisfaction in work reflects the general prosperity of the post-war era. It is probably also a function of the rising general level of education. A 1978 survey, which received responses from 29,609 persons who had graduated from Canadian universities and colleges in 1976, found that only 12 per cent were not satisfied with their jobs.[2] Two-thirds of this group were underemployed and/or working in jobs which had nothing to do with their post-secondary programs. Respondents who were most satisfied were graduates of master's and Ph.D. programs, presumably because they had been able to obtain interesting work.

The tendency to emphasize job satisfaction is not, however, restricted to highly educated or professional workers. A more general survey in the 1970s of Canadians' feelings about their jobs found that the single most important consideration was interesting work.[3] This factor ranked ahead of such other job characteristics as enough authority, clearly defined responsibilities, competent co-workers, a lot of freedom, or good job security. Of the 34 characteristics listed, good pay ranked 17th and good fringe benefits 26th. The importance of interesting work did increase with the respondent's income level, but a very high percentage of low-income workers indicated that they put much value on job satisfaction. Of the respondents whose incomes were at or near the poverty line, 72 per cent felt interesting work was important, compared to more than 85 per cent of those whose incomes were at middle-class levels.

The realities of the recession of 1982 may have tempered short-term aspirations, but they have not changed basic societal attitudes. The career orientation of labour force entrants was evidenced in the 1981–82 *Career Planning Annual*;[4] most organizations advertising in this publication emphasized opportunities for career growth and development. A glance at recruitment ads in fall 1982 suggested that not even that season's high unemployment rates had obviated the perceived importance of work as a challenge and a career. In just one edition of one daily paper, ads for many different jobs emphasized their potential for growth: "challenging, demanding, rewarding career opportunity" (caregiver for disturbed children); "ground floor opportunity to work yourself into the personnel department of a downtown hospital" (receptionist/clerk); "chance to grow with young company" (copy preparer for a typesetting and printing firm); "excellent dynamic opportunity" (telephone salesperson); and so on.

If frustrated, employee needs for growth and advancement can lead to dissatisfaction and voluntary turnover. A recent study comparing employee satisfaction in 1981 versus 1977 found a decline in satisfaction over the four-year period for both men and women. Decline in

[2] W. Clark and Z. Zsigmond, *Job Market Reality for Post-Secondary Graduates*, Statistics Canada (Ottawa: Minister of Supply and Services Canada, 1981).

[3] M. Burstein, N. Tonhaara, P. Hewson, and B. Warrander, *Canadian Work Values*, Manpower and Immigration (Ottawa: Information Canada, 1975).

[4] University and College Placement Association, *Career Planning Annual* (Toronto: UCPA, 1981).

satisfaction was attributed to two factors: lack of perceived opportunities for advancement and perceived inability to influence the decisions of superiors. Women experienced the greatest declines in satisfaction over the four-year period. Among men, the greatest declines were found among professional, managerial, and skilled workers.[5] Another study found that 42 per cent of executive job changers quit because they perceived better opportunities for career advancement elsewhere. An additonal 23 per cent left to assume greater responsibilities immediately.[6] Lack of advancement opportunities has also been linked to turnover among nurses, clerical workers, salesmen, and nonsupervisory plant workers, among others. Thus, career planning programs that help employees advance serve to facilitate retention and reduce one source of employee dissatisfaction.

Effective Utilization of Human Resources

A primary reason for career planning is the need of organizations to make the best possible use of their most valuable resource—people—in a time of rapid technological growth and change. By developing employees for future positions, an organization is assured a supply of qualified, committed employees to replace higher-level employees who either terminate or advance. This facilitates internal staffing of the organization and reduces the costs of external recruiting and selection. In addition, a career planning strategy enables organizations to develop and place employees in positions compatible with their individual career interests, needs, and goals, thus promoting employee satisfaction and optimal use of employee abilities.

While career planning programs can help employees channel their energies toward higher-level positions (giving them a sense of striving and upward mobility), they cannot be expected to guarantee higher-level positions for all who choose to pursue them. For one thing, the number of higher-level positions, especially in management, is limited. For another, the number of experienced and deserving workers vying for limited positions has grown due to aging of the work force. The realities of a sluggish economy, requiring staff cutbacks in many cases, has only made matters worse.

Problems of career blockage are especially acute among executives who find their paths blocked due to corporate reorganization, office politics, and sluggish company growth. Because of the lack of advancement opportunities, many such "blocked" executives actively seek alternative employment.

Another group that is especially affected by career blockage is women. One of the reasons for this is that women tend to be concentrated in

[5] T. Atkinson, "Differences Between Male and Female Attitudes toward Work," *The Canadian Business Review*, Summer 1983, pp. 47–51.

[6] P. Meyer, "Why Executives Change Jobs," *The Personnel Administrator*, October 1979, vol. 24, no. 10, pp. 59–64, 72.

domestic occupations, such as nursing, food service, and clerical work, which provide little opportunity to climb a ladder of success.[7]

The realities of affirmative action, slowed economic growth, and downsizing mean that career planning must identify logical job sequences and activities which have less of the traditional emphasis on upward mobility. With upward mobility less of an option, career planning increases in importance as a vehicle for meeting employee demands for more satisfying work.

Career Planning: Relation to Other Functions

From an employee's perspective, career planning takes place after some amount of time on the job and after the organization has had a chance to appraise his or her performance. From an organizational perspective, career planning is an ongoing management function with close ties to performance appraisal, human resource planning (HRP), job analysis, and employee development (see Exhibit 11.1).

Performance Appraisal

Performance appraisals inform employees of their strengths and weaknesses, their relative standing in the organization, and their chances for promotion or advancement. This information is essential to deciding on realistic individual career goals.

Such goals are often set within developmental performance appraisal interviews. Traditionally, organizations have used performance appraisal, formal or informal, to identify employees with the potential to advance to positions of greater responsibility. The underlying assumption is that employees with good performance records in one capacity will be good performers in another. Because of their past performance records, high-potential employees gain access to career planning and development opportunities which will prepare them for future positions in the organization.

Human Resource Planning

From an organizational perspective, career planning reconciles individual career planning needs, interests, and goals with the organization's future staffing needs. In this way the organization ensures that an adequate supply of well-trained and motivated employees will be available to fill job vacancies. Human resource planners provide predictions of expected job vacancies, data which career planners use to

[7] M. Boyd, "Occupational Segregation: A Review," in *Sexual Equality in the Workplace* (Ottawa: Labour Canada, Women's Bureau, 1982).

EXHIBIT 11.1

Career planning: relation to other functions

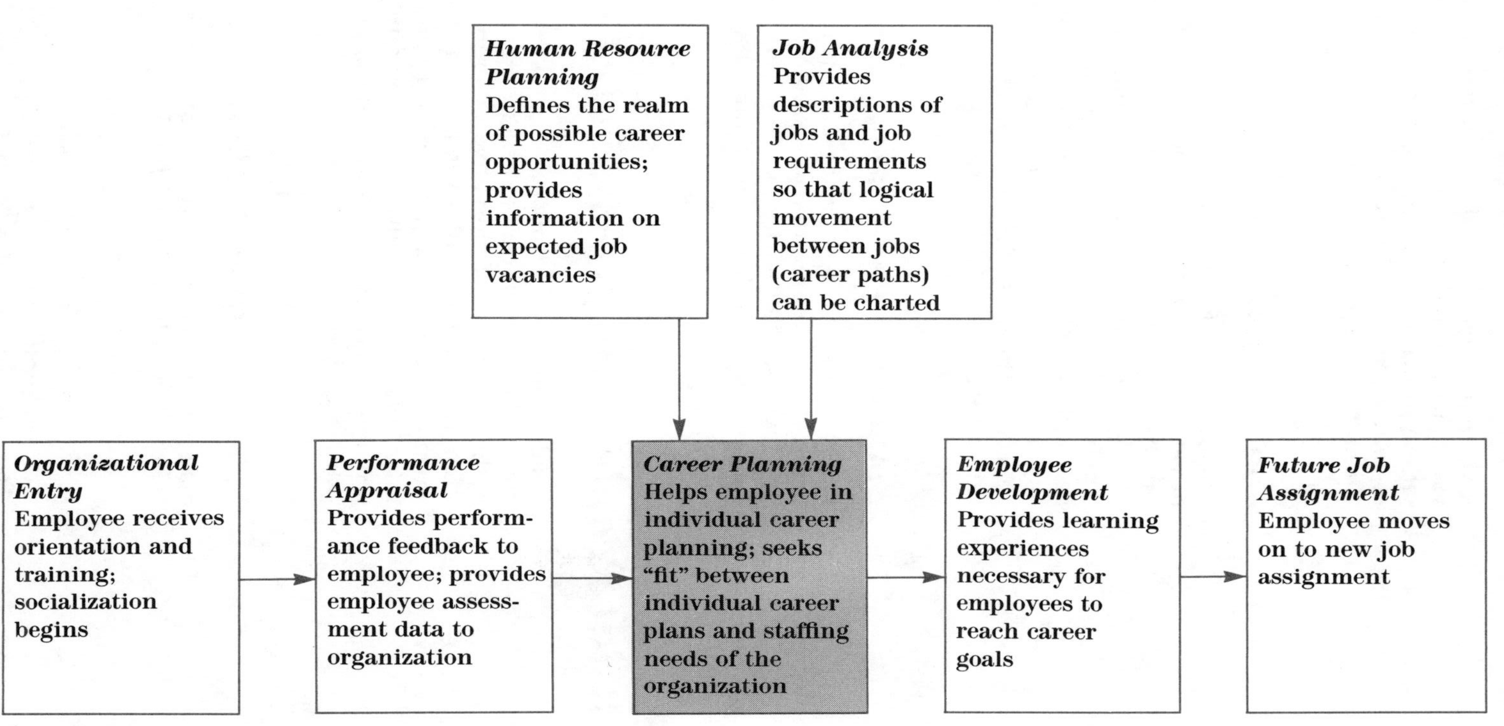

Human Resource Planning
Defines the realm of possible career opportunities; provides information on expected job vacancies
Job Analysis
Provides descriptions of jobs and job requirements so that logical movement between jobs (career paths) can be charted
Organizational Entry
Employee receives orientation and training; socialization begins
Performance Appraisal
Provides performance feedback to employee; provides employee assessment data to organization
Career Planning
Helps employee in individual career planning; seeks "fit" between individual career plans and staffing needs of the organization
Employee Development
Provides learning experiences necessary for employees to reach career goals
Future Job Assignment
Employee moves on to new job assignment

give employees reasonable expectations of their opportunities for advancement. Career planning also has valuable inputs for HRP. By providing information on the career plans of individuals, it contributes to management's knowledge of probable human resource flows throughout the organization.

Job Analysis

One of the responsibilities of career planners is to inform employees of career opportunities within the organization. This responsibility involves the charting of *career paths*, logical movements between jobs or from one job to a target position. A *target position* is one which an employee is striving to attain or one which the organization is preparing him or her to assume in the future. Target positions are the objects of individual career goals and the subjects of developmental efforts on the part of the organization. In order to chart career paths, career planners need job analysis information.

Employee Development

Career planning provides goals for the systematic development of employees. When mutually agreed-on career objectives are specified, developmental activities can be selected and channelled in a direction meaningful to both the individual employee and the organization.

What People Want from Their Careers

In addition to opportunities for growth and development, what do people want from their careers? Making generalizations is difficult because of the wide range of individual differences. Further, what people want from their careers tends to change over time: career advancements and advancing age spark new interests and change needs. Nonetheless, E.H. Schein has identified five dominant motives which underlie people's career choices and long-range goals. He refers to them as "career anchors."[8]

Schein's Career Anchors

Schein's career anchors represent aspects of work that people especially value or need for personal fulfillment. They include:

[8] E.H. Schein, "How 'Career Anchors' Hold Executives to Their Career Paths," *Personnel*, May–June 1975, vol. 52, pp. 11–24.

1. Managerial competence—the individual desires opportunities to manage.
2. Technical/functional competence—the individual wants to use various technical abilities and special competencies.
3. Security—the individual is basically motivated by a need for job security or stability in the work situation.
4. Creativity—the individual is motivated by a need to create or build something.
5. Autonomy and independence—of primary interest to this person is the opportunity to work independently, without organizational constraints.

Career planning and development activities allow employees to grow in any of these desired directions.

Career Stages

What people want from their careers also varies according to the stage of their careers. What may have been important in any early stage may not be in a later one. Researchers have identified four distinct career stages: trial, establishment/advancement, mid-career, and late career.[9] Each stage reflects different career needs and interests of the individual (see Exhibit 11.2).

Trial Stage. The trial stage begins with an individual's exploration of career-related matters and ends, usually at about age 25, with a commitment to a particular occupation. Until that decision is made, the individual may try a number of jobs and a number of employers. Unfortunately for many organizations, this trial and exploration stage results in high levels of turnover among new employees. Employees in this stage need opportunities for self-exploration and a variety of job activities or assignments.

Establishment/advancement. The establishment/advancement stage tends to occur between ages 25 and 44. The individual has made his or her career choice and is now concerned with achievement, performance, and advancement. This stage is marked by high productivity and career growth, as the individual is motivated to succeed in the organization and in his or her chosen occupation. Opportunities for job challenge and use of special competencies are desired in this stage. These employees strive for creativity and innovation through new job assignments. They also need a certain degree of autonomy so that they can experience feelings of individual achievement and personal success.

[9] D.T. Hall and M.A. Morgan, "Career Development and Planning," in M. Jelinek, ed., *Career Management for the Individual and the Organization* (Chicago: St. Clair Press, 1979).

EXHIBIT 11.2

Career Stages

Stage	***Task needs***	***Emotional needs***
Trial	1. Varied job activities 2. Self-exploration	1. Make preliminary job choices 2. Settle down
Establishment/ advancement	1. Job challenge 2. Develop competence in a specialty area 3. Develop creativity and innovation 4. Rotate into new area after 3–5 years	1. Deal with rivalry and competition; face failures 2. Deal with work-family conflicts 3. Support 4. Develop autonomy
Mid-career	1. Technical updating 2. Develop skills in training and coaching others (younger employees) 3. Rotation into new job requiring new skills 4. Develop broader view of work and own role in organization	1. Express feelings about mid-life 2. Reorganize thinking about self in relation to work, family, community 3. Reduce self-indulgence and competitiveness
Late career	1. Plan for retirement 2. Shift from power role to one of consultation and guidance 3. Identify and develop successors 4. Begin activities outside the organization	1. Receive support and counselling to see work as a platform for others 2. Develop sense of identity in extraorganizational activities

SOURCE: Adapted from D.T. Hall and M.A. Morgan, "Career Development and Planning," in W.C. Hammer and Frank L. Schmidt, eds., *Contemporary Problems in Personnel*, rev. ed. (Chicago: St. Clair Press, 1977).

Mid-career stage. The mid-career stage, which occurs roughly between ages 45 and 64, has also been referred to as the maintenance stage. It is typified by a continuation of established patterns of work behaviour. The person is no longer trying to establish a place within the organization but to maintain his or her position. This stage is sometimes viewed as a plateau,[10] but the individual in it may need some technical updating and should be encouraged to develop new job skills in order to avoid early stagnation and decline.

[10] D.E. Super, J. Crites, R. Hummel, H. Moser, P. Overstreet, and C. Warnath, *Vocational Development: A Framework for Research* (New York: Teachers College Press, 1957).

Late-career stage. D. E. Super, whose work has defined career stages, refers to the late-career stage from age 65 on as one of decline. He states: "You call it what you want—the Golden Years, the Sunshine Years, whatever. But I'm there; take my word for it, it's decline!"[11] In this stage, the career lessens in importance and the employee plans for retirement and seeks to develop a sense of identity outside the work environment.

MBA survey results. A 1977 survey of readers of MBA magazine, whose audience includes students and graduates of master's degree programs in business administration, drew 5,519 responses. Among other career-related questions was "What is the single most important thing you want from your career?" When the responses were analyzed according to age of the respondents, it was found that intellectual challenge was most important to the under-30 age group and to those between ages 40 and 45. Money was most important to those aged 35–39, followed by intellectual challenge. Those in the over-45 age group did not rank challenge among their top three desires but were more concerned with security, the opportunity to contribute to society, and money.[12] These responses document the fact that what people value in their careers may change over time.

Elements of Career Planning Programs

In practice, career planning is a poorly defined function whose responsibilities often span a number of other HRM functions. For example, human resource planners may describe career opportunities in terms of estimates of projected job vacancies at time X. Supervisors may handle career counselling within the context of performance appraisal interviews. Developmental activities for reaching career goals may be prescribed by training and development specialists. Career planning is not necessarily new to organizations; what is new is an increased awareness of its potential value and the attempt by some organizations to integrate its diverse elements into a separate and definable HRM function.[13]

Though career planning programs differ, four distinct elements emerge: (1) individual assessments of abilities, interests, career needs, and goals; (2) organizational assessments of employees' abilities and potential; (3) communication of information about career options and opportunities with the organization; and (4) career counselling to set realistic goals and plan for their attainment. Effective career planning programs provide opportunities for employees to engage in all four elements.

[11] D.E. Super, personal communication to D. T. Hall.
[12] "MBAs Look at Their World," *MBA*, July/August 1977.
[13] M.A. Morgan, D.T. Hall, and A. Martier, "Career Development Strategies in Industry—Where Are We and Where Should We Be?" *Personnel*, March–April 1979, pp. 13–30.

In order to aid individual career planning, HRM professionals may be responsible for providing materials and opportunities (workbooks and workshops) for employees' self-exploration and analysis. They make career counselling available to employees. They should support a system of periodic performance appraisals and feedback to employees, maintain personal assessment data in human resource information systems or personnel files, and perhaps sponsor assessment centres. Their responsibilities for communicating career options and opportunities include developing career paths in accord with the organization's human resource needs and disseminating information to employees via written materials, workshops, job posting, or other means. HRM professionals' primary responsibility for career counselling is to provide counsellors with information and perhaps training to function effectively as counsellors.

Individual Assessments

Many employees begin their working lives in an organization without any formal assessment of their abilities, interests, career needs, and goals. This phenomenon of entering jobs, occupations, and careers with little attention to planning is known as *career drift*. A 1978 *Psychology Today* survey of 2,300 readers found that career drift explained the job choice of many respondents: 40 per cent had happened into their present occupation by chance; fewer than 25 per cent were in an occupation of their choice, and the majority were thinking of making a major career change in the next five years. Further, nearly half the sample felt "locked into" their jobs with no avenues of escape other than termination. The authors of the survey concluded that the needs, desires, and dissatisfactions represented in this sample meant potential turnover and other problems for organizations unless they could provide more interesting and challenging jobs and careers.[14] The plant closings, layoffs, and relatively slow economic growth of the 1980s suggest that today's employees may have similar or even more pessimistic attitudes. Regardless of the economic climate, managers and HRM professionals must attempt to create opportunities for employees to do interesting and challenging work.

Since definitions of "interesting" and "challenging" vary from one employee to another, the career planning process must begin with the individual and an assessment of his or her abilities, interests, career needs, and goals.

Individual assessment of abilities, interests, career needs, and goals is basically a process of self-exploration and analysis. Individuals are frequently guided by self-assessment exercises (see Exhibit 11.3). The self-assessment process is primarily viewed as an individual responsibility; however, organizations can aid in it by providing the employee

[14] P.A. Renwick, E.E. Lawler III, and the *Psychology Today* staff, "What You Really Want from Your Job," *Psychology Today*, May 1978, vol. 11, pp. 53–8, 60, 62, 65, and 118.

with materials and opportunities for self-exploration and analysis. A variety of self-assessment materials are available commercially, but a number of organizations, including Ontario Hydro, IBM, General Motors, and General Electric, have developed tailor-made workbooks for employees' career planning.

Individual career planning exercises can be done independently by employees or in workshops sponsored by the organization. Workshops have the advantage of combining a number of career planning elements, including self-assessment, communication of organizational career and development opportunities, and one-on-one counselling to ensure that career goals are realistic. Planning for the accomplishment of career objectives, sometimes called "strategizing," may also be done at this time. Although workshops are a useful aid in individual career planning, they are still quite uncommon.

Organizational Assessments

A key issue in career counselling is whether an employee's goals are realistic in terms of organizational possibilities and the organization's assessments of his or her abilities and potential. Thus, accurate assessments of an employee's abilities and potential are important to both the organization and the individual.

Organizations have several sources of information for making assessments of their employees' abilities and potential. The first is selection information, including ability tests, interest inventories, and biographical information, such as education and work experience. The second is current job history information, including performance appraisal information, records of promotions and promotion recommendations, salary increases, and participation in various training and development programs.

Organizations have traditionally relied on performance appraisal data as the primary basis for assessing employee potential. This reliance assumes that past performance is a good predictor of future performance in a different capacity, an assumption that may be faulty for a number of reasons. First, performance appraisals do not always accurately reflect employees' abilities and actual performance. They are often coloured by evaluators' biases and by faulty instruments. Second, if the job requirements of the future position are substantially different from those of the present job, one cannot assume that the employee will be equally successful in the new role. Despite these potential problems, performance appraisal data will continue to be used in organizations. Effectiveness of performance appraisal for this purpose may be maximized both by training raters and through use of performance dimensions relevant to the job for which an employee is being considered.

A number of organizations have turned to methods such as psychological testing and assessment centres to assess more directly employees' potential for future positions.[15] Assessment centres evaluate

[15] J. Koten, "Career Guidance: Psychologists Play Bigger Corporate Role in Placing of Personnel," *Wall Street Journal*, July 11, 1978.

EXHIBIT 11.3

Items from a self-assessment exercise to determine personal wants

1. Select the three personal wants which are most important to you in your next job assignment and circle them below.
2. Select the three personal wants which are least important to you in your next career step and draw a line through them.
3. Add personal wants you don't find on the list.

Personal wants

Free time	Power	Fun work
Money	Independence	Security
Professional stature	Challenge	Freedom from worry
Friends	Prestige	Cultural opportunities
Geographic location	Recreation	Visibility
Climate	Educational facilities	Leadership
Expertness		Time with family

4. Does your present job setting offer possibilities for satisfying what you want most in your next step? If yes, describe how. If no, what setting is indicated?
5. Do you want your next job assignment to satisfy your wants? If yes, how? If no, why not?
6. Decide what you want most in your next job assignment and describe it.
7. Describe the major activities you can do and will do to gain what you want, but don't use job titles or positions to describe what you will do. Describe the type of activities you'll perform to achieve what you want. List at least five activities you can perform now.

   Examples: I'll analyze data for financial records.
   I'll collect more from creditors.
   I'll marry the boss's daughter.
8. Do you need to develop some new skills or abilities to improve your potential for your next step? If so, what skills or abilities would you develop?
9. Can or must some of your wants be satisfied off the job? If so, what does this mean in terms of how you would consider any future positions?
10. Summarize what you personally want and what you can do and will do to satisfy your wants.

SOURCE: Adapted from General Electric's *Career Action Planning Workbook* (Ossining, N.Y.: Corporate Education Services, 1973). (©)

employees on their abilities to perform tasks required in future positions. Assessors are trained; they tend to be managers familiar with the position for which centre participants are being evaluated. The methods used may include group discussions, role play, interviews, and an assortment of tests, but they always also use at least one simulation exercise.[16] For example, J. C. Penney Company's assessment

[16] Task Force on Assessment Center Standards, "Standards and Ethical Considerations for Assessment Center Operations," *Personnel Administrator*, February 1980, vol. 25, no. 2, pp. 35–8.

centre in the United States has used phone calls from irate customers as a simulation exercise to assess participants' ability to handle complaints.[17] Each participant's behaviour is observed and evaluated. An overall evaluation is the result of the process.

Almost all employees who participate in assessment centres do so to determine whether they have any potential for management positions. Exhibit 11.4 lists and describes ten common performance dimensions on which centre participants are assessed.

EXHIBIT 11.4

Common assessment centre dimensions

1. Oral communication skill—effective expression in individual or group situations (includes gestures and nonverbal communications)
2. Oral presentation skill—effective expression when presenting ideas or tasks to an individual or to a group when given time for presentation (includes gestures and nonverbal communication)
3. Written communication skill—clear expression of ideas in writing and in good grammatical form
4. Job motivation—the extent to which activities and responsibilities available in the job overlap with activities and responsibilities that result in personal satisfaction
5. Initiative—active attempts to influence events to achieve goals; self-starting rather than passive acceptance; taking action to achieve goals beyond those called for; originating action
6. Leadership—utilizing appropriate interpersonal styles and methods in guiding individuals (subordinates, peers, superiors) or groups towards task accomplishment
7. Planning and organization—establishing a course of action for self and/or others to accomplish a specific goal; planning proper assignments of personnel and appropriate allocation of resources
8. Analysis—relating and comparing data from different sources, identifying issues, securing relevant information, and identifying relationships
9. Judgement—developing alternative courses of action and making decisions that are based on logical assumptions and reflect factual information
10. Management control—establishing procedures to monitor and/or regulate processes, tasks, or the job activities and responsibilities of subordinates; taking action to monitor the results of delegated assignments or projects

SOURCE: Adapted from W.C. Byham, "Starting an Assessment Center the Correct Way," *The Personnel Administrator*, February 1980, pp. 27–32.

A number of organizations created assessment centres during the 1970s, largely because of their usefulness in managerial selection. However, assessment centres are also a valuable tool in career planning. Assessment helps organizations determine possible avenues for

[17] Koten.

employee development, and also aids employees in understanding their strengths and weaknesses so they can set more realistic career goals. If affirmative action programs grow in Canada, more employers may use assessment centres to identify women and minorities with the potential for development.

Assessment centres can, however, create some problems for an organization. Bell Canada, a pioneer in company-sponsored career planning, discontinued its use of appraisal centres in the 1960s because it found that results tended to categorize employees as having or not having potential, and persons in the latter group became demoralized.[18]

Career Information within an Organization

Before an employee can set realistic career goals, he or she needs to know about options and opportunities, including information about possible career directions, possible paths of career advancement, and specific job vacancies.

Job vacancies are announced in company newspapers, by word of mouth, or through job posting. In organizations where career planning is informal, employees learn about career options and opportunities from their supervisors within the context of developmental performance appraisal interviews.[19] Organizations with more established career planning programs make greater use of workbooks, workshops, and even recruiting materials to communicate career options and opportunities. Ontario Hydro is an example of an organization that has developed a career planning workbook for interested employees in managerial, professional, supervisory, and clerical jobs.

Career paths chart possible career directions and paths of advancement in an organization. They can be defined as logical movements between jobs or from one job to a target position. Career paths can be either traditional or behavioural.

Traditional career paths are based on past patterns of actual movement by employees. They tend to be limited to advancement within a single function or organizational unit, such as purchasing, sales, or customer relations. Years of service to the organization largely determine the rate at which advancement can occur. For example, a salesman might expect to advance to the position of account supervisor after 5 years, to sales supervisor after 10, to district manager after 15, and to regional manager after 25.[20] A basic problem with traditional career paths is that they are based on an organization's past needs for human resources, which may not suit present and future purposes. With needs for human resources always changing because of technological advances and legal requirements, today's organizations should develop more flexible, progressive patterns of career growth and development.

[18] Personal communication from Herbert Clappison and Margaret Briere, June 15, 1982.

[19] J.W. Seybolt, "Career Development: The State of the Art among the Grass Roots," *Training and Development Journal*, April 1979, vol. 33, no. 4, pp. 16–21.

[20] J.W. Walker, *Human Resource Planning* (New York: McGraw-Hill, 1980), p. 311.

More flexible patterns of career movement are described by *behavioural career paths*, which are based on analyses of similarities in job activities and requirements. Where similarities exist, jobs can be grouped into job families, or clusters. Thus, all jobs involving similar work activities and levels of required skills and abilities form one job cluster, regardless of job title. Consider Ted Maxwell's position of Medical Records Clerk I at City General Hospital. Although Maxwell is in the Medical Records Department, his position is in the same job cluster as Personnel Records Assistant I, located in the Human Resources Department. The two positions require similar levels of skill and have similar work activities. Medical Records Clerk II and Personnel Records Assistant II constitute another job cluster; they require somewhat higher levels of skill and entail somewhat greater responsibility.

After job clusters have been identified, lines of logical progression between them can be charted. Career paths can be very complex networks of lines of progression between jobs. Exhibit 11.5 presents two very simple career paths for Ted Maxwell's Medical Records Clerk I position.

EXHIBIT 11.5

Traditional and behavioural career paths for a Medical Records Clerk I

Traditional career path: Medical Records Clerk I, Medical Records Department	***Traditional career path: Personnel Records Assistant I, Human Resources Department***

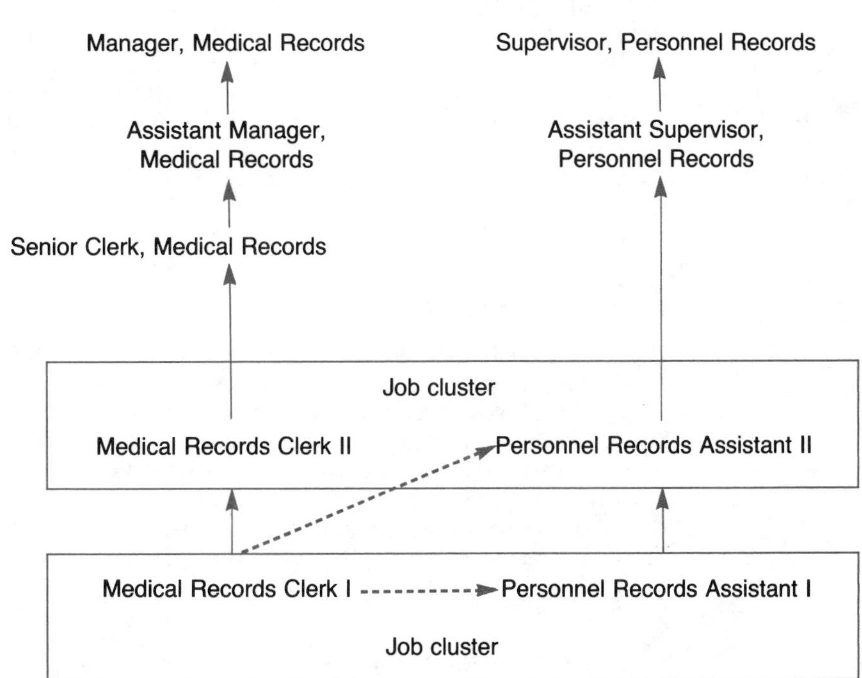

The traditional career path for a person in Maxwell's position is straight up on the diagram, from Medical Records Clerk I to Medical Records Clerk II to Senior Clerk, Medical Records to Assistant Manager, Medical Records and finally to Manager, Medical Records.

However, since the Medical Records Clerk I position is in the same job cluster as Personnel Records Assistant I, another career option for Maxwell is to make a lateral move and assume a Personnel Records Assistant I position. This transition would be quite easy as the job requirements are similar. Lateral moves such as this need not be limited to the same job cluster; they are moves across functions and organizational units at the same level. Strictly speaking, they are not career advancements, but they afford employees a chance for variety and growth in new career directions. By making the lateral move, Maxwell would gain access to a new career path in a different department. The value of lateral moves, as a means of providing employees with growth opportunities, is increasing as layoffs and early retirements leave relatively young employees in many higher level jobs. Thus, lateral moves are especially useful when opportunities for upward advancement in the organization are limited or blocked.

Exhibit 11.5 shows another career option for Maxwell. Since Medical Records Clerk I is in the same job cluster as Personnel Records Assistant I, it may be possible for him to advance directly to the Personnel Records Assistant II position. This move may require developmental efforts to acquaint him with the new job skills in the higher-level position.

Focussing on job similarities across functions and organizational units brings to light new career options for employees and greater flexibility for the organization in using the human resources it has available. One organization, for example, was able to shift a number of its sales personnel to purchasing positions when sales declined in a major product line and opportunities became available in the purchasing department. This shift was undertaken when a job anlaysis showed behavioural similarities between the two previously distinct functions.[21]

Career Counselling

It is in counselling sessions, most often with supervisors and managers in developmental performance appraisal interviews, that most employees explore career goals and opportunities in the organization. For these sessions, supervisors and managers need accurate assessments of employees' abilities and potential, as well as information about career options and opportunities in the organization. HRM professionals may be involved in some informal career counselling activities, but basically their role is to support the counselling activities of supervisors

[21] E.H. Burack and N.J. Mathys, *Career Management in Organizations: A Practical Human Resource Planning Approach* (Lake Forest, Ill.: Brace-Park Press, 1980), p. 127.

and managers. Thus, they must provide supervisors and managers with information as well as with the training they need to function effectively as counsellors.

In career counselling sessions, employees seek answers to questions such as:

1. What are my skills and what are the possibilities for developing them or learning new ones?
2. What do I really want for myself insofar as work is concerned?
3. What's possible for me, given my current abilities and skills?
4. What's really required for certain jobs?
5. What training will be required if I choose to pursue a certain career objective?[22]

When counsellors are equipped to help employees find the answers to such questions, realistic career goals can be set. Next, development strategies must be devised.

Career Planning Programs

Programs vary in the degree to which they emphasize the four elements of career planning. Some offer employees little assistance in self-assessment, while others aid this process by providing workbooks and workshops. Assessment centres are part of some programs, but most organizations rely on the judgement of supervisors and managers in assessing employee potential. Career path information is provided by some organizations, while others simply post job vacanices. Counselling in many organizations is informal, although some established programs provide staff positions for career counsellors. The ways in which organizations assemble career planning elements result in a variety of career planning programs.

International Business Machines (IBM)

IBM's employee development program is based on voluntary annual discussions between employees and managers regarding the subordinate's career and growth interests. Managers receive training in counselling, and employees are encouraged to do some self-exploration before the career counselling session. In some locations, career planning workbooks facilitate this process. The counselling session between employee and manager results in an "action plan" for employee development in mutually agreeable directions.[23]

[22] Ibid., p. 301.

[23] D.B. Miller, "Career Planning and Management in Organizations," in M. Jelinek, ed., *Career Management for the Individual and the Organization* (Chicago: St. Clair Press, 1979).

Bell Canada

Career planning was introduced at Bell Canada in the early 1940s by Clarence Fraser, author of the book *A Plan for Every Man*. Today the Bell program includes career counselling as part of its regular employee appraisal system, with recommendations included on the annual appraisal form. (The career planning appraisal is, however, separate from the annual job performance appraisal.) A managers' manual assists them in career planning discussions with subordinates. Information garnered in these sessions is fed into a computer system, which matches potential candidates with job openings.

Ontario Hydro

One of the most sophisticated career planning programs in Canada has been functioning at Ontario Hydro since 1980. An unusual aspect of this program is its integration with the corporation's human resource planning program.

Career planning at Ontario Hydro is a voluntary program available to managerial, professional, and clerical employees; all the materials used have been tested with office supervisory staff. The process begins with a self-assessment workbook, which helps employees examine their career plans, life satisfaction, and goals and priorities. Two additional workbooks follow: one helps the employee identify his or her reactions to the current job, individual skills and aspirations, and the desired characteristics of future positions; the other is aimed at selecting job goals and development needs and at making an action plan. At any point in the process, the employee may talk with the head of career planning, the supervisor, or an HRM professional. Workshops and seminars are also provided. HRP information, such as job vacancy forecasts with a five-year horizon, job specifications for vacancies, and career paths to desired positions are provided so that employees have a realistic understanding of where the career planning process can take them. While all career planning programs should provide this information, Hydro is unusual in making it available to employees engaged in the career planning process.

Sears

Sears uses a system in which employees progress through a well-defined sequence of job assignments (career paths) in order to maximize their career development. The system is based on an evaluation of job content that scores jobs on various skill dimensions, including know-how, problem-solving, and accountability; in addition, an overall point value is assigned to each job. Job assignments are ordered according to these point values in terms of lesser to greater degrees of skill required. An employee progressing through a logically developed sequence of job assignments is, therefore, able to acquire gradually the greater degrees of skill required for higher-level jobs. Since point values are assigned to jobs in different functional areas, it is possible for an employee to progress logically from a job in one area to a job in another.[24]

Aluminum Company of Canada (Alcan)

Alcan offers its staff considerable career planning; the program extends beyond organizational boundaries by providing an outplacement service for terminated employees. They visit an assessment centre to identify their strengths and weaknesses and also receive instruction in skills such as job-searching and résumé-writing to help them find a new job or career.[25] Exxon, General Electric, and Corning Glass Works are among the U.S. companies that offer similar outplacement programs.

CEIC Aids for Career Planning

Materials for the career planning programs just described were developed by large organizations for their own use. Companies, large and small, can also purchase aids for career planning. Canadian organizations also have access to excellent career guidance materials prepared by the Occupational and Career Analysis and Development Branch of the Canada Employment and Immigration Commission (CEIC).[26] These materials include booklets profiling particular occupations; they describe the preparation, training, and personal qualities required for jobs in these occupations, along with their outlook for the future. The Careers Canada series of the booklets focusses on particular provinces.

Detailed information has been compiled by Employment and Immigration Canada (EIC) on the fields of work of University and Community College graduates along with the projected labour market situation in a sizeable number of occupations. The information was prepared by EIC's Canadian Occupational Projection System (COPS) in its volume *Job Futures, An Occupational Outlook to 1992.*[27]

Job Futures is divided into two parts. Part one lists the major occupations held two years after graduation by 23 university fields of study and 18 community college fields. Part two presents the labour

[24] H.L. Wellbank, D.T. Hall, M.A. Morgan, and W.C. Hamner, "Planning Job Progression for Effective Career Development and Human Resource Management," in M. Jelinek, ed., *Career Management for the Individual and the Organization* (Chicago: St. Clair Press, 1979).

[25] B.R. Cuddihy, "How to Give Phased-Out Managers a New Start," *Harvard Business Review*, 1974, vol. 52, pp. 61–9.

[26] CEIC also has a short book discussing how to approach career choice: Catherine V. Davidson and L. Glen Tippett, *A Career Planning Guide* (Ottawa: Manpower and Immigration Canada, 1977).

[27] *Job Futures, An Occupational Outlook to 1992*, 1986–87 Edition (Ottawa: Minister of Supply and Services Canada, 1986).

market outlook in 174 occupations in 1992 as compared with the situation in 1981. For example Personnel and Industrial Relations Management Occupations (CCDO Code 1136) are expected to grow at an average rate from 25,600 in 1981 to 29,200 in 1992. In 1981 there were seven males for every three females in the occupation. Since an average proportion of this group was older than 54 in 1981, increases in labour demand owing to retirement may be moderate. Employment in this occupation group is somewhat sensitive to economic conditions.

Personnel and Related Officers (CCDO Code 1174) are also expected to grow at an average rate from 31,500 in 1981 to 36,000 in 1992. This occupation too is moderately sensitive to changing economic conditions and had an average number of persons over 54 years of age in 1981. The major difference between the two groups is that females and males were almost equally distributed in the personnel officer category whereas males far outnumbered females in the managerial group. It is to be expected that the female percentage of personnel/human resource managers will increase by 1992.

In addition, individual employees can also be referred to a computerized career information and exploration system called CHOICES. Since a person using it has to understand what he or she wants from a job, the first step is completing a questionnaire that pinpoints the individual's interests, aptitudes, and temperament; what environment, earnings, and other conditions of work he or she wants; and what education and training the person has. This information is fed into the computer, setting some parameters. Next, the person answers a series of questions set by the computer. The responses set up a path and lead eventually to a suggested set of compatible occupations.

The CHOICES model is available in some Canada Employment Centres, where it can also be used to explore possible occupations, to obtain detailed information about specific occupations, or to compare two or three occupations that share characteristics with a particular one in which a person is interested. The program's background material comes from the job characteristics set out in the *Canadian Classification and Dictionary of Occupations* (see Chapter 5).

Facilitating Career Planning and Development

Organizations can facilitate career planning in a number of ways. D. T. Hall categorizes the pertinent areas as: (1) organizational entry; (2) the job; (3) the boss; (4) organizational structure and procedures; and (5) human resource policy. Exhibit 11.6 presents ways the organization can facilitate career planning within each of these areas.

Organizational Entry

Efforts to facilitate career planning can begin before or at the time an individual takes a job. One of the earliest pre-entry points of influence

EXHIBIT 11.6

Facilitating career planning

Organizational entry:

1. Provide information on jobs and career opportunities to placement offices, career counsellors
2. Provide career planning information in recruiting materials

The job:

1. Make first job challenging
2. Sequence jobs so progression provides gradual acquisition of skills
3. Use job rotation to provide new challenge and growth opportunities

The boss:

1. Provide training to increase boss's ability to be an effective agent of career planning
2. Reward boss for career planning activities

Organization Structure and procedures:

1. Offer career planning services and programs
2. Work closely with human resource planning arm of the organization
3. Institute human resource accounting procedures

Human resource policies:

1. Institute policies that promote career planning
2. Legitimize downward transfers and fallback positions
3. Provide incentives for employees to leave the organization
4. Involve families in career decisions

SOURCE: Adapted from D.T. Hall, *Careers in Organizations* (Pacific Palisades, Calif.: Goodyear Publishing Company, Inc., 1976), p. 177.

is contacts between an employer and school placement staff or faculty, job counsellors, and others who may discuss career planning with potential job applicants. Increasingly, organizations are including career planning information in their recruiting messages and materials.

For example, Bethlehem Steel Corporation's career planning activities play a large part in its recruiting and selection. The company's Loop Program, in existence since 1922, guarantees top university graduates a chance at managerial-level positions. Trainees begin with a two-week orientation session, then are "looped" through all the company's operations by a system of rotating job assignments. The program's objective is to have all participants rise at least to the level of department head during their careers.

Bethlehem Steel is unusual in its belief that managerial potential can be identified before a new employee spends time on the job. Thus, the Loop Program provides selected individuals with excellent career development opportunities, while assuring the company a supply of high-ability and highly motivated people. More than half the top-level management at Bethlehem are "graduates" of the Loop.[28] Futhermore, turnover is much lower among Loop trainees than among recent university graduates in general.

The Job

Career planning and development can be facilitated in the job itself. Evidence from a number of different organizations and occupations, including an automobile manufacturer, AT&T, the Roman Catholic Church, managers in eight large organizations, and a sample of engineers, demonstrates the importance of a challenging and demanding first job.[29] Research shows that employees who have such an experience tend to be more successful later in their careers. Despite this evidence, however, most organizations are unwilling to give challenging jobs to young, new employees. Some managers hold negative stereotypes of recent graduates as too theoretical, over-ambitious, immature, and inexperienced. One survey of 22 research and development organizations found that only one had a policy of giving new professional employees a difficult first job.[30]

Another use of the job as a development agent is logical sequencing of work experiences, like the Sears program discussed earlier. By progressing through the logical sequences, Sears' employees acquire ever-increasing levels of skill and responsibility.

Related to the job progression concept is job rotation, which allows employees to work in a variety of capacities and provides growth and development opportunities at any stage of career development. A carefully planned and sequenced job rotation program can help meet employees' needs even when upward mobility is limited.

Job rotation is a fairly common method of management development at all levels. Bethlehem Steel's Loop program is a form of job rotation. Another organization that uses job rotation is Bell Canada, whose program includes rotating line managers into the personnel department and personnel officers into line management positions.

[28] D.R. Sease, "Grads Trained for Fast Track at Bethlehem," *Wall Street Journal*, July 29, 1980.

[29] M.D. Dunnette, R.D. Arvey, and P.A. Banas, "Why Do They Leave?" *Personnel*, May/June 1973, pp. 25–39; D.W. Bray, R.J. Campbell, and D.L. Grant, *Formative Years in Business* (New York: Wiley, 1974); D.T. Hall and B. Schneider, *Organizational Climate and Careers: The Work Lives of Priests* (New York: Seminar Press, 1973); B. Buchanan II, "Building Organizational Commitment: The Socialization of Managers in Work Organizations," *Administrative Science Quarterly*, 1974, vol. 19, pp. 533–46; H.G. Kaufman, "Relationship of Early Work Challenge to Job Performance, Professional Contributions, and Competence of Engineers," *Journal of Applied Psychology*, 1974, vol. 59, pp. 337–79; and D.E. Berlew and D.T. Hall, "Socialization of Managers: Effects of Expectations on Performance," *Administrative Science Quarterly*, 1966, vol. 11, pp. 207–23.

[30] D.T. Hall and E.E. Lawler III, "Unused Potential in Research and Development Organizations," *Research Management*, 1969, vol. 12, pp. 339–54.

Several other large organizations also rotate promising managers through the human resources department, and not merely as observers.[31] Job rotation is useful in providing managers with both knowledge and experience in different areas. Such moves both facilitate interdepartmental or divisional cooperation and have the potential of affording managers new challenges and opportunities to learn and grow in their careers. Programs of job redesign such as job enrichment also have the potential to satisfy employee development needs.[32]

The Boss

Another agent of career planning in organizations is the boss. The importance of the immediate supervisor, especially an employee's first boss, must not be underestimated. The boss assigns tasks, judges performance, provides feedback, rewards and punishes, and by such actions, defines the criteria for success. Exhibit 11.7 illustrates the important role of the boss and the anxiety and frustration that results when he or she fails to clarify success criteria.

The boss is also important because he or she serves as a model for the employee's own behaviour and future leadership style. Ironically, there is evidence that employees learn valuable lessons not only from "good" bosses, but also from "intolerable" ones. A recent *Psychology Today* survey asked 73 successful executives to describe intolerable bosses they had worked for in the past. Fifty of the executives had had an "intolerable" boss, and four had worked under two. The resulting 58 descriptions were collapsed into nine general types of intolerable bosses. The Rogues Gallery of Intolerable Bosses is presented in Exhibit 11.8. Interestingly, only 11 of the executives with intolerable bosses quit their positions. Another seven tried to get their bosses removed, but only two succeeded. The remaining 36 executives learned patience, coping behaviours, and how NOT to manage. Positive managerial guidelines that came out of the executives' negative experiences include: (1) give people recognition for what they accomplish; (2) give people responsibility, a chance to show what they can do; (3) look below the surface to understand people's actions; and (4) accept your responsibilities.[33]

Besides assigning tasks and rewards and serving as a role model, bosses often counsel individuals in career planning. Any one of these factors can have a strong impact on employee careers, but taken together they make the boss, especially the first boss, a key to career progress. Research has shown that even the boss's expectations can have a substantial impact on a new employee's career expectations and

[31] H.E. Meyer, "Personnel Directors Are the New Corporate Heroes," *Fortune*, February 1976, vol. 93, pp. 84–8.

[32] J.R. Hackman and G.R. Oldham, *Work Redesign* (Reading, Mass.: Addison-Wesley, 1980).

[33] M.M. Lombardo and M.W. McCall, Jr., "The Intolerable Boss," *Psychology Today*, January 1984, pp. 44–8.

EXHIBIT 11.7

Criteria for success at NASA

Astronauts unclear on selection process

By Paul Recer
The Associated Press

SPACE CENTER, Houston — The rule in the astronaut corps is simple: Please the boss and you can fly. Annoy him and you stay on Earth. The trick is figuring out how best to play the game and that's one of the mysteries of NASA.

Astronauts universally claim they have no idea why some are selected for flight after flight and others only rarely, but for the 95 active members of America's space corps there is a feeling of intense competition that touchs every phase of their life.

It's a pressure that some credit with breaking up marriages and disrupting family life. Some astronauts drop out, deciding it's not worth it. Others hang on for decades, trying to find the formula that will put them into space.

"You never really know what the criteria are," said Alan A. Bean, a former astronaut who says he walked on the moon only after learning how to play the game. "You know that certain people get good assignments and others get bad ones and you learn to read the winds."

Bean said the pressure comes from the fact that if one wants to fly in space "NASA is the only game in town." Astronauts, he said, can't quit and go to another space agency.

"If you're going to play the game, you have to figure out the rules," he said. "Nobody will tell you the rules."

Some astronauts, he said, "catch on right away. Some never did catch on."

SOURCE: "Astronauts Unclear On Selection Process" by Paul Recer.

performance. When the boss expects and demands more from the employee, the employee comes to expect and demand more from himself or herself.[34]

[34] J.S. Livingston, "Pygmalion in Management," *Harvard Business Review*, 1969, vol. 47, pp. 81–9.

EXHIBIT 11.8

Rogues Gallery of Intolerable Bosses

ROGUES GALLERY

Snakes-in-the-grass: The most frequently mentioned failing in our catalogue of bossy sins is lack of integrity. These men lie, fail to keep their word, employ their authority to extort confidential information and then use it to a subordinate's disadvantage and just generally can't be trusted.

Attilas: The dictators, little Napoleons or martinets, as they were also called by our executives, are not dismayed by a string of mistakes, and take offense if anyone else makes decisions or stands out in any way. They are both the easiest to spot of the intolerable types and the hardest to cope with; they simply sit on people.

Heel-grinders: "They treat others like dirt," one man said. They belittle, humiliate and demean those beneath them, showing their insensitivity in many ways. One popular sport: "raking people over the coals in front of a group."

Egotists: These blowhards know everything, won't listen and parade their pomposity proudly. One boss we heard about plays a ruthless game in which he brings up a seemingly insurmountable problem and then disparages every solution proposed. When his subordinates run out of ideas, he presents them with the solution he had in mind all along.

Dodgers: These bosses are the antitheses of Egotists. They are unable to make decisions and shirk responsibilities whenever possible. They have never heard of the saying, "Lead, follow or get the hell out of the way."

Incompetents: The men in this group don't know what they are doing and won't admit it. They are prime examples of the Peter Principle, men who have risen to the level of their incompetence.

Detail drones: They go strictly by the book, delight in detail—the pettier the better—and love to make big issues out of little ones.

Rodneys: For reasons that sometimes aren't clear, Rodneys just don't get no respect from anybody around them: subordinates, bosses or strangers in the street.

Slobs: Their personal habits, appearance or prejudices are intolerable to others. One described to us is a drunk; another sleeps on the job.

Miscellanies: There are few cases in which the boss doesn't seem especially villainous, but some personality clash or poor chemistry between between boss and subordinate causes problems the latter can never overcome.

SOURCE: "The Intolerable Boss," by M.W. Lombardo & M.W. McCall, Jr.

Unfortunately, many supervisors and managers fail to make the most of their potential to influence employees' careers in a positive direction. Some may feel unequal to the task, thinking they lack the ability to help develop their subordinates. This problem can be remedied through training. Hall suggests that managers receive training in job analysis and restructuring so that they can identify a challenging job or restructure one to make it more challenging. Additionally, they should receive training in interviewing and counselling skills, interpersonal skills, and performance appraisal, including providing constructive feedback.[35]

Supervisors and managers may be ineffective agents of career planning and development because they are not rewarded for such activities. Hall suggests that career planning be facilitated by rewarding managers for their career development activities. Or career development could be incorporated into an MBO program, with successful goal attainment resulting in a pay increase or bonus. Also, organizations must ensure that managers are not unintentionally punished for career planning efforts. For example, time and money for employee assessment, career counselling, and training courses are sometimes charged against the manager's operating budget. Or, if career development results in subordinates' transferring, moving upwards, or perhaps even leaving the organization, these events may be perceived as a turnover problem for the organization.[36]

Organizational Structure and Procedures

The most obvious way to facilitate career planning is, of course, to provide career planning services and programs. Although many organizations do this on an informal basis, established programs are still rare. Some organizations hesitate to involve themselves in career planning, believing that it would raise employees' expectations for advancement and thus lead to dissatisfaction and possible turnover. These risks may well exist, but they can be minimized. It depends to a large extent on the success of career counselling efforts and on the information provided by human resource planners. If expected job vacancies fail to materialize or if unforeseen changes force alterations in job structure, someone is likely to be disappointed. To avoid this, career planners and human resource planners need to keep lines of communication open. Finally, it is important for organizations to emphasize that the purpose of career planning is to provide employees with development and growth opportunities and not simply a means of upward mobility. When economic conditions restrict upward mobility, career planning activities may still increase quality of working life for employees and skill level and flexibility of an organization's work force.

[35] D.T. Hall, *Careers in Organizations* (Pacific Palisades, Calif.: Goodyear Publishing, 1976).

[36] Ibid.

Human resources accounting is an organizational procedure with potential for facilitating career planning. Its methods reflect both the costs and the assets of human resources development. On the cost side, B.A. Macy and P.H. Mirvis and others have demonstrated that the financial effects of employee behaviour can be measured.[37] Behaviour resulting in absenteeism, accidents, turnover, grievances, and low quality and quantity of products can be assigned estimated costs. Changes in these costs can be used as criteria for evaluating managerial performance and the effectiveness of managerial efforts for developing subordinates. On the input side, human resources are treated as an asset.[38] The basic point is that investments in human resources have value or produce benefits beyond the accounting period in which the investment is made.

In the United States, the accounting firm of Lester Witte and Company is using a relatively new approach to human resources valuation. The *stochastic rewards model* includes an assessment of the value and promotability of employees, from beginning staff accountants to partners, and judgements of the probability that they will remain with the firm for various lengths of time. Thus, the adoption of a human resources valuation model at Witte compels managers to consider both career and human resource planning dimensions for their subordinates.[39]

Human Resource Policy

Human resource policies can also facilitate career planning. An internal recruiting policy, for example, enables employees to plan their careers with greater certainty than does a policy of external recruiting. Additionally, a policy of job posting promotes employees' awareness of openings and the qualifications for jobs. Making human resource forecasts available to employees also facilitates career planning. Compensation policy can also affect career planning activities. For example, secrecy about compensation may reduce the financial incentives of higher-level jobs. Periodic, objective appraisals of performance are important to growth and should be encouraged by human resource policy.

A human resource policy legitimizing downward transfers and fallback positions can also promote career planning. A *downward transfer* is a move from an organizational level to a lower one. A *fallback position* is simply a job to which an employee can return if a new assignment does not work out. When organizations have a policy legitimizing downward transfers and fallback positions, employees can

[37] B.A. Macy and P.H. Mirvis, "A Methodology for Assessment of Quality of Work Life and Organizational Effectiveness in Behavioral-Economic Terms," *Administrative Science Quarterly*, 1976, vol. 21, pp. 212–26.

[38] P.H. Mirvis and B.A. Macy, "Human Resources Accounting: A Measurement Perspective," *Academy of Management Review*, 1976, vol. 1, pp. 74–83.

[39] E. Flamholtz and J.B. Wollmen, "The Development and Implementation of the Stochastic Rewards Model for Human Resources Valuation in a Human Capital Intensive Firm," *Personnel Review*, 1978, vol. 7, no. 3, pp. 20–34.

afford to accept more challenging assignments without risking the stigma of failure. Fallback positions are used in a number of progressive organizations, such as Continental Can and Procter and Gamble. Universities usually provide academic administrators a form of fallback position by allowing them to return to tenured teaching positions. While this is a well-accepted practice in academe, business organizations often regard downward transfers as failures. Perhaps they would be more accepted if more organizations adopted Robert Townsend's recommendation that top executives step down after five years.[40]

Hall suggests two additional human resource policies to facilitate career planning: (1) providing incentives for an employee to leave the organization; and (2) involving families in career decisions.[41] Too often, retirement and benefit programs, as well as seniority systems, reward people for mere long-term organizational membership. The result is that employees who might benefit both themselves and the organization by leaving end up staying. As alternatives, organizations could offer such incentives as reimbursement for continuing education, career counselling, or "mid-life transition" training sessions such as those held by the Menninger Foundation.[42]

As people's needs for job satisfaction increase, so does the family's role in affecting career decisions. This phenomenon is encouraged by the relatively recent emergence of the dual-career marriage. A *Psychology Today* survey found that, of married respondents, 93 per cent of the women and 59 per cent of the men had spouses who were fully employed and pursuing a career.[43] The increasing number of female professionals in the work force has brought dramatic changes to North American life, introducing a new dimension of thought on job change. As recently as the early 1970s, it was commonly accepted that if a man were transferred, his family would simply move with him. Times have changed. The number of individuals who turn down job offers to avoid uprooting their families or working spouses is steadily rising. Since family considerations are important to today's employees, organizations should maintain a policy of actively seeking to involve family members in significant career decisions. More emphasis must be placed on growth opportunities that do not involve relocation.

Career Planning Issues

Employers face many career-related challenges in the years ahead. For example, increased levels of participation by women in the labour force have already forced many employers to examine problems of dual-

[40] R. Townsend, *Up the Organization* (New York: Knopf, 1970.)
[41] Hall.
[42] B. Rice, "Midlife Encounters: The Menninger Seminars for Businessmen," *Psychology Today*, 1979, vol. 12, no. 11, pp. 66–77.
[43] Renwick et al.

earner and dual-career families. Affirmative action legislation may compel many employers to develop women and minorities for jobs and career paths that have traditionally been occupied by white males. As mandatory retirement becomes a thing of the past, employers must find ways to make longer working lives both productive and satisfying. Finally, the higher education and aspiration levels of today's employees suggests that they will demand more career planning and development from employers.

Of the many issues suggested above, dual-careers have attracted considerable interest. To understand career issues, one must distinguish the *dual-career family* from both the traditional and the dual-earner family. In the *traditional family*, one spouse, usually the husband, engages in paid work while the other spouse works as homemaker and parent. Wives or husbands may help to facilitate their spouse's promotion and career progress through career support activities such as entertaining colleagues or clients and participation in community affairs.

In *dual-earner families*, both spouses work outside the home for pay. One spouse may pursue a career while the other regards working as a temporary activity pursued for economic reasons.[44] This shift from the traditional family pattern is often caused by high levels of inflation, layoff or desires for a higher standard of living. This pattern typically leaves the primary responsibilities for homemaking and/or parenting to the wife. From an employer's perspective, dual-earner families mean that wives may seek part-time jobs or jobs with convenient or flexible hours at organizations located near their residence. Wives of dual-earner families may have little interest in career planning and development activities due to their lower commitment to the labour force. Another consequence of this pattern is that the spouse is not available to support the career activities of the career-pursuing spouse.

A *dual-career family* is one in which both spouses have a commitment to careers as well as to a family life together.[45] The implication of this pattern is that neither spouse will subordinate his or her career to family demands but both maintain a commitment to family activities. Organizations encounter numerous career planning challenges with respect to dual-career employees. One of the most common challenges is dealing with a spouse's promotion opportunity that requires relocation. In the traditional career and the dual-earner families, the promotion opportunity would likely be readily accepted. In the case of the dual-career family, acceptance of the promotion and relocation may depend upon obtaining a comparable job for the other spouse. In reality, this is often difficult or impossible and the couple is forced to choose between the relative gains of accepting the new position versus the consequences of not relocating. Large employers located in urban areas

[44] L.A. Gilbert and V. Rachlin, "Mental Health and Psychological Functioning of Dual-Career Families," *The Counseling Psychologist*, 1987, vol. 15, no. 1, pp. 7–49.

[45] R. Rapoport and R.N. Rapoport, *Dual-Career Families* (Middlesex, England: Penguin, 1971).

may have less difficulty locating alternative positions for spouses than small employers in rural areas. Other problems associated with dual-careers include conflicts in work and vacation schedules, career-family role conflicts regarding child care, and the stress of managing two careers.

Summary

Career planning as a separate HRM function is a relatively new but growing phenomenon. Established programs are rare but increasing because of organizations' desire to ensure a supply of qualified replacements and to satisfy the desires of employees for career and growth opportunities.

While programs differ, career planning has four elements: (1) individual assessment of abilities, interests, career needs, and goals; (2) organizational assessment of employees' abilities and potential; (3) communication of information concerning career options and opportunities with the organization; and (4) career counselling to help individuals set realistic goals and plan their attainment. HRM professionals provide materials and opportunities for individual career planning, conduct assessments of employee potential, develop career paths, and inform employees and those acting as counsellors of career opportunities in the organization. HRM professionals also aid managers and supervisors in career planning and development efforts. Support functions include providing needed information, encouraging periodic and objective appraisals of employee performance, and training supervisors and managers to function effectively as career counsellors and agents of employee development. Career planners should develop a close working relationship with human resource planners so that employee expectations for advancement are reasonable and career goals realistic.

Project Ideas

1. Visit your university or college placement office, student counselling centre, or any other agency offering career planning and counselling services. Prepare a brief report describing the services it offers. For example, what are its standard operating procedures? Is a battery of tests given before the meeting with a counsellor? Is more than one trip required? What kinds of tests are given? What kind of feedback does the student receive? What qualifications do counsellors possess?
2. Work through the self-assessment exercise on personal wants in Exhibit 11.3. Record your responses. After you have finished, write

a short paper evaluating the exercise. What do you think of it? Did it help you to clarify your wants and needs? Submit both your self-assessment report and your evaluation of the exercise to your instructor.

3. Try to obtain a career planning workbook or other materials from a large organization that has some kind of career planning program. Prepare a written or oral report on the organization's career planning activities as described in the materials. If a workbook is available, describe its contents, including the nature of some of the career planning exercises.

Cases

Case 11.1: Tuition Aid and Turnover at Westfield Construction

From his office in mid-town Calgary, Howard Flanders, human resource manager for Westfield Construction Company, gazes at the setting sun as he contemplates Sims' report. Sims is manager of career planning and development at Westfield, and her report describes the past six months of the company's career development and tuition reimbursement program. Flanders finds the report disturbing. Basically, it documents an increased use of the company's tuition aid program, but also a 15 per cent increase over last year in quit rates among tuition recipients. Tuition recipients tend to be workers of high ability and motivation—ones Westfield would choose to retain even in the worst of times. Quit rates seem to be higher among engineers than other types of workers, including project and cost analysts. Career paths for these two types of employees are given in Table 1.

Not surprisingly, Sims' report also documents an increase in dissatisfaction with promotion and growth opportunities among engineers, the company's most vital human resource. Several engineers complained, for example, that they had not even learned of some vacancies until others had been promoted to fill them. The following quotes are illustrative of the engineers' discontent:

"We're trained for construction, but now we 'build' pre-fabricated burger joints" (engineer I);

"We used to do big projects, but now we do simple jobs an engineer I could handle" (engineer II);

"The tuition aid program is fine, but Westfield can't seem to utilize our added knowledge" (engineer III, who quit six months after completing an MBA degree);

"When I first came here, the work was tough and challenging, and good engineers could move up quickly; now even good engineers are stuck with routine projects and slow promotions" (engineer IV, who left after 10 years with the company).

Flanders understands why his engineers might miss the "boom" times. Still, he was hoping they would understand that business was slow in the entire construction industry. He also hoped that employees would appreciate Westfield's policies of reducing hiring and offering early retirements in order to avoid layoffs.

In light of Sims' report, Flanders now wonders whether Westfield should modify its $250,000 per year tuition aid program or discontinue it entirely. Currently, the program allows employees who receive at least a B grade to receive reimbursement for work-related undergraduate and graduate-level courses. In the past, entry-level engineers have typically pursued undergraduate degrees, while higher-level engineers pursued MBA or graduate engineering degrees.

Table 1:

Career paths for engineers and project and cost analysts at Westfield

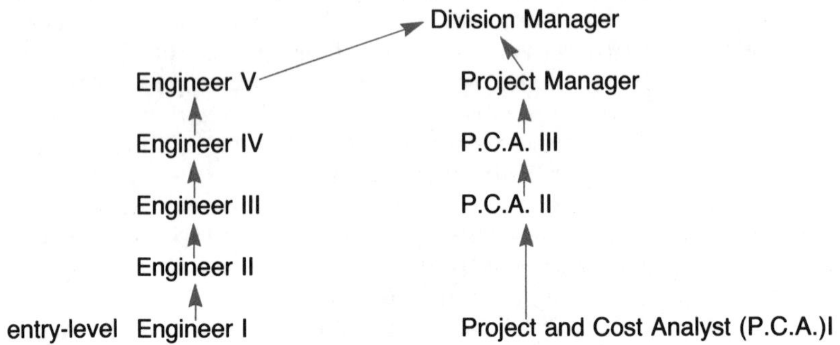

Note: Engineer I requires at least two years of college engineering; Project and Cost Analyst I requires a Bachelor's degree in commerce with a finance and/or accounting major. Education requirements increase for higher levels in each career path.

Questions:

1. How has the slowdown at Westfield affected career planning and career-related issues? What actions might Flanders take to ease the situation, other than modifying or discontinuing the tuition aid program?

2. What are some possible consequences of discontinuing the tuition aid program? What are some possible consequences of continuing or modifying it?
3. What do you feel Flanders should do about the tuition aid program? Why? What, if any, additional information would be useful in answering this question?

Case 11.2: No Room at the Top

For six years Lowell Honeycutt, age 37, has been a middle manager at Brooks-Jennings Corporation, a large retailer of lumber and hardware supply. Honeycutt is a well-liked and respected employee whose performance has always been excellent. However, due to slowdowns in the construction industry and low turnover in the organization, Honeycutt's plans for advancing to one of the company's 60 top management spots have been thwarted, perhaps indefinitely. In short, Honeycutt's career has "plateaued."

An individual's career is said to "plateau" when additional upward mobility within the organization is unlikely, even though performance may be adequate to very good. Most employees who stay with a company long enough reach a career plateau at some point in time. This is inevitable due to the classic pyramidal shape of organizational structures. There are limited spots at the top.

Brooks-Jennings is aware of the plight of Honeycutt and others and is exploring ways to solve or ease the problem. Specifically, HRM professionals are considering how the company's career planning resources might be used or modified in order to effect a solution. These resources include the following:

1. A series of workbooks designed to help employees analyze their present positions, identify desired characteristics of future positions, and determine job goals, development needs and plans of action;
2. A number of career planning seminars focussing on current job requirements and self-assessments of values, skills, preferred work characteristics, and areas for development;
3. Vacancy forecasts for the next five years produced and updated annually. These are broken down by functional groups, by salary levels, and year;
4. Position descriptions and requirements of advertised vacancies organized by occupational code within a reference binder;
5. Pathways to target positions based on historical career paths, plus future directions suggested by appropriate managers;
6. Career reference library containing theoretical texts, "how-to" books, other firms' workbooks, and selected journal articles;
7. Reference list of courses related to career planning offered by the company and the community;
8. List of available career counselling services in a number of communities.

Questions:

1. How might Brooks-Jennings' career planning resources be used or modified to help solve or ease the career plateauing problem?
2. Besides career planning, what other approaches could the company take to this problem?
3. What are the likely consequences of not taking steps to deal with career plateauing?

IV Employee Maintenance

12

Compensation

Walt Lester, human resource manager at Supply Unlimited, a manufacturing firm, has decided to re-evaluate the pay level of the drill press operator job. Turnover among drill press operators has been high and exit interviews point to insufficient pay as the likely culprit. To re-evaluate the job's pay, Lester compares the drill press operator job at Supply Unlimited with similar jobs in other companies nearby. When he discovers that competing firms are paying drill press operators more, Lester raises the job's pay from Level 3 to Level 4. In the weeks immediately following the raise in pay level, Lester receives approximately 60 formal complaints, mainly from employees one pay grade below the 20 drill press operators whose pay rate was increased. The complaining employees believed that their jobs should also receive more pay.

Walt Lester's experience illustrates the difficulty of determining and maintaining pay structures which meet the demands of both external and internal equity. External equity is the fairness of pay and other rewards as perceived in relation to similar jobs outside the organization. Internal equity is the fairness of pay and other rewards as perceived in relation to other jobs within the organization. In raising the pay grade of the drill press operator job, Lester had increased its external equity, but disrupted the internal equity of the pay structure. An organization's pay structure is the set of pay levels associated with jobs in the organization. As such, it defines the relationships between jobs in terms of pay. For example, a Labour Grade 4 job might pay $1 per hour more than a Labour Grade 3 job. Such relationships are known as pay differentials.

Compensation: A Definition

Compensation is any form of payment given to employees in exchange for work they provide their employer. Financial payment made at or near the time work is performed is called *direct compensation*. Examples of direct compensation are wages, salaries, overtime pay, commissions, and bonuses. *Wages*, which are usually distinguished from salaries, are direct compensation received by employees who are paid according to hourly rates. Employees paid on a monthly, semimonthly, or weekly basis receive salaries; their pay does not vary with number of hours worked.

Besides earning a wage or a salary, most employees are also compensated for their efforts by certain benefits, such as paid vacation days and holidays, various forms of insurance, and pensions. These are forms of *deferred*, or *indirect*, compensation.

This chapter discusses direct compensation. The following chapter deals with forms of indirect compensation.

Compensation and Organizational Effectiveness

Organizational effectiveness has been defined as "an organization's capacity to acquire and utilize its scarce and valued resources as expeditiously as possible in the pursuit of its operational goals."[1] Compensation contributes to organizational effectiveness in five basic ways. First, it can attract qualified applicants to the organization. Other things being equal, an organization which offers a higher level of pay can attract a larger number of qualified applicants than its competition. Thus, it benefits from a lower selection ratio, which enables it to hire the most highly qualified of a relatively large number of applicants. Of course, this assumes that the organization uses valid selection procedures. More highly qualified applicants are more likely to be highly productive employees. When worker productivity is high, a smaller

[1] R.M. Steers, *Organizational Effectiveness: A Behavioral View* (Santa Monica, Calif.: Goodyear Publishing Co., Inc., 1977), p. 5.

number of workers can achieve the same output, thus reducing the employer's total labour costs and increasing organizational profitability.

Second, compensation helps to retain competent workers in the organization. Although retaining workers is contingent on many factors, compensation policies help by maintaining a fair internal pay structure, as well as by keeping pay and benefits competitive (ensuring external equity). Turnover is thus reduced, along with costs associated with recruiting, selecting, and training replacements. ISECO Safety Shoes of Mississauga, Ontario is one company which credits its record of low turnover to a compensation plan featuring profit sharing, bonuses, and generous benefits. ISECO's compensation plan is described in Exhibit 12.1.

EXHIBIT 12.1:

ISECO reaps benefits from compensation plan

If low turnover is a key measure of employee satisfaction, ISECO Safety Shoes of Mississauga, Ont., is a very satisfying place to work. It's a rare year when even one of the national staff of 100 leaves ISECO, says Randy Munnings, the company's secretary treasurer. He attributes a good deal of the record for low turnover to a compensation schedule featuring cash and benefits. Then there are the special perks for sales staff, such as merchandise and vacation trips.

Munnings's uncle George founded the company 45 years ago (his father, Bob, joined the company two years later) to sell steel-toed safety shoes directly to customers from specially equipped trucks. ISECO currently has about 40 trucks and 11 stores across the country and distributes products from about 10 safety-shoe manufacturers. With annual sales of about $14 million, the company has earned its own rewards by paying close attention to how it compensates employees. "Our attitude is that we're a privately owned company and we don't have to satisfy shareholders," says Munnings. "So we share as much of the profit as possible with the employees." The standard profit-sharing plan is based on a percentage of the previous year's after-tax profits. It generally amounts to about 8% of an employee's salary.

The noteworthy difference in ISECO's approach is its deliberate emphasis on relating individual performance directly to company performance. Instead of sharing profits in one lump sum after the year-end, Munnings says the company gets maximum psychological benefit from the payment by distributing it quarterly, that way employees get four reminders annually. Although each employee is entitled to a different amount in the profit-sharing scheme based on individual salary, Munnings figures profit sharing linked to salary works in a company the size of ISECO, since it removes the need for complex calculations, and since salaries already reflect employee value and years of service.

In most heavily sales-oriented companies, commissions earned are in themselves an incentive. ISECO gives its sales staff a guarantee of about $200 a week and a percentage of sales and looks after maintenance of the trucks. In addition, Munnings started a special bonus plan two years ago, enabling the sales force to earn points based on performance. "The main feature is that we don't pay cash," he says. "After a certain number of points are accumulated, employees can exchange them for merchandise or a trip or something like that." Again, he figures ISECO gets maximum results for its outlay through the plan. "Our thinking was that, if we paid them in cash, it would go to pay grocery bills or something," he says. "But if we pay in merchandise or other goods, the incentive is there as a reminder for a longer time."

Because top management at ISECO is family—Munnings's father is president, and his cousin Garry is vice-president—the company doesn't have a special executive-compensation plan. However, ISECO looks after salaried people well. The company pays half of their provincial medical coverage, all of their major medical coverage for prescription drugs and semiprivate hospitalization and all of a long-term disability insurance plan. ISECO also matches employee contributions to the company's pension plan and covers the administrative costs for a group registered retirement savings plan.

With a far-flung work force, Munnings says communications can sometimes be a problem, especially since most of the sales-people are on the road every day. But he points out that the low turnover resulting from a good compensation package itself leads to good communications. "It's sort of a joke that we try to make things so good for employees that they can't afford to leave," he says. "But because few of them do, we know most employees personally."

SOURCE: From "More Money" by Wayne Lilley, *Canadian Business*, April 1985, pp. 52. Reprinted by permission of the author.

Third, compensation can motivate employees to put forth their best efforts. For example, many manufacturers and sales organizations use monetary incentives to attain higher levels of production or sales without hiring additional employees. Monetary incentives provide employees with additional pay as a reward for higher levels of performance. When employees put forth their best efforts, the average productivity of labour increases. With increased productivity, fewer employees are needed to achieve the same level of output. Thus, labour costs are reduced and organizational profitability increased. Note the way ISECO's plan serves to motivate workers.

Fourth, compensation systems are important to the effectiveness of organizations since they help to define organization structure and culture.[2] For example, when an organization adds a new line of business, it may need to change its compensation system. New lines of business often require a different set of behaviours and culture than current business lines, and the compensation system can redirect behaviours to meet changed conditions. Additionally, an organization seeking to downsize and have a more flexible work force may seek to change from a traditional job-based pay system to a skill-based pay system. Job-based systems pay people for the job they occupy, while skill-based systems reward job-related knowledge and skill. Thus, the change in reward systems is consistent with and supports the new strategy and related structure and culture changes.

[2] E.E. Lawler III, "The Strategic Design of Reward Systems," in R.S. Schuler & S.A. Youngblood, *Readings in Personnel and Human Resource Management*, 2nd ed. (St. Paul, Minn.: West Publishing Co., 1984), pp. 253–69.

Finally, minimizing the costs of compensation can also contribute to organizational effectiveness since compensation is a significant cost for most employers.

Compensation Responsibilities

HRM professionals engage in a number of compensation activities to facilitate the goals of attracting, retaining, and motivating employees while trying to control compensation costs.

First, in order to ensure that compensation packages are competitive, HRM professionals conduct pay or wage surveys. Pay or wage surveys are a way of collecting and analyzing information about jobs and their pay for the purpose of making pay comparisons between similar jobs in different organizations. Second, to facilitate retention, compensation specialists conduct job evaluations. Job evaluations use selected criteria to compare jobs within an organization, providing a rationale for paying one job more than another. Third, in order to motivate employees, compensation specialists design incentive systems, which attach rewards to desired levels of performance. Chapter 2 presented an incentive system used at Mary Kay Cosmetics, Inc. (see Exhibit 2.9). Finally, HRM professionals implement systems of compensation cost control, including budgets, audits, and compensation guidelines.

Compensation: Relation to Other Functions

Compensation is related in some way to almost every other HRM function. The most direct relationships are portrayed in Exhibit 12.2.

An employee receives his or her pay after a period of time on the job, usually a week to a month. However, the typical employee's first contact with compensation is during recruiting. Pay can be an important factor in whether an applicant accepts a job offer.

Four HRM functions that directly influence compensation policies and practices include: (1) human resource planning, (2) job analysis, (3) performance appraisal, and (4) labour relations. Also, compensation directly influences three functions: (1) recruiting/selection, (2) benefits, and (3) career planning and development.

Human Resource Planning

Human resource planning specifies human resource goals, which can be furthered by compensation policies and programs. The number and type of employees needed have a substantial effect on an employer's compensation costs. If, for example, human resource planners project a need for a scarce type of labour, such as tool and die makers,

EXHIBIT 12.2

Compensation: relation to other functions

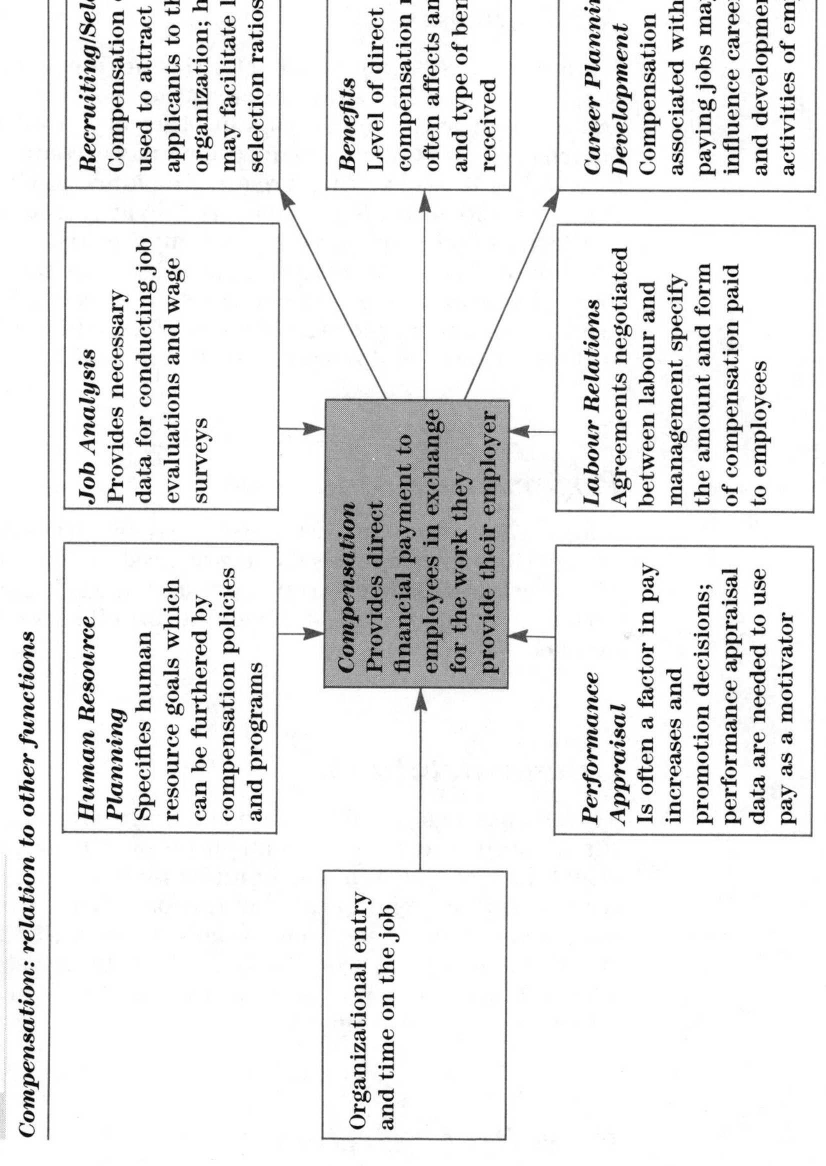
Organizational entry and time on the job
Human Resource Planning
Specifies human resource goals which can be furthered by compensation policies and programs
Job Analysis
Provides necessary data for conducting job evaluations and wage surveys
Recruiting/Selection
Compensation can be used to attract applicants to the organization; high pay may facilitate low selection ratios
Compensation
Provides direct financial payment to employees in exchange for the work they provide their employer
Benefits
Level of direct compensation received often affects amount and type of benefits received
Performance Appraisal
Is often a factor in pay increases and promotion decisions; performance appraisal data are needed to use pay as a motivator
Labour Relations
Agreements negotiated between labour and management specify the amount and form of compensation paid to employees
Career Planning and Development
Compensation associated with higher-paying jobs may influence career plans and development activities of employees

compensation budgets have to allow for high starting salaries. Compensation policies and programs can also have an effect on the goals of human resource planners. If, for example, pay incentive systems increase worker productivity, then HRP goals for external recruiting may be reduced.

Job Analysis

Job analysis is basic to two activities of the compensation function: wage surveys and job evaluations. Wage surveys compare jobs in the organization with similar jobs in other organizations. They are conducted to ensure that an organization's pay is competitive and equitable in relation to what other organizations are paying for similar jobs. Complete and accurate job analysis data are essential to determine the similarity of jobs for making pay comparisons.

Job analysis information is also basic to conducting job evaluations. Job evaluations compare jobs on selected criteria so that they can then be ordered for the purpose of assigning differential pay. Job evaluations are conducted to ensure internal pay equity.

Performance Appraisal

If an organization chooses to use a pay-for-performance or merit system, performance appraisals may be used to determine the magnitude of pay increases or who receives promotion to a higher-paying job. Valid performance appraisals are essential for effective utilization of merit increase dollars.

Labour Relations

Agreements negotiated between labour unions and management affect the amount and form of compensation. Under provisions of labour relations acts, unionized employers must negotiate with union representatives who speak for the organized workers. Specifically, management must negotiate wages, benefits, and the conditions of employment such as working hours, production standards, and so on. The unionized employer thus has less flexibility in compensation than does the nonunion employer.

Recruiting/Selection

Compensation can be used to attract applicants to the organization; attractive pay packages may facilitate low selection ratios and the hiring of high-quality personnel.

Benefits

A form of indirect compensation, benefits are closely tied to the compensation function. In some instances, the amount of direct compensation an employee receives affects the amount and type of benefits received. The Unemployment Insurance Act, for example, uses the employee's pay to determine the amount of benefits.

Career Planning and Development

Compensation influences an employee's career plans. The higher pay associated with higher-level jobs can motivate an employee to prepare for a position of greater responsibility in the organization.

Major Laws Affecting Compensation

In using compensation to serve its various organizational purposes, employers must work within the framework of many laws and regulations. Among the most important are labour standards legislation, human rights legislation, and income tax laws.

Employment Standards and Human Rights Legislation

Chapter 3 included a survey of legislation related to labour standards and human rights. Labour or employment standards acts mandate and regulate minimum wages, maximum hours of work and overtime pay, paid vacations and holidays, and so on. Their provisions are normally enforced by the appropriate department of labour.

In Alberta overtime begins after 8 hours per day and 44 per week, while in Ontario and Quebec overtime begins after 44 hours per week. Equal pay provisions apply to male and female employees performing the same or similar work under the same or similar conditions. In some provinces these provisions are in the human rights acts; others include them in employment standards legislation. Provisions for equal pay for work of equal value apply in Quebec, Manitoba, and the federal jurisdiction. The criterion is an assessment of the value of work performed by employees in the same establishment.

Human rights legislation prohibits various types of discrimination in employment practices. Except as provided in minimum wage legislation, forbidden practices include paying different wages to persons on the basis of race, religion, ethnic or national origin, marital status, or age. Human rights provisions are normally enforced by human rights commissions.

All these laws exist in each of Canada's 13 jurisdictions (the ten provinces, the two territories, and the federal jurisdiction, which covers industries such as transportation and communications). Since the laws and their interpretations by regulatory bodies are different in each jurisdiction, and since the legislation and regulations undergo frequent revision, HRM professionals must continually monitor the changing legal environment as it relates to compensation.

Income Tax Laws

Federal and provincial laws have an important impact on employee take-home pay and often affect an employer's compensation policies and practices. The effect of income tax laws has been a major factor in developing compensation programs for highly paid executives. Because such employees are in high income tax brackets, salary increases often result in very little additional take-home pay. For this reason, executive pay specialists have developed forms of compensation that reduce the impact of taxes on executive income. Examples include stock options and methods of deferred pay, such as profit-sharing plans and generous pensions.

Continued inflation may increase the impact of tax laws on the pay of all employees. Until 1982, the federal government fully indexed tax brackets to prevent the erosion of income through inflation's pushing people into higher brackets. In that year, however, the adjustment was held to 6 per cent, less than the rate of inflation. In the middle-income brackets especially, a pay increase can move an employee into a higher tax bracket. These circumstances reduce the effectiveness of the pay raise as a means of motivating employees.

Pay Surveys

Traditionally, employers have used money to attract an adequate supply of qualified applicants. Whether an organization chooses to be a wage leader or to offer only the market rate for new employees, it must have accurate information about the pay rates for relevant jobs in other organizations. This information is obtained through pay surveys, which enable an employer to learn the going rates for jobs included in the survey. Most organizations obtain pay survey data for only their "key jobs." Key jobs have the following characteristics: (1) they are representative of the organization's pay structure; (2) their job content is relatively stable and well-known; (3) they include substantial numbers of employees; and (4) they have not recently undergone large changes in pay level. Data from pay surveys are used both to attract employees and to retain them by ensuring external equity.

Pay surveys are particularly important to employers since they are a major means of determining not only the worth of jobs, but the validity of job evaluation methods. Though pay surveys and job evaluation are separate components of compensation, it is common practice for employers to compare the rankings of jobs produced by job evaluation to that found in pay surveys. Several researchers have recently argued the importance of pay surveys and how they are done in determining the comparable worth of jobs.[3]

Many pay surveys are published by private and government agencies. An employer can also gain such information by participating in local pay surveys conducted by other organizations. If existing pay surveys prove ill-suited to an organization's purposes, it can conduct its own pay survey.

Conducting a Pay Survey

In order to provide maximum benefit, the makers of a pay survey must follow six steps:

1. Specify purpose of the survey.
2. Specify jobs to be surveyed and information needed from survey participants.
3. Select comparison employers for inclusion in the survey.
4. Select survey method and design survey instrument.
5. Administer the survey.
6. Analyze and display survey data.

An employer can have a number of reasons for wanting to conduct a pay survey. One very common one is to examine the competitiveness of hiring wage rates for entry-level jobs. Another common purpose is to compare pay levels for higher-level jobs with those in other organizations. The intended purpose of a pay survey has implications for its design and administration. For example, one must pose different questions in a survey to examine the competitiveness of hiring wages for entry-level jobs and in a survey to investigate the appropriateness of pay differentials among jobs.

Depending on the intent of the survey, different jobs are selected for comparative purposes. If the purpose of the survey is to evaluate a firm's competitive position in the labour market, only entry-level jobs need be included. However, if the survey's purpose is to compare the pay structure to competitors', it is important to include a representative sample of jobs throughout the firm. Information commonly requested in pay surveys includes the number of employees in each surveyed job; pay ranges and mid-points for each job; the basis for advancement to higher pay levels; and the actual pay for each job occupant. Surveys sometimes also seek additional information, such as the nature of fringe benefits provided for various jobs.

[3] S.L. Rynes and G.T. Milkovich, "Wage Surveys: Dispelling Some Myths About the 'Market Wage'," *Personnel Psychology*, 1986, vol. 39, pp. 71–90.

HRM managers may also telephone other managers to check whether they have adjusted the pay level for one or more jobs since the last pay survey.

Employers selected for a pay survey are generally in the same industry and local labour market as the employer conducting the survey. When private or public surveys are used, employers may utilize pay data from other companies within either their industry or their local or regional labour market. Labour unions generally prefer that employers compare wage rates with other unionized firms in the same industry. This is because pay levels of such jobs are often higher than for the same or similar jobs in local, nonunion firms. Generally, it is necessary to utilize competitors in other geographic areas in order to make pay comparisons for highly skilled and specialized jobs.

In theory, organizations could use industry surveys for jobs that are unique to their industry, while also using local wage surveys for jobs that are common to many employers, such as secretaries, truck drivers, and custodians. In practice, however, many industries, such as banking, hospitals, and breweries, use industry wage survey data for all jobs, not just those specific to the industry. This may result in problems of external equity, since some common jobs tend to be paid more in some industries than in others. For example, a secretary may be paid more at a bank or a brewery than at the hospital down the street.

In deciding how many organizations to include in a pay survey, the designer must consider the number of organizations with which the employer actually competes for various types of labour. Cost and time considerations also affect the decision of how many organizations to survey. One compensation manager suggests that a pay survey include at least ten, but no more than 30, organizations.[4]

Since employers often use the results of pay surveys to demonstrate to employees the fairness of their pay in relation to that given by other organizations, it may be beneficial to give employees a voice in selecting the organizations to be included in such surveys. Employee participation of this sort can tend to persuade employees of the external equity of their pay. Of course, employers who cannot afford to pay at or above the market wage level may choose not to allow employee involvement in the survey process.

The choice of a survey method depends on the number of jobs to be surveyed, the geographic area of the potential respondents, and time and cost constraints. In some cases, employers may find that surveys available from government or private compensation firms are adequate for their needs. However, government surveys may not be available when needed. Surveys by private firms tend to be more timely, but may cost several hundred dollars or more. Both types of survey have the disadvantage that an employer is not able to choose or even know which organizations are included in the survey. For these reasons,

[4] B.R. Ellig, "Salary Surveys: Design to Application," *The Personnel Administrator*, 1977, vol. 22, no. 8, pp. 41–8.

many employers choose to conduct their own survey using one or more survey methods.

Mailed questionnaires are the most common survey method. Questionnaires are most appropriate for surveying large numbers of jobs. When a relatively small amount of information is needed quickly, a telephone survey may be practical. One seldom-used but potentially valuable method of gathering pay information is a conference at which managers from different companies exchange wage and salary information. This method is superior to the questionnaire since ambiguities can be clarified on the spot and data collected rapidly. Further, pay data are easily exchanged in the conference situation.

The survey instrument must be simple, understandable, and easy to complete to encourage cooperation from respondents. It must include adequate descriptions of the jobs being surveyed so that respondents can provide information for comparable jobs in their organizations. Comparability of jobs is crucial to the usefulness of the pay survey, since differences in pay are meaningful only when jobs are similar in content.

The first step in the administration of a pay survey is to notify potential participants that the survey is being conducted and that they are being included. An explanation of the purposes of the survey should be provided. To encourage participation, employers who participate should be promised survey results. In the case of mailed questionnaires, follow-up phone calls are often required to ensure an adequate response rate.

The final step in a pay survey is to analyze and display the data. Data from the pay survey must be summarized and presented to management and/or employees in an understandable and useful way. Exhibit 12.3 is an example of the results of a pay survey for a secretarial job. Notice that it includes both a description of the job and job specifications. One can also easily see that the survey results are based on the pay of 95 secretaries from 20 different employers. The data show both the minimum and maximum pay for the job in each of the 20 companies, as well as that of Brucell Company, the organization conducting the survey. Both the weighted and the unweighted averages show that Brucell pays less for the job of secretary than do most other employers in the pay survey. *Unweighted averages* provide equal weight to each employer, while *weighted averages* are based upon the number of employees in a surveyed job. This survey also shows that most of the surveyed firms use merit as the basis for pay progression in the secretarial job, though Brucell uses a combination of seniority and merit.

Conducting a pay survey is a complex, costly, and time-consuming process. For this reason, employers should thoroughly examine existing pay surveys before deciding to conduct one of their own.

Major Pay Surveys

Employers can use a number of existing pay surveys to learn the market rates of pay for certain jobs. Labour Canada and the federal govern-

EXHIBIT 12.3

Results of a pay survey for a secretarial job

JOB TITLE

SECRETARY

REQUIREMENTS

This position requires the equivalent of a high school education or specialized training in secretarial duties. It requires proficiency in typing and shorthand/speedwriting and approximately one year of secretarial experience.

DESCRIPTION

This is not a recent graduate job. It is the second level of secretary with at least one year of experience. The incumbent would typically work for a staff specialist or a group of junior executives, typing letters, reports and memos from rough or corrected copy and dictation notes. The incumbent sets up and maintains files and arranges meetings and travel accommodations for the principal/s. The next promotional step would be to senior secretary which would require a minimum of three years of secretarial experience and would involve a principal who is a department or function head but not a senior executive.

SUMMARY STATISTICS

RANK	CO. CODE	NO. OF EMPLOYEES	ESTABLISHED RANGE MIN	MAX	PROG. BASIS	WGHTD AVG PAY
1	M	2	$213.00	$289.00	M	$260.00
2	R	7	$175.00	$242.00	M	$241.33
3	D	16	$187.00	$263.00	M	$241.00
4	P	4	$205.00	$264.00	M	$237.00
5	J	2	$194.00	$260.00	S/M	$235.00
6	B	4	$172.00	$242.00	M	$231.00
7	Q	8	$165.00	$242.00	M	$229.25
8	O	4	$172.00	$235.00	S	$224.00
9	K	2	$175.00	$238.00	M	$221.50
10	E	11	$184.00	$255.00	M	$217.00
11	C	2	$159.00	$219.00	M	$213.50
12	G	7	$195.00	$249.00	M	$212.23
13	N	2	$189.00	$254.00	M	$211.50
14	S	3	$178.00	$236.00	M	$211.33
16	A	6	$175.00	$230.00	S/M	$189.47
17	F	5	$181.00	$251.00	M	$185.20
18	L	3	$175.00	$227.00	M	$181.33
19	H	3	$145.00	$202.00	S/M	$162.33
20	I	4	$155.00	$212.00	M	$160.00
	TOTAL	95				
SURVEY RATIOS			1.47	1.43		1.62
WEIGHTED AVERAGES		*****	$179.48	$245.77	***	$217.59
UNWEIGHTED AVERAGES		5	$178.63	$242.63	***	$213.89
15 BRUCELL		3	$171.00	$233.00	S/M	$208.33

2915

SOURCE: B.R. Ellig, "Salary Surveys: Design to Application," *The Personnel Administrator*, 1977, vol. 22, no. 8, p. 45.

ment's Pay Research Bureau (PRB) are important sources of pay surveys for many types of jobs (see Exhibit 12.4). Most provincial government departments of labour publish the pay rates contained in collective agreements within their jurisdictions. In addition, various private groups and associations conduct their own surveys, which usually focus on selected occupations or industries. These include the Administrative Management Society, Bell Canada, and the Conference Board in Canada. The cost of obtaining a pay survey's results ranges from mere participation in the survey to over $600. A complete listing of sources of pay information, along with a summary of the contents and the cost of each, is in Labour Canada's *Collective Bargaining Information Sources*.[5]

An employer can sometimes obtain information regarding local pay surveys from a local board of trade or chamber of commerce. Many unions conduct periodic pay surveys; it is useful for employers who operate under collective agreements to have detailed information about such surveys, especially during contract negotiations.

Before deciding to use an existing survey, an employer should consider a number of factors. First, does it provide the information the organization needs? If one survey does not meet an employer's needs, perhaps several surveys can provide the needed information. Second, to what degree are the surveyed organizations representative of those with which the employer wishes to make pay comparisons? If the fit is not close, using the survey data can lead to false conclusions regarding the competitiveness of pay levels. Third, does the existing survey provide job descriptions that are detailed enough to permit comparison with jobs in the organization? Most standard pay surveys include only "key jobs," those that are relatively common among a given group of employers. For example, machinist is a key job for metal fabricating firms, while clerk/typist is a key job for many different types of employers. Although the content of key jobs is usually similar to related jobs in many organizations, reliance upon a general pay survey means that an employer may have to interpolate pay ranges for jobs which are not included in the standard list. Many employers have at least a few jobs that are unique to their organizations and are, therefore, impossible to compare to identical jobs elsewhere. Finally, in using an existing survey, attention must be given to the form of pay specified in the survey. For example, most surveys use an *average wage rate*, which is defined as the "weighted average or 'mean' of straight-time rates paid on a time basis in an occupation. . . The wage rates. . . in an occupation are multiplied (weighted) by the number of employees receiving each rate, the sum of these products then being divided by the total number of employees reported in the occupation."[6] To make a valid pay comparison with surveys reporting this form of pay, the employer must use the same definition.

[5] Labour Canada, *Collective Bargaining Information Sources* (Ottawa: Minister of Supply and Services Canada, 1978 and periodic updatings), section 1.

[6] Labour Canada, *Wage Rates, Salaries and Hours of Labour, Canada, 1980* (Ottawa: Supply and Services Canada, 1981), Appendix A, p. 6.

EXHIBIT 12.4

Federal government's wage and salary surveys

Sponsoring organization	*Type of employees &/or industries surveyed*	*Geographical areas surveyed*	*Frequency of survey*
Labour Canada Wage and Salary Survey	Forty-seven industries: selected office occupations, maintenance trades, service occupations, nonproduction labourers	Canada-wide; separate reports for 30 communities	Annual
Labour Canada Collective Bargaining Review	All (except construction) for lowest labour classification and top rated nonsupervisory tradesmen	Federal labour jurisdiction and provinces	Monthly
Pay Research Bureau (PRB) Rates of Pay in Industrial and Other Organizations	Mining, manufacturing, transportation and communication, public utilities, trade, finance and insurance, service; 14 occupational groups in five classes	Atlantic, Quebec, Ontario, Prairies, British Columbia, plus major metropolitan areas	Annual
Pay Research Bureau (PRB) Remuneration of Elected Officials	Federal, provincial, territorial, and municipal governments	Federal, provincial, and territorial governments, plus eight major cities	Annual
Pay Research Bureau (PRB) Anticipated and Actual Recruiting Rates for University and Community College Graduates	No industry breakdown; various engineering, science, arts and commerce, and business administration graduates	Canada-wide	Annual

Using Pay Survey Information

While procedures for conducting pay surveys and for analyzing and displaying survey data are fairly standard, little is known about how managers actually use pay survey information to determine levels of pay. It is likely that different compensation policies affect the use that is made of pay survey information. For example, one HRM manager of a unionized auto parts plant adheres to a corporate policy of keeping pay levels at or only slightly below that of his average-paying local competitors. This manager surveys only a few competitors several months before negotiations and disregards pay levels of the highest and lowest-paying among them. On the other hand, a highly profitable, nonunion manufacturer surveys only the better-paying employers in its local labour market. It does this at least twice per year because it has a policy of being a wage leader. This employer grants a pay increase anytime a competitor gets close to their pay levels. Thus, the different compensation policies of these two organizations lead one employer to take a vital interest in its highest-paying competitor, while the other chooses to ignore it.

Job Evaluation Systems

The major factor contributing to retention of employees is job satisfaction. As we saw in Chapter 2, job satisfaction has several components, one of which is pay. Dissatisfaction with pay is one factor leading to employee turnover.

One theory used to explain satisfaction with pay is equity theory, also discussed in Chapter 2. Equity theory postulates that people compare their inputs (abilities, effort, experience, education) and outcomes (pay, benefits, and other rewards) to the inputs and outcomes of other, comparable persons.[7] The amount of a person's inputs in relation to his or her outcomes is the *ratio of exchange*. An employee who believes that his or her ratio of exchange is not equal to that of a comparable person is likely to perceive the situation as inequitable.

Inequities can be perceived among the pay of co-workers in the same job and among employees in different jobs in the same organization. For example, many employees feel it is inequitable that co-workers receive more pay for the same work simply because they have been on the job longer. In the second kind of perceived inequity, a university-educated reporter might complain about making less money than a printer who works for the same newspaper.

Job evaluation systems are useful in achieving internal equity of pay between different jobs in the organization. Internal equity may be

[7] J.S. Adams, "Inequity in Social Exchange," in L. Berkowitz, ed., *Advances in Experimental Social Psychology*, vol. 2 (New York: Academic Press, 1965).

distinguished from employee equity, which is the perceived fairness of pay among workers in the same job or pay grade. Employee equity, which is discussed in a later section, is maintained through seniority, merit, and pay-for-performance systems.

The Job Evaluation Process

The process of ***job evaluation*** uses selected criteria to compare jobs within an organization so that they can be ordered for the purpose of assigning differential pay. Job evaluation systems provide a rationale for paying one job in an organization more or less than another. The job evaluation process involves five steps:

1. Collect job analysis data.
2. Prepare job descriptions and job specifications.
3. Choose compensable factors.
4. Develop or choose a job evaluation method.
5. Evaluate jobs.

The first step is to collect job analysis data. This information must be collected through a method of job analysis that completely and accurately captures the content and employee requirements of the jobs. Since job evaluation compares the content of jobs, it is also important to use a job analysis method that captures the similarities and differences between jobs. Some methods of job analysis are better suited than others to conducting job evaluations; methods that are well suited are functional job analysis (FJA), the Position Analysis Questionnaire (PAQ), and work analysis methods for manual, repetitive jobs.

The job descriptions and job specifications that result from job analysis should state clearly and completely the content and employee requirements of jobs. Ambiguous, incomplete job descriptions can result in some jobs being incorrectly evaluated.

The third step in job evaluation is choosing the compensable factors on which jobs will be compared. ***Compensable factors*** are those factors an organization values and chooses to reward through differential pay. Examples of common compensable factors are skill, knowledge, responsibility, effort, and working conditions.

If a factor is to be useful in job evaluation it must meet four conditions.[8] First, it must be present in different amounts among jobs. For example, working conditions may be a useful compensable factor for comparing jobs that do actually have different working conditions, say those of a mining company with employees working underground, above ground, and in offices. On the other hand, working conditions would not be a useful compensable factor for evaluating clerical jobs in an air-conditioned insurance office in which all workers are exposed to the same temperature, humidity, lighting, and noise levels.

[8] D.W. Belcher, *Compensation Administration* (Englewood Cliffs, N.J.: Prentice-Hall, 1974), p. 136.

The second condition is that there be no overlap in meaning between factors. If all jobs are consistently evaluated at the same level on two different factors, a high degree of overlap between the two is likely. Thus, the two factors measure essentially the same aspect of a job and receive an inappropriate weight in relation to other aspects. An example of overlap occurred in an evaluation done by a large retail clothing company. It used financial responsibility and decision-making as two of its compensable factors. When the evaluators discovered that most jobs had nearly identical levels of these two factors, the decision-making factor was retained and slightly modified to include financial decisions. Thus, the two factors were combined into one and the overlap problem was solved.

The third condition is that some degree of the factor must be present in all jobs. Quite simply, it is unfair to compare jobs for pay purposes on a factor appropriate to some jobs but not to others.

A fourth condition for the usefulness of compensable factors is that management, employees, and the union should be involved in choosing the ones that will affect pay. Recent research shows that employees have considerable interest in participating in decisions affecting their pay.[9] Compensation specialists agree that when management begins a job evaluation program, employees and their union representatives should be included on an evaluation committee. Since job evaluation involves many value-laden decisions and has a significant impact on pay, it is generally better to include employees in the inevitable discussions and arguments before a job evaluation system is implemented rather than afterwards. Some unions, however, resist becoming involved in the job evaluation process, fearing that their involvement may be interpreted as support and acceptance of the results of job evaluation. Such unions often prefer to let management conduct the job evaluation; then, if aspects of the job evaluation prove objectionable, the union can file a grievance.

If an organization develops its own job evaluation system, it must select compensable factors. If, on the other hand, it chooses to use one of the many ready-made systems available from compensation consulting firms, government agencies, or industry associations, the compensable factors will already have been selected. For example, the Hay Guide Chart-Profile method employs three factors: know-how, problem solving, and accountability. Though ready-made plans have established compensable factors, modification of factor weights or other details may be made to fit a particular employer's situation. Although ready-made systems have such benefits as savings in time and effort, these advantages should not prevail over developing a more appropriate, custom-made system if necessary. Whether an employer chooses a custom-made or a ready-made system depends upon: (1) the uniqueness of the organization's jobs; (2) the number and variety of jobs to be evaluated; and (3) the financial resources available.

[9] E.E. Lawler III, "The New Pay," in R.M. Fulmer, *New Management* (New York: MacMillan, 1987).

After an evaluation method is developed or chosen, it is implemented and jobs are evaluated. Employers purchasing ready-made plans typically receive professional assistance in all aspects of the evaluation process, including job analysis, training in use of the system, and advice on administrative problems following plan implementation. Though methods of evaluating differ, they all basically involve determining how much of each compensable factor is present in each job. Thus, jobs can be ordered in terms of their relative worth to the organization.

Even with an excellent job evaluation system, the evaluation process contains subjective value judgements. Since a major criterion of the effectiveness of a job evaluation system is how well it is accepted by employees, compensation experts advocate using a compensation committee with employee representation. Compensation committees are used in the implementation stage to determine how many points or what relative value should be assigned to each job. Disagreements or grievances regarding evaluation of particular jobs are also sometimes resolved by compensation committees consisting of management, HRM professionals, and employee representatives.

Job Evaluation Methods

There are five basic methods of job evaluation: (1) ranking; (2) level description; (3) factor comparison; (4) point method; and (5) market pricing. While many variations of these methods exist in practice, the five basic approaches are described here.

Ranking. The simplest and most basic form of job evaluation is ranking. *Ranking* is a method of ordering jobs from least valued to most valued in an organization. It involves subjective judgements of relative value. The judgements are made by the chief executive officer, perhaps with the assistance of other managerial personnel. Ranking does not require a set of complete job descriptions because those doing it should be thoroughly familiar with the content of the jobs. The compensable factors are not explicit but underlie the subjective judgements about the relative worth of jobs.

The ranking method is most appropriate for small organizations and for those with a limited number of different jobs. It has advantages in that it can be done quickly and inexpensively. An obvious disadvantage is that it is entirely subjective and has no explicit rationale or documentation for the results. This makes the method less useful for establishing internal equity in an organization's pay structure and also less useful for defending against pay discrimination suits.

Level description. The *level description* or *classification method* places jobs in a hierarchy, which is a series of descriptions of job grades. *Job grades* are general descriptions of types of jobs. Grades are differentiated according to the degree to which the jobs possess a set of compensable factors. For example, the federal government identifies 74 occupational groups and 153 subgroups, each with different factors that are important for determining levels of pay for different jobs. Thus, evaluation of a job analyst (classification officer), which belongs to the personnel administration group, considers three: knowledge, decision-making, and managerial responsibility.[10] Each factor is assigned points, and their sum determines the job's level within the government's seven-level system. Jobs in other occupations receive points for different factors; for example, hazard and environment are weighed for general labour and trades.

In using a level system, a job evaluator compares the job's description to descriptions of job grades in the job classification system. When a close match is found between the job's description and one of the job grade descriptions, the job can be placed in the hierarchy and assigned a pay scale. To illustrate how the level system is used, suppose you are considering the purchase of a new General Motors car. You have a brochure which has a description of all GM models ranging from the bottom of the line to the top. Assume that a new GM model is introduced which is not included in the brochure. In order to determine where the new model fits into the existing hierarchy of models, you could obtain a description of the new model and compare it to the descriptions of other GM models in the brochure.

The level description method of job evaluation is available to employers at minimal cost from the *Canadian Classification and Dictionary of Occupations*, published by Employment and Immigration Canada. Nevertheless, very few private employers use the method, perhaps because they find its two volumes of job descriptions cumbersome.

Factor comparison. *Factor comparison* is a quantitative method of job evaluation which evaluates jobs according to several compensable factors. It is a sophisticated method of ranking in which jobs are compared to each other across several factors.

The method has five steps. In the first, a job evaluation committee selects and rank-orders the key jobs in the organization. Key jobs represent the full range of jobs, from the highest to the lowest levels, and are typical of the various job families. When the key jobs have been ranked, each is assigned a monetary value which is its current going wage. Exhibit 12.5 shows the monetary values assigned to six key jobs in a machinery manufacturing plant and their compensable factors. In this first step, monetary values ranging from $3.54 to $7.00 have been assigned to the six key jobs.

In the second step, the evaluation committee rank-orders compensable factors according to their relative importance in each job. Though the committee may select its own compensable factors, the most commonly used are mental requirements, skill requirements, physical effort, responsibility, and working conditions. In the example, skill is ranked most important in the machinist's job and working conditions are least important. In the labourer's job, physical effort is most important and mental requirements are least important.

[10] *Classification and Selection Standard for the Personnel Administration Group* (Ottawa: Information Canada, 1975).

EXHIBIT 12.5

Monetary values assigned to key jobs and compensable factors

Job	*Monetary value of key job*	*Monetary value assigned to compensable factors*				
		Mental requirements	*Physical effort*	*Skill*	*Responsibility*	*Working conditions*
Machinist	$7.00	$ .98	$ .82	$3.72	$ .81	$ .67
Electrician	6.82	1.00	.94	3.13	.83	.92
Drill press operator	5.32	.82	.76	2.39	.75	.60
Inspector	4.79	.81	.63	2.24	.63	.48
Tool crib attendant	4.27	.60	1.03	1.35	.60	.69
Labourer	3.54	.45	1.02	.73	.46	.88

The third step involves the assignment of a monetary value to each factor for each key job so that the total equals the overall value assigned to the job in the first step. For example, of the $7.00 monetary value assigned to the machinist's job, $0.98 is allocated to mental requirements, $0.82 to physical effort, $3.72 to skill, $0.81 to responsibility, and $0.67 to working conditions.

The fourth step is development of job factor comparison scales based on information from step three. Exhibit 12.6 shows job factor comparison scales for physical effort, mental requirements, and skill for the key job in the machinery manufacturing plant. Note that each scale is weighted by the highest monetary value assigned to it. Skill is the most heavily weighted, and physical effort and mental requirements are weighted approximately equally. Thus, skill is the most important of the compensable factors.

EXHIBIT 12.6

Three job factor comparison scales

Monetary value	*Physical effort*	*Skill*	*Mental requirements*
$3.75		Machinist	
3.60			
3.45			
3.30			
3.15		Electrician	
3.00			
2.85			
2.70			
2.55			
2.40		Drill press operator	
2.25		Inspector	
2.10			
1.95			
1.80			
1.65			
1.50			
1.35		Tool crib attendant	
1.20			
1.05	Tool crib attendant		
	Labourer		Electrician
.90	Electrician		Machinist
	Machinist		Drill press operator
.75	Drill press operator	Labourer	Inspector
.60	Inspector		Tool crib attendant
.45			Labourer

The final step in the factor comparison method is to use the factor comparison scales to evaluate other, non-key jobs in the organization.

There are advantages to this method. First, it "fits" the organization very well because it must be custom-built by each employer. Second, it is easy to use because evaluators rate jobs in terms of well-known jobs in their own organization.

The factor comparison method also has several disadvantages. The most important is that as the content of key jobs changes, the system becomes less accurate. And this method may formalize any existing pay inequities since it assumes that the existing pay rates for key jobs are correct. Finally, the complexity of the factor comparison method makes it difficult for employees to understand and accept.

This method is limited primarily to manufacturing and manual, blue-collar jobs. The disadvantages mentioned above, as well as the applicability of the method to a declining occupational group, mean that factor comparison is not commonly used. In fact, the authors of one compensation text have estimated that this method is used by less than 10 per cent of all employers using formal job evaluation.[11]

Point method. The most complex and yet most frequently used of the major job evaluation methods is the *point method*, which is similar to the factor comparison method in that separate scales are developed for each compensable factor. The two methods differ primarily in that the factor comparison method is based upon a set of key jobs existing in one organization at one point in time, while the point method is independent of jobs in a particular organization. Since point systems are usually not unique to a specific organization, they are used in many ready-made job evaluation systems.

Scales based on the point method are more precise and accurate than factor comparison scales because point systems use universal compensable factors which are further divided into subfactors and degrees. *Universal factors* are compensable factors common to many different jobs in an occupational group, such as management or manual labour jobs. Typically, the factors receive different weights to reflect greater or lesser degrees of importance, as compared to other factors. A common method of assigning different weights to factors is by allocating a larger number of maximum possible points to one factor as opposed to another. For example, if a job evaluation system had 1,000 possible points, a professional services employer, such as a CPA firm, might emphasize responsibility by assigning 400 points to the highest level of responsibility, 300 to skill, 200 to effort, and 100 to working conditions.

One example of a ready-made point system from the U.S. is the American Association of Industrial Management's National Position Evaluation Plan. As shown in Exhibit 12.7, it has four universal factors: (1) skill; (2) effort; (3) responsibility; (4) job conditions. Each of these

[11] A.N. Nash and S.J. Carroll, Jr. *The Management of Compensation* (Belmont, Calif.: Wadsworth, 1975).

factors is further divided into subfactors. For example, "skill" is divided into the subfactors "knowledge," "experience," and "initiative and ingenuity." Subfactors are further divided into degrees which are defined so that the job evaluator can determine how much of each is present in the job or jobs being evaluated. Under the National Position Evaluation Plan, each degree of a subfactor has a fixed point value. For example, a job with fifth-degree knowledge requirements receives a point value of 70; a job with first-degree knowledge requirements receives a point value of 14.

The point values assigned to each subfactor of a job are then totalled across factors, allowing jobs to be placed in a hierarchy according to their total point value. For pay administration purposes, jobs within certain point ranges are grouped together and assigned labour grades.

The federal government uses the point method, also called point-rating, to evaluate some of its jobs. One reviewer explained, "In general, point-rating is used where the duties and responsibilities of positions in an occupational group or sub-group are heterogeneous. Level description is used if they tend to be homogeneous."[12]

The point method is the most accurate of the job evaluation systems. It remains relatively stable over time, unlike the factor comparison method, whose key jobs are subject to change. The accuracy and comprehensiveness of the point method mean that employee acceptance is relatively high, increasing the chances that workers will perceive their pay as internally equitable. One disadvantage of the method is that administrative costs may be too high to justify its use in small and medium-size organizations.

Market pricing. The *market pricing method* is entirely different from the other four methods of job evaluation; it relies entirely on the labour market to determine how much jobs should be paid. It is not concerned with internal equity of pay, compensable factors, or assigning relative worth to jobs except in relation to the going rate in the labour market. In order to evaluate jobs using the market pricing method, an employer must conduct a pay survey to determine the market price for each job.

The market pricing method may be impractical for a number of reasons. First, going rates may vary depending upon what comparison firms are included in the survey. The inclusion or exclusion of one high or low-paying firm in the pay survey, for example, could make hundreds of dollars difference in pay for a job. Second, it may prove difficult to obtain pay information about some of the less common jobs in an organization. Third, market prices of jobs vary from time to time, making it difficult to maintain a stable pay structure or predict labour costs with this method. Finally, the market pricing method may cause problems with internal equity, especially for persons in jobs for which demand has declined. When demand declines, the going rate for the job declines. This situation could actually result in pay *reductions* for

[12] L.J. Nozzolillo, "The Classification and Pay System in the Public Service of Canada," *The Labour Gazette*, May 1976, p. 262.

EXHIBIT 12.7

Point system of the American Association of Industrial Management

Points assigned to factor degrees and range for grades

Factor	1st Degree	2nd Degree	3rd Degree	4th Degree	5th Degree
Skill					
1. Knowledge	14	28	42	56	70
2. Experience	22	44	66	88	110
3. Initiative and ingenuity	14	28	42	56	70
Effort					
4. Physical demand	10	20	30	40	50
5. Mental or visual demand	5	10	15	20	25
Responsibility					
6. Equipment or process	5	10	15	20	25
7. Material or product	5	10	15	20	25
8. Safety of others	5	10	15	20	25
9. Work of others	5	10	15	20	25
Job conditions					
10. Working conditions	10	20	30	40	50
11. Hazards	5	10	15	20	25

Score Range	Grades	Score Range	Grades
139 and under	12	250–271	6
140–161	11	272–293	5
162–183	10	294–315	4
184–205	9	316–337	3
206–227	8	338–359	2
228–249	7	360–381	1

SOURCE: Midwest Industrial Management Association, Westchester, Illinois.

1. Knowledge

This factor measures the knowledge or equivalent training required to perform the position duties.

1st Degree

Use of reading and writing, adding and subtracting of whole numbers; following of instructions; use of fixed gauges, direct reading instruments and similar devices; where interpretation is not required.

2nd Degree

Use of addition, subtraction, multiplication and division of numbers including decimals and fractions; simple use of formulas, charts, tables, drawings, specifications, schedules, wiring diagrams; use of adjustable measuring instruments; checking of reports, forms, records and comparable data; where interpretation is required.

3rd Degree

Use of mathematics together with the use of complicated drawings, specifications, charts, tables; various types of precision measuring instruments. Equivalent to 1 to 3 years applied trades training in a particular or specialized occupation.

4th Degree

Use of advanced trades mathematics, together with the use of complicated drawings, specifications, charts, tables, handbook formulas; all varieties of precision measuring instruments. Equivalent to complete accredited apprenticeship in a recognized trade, craft or occupation; or equivalent to a 2 year technical college education.

5th Degree

Use of higher mathematics involved in the application of engineering principles and the performance of related practical operations, together with a comprehensive knowledge of the theories and practices of mechanical, electrical, chemical, civil or like engineering field. Equivalent to complete 4 years of technical college or university education.

some employees. Furthermore, many employees might be disturbed to know that their pay is determined by the going rate in the labour market and not by factors more under their control.

The theoretical advantage of the market pricing method is that employees are paid their market value and employers can obtain needed labour at current market prices. In reality, use of market pricing is probably limited to both unskilled, nonunion labour and independent professionals, such as lawyers and architects. Market forces were used to some employers' advantage in the recent recession when they negotiated wage concessions from unions.

Job evaluation methods are summarized in Exhibit 12.8.

Pricing the Pay Structure: Assigning Pay to Jobs

The result of any job evaluation process is a hierarchy of jobs in terms of their relative value to the organization. The practice of assigning pay to this hierarchy of jobs is called pricing the pay structure. This practice involves a number of policy issues including: (1) how the organization's pay levels relate to the market; (2) what the organization pays for; (3) how it pays; and (4) what steps the organization takes to assure that pay is administered in a bias-free manner.[13]

How should an organization's pay levels relate to the market? An organization can choose to be a wage leader, to match the going rates in the market, or to pay less than the market. We have already discussed implications of this policy decision for the recruiting and selection functions. An implication of the earlier discussion is that the wage policy decision is substantially affected by an employer's ability to pay high wages. Ability to pay is related to many factors, including profitability, industry, organization size, and others. Some employers recognize the need to be wage leaders for some occupations or jobs that are vital to their business, while they cannot afford to be wage leaders for all jobs. In such situations a mixed wage policy may be adopted in which a firm is a wage leader for some jobs, while only matching the going rate for others. Though a mixed wage policy has the advantage of controlling labour costs, it runs the risk of creating internal inequity.

What does an organization want to pay for? Most organizations use a combination of factors, with job content being a major one. Basing pay on job content means that rates are determined on the basis of the presence of certain compensable factors in jobs. Once pay rates for jobs have been established, individuals may receive increases based on other factors, such as seniority, performance, and cost of living.

How does an organization pay? Basically, an organization has to decide whether to have a single rate or a range of pay for each job. A

[13]American Society of Personnel Administration/American Compensation Association, *Elements of Sound Base Pay Administration* (Scottsdale, Ariz.: American Compensation Association and ASPA, 1981).

EXHIBIT 12.8

Major job evaluation methods

Method	*What facet of job is evaluated?*	*How is job evaluated?*	*Type of method*	*Major advantage(s)*	*Major disadvantage(s)*
Ranking	Whole job (compensable factors are implicit)	Ordered subjectively according to relative worth	Non-quantitative	Relatively quick and inexpensive	Entirely subjective
Level description	Whole job	Compared to descriptions of job grades	Non-quantitative	Readily available and inexpensive	Cumbersome system
Factor comparison	Compensable factors of job	Compared to key jobs on scales of compensable factors	Quantitative	Easy to use	Hard to construct; inaccurate over time
Point method	Compensable factors of job	Compared to standardized descriptions of degrees of universal compensable factors and subfactors	Quantitative	Accurate and stable over time	May be costly
Market pricing method	Whole job	Compared to similar jobs in terms of going rate of pay	Quantitative	Avoids management bias; simple to use	Promotes instability of pay structure; may lead to perceived inequities

single rate of pay means that all employees in a job receive the same rate of pay regardless of other factors. In practice, single pay rates are rare. Most employers prefer to use pay ranges, which allow for variations in pay to individuals in the same job. Such variations can be based on differences in performance, on employee qualifications, and/or on seniority. Whatever the basis for difference in pay between employees in the same pay grade, they must be perceived as fair in order to maintain employee equity. When pay ranges are used, an employer must decide the basis both for starting pay and for how employees progress through pay ranges. Once such policy decisions have been made, pay can be assigned to the hierarchy of jobs.

Pricing jobs is difficult because there are many factors to be taken into consideration. For example, the American Society of Personnel Administration (ASPA) says, "The resulting pay structure should reflect the organization's objectives; the market place; internal job values; the mix of pay and benefits; its philosophy on how it wishes to pay versus the market; compensation policies, practices, and procedures; the entity's approach to organizational structure; and the economic ability of the organization to pay at a given level."[14] While the complexities of pricing jobs are beyond the scope of this book, we can discuss the basics of developing a pay structure.

In developing a pay structure, similar jobs are grouped together in pay grades. Pay grades determine the magnitude of difference between levels of work and make compensation administration easier for employers. But employees must perceive the pay grades as equitable, and this can be a problem because jobs in the same pay grade can be fairly different from one another. For example, a secretary, a security guard, and an assembler may be in the same pay grade.

A major decision is determining the number of pay grades in the structure. Two factors affecting this decision are the number of different work levels the organization chooses to recognize and the difference in compensation for the highest-paid and the lowest-paid jobs in the pay structure. The larger the difference, the more grades the organization needs. The number of pay grades in an organization also has implications for employees' career advancement. A pay structure with relatively few grades provides limited financial incentives for advancement.

Each grade has a midpoint and a range of pay. The *midpoint* is usually paid to an employee who is performing at an acceptable and fully competent level; it is usually determined by wage survey data from similar jobs. The *pay range* defines the upper and lower limits of pay for jobs in a grade. Individual levels of pay within the range reflect differences in seniority and/or performance. The size of a pay range may vary, but it is often about 20 per cent from the midpoint in both directions. For example, if the midpoint for a secretary is $12,000 per year, the pay range might be $9,600 to $14,400. In many organizations, the size of the pay range increases for higher-level jobs. For example, a pay range of 30 per cent from the midpoint may be used

[14] Ibid., p. 13.

for supervisors. The rationale is that higher-level jobs have a greater performance potential and that employees tend to remain in higher-level positions longer.

Most employers have some degree of overlap among their pay grades. The highest-paid employees in one pay grade may receive more than the lowest-paid of the next-higher grade. Such an overlap allows an organization to reward employees for performance or seniority without promoting them.

Developing a basic pay structure usually has to be done only once, but periodic assessments must be made to determine the competitive position of the pay structure over time. One way to compare two or more organizations' wage or pay levels is to portray each one's pay grades graphically and draw a line between the midpoints. This line, called a *pay policy line*, represents an organization's pay level. The pay policy lines can then be compared to ascertain each organization's competitive position in the labour market. A common way organizations respond to increases in cost of living or competitors' pay increases is simply to raise their pay policy line. This results in an increase in the midpoints of pay ranges.

Exhibit 12.9 is a graphic portrayal of one firm's pay grades and their pay policy line. In this case, although there is some overlap between pay grades, the size of the pay range does not increase for higher-level jobs.

Using Pay to Motivate Employees

Most employees are paid for their time or the number of hours they work. In this case, pay is not contingent upon levels of individual performance. What, then, motivates employees to perform even to acceptable levels?

Employees can be motivated by their boss, by co-workers, or by the nonfinancial rewards of work, such as intrinsic satisfaction derived from the job. This section deals with an alternative approach to motivating employees: pay for performance.

Pay for performance means that an employee's pay is contingent upon some level of performance specified by the organization. There are three basic approaches to pay for performance. The first is *merit pay*, in which pay increases are based on subjective evaluations of employees' performance. In determing merit pay for individual employees, superiors usually fill out performance evaluation forms, such as those described in Chapter 10.

The second approach makes promotion to higher-paying jobs contingent upon superior performance. Again, superior performance is usually judged by the employee's boss, using a system of performance appraisal. This approach is most commonly used for white-collar, professional, and managerial employees. As a pay-for-performance method, promotions have two major disadvantages. First, employees

EXHIBIT 12.9

One organization's pay grades and pay policy line

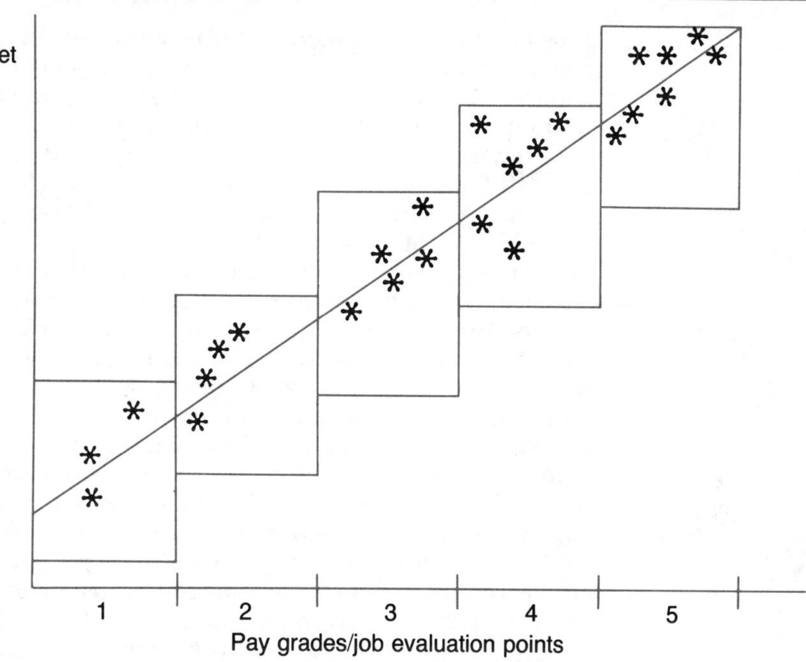

SOURCE: American Society of Personnel Administration/American Compensation Association, *Elements of Sound Base Pay Administration* (American Compensation Association, Scottsdale, Ariz. and ASPA, Berea, Ohio, 1981).

compete against one another for promotions, which may reduce cooperation among employees. Second, a high level of performance may not lead to promotion because such opportunities are limited. In many Canadian organizations, there are likely to be less promotion opportunities than in the past due to leaner organizations with flatter structures, fewer retirements due to successful early retirement programs, and lower turnover due to high unemployment.

The third approach to linking pay to performance is to make pay directly proportionate to criteria such as the number of units produced, sales volume, or the profitability of the organization. This type of system is called an incentive pay system because the level of monetary reward associated with different levels of performance is specified in advance.

If linking pay to performance is to be useful in motivating employees, the work situation must meet five conditions:

1. The jobs must have the potential for meaningful performance variation.
2. Employees must have—and *believe* they have—the ability to perform at higher levels.

3. Employees must be motivated by money.
4. Employees must perceive an equitable pay-effort bargain.
5. Employees must perceive that the system is fairly administered.

Jobs must have the potential for meaningful variations in performance if pay is to be used as a motivator. Some jobs have very little of this potential because of their narrow scope and/or because employees have limited control over work activities. For example, jobs with a low standard deviation of performance (SD_y) have little potential for variation. In such jobs, performance variations have relatively little impact on the firm's profitability. Examples include library assistants, janitors, and garbage collectors. A job with a low SD_y is not a good candidate for an incentive pay system because performance cannot be greatly influenced by linking it to pay. On the other hand, a job with a high SD_y may be an effective place to link pay to performance. For example, significant differences in performance can result if pay is used to motivate sales representatives, human resource and production managers, and individually-paced production workers.

Pay-for-performance systems are useful only if employees have the ability to peform at higher levels and believe that they can achieve higher levels of performance. Since performance is a combination of abilities and effort, pay-for-performance systems have only limited effectiveness with low-ability employees. This points up the importance of the recruiting and selection functions in hiring high-ability employees and of the training function in developing skills. Employees themselves must believe that they have the abilities necessary to perform at higher levels. If employees do not believe this, they will not be motivated to achieve higher levels of pay.

Pay-for-performance systems offer employees the opportunity to obtain money beyond their standard level of pay. To be useful as a motivator of performance, money must be a valued reward. Individuals differ in the value they assign to money. Even employees who view money as a valued reward may choose not to pursue it because they value other rewards or outcomes more highly.

People are motivated by money for many different reasons. The need to provide the basic necessities of life motivates most people. Some also view money as instrumental in satisfying noneconomic needs, such as status, power, and affiliation with desired groups. It is often seen as a symbol of personal success and achievement.

The power of money to motivate individuals varies from time to time. A survey of over 5,000 MBA magazine readers reported that money was the most important thing wanted from a career by the 35 to 39 age group but not by the under 30s or the over 45s.[15] For some employees, money is a more powerful motivator in times of greater financial need. One Canadian manufacturer found that employees transferred into and out of pay-for-performance jobs as a function of their need to pay for large items they had purchased. Although em-

[15] "MBAs Look at Their World," *MBA*, July/August 1977.

ployees must value money if pay-for-performance systems are to be effective, employers have very little control over this factor.

Employees must also feel that the additional pay offered is worth any extra effort they have to expend to get it. The ratio of pay to effort is known as the *pay-effort bargain*. Each employee has a certain ratio of exchange between pay and effort which he or she considers equitable. For example, one employee may believe it is fair to be paid $1 for each unit produced above standard, while another employee may perceive that amount to be too low and hence unfair. The employee who perceives the ratio of pay to effort as unfair may have a lower level of ability which would require him or her to exert more effort to produce each additional unit. How an employee perceives the pay-effort bargain is also influenced by how much the employee needs and desires money.

Management determines the amounts of additional pay offered to different levels of performance on the basis of product costs, considering the value of additional production in relation to the costs of the pay-for-performance system. Such considerations set upper limits on what an employer can pay for higher levels of performance and additional levels of production.

A final condition to be met in using pay to motivate performance is that employees must perceive that the system is administered fairly. They must believe that if they achieve the specified levels of performance, they will receive the promised rewards. The method of measuring performance must be reliable and valid. If performance measures are inconsistent or inaccurate, employees regard the system with distrust and suspicion.

Employees working under pay-for-performance systems often fear that standards will be raised if they consistently produce at high levels or earn too much. These fears are heightened by the changes that the introduction of new equipment and methods frequently requires in these systems. When such changes become necessary, employees must fully understand them and why they are necessary. One way of facilitating understanding is to involve employees via compensation committees in decisions affecting their pay.

Pay-for-performance systems are summarized in Exhibit 12.10.

Merit Pay Systems

The most commonly used pay-for-performance system is merit pay. Under merit pay systems, superiors make subjective appraisals of their subordinates' performance. These appraisals are then used to determine the magnitude of an employee's pay increase. Merit pay systems have been criticized by many authors as unreliable, invalid, and unfair.[16] Additionally, the size of merit budgets fluctuates, increasing in good times and decreasing in lean times. This means that the amount

[16] N.B. Winstanley, "Are Merit Increases Really Effective?" *Personnel Administrator*, April 1982, pp. 37–41.

EXHIBIT 12.10

Summary of pay-for-performance systems

Level of performance measurement	*Types of plans*	*Method of pay determination*
Individual	Merit	Performance appraisal data Merit guidechart
	Promotion	Performance appraisal data
	Straight piece rate	# units produced × $ per unit
	Standard hour plan	Standard time for task × hourly rate of pay
Group	Group piece rate or group standard hour plans	Same as individual plans, but members receive equal pay
Company	Gain sharing plans — Scanlon — Rucker	Employees share in cost savings in proportion to their job classification or pay
	Profit sharing plans — Current distribution — Deferred payment — Combination	Employees receive some portion of profit based on set formula

of merit pay an employee receives may depend more on the financial status of the employer than on the employee's performance.

Assuming that an employer has an adequate performance appraisal system, some mechanism must be developed to translate appraisals into merit increases. One frequently used mechanism is the merit increase guidechart. Guidecharts, which are developed by individual employers, vary in complexity, but most include two dimensions: performance level and position in the pay range relative to the midpoint of the pay range. Position in the pay range (whether above or below the midpoint) is important because employers use this information to assign pay and control compensation costs. For example, most employers try to move excellent performers to the midpoint of the pay range rapidly, whereas employees above the midpoint generally receive smaller percentage pay increases in order not to exceed the pay range maximum. Therefore, as shown in the example of a simplified guidechart in Exhibit 12.11, employees below the pay range midpoint receive larger merit raises than those above the midpoint. Excellent performers at the top of the pay range are prime candidates for promotion.

Note that in the guidechart, performance level is specified in terms of distribution of performance, from below average (bottom 10%), to average (70%), to excellent (top 20%). A Conference Board of Canada survey found that over 75 per cent of the surveyed firms had a perfor-

EXHIBIT 12.11

A simple merit increase guidechart

Current Salary	*Below average performance (lowest 10%)*	*Average performance (middle 70%)*	*Excellent performance (upper 20%)*
Above midpoint	0	4%	8%
Below midpoint	0	5%	10%

mance appraisal system that linked pay to performance. This same survey found that more than one-third of the firms that linked pay to performance used a forced distribution system which limited the proportion of above-average pay increases that could be given.[17] While performance level and position in the pay range are important to merit pay decisions, other factors, such as financial resources and state of the labour market, may also affect decisions.

Incentive Pay Systems

All incentive pay systems link pay directly to measured job outcomes. Such systems can be categorized in terms of the level at which performance is measured, including (1) individual-level; (2) group-level; and (3) plant-wide or company-level. In each case, additional pay is awarded when the performance or production levels exceed some minimum specified by the organization.

Individual-level incentive pay systems. Under an individual-level system, employees who perform at minimal levels receive their standard pay for the job, but those who perform above these levels receive incentive pay. Two common examples of individual incentive pay plans are the straight piece rate and the standard hour plan. Standard hour plans are used when the time to complete one unit is relatively long, while piece rates are used for parts which can be rapidly made.

For straight piece rates, pay is determined by multiplying the number of units produced by a number of dollars or cents. If, for example, a job pays $0.50 per unit and an employee produces 100 units, he or she earns $50. Piecework is the most frequently used incentive system because it is the most easily understood and accepted by employees. One disadvantage of this method is that setting the rate of pay requires careful study and must often be negotiated with the union. And, since the rate is expressed in monetary terms, it must be changed whenever wage rates are increased.

[17] S.R. Luce, "Paying for Performance," *The Canadian Business Review*, Winter 1983, pp. 19–22.

The standard hour method is essentially the same, but standards are set in terms of hours. Industrial engineers determine standard times to complete various jobs or tasks. Also specified is the amount an employee is to be paid for the standard level or 100 per cent of production. For example, if the standard for assembling a compact disc player is 30 minutes and assemblers work eight hours, 16 players should be assembled in an eight-hour day. Assuming employees are paid $10 per hour, an employee assembling the standard 16 would earn $80. The standard hour plan rewards faster employees by paying them at their hourly rate for additional units produced. Thus, an employee assembling four units above standard in an eight-hour day would be paid for two extra hours of production, or a total of $100.

The John Deere Company, a major U.S. manufacturer of construction and farm equipment, has had great success with the standard hour system. It is not uncommon to find some Deere employees producing consistently at 150 to 180 per cent of standard. The company's success with the system has come about through use of a large staff of well-trained industrial engineers who have developed and monitored the system.

Incentive pay systems have proven effective in increasing productivity. Conservative estimates indicate that they can increase productivity by 10 to 20 per cent.[18] Because the link between individual performance and incentive pay is most direct in individual incentive systems, they result in larger increases in productivity than do group or company-wide systems. However, individual incentive pay systems are costly to set up and to monitor. Further, they are limited to jobs in which individual performance can be measured objectively and to jobs which require little interdependency of workers to accomplish a common task.

Individual wage incentive systems are becoming less common in Canada. Data on collective agreements covering 500 or more employees in industries other than construction showed that the percentage with wage incentive provisions declined from 19.8 to 13.7 per cent between 1973 and 1980. Similarly the number of employees covered by such provisions declined during this period from 14.5 to 11.9 per cent.[19] The economic woes faced by many Canadian employers in the early 1980s may, however, result in a reversal of this trend as employers seek ways to both increase productivity and control labour costs.

Group-level incentive pay systems. If it proves difficult or impossible to measure individual output or if the need for cooperation within work groups is high, employers can use group-level incentive pay systems. Such a system links incentive pay to group performance. All members of a work group receive the same amount of incentive pay, which is determined by the level of group output. The measurement of output

[18] E.E. Lawler III, *Motivation in Work Organizations* (Monterey, Calif.: Brooks/Cole Publishing Company, 1973).

[19] W.D. Wood and Pradeep Kumar, eds, *The Current Industrial Relations Scene in Canada, 1981* (Kingston, Ont.: Industrial Relations Centre, Queen's University, 1981), p. 352.

is similar to that used for individual incentive systems, but what is measured represents the collective efforts of a number of workers.

Research shows that the productivity gains of group-level incentive systems are not as high as those of individual-level systems. One explanation is that as the size of the work group increases, each employee has less influence on the output. Thus, the relationships between any one individual's effort and the group's performance and pay are less direct than the relationships between individual effort and individual performance and pay. If an employee feels that he or she is working harder than another member of the work group, feelings of inequity are created. If an employee resolves this inequity by reducing his or her contribution, the group's performance will suffer. While gains in productivity are higher under individual-level systems, group-level incentive systems are usually less expensive to administer. Research has shown that productivity levels under group incentive systems are higher than productivity levels in organizations with no incentive pay system.[20]

Plant-wide or company systems. Plant-wide or company systems base incentive pay on the performance and organizational results of all employees. The goal of plant-wide systems is not only to motivate employees, but also to improve cooperation and participation in organizational decision-making. Plant-wide incentive systems are appropriate where individual-level incentive systems have failed or are not possible, where close supervision and close monitoring of quality is difficult, and particularly where cooperation and teamwork are important to organizational success.

There are two basic types of plant-wide systems: gain sharing plans and profit sharing plans. Gain sharing plans share productivity gains and/or cost savings with employees; profit sharing plans provide employees with some share of a company's profits.

Gain sharing plans. All gain sharing plans are similar but use different formulas to calculate productivity or labour savings. Unlike individual incentive systems, the amount an individual receives is based on his or her job grade or classification, rather than on contribution. Thus, all employees in the same job receive the same amount of incentive pay, and employees in lower-paying jobs receive a smaller share of the incentive pay fund than do those in higher-paying jobs.

Two well-known gain-sharing plans are the Scanlon and the Rucker plans, which have similar formulas for calculating labour savings, though the Rucker formula is somewhat more complex. We will discuss only the Scanlon Plan here. In the Scanlon Plan, a ratio of the total labour costs to the sales value of production is obtained from past company data. If, through suggestions, changes, and effort, employees either reduce payroll costs or increase production, they receive a share of the resulting savings.[21] The amount an individual employee receives is based on his or her job classification and pay.

[20] E.E. Lawler III, p. 111.

[21] B.E. Moore, "A Plant-wide Productivity Plan in Action: Three Years of Experience with the Scanlon Plan" (Washington, D.C.: National Center for Productivity and Quality of Working Life, 1975).

The Scanlon Plan requires two committees: a production committee and a screening committee. A production committee, which includes several employees and a management representative, is usually installed in each major department. Its function is to produce suggestions for improvements and cost reductions. The screening committee consists of members of top management and worker representatives who discuss problems and changes in the plan and the company's competitive position. Labour's share of the savings, usually 50 to 75 per cent, is often a matter for bargaining with management.

Gain sharing plans, such as the Scanlon and Rucker plans, work best when high levels of interdependence are necessary between employees and departments, and when individual or small-group incentive systems are too difficult or costly to install. Case studies suggest that such systems are successful in small organizations which have stable product lines, good supervisors and good union-management relations, and committed top managers who are willing to work with employees on problems.[22]

Profit sharing plans. Profit sharing plans have been in existence for nearly 100 years, but have only recently received renewed interest. There are three basic types of profit sharing plans: the current distribution or cash plan; the deferred payout plan; and the plan combining both cash and deferred payout. Discussion of current distribution plans is appropriate to this chapter.

Current distribution plans distribute some portion of company profits in cash or stock to eligible employees on a regular basis, such as quarterly or annually. For example, ISECO Safety Shoes, distributes profit shares quarterly to get "maximum psychological benefit from the payment."[23]

One of the foremost advocates of all forms of profit sharing, Don Nightingale, Professor of Management at Queen's University, argues that there is a need for such plans in today's economy. Specifically, he views profit sharing as an important means to greater participation, cooperation, and commitment in organizations.[24] Higher levels of commitment and cooperation are likely to make Canadian businesses more competitive with foreign companies.

A survey of 83 member firms of the Proft Sharing Council of Canada found profit sharing an excellent means of improving employee morale as well as profitability. And 84 per cent of the surveyed firms said that the plan was a good means of attracting and retaining desirable employees.[25]

While most profit sharing plans are deferred plans, which often

[22] T.H. Patten, Jr., *Pay: Employee Compensation and Incentive Plans* (New York: The Free Press, 1977).

[23] W. Lilley, "More Money," *Canadian Business*, April 1985, pp. 48–62.

[24] D. Nightingale, "Profit Sharing: New Nectar for the Worker Bees," *The Canadian Business Review*, Spring 1984, pp. 11–14.

[25] D. Nightingale, *Workplace Democracy* (Toronto: University of Toronto Press, 1982), pp. 159–60.

EXHIBIT 12.12

Profit sharing at IPSCO Inc.

Until this past winter, Roger Phillips, the gruff CEO of Ipsco Inc. of Regina, was not a fan of profit-sharing plans. Since developing his own profit-sharing scheme, however, Phillips has become a believer. And if the steel manufacturer's novel program works as well as he envisions, its components may soon turn up in other companies' compensation programs as well.

One of the approaches that Phillips found attractive was the idea that profits could be shared in the form of Ipsco stock instead of cash. Equally appealing was the idea of getting participants to contribute money to the profit pool used to buy Ipsco shares. "We think people will appreciate the plan more if their own money is invested," says Phillips. Ipsco asks profit-sharing participants to put from $200 to $500 of their own money into the plan through payroll deductions. The employees' money is then put together with the profit-sharing pool to buy Ipsco shares on the open market. The $200 contributor gets two-fifths of the shares allotted to a $500 contributor. "Most employees can handle that much," says Phillips, "and those who are eligible can shield their share purchase in a group registered retirement savings plan, so there's a tax deduction involved."

The Ipsco plan differs from conventional approaches in other ways as well. For one thing, all participants share equally in the profits. "Most plans divide up what's going to be shared according to salary," says Phillips. "But that means the more you make, the more you earn from profit sharing, and we didn't think that was necessarily equitable." Another uncommon variation is that the shares bought by the plan are vested right away. "Naturally, we hope they hang on," Phillips says. "But employees are able to sell their shares at any time."

One of Phillips' initial objections to profit-sharing plans was the suggestion by some consultants that there should be a guaranteed payout whether there were profits or not. He has skirted that condition and, at the same time, attempted to impress profit-sharing participants with the role of Ipsco's nonemployee shareholders who risked investment money in the company. "Most of the plans we looked at designate a certain percent of profit for sharing, but they start at zero," says Phillips. "We recognize that our shareholders have first call on dividends, so we based our pool formula on after-tax dollars less dividends; 10% of that net figure is allocated to the profit-sharing plan." Of course, once the Ipsco plan is up and running, employees will benefit from those dividends.

SOURCE: From "More Money," by Wayne Lilley, *Canadian Business*, April 1985, p. 55. Reprinted by permission of the author.

substitute for pensions, both types of plan have been growing rapidly. Exhibit 12.12 describes the profit sharing plan of IPSCO Inc. of Regina. The IPSCO plan illustrates both some typical and some unique features of profit sharing plans.

Profit sharing plans are appropriate in many situations, but are likely to be unsuccessful when profit levels fluctuate substantially from year to year due to factors beyond the control of employees and managers. Profit sharing may also not work well in capital-intensive industries or in large organizations.[26] However, a number of large organizations have used profit sharing successfully.

The many different plant and company-wide incentive pay systems all have the disadvantage of a weak link between each employee's efforts and his or her share of the incentive pay fund. Also, some methods are complex and difficult to explain to employees. Incentive pay may be relatively infrequent; when it comes, it is often included in a regular cheque, and the employee is unable to differentiate between regular pay and incentive pay, a fact that can reduce the ability of incentive pay to motivate employees. One way to overcome this disadvantage is to keep incentive pay separate from regular pay. For example, in the U.S., Procter and Gamble issues incentive pay cheques on a quarterly basis. It also communicates to employees the formula on which incentive pay is based. Clearly identifying incentive pay and making sure that employees know how they earned it is important to success of plant and company-wide incentive systems. Also, management's philosophy must encourage employee participation and sharing in organizational decisions.

Controlling Compensation Costs

Since compensation costs represent a major part of an employer's labour costs, minimizing them is one way to facilitate organizational effectiveness. Recessionary pressures and strong competitive pressures have made control of labour costs a major goal at many organizations. Efforts to control labour costs can create difficulties for the compensation objectives of attracting and retaining quality employees and effectively using pay to motivate employees toward higher levels of performance. Even when there is less pressure toward cost control, there are large differences between employers in terms of their ability to pay high wages.

Factors Affecting Budget Allocations

Whatever the size of an employer's compensation budget, certain portions of it must be allocated to wages and salaries, benefits, overtime, and special programs, such as pay-for-performance systems and attractive recruiting packages. The allocation of compensation funds to these areas is influenced by several factors: (1) laws and regulations affecting compensation; (2) unions; and (3) human resource policies. We have already seen how laws and regulations and unions pose constraints on compensation. Let us now consider the impact of human resource policies.

[26] Nightingale, 1984.

An organization's human resource policies have a major effect on how compensation is allocated since they determine the relative importance of alternative goals. For example, does an employer choose to be a wage leader and attract the best-qualified applicants, or to pay less and allocate the difference to an incentive pay system for the purpose of increasing productivity? In times of increased product demand, are compensation funds allocated to the hiring of new employees or are present employees paid overtime for extra hours worked? Such policy questions affect how compensation funds are allocated.

Although human resource policies influence the allocation of compensation dollars, these policies themselves are often influenced by budgetary constraints. Situations often arise that force employers to choose which human resource goals are most important to the organization.

A common conflict in human resource policies is that between offering competitive wages for hiring positions and maintaining internal equity. Organizations must offer competitive pay in order to attract adequate numbers of competent employees. However, a competitive hiring wage often conflicts with the goal of maintaining internal equity in the pay structure. The problem is caused by market forces pushing up the pay rates of certain jobs more rapidly than many employers can afford to increase the pay of experienced employees in the same or similar jobs. Thus, experienced employees often find themselves earning an amount very close to the starting pay of a new employee. This narrowing of the pay differentials between jobs is called *compression*. It often results in experienced employees' feeling that the pay structure is inequitable, that their years of experience and service count for very little. Compression was found to be a problem in 90 per cent of the organizations in a recent survey.[27] Ideally, employers would simply raise the pay of experienced employees to meet the higher rates of the labour market, but such a policy would greatly increase costs and would also disrupt internal pay relationships, which have been carefully constructed through job evaluation.

Monitoring Compensation Administration

After compensation budgets have been allocated, steps must be taken to ensure that the compensation system is achieving its goals and that compensation costs remain within allocated amounts. The mechanisms commonly used for this purpose include: (1) the compa-ratio and other indices, (2) budget, and (3) periodic audits of wages.

Compa-ratio and other indices. The compa-ratio is an index of the relationship of an employee's actual pay to the midpoint of their pay grade. In order to calculate a compa-ratio, divide current pay by the midpoint of the pay grade. This index may be used to indicate the

[27] R.W. Merry, "Labor Letter," *Wall Street Journal*, March 21, 1978.

relative position of an individual employee's pay or the relationship of the average employee pay to the pay grade midpoint. A compa-ratio for a company could also indicate the relationship between the average of all employees' pay to the average midpoint of all pay grades in the company. Though compa-ratios of 1.0 are often desirable, there are many valid reasons why the compa-ratio for a pay grade or company may be above or below 1.0. A compa-ratio of below 1.0 may result from many newly-hired employees in a pay grade, many poorly-performing employees, or rapid promotion of employees to higher pay grades. Compa-ratios of above 1.0 may result from the opposite conditions of low ratios, namely, many high-seniority employees, high-performing employees, low turnover, and slow promotions. A rapidly growing organization is more likely than a stable or declining organization to have low compa-ratios.

Other potential indices of the effectiveness of a company's compensation policies and practices include labour costs to total product or service costs, voluntary turnover rate, average number of applicants per vacancy, and the average length of time to fill a vacancy.

Budgets for managers. Managers can be required to hold compensation costs in their departments to specified limits. Within these limits, the managers must decide how to allocate funds among their subordinates. For example, if product demand increases, a manager can choose either to allocate funds to additional personnel or to pay present employees overtime for extra hours. Some employers have separate budgets for pay increases. Budgets often force managers to choose between rewarding high-performance employees with large pay increases and providing smaller increases to a larger number of employees. As a part of their cost control and performance appraisal systems, some organizations periodically review managerial decisions relating to pay increases. Such reviews also help maintain some degree of consistency in the compensation administration of managers in a single organization.

Periodic audits of wages and hours. Detailed records document proper and fair compensation practices and provide useful data for monitoring the way in which pay is used. For example, periodic audits may reveal incomplete or inaccurate compensation records or excessive use of overtime. Excessive use of overtime sometimes indicates that a particular department is not functioning as efficiently as it should. When compensation problems are discovered, steps can be taken to alleviate them.

Pay Equity

Pay equity, also known as *equal pay for work of equal value* or *comparable worth*, refers to the concept of paying equal wages to men and women for jobs of equal or comparable value to an employer. It is an extension of the concept of equal pay for equal work which underlies legislation prohibiting sex discrimination in pay for equal work on jobs requiring equal skill, effort, and responsibility performed under similar working conditions. Advocates of the concept of equal value have argued that employers should pay equal wages to employees who hold jobs that are substantially different but that have comparable economic value in order to abolish sex discrimination in pay that may be due to traditional or market-based pay differences between predominantly female- versus male-dominated jobs.

The application of pay equity legislation is illustrated in the following example from a clothing factory. Marg schedules and supervises the work of 15 sewing machine operators. Her job requires five years of experience and the ability to repair machines when they breakdown. She earns $20,000 a year. John ships the finished goods made in the factory. His job requires the ability to lift heavy boxes and no experience. He earns $23,000 a year. Under pay equity legislation, the employer of Marg and John would have to examine carefully how both salaries are determined. If it is decided that their work is of comparable worth, then they would have to be paid equally.[28]

The federal government, Quebec, and then Manitoba first introduced equal value (comparable worth) legislation. In 1986, Ontario proposed two pay equity bills, one to cover government employees and one to apply to the broader public sector and the private sector (Bill 154). In the spring of 1987, it was proposed that Ontario government employees be included within the coverage of Bill 154. The proposed legislation would be the most comprehensive in Canada. The key aspects of Bill 154 are the establishment of a criterion for determining value; tests for the achievement of pay equity; the requirement that the employer and the bargaining agent for employees negotiate a pay equity plan for the bargaining unit (in a nonunion situation the employer prepares the pay equity plan); and creation of a pay equity commission whose review officers would investigate and attempt to settle disputes between employers and bargaining agents or investigate objections and complaints concerning the implementation of plans.[29]

Opponents of pay equity fear that the legislation will result in increases in wages of billions of dollars without any increases in productivity.[30] Results to date elsewhere have shown increases in costs but less than anticipated. In Minnesota, a pay increase for 9,000 of the state's 29,000 employees raised state payroll costs by 3 per cent.[31] For the Government of Canada, the cost of a 1980 pay equity settlement covering 470 librarians was $2.3 million. This settlement between the Treasury Board and the Public Service Alliance of Canada followed an

[28] Patricia Orwen, "How Pay Equity Proposal Might Work. Three Examples Show Ways Companies Could Compute Work Values," *Toronto Star*, March 21, 1987.

[29] Ontario Women's Directorate, "Pay Equity Act 1986," Explanatory Notes.

[30] Joan Breckenridge, "Equal Pay's Unequal Effect," *The Globe and Mail Report on Business Magazine* (Toronto), December 1985, vol. 2, no. 6, pp. 110–18.

[31] R. Arnold, "Why Can't a Woman's Pay Be More Like a Man's?", *Business Week*, January 28, 1985, pp. 82–3.

equal pay for work of equal value complaint to the Canadian Human Rights Commission. The Commission approved the settlement, which included back pay for the two years from the day the Canadian Human Rights Act came into effect.

The Ontario Pay Equity Act would require employers to make annual adjustments in rates of compensation to at least 1 per cent of the employer's payroll for the preceding year until pay equity is achieved. It is important to note that the legislation does not attempt to raise women's wages in general, but only in those cases where women's jobs and men's jobs in the same factory, office, business, or public institution are of comparable value but command different salaries. The legislation only requires the preparation of pay equity plans by employers with at least 100 employees.

The Ontario Pay Equity Act was passed in the spring of 1987. Given the commitment of all three political parties to the concept of pay equity, it was certain that something would have been implemented. For HRM professionals, this means a key role in the evaluation of jobs and the preparation and implementation of pay equity plans.

Compensation Issues and Innovations

By its very nature, compensation is an HRM function subject to conflicting pressures from many sources, including management seeking to control labour costs, employees and unions seeking higher pay, the government seeking to control inflation and ensure minimum, nondiscriminating pay, and the forces of product and labour markets. From these conflicting pressures emerge problems such as cost of living adjustments and pressures to move away from a single wage system.

In the latter 1970s, inflation spiralled upwards, pushed in part by small or negative growth in productivity. Since employers' labour costs rose more quickly than they would have if productivity had increased, they kept raising prices in an effort to pass their added costs along to consumers. Then, the dramatic economic slump of 1981–82 made this pass-along more difficult. The result was pressure on workers to bring the growth rate of compensation below the inflation rate. For example, the federal government announced that it would hold its own employees' increases to 6 and 5 per cent respectively in 1982–83 and 1983–84; it pleaded with the private sector to do the same, and several provincial governments followed suit. Unionized workers met increased resistance at the bargaining table, resulting in smaller wage increases and benefits packages. Forecasts for the years to the mid-1980s predict a continuation of slow or negative productivity growth, so HRM professionals can expect a continuing need to monitor compensation costs closely.

A number of innovative compensation practices have developed over the past decade as organizations have changed to meet competitive and recessionary pressures. Examples of innovations include two-tier wage systems, lump sum pay increases, and skill-based pay.

Two-Tier Wage Systems

In the early 1980s, as a way of reducing labour costs, a number of unionized U.S. employers negotiated contracts with two-tier wage systems. Some Canadian employers followed the American lead. A two-tier system reduces starting pay for new employees hired after some date, while maintaining or raising pay for current employees. In some two-tier systems, the pay levels of newly hired employees never reach the level of current employees; in others, the two pay scales meet after a number of years.

The 1985 agreement between Sunbeam Corporation (Canada) and the United Electrical Workers is an example of a two-tier wage system in which the two scales do not meet. The agreement reduced the hiring rate for new employees by $2.00 an hour to $5.42. The 60 laid-off employees are to be recalled before there are any new hires.[32] Those persons who are recalled will return at their old rates. An example of a two-tier agreement in which the new hire rates rise toward the rates of previously hired employees is the 1986 agreement between Air Canada and the International Association of Machinists. New employees in eight unskilled jobs will have their starting pay reduced to $7.00 an hour for their first year. In the second year they will earn a rate half-way between $7.00 and the previous entry rate. After two years they will move to the previous entry rate and progress at six-month intervals from there.[33] The eight jobs are:

Job	*New entry rate*	*Old entry rate*
Cleaner blaster	$7.00	$10.42
Toolroom issuer	$7.00	$10.27
Cleaner	$7.00	$10.19
Commissary attendant	$7.00	$ 9.96
Building attendant	$7.00	$ 9.77
Station attendant	$7.00	$ 9.58
Stockkeeper	$7.00	$ 9.58
Cargo communications operator	$7.00	$ 8.09

Hughes Aircraft, which used a two-tier system, found that morale, productivity, and quality declined to such an extent that they had to raise starting pay and modify the plan. Other companies have had fewer difficulties, with more than 10 per cent reporting gains in productivity.[34] Two-tier wage systems are more likely to work when wages for new hires are generally competitive and when workers realize they would not have jobs if it weren't for the system.

[32] CLV Reports, *Facts and Trends in Labour Relations*, 1985.
[33] CLV Reports, *Facts and Trends in Labour Relations*, February 3, 1986.
[34] D. Wessel, "Split Personality," *Wall Street Journal*, October 14, 1985.

Lump Sum Pay

Lump sum pay means giving an employee the total annual dollars of his or her pay increase at one point in time. Compensation expert Edward E. Lawler III has argued for such increases as a way of making rewards for increased performance more visible to employees.[35] More recently, some employers have used lump sum increases as a cost control mechanism. By using lump sum pay rather than raising base pay by some fixed percentage, the employer is not committed to a higher base pay in the future. A compromise may be the best approach; for example, a small increase in base pay could be accompanied by a lump sum payment that is contingent upon accomplishment of a certain performance goal.

Skill-Based Pay

A final innovation, skill-based pay, is a substantial departure from the traditional job evaluation method of establishing pay differentials. In a skill-based pay system, employees are paid on the basis of the number and level of jobs they can perform. All new employees earn a starting rate until they have mastered one job. At this point, they are paid a "one-job" rate. The process continues until the employee has learned to perform all jobs in the organization, which entitles him or her to receive the highest rate of pay. Thus, employees are paid on the basis of what they know and the skills they possess, rather than on the particular job to which they are assigned. The advantage of this type of system is that it encourages employee growth and development and provides the organization with a skilled, flexible work force. The Gaines dog food plant in Topeka, Kansas was one of the first plants to use skill-based pay. Since this early 1970s experiment, a few companies, such as Shell Canada, have used skill-based pay in some form. Shell Canada's skill-based pay system, used in their Sarnia, Ontario chemical plant, is described in a case at the end of this chapter. One obvious disadvantage of skill-based pay is that labour costs may be relatively high if a large proportion of the work force has reached the top skill-pay level.

Summary

This chapter has discussed the role of compensation in facilitating the human resource goals of attracting, retaining, and motivating employees. The related activities of HRM professionals and compensation

[35] E.E. Lawler III, "Workers Can Set Their Own Wages—Responsibly," *Psychology Today*, February 1977, pp. 109–12.

specialists include pay surveys, job evaluations, pricing jobs, and pay-for-performance systems. As employees' needs and desires change and as organizations experience continuing competitive, technological, economic, and legal pressures, attaining the goals of attracting, retaining, and motivating employees will become increasingly difficult. HRM professionals must work with management to develop new and innovative pay methods to meet these goals while controlling compensation costs.

Project Ideas

1. Have you ever experienced dissatisfaction with pay or other rewards received from an employer? Discuss your experience. Why were you dissatisfied? Describe your dissatisfaction in terms of the ratio of exchange between inputs and outcomes. To whom did you compare yourself? What could your employer have done to alleviate the inequitable situation? What did he or she do? What could you have done to resolve the inequity? What did you do?

2. Search through recent newspapers or news magazines for incidents revealing workers' dissatisfaction with pay or other rewards. Find at least three incidents related to dissatisfaction with different aspects of pay—for example, the amount of pay, the form of pay (direct versus benefits), the administration of pay (not receiving due pay or other rewards). For each incident, describe the nature of the complaint, the employees' demands, and the resolution of the situation, if any. Note the type of employee making the complaint (labour type, sex, individual or group, union or nonunion). What would be the implications for the organization of meeting the employees' demands as stated?

3. Interview a compensation manager or HRM professional who has major compensation responsibilities. Ask about pay problems he or she has encountered. How have they been handled? If a number of students do this project, half should visit unionized employers and half nonunionized. If different types of organizations are visited, a range of compensation problems should be revealed. This variety can be demonstrated to the class as a whole by each student's giving a brief oral report.

4. One major issue in compensation is whether pay rates or levels for jobs should be open or secret. Some employers feel so strongly about keeping pay secret that they have policies prohibiting employees from discussing pay; in some cases, workers have been fired for talking about their pay with others. Research regarding the effects of open and secret pay has not provided definitive answers on which is the better approach. Discuss in a short report the possible pros and cons of each approach. Do not limit your discussion to the compensation area; include the implications of open and secret pay

for other HRM functions, such as career planning, training and development, worker satisfaction, and so on. If several students choose this project, a debate could be arranged.

5. Several organizations, including a Shell plant in Sarnia, Ont., and four Procter and Gamble plants, have used a new basis for pay called *skill evaluation*. Skill-based evaluation plans pay employees for their job-related skills and abilities, rather than for hours worked or units produced. A new employee working under a skill-based plan begins at a standard rate. After mastering several jobs in the plant, he or she moves to a higher rate of pay. When all the production jobs in the plant have been mastered, the employee receives the top rate. Additional pay can be obtained through a specialty rate, which rewards an employee for expertise in a skilled trade, such as electricity, or a technical area, such as computer programming. This system requires much job rotation so that employees can learn the various jobs. At the Shell plant in Sarnia, members of an employee's work team decide when the employee should receive a higher rate of pay. Discuss the pros and cons of the skill-based approach as opposed to the traditional approach in which pay is based primarily on the characteristics and demands of the job rather than on the person. Evaluate each approach in terms of the four human resource compensation goals of attracting, retaining, and motivating employees, and controlling costs.

Cases

Case 12.1: Merit Pay Crunch at Wunderkind Toys

A.B. Walnut, chairman of the board of Wunderkind Toys, is concerned about this year's merit awards to top people, those who report to him and to President G.H. Prexy. Due to large drops in company profits over a two-year period (23 per cent in 1985 alone), the merit budget is tight. Wunderkind's top people, accustomed to generous awards, will have to share a meager $70,150 between them. This represents only 5 per cent of the executive group payroll excluding the chairman, who will not receive a raise this year.

To advise on the difficult task of allocating the merit budget, Walnut has called in consultant Thomas Tweedy. Tweedy is to make recommendations on which of Wunderkind's key executives should receive increases and on the size of those increases, considering the difficult circumstances facing the industry and the company. The economic environment is one of cautionary recovery in the midst of slowed but continuing inflation. The current unemployment rate is 6.5 per cent and has ranged between 6 and 6.5 per cent for the past six months. The inflation rate has been 6 per cent for the past 12 months and the annualized rate for the recent month was 5.5 per cent.

Walnut's basic objectives are to provide the maximum motivation possible through the merit program under the difficult circumstances. He does not want to lose any of his key people. Traditionally, all top executive increases have at least exceeded the inflation rate, but that is not possible this year.

Walnut gives Tweedy an organization chart and brief data on salary grade; age; years of service with the company; years in the present job; base salary; Compa/Ratio (an index of an individual's relative position in their pay grade, calculated by dividing current pay by the midpoint of the pay grade); peformance-potential-exposure rating; and an indication of whether there is a qualified back-up for each of the key executives.

The performance rating system is a good one and ratings on all key people were recently completed. The system uses an A-B-C-D coding: A is the highest peformance rating, the highest potential rating, and the highest level of exposure to the possibility of the individual's being attracted away from the company; B is a good rating and C is considered adequate. Anyone who receives a D rating must bring it up by the end of the next rating period or face termination or demotion.

The company has a formal job evaluation program. Salary ranges are set by competitive survey and the salary administration structure is in good shape. Jobs were evaluated and regraded and the structure was revised only a few months ago.

The company does not have a bonus plan and is not in a position to establish one in the near future. So the salary structure is essentially a total compensation structure, which must match competition that, in some cases, uses bonuses. Wunderkind has few special fringe benefits and is not in a position to inaugurate any new ones at this time, if any cost is involved. There is a stock option program, but it has been relatively ineffective in recent years because of the drop in the company's stock price. Few shares are available for grant under the plan and management cannot go to the shareholders for more shares for two years. So the option program offers little opportunity for augmenting the merit program.

Walnut tells Tweedy that no promotions or retirements are expected this year from among his top people. The only rule Tweedy must follow in allocating the $70,150 merit budget is: no increases to pay levels above the maximum of the range.

Questions:

1. Assume you are Tweedy. What recommendations will you make to Walnut regarding allocation of merit increases between top people at Wunderkind? Base your recommendations on a merit pay policy or system designed to reward high performers and retain good, needed managers. Assign pay increases (in both per cent and dollars) in accordance with your system and explain any deviations from policy which may occur.

2. **From an employee relations standpoint, how might Walnut increase acceptance of difficult merit pay decisions among his key personnel?**

SOURCE: Adapted from an exercise in K. Foster and V. Lynn, "Dividing Up the 'Merit' Increase Pie for Top Management," ***Personnel Administrator*****, May 1978, pp. 42–8.**

Table 1:

Organization Chart, Wunderkind Toys

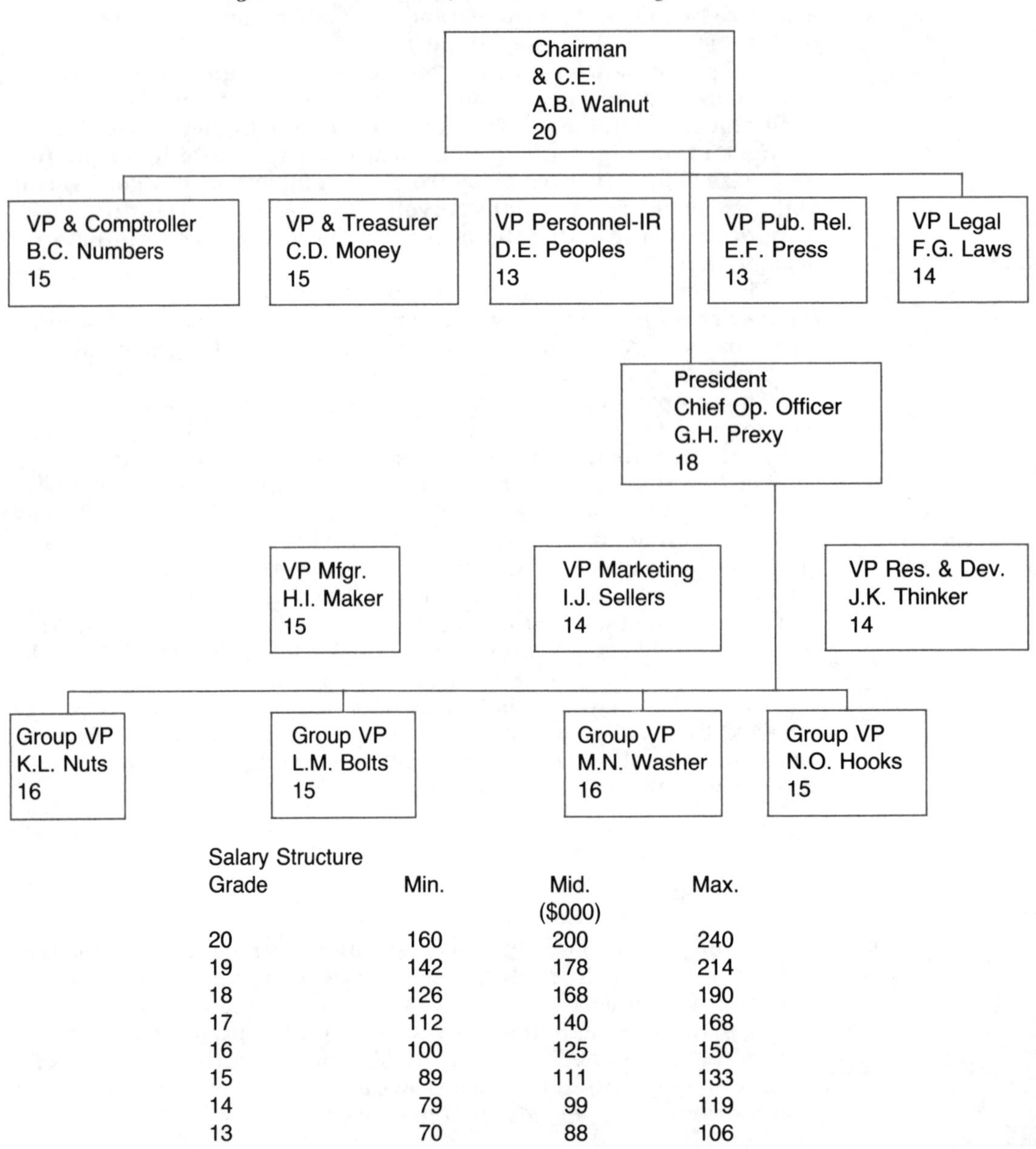

Salary Structure

Grade	Min.	Mid. ($000)	Max.
20	160	200	240
19	142	178	214
18	126	168	190
17	112	140	168
16	100	125	150
15	89	111	133
14	79	99	119
13	70	88	106

Table 2: *Pertinent Data, Wunderkind Toys*

Name	Title	Salary Grade	Age	Years Service	No. Of Employees Supv.	Years In This Job	Base Salary	Compa Ratio	Perf.	Pot.	Expo-Sure	Back-Up
Walnut	Chairman	20	62	24	20,000	5	210,000	105.5	—	—	—	—
Prexy	President	18	57	8	20,000	7	180,000	107.1	B	B+	B−	Yes*
Numbers	VP-Compt.	15	42	3	40	1	85,000	76.6	A	A−	A	No
Money	VP-Treas	15	48	12	15	4	100,000	90.1	B	B−	B	No
Peoples	VP-Pers IR	13	51	17	25	7	80,000	90.1	A	C+	B+	Yes
Press	VP-P.R.	13	46	6	7	2	92,000	104.5	C+	C	B	Yes
Laws	VP-Legal	14	45	5	10	5	110,000	111.1	B	B+	A−	No
Maker	VP-Mfg	15	59	20	15	6	113,000	101.8	B	B−	B−	Yes
Sellers	VP-Mkt	14	54	13	10	3	84,000	84.8	A	B	A−	Yes
Thinker	VP-R&D	14	50	14	50	8	102,000	103.0	B	C	B	Yes
Nuts	GR V.P.	16	42	4	5,500	4	115,000	92.0	A	A	A	No
Bolts	GR V.P.	15	46	10	4,000	3	112,000	100.9	B+	B+	A	No
Washer	GR V.P.	16	59	19	7,400	11	130,000	104.0	B	B−	B−	No
Hooks	GR V.P.	15	49	15	2,900	8	100,000	90.0	C	C	C	Yes
*Nuts		Total Excluding Chairman					$1,403,000					

Case 12.2: Salary Progression at Shell Canada's Sarnia Chemical Plant

In the Sarnia chemical plant of Shell Canada, the salary progression is based on demonstrated knowledge and skill rather than on specific tasks being performed. This includes process operating areas, craft skills, laboratory and warehousing.

As set out in the *Good Work Practices Guidebook*, the plant has been divided into ten process areas each with a particular job knowledge cluster (JKC). An individual progresses through the compensation system in 12 phases. The skill and experience required in a phase depend on the nature of the particular process. The table presented below provides an example of a typical progression for a new team member. Also included in the table is the schedule of basic monthly salaries for each phase as set out in the collective agreement between Shell Canada (Sarnia Chemical Plant) and The Energy and Chemical Worker's Union, Local 800, February 1, 1983 to January 31, 1984.

A phase level increase can be obtained by demonstration of knowledge and skill in the JKC area. The team member must, however, spend 12 consecutive months in the area even though qualified sooner.

These JKC's have been grouped into sections, the intent being that a team member who begins his process training in a particular section will complete all JKC's in that section before moving to a new section. Exceptions to this may have to be made depending on team requirements.

If because of circumstances beyond a team member's control (e.g., team member attrition), a change of this nature must be made, and the team member is not meeting his progression timetable, an accommodation will be made on an individual basis. Guidelines have been developed to handle these special situations.

The Shell Chemical Plant introduced this compensation system when the chemical plant was built. The principle for payment was developed with the union and is set out in a document separate from the collective agreement. The document is called "Philosophy Statement" and it includes the following key criteria to be incorporated into the organization:

1. a. Employees are responsible and trustworthy.
   b. Employees are capable of making proper decisions given the necessary training and information.
   c. Groups of individuals can work together effectively as members of a team.
2. Advancement and growth to each individual's fullest potential and capability.
3. Compensation on the basis of demonstrated knowledge and skill.
4. Direct, open and meaningful communications amongst individuals.

Table 1

Phase	Monthly salaries from February 1, 1983	Equivalent hour salary rate
1. Entry	$1,841	($11.35)
2. "Basic A" and 18 weeks' service	1,902	(11.73)
3. 1 Process JKC and "Basic B"	1,989	(12.26)
4. 2 Process JKCS	2,078	(12.81)
5. 1 Other skill JKC + 24 months in that other skill	2,165	(13.35)
6. 3 Process JKCS	2,254	(13.90)
7. 4 Process JKCS	2,338	(14.41)
8. 2 Other Skill JKCS + additional 24 months after completion of JKC-1	2,450	(15.10)
9. 5 Process JKCS	2,559	(15.78)
10. 5 Process JKCS + 1 year minimum on 5th Process JKC	2,644	(16.30)
11. 6 Process JKCS	2,734	(16.86)
12. 6 Process JKCS + 1 year minimum on 6th Process JKC	2,823	(17.40)

Note I: All persons being paid at a rate higher than that to which they are entitled according to the progression qualifications will be expected to complete those qualifications before further increases are forthcoming.

Note II: Although obtaining the top rate in Sarnia's plant is through the acquisition of Basics, 6 Process JKCS and 2 Other Skill JKCS, it is understood that team members at the top rate will be expected to train on and learn all the process areas in the plant in time. There is also an expectation that team members will acquire more than the minimum standards in the other skills areas if the opportunity is available.

5. Information flow directed to those in position to most quickly act upon it.
6. "Whole jobs" to be designed to provide maximum individual involvement.
7. System that provides direct and immediate feedback in meaningful terms.
8. Maximum amount of self-regulation and discretion.
9. Artificial, traditional, or functional barriers to be eliminated.
10. Work schedules that minimize time spent on shift.
11. Early identification of problems and collaboration on solutions.
12. Errors reviewed from "what can we learn" point of view.
13. Status differentials to be minimized.

The application of the principle is set out in the *Good Work Practices Guidebook.*

In Shell's other operating plants, including a neighbouring refinery with the same union, there are in place modified versions of progression. The main differences are that progression is only permitted part way to the top. The top compensations are still filled by promotion through vacancies. In addition, in these other plants compensation by skill is only for process operations. Crafts and laboratories are excluded. One of the factors in this difference is that there is still an operator in charge versus self-regulating teams. Another factor is that the other plants have jurisdictional divisions and the multiskilling features.

Questions:

1. Discuss the pros and cons of a system of compensation based on acquired skill rather than one based on type of work performed.
2. The Sarnia Chemical plant has found that it must maintain an awareness of the principles which underline the compensation system. This is accomplished through regular meetings with union representatives to monitor the progress of the system. In addition, there is a team norm review board comprised of union and management representatives who deal with any aspects of change in the system as well as resolution of problems which cannot be resolved at the team level. Discuss why a stated philosophy is so important to this type of compensation system.

NOTE: For a discussion of the Shell program see N. Halpern, *Sustaining Change in the Shell Sarnia Chemical Plant, QWL Focus*, vol. 2, no. 1, May 1982. (Toronto: Ontario Ministry of Labour, Quality of Worklife Centre, 1982).

13

Benefits

Leah Holstein has been a research chemist at Monsanto Canada for the past six years. She has never considered leaving Monsanto because she enjoys her work, has opportunities for growth and advancement, and feels she is compensated fairly. Besides an ample paycheque, Holstein receives a generous benefit package, including paid vacations and holidays, supplemental medical benefits, dental assistance, life insurance, a pension plan, a tuition payment program and more. Monsanto's benefit package for management and professional employees is shown in Exhibit 13.1 Note that career development is included as a benefit in Monsanto's package.

Holstein is unusual in one sense: she understands and appreciates the value of the wide range of benefits provided by her employer. Most employees don't, as evidenced by a recent survey of 850 employees which revealed that only 5 per cent had any idea how large a proportion of company payroll went to pay for their benefits.[1] An important

[1] Brent King, "Many Employees Don't Know What Their Firm's Benefits Are Worth," *Financial Post*, December 3, 1983.

EXHIBIT 13.1

A benefit package

A Benefits Program Checklist

Benefits for today	
Paid Vacations	Up to six weeks a year
Paid Holidays	At least 10 a year
Supplemental Medical Benefits Plan	Financial security against illness
Dental Assistance Plan	Preventive dental care
Disability Income Plan	Works when you can't
Relocation Program	Pays your normal moving expenses
Leaves of Absence	For many reasons, some with pay
Matching Gift Program	Dollar-for-dollar, up to $5,000
Benefits for tomorrow	
Life Insurance	2½ times annual base pay plus another 2½ times if killed while on company business plus 1 if death is accidental (to maximum of 5 times pay)
Pension Plan	Paid entirely by company
Stock Purchase Plan	In payroll deduction instalments
For your career development	
Tuition Payment Program	Pays tuition for job-related courses
In-House Training	Continues your education
Organization Memberships	Your choice of one professional membership—paid by company

SOURCE: Monsanto Canada, Inc.

function of HRM professionals and benefits specialists is to help employees understand and appreciate the value of their benefit packages. Such understanding is necessary if organizations are to achieve maximum benefit from the benefits they offer.

In addressing benefits as an HRM area, this chapter deals with five categories: (1) those provided directly by government; (2) those mandated by federal and provincial law for total or partial provision by employers; (3) those provided at an employer's discretion; (4) those providing pay for time not worked; and (5) those providing employees with a variety of services. Within certain constraints, each organization chooses from among the wide range of benefits available to assemble a benefit package uniquely its own.

Growth of Employee Benefits

Benefits first gained popularity during World War II when the imposition of wage ceilings made it necessary for employers to find alternate means of attracting, rewarding, and retaining employees. Since that time, the scope and importance of benefits have grown tremendously. According to data from private surveys, in 1984 the average Canadian employer's outlay on fringe benefits was 32.5 per cent of direct labour costs; it had been 15.1 per cent in 1953/54.[2] This increase reflected particular growth in two types of benefits: in paid time off (vacations, holidays, coffee breaks, and rest periods), to 14.9 per cent of the total; and in pension and welfare plans, to 9.4 per cent. There was less growth in the proportion attributed to payments required by law and to such things as bonuses and profit sharing. The findings of an earlier Statistics Canada survey were simiiar: it set the costs of benefits in 1978 at 34 per cent of the basic pay for regular work.[3] The largest items were paid absences (12.8 per cent) and welfare and benefit plans (11.5 per cent).

The growth of benefits has two major causes. First, the growth of unions and collective bargaining has spurred benefit expansion. Second, as we shall see in the next section, certain benefits have inherent cost advantages to the organization. Moreover, some benefits provide forms of compensation that are not taxable to employees; recent changes in the tax laws have reduced some of these possibilities, but a number remain.

How Benefits Contribute to Organizational Effectiveness

Benefits contribute to organizational effectiveness by:

1. Helping to attract and retain employees;
2. Controlling costs by making an organization's compensation dollars go further;
3. Enhancing an organization's image as a caring employer.

[2] *Employee Benefit Costs in Canada 1984* (Toronto: Thorne, Stevenson and Kellogg, 1984), p. 22; and Sylvia Ostry and Mahmood A. Zeidi, *Labour Economics in Canada*, 3rd ed. (Toronto: Macmillan of Canada, 1979), pp. 202–3.
[3] Statistics Canada, *Employee Compensation In Canada: All Industries, 1978* (Ottawa: Minister of Supply and Services Canada, 1980), p. 46.

Attracting and Retaining Employees

Most organizations use benefits as they do direct compensation to attract and retain a qualified work force. However, very little research evidence exists to support the view that benefits are useful in achieving this purpose. In fact, several investigations of pensions and turnover in the U.S. found very little relationship between them.[4]

The need to provide an attractive benefit package stems largely from an organization's need to remain competitive. Many employers find that they must frequently add to their benefit packages in order to remain competitive. Also, "pattern bargaining," in which a single large union negotiates a contract with a major employer, then uses it as a model for other employers, tends to make benefits proliferate. For example, dental insurance is an increasingly common demand of employees and their unions.

Unlike direct pay, benefits are rarely used to motivate employees to desirable work behaviour and performance. In order for benefits to be used as motivators, they must be contingent upon certain levels of job performance or work behaviour. But benefits are generally provided to all employees as a condition of employment, without regard to level of performance or contribution to the organization. (An exception is some kinds of benefits provided executives in lieu of increases in direct compensation.)

Benefits which are perceived as inadequate can be a source of dissatisfaction, contributing to poor job performance and possible turnover. One waitress, for example, was very upset when she learned that her five-day absence from work because of illness had cost her two paid vacation days. The employee was eligible for ten "sick days," but the employer's policy was that the first two days of any absence had to be covered by accrued vacation days unless hospitalization occurred on the first day of absence. This policy, which was designed to reduce abuse of sick pay benefits, provoked such negative feelings in the employee that she left to take a position in a restaurant with a more lenient sick pay policy.

This is admittedly an extreme example: most employees do not terminate simply because they are dissatisfied with their benefit package. However, it does illustrate the importance of maintaining benefit programs and policies that employees perceive as adequate and desirable.

Cost Savings

A second purpose served by benefits relates to cost control. Both employer and employee gain when a proportion of the organization's compensation dollars is allocated to benefits. The major advantage is that payments for benefits are often tax-deductible for the employer but the benefits are not taxable income to the employee.

[4] D.J. Wynne, "Employee Mobility: Relationship to Pensions," *Public Personnel Review*, 1971, vol. 32, pp. 219–22.

A further cost advantage is an economy of scale. An organization can provide its employees with certain benefits which might otherwise have to be purchased out of their take-home pay and at a higher cost to them than to the organization. For example, an organization can purchase life, disability, and supplementary health insurance at reduced group rates, whereas an individual would pay more for this protection. Thus, an organization's compensation dollars can go further in terms of what an employee receives when a certain percentage is set aside for benefits. Of course, insurance protection provided by an employer out of available compensation funds is a bargain for the employee only if he or she values and desires the protection.

This points up one disadvantage of employee benefits: inasmuch as employees do not have a say in selecting their individual benefits, benefits can be regarded as a forced allocation of their income. Given the option, the employee might not have chosen to spend that amount in the prescribed manner, preferring to allocate the cash in a different way. Life insurance is a good example. In many instances, an unmarried employee has no need for life insurance yet must accept it as part of the total compensation. Pension funds are another example. While it is generally agreed that individuals should provide for their own retirement, they vary widely in the relative weights they assign to current income and future security.

The Organization's Image

Benefits also serve to enhance an organization's image as a caring employer, concerned with the welfare of its employees, an image that can be very useful in recruiting. Benefits are essentially a means of providing for certain needs of employees and protecting them against certain risks. While an employer's motives for providing benefits may not be entirely altruistic or humanitarian, they can at least be regarded as an exercise in enlightened self-interest: that is, in pursuing the organization's own best economic interests, the employer also accomplishes something which is of benefit to others and to society in general.

Benefits: Relation to Other HRM Functions

The relationship of benefits to other HRM functions is portrayed in Exhibit 13.2. The benefits area is related in varying ways to compensation, recruiting, orientation, and labour relations.

Direct Compensation

Since benefits are a form of compensation, benefits as an HRM function is closely related to the direct compensation function. The proportion of total compensation spent on benefits as opposed to wages and salaries is determined by the employer. The typical range is 10 to 40 per cent,

EXHIBIT 13.2

Benefits: relation to other functions

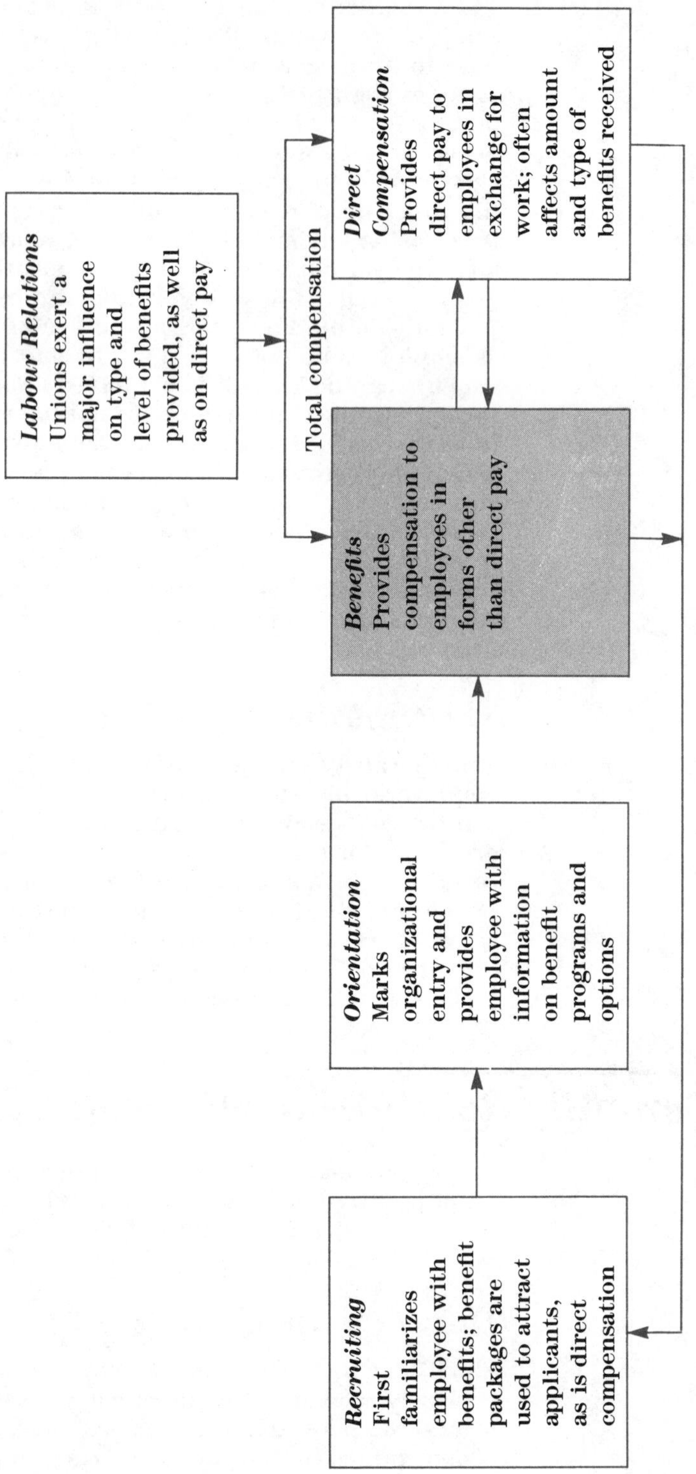

Recruiting
First familiarizes employee with benefits; benefit packages are used to attract applicants, as is direct compensation

Orientation
Marks organizational entry and provides employee with information on benefit programs and options

Benefits
Provides compensation to employees in forms other than direct pay

Labour Relations
Unions exert a major influence on type and level of benefits provided, as well as on direct pay

Total compensation

Direct Compensation
Provides direct pay to employees in exchange for work; often affects amount and type of benefits received

although some organizations pay as much as 50 per cent of their compensation costs in the form of benefits.[5] Like direct pay, benefits are usually received only after organizational entry and some amount of time on the job. However, some benefits, such as relocation expenses, are commonly provided before organizational entry.

Recruiting

An employee generally first gains familiarity with an employer's benefit package during the recruiting process. There is very little research examining the influence of benefits on an employee's decision to join an organization, but it is generally believed that employers must offer packages competitive with those of their competitors in the labour market if they are to be successful in recruiting qualified applicants.

Orientation

Company benefits, including those options that require employees' decisions and signatures, are explained in greater detail during orientation sessions, which are usually held on the first day at work or shortly thereafter. Presentations by benefits specialists are quite common at this time. Although an orientation session may be a convenient time to acquaint employees with their benefit programs and options, it may not be the best time to do so. Research has shown that employees' concerns at this time focus mainly on what is expected of them and whether they will be able to perform successfully.[6] For this reason, some organizations schedule separate orientation sessions, dealing specifically with benefits, at a somewhat later date.

Labour Relations

Unions exert a major influence on the type and level of benefits an employer provides. Benefits are as important an area of labour-management negotiations as are wages. The addition of particular benefits, such as a dental care plan or an extra holiday, can be the key to settling a collective agreement. For example, in a strike at Bata Footwear in 1980, a company pension plan was a major issue, along with demands for a wage increase and a cost-of-living allowance (COLA). According to a *Globe and Mail* report of the strike: "The company's offer on pensions—$260 a month for workers with 40 years' service—has been the crowning insult in the contract dispute." The story further noted that pensions seemed to be a "priority item" with many of Bata's longer-service employees, while younger workers emphasized the wage and

[5] *National Underwriter*, December 29, 1979, p. 1.

[6] E.R. Gommersall and M.S. Myers, "Breakthrough in On-the-Job Training," *Harvard Business Review*, July-August 1966, vol. 44, pp. 62–71.

COLA provisions. Younger workers were also cited as "ridiculing the pension offer as being completely inadequate."[7]

Benefits and the HRM Professional

Many medium- and large-sized organizations employ benefits specialists to handle the unique problems of the benefits area. Exhibit 13.3 is an example of a recruitment ad for a pensions supervisor, a particular kind of benefits specialist. It is amusing to note that this ad seeks to attract applicants by offering "a competitive compensation package including pension, dental, supplementary health, OHIP and group life insurance plans."

According to the ad, the job includes responsibilities "for the maintenance of pensions and benefits data, as well as analysis and reporting of this information to management, insurers and government authorities." This is consistent with the organization's need to administer its benefit package and to comply with government regulations.

Many small- and medium-sized organizations do not employ benefit specialists but assign these responsibiliies to HRM generalists. HRM generalists are sometimes aided by plan fiduciaries (representatives of organizations that hold plan assets) and outside benefits consultants.

Categories of Benefits and Types of Protection

The wide variety of employee benefits can be divided into five major categories: (1) universal benefits; (2) mandatory benefits; (3) discretionary benefits for employee protection; (4) pay for time not worked; and (5) employee services. Benefits in the first category cannot truly be called employee benefits because employment (or lack of employment) is not what entitles an individual to receive any of them. They are discussed here, however, because, with mandatory and discretionary benefits, they offer employees protection against certain risks, including risks of superannuation, untimely death, disability, medical expenses, and unemployment.

Superannuation

Superannuation refers to the risk of outliving one's ability to earn an income. Protection against this risk reduces the economic loss associated with retirement by providing a regular source of income to former employees in their retirement years. Superannuation is a risk faced by virtually everyone who depends upon his or her personal

[7] *The Globe and Mail* (Toronto), November 19, 1980.

EXHIBIT 13.3

Ad for a pensions supervisor

ABITIBI-PRICE

PENSIONS SUPERVISOR

A large Canadian resource-based manufacturer offers a challenging opportunity for an experienced Pensions Specialist. This individual will be responsible for the maintenance of pensions and benefits data, as well as analysis and reporting of this information to management, insurers and government authorities. A major aspect of this work is the annual updating of employee pensions records. The successful candidate will become an important resource to management.

You should have a good knowledge of computer applications and accounting principles as related to pensions and administration. Five or more years of related work experience, preferably at a supervisory level, is desired. Excellent oral and written communication skills are essential. Early advancement potential for a high performer.

The Company offers a competitive compensation package including pension, dental, supplementary health, OHIP and group life insurance plans.

Interested applicants may call:

(416) 866-4328
Abitibi Price Inc.
TD Centre.

efforts to provide the resources for life, and the employment situation provides an opportunity to protect against it. Protection against this risk is provided under the Canada and the Quebec Pension Plan (CPP and QPP), the federal government's Old Age Security benefits, and employer-sponsored pension and retirement plans, as well as by personal savings and investments.

Untimely Death

Death is said to be untimely when it occurs before an individual's productive years are over, thus causing an economic loss to the survivors. The untimely death of a single employee with no dependents is associated with no risks except funeral expenses.

Certain programs protect against untimely death, in the form of payments to eligible survivors. Protection is provided by the mandatory Canada (or Quebec) Pension Plan and by voluntary programs, such as group life insurance and the death benefit in private pension plans.

Disability

Disability can take two forms: total or partial. A totally disabled worker is one who cannot undertake any employment; a partially disabled worker cannot perform the job held before the accident or illness but can perform some work for the same or another employer.

The risk of disability poses a far greater threat than does untimely death. First, all employees face this risk. Only those who have dependents need protection from death, but everyone is his or her own dependent in cases of disability. Moreover, from an economic standpoint, the loss associated with disability is greater than that resulting from death since a disabled employee still incurs living expenses, often greatly increased expenses. Further, disability may be partial, permitting some work—but often only with aids and after retraining, which can be very expensive. Finally, the likelihood of becoming disabled exceeds that of dying. Statistics indicate that young workers are approximately three times more likely to become disabled before retirement age than they are to die.[8] Protection against disability is provided by the mandatory Canada (or Quebec) Pension Plan, and workers' compensation, and by group disability plans, which are provided at an employer's discretion. Unemployment insurance also provides short-term protection against the loss of earnings because of accident or illness.

Medical Expenses

Modern health care is expensive, and costs are increasing rapidly. Services are available today that could not be purchased at any price a decade ago. Basic protection against the risks of health care costs is provided by provincial government insurance plans under a federal-provincial cost-sharing agreement. Additional protection may be afforded by supplementary health insurance, offered at an employer's discretion.

Unemployment

People are unemployed for numerous reasons. Some, such as quitting or dismissal for misconduct, are generally within an employee's control. Others, such as market shifts or automation, are not. Unemployment Insurance (UI) offers compensation for unemployment that is outside a person's control. It also provides benefits when a worker's

[8] O.D. Dickerson, *Health Insurance* (Homewood, Ill.: Richard D. Irwin, 1968), p. 16; and material compiled by the Life Underwriters Training Council, Washington, D.C.

ability to earn is interrupted by sickness, nonoccupational accident, pregnancy, or quarantine.

Universal Benefits

Universal benefits are those that governments provide without requiring direct contributions from either employees or employers. As shown in Exhibit 13.4, the universal benefits in Canada that protect against the risks discussed are: Old Age Security; the Guaranteed Income Supplement to Old Age Security; and provincial supplements to these programs. In addition, basic health insurance is a universal benefit in five provinces; in the others, the premiums are paid by individuals and/or employers.

Old Age Security

On January 1, 1952, the federal government's Old Age Security Act first gave Canadians universal pensions as a matter of right, with no means test. Initially, the program provided a pension of $40 a month to everyone from age 70. The benefit has since been raised in amount (it is indexed to the Consumer Price Index), and the commencement age has been reduced to 65. A full pension requires residence of 40 years after age 18; persons whose adult residence in the country has been shorter receive a proportionate pension. This benefit is taxable to the persons who receive it.

Guaranteed Income Supplement

A guaranteed monthly income supplement (GIS) was added to the Old Age Security plan effective January 1, 1967. It was intended as a transitional support to ensure that all recipients of the OAS pension would receive a minimum monthly income until the Canada and Quebec Pension Plans matured. Instead, the GIS became a permanent part of the social security system because full indexing in a time of inflation increased the number of pensioners who could qualify under the required income test.

The GIS is reduced by $1.00 for each $2.00 of income an elderly person receives in addition to the OAS benefit. A pensioner's husband or wife age 60 to 65 may qualify for a Spouse's Allowance, subject to an income test that reduces it $4.00 for every $400 of the couple's income.

As of July 1, 1986, the basic OAS pension was $291.51 monthly while the GIS was $346.45 for a maximum federal pension of $637.96. For a married couple, the maximum, including the GIS, was $1,034.08 per month. Cost-of-living adjustments are made quarterly.

Several provinces provide *minimum income supplements* to old people in addition to federal benefits, subject to a means and a residence test.

EXHIBIT 13.4

Universal benefit programs

Program	*Regulatory body*	*Risk covered*	*Nature of benefits*	*Funding*
Old Age Security (OAS)	Federal government	Superannuation	Universal pension; monthly payments from age 65 (indexed to Consumer Price Index); subject to residence requirements	Federal government
Guaranteed Income Supplement (GIS) to Old Age Security	Federal government	Superannuation	Monthly payments from age 65 to ensure that all recipients of OAS receive a minimum income; subject to income test	Federal government
Provincial supplements	Ont., N.S., Man., Sask., Alta., B.C.	Superannuation	Monthly payments to guarantee minimum income to old people; subject to residence test	Provincial governments
Provincial health insurance plans in Nfld., P.E.I., N.S., N.B., Man., and Sask.	Provinces	Hospital and medical expenses	Most basic hospital and medical-care costs	Federal block and per capita grants, plus general tax revenues in these provinces (federal money supplemented by payroll tax in Quebec and Manitoba, and by individually paid premiums in other provinces)

Provincial Hospital and Medical Insurance Plans

Basic health care in Canada is covered by provincial insurance plans, which receive considerable federal funding. The system began July 1, 1958, when the federal government began sharing the cost of provincial hospital insurance plans which were available to all residents and operated by a public nonprofit agency. It was extended to providing insured medical care services in 1966.

The method of financing under the Canada Health Act, which became effective on April 1, 1984, sets out six conditions that a provincial health program must meet to be eligible for the full cash portion of the federal contribution for insured health services. The six conditions are: administration on a nonprofit basis by a provincial public authority; comprehensiveness (coverage of all necessary hospital and medical services, including surgical-dental services provided in hospitals); universality; portability within Canada and for services out-of-Canada at the home province rates; accessibility; and the banning of extra-billing and nonpermitted user charges.[9] The federal government can impose financial penalties on provinces that do not abide by these rules.

The hospital plans provide unlimited time in hospital which is medically necessary but do not cover private duty nurses or semiprivate accommodation. The medical plans cover services by physicians, surgeons, and anaesthetists, as well as diagnostic X-rays and laboratory tests. Limited coverage is provided for optometrists and practitioners such as chiropractors, osteopaths, and podiatrists. Many provinces have added dental care for children and/or prescription drugs for elderly people.

The provincial funding mechanism varies. Saskatchewan, New Brunswick, Nova Scotia, Prince Edward Island and Newfoundland finance their plans from general revenues, plus the federal grants. Quebec and Manitoba levy a special tax on employers equal to 3.0 and 1.5 per cent of total payroll respectively. British Columbia, Alberta, Ontario, and the Yukon require monthly premiums from individuals or families. If an employer pays the premium in those provinces, the amount is considered taxable income for the employee.

Because of this variation in funding mechanisms, provincial health insurance must be regarded as a true universal benefit only in those provinces that finance their share of costs from general revenues. In Quebec and Manitoba the payroll tax makes it a mandatory benefit, and in the other jurisdictions it is a government-offered service with economies of scale and other benefits.

Mandatory Benefits

Mandatory benefits are those that an employer must provide under federal and/or provincial laws. Mandatory benefits include: retirement, disability, survivors' and death benefits under the Canada (or Quebec) Pension Plan; disability benefits and spouses' and dependents' pensions under workers' compensation; unemployment compensation; and health insurance in Quebec (see Exhibit 13.5). The payment of mandatory benefits amounted to 4.4 per cent of the average employer's gross annual payroll in 1984.[10]

[9] Lawrence E. Coward, *Mercer Handbook of Canadian Pension and Welfare Plans*, 8th ed. (Don Mills, Ont.: CCH Canadian Ltd., 1984), pp. 213–15.
[10] *Employee Benefit Costs in Canada 1984.*

Canada (or Quebec) Pension Plan

The Canada and Quebec Pension plans (CPP and QPP) were introduced on January 1, 1966. (Quebec opted out of the federal plan but introduced its own with identical main features.) The plans are not subsidized by the government; they are based on contributions by the employer and the employee, each of whom contributes 1.8 per cent of pensionable earnings up to a maximum, which was $25,800 in 1986.[11] Contributions are deducted from employees' pay and remitted once a month by the employer, together with his or her contributions. All employees and the self-employed (who remit 3.6 per cent of earnings themselves) pay into the fund between the ages of 18 and 65; a person may continue to contribute to age 70.

The retirement pension, equal to 25 per cent of the contributor's earnings in the previous three years, is paid at or after the age of 65; in 1986, the maximum pension was $486.11 per month. A disability pension, with a maximum of $455.64 per month in 1986, is payable to a person who has contributed for at least five years and is suffering from a disability which prevents gainful occupation. It is paid for the duration of the disability or until age 65, when the person receives the retirement pension. Survivors' benefits vary with the age of the surviving spouse and whether there are any dependent children. There is also a death benefit.

Workers' Compensation

Every province and territory in Canada has a workers' compensation act which mandates compensation to a worker (or the family) for injury or death arising from employment. Hospital, medical, and related expenses are also paid, and disabled workers receive full rehabilitation services from workers' compensation boards. The funding mechanism is a premium levied on employers. It is calculated on the statement of wages for the previous year and an estimate of payroll for the present year. The rates vary with the type of industry and hence the hazards involved. In 1984 they ranged from 20¢ per $100 of annual payroll in nonhazardous work up to $10 or more per $100 for various types of mining and nearly $21 for stevedoring.

Disability compensation for an accident or illness is 75 per cent of average gross earnings, subject to minimums and maximums which vary among provinces. In 1984, the lowest maximum was $17,000 in Prince Edward Island, and the high was $45,000 in Newfoundland.[12]

The employer's contribution is a deductible operating expense, but it is not taxable income for workers. Workers' compensation payments are not taxable to the recipients.

[11] Ten per cent is deducted from earnings to calculate the contribution.
[12] Coward, p. 208.

EXHIBIT 13.5

Mandatory benefit programs

Program	*Regulatory body*	*Risk covered*	*Nature of benefits*	*Funding*
Canada (and Quebec) pension plans	Federal (Quebec) government	Superannuation	Monthly payment	Payroll tax paid by employer and employee
		Disability	Monthly payment	
		Untimely death	Percentage of deceased spouse's monthly retirement benefit	
		Costs of raising orphans	Monthly payment	
		Death	Lump sum six times the monthly retirement benefit	
Workers' compensation	Provinces	Injury	Weekly benefit	Employer premiums levied on the statement of wages for the previous year and estimate of payroll for current year
		Untimely death resulting from employment	Dependents receive a pension plus lump sum	
		Disability resulting from employment	Weekly benefit	
		Medical, hospital, all related expenses (work-related injuries or illnesses)	Expenses covered	
Quebec health insurance Manitoba health insurance	Province of Quebec Province of Manitoba	Hospital and medical expenses	Most basic hospital and medical-care costs	Federal block and per capita grants, plus 3% payroll tax in Quebec and Manitoba (federal money supplemented by general tax revenues in Nfld., P.E.I., N.S., N.B., and Sask., and by individually paid premiums in other provinces)
Unemployment insurance	Canada Employment and Immigration Commission	Interruption in employment due to: work shortage, sickness, non-occupational accidents, pregnancy, quarantine	Payments for a limited period of time	Premiums levied on employees and employers

Unemployment Insurance

Unemployment insurance (UI) was introduced to Canada in 1942. While most social welfare measures are a provincial responsibility, the British North America Act was amended in 1940 to give the federal government exclusive jurisdiction in matters relating to unemployment insurance.

The program now covers all employees under age 65, except employees of a provincial or foreign government and casual workers. Funding is through premiums levied on both employers and employees. In 1986, an employee paid 2.35 per cent of gross pay of up to $495 per week, and the employer paid 1.4 times that amount. The premiums are tax-deductible for both employers and employees. On the other hand, UI benefits are taxable.

UI benefits cover interruptions in employment income caused by loss of a job or by a layoff, but not by a strike or lockout. A claimant must be genuinely unemployed and cannot, without good cause, refuse to apply for a suitable situation or a designated training program.

To qualify for benefits, the worker must usually have made regular contributions to the fund for at least 20 weeks during the "qualifying period," which is the lesser of the 52 weeks preceding the claim or the number of weeks since the start of the last claim. After a two-week waiting period, the claimant receives 60 per cent of his or her average weekly insurable earnings. (In 1986, given maximum weekly insurable earnings of $495, the maximum UI benefit was $297.) An "initial benefit" is payable for the lesser of the number of weeks of contributions in the qualifying period, or 25. This may be extended to as much as 50 depending on the contribution record, the regional unemployment rate, and whether layoff was the cause of unemployment.

Major revisions to the Unemployment Insurance Act in 1971 increased benefits, reduced the qualifying period for layoff benefits; shortened the waiting period; and introduced 15-week coverage for interruptions in employment caused by sickness, nonoccupational accident, quarantine, or pregnancy. A controversy soon arose over whether the more generous provisions had resulted in a higher measured rate of unemployment. Economists estimated that they had raised it 0.8 to 1.9 percentage points, a finding based on the fact that between 1971 and 1972 the job vacancy rate doubled, indicating a strong demand for workers, yet the unemployment rate remained unchanged.[13] The suggestion that the UI revisions might have affected unemployment so incensed trade unionists that their representatives on the Economic Council of Canada refused to sign a study that reached this conclusion.[14] (The Council had noted that the increase in unemployment could have positive aspects from society's perspective if workers used their unemployment time to search for better jobs, ones which they would presumably hold for a longer duration.) In 1975, the regulations for drawing UI benefits were tightened by extending the qualifying period.

In 1981, another controversy arose when the government introduced a program of worksharing through UI. Employers who would otherwise have to lay off some employees could put all of them on a part-week basis; all of them could receive UI benefits without using up

[13] Frank Reid and Noah M. Meltz, "Causes of Shifts in the Unemployment-Vacancy Relationship: An Empirical Analysis for Canada," *Review of Economics and Statistics*, 1979, vol. 61, pp. 470–75.

[14] Economic Council of Canada, *People and Jobs* (Ottawa: Information Canada, 1976).

any of their UI eligibility. Both central union and central employer associations were critical of the program. The former felt that by reducing measured unemployment, it took pressure off the government to fight the recession, and the latter worried about its effects on productivity. But the evident popularity of worksharing with the workers and employers who participated in it eventually reduced the opposition, and the program was expanded to 8,780 firms and over 200,000 employees.[15] As expected, the number of firms and employees involved in worksharing has declined following the general decrease in unemployment in the period following the 1982–83 recession. For current controversy surrounding UI, see Exhibit 13.6.

Supplementary Coverage

Some employers, at their own discretion, supplement government unemployment insurance by offering plans which provide additional weeks' coverage. The best-known examples have been in the auto industry. The ultimate expansion of such plans is the guaranteed annual wage provided by some large U.S. employers such as Hormel and Procter and Gamble. Under such plans, an employee is entitled to a full year's pay, whether continuously employed or not.

Health Insurance

As we have already noted, basic health insurance is, strictly speaking, a mandated benefit only in Quebec and Manitoba where the provincial financing for the plan is raised by a payroll tax. Other provinces augment federal funding from general tax revenues (making the insurance a universal benefit) or through premiums paid by individuals and families. The latter jurisdictions, however, usually use payroll deductions to collect the premiums. The cost to employers of administering these deductions may be considered a mandated benefit to employees.

Discretionary Benefits for Employee Protection

In addition to mandatory benefits, many employers provide discretionary benefits for employee protection. These include private pension plans, and group life, disability, and supplementary health insurance, among others. Such benefits accounted for 9.4 per cent of the average employer's total compensation costs in 1984.[16]

[15] Frank Reid and Noah M. Meltz, "Canada's STC: A Comparison with the California Version," in Ramelle MaCoy and Martin V. Morand eds. *Short-Time Compensation: A Formula for Work Sharing* (New York: Pergamon Press, 1984) pp. 106–19.

[16] *Employee Benefit Costs in Canada 1984.*

EXHIBIT 13.6

Unemployment insurance: at issue

It's time for some $12-billion questions:

- Do you think the federal government should encourage companies to lay off workers?
- Do you think the feds should encourage workers to seek out unstable jobs instead of stable ones?
- Do you think Ottawa should take billions of dollars annually from workers who have stable jobs and employers who offer such jobs, and use that money to reward companies that generate unemployment?

These are $12-billion questions because that was the cost last year of unemployment insurance, the biggest program in the federal government. If you answer no to these questions, then you want to reform UI because UI does all of these things.

Jonathan Kesselman is an economist at Vancouver's University of British Columbia who recently published a major study of UI financing. He says the current system, in which all employers pay the same premiums, whether their layoff records are bad or good, is unjust and harmful to the Canadian economy. Just as accident-prone drivers pay more for car insurance, Kesselman says layoff-prone firms should pay higher UI premiums. (In his scheme, employees would pay uniform premiums regardless of occupation.) This system is called experience rating, or ER, and a form of it is used in the U.S. It would have been introduced here in 1971, says Bryce Mackasey, who, as minister of labour brought in a major revision of UI that year, but strong opposition, especially from the highly seasonal construction industry, caused the Cabinet to back off.

Yet the reasons for adopting ER are so compelling that it will be hard to ignore them as UI reform is debated in the coming years. "It makes no sense at all," says Richard Lipsey, senior economic adviser with the C.D. Howe Institute, "for the average ordinary worker to be subsidizing companies in the forestry industry." Yet that is what payers of UI premiums are doing.

In the current system of uniform premiums, firms have no incentive to stabilize their work forces; instead, the system encourages them to use temporary layoffs to cope with sales fluctuations. Despite seasonal and cyclic swings, businesses can find ways to avoid layoffs if they really want to, Kesselman argues. Japanese firms do it and so do a few Canadian companies. E.D. Smith and Sons Ltd. of Winona, Ont., for instance, makes jams and pickles in summer, then uses its workers to bottle Worcestershire and HP sauces in winter.

But wait a minute. Construction companies can't bottle HP sauce in the winter. Is it fair that they should pay higher premiums than companies that easily operate all year round? Is it fair, counters Kesselman, that milk costs more in Tuktoyaktuk than in Toronto? "Firms and industries that have unavoidably high unemployment risks should bear the costs as a matter of economic efficiency," he says. "Whether high UI costs are borne by the firms, their workers or customers, this reduces the portion of the economy's resources devoted to unstable activities."

SOURCE: "The Real UI bill," by D. Stoffman. From *Canadian Business* (March 1984), pp. 43–52. Reprinted by permission of the author.

Private Pension Plans

Some employers sponsor private pension plans that supplement CPP (or QPP) benefits. Although the primary purpose of a pension plan is to protect against the risks associated with retirement, many plans also pay a death benefit if the employee dies before retirement.

Basically, private pension plans operate as follows. During the course of employment, contributions are made to the pension fund, either by the employer alone or jointly by employer and employee. The accumulated money, representing contributions on behalf of many employees, is invested and allowed to accumulate interest, dividends, and/or capital gains. Upon retirement, an employee receives income from the fund. The amount received is calculated on some combination of the employee's years of service to the company and his or her average earnings, usually in the few years just prior to retirement.

Pension plans may have been prompted by humanitarian reasons, but their growth can be attributed to the inherent tax advantages for both employer and employee. Employers may usually deduct contributions to the plan from income before taxes.

Private pension plans are regulated by the Canadian Association of Pension Supervisory Authorities (CAPSA), which was established to promote uniformity and ease in the administration of provincial pension benefits acts. The acts are uniform in their essentials, although Manitoba's, Ontario's, and Saskatchewan's have some variations to give employees further protection. An organization that operates a pension plan covering its employees must register the plan with provincial authorities.

Pension plans are either vested or nonvested. A plan is said to *vest* for an employee when that employee obtains the right to the pension contributions made on his or her behalf even *if employment is terminated before retirement.* In most jurisdictions, a private pension plan must vest for an employee who has at least ten years of service with an employer and has attained age 45. The employee who terminates before retirement age and meets these conditions is entitled to a deferred annuity. In Manitoba, vesting occurs after five years of service regardless of age, while in Saskatchewan vesting applies when the years of service plus age add to 45 or more.

Private pension plans may, of course, vest more quickly than required by law. A plan in which the employee obtains a nonforfeitable right as soon as participation begins is said to vest immediately.

Once the pension plan becomes vested, the contributions are "locked-in"; that is, they cannot be withdrawn as a cash sum before a terminated employee is eligible to receive the deferred annuity, except in cases of mental or physical disability or if the deferred benefit is less than some minimum ($25 per month in most provinces). Before vesting takes place, contributions can be withdrawn.

The regulations provide that private plans be funded so as to meet various solvency tests and that their benefits, conditions, and financial arrangements be well disclosed to the participants. Manitoba goes the furthest in terms of disclosure, requiring that employees receive an explanation of rights and duties, an annual financial statement, and the right to inspect financial and actuarial aspects of the plan. In 1980, Ontario added provisions to its act to protect pension rights of employees in the event of plant closure. If the employer is insolvent, payments are to be made from a Pension Benefit Guarantee Fund financed by contributions from all employers in the province.

Group Insurance Programs

Group insurance programs are another way in which employers can voluntarily provide protection to employees. Under them, an employer contracts with an insurance company to provide certain protection for employees, including life, disability, or supplementary health insurance. A wide variety of group policies are available. Many are paid in full by employers (noncontributory plans), but others require employee contributions (contributory plans). Group plans do not allow for individual selection of benefit levels. Rather, a prearranged formula, such as a percentage of annual income, determines how much of a particular benefit each employee can receive under the plan.

The major advantage of group insurance is its cost. Administrative costs are reduced when the agent deals with a group rather than with individuals. And since the agent is handling a large amount of insurance at one time, acquisition costs are much lower. The agent's commission, which is figured as a percentage of the annual premium, is often 40 to 60 per cent in individually written business but generally only about 5 per cent of group business. A final cost savings to the organization is realized through operation of income tax laws. An employer can deduct the cost of group term life insurance (up to $25,000 per employee) as a necessary business expense, but the employee need not report it as income.

Automatic availability may be the primary advantage of group insurance for those employees who would be unable to acquire coverage otherwise. From an insurance company's perspective, it is reasonable to provide coverage to "uninsurable" individuals because the larger number of "good" risks being insured at the same time offsets them. This "risk pooling" is a major advantage of the group technique.

Group life insurance. Several types of group life insurance are available but the primary choice is between a term and a cash-value policy. Term insurance provides the beneficiary with the face value of the policy upon the death of the insured. Cash-value (or whole life) insurance pays the face value and also accumulates cash values, which are also payable to the beneficiary. The premiums for term insurance are considerably lower than those for cash-value, and term is the type often offered by employers. In fact, insurance companies often insist on term insurance's being part of a benefits package that includes other kinds of group insurance.

A relatively recent and increasingly popular development in group life insurance has been the addition of survivors' benefits, which are payable periodically to a surviving spouse. They may be payable for life or until remarriage, perhaps being limited by length of service of the deceased worker. A policy may also include contingent benefits, which are payable to children in the event of the death of the surviving spouse.

Group disability insurance. Group disability coverage is needed to fill gaps left by CPP (or QPP) and workers' compensation. The government pension plans cover only total disability and provide only a "floor" of protection. Workers' compensation pays only for work-related disabilities. UI benefits for sickness or accident are available only for a short time. Group disability benefits are desirable to increase available benefits, to provide for temporary and partial disability, and to provide some medium-term benefits, particularly for nonoccupational disabilities.

Disability benefits are generally determined as a percentage of salary. One common alternative is to have this percentage increase as years of service with the organization increase. For example, employees with five years of service could be awarded benefits equal to 80 per cent of predisability income, while those with one year of service would get 20 per cent of this amount, those with two years 40 per cent, and so on.

Group health insurance. Since basic hospital and medical services are provided under provincial plans, the private health insurance offered in Canada is what is frequently referred to as supplementary or extended health care plans. Typical plans cover private hospital rooms, nursing home accommodations, the cost of private duty nursing and other paramedical services, ambulances, emergency health expenses in foreign countries, prescription drugs, and medical supplies and appliances, including hearing aids and eyeglasses. Such plans usually specify a certain deductible and may pay less than 100 per cent of the remaining expenses.

Recently, dental plans have become a popular new offering; their benefits range from basic dental care to major restorative care (crowns, inlays, fixed bridges, and dentures) and orthodontics. Vision care is a less common feature of benefit packages, but coverage is increasing.

Employers' contributions to health insurance plans may be charged as operating expenses for tax purposes. However, employees' contributions to nongovernmental plans are not deductible from taxable income, and several types of employer contributions are added to it for tax purposes.

Holiday and Vacation Pay

Employees receive benefits in the form of pay for time not worked, such as paid vacation days, paid holidays, paid "sick days," lunch or rest periods, coffee breaks, and paid leaves of absence for jury duty. Some of these benefits are mandated by the relevant jurisdiction's employment standards legislation. Others are given at the employer's discretion. Some discretionary benefits may, however, be virtually required by common practice in the industry or locality. In unionized organizations, collective agreements normally specify benefits in detail. Pay for time not worked cost the average Canadian employer 14.9 per cent of gross annual payroll in 1984.[17]

Holidays

As we saw in Chapter 3, employment standards in all jurisdictions require specified paid holidays—from five in Newfoundland to nine in the federal jurisdiction. Many employers go beyond the legal minimum, particularly employers covered by collective agreements. Industry or local practice is also important—even clerical workers in the oil industry claim their "Golden Fridays," and many offices in large metropolitan centres close on Friday afternoons in the summer, despite ubiquitous air conditioning, because of employees' demands for time off during the short Canadian season. Not unrelated is the particularly Canadian trend of setting holidays on Mondays so that employees may have long weekends.

Also growing in popularity is the "floating holiday," which varies from year to year or from employee to employee. One type, a "personal" holiday, allows an employee to take off any day with supervisory approval. Another type is chosen by an employer, usually to give employees a long weekend or extra days off during the holiday season.

Vacations

Even the newest employee is generally entitled to holiday benefits, but paid vacations must be earned through length of service to an employer. In most jurisdictions, vacation days accrue at a rate of about one day per month of service, entitling an employee to two weeks of paid vacation after one year's employment. It is common to require an employee to work six months to a year before vacation can be taken. Generally, office and managerial employees become eligible for paid vacation days sooner than do production and maintenance employees. Regardless of job level, the length of paid vacations increases with length of service, and many firms go beyond the legal minimums. Many offer three weeks after three, four or five years of service (depending upon job type), four weeks after nine to 12 years, and five after 15 to 20 years. Fifty-five per cent of nonoffice employees who were included in a recent survey were entitled to six weeks after 25 to 30 years' service, and 18 per cent received seven weeks.[18]

Many firms provide additional vacation entitlement in various circumstances. Some reward long-service employees with additional days of leave after specified years of service. Others offer additional paid

[17] *Employee Benefit Costs in Canada 1984.*

[18] *Employee Benefits and Working Conditions in Canada 1984* (Ottawa: Pay Research Bureau, Public Service Staff Relations Board, Canada, 1984), pp. 106–7.

days for special reasons, such as an employee's taking the vacation in the winter, working in an isolated region, or reaching a given age. These additional vacation days are usually available only for the particular period or occasion and are not an annual entitlement.[19]

The 1982 collective agreement between the United Auto Workers and General Motors of Canada moved in the other direction. In response to the recession of the early 1980s and numerous layoffs and plant closings in the industry, it eliminated nine days of paid personal holidays. In the 1984 agreement, two and one-half days of paid absence allowance were added.

Employee Service Benefits

In addition to compensation for time not worked and mandatory and discretionary benefits, employees frequently receive various kinds of service benefits, ranging from savings plans, stock purchase plans, credit unions, and tuition loans to recreational facilities and programs, use of company cars and parking privileges, and company discounts. This type of benefit accounted for 3.8 per cent of the average Canadian employer's total compensation costs in 1984.[20]

Employee service benefits generally differ according to job level. For example, stock options and deferred pay plans are especially attractive to employees in higher-paying jobs. Executives commonly have their own special benefits, called perquisites or "perks," which include such items as physical examinations, special parking and company cars, transportation for spouses who travel on company business and memberships in luncheon clubs and country clubs.[21]

Increasingly organizations are providing career counselling services and educational assistance as employee service benefits. Many offer employees time off the job with pay for participation in developmental activities, such as workshops and professional meetings, and some make low-interest loans available to employees who wish to continue their education. For example, Imperial Oil provides its employees with tuition for any job-related courses, as well as a 75 per cent refund (to a maximum of $275 a year) on fitness club memberships and full tuition for children's university education.[22]

Another form of service that has been growing rapidly in Canada is Employee Assistance Programs (EAPS). Initially EAPS tended to focus on alcoholism but have since been broadened to include drugs and psycho-social problems. Unions and management have increasingly been cooperating in dealing with these problems. Types of approaches used by EAPS will be discussed in Chapter 14, Employee Health and Safety.

[19] Ibid., p. 109.

[20] *Employee Benefit Costs in Canada 1984.*

[21] L. Maloney, "Business Perks That Rile the White House," *U.S. News & World Report*, March 27, 1978, pp. 33–4.

[22] Helen Kohl, "Surprise Packages," *Canadian Business*, August 1982, p. 83.

Cafeteria Benefits: An Individualized Approach

While most employers offer a variety of benefits, their employees very rarely have any choice in what they receive as a part of their total compensation. Benefits are generally selected for employees by management or, in the case of unionized employers, by union representatives. One study found that many union representatives do not have a good idea of the benefits desired by their constituents.[23] Another study reported that when given the opportunity, 80 per cent of the respondents had made changes in their benefit packages.[24]

The benefits in benefit packages and the options in group insurance plans are geared to the needs and interests of the "average" employee. Even if such an employee really existed, there would be many others whose individual needs and interests were poorly met by benefits selected for them.

A moderate amount of research in the U.S. has examined employees' preferences for various forms of benefits. Several studies of blue- and white-collar workers found as much or more interest in some types of benefits, especially more vacations and increased medical insurance, than in additional increases in wages and salaries.[25] Canada's universal health insurance plans undoubtedly remove much pressure for that benefit.

At the executive levels, Canadians receive a smaller percentage of their total compensation in the form of benefits than do their U.S. counterparts. However, 58 per cent of Canadian-managed companies offer supplemental pensions for executives, compared with 17 per cent of U.S.-controlled companies. In addition, as one commentator says, Canadian companies are also far more generous with executive disability benefits and with medical and dental plans. And they're more likely to offer such perks as company cars right down to middle-management level because perks have had preferred status in this country.[26]

Several studies have found that age, sex, number of children, and job type affect employees' preferences for benefits. For example, preference for pensions increase with age, and employees with children rate medical insurance higher than employees without children.[27] Also, younger workers favour dental plans more than do older employees.[28]

[23] E.E. Lawler III and E. Levin, "Union Officers' Perceptions of Members' Pay Preferences," *Industrial and Labor Relations Review*, 1968, vol. 21, pp. 509–17.

[24] Berwyn N. Fragner, "Employees' Cafeteria Offers Insurance Options," *Harvard Business Review*, November-December 1975, pp. 7–10.

[25] S.M. Nealey, "Pay and Benefit Preference," *Industrial Relations*, 1964, vol. 3, pp. 17–28; S.M. Nealey and J.G. Goodale, "Worker Preferences among Time of Benefits and Pay," *Journal of Applied Psychology*, 1967, vol. 52, pp. 357–61; J.R. Schuster, "Another Look at Compensation Preferences," *Industrial Management Review*, 1969, pp. 1–18; and J.B. Chapman and R. Ottemann, "Employee Preferences for Various Compensation and Fringe Benefit Options," *The Personnel Administrator*, 1975, vol. 20, pp. 31–6.

[26] Kohl, p. 84.

[27] Nealey; Nealey and Goodale; and Schuster.

[28] Chapman and Otteman.

One means of allowing employees to have some say in the type of benefits they receive is a system known as cafeteria benefits, in which employees can choose the combination of cash and benefits they want included in their total pay packages. It is highly unusual for an organization to allow an employee to decide the proportion of total compensation that will be spent on benefits. It is somewhat more common, however, to allow employees to choose from various benefit alternatives. This system known as flexible compensation or employee choice benefits, generally places a limit on the total dollar value of benefits which can be selected; sometimes the employee is entitled to cash payments to the extent that the value of selected benefits does not reach the limit.

Cafeteria or flexible benefits are very uncommon, though most experts agree that, in theory, they are a good idea and they are likely to be gradually introduced by more companies.[29] Several U.S. organizations have used the approach successfully, among them American Can and TRW.[30] These companies allow employees to choose whether they want more or less of certain types of benefits after a predetermined core of coverage has been provided. This type of system is also used at Cominco Ltd. for its nonunionized staff. Cominco is a large Vancouver-based mining operation. Its flexible compensation system is described in Case 13.2 at the end of the chapter.

The fact that cafeteria benefits are not more widely used is partly because of the costs of developing and administering such a system and also because certain cost advantages of group insurance may be lost. Also, allowing individuals to choose their own packages may make it more difficult to predict and budget for benefit costs.

A cafeteria-style approach has, however, two important advantages. First, it allows employees to have the benefits they need and desire most. Second, by their active involvement in benefits selection, employees become more aware of the benefits they have and of their costs. Such awareness can increase employees' appreciation of an employer's financial contribution on their behalf. Use of such a system does, however, impose a substantial responsibility upon the employer and, more specifically, on HRM professionals to see that the nature of the program and of each optional benefit is adequately communicated to employees. It may be necessary to hold a number of meetings, to prepare brochures and/or videotapes, and perhaps to hold individual conferences to answer questions and record choices and changes in them. Changes in tax legislation can have a significant effect on the choice of benefits in a cafeteria program.

Controlling Benefit Costs

Benefit costs, like any other costs, must be controlled if an organization is to remain profitable. The costs of employee benefits and services

[29] Brent King, *op. cit.*

[30] A. Schlachtmeyer and R. Bogart, "Employee-Choice Benefits—Can Employees Handle It?" *Compensation Review*, third quarter, 1979, pp. 12–19; and Fragner.

have risen to nearly 35 per cent of total compensation costs and appear to be increasing further. While some costs are for government-mandated programs, many benefits and services are provided at the discretion of an employer or are negotiated through collective bargaining. Most employers find it difficult to eliminate existing benefits and to control the amounts which must be spent if certain benefits are to be made available. Some steps can be taken, however, to reduce benefit costs and get the most from benefit dollars. An obvious one is to provide benefits which the majority of employees value and eliminate those in which they have little interest. A questionnaire survey can be used to elicit employees' preferences for various benefit offerings. If a new benefit appears attractive to them, instead of simply adding it to the list, an employer might use it to replace a less-attractive one in the package.

A second approach, used increasingly, is to have employees contribute a certain amount towards the purchase of discretionary benefits. This system accomplishes two purposes. First, the desired coverage can be provided at a lower cost to the organization but still as a bargain to the employee, who would pay more for it as an individual purchaser. Second, using a contributory approach promotes communication and creates an awareness and appreciation of the employer's contributions to benefits coverage on the employees' behalf.

Issues in the Benefits Area

HRM professionals face a number of issues and problems in the benefits area. Foremost among these are avoiding sex and age discrimination in benefits administration, controlling rising benefit costs, and keeping up with changes in the tax laws.

As a form of compensation, benefits must be provided equally to all employees regardless of sex, age, race, religion, or ethnic origin. For many benefits, maintenance of equality is relatively straightforward. However, in areas such as pensions and disability and health insurance, the road to equality between men and women is less clear. One problem with relation to pension plans is that women have a longer lifespan than men. Thus, they reap the benefits of pension plans for a longer time after retirement than do men, increasing benefit costs to employers.

Another problem is remaining aware of the current costs of benefits. While benefit packages can offer incentives for employees to remain with a company, the costs of these incentives can change, sometimes quite suddenly. The June 1982 federal budget, by making many benefits taxable, reduced many of the advantages of using benefits to reward certain groups of employees. Thus, a government effort to close what were viewed as tax loopholes forced employers to realize that nonsalary forms of compensation have to be examined continually for their cost implications to both companies and employees.

There are a number of deficiencies in the pension system in Canada which are likely to grow unless the implications of changes occurring on the structure of the work force are addressed. The continuing increase in employment in the service industries and the gradual aging of the population are the two primary underlying factors affecting the pension system. Growth in the service sector has carried with it the bulk of the increases in female employment and in part-time work (which is largely by females). Private pensions have not generally been available to most part-time workers and even those women who work full-time end up with lower private pension benefits than men because, on average, their salaries are lower.[31] Hence, issues for the future include the extent to which pensions are insufficient and the extent to which coverage of the system is uneven.

Aging of the population will increasingly put upward pressure on pension benefits which will not be fully offset by a decline in the costs of schooling and other child-related expenditures. The lack of protection of private pensions from inflation is also an issue which has to be considered.

A final pension issue concerns the ability of firms to withdraw money from pension funds over and above what is deemed necessary to meet anticipated employee pension needs. The courts have held in the Dominion Stores case[32] and the Dominion Securities Pitfield case[33] that money which was withdrawn from employee pension plans must be returned. In the case of Dominion stores, the amount was $38 million and for Dominion Securities, $1.7 million. There are likely to be changes in the rules, which in these cases permitted the Ontario Pension Commission to allow withdrawals of the funds. HRM professionals should follow these developments.

Cost issues also arise in the case of workers' compensation. It has recently been observed that Canada's 12 workers' compensation boards are underfunded by an estimated $5 billion.[34] In addition, there has been a rapid increase in the cost of the average claim, although the number of claims has been reduced. Some boards have attempted to raise assessment rates by as much as 21 per cent (British Columbia, 1984), but others such as Ontario have run into such sharp opposition from employees that they rolled back their proposed increase in 1984 assessment rates to a maximum of 15 per cent. With an existing underfunding situation and costs increasing rapidly something has to give. One proposal emerging from a Harvard study of workers' compensation is that experience ratings of companies be instituted; less accident-prone companies would pay lower rates. Given the cost pressure on compensation systems, it is likely that a more widespread form of experience rating will be used than the broader industry categories

[31] Virginia Galt, "Action Urged to Remedy 'Holes' in the Pension System," *The Globe and Mail* (Toronto), June 5, 1985.

[32] Mark Kingwell and Lorne Slotnick, "Return Pension Funds, Dominion Stores Told by Court," *The Globe and Mail* (Toronto), August 19, 1986.

[33] Rick Haliechuk, "Firm Accused of 'Pirating' Pension Fund," *Toronto Star*, August 30, 1986.

[34] Margaret Wenk, "The Coming Crisis in Workers' Compensation," *Canadian Business*, February 1984, pp. 46, 48–50.

used in such provinces as Ontario and British Columbia. For HRM professionals, this issue signals the need to monitor the extent and cost of accidents and industrial hazards.

Summary

This chapter has focussed on five categories of benefits provided employees: universal benefits; mandatory benefits; discretionary benefits; pay for time not worked; and employee service benefits. While many organizations provide very generous benefit packages, most employees have very little control over the type of benefits they receive. The cafeteria approach, which seeks to remedy this problem by giving employees a choice in benefit selection, has rarely been used by organizations. Though benefits are used by organizations to attract and retain employees, there is little research evidence that they are successful in achieving this purpose. However, it is generally accepted that attractive pay and benefit packages are necessary if an organization is to maintain a competitive position. In the past, because of the favourable tax treatment afforded a number of benefit programs, both employers and employees could benefit by having a certain proportion of an organization's compensation dollars set aside for benefits. Cost advantages still exist, even though changes in the 1982 tax laws have reduced the value of many benefit programs.

Project Ideas

1. Design an optimal benefit and service program to fit your own needs. Explain why you selected particular benefits and services and why you rejected other options. Compare your benefit preferences with those of other students.

2. Acquire a booklet describing employee benefits from a local employer (perhaps from your university or college). Relate the plans discussed therein to the material presented in the chapter, noting where applicable the choices that had been made by the employer. Comment on the extent to which the programs are clearly described.

3. Find a firm with a pension plan. Discuss with the employee benefits manager the reasons for the provisions of the plan (for example, the amount of contributions by employer and employee, the basis for calculating benefits, and who administers the plan).

4. Interview an HRM professional of a local organization. Ask about its benefit program, its changes in the past several years, the implications of any recent tax changes, and what methods are used to communicate the program to employees. Be sure to find out if the organization is unionized.

5. Develop a hypothetical company and ask one or more insurance companies or agents to recommend benefit coverages and perhaps provide cost estimates. (If this activity is done as a class project, many insurance companies may be willing to go to this trouble, particularly since they will be assisting individuals who may well be their corporate clients in the near future.)

Cases

Case 13.1: High Health Care Costs at Chrysler

When Lee Iacocca asked Joseph Califano to join the Chrysler board in 1981, he told Califano that health care costs alone could block the company's recovery. Iacocca asked Califano to chair a committee to examine health care expenditures and possible cost-cutting measures. Califano was joined on the committee by Doug Fraser, then president of the United Auto Workers, and Iacocca himself.

Califano describes the work of his committee and some of its findings as follows:

> The first thing our committee did was ask questions about what we were getting for our health care dollars. Then we discovered that we didn't know. Chrysler was spending more than $300 million for health care in 1982, and had no idea what it was buying or from whom. We didn't know who the efficient suppliers were. We had no quality controls. We didn't have the slightest idea what health care our employees needed.
>
> So the first step was to get the facts—the kind of information any businessman or individual buyer should get from any seller. We went to work with our insurer, Blue Cross/Blue Shield of Michigan, and the United Auto Workers. We took a 30-month snapshot of our health care purchases. We examined more than 67,000 hospital admissions, and more than $200 million in charges, incurred over a 30-month period. We catalogued each incident of inpatient and outpatient care for each Chrysler employee, retiree, and dependent. What we found was appalling: unnecessary care, inefficiency, waste, even abuse and fraud.
>
> Here are a few of the things we discovered for the year 1981 alone:
>
> • Chrysler insureds got more than 1 million lab tests at a cost of $12 million. That's more than five for every man, woman, and child we insured.
>
> • Chiropractors increased their diagnostic X-rays almost 15% for each employee over the prior year. Each chiropractor billed our insureds an average of $10,000 annually, just for X-rays.
>
> • The single most costly medical procedure Chrysler paid for turned out to be the $4 million doctors billed the company

for post-admission visits to hospitalized patients—$4 million for those bed visits doctors make as they walk down the hall.*

By 1984, with a projected health care budget of $460 million, Califano's committee had uncovered other problems and abuses in the system, including inappropriate hospital admissions and unnecessarily lengthy stays. In a study of eight major suppliers of hospital care, for example, two-thirds of the admissions for non-surgical low back pain were deemed inappropriate, as were 85 per cent of the days spent in hospital for treatment of the ailment. Hospital stays for maternity were also longer than necessary in over 80 per cent of maternity cases studied.**

Commenting on abuses in the system, Iacocca declares: "The real nut of the problem is there's no buyer/seller relationship left in the delivery of medical goods and services. The attitude is always to let Uncle Sam or Uncle Lee pick up the tab. 'So what if you're charging me too much for the tests or the surgery—*I'm not paying for it.*' "***

Iacocca goes on to say that while medical plans began modestly, Chrysler now pays for "everything you can think of: dermatology, psychiatry, orthodontics—even eyeglasses. To make matters worse, there's no deductible for doctor's fees or hospital costs. There is one small fee for prescription medicines: the guy has to pay the first $3.00 himself."****

Questions:

1. A number of factors led to high health care costs at Chrysler. Which of these factors were beyond Chrysler's control and which could have been controlled by the company? How might they have been controlled?
2. What steps might Chrysler take to reduce its high costs of health care? What are the possible implications of each alternative for the company and its employees?

* From a speech by J.A. Califano, excerpted in "Chrysler Reports Success with Benefit Cost Control," *Employee Benefit Plan Review*, October 1985, pp. 114–20.
** Ibid., pp. 116–17.
*** L. Iacocca with W. Novak, *Iacocca: An Autobiography* (Toronto: Bantam Books, 1984), p. 307.
**** Ibid., p. 307.

Case 13.2: Flexible Compensation at Cominco Ltd.

Along with compensation consultants Hewitt Associates of Toronto, Cominco designed a plan that began with a core of mandatory benefits. The core includes provincial medical plan payments, extended medical coverage with a $500 deductible, life insurance offering one year's salary to the beneficiary, accidental death and dismemberment coverage equal to three times annual salary, short- and long-term disability insurance, vacations, a company pension, and a group registered retirement savings plan.

Core coverage is offered to all salaried employees. But since it doesn't cost the company as much as the previous plan, the difference between the core and the previous plan is given to each employee as "flexible dollars." The employee can use these flexible dollars to buy back the former benefits or additional coverage from certain options offered. As well, some core benefits can be "sold" back to Cominco to add to the cash account. For instance, if an employee's spouse is covered at work for the provincial hospital plan, the employee can obtain a credit in flexible dollars for the core hospital plan. And, depending on years of service with the company, a maximum of five holidays can be converted to flexible dollars to purchase other benefits. The options include extended medical coverage with a $25 deductible, three ranges of dental insurance, life insurance upgraded by six increments and increased insurance for accidental death, dismemberment and long-term disability. In addition, Cominco operates a basic retirement income plan for employees. Fully paid for by Cominco, it provides a pension based on preretirement salary and years of service. Since 1979 the company also has offered a retirement income savings plan (RISP) through which employees pay a minimum of 5 per cent of salary up to $3,500 and Cominco pays 1 per cent of salary up to $700. The savings are invested in company stock. Under the flexible plan, members of the RISP are able to direct some or all of the contributions to a spousal RISP account. Interestingly, any employee who doesn't use his flexible dollars to purchase benefits can withdraw the money from the cash account (and pay taxes on it) at year-end or roll it over into a retirement savings plan.

While all the options may seem complex, Kuntz (Cominco's compensation manager), says that Cominco has had no disasters to date, partly because of planning and partly a function of testing conducted by Hewitt prior to implementing the flexible plan. Says Kuntz: "The biggest single factor that won approval was that there was some choice involved."

Questions:

1. What do you think Cominco gained by adoption of its flexible benefits plan?
2. Can you think of any potential problems with the plan or ways in which to improve it?

14

Employee Health and Safety

The role of health and safety as an HRM function is to maintain a safe and healthy work environment for employees. Nowhere is the challenge greater than on Canada's hazardous oil-drilling rigs. As one reporter has observed, "A worker can be badly injured (on the rigs) in countless ways: crushed by falling 30-foot lengths of 3- to 5-inch-diameter steel pipes, caught in an explosion, blown off the derrick by wind, sliced by fast-moving chain used to lift and tighten pipe, or felled instantly by lethal hydrogen sulfide gas."[1]

In the first half of 1980, one out of five crew members manning the 400 oil-drilling rigs in Alberta sustained an injury serious enough to draw compensation. From 1975 to 1979, 63 men died on Alberta's rigs. Various sources attributed that poor safety record to the use of inexperienced and untrained workers in a high-hazard occupation; poor maintenance of equipment; fatigue and tedium from long stretches of 12-hour shifts; and the lack of a collective voice for the rig workers.[2]

[1] K. Makin, "Casualties—The Bad Side of the Alberta Oil Boom," *The Globe and Mail* (Toronto), December 1, 1980.
[2] Ibid.

In February 1982, one of Canada's most publicized disasters occurred with the sinking off Newfoundland of the Ocean Ranger, an oil-drilling rig, and its entire 84-man crew. According to the commission investigating the tragedy:

> The problems began when a wave broke a porthole in the rig's nerve centre, the ballast control room, soaking the electrical controls that kept the vessel upright in the water.
>
> As a result, four hours later the control panel malfunctioned and allowed water to surge into one of the two gigantic underwater pontoons that supported the rig. When the Ocean Ranger then began to tip forward, untrained crewmen tried to correct the alarming list, but instead made it worse. As the rig leaned into the sea, water rushed inside through openings in two anchor chain compartments. By 1:30 a.m. on Feb. 15, roughly $5^1/_2$ hours after the control centre porthole had broken, the crew began to abandon ship. But one of the four lifeboats was already underwater, and, lacking the protection of cold-weather survival suits, all hands perished.[3]

The commission blamed the rig's owner "for a variety of lapses, including ignoring regulations, training crewmen inadequately, and not providing survival suits."[4] Two years after the accident, the owner agreed to an out-of-court settlement of $440,000, tax free, to each crewman's family.[5] This incident illustrates not only the high human costs of inattention to safety, but also some of their financial repercussions to employers.

Organizational Benefits of a Safe and Healthy Workplace

A safe and healthy workplace helps to maintain a productive and satisfied work force. A safe work environment facilitates productivity by reducing time lost due to work-related accidents and illnesses, as well as time lost due to labour disputes and work stoppages focussed on safety concerns. In just one year in British Columbia, for instance, 46 labour disputes with some of the province's largest public and private employers involved health issues such as first aid facilities, train manning levels, inspections, personal safety equipment, and pollutant levels. Disputes on these issues resulted in 75,000 lost days of worker production.[6]

[3] M. Clugston, "A Preventable Tragedy," *Maclean's*, August 27, 1984, p. 45.
[4] Ibid.
[5] B. Woodworth, "Settling the Rig Disaster," *Maclean's*, January 9, 1984, p. 25.
[6] C.E. Reasons, L.L. Ross, and C. Paterson, *Assault on the Worker*, Occupational Health and Safety in Canada (Toronto: Butterworths, 1981), p. 243.

A safe and healthy workplace can eliminate worker dissatisfaction with unsafe and unhealthy working conditions. That workers care about health and safety is evidenced by the large number of labour disputes arising from safety concerns and the recent statement of one occupational health and safety agency administrator: "Health and safety is now the 'No. 1 priority' of unions."[7]

Besides facilitating productivity and worker satisfaction, maintaining a safe and healthy workplace helps reduce costs associated with work-related accidents and illnesses. An *accident* is defined as an unexpected or unplanned event that results in an injury, property damage, or material loss at a workplace.[8] According to the Occupational Health and Safety Branch of Labour Canada, in 1982 Canada had 854 work-related accidents that resulted in death and 518,790 disabling injuries. The total direct cost of these accidents, including medical and related costs, compensation for lost earnings, and pensions, was $1.97 billion, or an estimated $217 per worker. Actual costs to organizations are even higher, since accidents and illnesses invariably result in production losses. A study by the Economic Council of Canada suggests that indirect costs could range from two to ten times the direct costs. For 1981, for example, the total cost of employment injuries and illnesses would be between $5.7 and $20.9 billion or 1.7 to 6.3 per cent of the Gross National Product.[9]

Maintaining a safe and healthy workplace also helps control health care costs, since employers experience a rise in disability and other health and accident-related insurance expenditures as the number of work-related injuries increases. And since premiums for workers' compensation are rated by industry, inattention to matters of health and safety can result in all employers in an industry having to pay more.

Disabling injuries and illnesses also deprive an employer of the full working life of an employee. A copper refinery recently lost the services of one loyal and enthusiastic worker when a platform collapsed under her. According to one of her co-workers, "Out of ten guys, Sally did more work than nine of them."[10] Furthermore, unsafe working conditions often lead to voluntary turnover when employees become anxious about work-related hazards. Having to replace workers who die, become disabled, or quit because of unsafe working conditions increases an organization's recruiting, selection, and training costs.

Finally, accidents often result in physical damage to material, equipment, and property, as well as in loss of life to employees, customers, and other nonemployees. The actual costs of such damage can be quite high, but even costlier is the damage done to an organization's image. An organization found guilty of practising or perpetuating unsafe or unhealthy working conditions often pays a price in business losses and in the ability to attract qualified applicants for job vacancies.

[7] K. Govier, "Eminence Gray," *Canadian Business*, March 1986, pp. 31–4, 107–12.
[8] Labour Canada, *Canadian Employment Injuries and Occupational Illness, 1972–1981 ed.* (Hull, Que.: Minister of Supply and Services Canada, 1984), p. xiii.
[9] P. Manga et al., *Occupational Health and Safety: Issues and Alternatives*, Technical Report Series No. 6 (Ottawa: Economic Council of Canada, 1981).
[10] A. Moses, "Mine Worker Remembered as Extraordinary Woman," *The Globe and Mail* (Toronto), December 19, 1980.

Health and Safety: Relation to Other Functions

Seven HRM functions are directly related to the health and safety function, including selection, training, performance appraisal, job analysis, recruiting, benefits, and labour relations. These relationships are portrayed in Exhibit 14.1.

Selection

The selection function facilitates health and safety by selecting applicants who are physically and mentally able to perform the job. While research shows very little support for an identifiable personality trait predictive of unsafe work behaviour ("accident proneness"), selection procedures can screen applicants for physical and mental impairments that could conceivably increase the likelihood of accident or illness.[11] For example, a relationship has been established between vision and accident occurrence: employees who passed vision standards for their jobs had significantly fewer accidents than employees who failed vision requirements.[12] It is safe to assume that an employee who fails any selection standard important to performance in his or her job (such as coordination, hearing, or physical strength test) has a greater risk of accident or injury in the performance of job duties. Research also indicates that older workers are much less likely than younger workers to have an accident.[13] Though younger applicants may not be rejected simply because of their age, in the interest of safety they could be assigned to less hazardous jobs.

Training

Training facilitates health and safety by educating workers in safe work procedures and behaviour. Training is one of the major components in organizational programs to promote safety awareness among employees. The value of safety training for new employees or employees on a new job is supported by data indicating that accidents are highest during the first months on a new job. This relationship holds regardless of age or sex of the worker.[14]

Training programs should be conducted for both supervisors and their subordinates. Program content for supervisors should emphasize knowledge and enforcement of safety rules and regulations, as well as

[11] F. Lindsay, "Accident Proneness—Does It Exist?" *Occupational Safety and Health*, February 1980, vol. 10, no. 2, pp. 8–9.

[12] N.C. Kaphart and J. Tiffin, "Vision and Accident Experience," *National Safety News*, 1950, vol. 62, pp. 90–1.

[13] N. Root, "Injuries at Work are Fewer Among Older Employees," *Monthly Labor Review*, 1981, vol. 104, no. 3, pp. 30–4.

[14] F. Siskind, "Another Look at the Link Between Work Injuries and Job Experience," *Monthly Labor Review*, 1982, vol. 105, no. 2, pp. 38–40.

EXHIBIT 14.1

Health and safety: relation to other functions

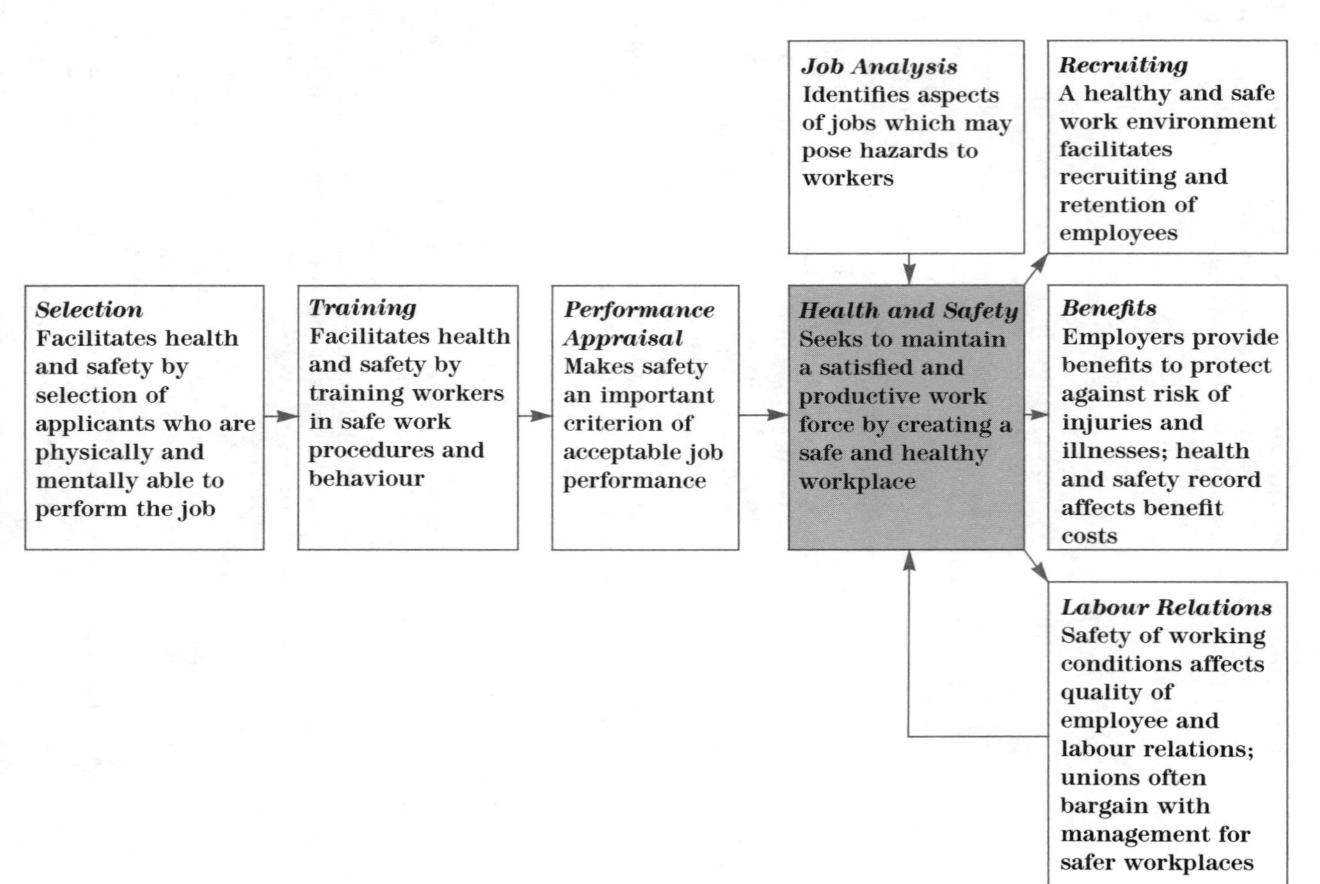
Selection
Facilitates health and safety by selection of applicants who are physically and mentally able to perform the job
Training
Facilitates health and safety by training workers in safe work procedures and behaviour
Performance Appraisal
Makes safety an important criterion of acceptable job performance
Job Analysis
Identifies aspects of jobs which may pose hazards to workers
Health and Safety
Seeks to maintain a satisfied and productive work force by creating a safe and healthy workplace
Recruiting
A healthy and safe work environment facilitates recruiting and retention of employees
Benefits
Employers provide benefits to protect against risk of injuries and illnesses; health and safety record affects benefit costs
Labour Relations
Safety of working conditions affects quality of employee and labour relations; unions often bargain with management for safer workplaces

recognition and control of hazards in the workplace. Programs for subordinates should be more specific, emphasizing rules and safe work behaviours.

Performance Appraisal

Safe work procedures and behaviour can also be encouraged by performance appraisal systems that make safety an important criterion of job performance. For example, if the safety record of a unit is one dimension for appraising managerial performance, the unit's manager is motivated to demand subordinates' attention to safety. Holding managers responsible for the safety records of their units is one factor associated with effective safety management programs.[15] Alternatively, appraisal and reward systems that emphasize productivity over safety may lead to a disregard for safe work procedures. Employees and union leaders claim that this had been the case in the deaths of several miners working under a production bonus system which encouraged production at the expense of safety.[16]

Performance feedback can also be used in programs that encourage safe work behaviour. The behaviour of employees in a vehicle maintenance department was observed and recorded with attention to safety. Feedback was in the form of a posted graph comparing the observed safety behaviour of the department against the desired behaviour. The study found that a combination of training and performance feedback on safety dimensions resulted in improved work behaviour and a substantial reduction over previous years in time lost because of accidents.[17]

Job Analysis

Job analysis identifies aspects of jobs that may pose hazards to workers. Following the identification of such hazards, jobs may be modified to eliminate hazards, or safe work procedures can be developed and specified in job descriptions. The use of required safety equipment and protective devices, such as goggles, ear protectors, and hard hats, should also be specified in job descriptions.

Job descriptions that identify hazards and specify safe work procedures provide guidelines and objectives for safety training programs. A job safety analysis training guide is given in Exhibit 14.2. The analysis has three steps:

[15] M.J. Smith, H.H. Cohen, A. Cohen, and R.J. Cleveland, "Characteristics of Successful Safety Programs," *Journal of Safety Research*, 1978, vol. 10, pp. 5–15.

[16] M. Lowe, "Union Leaders Suspect Bonus Hinders Safety," *The Globe and Mail*, September 18, 1980.

[17] J. Komaki, A.T. Heinzmann, and L. Lawson, "Effect of Training and Feedback: Component Analysis of a Behavioral Safety Program," *Journal of Applied Psychology*, 1980, vol. 65, no. 3, pp. 261–70.

1. Break the job down into its basic steps.
2. Identify potential accidents and hazards associated with each step.
3. Recommend safe job procedures for each job step.

When completed, the job safety analysis serves as an aid in instructing employees in safe work behaviour. Exhibit 14.3 shows the safety analysis guide completed for a vertical lathe operation job.

Recruiting

Recruiting and retention of employees is facilitated when organizations demonstrate a protective concern for the safety and well-being of their employees. Whereas a good health and safety record may facilitate recruiting, a reputation for dangerous or unhealthy working conditions will surely discourage many potential applicants.

Benefits

Concern for health and safety has prompted employers and governments to provide a variety of benefits to protect workers against the risks of untimely death, disability, medical expenses, and unemployment from causes outside an employee's control (for example, shutdowns because of accidents, termination for health reasons). The cost of many discretionary benefits is affected by an employer's health and safety record since employers with poorer records must pay higher rates. Mandatory workers' compensation is industry-rated; a poor record by a few employers can force up the rate for every employer in the industry.

Some organizations also provide employee service benefits geared to maintaining a healthy work force. Examples include periodic physical examinations, fitness programs, anti-smoking campaigns, workshops on stress, and alcohol and drug abuse programs.

Labour Relations

Relations between labour and management can be strained by employees' concerns about health and safety. Worries about safety may give rise to strikes, as noted earlier. During labour negotiations, unions often voice employees' safety concerns to management and bargain for safer working conditions and other safety measures. For example, the Canadian Automobile Workers' collective agreements with Canadian automobile manufacturers now include provision for a full-time worker-inspector in all plants with more than 600 employees. Plants with more than 10,000 workers have two health and safety inspectors. This representative, who is appointed for an indefinite term by the president of the union, must be given an office by the company; he or she maintains a close but independent relationship with the company's safety committee.

EXHIBIT 14.2

A form for a job safety analysis training guide

JOB:			DATE:
JOB SAFETY ANALYSIS TRAINING GUIDE	TITLE OF PERSON WHO DOES JOB:	FOREMAN/SUPR:	ANALYSIS BY:
DEPARTMENT:	SECTION:		REVIEWED BY:
REQUIRED AND/OR RECOMMENDED PERSONAL PROTECTIVE EQUIPMENT:			APPROVED BY:

SEQUENCE OF BASIC JOB STEPS	POTENTIAL ACCIDENTS OR HAZARDS	RECOMMENDED SAFE JOB PROCEDURE
Break the job down into its basic steps, e.g., what is done first, what is done next, and so on. You can do this by 1) observing the job, 2) discussing it with the operator, 3) drawing on your knowledge of the job, or 4) a combination of the three. Record the job steps in their normal order of occurrence. Describe what is done, not the details of how it is done. Usually three or four words are sufficient to describe each basic job step.	For each job step, ask yourself what accidents could happen to the man doing the job step. You can get the answers by 1) observing the job, 2) discussing it with the operator, 3) recalling past accidents, or 4) a combination of the three. Ask yourself: can he be struck by or contacted by anything; can he strike against or come in contact with anything; can he be caught in, on, or between anything; can he fall; can he overexert; is he exposed to anything injurious such as gas, radiation, welding rays, etc? For example, acid burns, fumes.	For each potential accident or hazard, ask yourself how should the man do the job step to avoid the potential accident, or what should he do or not do to avoid the accident. You can get your answers by 1) observing the job for leads, 2) discussing precautions with experienced job operators, 3) drawing on your experience, or 4) a combination of the three. Be sure to describe specifically the precautions a man must take. Don't leave out important details. Number each separate recommended precaution with the same number you gave the potential accident (see center column) that the precaution seeks to avoid. Use simple do or don't statements to explain recommended precautions as if you were talking to the man. For example: "Lift with your legs, not your back." Avoid such generalities as "Be careful," "Be alert," "Take caution," etc.

SOURCE: This form is copyright by and available from the U.S. National Safety Council, Chicago. Used with permission.

Health and Safety Responsibilities

Large organizations in industries with potentially hazardous equipment or materials (such as manufacturers and chemical producers) often have separate safety departments headed by a safety engineer. In the majority of companies, however, health and safety responsibilities are assigned to HRM professional staff, which sometimes includes safety specialists and medical professionals, such as industrial nurses or hygienists. Full-time safety specialists are most common in large manufacturing companies, public utilities, and transportation and distribution industries. They are least common in banks, nonprofit organizations, and insurance companies. In general, HRM professionals

EXHIBIT 14.3

A completed job safety analysis training guide for a vertical lathe operator

	JOB: VERTICAL LATHE OPERATION	DATE: AUGUST 29, 19——
JOB SAFETY ANALYSIS TRAINING GUIDE	TITLE OF PERSON WHO DOES JOB: LATHE MACHINIST; FOREMAN/SUPR:	ANALYSIS BY:
DEPARTMENT: SV-SHOP	SECTION: MACHINE SHOP	REVIEWED BY:
REQUIRED AND/OR RECOMMENDED PERSONAL PROTECTIVE EQUIPMENT: SAFETY GLASSES, HAND & FOOT PROTECTION		APPROVED BY:

SEQUENCE OF BASIC JOB STEPS	POTENTIAL ACCIDENTS OR HAZARDS*	RECOMMENDED SAFE JOB PROCEDURE
1. PLACE RAW STOCK BLANK IN LATHE CHUCK.	1. (SA) Sharp edges of stock blank.	1. Wear gloves or protect against sharp edges as required when handling raw stock.
	2. (CB) Stock and lathe	2. Watch position of hands, arms and body to keep clear of pinch points.
	3. (SO) Lifting raw stock blank	3. Use proper lifting procedures. Get help if blank is too large for one man.
	4. (CO) Moving parts while rotating blank	4. Keep hands clear when rotating chuck to position part. Use jogging control or slow speed. Wear short sleeves. Do not wear gloves or rings.
	5. (SB) Falling objects	5. Wear foot protection.
2. FABRICATE AND/OR INSTALL TEMPLATE ON STYLUS PLATEN.	1. (F) Slips on oily surface at same or different level. Climbing for access to elevated controls of equipment.	1. Keep oil spills wiped up. Apply non-skid material to elevated steps. Use work platform engineered for job, including hand rail protection.
3. SELECT AND INSTALL TOOL CUTTER.	1. (SB) Falling objects, oily	1. Keep parts free of oil when handling, wear foot protection.
	2. (SA) Sharp tools	2. Be aware of handling sharp objects.
4. SELECT MACHINE MODE	1. (CW) Electrical controls	1. Be sure machine is properly grounded and all electrical controls are in good repair.
5. MACHINE PART	1. (SB) Metal particles	1. Wear eye protection.
6. REMOVE TURNINGS AND CHIPS AS MACHINING PROGRESSES	1. (SB) Turnings and chips	1. Wear eye protection. Use correct tools to clean turnings from table.
	2. (CO) Turnings	2. Break turnings before they become unwieldy. Do not wear long sleeve work clothes.
	(More)	

*Abbreviations: CB — caught between; CO — caught on; CW — contact with; F — falls; SA — struck against; SB — struck by; and SO — strain or overexertion

SOURCE: *Handbook of Occupational Safety and Health,* copyright 1975 by the U.S. National Safety Council, Chicago. Used with permission.

help organizations comply with health and safety standards set by legislation, as well as by employers.

All Canadian jurisdictions have health and safety legislation that requires employers to accept certain responsibilities for workers' safety and take various actions towards maintaining it. Most of the laws mandate an employer with a specified number of employees in a workplace—Ontario's act sets the number at 20—to establish a joint management-worker health and safety committee.

This legislation affects HRM professionals in a number of ways. When an employer is required to provide information, instruction, and supervision to a worker to protect his or her health and safety, this task often falls on HRM staff. So does meeting the requirements of giving assistance, cooperation, and certain information to the joint health and safety committee or to the safety representatives in smaller workplaces. Other major responsibilities of HRM staff, often HRM generalists, include record-keeping, posting of notices, communicating and enforcing health and safety rules, monitoring the work environment, and safety training.

Safety management also includes identifying and changing hazardous working conditions, as well as evaluating the effectiveness of health and safety efforts. Some related activities extend beyond HRM department boundaries. For example, the purchasing department must include the criterion of safety when purchasing new equipment. The comptroller and top management must be willing to support health and safety training and the costs of purchasing and installing safety equipment.

The Ontario Occupational Health and Safety Act

All Canadian jurisdictions have legislation dealing with occupational health and safety. Their regulations are similar except that Prince Edward Island's and Nova Scotia's have no provision for joint health and safety committees. For the most part, we will discuss the Ontario Occupational Health and Safety Act because it is generally regarded as the country's most comprehensive.[18]

History of the Ontario Legislation

In 1974, following union allegations of serious health and safety problems in the mining industry, Ontario established the Royal Commission

[18] G.B. Reschenthaler, *Occupational Health and Safety in Canada: The Economics and Three Case Studies* (Montreal: Institute for Research on Public Policy, 1979), p. xiv; and Albert Broyles and Gil Reschenthaler, *Occupational Health and Safety: Issues and Alternatives*, Technical Report no. 6 (Ottawa: Economic Council of Canada, 1981).

on the Health and Safety of Workers in Mines, chaired by Professor (later President) James Ham of the University of Toronto. The commission's report in 1976 made sweeping recommendations, including the following:

1. The consolidation with the Ministry of Labour of various inspection, health, and safety units from various other ministries.
2. Mandatory establishment of joint worker-management health and safety committees.
3. Safety-related qualifications for supervisors and workers.
4. Safety-related duties of employees.
5. The provision of defined medical surveillance and services and the keeping of occupational health and safety records.[19]

In addition, the Ham Report found "a serious lack of openness on matters of the health and safety of workers in mines . . . Workers have a right in natural justice to know about the risks and consequences of the risks that they undertake at work."[20]

Because the commission felt workers had too few opportunities to contribute their insights to the assessment of work conditions and decision-making on issues of health and safety, it recommended removing these issues from the "adamantly confrontational character of Canadian labour-management relations" and establishing joint committees in the hope that "a new measure of labour-management cooperation can emerge."[21]

The Ham Report provided the major impetus for the Ontario Occupational Health and Safety Act of 1978 (OHSA), which consolidated previous legislation and introduced new principles concerning the control of toxic substances and the participation of workers in health and safety programs.

Provisions of the Ontario Legislation

OHSA covers all workplaces except those of domestic workers, farm workers, teachers, and the academic staff of a university or related institution. As described in explanatory material published by the Industrial Accident Prevention Association,[22] the act sets out the respective responsibilities of employers, supervisors, and workers for maintaining occupational health and safety. It also mandates the formation of joint committees and sets procedures for inspection and record-keeping.

[19] *Report of the Royal Commission on the Health and Safety of Workers in Mines* (Toronto: Ministry of the Attorney General, Province of Ontario, 1976), pp. 254–55.

[20] Ibid., pp. 249–50.

[21] Ibid., p. 250.

[22] *A Guide to the Provisions of Ontario's Occupational Health and Safety Act*, 7th ed. (Toronto: Industrial Accident Prevention Association, 1986).

Employers' responsibilities. An employer is required to inform workers and supervisors of any health or safety hazards in a job. The employer must also provide workers with information concerning measures to be taken for their protection. It is also the employer's duty to ensure that equipment, materials, and protective devices are provided, maintained, and used as prescribed. Employers must also be sure that all supervisors are "competent persons"—qualified because of knowledge, training, and experience to organize work and its performance; familiar with regulations that apply to the work; and knowledgeable about actual or potential dangers in the workplace.

Copies of the act must be posted in both English and the majority language of the workplace; explanatory material produced by the Ministry of Labour must also be posted. Assistance, cooperation, and certain information must be given to the joint committee or to workers' health and safety representatives. An occupational health service must be maintained and records kept of exposure to toxic substances. Where so prescribed, an employer may permit in the workplace only those employees who have undergone specified medical examinations, tests, or X-rays and are physically fit to do the work.

Supervisors' responsibilities. A supervisor, defined as a person who has charge of a workplace or authority over a worker, is required to ensure that employees work in the manner prescribed and use prescribed protective devices and equipment. He or she also has the duty of advising workers of potential or actual hazards "of which he is aware."

Employees' responsibilities and rights. Employees are required to use or wear the safety equipment, protective devices, or clothing that their employers require. They must work in compliance with the provisions of the act and regulations, which include reporting to the employer or supervisor any absence of or defect in equipment or protective devices which might endanger themselves or other workers. Employees may not operate any equipment in a manner that might endanger themselves or other workers. (This prohibition includes pranks or other unnecessary conduct which could pose a danger.)

On the other side of the coin, an employee has the right to refuse work which he or she believes would endanger himself or herself or another worker. This right applies to danger perceived from the physical condition of the workplace or any machine.

When a worker invokes the right of refusal, an established procedure, diagrammed in Exhibit 14.4, is set in motion. The worker reports the circumstances to the supervisor, then remains in a safe place near the work station. The supervisor must investigate in the presence of the complainant and a workers' representative. If the problem is not resolved, it is reported to a Ministry of Labour inspector, who investigates as soon as possible. Meanwhile, the worker may be assigned other duties, subject to the terms of any collective agreement, and another worker may be assigned to the work, provided he or she has been informed of the first worker's refusal and the reasons for it.

Saskatchewan's legislation, in contrast to Ontario's, has the joint health and safety committee itself investigate when an individual refuses unsafe work. If the members decide unanimously that the refusal is justified, the matter is settled. Otherwise, an inspector can be called in.

Joint health and safety committees. With some exceptions, all workplaces where 20 or more persons are regularly employed or where workers are involved with toxic substances must establish a joint health and safety committee. It must have at least two members, at least half of whom are nonmanagerial workers selected by the workers or, where applicable, by the union. The members are to identify hazardous situations and make recommendations to the employer on issues of health and safety. In addition, they are to obtain information from the employer concerning the identification of health and safety hazards and the experience of similar industries of which the employer has knowledge. One of the worker-members of the committee is to inspect the physical condition of the workplace not more than once a month. A worker-member is also to investigate cases of critical injury or fatality and report the findings to the Ministry of Labour, as well as to the joint committee.

The committee meets at least once every three months. Its members must be paid for the time they spend attending meetings and carrying out other OHSA duties.

Workplaces excluded from the requirement for joint committees include construction projects, offices, shops, libraries, museums, art galleries, restaurants, hotels, theatres, and private clubs. The Minister of Labour can order the establishment of joint committees in any of the excluded workplaces.

Inspection and enforcement. The Ministry of Labour appoints inspectors to enforce OHSA regulations. Inspectors have the power to enter any workplace at any time without notice; to inspect and copy records and other material; to conduct tests; and to require an organization to provide, at its expense, reports from a professional engineer on the load limits of a floor, roof, or temporary structure. If an inspector finds that a provision of the act has been contravened, he or she can direct compliance, limit or stop work, or clear a workplace and isolate it by barricades, depending on the degree of hazard.

Any person within an organization, regardless of position, who fails to comply with any part of the legislation is liable to a fine and/or a jail sentence. However, strict liability has been modified by allowing accused employers, supervisors, and constructors to defend themselves by proving that they have "taken every precaution reasonable in the circumstances."[23]

Information and record-keeping. To encourage the active participation of workers and their representatives in workplace health and safety programs, OHSA requires employers to provide health and safety information to workers and their representatives. Exhibit 14.5 provides a list of types of information, when and how it is to be provided, and

[23] Ibid., pp. 30–1.

EXHIBIT 14.4

Ontario's procedure when a worker has reason to believe work is likely to endanger self or another person

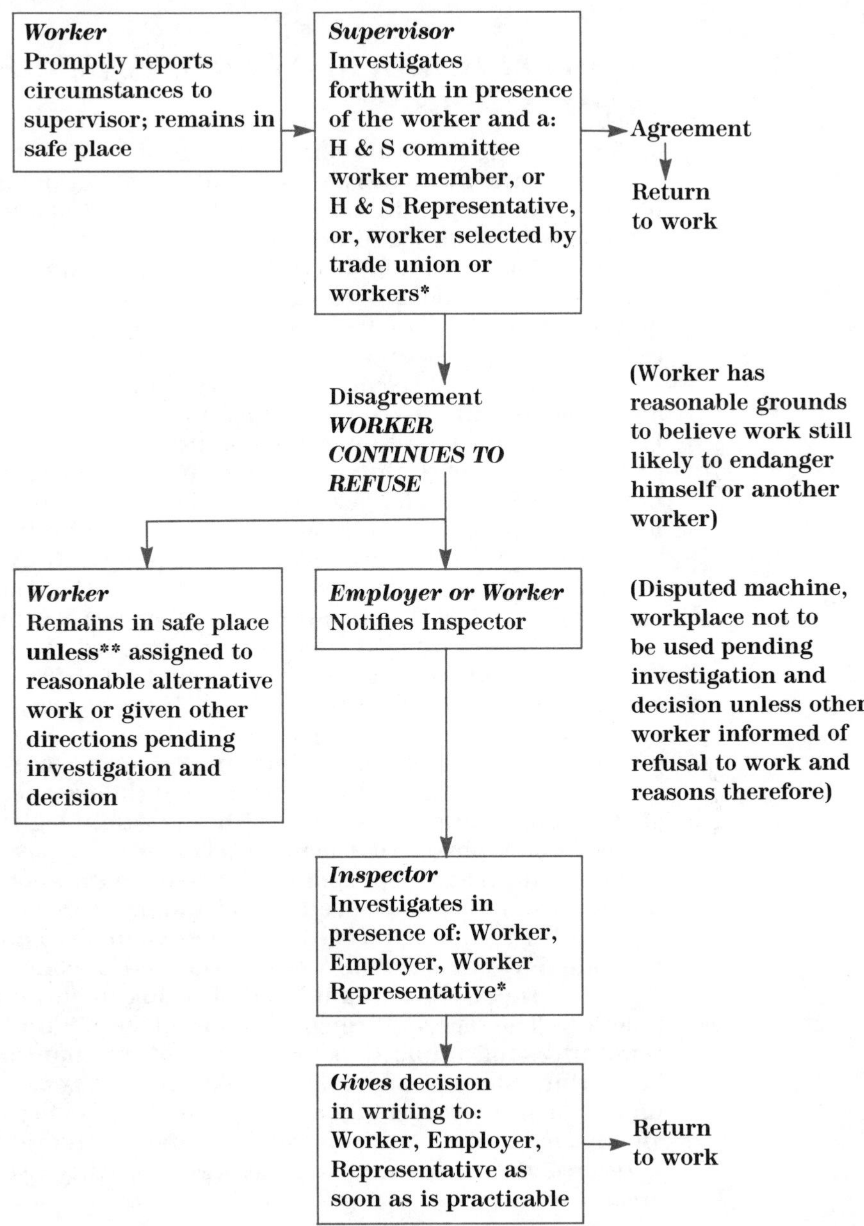

*One of whom must be made available, the representative entitled to pay for time spent here.
**Subject to terms of any collective agreement.

SOURCE: *A Guide to the Provisions of Ontario's Occupational Health and Safety Act*, 7th ed. (Toronto: Industrial Accident Prevention Association, 1986), p. 16.

to whom. The act also requires that reports be sent to the Ministry of Labour and to the joint labour-management committee concerning fatal or critical injuries, disabling injuries, other injuries that require medical attention, occupational illnesses, and toxic substances.

Impact of Health and Safety Legislation on Organizations

OHSA and parallel legislation in other Canadian jurisdictions have tended to increase the awareness of health and safety among employees, employers, and the public. However, a 1981 report of a federal-provincial commission enquiring into safety in the mines found that several companies had failed to establish clear goals or accountability for accident prevention and did not recognize the value of consulting with employees either for input into decision-making or as a mechanism to improve workers' attitudes.[24]

Moreover, disagreements exist over how much certainty of hazard an employee must have to exercise the right to refuse to work. The labour relations board in the federal jurisdiction, which has a refusal provision similar to Ontario's, ruled in a recent case that a possible hazard in the normal operation of a job is not sufficient justification for refusal to work. A Bell Canada employee had refused to work with a sealant used in cable systems; initial tests at the University of Western Ontario had been inconclusive as to whether the compound was carcinogenic. A federal safety office found there was no imminent danger, and the worker's refusal was ruled unjustified. The union staff representative said the board's decision contained the dangerous implication that "if scientific research discloses hazards in chemicals or compounds that have been used normally for years, workers would be precluded from invoking the imminent danger clause."[25]

Another problem is that workers and their representatives do not always understand or follow health and safety legislation. The 1981 commission reported that many workers were bypassing first-line supervision in firms' responsibility systems (with apparent approval of union locals) and that several local unions were failing in their responsibilities by not recognizing the extent of their influence over individual workers. Unions were also faulted for concentrating on identifying workplace hazards instead of trying to eliminate unsafe work practices. The report affirmed the importance of joint health and safety committees but found that they were not functioning as they should be. Noting that the role of a safety department is essential, but rarely understood, the report recommended that the safety department play an advisory and an auditing role, facilitating the integration of what it termed the direct and indirect responsibility systems within an organization.[26]

[24] *Towards Safe Production: The Report of the Joint Federal-Provincial Inquiry Commission into Safety in Mines and Mining Plants in Ontario*, vol. 1 (Toronto: Ontario Ministry of Labour, 1981), pp. 14–15.

[25] Wilfred List, "Worker Can't Refuse Normal Job if Safety in Dispute, Board Rules," *The Globe and Mail* (Toronto), December 17, 1981.

[26] *Towards Safe Production*, pp. 14–15, 19.

EXHIBIT 14.5

Ontario regulations on access to health and safety information

Type of information	*Provided by*	*When & how*	*To whom*
Names and work locations of joint Health and Safety Committee members	Employer	Permanently posted in workplace	(Workers)
Copy of Act and any explanatory material published by Ministry	Employer	Permanently posted in workplace in English and majority language	(Workers)
If prescribed to keep exposure records of workers, access to those records	Employer	Make available:	Each worker, his or her exposure record
Where required to do air sampling under regulation, air sampling results	Employer	Post in workplace	(Workers)
Written measures and procedures where required to have by regulation	Employer	When applicable, to:	Workers affected
A Director's order made under S. 20	Employer	Posted in workplace on receipt from director; copies to:	(Workers): Trade union Health & Safety Committee Health & Safety representative
A Ministry Inspector's order or report	Employer	Posted in workplace and copies to:	(Workers): Health & Safety Committee Health & Safety representative, trade union
Notices required to be sent to Ministry in cases of injury, death, or accident	Employer	Copies to: (same time as provided to Ministry)	Health & Safety Committee members Health & Safety representative, trade union

EXHIBIT 14.5–Continued

Ontario regulations on access to health and safety information

Type of information	*Provided by*	*When & how*	*To whom*
Necessary information for carrying out of workplace inspection by Health & Safety Committee member or representative	Employer	As required for inspection	Health & Safety Committee members or Health & Safety representatives
Health & Safety experience and work practices of similar industries of which Employer is aware	Employer	as requested	Health & Safety Committee members
Annual summary of workplace injury experience	WCB	As requested by trade union, Health & Safety Committee, representative, or worker. Post in workplace	Person or body requesting the information and employer, who should post. (Workers)
Where a designated substance regulation applies, assessment results	Employer	Copies to:	Members of Health and Safety Committee
Control program for the designated substance, where applicable	Employer	Copies to:	Members of Health and Safety Committee. All workers affected

SOURCE: *A Guide to the Provisions of Ontario's Occupational Health and Safety Act*, 7th ed. (Toronto: Industrial Accident Prevention Association, 1986), p. 23.

Ensuring a Safe and Healthy Workplace

This section focusses on strategies used by organizations and HRM professionals to ensure a safe, healthy workplace, including (1) controlling physical hazards, (2) promoting safety awareness, and (3) promoting good health.

Controlling Physical Hazards

The most direct approach to controlling physical hazards is to eliminate them, but this is not always possible. Some hazards, such as those inherent in oil-drilling equipment and locales, cannot be eliminated. However, steps can be taken to reduce their potential for causing accidents. For example, drilling operations can be suspended in periods of high wind; equipment can be maintained so that it functions properly; crew members can be alerted to the potential hazards of operating equipment; and shifts can be shortened so as to reduce the fatigue and tedium which contribute to accidents. In oil drilling and other industries, safety inspections can ensure that employees follow safety rules and use protective devices, and that machinery and the workplace are free from hazards.

Accident-causing hazards have been recognized for some time, but only in recent years have occupational threats to employees' health, both physical and mental, been recognized. Occupational illnesses are difficult to analyze and control because they develop relatively slowly. However, it has been estimated that in 1980 there were 10,000 workers in Canada suffering from job-related diseases such as cancer, silicosis and asbestosis.[27] While it is generally known that exposure to radioactive materials, coal dust, asbestos, and other substances can lead to illness and often death, there are literally thousands of other materials and substances which the United States' National Institute for Safety and Health has identified as hazardous. Indeed, medical research has uncovered health hazards in most occupations in modern society.

Employers' efforts to control physical health hazards should include regular monitoring of the work environment and regular physical examination of employees. For example, underground mining requires constant checking of the air quality and levels of coal dust. Grain milling and processing also require testing of dust levels not only for health reasons, but also to avoid explosions and fires. Company physicians and medical personnel should monitor a wide range of matters relating to employees' health, from routine hearing tests and chest X-rays to incidents of infertility and abnormal childbirths. The latter is a particularly sensitive issue since employers are prohibited from discriminating against women. Although an employer must not deny a pregnant woman access to any job, certain jobs, such as video display terminal operator, may involve exposure to materials or conditions known to be hazardous to unborn children.

As employers discover that certain processes and materials are hazardous to the health and well-being of employees, they must develop ways to eliminate or reduce the danger. Recently, some organizations have eliminated hazards by a very obvious and direct approach: they

[27] Reasons, Ross, and Paterson, p. 38. The estimate is attributed to Dr. Gordon Ackerley, president of the Canadian Centre for Occupational Health and Safety, as reported in Linda M. Quaig, "Occupational Death," *Maclean's*, May 19, 1980, p. 45.

have substituted robots for people in high-risk jobs ranging from feeding metal blanks into a furnace and removing hot castings, to shearing sheep and welding and painting automobiles. The cost of robots is lower than one might expect. A Goodyear tire plant gave a robot the job of carrying heavy wheels from one line to another. The robot cost $23,000 and replaced two workers on each of two shifts, creating a direct savings in wages of $28,000 per year and eliminating risks of back injuries.[28] The possibilities for improving employees' health and safety through "smart" robots look very promising.

The primary means used by organizations to reduce physical hazards is requiring the use of safety devices and protective equipment. A Bureau of National Affairs (BNA) survey of 124 U.S. organizations found that all manufacturers in the sample and more than half the nonmanufacturers required some type of personal safety equipment. The more common types required included safety glasses or goggles, face shields (including welders' helmets), safety shoes or boots, hard hats, respiratory equipment, and protective clothing. In only half the surveyed organizations did the employer pay for the entire cost of this equipment.[29]

Safety devices should meet three criteria. They should be foolproof, should not become disengaged, and should not interfere with production. In many cases, new equipment meets these criteria better than do "add-on" safety devices for existing equipment.

Unfortunately, personal safety equipment is sometimes unpopular with employees, and they object to using it. Despite the unpopularity of safety devices and equipment, nearly all employers require their use to protect employees against work-related injuries and illnesses. In most organizations, employees can be disciplined and even fired for failure to use required safety equipment. Also not uncommon are disagreements between employers and employees about whether safety equipment reduces hazards more than it imposes additional dangers. For example, in 1982, garbage collectors in Toronto went on an illegal strike against the imposition of wearing fluorescent red and yellow vests. The workers claimed the jackets were a safety hazard, while management said they would reduce injuries from passing automobiles, as they had in a neighbouring jurisdiction. The strike was resolved by an agreement to have the Ontario Labour Relations Board decide the issue and, in the interim, to have the garbage collectors wear strips of reflective tape on their uniforms in lieu of the vests.[30]

Clearly, rules and regulations about the use of safety equipment, unless accepted by most employees, can strain supervisor-subordinate relations. Increased acceptance of safety rules and regulations, including the use of safety equipment, is a common goal of organizational safety programs.

[28] G. Bylinsky, "Those Smart Young Robots on the Production Line," *Fortune*, December 17, 1979.

[29] Bureau of National Affairs, *Safety Policies and the Impact of OSHA*, Personnel Policies Forum Survey no. 117 (Washington, D.C.: BNA, May 1977).

[30] Ross Laver, "Compromise Reached, Garbagemen Returning," *The Globe and Mail* (Toronto), May 26, 1982.

Promoting Safety Awareness

There are a number of ways organizations focus attention on matters of safety, including safety committees; recording and posting safety performance records; providing recognition and awards to individuals and units with good safety records; creating rules and regulations regarding work behaviour and the use of safety equipment; and safety training programs. In addition to these company-sponsored efforts, a number of organizations, such as the Industrial Accident Prevention Association and the Construction Safety Association, actively promote safety consciousness through seminars, television advertising, joint meetings with various organizations, and safety programs in schools.

Most organizations with safety programs combine a variety of approaches. Whatever methods are used, the commitment and participation of top management are key ingredients in the success of occupational safety programs.[31] Managerial commitment to safety is in evidence at Du Pont, whose highly successful program is described in Exhibit 14.6.

EXHIBIT 14.6

Safety first at Du Pont

Du Pont started a safety tradition at his powder mill that has long outlived its founder or the mill and become a core value of the company. He designed his first powder mills to minimize the danger in the event of an explosion. He tested new gunpowder formulations himself before permitting other employees to handle them. He established a rule that no employee was allowed to enter a new mill until he or his general manager had first operated it safely. But more than all these precautions, he demonstrated his commitment to safety by living with his family on the plant site beside the mills along with his employees.

Two hundred years later Du Pont's safety record is truly impressive. Its workdays-lost rate (related to accidents) in the United States is 69 times better than the average for all U.S. industry and 17 times better than the average for the U.S. chemicals industry. Even the worldwide rate for Du Pont's 146 facilities is 67 times better than the U.S. average. In the wake of the recent disaster in Bhopal, India, where 2,500 people died and more than 100,000 were injured due to leakage of gas from a chemicals plant, Du Pont's performance takes on far greater significance. During the past five years, Du Pont's 157,000 employees have been involved in only 253 lost-workday injuries. If the company had been typical of U.S. industry, it would have had more than 12,000 such injuries.

How does Du Pont do it? It begins by converting the corporate *value* of safety into an explicit *objective*—zero accidents. This objective is based on the *belief* that all accidents are preventable. One Du Pont plant with 2,000 workers

[31] F.C. Rinefort, "A New Look at Occupational Safety," *The Personnel Administrator*, November 1977, vol. 22, pp. 29–36. Smith, Cohen, Cohen, and Cleveland; and D. Zohar, "Safety Climate in Industrial Organizations: Theoretical and Applied Implications," *Journal of Applied Psychology*, 1980, vol. 65, no. 1, pp. 96–102.

actually went for 445 days without a recordable injury. At Du Pont safety is a line management responsibility. All managers, from the chairman of the board to the supervisors who manage groups of workers in plants or offices around the world, are responsible for safety in their departments. If an injury occurs in any Du Pont plant, it is reported to world headquarters within 24 hours. If a death occurs, it is reported to the chairman. At Du Pont the CEO is also the chief safety officer, and at all executive committee meetings, safety is first on the agenda.

The same importance is given to safety by plant managers. Every plant defines standards, sets goals, designs a safety program, and conducts regular safety audits. Training is a key element. The first thing taught in every training program is safety. Studies have shown that safety performance is proportionate to the level of training of the workforce, so training is continued as an ongoing activity. More impressive than all these things is the fact that all supervisors in Du Pont facilities must review one safety feature every single day with each of their subordinates. Every sales and administrative department also conducts regular safety meetings. An open file drawer in a Du Pont office is considered a safety hazard and attracts immediate attention.

There is also a specific set of safety-related rules. Wearing seat belts in company vehicles while on company business is mandatory. Defensive-driving courses are given to employees who travel on the job by car. When one traveling employee in Florida was identified by his manager as a problem driver, an outside driving expert was flown down from Wilmington the next day to give him special instruction.

Safety is the responsibility of every employee at Du Pont, not just managers. Rules are enforced by discipline, and violations are a serious matter. Leon C. Schaller, section manager in the employee relations department, says, "Anyone working for Du Pont knows the fastest and surest route to getting fired is to repeatedly violate safety rules and procedures." The company tries to positively involve workers in the safety program.

SOURCE: Reprinted by permission of the publisher, from *The Vital Difference*, by F. G. Harmon & G. Jacobs, pp. 59–60,

Safety committees. As already noted, most jurisdictions require joint worker-management safety committees in most workplaces. Where these committees are not required, organizations often have their own safety committees, which have worker members but are usually headed by a safety specialist, the HRM department head, or an operations manager. Depending on the relevant legislation, the union situation, and company policy, these committees usually focus on one or more of the following functions:

1. Safety policy—reviewing safety and health records, investigating accidents, and making recommendations for safety procedures and expenditures.
2. Inspection—conducting periodic safety inspections of the establishment.
3. Education—promoting interest in and compliance with safety rules and methods.

Recording and posting safety performance records. Most health and safety laws require that an employer post notices of pertinent regulations and related information. In addition, employers can also use posting as a form of feedback to employees on their safety performance. One study credited the public posting of departmental safety performance levels with improving the safety record in a wholesale bakery.[32]

Safety recognition and awards programs. These programs reward individual or group safety performance, or both. Typical rewards are plaques, certificates, and recognition in in-house publications. In the bakery mentioned above, subordinates demonstrating safe work behaviours received verbal praise from their supervisors, who, as a part of the safety program, had received training in positive reinforcement techniques.

Safety rules and regulations. Almost all organizations have some rules and regulations regarding safe work behaviour. They are communicated to employees via supervisors, bulletin boards, and employee handbooks.

Rules and regulations should be developed from the results of detailed job analyses. The job safety training guide shown in Exhibits 14.2 and 14.3 provides an excellent source of specific safe job procedures which may be used to prepare rules and regulations. For example, Exhibit 14.3 suggests that vertical lathe operators and others using this equipment should be required to wear short-sleeved shirts and eye and foot protection. Also, employees should be required to clean up oil spills promptly. Safety rules and regulations developed in this way are specific to jobs rather than overly general, and they are also consistent with training. It is also easier to develop incentive programs for safe work behaviour when proper and safe work behaviours have been specified in this way.

Employers are responsible for compliance with the relevant health and safety act, and they must make certain that employees know and follow its regulations and other safety rules. Many organizations impose penalties on employees for violation of safety rules and terminate for serious or repeated infringement. Of course, as with any rules and regulations, those responsible for ensuring compliance must consider specific cases. For example, violations of some rules represent considerable danger to many people, while others may involve only a very low risk of minor injury. Some rule violators may be new employees who are unfamiliar with the rules or good employees who usually obey the rules, while others are frequent violators. Most supervisors would treat these different cases differently. One of the more effective means of obtaining compliance with health and safety regulations is through employees' knowledge and commitment, which can often be obtained through safety training programs.

[32] J. Komaki, K.D. Barwick, and L.R. Scott, "A Behavioral Approach to Occupational Safety: Pinpointing and Reinforcing Safe Performance in a Food Manufacturing Plant," *Journal of Applied Psychology*, 1978, vol. 63, pp. 434–45.

Safety training programs. Safety training programs identify hazards and teach workers how to avoid or handle them. The role of safety training is generally the same as that of any other training program: to ensure employee performance at a specified level. In this case, specified levels include attention to safety.

Safety training programs are developed and conducted like any other training program. First, problems are identified via job analysis, as discussed above, or by inspection, monitoring of the work environment, and/or by accident and injury reports. Next, problems are examined to determine appropriate solutions, either training or elimination of the hazard. If training is indicated, and some training will be appropriate for most jobs, a program may be designed. In such programs, mastery of safe behaviour on the job is the objective of training.

Workers learn safe work procedures through any number of training methods. To facilitate transfer and maintain desired levels of safety performance after training, arrangements should be made to reinforce or otherwise reward employees for safe behaviour on the job. The importance of trained supervisors and committed top management has already been mentioned. In addition, research suggests that incentive systems encourage the continued use of safe work behaviours.[33]

According to the BNA survey referred to earlier, most organizations have safety training programs for both supervisors and employees, and participation in these programs is mandatory in nearly all cases. Training sessions are conducted by safety specialists in about half the organizations, by supervisors and others; they are given monthly, "as needed," once a year, and at the time of hiring or transfer. Most safety training programs require employees to pass a proficiency test before they are allowed to use hazardous equipment.[34] This criterion provides an excellent means of determining both the effectiveness of the program and which employees need further training.

Training for job safety can begin as early as orientation. Research shows that new employees are most susceptible to accidents and should be informed at the earliest opportunity of hazardous areas and practices.[35] During orientation, they can be informed of health and safety regulations and told of their importance to personal health and safety. A new employee can also be encouraged to ask for assistance from the supervisor or an experienced employee, should a potentially hazardous situation arise. Orientation is also a good time to convey proper attitudes towards health and safety matters. Attention to health and safety at this stage lets employees know about management's concern for their safety and well-being. However, since orientation is a time when em-

[33] R.S. Haynes, R.C. Pine, and H.G. Fitch, "Reducing Accident Rates with Organizational Behavior Modification," *Academy of Management Journal*, 1982, vol. 25, pp. 407–16; and R.A. Weber, J.A. Wallin and J.S. Chhokar, "Reducing Industrial Accidents: A Behavioral Experiment," *Industrial Relations*, 1984, vol. 23, pp. 119–25.

[34] Bureau of National Affairs.

[35] N. Root and M. Hoefer, "The First Work-Injury Data Available from New BLS Study," *Monthly Labor Review*, 1979, vol. 102, no. 1, pp. 76–80.

ployees must absorb a great deal of information, it is advisable to also include safety in job training programs.

Ideally, safety training should be an integral part of job training, whether on or off the job. It is easier to teach employees how to do the job safely in the first place, rather than expect them to "unlearn" old habits and replace them with new ones. Special safety training programs may, of course, be helpful at any time during the course of employment. Periodic safety training programs help to renew employees' attention to health and safety concerns and are especially useful when new equipment or procedures are introduced or safety regulations change.

Another common goal of safety training programs is to encourage managers and supervisors to concern themselves with matters of health and safety by developing safe working conditions, spending time and money on safety training for employees, and creating and enforcing safety rules and procedures. Managers and supervisors often need to be "sold" on health and safety interests, since they sometimes interfere with short-run production and profitability goals. For example, the "push for production" in the Alberta oil fields was cited as a reason for the lack of on-the-job safety training for new recruits. Given high labour demands coupled with high turnover, the industry could barely keep up with the demand for its product and sacrificed safety training in the interests of attaining production goals.[36] While such a human resource management policy may be effective in the short run, it is clearly costly and ineffective in the long run. In another case, the deaths of seven young Ontario forestry workers in a prescribed burn in 1979 were blamed on the failure of supervisors to follow basic safety rules. An official enquiry into the accident concluded that "fire bosses may have been more concerned with filling their quota of prescribed burns for the season than for safety."[37] A real problem in encouraging managerial commitment to safety is that managers and supervisors are often rewarded not for attention to safety but for controlling costs and promoting production and profitability. Therefore, many prefer to avoid the certain costs of a safety program, gambling that few or no accidents will occur. When this attitude prevails at managerial levels, it is likely to filter down to employees at all levels.

Training or education directed towards "selling" management on the value of safety programs and training is a key first step in creating an awareness of health and safety among employees. They can be taught to take a positive attitude towards safety through positive reinforcement from their superiors for safe work behaviour. Through performance appraisal and reward systems, management can ensure that employees are not forced to choose between safe and highly productive work behaviour.

[36] Makin.

[37] M.K. Rowan, "Ignoring Rules Led to Seven Deaths, Ministry Tells Inquest into Test Burn," *The Globe and Mail* (Toronto), December 18, 1980.

Promoting Good Health

Besides efforts to control physical hazards in the workplace and to promote safety awareness, some organizations sponsor programs that promote good health among workers. A recent Ontario study by Danielson and Danielson explored health promotion activities in a random sample of 680 organizations of 50 or more employees.[38] Exhibit 14.7 shows the prevalence of certain types of programs across all surveyed organizations and among a subset of organizations with 500 employees or more. Note that most common are drug and alcohol counselling, exercise and fitness programs, and mental health counselling; these and other health promotion programs are more prevalent in large organizations (>500 employees).

EXHIBIT 14.7

Types and prevalence of health promotion programs

Type of Program	*Organizations with >50 employees %*	*Organizations with >500 employees* %*
Smoking cessation	4.1	11.9
Weight control/nutrition	6.4	18.5
Mental health counselling	10.4	29.7
Exercise and fitness	13.0	36.0
Drug and alcohol counselling	13.6	39.0
Stress management	5.3	15.2
	(n = 680)	(n = 48)

* This column of figures is a subset of the column directly to the left of it, that is, the 48 organizations with more than 500 employees are a subset of the 680 organizations with more than 50 employees.

SOURCE: Reprinted by permission of the publisher, Lexington Books, Lexington, Ky., from *Healthier Workers: Health Promotion and Employee Assistance Programs*, by Martin Shain, Helne Suurvali, and Marie Boutilier.

Programs that provide counselling and other forms of assistance to employees on a variety of topics, primarily alcoholism and drug abuse, are known as *employee assistance programs* (EAPS). One drug expert with Health and Welfare Canada has estimated that EAPS are

[38] D. Danielson and K. Danielson, *Ontario Employee Programme Survey*. (Toronto: Ontario Ministry of Culture and Recreation, 1980).

available to 12 per cent of employees in the private sector and as many as 40 per cent of all employees.[39] An important component of EAPs is often the identification of workers in need of assistance. In a survey of 45 Ontario organizations known to have EAPs, researchers talked with respondents "who held the greatest day-to-day responsibility for EAP." This person was likely to be a nurse, an EAP coordinator, a medical director, or human resource manager. EAPs were under the auspices of HRM departments in nearly half the organizations and in medical departments in nearly a third.[40] Exhibit 14.8 presents the type of problems EAPs in these organizations are equipped to handle. Note that most programs address a variety of concerns, but all assist employees with alcohol and drug-related problems. Programs have also been established for some professions. Exhibit 14.9 discusses British Columbia's Interlock program for lawyers and chartered accountants.

EXHIBIT 14.8

Problems EAPs are meant to handle

	Number and Percent of EAPs Handling Problem (n = 45)	
Type of Problem	*n*	*%*
Alcohol	45	100
Drugs	45	100
Cross addiction	45	100
Domestic	32	71.1
Mental health	32	71.1
Legal	30	68.2
Financial	33	73.3
Housing	30	68.2
Daycare	31	70.5
Work problems	31	68.9
Other*	25	64.1

*Other problems include physical health, retirement and career planning, leisure, education, anxiety, "life-style-related" problems, bereavement, and wife abuse.

SOURCE: Reprinted by permission of the publisher, Lexington Books, Lexington, Ky., from *Healthier Workers: Health Promotion and Employee Assistance Programs*, by Martin Shain, Helne Suurvali, and Marie Boutilier.

[39] D. Lees, "Executive Addicts," *Canadian Business*, February 1986, pp. 52–6, 105–6.
[40] M. Shain, H. Suurvali, and M. Boutilier, *Healthier Workers: Health Promotion and Employee Assistance Programs* (Lexington, Ky.: Lexington Books, 1986), pp. 76–9.

EXHIBIT 14.9

British Columbia's Interlock program for lawyers and accountants

The argument got heated and Charles lost control. It didn't help at all that Charles, a lawyer, was suffering emotional problems during the dispute with his client. The upshot was that Charles struck the client, and in short order the Law Society of British Columbia was involved.

For Charles, the consequences could have been serious. If the law society ruled against him, it had the power to impose a fine and suspend his licence to practice. But Charles was spared such an ordeal because of an arrangement between the legal body and Interlock, a pioneer in the employee assistance movement in B.C.

Interlock is a non-profit diagnostic, counselling and referral service to which the law society's 5,800 members can turn for help in dealing with their personal problems. Although Charles was given the option of seeking help as an alternative to disciplinary action, most lawyers who use Interlock's services do so voluntarily and anonymously, with complete assurance of confidentiality.

Similarly, British Columbia's 5,000 chartered accountants have access to Interlock through a contract between the B.C. Institute of Chartered Accountants and the privately operated mental health care service. The institute has not followed the law society model of linking its disciplinary process to a counselling program, although it is being considered.

Interlock, which grew out of a government-financed alcoholism and drug abuse treatment organization, now serves 35,000 employees and members of about 60 companies, institutions and professional groups in British Columbia. Its board of directors is drawn from the ranks of labor, management and community representatives. Interlock's focus is on diagnosis, referral to appropriate community agencies for treatment, and followup by Interlock's staff. The clinic's counsellors also provide therapy for about 30% of the people they see in Interlock's facilities in Vancouver, Kelowna, Victoria and Prince George.

Fees are usually based on the number of employees within a firm. However, the agreements with the law society and the institute provide for fee for service, with the costs paid by the two organizations, which are billed without any disclosure of the names of the clients.

The arrangement between the Institute of Chartered Accountants and Interlock had its genesis in a fund established by an institute member for the prevention of alcoholism and treatment of alcoholics. Before selecting Interlock, the fund's trustees interviewed health care agencies and firms specializing in psychological counselling. After discussions with Interlock, the plan was enlarged to deal with a whole range of emotional problems—from marital difficulties to general depression and even financial woes.

Barrie Jones, secretary to the trustees who administer the fund, says a professional who is addicted to alcohol either denies he has a problem or feels he is intelligent enough to handle it on his own. The institute's monthly publication has carried articles designed to shatter that belief and to draw attention to the availability of help through Interlock. A recent article offered a personal account of an accountant's drift to alcoholism. It began: "My name is X and I am an alcoholic. I am also a chartered accountant." The article prompted a surge of interest in Interlock.

The accountants have had four years' experience with Interlock and the lawyers nearly three and a half years. For both groups the success of the program can be measured by the rehabilitation of alcoholics, and assistance provided in dealing with personal problems of lawyers and accountants that often interfered with the quality of service to clients. Says Frank Maczko, secretary of the law society: "A disrupted personal life makes for an impaired practitioner." Among cases where lawyers were referred to Interlock by the law society was one involving a lawyer who turned up drunk in court, and another of a lawyer who had been convicted on a drug charge. "If we hadn't intervened they might have found themselves in even worse trouble," Maczko says.

But there is still the nagging question of how far an organization should inject itself into a member's or employee's personal life. "Rehabilitation is certainly better than punishment," notes Maczko. "The issue is one of balancing individual rights and our duty to protect the client's interests. No one is forced to take treatment. But we have a right to prevent someone from practicing if the use of drugs or alcohol addiction is a threat to clients."

Still, of 34 law society members who used Interlock's services last year only five were directed to the clinic by the society. The level of voluntary referrals for all 650 persons among Interlock's client firms and organizations is even higher at 95%.

A survey by Interlock of its clients suggests that the vast majority were pleased with the help they had received. Says Interlock executive director David Ayers: "Employees are being helped in resolving their personal problems, and in the process their life at home and at work is being made more productive and pleasant. What more could you ask for?"

SOURCE: Wilfred List, "Helping Out the Problem Employee," *The Globe and Mail Report on Business Magazine* (Toronto), September 1986, p. 72.

We will now take a closer look at several health problems that are of special concern to today's employers: job stress, smoking, alcoholism, and use of drugs.

Special Health Problems

Job Stress

The Canadian Institute of Stress in Toronto has estimated that in 1984, job stress cost Canadian employers almost $8 billion in health care and $10 billion in lost productivity.[41] Job stress occurs when some element of the work environment has a negative impact on an employee's mental health and well-being. For example, stress may occur when role and job expectations are unclear, or when a job makes

[41] B. Shein, "Bright Lights that Fail," *Canadian Business,* July 1985, pp. 61–64, 69–72.

demands that an employee cannot meet. The boss can be a source of stress, as can a demanding work schedule. Interruptions, lack of advancement opportunities, lack of input into decisions, and lack of communication from the supervisor are common stressors among secretaries.[42]

The factors related to stress and employee health are numerous and their relationships complex. While certain occupations are recognized as being more stressful than others, stress is largely an individual matter: what is stressful to one may not bother another.

Job stress often results in physical complaints, such as ulcers, headaches and backaches, and increased use of alcohol and drugs. The end result for organizations is increased absenteeism and reduced worker productivity. In high-stress occupations, such as air traffic control, health care, and high-tech, prolonged job stress often leads to burnout, a three-phase process characterized by emotional exhaustion, negativism, and lowered self-esteem. Recently, a labour arbitrator in Nova Scotia ruled that burnout is a form of work-related injury, compensable under workers' compensation.[43]

To counter the effects of job stress and burnout, a growing number of organizations are sponsoring stress-management workshops and exercise programs for workers. Employee assistance programs also help employees deal with stress related to a variety of concerns. Another more basic approach is to reduce, as much as possible, the number of stressors in the workplace. For example, noise levels might be reduced and job expectations clarified; supervisors might be provided with interpersonal skills training, and work loads might be reduced.

Smoking

It has been estimated that smokers cost their employers $200 to $500 more per year than nonsmokers. Smokers have higher rates of accidents and absenteeism, receive more disability payments, and are 50 per cent more likely to need health care. Furthermore, smoking greatly increases the risks of developing lung cancer and chronic lung disease among those exposed to asbestos and coal dust.[44] One employee relations manager in British Columbia recently calculated the cost of smoking to his company at $3 million annually, or $3,750 per smoker. This figure included $1,750 for time spent smoking daily (estimated at half an hour), $500 for property damage, $330 for absenteeism, and $53 for additional maintenance.[45]

[42] "Secretaries and Stress," *Wall Street Journal*, March 18, 1986.

[43] M. Strauss, "Burnout Compensable as Work-related Injury, N.S. Arbitrator Rules," *The Globe and Mail* (Toronto), June 4, 1985.

[44] 17th Report of the U.S. Surgeon General, as referenced by H.F. Rosenthal, "Employers Pick up $200–$500 Yearly Tab for Smokers," *Iowa City Press Citizen*, December 19, 1985.

[45] T. Falconer, "No Butts About It," *Canadian Business*, February 1987, pp. 66–70.

To reduce the costs and risks associated with smoking, and also to appease growing numbers of nonsmokers who object to "second-hand smoke," many organizations have established policies on smoking. Health and Welfare Canada, for example, has recently restricted smoking in all of its offices. The cities of Vancouver and Toronto have passed bylaws curbing smoking, and many organizations such as Bowater Mersey Paper Co. Ltd. of Liverpool, Nova Scotia, and Maritime Telegraph and Telephone Co. Ltd. of Halifax, are voluntarily choosing to limit smoking to designated areas. Such actions have led to predictions that "smoke (will be) out of the workplace within five years."[46]

Companies that have implemented smoking policies report little employee resistance, but experts agree that successful programs require commitment from top management and consultation with employees prior to policy implementation. In order to obtain employee input, organizations often conduct surveys or establish employee committees.

Alcoholism

Alcoholism is both a health problem and a performance problem in organizations. The alcohol addicted population in Canada was estimated at 635,600 in 1978, or 1 in 20 Canadian adult drinkers, up from 400,000 in 1970.[47] It has been estimated that in 1979 alcohol-related problems cost the Canadian economy $900 million in reduced productivity and $35 million in wages and salaries paid for time off work.[48] According to an estimate by the Harvard School of Public Health, problem drinkers miss an average of 22 work days per year and are at least twice as likely as nondrinkers to have accidents.[49] The direct and indirect costs of alcoholism to employers include the costs of absenteeism, accidents, bad decisions, fighting, discharges, garnishment of pay, increased benefit costs, lower productivity, and supervisors' lost time in dealing with alcoholic workers.

Managers are slightly more likely than other employees to become alcoholics since it is often easier for a manager to conceal a drinking problem. Managers also come into more frequent contact with alcohol in the context of business luncheons, dinners, and meetings. Several years ago, a Ford Motor Company executive sued his employer, arguing that his job, which involved many luncheons and parties at which virtually everyone drank, had caused his drinking problem.

Employers should have a policy regarding alcoholism, and it should be applicable to both managerial and nonmanagerial employees. The

[46] Ibid.

[47] *Special Report on Alcohol Statistics* (Ottawa: Minister of National Health and Welfare and Minister of Supply and Services Canada, 1981).

[48] Keith Thompson, "Alcoholism and Drug Abuse in the Workplace," *IR Research Reports*, January-February 1980, vol. 4, p. 11.

[49] C.A. Filipowicz, "The Troubled Employee: Whose Responsibility," *The Personnel Administrator*, June 1979, p. 18.

policy should be a realistic and supportive one, since strict, punitive policies often cause an alcoholic to hide the problem as long as possible, rather than ask for help. Employers, of course, cannot tolerate alcoholic employees, especially those in responsible or potentially hazardous jobs, and should terminate any who fail to respond to rehabilitation.

In addition to offering supportive policies, employers can make available employee assistance programs on alcohol abuse. Evidence shows economic as well as ethical benefits are inherent in establishing such programs. In the U.S., Kennecott Copper experienced a 52 per cent improvement in attendance, a 75 per cent drop in worker compensation costs, and a more than 50 per cent decline in health care costs through the use of an alcohol abuse counsellor; a General Motors study found similar results.[50] One of the largest employee assistance programs is jointly run by GM and the United Auto Workers; it is available to 600,000 employees and involves 100 alcoholism committees in plants. In two years, this program handled 9,000 alcoholic employees with a "cure rate" of 80 per cent.

Finally, employers should examine their policies and practices in other areas to be sure that they are not contributing to an alcohol problem. For example, the human resource manager of a large personal-products manufacturing plant became concerned at the number of "hung over" employees at work on Fridays, then discovered that the major cause was the company-sponsored bowling league, which met on Thursday nights. The manager handled the problem by announcing that if employees did not come to work in better condition on Fridays, the bowling league would have to be discontinued.

Drug Use

Drug use, including abuse of prescription drugs, is a growing problem for employers in Canada and the United States. In the U.S., drug abuse is estimated to have cost the economy $60 billion in 1983; annual productivity losses alone are estimated at $25.7 billion.[51] Drug use can be costly to employers; as an example, TIME Magazine reported the following anecdote:

> Last year, according to Dr. Robert Wick, corporate medical director for American Airlines, a computer operator who was high on marijuana failed to load a crucial tape into a major airline's computer reservations system. Result: the system was out of service for some eight hours, costing the company about $19 million. Says Wick: "That was an awfully expensive joint by anybody's standards."[52]

[50] R. Witte, "Employee Assistance Programs: Getting Top Management's Support," *The Personnel Administrator*, June 1979, p. 24.

[51] Estimate of the Research Triangle Institute, North Carolina, as reported in J. Castro, "Battling the Enemy Within," TIME, March 17, 1986, pp. 52–61; and Estimate of the U.S. Alcohol, Drug Abuse and Mental Health Administration, 1984, as reported in D. Lees, "Executive Addicts."

[52] J. Castro, p. 55.

Besides not performing as well as they otherwise might, drug users have higher rates of accidents and absenteeism and receive three times the average level of sick benefits.[53] Drug use may also lead to theft and drug dealing in the workplace, as users are driven to support their expensive habit.

No industry or occupation is immune to drug use; it is especially prevalent among young adults, with cocaine being the preferred drug of professionals and executives. As stated in TIME, "Cocaine is an increasingly popular drug to use at work, partly because the intense high it generates often gives users the false feeling that they can do their jobs better and faster. Moreover, cocaine is easy to hide. It is generally snorted rather than smoked, and does not give off an odor as marijuana does.[54]

Many Canadian and U.S. companies are having to come to terms with drug use in their organizations. Most companies have rules against drug use and many have begun employee assistance programs or equipped existing programs to deal with problems of drug abuse and cross addiction, addiction to both drugs and alcohol. Programs generally involve both counselling and referral to hospital for treatment. Mobil Oil's drug treatment program, described in Exhibit 14.10 is typical of one such program.

EXHIBIT 14.10

Mobil Oil's drug treatment program

Mobil employees with a drug problem can call or stop by the medical departments at any of the oil company's facilities around the world. Supervisors who spot unusual behavior that is affecting job performance can encourage workers to contact an employee-assistance counsellor. After initial medical examinations and counseling sessions, patients are generally referred to a hospital or outpatient drug clinic for treatment, which may take from four to six weeks. During that period the employees are given sick leave with pay, and their status is kept confidential. Company health-insurance benefits pay all the treatment costs. Once employees return to the job, they are allowed to attend follow-up counseling sessions during work hours. Says Dr. Joseph M. Cannella, Mobil's medical director: "We like to identify people, get them treated and back to work." He claims that Mobil's rehabilitation efforts have been 70% to 75% successful.

SOURCE: J. Castro, "Battling the Enemy Within," TIME, March 17, 1986, p. 57.

A popular strategy in the U.S. is to weed out users in the selection process by requiring urinanalysis tests for job applicants. In early 1986, such tests were required by almost one-fourth of the largest, most prestigious companies in the U.S., with another 20 per cent expected

[53] Ibid.
[54] Ibid., p. 54.

to begin drug screening by year's end.[55] Less common strategies are drug testing of current employees (which often meets with strenuous objection from employees and their unions), use of undercover agents posing as employees, and use of dogs to sniff out drugs in the workplace.

Health and Safety in the Chemical Industry

As an example of a comprehensive and well-integrated approach to employee health and safety, we will briefly examine the U.S. chemical industry's worker safety protection system. Elements in the industry's five-pronged approach include:

1. Improving detection techniques for monitoring the environment.
2. Upgrading educational programs in safety and health.
3. Expanding laboratory studies into the long-term effects of chemicals.
4. "Engineering out" risks by substituting safer chemicals and redesigning manufacturing processes, if necessary.
5. Closer monitoring of employee health, including the use of interdisciplinary teams and of computer technology to process and study the data they collect.[56]

The U.S. chemical industry's worker safety protection system is shown in Exhibit 14.11. The system monitors hazardous levels of contaminants, the air quality, and the health of workers. These data, along with data from laboratory investigations of the effects of chemicals, are analyzed by computer. Results of the analyses indicate needs for changes in process design (choice of chemicals and manufacturing processes) and serve as focal points for safety training programs.

Summary

This chapter has examined the role of health and safety in organizations, the requirements and impact of legislation on employers and on human resource management, various approaches to health and safety, and the special health problems of job stress, smoking, alcoholism, and drug use. Organized labour has been promoting more stringent health and safety legislation. This activity has led to several government commissions, which, in turn, have led to more legislation in this field. With increasing awareness of the dangers to health and safety in both the workplace and the environment (including acid rain), it is likely that HRM professionals will face greater responsibilities in this area during the coming years.

[55] Ibid., p. 57.
[56] "Protecting Chemical Workers," *Time*, April 28, 1980.

EXHIBIT 14.11

The U.S. chemical industry's worker safety protection system

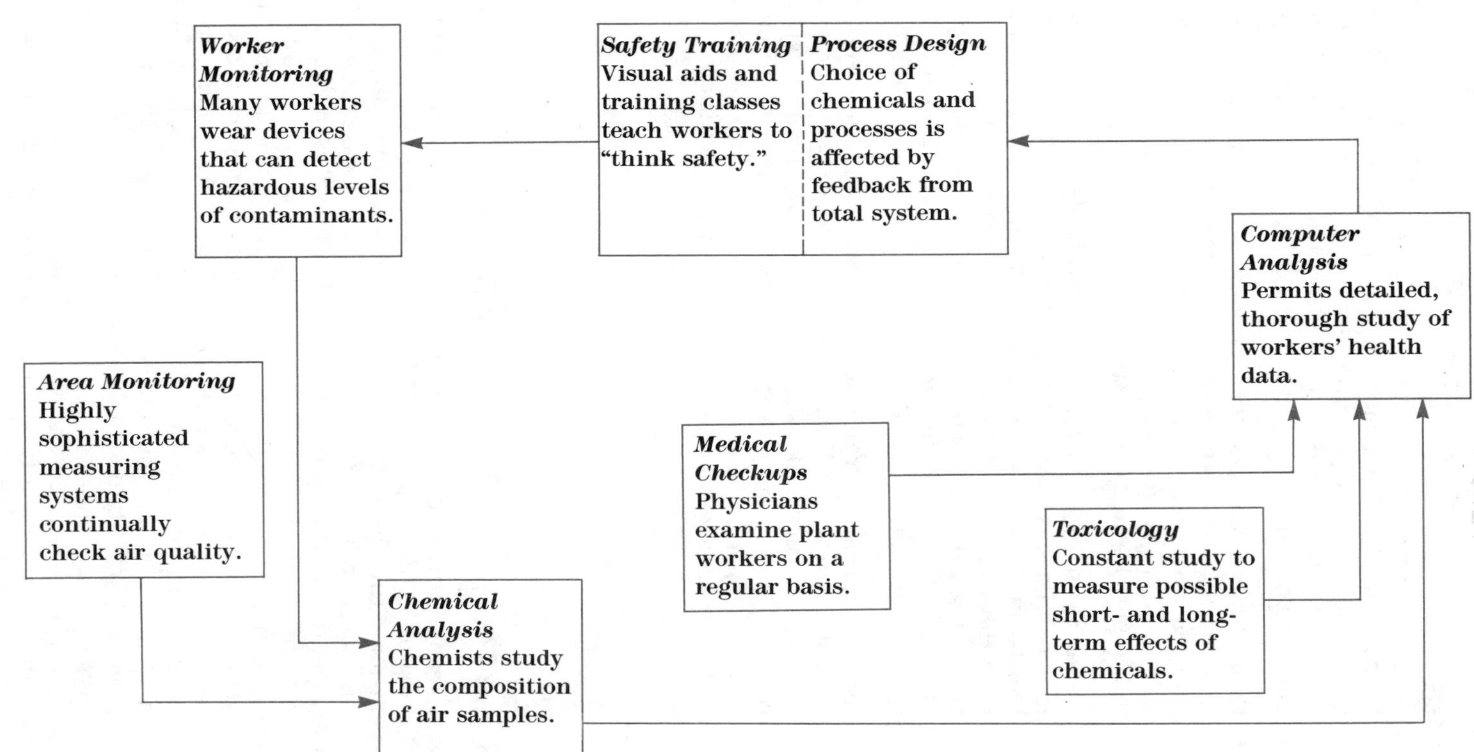

Worker Monitoring
Many workers wear devices that can detect hazardous levels of contaminants.
Safety Training
Visual aids and training classes teach workers to "think safety."
Process Design
Choice of chemicals and processes is affected by feedback from total system.
Computer Analysis
Permits detailed, thorough study of workers' health data.
Area Monitoring
Highly sophisticated measuring systems continually check air quality.
Medical Checkups
Physicians examine plant workers on a regular basis.
Toxicology
Constant study to measure possible short- and long-term effects of chemicals.
Chemical Analysis
Chemists study the composition of air samples.

Worker safety protection system: data from health exams, monitoring devices, and laboratory studies are continually analyzed to identify situations that may require immediate action and to provide information for possible improvements in process design and safety training.

SOURCE: "Protecting Chemical Workers," *Time*, April 28, 1980.

Project Ideas

1. Peruse some trade journals or journals related to safety, and locate an article on one organization's safety program. Make sure that the article you choose provides a good description, rather than a sketchy one. Describe the program in a short written or oral report.
2. Contact a company, either by phone or mail, and request copies of its rules and regulations relating to employees' health and safety. Find out what other measures the employer takes to ensure a healthy and safe workplace for employees. Share the information you obtain in a report to your classmates.
3. Obtain a copy of your province's health and safety regulations. (They may be in a special act or contained in the workers' compensation legislation.) Summarize the major provisions and compare them with those of Ontario's Occupational Health and Safety Act, which is discussed in this chapter. Write a short essay discussing the relative merits of each jurisdiction's approach to health and safety from the perspective of the employer and of the employee.
4. As a class project, arrange for a visit to a local employer, preferably a manufacturer or other organization where health and safety may be major problems. If possible, tour the organization with a person responsible for safety (arrangements will need to be made in advance). Pinpoint as many potential hazards as you can and find out how the organization protects its workers from them.

Cases

Case 14.1: Death at Tenerife

KLM's captain was 50-year old Jacob Veldhuyzen van Zanten. He was the airline's chief of pilot training, a prestigious post although he spent more time on training duties than on regular flights. "He was like a general with a lot of medals," one safety expert says. With his prestige, the captain wouldn't be likely to yield if questioned by a junior crew member.

The KLM pilot was affable while on the ground at Tenerife, but he also was under pressure. He had been on duty for more than nine hours. If he stayed at Tenerife much longer, crew members would reach the limit on their flying time before they got back to Amsterdam. Hence, the 747 would have to remain overnight in the Canary Islands, and KLM flight schedules and passengers' plans would be disrupted.

But if they hurried to leave, and there weren't any weather or air traffic delays enroute, the KLM crew might make it back to Amsterdam in time. If they were late in arriving at Amsterdam, they faced tough Dutch disciplinary measures, including possible fines and prison terms. As they awaited permission to depart, cockpit conversation went like this:

KLM engineer: "What are the repercussions (of exceeding flight limits)?"

KLM crew members: "You'll face the judge . . . "

KLM engineer: "Then you are hanged from the highest tree."

KLM captain: "Suppose you get a flat tire and you hit a couple of runway lights—then you are really hanging."

While the KLM and Pan Am planes were waiting, the weather at Tenerife deteriorated. "When we landed, the weather was beautifully clear and sunny; we could clearly see the surrounding mountains," Pan Am stewardess Joan Jackson recalled later. But, "as we sat there, we watched the fog roll in. It was amazing how fast the mountains were obliterated."

When it came time to leave, the KLM plane couldn't use taxiways to get to the end of the runway at Tenerife; most taxiways were jammed with other planes diverted from Las Palmas. So the KLM plane was cleared to taxi down the airport's only runway. The Pan Am plane was cleared to taxi down the runway behind the KLM jet. As the Pan Am plane began to move after a two-hour wait, happy passengers broke into applause.

The Tenerife controller had ordered the Pan Am plane to taxi part way down the runway to a turnoff and then exit to a taxiway that was clear. But the fog had become so thick the Pan Am crew could barely see; they missed their assigned turnoff and continued taxiing on down the runway.

Meanwhile, the KLM craft had reached the end of the runway and turned around. The captain still needed two separate clearances, for air-traffic control (ATC) and for takeoff, but the captain began to advance the throttles anyway.

KLM copilot: "Wait a minute, we don't have an ATC clearance."

KLM captain, retarding the throttles: "I know that, go ahead ask."

KLM copilot reads ATC clearance back to the tower, but even before he finishes, the pilot advances throttles again. The copilot tells the tower hurriedly: "We are now at takeoff." (That commonly means "takeoff position.")

Tower: "Okay—stand by for takeoff. I will call you."

But only the word "okay" was clear. The Pan Am crew, to inform everyone that their plane still was on the runway, radioed the tower. That transmission caused a squeal that partly blocked the rest of the tower's order to the KLM crew to stand by. Saying, "We go!" the KLM captain gunned the 747 down the runway. The next two transmissions were heard in the KLM cockpit.

Tower: "Roger Papa Alpha (Pan Am) . . . report the runway clear."

Pan Am: "Okay, we'll report when we're clear."

KLM engineer, in the KLM cockpit: "Is he not clear, that Pan American?"

KLM pilot: "Oh, yes."

In the dense fog, the Pan Am crew couldn't see the KLM jet roaring down the runway toward them, but the radio transmissions alarmed them.

Pan Am pilot: "Let's get the hell out right here . . . "

Pan Am copilot: "Yeh, he's anxious, isn't he?"

Pan Am pilot: "There he is—look at him—goddamn—that—that son of a bitch is coming."

Pan Am copilot: "Get off, get off, get off."

For about five agonizing seconds, the Pan Am pilot tried to steer his jumbo jet off the runway. The KLM jumbo, as it struck the Pan Am plane, was going about 130 miles an hour. Most of the 583 who died were killed on impact or in the subsequent searing fires.

Questions:

1. Identify the causes, both primary and contributory, to the accident.
2. What specific policy or procedure changes could be instituted to prevent such accidents?

SOURCE: *Wall Street Journal*, Nov. 2, 1979.

Case 14.2: Performance Problem at Lorax Steel

Tim Rainer, supervisor of maintenance at Lorax Steel, has just received a phone call from John Mayberry, an electrician at the plant. Mayberry says he's too ill to come to work; he complains of a headache and a queasy stomach, but it sounds to Rainer as though Mayberry had too much to drink the night before. This is somewhat unusual since Mayberry isn't known as much of a "drinker."

Rainer would think nothing of Mayberry's call except that Mayberry, a respected employee with no previous record of excessive absenteeism, has called in sick seven times in the past month, mostly with minor physical complaints. While each absence lasted only one day, each had a disruptive effect on production. The last time Mayberry was "out," the wiring in one production area went haywire and no one was able to fix it. Besides, Mayberry was especially valuable now that he was performing a mechanic's duties in addition to his own.

Mayberry was asked to assume a mechanic's duties following the layoff of several full-time mechanics. In a cost-cutting move, and for the sake of expediency, Lorax decided against providing any mechanic's training for Mayberry, despite the fact that accidents were known to happen even to trained mechanics. Why only last month, mechanic Whitney Marshall lost a finger to a hungry piece of machinery.

Rainer resolved to talk with Mayberry about his absenteeism before deciding on an appropriate course of action to deal with the problem.

Questions:

1. What do you suspect is at the root of Mayberry's absence problem? What factors in the work environment may have contributed to the performance problem? How could the situation have been avoided?
2. What are some possible strategies for dealing with Mayberry's situation? Decide on the best strategy and try to persuade Rainer of its advantages compared to other possible actions.

15

Labour Relations

It had been two days since Rob Williams, human resource manager of a medium-size manufacturing plant, received notice that the United Steelworkers had applied to the provincial labour relations board for certification to represent the plant's 80 hourly employees. Williams felt that unionization of the factory workers would limit his policy-making flexibility and authority by requiring agreement between management and the trade union on many HRM issues. He would have liked to try to persuade the employees not to support unionization, but he knew he had to be very careful.

First, labour relations boards in Canada prohibit employers from coercing, intimidating, or promising something to employees to prevent them from joining a union. Employers are allowed to voice their opinions on the advisability of unionization, but they must avoid any action or statement which could be deemed an unfair practice. Hence, Rob Williams realized he must not say too much. Second, a union usually applies for certification only when it has signed up at least enough employees to require a representation vote. And quite likely, the Steelworkers had a percentage so high that the board would certify without a vote. Rob Williams knew that if the union had the support of a majority of the employees and so won certification, he would simply have to make the best of it. An aggressive campaign on his part now might alienate the workers and poison the atmosphere when collective bargaining began.

Williams's estimate of the probabilities was correct. When the union submitted its list of members to the labour relations board, it did have a percentage of the bargaining unit sufficiently large to be certified without a representation vote. The employer filed no formal objection, and the board certified the new local of the United Steelworkers as the exclusive bargaining agent of the plant's hourly employees. The union then gave notice that it wanted to begin collective bargaining.

Incidents like this occur hundreds of times each year in Canadian places of employment that range from manufacturing plants to nursing homes. The union wins the right to represent employees in the majority of certification applications. For example, in Ontario during the fiscal year 1984–85, unions were certified in 673 out of 985 applications. Only 165 of them (17 per cent of the total) were cases in which the union had signed up 45 to 55 per cent of the employees in the prospective bargaining unit, and so a representation vote was conducted; the union won 91 of these votes and lost 74.[1] In most of the other cases, more than 55 per cent of the employees involved had signed with the union before the application for certification was filed.

Across the country, similar situations prevail, although there are variations in the percentages at which a representation vote must or is likely to be called. With the exception of Nova Scotia and British Columbia, a provincial labour relations board certifies a union whenever it has reason to believe a majority of the bargaining unit's employees favour it. And whether an application for certification is successful or not, the fact of the bid usually affects management's personnel policies.

Unions: A Definition

Trade unions are organizations of employees who have joined together to obtain a stronger voice in decisions affecting their wages, benefits, working conditions, and other aspects of employment than they would have as individuals. (In Canada, the terms "trade union" and "union" are used synonymously. For the sake of brevity, we often use "union.") There are two major types of unions: craft and industrial. Craft unions are organized around a particular skill or craft, while industrial unions are organized on the basis of product or industry. Union members elect officers and officials, who represent the group's collective views to management. Through collective bargaining, union representatives negotiate collective agreements which spell out the terms and conditions of employment with management. Collective agreements also structure and define the nature of the relationship between labour and management.

[1] Ontario Labour Relations Board, *Annual Report 1984–85* (Toronto, 1985), pp. 89, 94.

Collective bargaining is a rule-making process that seeks to maintain a balance of power between labour and management so that they can come to terms and resolve their differences. Unions provide a system of justice through the grievance procedure to assure that employees are treated according to terms specified in the collective agreement. If an employee feels that rights or privileges under the agreement have been violated, he or she may file a formal complaint, or *grievance*, against management. Union officials support and assist employees during the grievance process.

Like other organizations, a union depends upon its members for its continued existence and for financial support through the payment of dues. Therefore, a union attempts to persuade employees of its value by engaging in activities such as speeches, informal discussions, and dissemination of literature informing employees of what it can do to improve pay and other conditions of employment. Some unions also offer apprenticeships and a variety of educational and social programs.

Labour Relations and Public Policy

The term *labour relations* describes all interactions between labour and management in situations in which employees are represented by a trade union. Unionized employees are often referred to collectively as *organized labour*. In the absence of a union, the structure and nature of interaction between labour and management are called *employee relations*. Employee relations are characterized by managerial control over the making and interpretation of human resource policies. In employee relations, management deals with employees individually rather than collectively.

Labour relations in the 1980s can best be understood by examining the history of trade unions and labour laws. In the Canadian context, labour laws are primarily provincial laws since the provinces have jurisdiction over labour relations for approximately 90 percent of the Canadian work force. Federal government jurisdiction applies to federal government employees and employees of bank, air, rail and sea transportation, and grain elevators. Laws reflect the dominant values of society at a given point in time. Thus, the role of unions in society has changed as values and laws have changed. The history of unions can be traced from the free-market period, during which they were regarded as criminal conspiracies, to the era of World War II, when collective bargaining became the approved mechanism for labour-management negotiations and resolutions of conflict. In recent years the trend has been towards granting of the right to strike to more groups of employees, particularly employees in the public sector.

The Free-Market Period

The free-market approach regards the employee-management relationship primarily as an exchange in which each person bargains individually with management. During this early period in union history, public policy did not support organized labour. In fact, unions were regarded as criminal conspiracies. The Trade Unions Act of 1872 did exempt "registered" unions from the charge of criminal conspiracy, but since no labour organization apparently ever did register, the first "charter of Canadian labour rights" came to nothing.[2] Moreover, the Criminal Law Amendment Act passed at the same time provided severe penalties for most forms of picketing and union pressure.

The IDI Act of 1907

Despite their barely legal status, unions continued to grow in turn-of-the-century Canada. A landmark came in 1907, when the Industrial Disputes Investigation (IDI) Act introduced the principle of compulsory delay of work stoppages, a principle still present in most Canadian labour legislation. The act, which was passed after a coal-mining strike in the West resulted in a major emergency, provided for investigation and conciliation by a tripartite board—that is, a board with a representative of labour, a representative of management, and a neutral chairman. The board was given legal power to investigate disputes, to compel testimony, to determine the cause of dispute, and to recommend a settlement. This approach was developed by William Lyon Mackenzie King, who, as deputy minister of labour, found that publicity could be a useful weapon in settling a labour dispute. As historian Desmond Morton has said, "On the strength of the IDI Act, King entered Parliament in 1908 to become Canada's first fullfledged minister of labour."[3] He later became prime minister.

Although the IDI Act did give unions in the federal jurisdiction a form of recognition while the boards were conducting their investigations, it also undercut the power of the measures by which trade unionists attempted to achieve their goals. "Any arrangement which allowed employers to continue operations, stockpile, train strikebreakers, and victimize selected unionists could make an eventual strike much longer and probably hopeless."[4]

World War I and the IDI Act

During World War I, the IDI Act was extended to cover disputes between workers and employers in industries producing military supplies. However, with full employment and rampant inflation, labour unrest increased, and in October 1918, strikes and lockouts were simply prohibited in major war industries. While this prohibition was rescinded shortly

[2] See Desmond Morton with Terry Copp, *Working People: An Illustrated History of the Canadian Labour Movement*, revised edition (Ottawa: Deneau, 1984), p. 27.
[3] Desmond Morton, "The History of Canadian Labour," in John Anderson and Morley Gunderson, eds., *Union-Management Relations in Canada* (Don Mills, Ont.: Addison-Wesley, 1982), p. 101.
[4] Ibid.

after the end of the war, the scope of the IDI Act was extended to empower the federal minister of labour "to establish on the request of a municipality or on his own initiative, boards of conciliation and investigation to settle disputes in which strikes threatened, as well as to settle strikes already in progress."[5]

In 1925, in the Snider case (*Toronto Electric Power Commissioners v. Snider et al.*), the courts and the Privy Council declared that the federal government had acted beyond its proper constitutional jurisdiction. The Parliament of Canada then amended the act to make it apply only to disputes within its jurisdiction, but it also provided that the act could be extended to any province which passed enabling legislation. All the provinces except Prince Edward Island passed such legislation between 1925 and 1932.

The Wagner Act in the United States

Meanwhile, the union movement had had no better legislative support in the United States than in Canada from the 19th century through the 1920s. During the Depression, however, the Americans swung to a more pro-labour stance. Of the several labour laws they passed during this period, the most important was the National Labor Relations Act of 1935, often called the Wagner Act. As historian Stuart Jamieson has explained, its principles were eventually influential north of the border:

> The almost revolutionary change in government attitude and policy toward organized labour in the United States during the 1930s had a delayed impact in Canada. The Wagner Act of 1935 firmly established the by now well-known principles of guaranteeing workers the freedom to organize into unions of their own choosing, free from employer interference or attack; of establishing labour relations boards to investigate complaints of unfair labour practices, to prosecute offenders, and to conduct supervised elections to decide certification of unions representing the majority of workers in appropriate bargaining units; and of requiring recognition and bargaining by employers with properly certified unions. Notably absent from the act were measures to aid unions and employers to negotiate agreements, to regulate the contents of agreements, or to restrict the use of strikes or lockouts. Through the device of certification, however, it did have the effect of sharply reducing the issues of recognition and jurisdiction as major causes of strikes.[6]

The latter 1930s in Canada saw a considerable amount of new labour legislation, encouraged by changing attitudes and the support organized labour received from the States. Most provincial legislatures passed

[5] Stuart Jamieson, *Industrial Relations in Canada*, 2nd ed. (Toronto: Macmillan of Canada, 1973), p. 120.
[6] Ibid., pp. 120–21.

new labour laws; many of these adopted some of the Wagner Act principles, such as freedom of association and required collective bargaining where desired by a majority of a unit's workers. Most, however, retained the basic IDI Act restrictions, and most lacked effective mechanisms for enforcement. The federal government let the IDI Act stand but did make it an offence under the Criminal Code for an employer to discharge workers for union activity.

World War II and PC 1003

World War II brought another tight labour market, but the federal government again extended the IDI Act, with its compulsory conciliation and "cooling off" period, to industries deemed essential to the war effort. Wartime orders-in-council did add recognition of the right to join unions and encouragement of collective bargaining, but full employment plus vigorous organizing campaigns by industrial unions produced what Jamieson terms "a new peak of intensity and bitterness in 1943."[7] Time lost through strikes approached the heights reached in 1919.

The passage of the Ontario Collective Bargaining Act of 1943 led the way for subsequent federal legislation. It began in 1944 with a new, blanket order-in-council, PC 1003, which included the main principles of the Wagner Act: guarantees of labour's right to organize; selection of units appropriate for collective bargaining; certification of bargaining agents; compulsory collective bargaining; and labour relations boards to investigate and correct unfair labour practices. Nevertheless, the order retained the IDI Act's compulsory conciliation and "cooling off" procedures.

After the war, in 1948, Parliament passed the Industrial Relations and Disputes Investigation (IRDI) Act; it was almost identical to PC 1003 but applied only to the much smaller peacetime jurisdiction of the federal government. However, the provinces (except for P.E.I.) soon passed new labour relations acts modelled on PC 1003. Since then federal and provincial legislation has evolved to take into consideration the responsibilities of unions as well as their rights, following aspects of the Taft-Hartley and Landrum-Griffin acts in the United States.

The Public Service Staff Relations Act of 1967

Although some provincial governments' employees had won the right to strike earlier (Saskatchewan's in 1944 and Quebec's in 1964), the granting of this right by the federal government had a major impact on organized labour across Canada. In 1967, Parliament passed the Public Service Staff Relations Act (PSSRA), which enabled workers

[7] Ibid., p. 122.

in bargaining units to opt for compulsory conciliation or the right to strike. With the exception of Ontario and Alberta, the provinces followed in granting their employees the right to strike.

The Growth of Organized Labour

The history of unions and labour laws in Canada and the United States is portrayed graphically in Exhibit 15.1. As the graph shows, union membership in Canada has had two periods of rapid growth: the 1940s through the early 1950s, and the late 1960s through the 1970s. The first reflected the late-1930s establishment in Canada of industrial union-organizing committees, most as branches of the CIO (Congress of Industrial Organizations), followed by the wartime boom in employment and by legislation (PC 1003) which required recognition of unions and bargaining with them.

The second spurt in membership contrasts with the steady decline in the percentage of the labour force which is organized in the United States. Before 1955, the percentage of workers who were unionized in the U.S. exceeded that in Canada. By 1986, the Canadian rate (38 per cent) was double the American (19 per cent). The second growth period began in 1967 and has been dominated by the organization of public employees, including professional and white-collar workers. The spur has been the federal PSSRA and provincial legislation permitting the unionization of provincial, municipal, and other public-sector workers, such as teachers and hospital staff. By 1986, the public sector accounted for three of Canada's five largest unions: the Canadian Union of Public Employees (CUPE); the National Union of Provincial Government Employees (NUPGE); and the Public Service Alliance of Canada (PSAC). In 1965, NUPGE and PSAC had not even existed as unions.

While the growth of unionization in the public sector has been dramatic in Canada there has also been strong growth of union membership in this area in the United States. The big difference has been the falling U.S. membership rates in other sectors in contrast with the general stability in Canada. The most important factor which has been identified as the source for the difference has been more supportive labour legislation and much stronger enforcement in Canada than in the U.S..[8]

[8] Noah M. Meltz, "Labor Movements in Canada and the United States," in Thomas A. Kochan, ed., *Challenges and Choices Facing American Labor* (Cambridge, Mass.: MIT Press, 1985), pp. 315–37; J.B. Rose and G.N. Chaison, "The State of the Unions: United States and Canada," *Journal of Labour Research* (Winter 1985), pp. 97–112. Seymour Martin Lipsett, "North American Labor Movements: A Comparative Perspective," in Seymour Martin Lipsett, ed., *Unions in Transition, Entering the Second Century* (San Francisco: ICS Press, 1986), pp. 421–52. See also: Pradeep Kumar, "Union Growth in Canada, Retrospect and Prospect," in W. Craig Riddell, Research Coordinator, *Canadian Labour Relations* (Toronto: University of Toronto Press, 1986), pp. 95–160.

EXHIBIT 15.1

Union shares of the nonfarm labour force in Canada and the United States

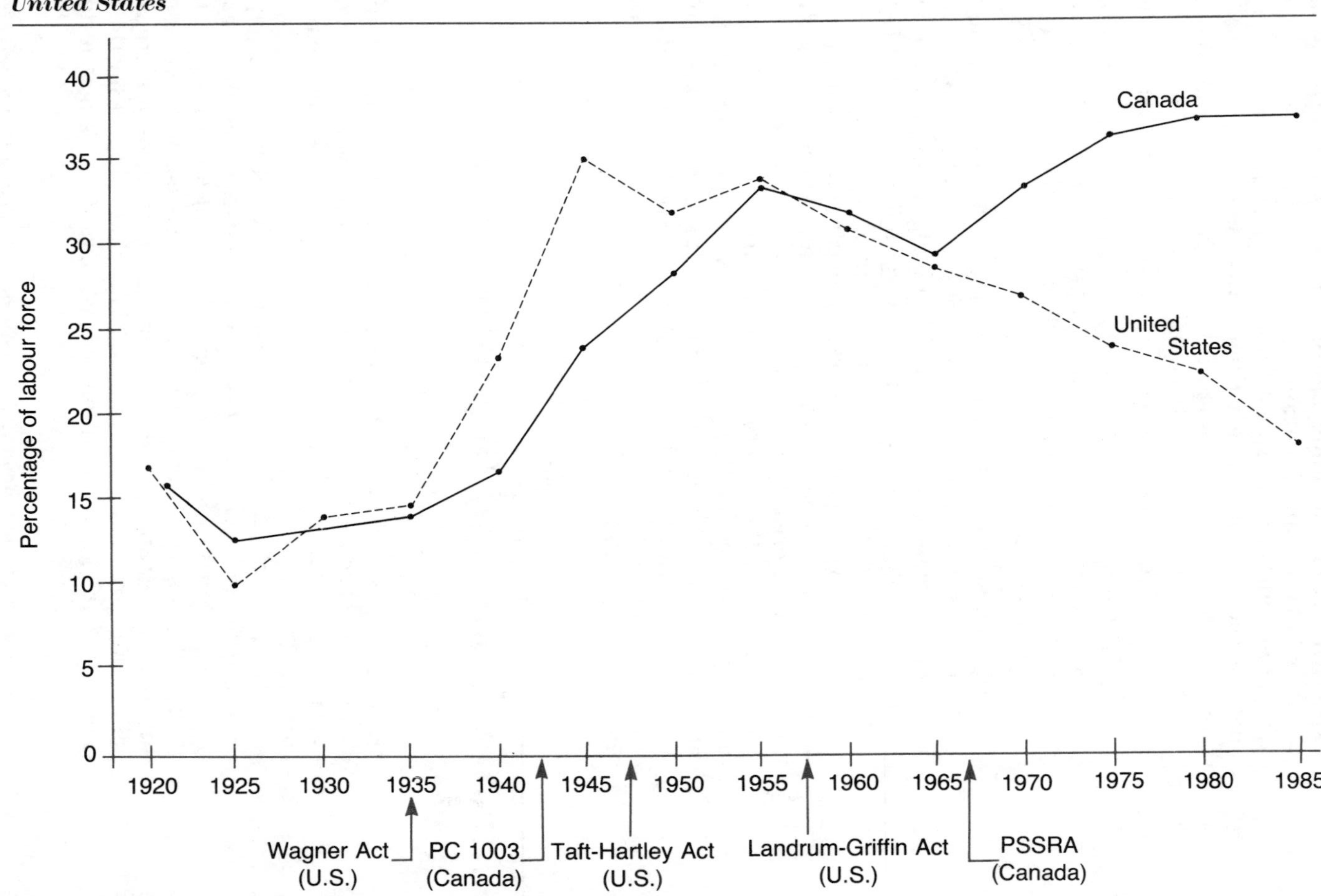

SOURCE: Noah M. Meltz, "Labor Movements in Canada and the United States," in Thomas A. Kochan, ed., *Challenges and Choices Facing American Labor* (Cambridge, Mass.: MIT Press, 1985), p. 318.

With unionization of the public sector well under way, many experts expect the Canadian union movement to attempt again to organize workers in banks and insurance companies, sectors where it has not yet had notable success. The one major gain in the banking sector was the first contract the Canada Labour Relations Board ordered be imposed in 1986 on the Canadian Imperial Bank of Commerce after its Visa unit workers were on strike for seven months. The contract was renewed in 1987 without a strike. One expert studying banks concluded:

> Collective action is more likely to emerge in heavily unionized centres than elsewhere, providing that bank employees are sufficiently dissatisfied to have considered collective means of solving work problems.[9]

Organizing also took place in the mid-1980s in department stores with the certification of retail workers in a number of branches of Eaton's and Simpsons. Since bargaining rights in all but one of the Eaton's locations were subsequently terminated, there is likely to be little momentum for further organization of this sector.

Whatever sector one considers, it is clear that Canadian organized labour faces many challenges, including uncertain job opportunities, the problems of organizing small groups of employees in widely scattered areas, and the example of the United States where the union movement has been slowed by some of the 1960s' and 1970s' social legislation (which has given government guarantees in areas affecting wages, benefits, and working conditions, where workers had depended on unions for protection) and by the increasing hostility of management and legislators.

Labour Relations and Organizational Effectiveness

Many managers feel, as Rob Williams did, that when a union represents some or all of their employees, the organization is less flexible and less effective and managers have less power. These feelings may not be entirely justified.

Opponents of unions argue that they have a negative impact on organizational effectiveness because they raise wages above competitive levels, impose inefficient work rules, and lower output through strikes. The opposite view is that unions increase effectiveness by reducing turnover and by inducing management to adopt more efficient policies and practices. A recent study provides support for the second view.[10] It found that the unionized workers it investigated did have

[9] Graham S. Lowe, *Bank Unionization in Canada: A Preliminary Analysis* (Toronto: Centre for Industrial Relations, University of Toronto, 1980), p. 104.

[10] R.B. Freeman and J.L. Medoff, *What Do Unions Do?* (New York: Basic Books, 1984), p. 166.

significantly lower turnover than comparable nonunion workers, and that productivity was 20 to 25 per cent higher in unionized manufacturing industries, although unionized bituminous coal industries had lower productivity than did their nonunionized counterparts. (During the period studied, the United Mine Workers Union suffered a number of internal problems, which may have resulted in the relatively low productivity.) Another study, of the cement industry, found productivity gains in unionized firms; it attributed one-fifth of the increase to reduced turnover and the remainder to changes in management personnel and in HRM policies.[11]

Of course, the effects of unionization on organizational effectiveness depend both on the development of an effective working relationship between labour and management and on management's ability to make efficient use of labour, capital, and technology. According to an old saying, "Management usually gets the union it deserves."

Labour Relations and Other HRM Functions

As shown in Exhibit 15.2, unions exert an influence on many HRM functions. Unions give employees a collective voice in bargaining for wages, benefits, and other conditions of employment. They also provide employees with a formal grievance procedure for disputes regarding the interpretation of the collective agreement or any other complaints regarding conditions of employment.

The major influence of unions on HRM policies relates to how human resources are used and maintained in the organization. In a unionized firm, policies on virtually all aspects of employment must be agreed upon by labour and management through the collective bargaining process. Since collective agreements specify rules and standard operating procedures, one result of unionization is increased consistency in HRM policies and practices. For example, when employees are unionized, pay is administered either "across-the-board" (everyone in a particular job category receives the same amount) or according to very objective criteria (everyone is paid according to, for example, the number of units assembled). Under some collective agreements, seniority is another dimension to be considered.

Human Resource Planning

Collective agreements affect human resource flows through the organization by specifying criteria for promotions, transfers, and layoffs—for example, who will be laid off first in the event of reductions in the work force, and who will qualify to fill job vacancies. (Ability usually

[11] K.B. Clark, "The Impact of Unionization on Productivity: A Case Study," *Industrial and Labor Relations Review*, July 1980, vol. 33, no. 4, pp. 451–69.

EXHIBIT 15.2

Labour relations and other HRM functions

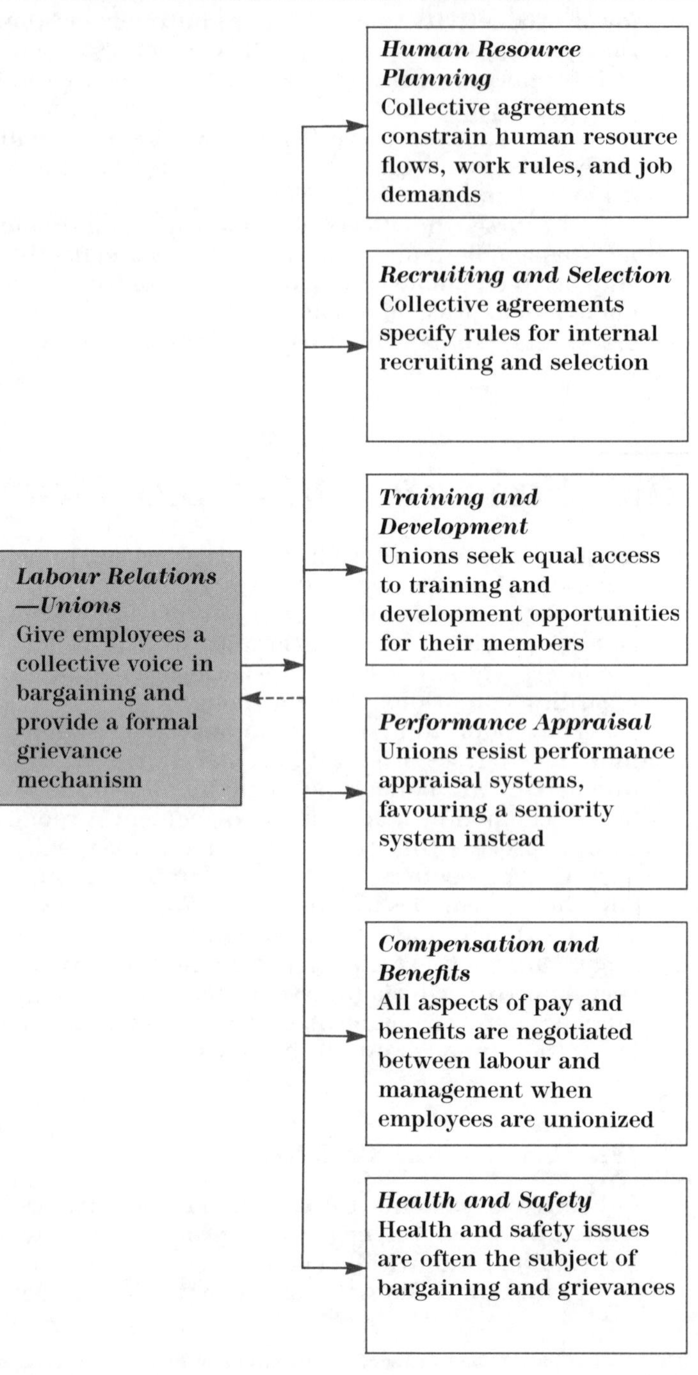
Human Resource Planning
Collective agreements constrain human resource flows, work rules, and job demands
Recruiting and Selection
Collective agreements specify rules for internal recruiting and selection
Training and Development
Unions seek equal access to training and development opportunities for their members
Labour Relations —Unions
Give employees a collective voice in bargaining and provide a formal grievance mechanism
Performance Appraisal
Unions resist performance appraisal systems, favouring a seniority system instead
Compensation and Benefits
All aspects of pay and benefits are negotiated between labour and management when employees are unionized
Health and Safety
Health and safety issues are often the subject of bargaining and grievances

remains an important criterion in such decisions, but management must be in a position to substantiate its judgement.) Some agreements allow unions to object to work rules such as production standards and the introduction of new equipment and work methods. Others specify and limit the tasks to be performed in some jobs. All of these factors and others impose constraints upon human resource planners.

Recruiting and Selection

The major impact of unions on recruiting and selection is on policies relating to internal movement. Generally, unions try to make seniority the major criterion of internal recruiting and selection, while management usually prefers promotions based on individual merit or past job performance. Collective agreements usually settle on a compromise: when two workers being considered for promotion have approximately equal ability and experience, preference must go to the one with more seniority. In some industries, most notably shipping and construction, unions also maintain substantial control over external recruiting since employers may hire only union members. Such agreements are called *closed shop agreements* or contracts. This control increases when unions, like the longshoremen's, run their own hiring halls.

Unions sometimes sponsor apprenticeship programs to train people in skilled occupations, and employers often recruit new employees from such programs.

Training and Development

Unions take an interest in training and development. They try to ensure that their members receive equal opportunities for programs because participation can lead to higher-level jobs and higher-level pay.

Performance Appraisal

Because unions favour seniority-based systems, they strongly resist all forms of performance appraisal based on individual merit or other performance measures. In regard to employee discipline, unionized employees have a formal mechanism for complaints or grievances. Although nonunion employers may also have a grievance procedure, only the presence of a union ensures that employee complaints are considered seriously and that no reprisals are taken by management.[12]

[12] The Canada Labour Code contains a provision for grievance by workers of nonunion employers in cases of unjust dismissal.

Compensation and Benefits

In a unionized firm, the employer must negotiate all aspects of wages and benefits, including increases, with union representatives. Most collective agreements also specify which workers should be offered overtime first (usually those with the most seniority). All aspects of wages and benefits are subject to the grievance procedure during the term of the agreement.

Health and Safety

Since matters of health and safety are conditions of employment, they are subject to negotiation with management, subject to the jurisdiction's health and safety legislation. Union representatives can also file grievances regarding health and safety during the term of a collective agreement. In jurisdictions that mandate joint worker-management health and safety committees, the regulations usually provide for worker representation through the union if one exists.

Influences on Unions

The dotted arrow in Exhibit 15.2 indicates that human resource policies also have an influence on union activities. For example, employees' dissatisfaction with certain aspects of employment may result in grievances and in contract demands at the bargaining table. Human resource policies exert another type of influence on unions: if policies are acceptable to employees who are not yet unionized, employees are less susceptible to union organizing attempts. On the other hand, policies that are poorly received may give rise to organizing attempts.

Responsibilities for Labour Relations

The major role of HRM professionals in labour relations is to preserve management rights and to ensure that an adequate supply of qualified labour is available at the least possible cost. The term *management rights* refers to management's freedom and autonomy to run the organization efficiently, including the right to hire, promote, discharge, or discipline employees for justifiable reasons; the right to determine production schedules and plant locations; and the right to make all other business decisions as long as they do not conflict with the other terms of the collective agreement. In unionized organizations, HRM labour relations specialists perform two major functions: they represent management in collective bargaining and they handle all grievances and contract-related disputes.

The major part of collective bargaining is contract negotiations, and labour relations specialists often begin preparing for them many months before an existing agreement expires. This preparation requires a great deal of planning and research in order to predict the employer's business future, anticipate union demands, and develop tentative offers to the union. Research may include examining other collective agreements in the same industry and/or geographical area; conducting wage and benefit surveys; analyzing organizational productivity, labour costs, and profitability; and forecasting future demand for the organization's products or services. Labour relations specialists often head the management bargaining team and always act as expert advisors in contract negotiations. When a tentative agreement has been reached, labour lawyers, who are often employed by large organizations, finalize the language of the collective agreement so that its conditions are properly stated. The agreement is very important to both management and labour since it specifies the terms and nature of labour-management relations for periods of up to three years.

While contract negotiations are a major part of labour relations, also important are the handling of grievances and the day-to-day administration of the collective agreement. Administration requires careful monitoring of all human resource policies and grievances to ensure that no precedents are set that would adversely affect management rights. Thus, supervisors must know the collective agreement, how to interpret it, and how to be consistent in its administration. Labour relations specialists also represent management in all grievances.

In order to illustrate some of the activities of HRM professionals in unionized organizations, the following typical day is described by John Duke, the industrial relations manager of a manufacturing plant of about 500 employees. Duke reports to the plant manager and manages a human resources department of five employees. A major part of his day is devoted to union-related activities.

7:30–7:45 A.M. Held meeting with employees of my department.
7:45–8:00 Read the day's mail.
8:00–9:00 Discussed problem with employee regarding workers' compensation claim. Met with maintenance supervisor regarding grievance filed in his department. Discussed problem with employee regarding scheduling and overtime.
9:00–10:00 Staff meeting.
10:15–10:30 Discharged employee for insubordination.
10:30–11:00 Held telephone conversation with lawyer regarding grievance arbitration case. Met with five employees regarding scheduled overtime.
11:00–12:00 Held telephone conversation with lawyer regarding a hearing before the provincial labour relations board. Discussed human resource problem with a department head. Prepared for grievance meeting later in the day with union.
12:00–12:30 Lunch.
12:30–1:15 P.M. Met with chief union steward regarding procedure for scheduling overtime. Met with a supervisor regarding new safety procedures.
1:15–2:00 Met with four supervisors regarding interpretation of

collective agreement. Met with union business agent to discuss meeting today plus other problems.
2:00–3:15 Union meeting (handled three grievances).
3:15–3:45 Dictation to secretary.
3:45–4:30 Met with three supervisors regarding interpretation of the collective agreement. Met with general manager of the plant.
4:30–5:15 Investigated and took disciplinary action against three employees on second shift.
5:15–6:00 Miscellaneous paperwork.

Comment: As on any typical day, I received 15 to 20 telephone calls from people inside or outside the plant. I also spent two hours in the evening preparing for a grievance arbitration.

Labour Union Goals

The goal of any trade union is to improve the welfare of its members, who are workers. It is possible, however, to take several approaches towards this goal. Broadly speaking, a union can concentrate on representing its members' interests to employers through collective bargaining, or it can attempt to better their lot through political action. Historically, unions in the United States have emphasized the employment relationship, and the AFL-CIO is not affiliated with any political party. The European labour movement, on the other hand, emphasizes social reform through the political process, often allying itself with or forming political parties. The split is by no means total: European unions do concern themselves with wages and other terms of employment, while American labour organizations lobby for or against specific legislation and attempt to influence the outcome of elections by supporting one party or another (an approach that Samuel Gompers, founder of the AFL, referred to as "rewarding your friends and punishing your enemies"). Nevertheless, the difference in approach is clear, with U.S. labour often being called "job conscious" and European "class conscious."

As in other fields of endeavour, Canadians have combined aspects of both the American and the European approaches, although their pattern comes closer to mirroring that of the United States, with the Canadian trade union movement being a somewhat tempered form of business unionism. Certainly, the goals of Canadian unions at the bargaining table can be described as "job conscious," rather than "class conscious," in that they emphasize wages, benefits, working conditions, and job security. On the other hand, central labour organizations, such as provincial federations of labour and the 2.1-million-member Canadian Labour Congress (CLC), have pressed for legislated improvements in minimum wages, social benefits such as pensions and health care, and health and safety standards in workplaces, and this pressure has been applied partly through affiliation with the New Democratic Party and its predecessor, the Co-operative Commonwealth Federation.

Support for the NDP has not, however, found favour with all Canadian unions, particularly the craft unions in the skilled construction trades. In 1982, ten of them left the CLC and formed a new congress, the Canadian Federation of Labour (CFL). Although the specific issue on which they broke away was a question of jurisdiction, the CFL has followed the American approach of not being formally linked with a political party.

Of course, in another sense, all Canadian unions, like unions everywhere, are political in that union leaders are elected by union members. To retain their positions, union leaders must not only bargain effectively with management; they must also satisfy the needs of those they represent.

Labour Unions: Structure

Labour organizations in Canada exist at three levels: (1) local unions; (2) national and international unions; and (3) central labour congresses. Although the organizational chart in Exhibit 15.3 shows the Canadian Labour Congress at the top of a pyramid, primary authority rests at the local level because individual unions have the responsibility for organization and collective bargaining.

Local Unions

A *local union* is the basic unit of labour organization formed in a particular plant or locality. Locals in Canada are of three kinds. By far the most prevalent is the *local of an international or national union*, which is affiliated with a national or international union. The local pays per-capita dues to the parent union and receives services in return. A second kind of local is one *directly chartered* by a central labour congress. Dues are paid directly to the congress and services are received from it. Directly chartered locals covered 0.7 per cent of all union members in 1986. *Independent locals* are units not formally affiliated with any other labour organization. Their membership totalled 3.0 per cent of organized workers in 1986.[13]

It is with local unions, no matter what their type, that individual employers and employees usually interact on a day-to-day basis. Though locals vary considerably, in membership size, they are usually confined to a specific municipality or other geographic area, representing workers in a single industry or kind of job and frequently bargaining with a single employer. Each has officials, including stewards, and elected officers. Stewards are the lowest-level officials; they act as the union's

[13] Labour Canada, *Directory of Labour Organizations in Canada, 1986* (Hull, Que.: Supply and Services Canada, 1986), p. 20.

EXHIBIT 15.3

The structure of the CLC-affiliated segment of the Canadian labour movement

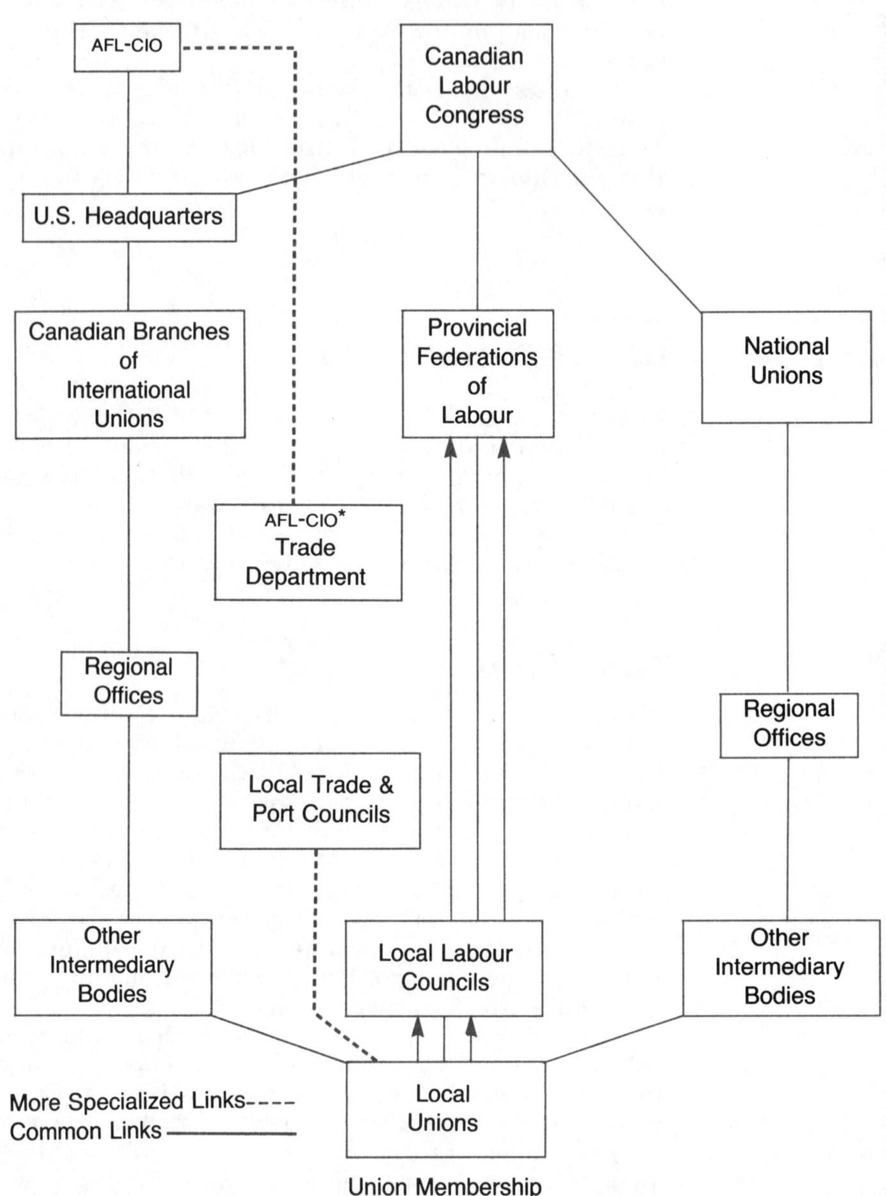

*Since the separation of the Building Trades from the Canadian Labour Congress, and the formation of the Canadian Federation of Labour in 1982, none of the unions in the AFL-CIO Trade Department are affiliated with the Canadian Labour Congress.

SOURCE: John Crispo, *International Unionism* (Toronto: McGraw-Hill, 1967), p. 167. By permission of the author.

representatives on a daily basis to be sure that management complies with the collective agreement. They also represent employees in grievances against management. Like most union officials, stewards are employees who are not paid for their union activities. Besides elected officials, unions have committees to handle functions such as organizing and membership, recreation, and community relations. An important committee is the executive committee, which often handles contract negotiations with management as well as major grievances.

Workers in unionized organizations have various degrees of freedom to join or not join the union. Under *closed shop agreements*, only union members can be hired for employment. In *union shop agreements*, employees must become union members within 30 days of their date of hire. Under *Rand formula*, or *agency shop agreements*, employees who do not wish to join a union must still pay union dues on the grounds that the union represents all the bargaining unit's employees, not just union members. No Canadian jurisdiction has an equivalent of American "right-to-work" laws, which make union membership completely voluntary.

Members' level of interest in local unions is often low. One U.S. study found that attendance at meetings was generally very poor but increased substantially for discussions of collective-agreement demands, ratification votes, and election of officers.[14] One author has suggested that most union members have little interest in participating in union activities, but just want the organization to function effectively as their representative in matters of pay, benefits, and working conditions.[15] On the other hand, the mechanism of the local union always exists to permit a great deal of grass-roots participation if members believe the situation demands it. This normally occurs at contract negotiation time since 60 per cent of collective bargaining in Canada is between single unions and single employers.[16] Whether they take advantage of it seems to depend on their perceptions of both the elected representatives and the organization that employs them. In one insightful paper, North American unions are depicted as combining features of the army and of an old-fashioned town meeting.[17]

National and International Unions

In most parts of the world, one can find unions that are restricted to one country as well as unions (or alliances of unions) that cross international boundaries. In Canada, however, the terms "national union" and "international union" have a specialized meaning. A *national union*

[14] L.R. Sayles and G. Strauss, *The Local Union*, rev. ed. (New York: Harcourt, Brace & World, 1967).

[15] J.A. Fossum, *Labor Relations: Development, Structure, and Process* (Dallas: Business Publications, Inc., 1979), p. 81.

[16] Alton W.J. Craig, *The System of Industrial Relations in Canada*, 2nd ed. (Scarborough, Ont.: Prentice-Hall Canada, 1986), p. 171.

[17] A.J. Muste, "Army and Town Meeting," in E. Wight Bakke, Clark Kerr, and Charles W. Anrod, eds., *Union, Management and the Public* (New York: Harcourt, Brace & World, 1967).

is an organization that charters locals only in Canada. Well-known examples are the Canadian Union of Public Employees (CUPE), the National Union of Provincial Government Employees (NUPGE), the Public Service Alliance of Canada (PSAC), Centrale de l'enseignement du Québec (CEQ), and the Canadian Paperworkers Union (CPU).

An *international union*, on the other hand, charters locals in both the United States and Canada. Well-known international unions include the United Steelworkers of America, the United Food and Commercial Workers International Union (UFCW), and the International Brotherhood of Teamsters, Chauffeurs, Warehousemen, and Helpers of America.

The United Automobile Workers (UAW) used to charter locals in both countries but in 1986 all but one of the Canadian locals formed a new national union, the Canadian Automobile Workers (CAW), with 140,000 members. The Canadian union received $43 million from the UAW as the Canadian share of strike funds and other resources which were held by the international.

Both international and national unions may be organized as craft unions, such as the United Brotherhood of Carpenters and Joiners or the CEQ; as industrial unions, such as the UAW or CUPE; or as a mixture of craft and industrial, such as the Teamsters. *Craft unions* attempt to organize all employees in a specific occupation, such as carpenters, machinists, musicians, printers, and others. *Industrial unions* organize employees in a specific industry, such as steel, automobiles, or government.

In many ways, national and international unions, craft or industrial, function alike. They are large groups—varying from 1,000 to 300,000 Canadian members—that provide structure and support for their local affiliates. Often they help locals in bargaining by providing experienced negotiators, and they fund and support many organizing campaigns. The structure and government of nationals and internationals are similar to those of locals, but their officers and professional staffs are paid, full-time employees of the union. Money to run the nationals and internationals comes from dues collected by the local affiliates.

The difference between national and international unions is basically one of the locus of power. All international unions have their headquarters in the United States, although most elect a Canadian vice-president or some other senior official to ensure Canadian representation at the executive-committee level. The relative merits of international versus national unions have been debated for almost a century in Canada. After a detailed examination of the subject in 1966, John Crispo concluded:

> Where effective alternative forms of unionism are available, Canadian workers sometimes look more critically upon the role played by international unions. To date, however, relatively few of them have chosen to abandon them. This attitude indicates that the Canadian workers who have become members of international unions remain convinced that they represent a good investment.[18]

[18] John Crispo, *International Unionism, A Study in Canadian-American Relations* (Toronto: McGraw-Hill, 1967), p. 322.

This statement is still valid more than 20 years later, although the creation of the CAW may suggest a greater possibility that other international unions will separate. The major development since the late 1960s is that national unions have grown rapidly, particularly in the public sector, sharply increasing their share of the organized labour force. In 1965, 70.8 per cent of Canadian union members belonged to international unions and 24.5 per cent to national unions. By early 1986, it was 39.1 per cent and 57.2 per cent respectively.[19] The creation of the Canadian Auto Workers from the Canadian branch of the United Automobile Workers (UAW) reduces the international percentage to 35 and increases the national to 60.

The CLC and Other Central Labour Congresses

Several large labour congresses serve as unifying bodies for Canadian labour unions. Most national and international unions belong to them; notable exceptions are the Teamsters and the Centrale de l'enseignement du Québec. The largest congress is the Canadian Labour Congress (CLC); in 1986, 58 per cent (2.2 million) of Canada's 3.7 million union members were affiliated with it. The country's next largest labour congress is the Confederation of National Trade Unions (CNTU) with 219,000 members. There are also two small groups, the Centrale des Syndicats Démocratiques (CSD), a CNTU breakaway with 35,967 members, and the Confederation of Canadian Unions (CCU) with 35,683 members. A recent addition is the Canadian Federation of Labour (CFL) formed in 1982 by ten international construction trade unions, totalling 209,000 members, which left the CLC after various contentious issues culminated in a jurisdictional dispute.

Resolution of jurisdictional disputes is one of a number of functions of the central labour congresses. Others include assisting affiliates in collective bargaining through technical expertise and support, furthering the political interests of organized labour, and representing Canadian labour in international organizations. The congresses also directly charter a few locals.

The Transition from Employee Relations to Labour Relations

This section examines the transition from nonunion status (employee relations) to union status (labour relations). It briefly discusses employee relations, then factors related to unionization; finally the union organizing process is described. Exhibit 15.4 illustrates the movement.

[19] Department of Labour, *Labour Organizations in Canada* (Ottawa: Queen's Printer, 1966), p. xii; and Labour Canada, p. 20.

EXHIBIT 15.4

From employee relations to labour relations

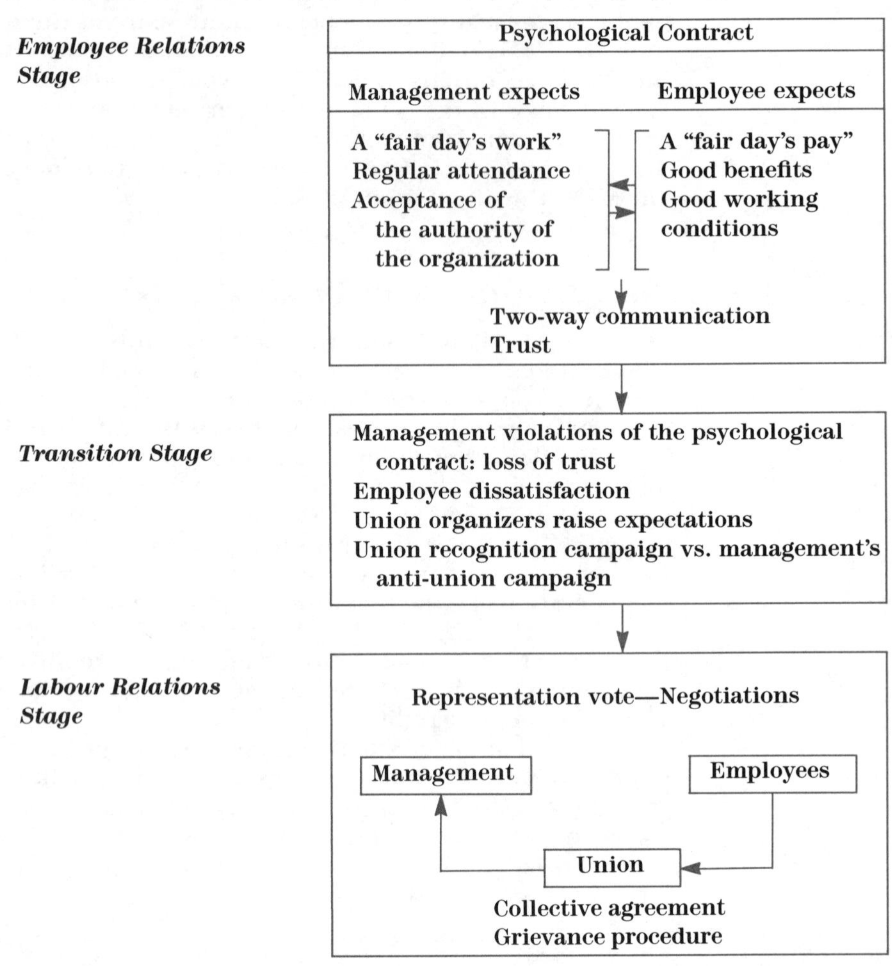

Employee Relations

The majority of employers are not unionized and less than 40 per cent of the paid labour force is unionized. Therefore, most employers and employees function in an employee relations environment, as opposed to a labour relations environment. *Employee relations* is a general term that describes the way in which management interacts and deals with nonunion employees. An employee relations environment is characterized by an employer, who is in a dominant power position, interacting with employees on an individual basis. It is the employer who dictates all the conditions of employment except those set by employee standards acts and other pertinent legislation. Some senior executives do have written, legal contracts, but in most nonunion situations, employer and employee develop an unwritten psychological contract.[20]

The psychological contract is a set of expectations held by both employer and employee. Employers expect employees to provide a "fair day's work," to accept the authority of the organization, and to come to work regularly. Employees expect, in return for their services, a "fair day's pay" and good working conditions and benefits. These expectations have been rising since the post-war era. Today's employees also expect many intangibles, including a mechanism through which unfair or biased actions by supervisors or other employees may be appealed; an equitable system of judging and rewarding job performance; an explanation of the employer's goals, policies, actions, and any changes affecting employees; at least some participation in decisions affecting their jobs; and more challenging jobs.

Maintaining the psychological contract is an essential part of good employee relations. The terms of a psychological contract require a period of interaction and communication between employer and employee. Over time, a climate of trust is developed if both parties are consistent and fair in their actions, keep their explicit and implicit promises, and maintain honest, two-way communication. It is especially important for management to be consistent and fair. A climate of trust is usually easier to develop and maintain in small organizations, since their managers can know employees personally. Of course, a climate of trust is not unique to nonunionized settings, but it is especially important in them. Repeated and serious violations of the psychological contract by management cause dissatisfaction, distrust, and a feeling of powerlessness among employees, which often lead them to seek a union to restore equity and fairness in the workplace.

Factors Related to Unionization

The previous section suggests that good employee relations reduce the tendency for employees to join a union. A number of other factors are related to unionization. Survey results indicate that the propensity to unionize is related to the following situations and attitudes:

1. Job dissatisfaction, especially with wages, benefits, and working conditions.
2. Perceived inequities in pay.
3. Lack of the desired amount of influence or participation on the job and perceptions of inability to influence working conditions.
4. Beliefs about how effective unions are in improving wages and working conditions.

[20] E.H. Schein, *Organizational Psychology*, 2nd ed. (Englewood Cliffs, N.J.: Prentice-Hall, 1970).

Exhibit 15.5 shows a model of the propensity for employees to support unionization. It begins with job satisfaction regarding pay, benefits, and working conditions. Dissatisfaction with these factors has been found to be highly related to pro-union behaviour.[21] Another study found that perceived pay inequities were as important as dissatisfaction with levels of pay in determining the propensity to favour unionization.[22] From the employee's perspective, both these forms of dissatisfaction may be viewed as the result of violations of the psychological contract. Additionally, some employees may have a high degree of interest in having some influence in aspects of their work. If the employer does not accommodate them, the result is job dissatisfaction.

When employees experience job dissatisfaction for any of these reasons, they may choose either to quit or to remain on the job and work to improve conditions. Those who have more commitment to the job generally remain, and some of them are likely to support union-organizing attempts. Within this group, the tendency to support a union depends upon another factor: the employee's perception of union effectiveness, of the likelihood that a union could improve wages and other working conditions. Moreover, the propensity to unionize is higher in medium-sized organizations (companies with more than 200 and fewer than 1,000 employees). As already suggested, a climate of trust is easier to maintain in small organizations. On the other hand, large employers, such as Dominion Foundries and Steel Company (DOFASCO), are more likely to be able to afford to pay high wages and benefits and to maintain good employee relations programs.

While the model suggests that only job dissatisfaction or a frustrated desire for influence on the job leads to unionization, this is not the case. Some employees choose to join unions for reasons completely unrelated to pay, benefits, or any aspect of job satisfaction. For example, an employee may join because his or her relatives or friends are union members. An employee may have been a union member at another place of employment. Or an employee's political persuasions may suggest the importance of unions. And, of course, if a company is already unionized, employees must join the union under a union shop agreement; in other situations, they may join because of peer pressure.

Certainly a factor affecting the propensity to unionize is union strength in certain industries and certain parts of the country. Unions have traditionally represented employees in approximately half of all manufacturing firms and have been strong in resource industries and construction. During the 1970s, union penetration remained stable in these areas. It was in the service industries and the public sector that it shot upwards, led by the growth of CUPE, NUPGE, PSAC, teachers' fed-

[21] J.G. Getman, S.B. Goldberg, and J.B. Herman, *Union Representation Elections: Law and Reality* (New York: Russell Sage, 1976); W.C. Hamner and F.J. Smith, "Work Attitudes as Predictors of Unionization Activity," *Journal of Applied Psychology*, 1978, vol. 63, pp. 415–21; and C.A. Schriesheim, "Job Satisfaction, Attitudes toward Unions and Voting in Union Representation Elections," *Journal of Applied Psychology*, 1978, vol. 65, pp. 548–52.

[22] T.A. Kochan, "How American Workers View Labour Unions," *Monthly Labor Review*, April 1979, vol. 10, pp. 15–22.

EXHIBIT 15.5

Factors affecting propensity to unionize

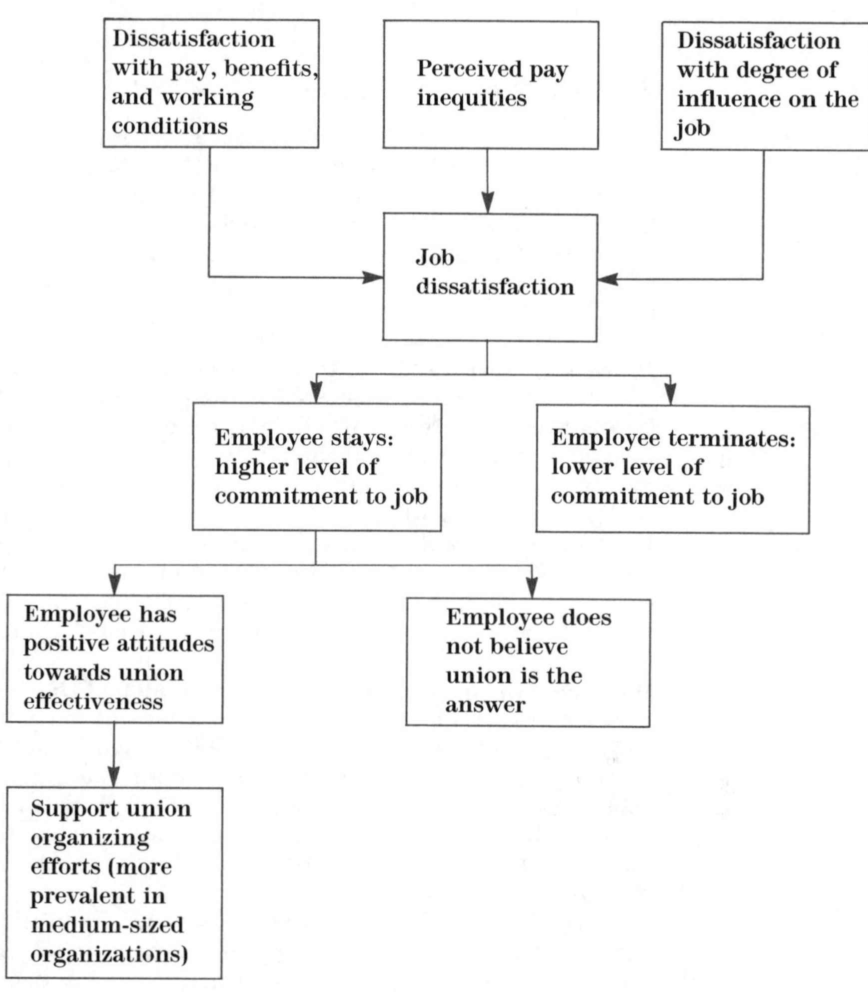

erations, nurses' associations, and the Service Employees International Union (SEIU). By 1979, the public sector was the most organized in Canada, with 67.7 per cent of its workers unionized. British Columbia and Newfoundland are the most highly unionized provinces in Canada, while Prince Edward Island and Alberta are the least.[23]

[23] W.D. Wood and Pradeep Kumar, eds., *The Current Industrial Relations Scene in Canada 1982* (Kingston, Ont.: Industrial Relations Centre, Queen's University, 1982), p. 227.

These data suggest that employees in industries and provinces which already have a high concentration of unionized employees are more likely to become unionized than are employees in industries and areas with low levels of unionization.

The Union Organizing Process

The previous section examined factors leading to employees' propensity to unionize. This section examines activities and legal constraints associated with union organizing campaigns. Exhibit 15.6 portrays the union organizing process in Ontario. Other jurisdictions vary only in detail, most notably in the percentage of union membership the labour relations board usually requires to call a representation vote or to certify without a vote.

Process initiation. The union organizing process is initiated in one of two ways. First, as suggested in the previous section, employees may become sufficiently dissatisfied with their pay and working conditions to seek help through a union. In the second case, representatives of a national or international union may contact employees at the local level. Established unions often allocate money to organize employees in specific geographical regions or in industries considered "good candidates" for unionization. Though unions need new members to grow, organizing campaigns can be expensive. Therefore, most unions try to organize only where they feel they have a good chance of success.

Membership campaign. In the second step of the organizing process, the union convinces members of a potential bargaining unit to join the group, obtaining a signed membership card from each. These cards are important because the relevant labour relations board will check each signature against a sample obtained from the employer. Some boards also require the filing of receipts to ensure the new members have made at least token payments as evidence of their wish to have the union represent them.

An organization can agree to recognize voluntarily the union as the exclusive bargaining agent for certain of its employees. If this recognition is given, collective bargaining may begin. However, employers rarely give voluntary recognition to a union; most wait for the appropriate labour relations board to make the decision for them.

Union organizers often face a difficult task in gaining access to employees in order to convince them to become union members. By law, employers need not permit any organizations to solicit on company property or time. Thus, membership campaigns often depend on organizers who are already company employees.

Determining the bargaining unit. In organizing employees, a union must define what it considers the *bargaining unit*, which is the group or type of employee which it seeks to represent. As we already mentioned, each union seeks to organize employees within its traditional jurisdiction, along certain craft and/or industry lines. Unions also try

EXHIBIT 15.6

Union organizing process under the Ontario Labour Relations Act

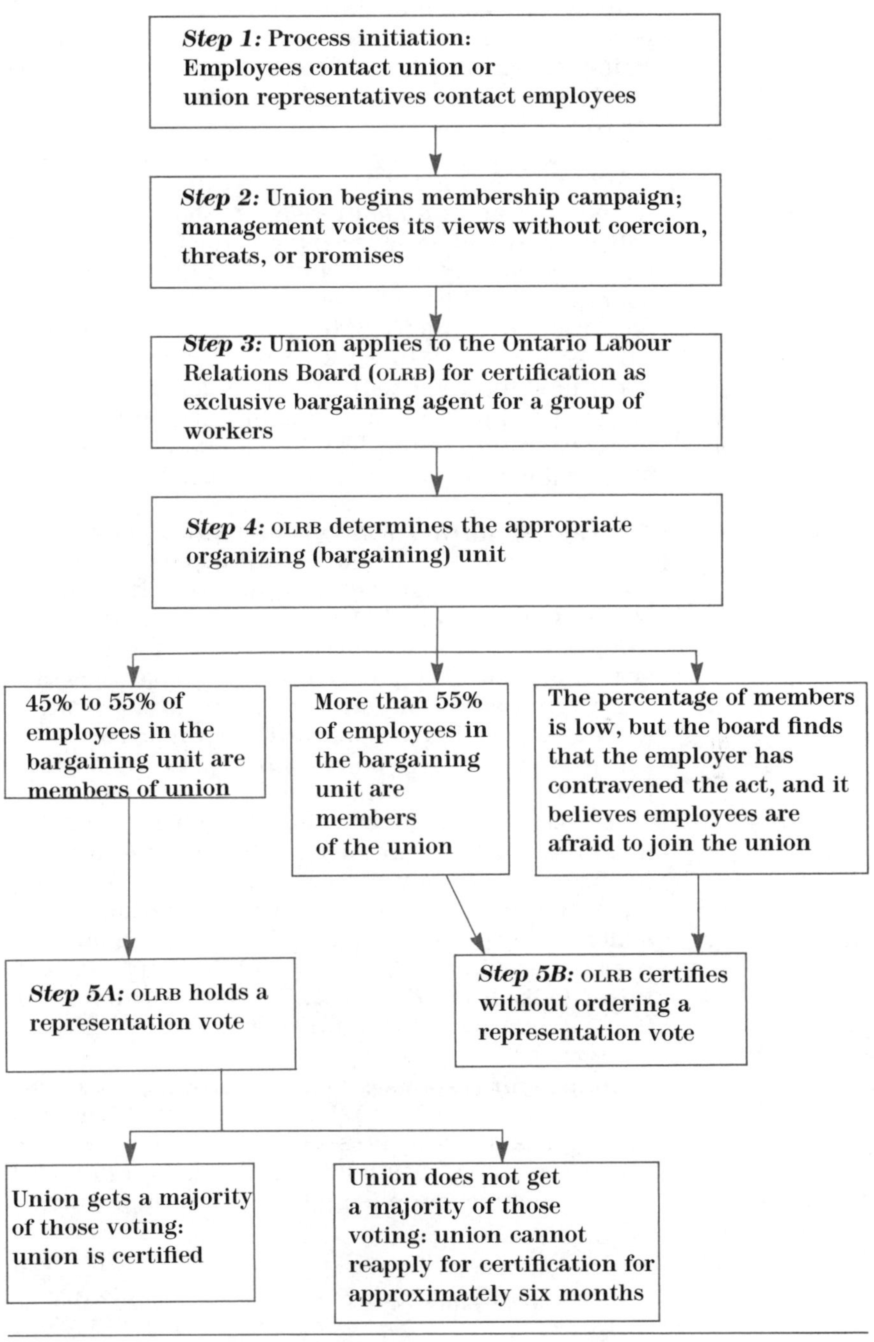

to define the bargaining unit in a way that favours winning certification (by including job categories in which a high proportion of workers favour unionization and excluding those in which unionization is unpopular) and that will give it the most bargaining power if the union is certified. Thus, the union prefers a bargaining unit in which employees have common skills, needs, and work experiences and are important enough to the employer to disrupt the organization through a strike. Management, on the other hand, prefers a bargaining unit defined so as to make it less powerful and less likely to win certification for the union.

Because union organizers and management each have vested interests in defining the bargaining unit, the final determination is left to the appropriate labour relations board. The complex decision involves many factors. For example, the Ontario Labour Relations Board only occasionally carves out craft units; in general, it decides on an appropriate industrial unit by considering: (1) the desires of the employer and the union; (2) the community of interest among employees (that is, the nature of work performed, the conditions of employment, and the skills required); (3) the organizational structure of the employer; (4) the desire not to split one employer's work force into too many bargaining units; (5) the general policy of not putting office staff and production workers in the same bargaining unit.[24]

The representation vote. Before certifying a union as a bargaining agent, the relevant labour relations board needs to ascertain that a majority of the workers in the unit favour the union. If the membership count alone gives it this certainty, it will certify the union automatically. If there is some question, it calls for a representation vote. The percentages of workers needed for automatic certification and for calling a representation vote vary from jurisdiction to jurisdiction. The Canada Labour Relations Board (federal jurisdiction), for example, certifies automatically if more than 50 per cent of the workers have taken membership in the union, and it orders a representation vote if 35 to 50 per cent are members. Ontario's board, however, usually requires more than 55 per cent membership for automatic certification and 45 to 55 per cent for a representation vote.

If the board does require a representation vote, it is taken by secret ballot under the supervision of a returning officer sent by the board. In many provinces, the union and the employer may each send a scrutineer to each polling place. The union wins the representation vote if more than half of those voting favour it.

Management responses to unionization. No employer may interfere with the formation or selection of a union by employees. While an employer is free to express his or her views, that expression must not involve coercion, intimidation, threats, or undue influence. Undue influence includes promising benefits to employees if they do not join a

[24] *A Guide to the Ontario Labour Relations Act* (Toronto: Ontario Ministry of Labour, 1986), p. 21.

union. It also includes making threats against employees, such as threats of closing down, of moving the firm's facilities elsewhere, or of ending certain employee benefits. "If the board feels that a vote is not likely to disclose the true wishes of the employees because of undue coercion, it will grant certification;"[25] illegal anti-union statements by an employer may be sufficient evidence of undue coercion. Once a union has applied for certification, the terms and conditions of employment cannot be changed without its approval.

Additionally, an employer may not fire or penalize an employee for organizing or other union activity; if a complaint of this sort of harassment is upheld, the employee can be ordered reinstated with back pay or reimbursed for lost wages. Moreover, a labour board may order remedies, including access to the employees for the union, to moderate the impact of this or other illegalities by the employer. Management may, however, use labour lawyers to disallow, delay, or block the signing of members of certification votes. Generally, the longer the time between the membership campaign and the vote, the less likely the union is to win certification.

Alternatively, an employer is forbidden to support a union in any way. If there has been such support, the union will not be certified. (This regulation prevents company, or employer-controlled, unions.)

Organizing campaigns are a very difficult and stressful time for most HRM professionals and management. Many employers view the organizing process as an invasion of their territory and rights. In fact, management resistance to unionization has produced a lucrative consulting business for many labour lawyers and consulting firms.[26]

One popular seminar for managers, entitled "Making Unions Unnecessary," focusses on the following areas:

1. Management commitment to and communication of a nonunion objective.
2. Basic assumptions of nonunion companies, including shaping employee thinking and avoiding human resource policies that teach people to "think union."
3. Pay policy, including avoiding problems in performance reviews and the danger of poorly handled merit reviews.
4. Benefit programs, including overcoming communication and administrative problems.
5. Problem-solving, including consistency and due-process approaches to discipline.
6. Communication programs, including discussion methods such as meetings, employee handbooks, newsletters, attitude surveys, and the use of survey results.
7. Value system analysis, including management and employee values and a workshop on management flexibility.[27]

[25] Ibid., pp. 35, 48–49.

[26] D. Martin, "Labor Nemesis," *Wall Street Journal*, November 19, 1979.

[27] C.L. Hughes, "Making Unions Unnecessary," Executive Enterprises Seminar, New York, 1979.

In brief, this seminar covers many of the aspects of good employee relations that we discussed earlier. It is interesting to speculate whether such programs, which basically teach good employee relations, would be nearly as successful if they were marketed as "employee-relations-improvement" programs rather than as "union-prevention" programs.

Perhaps it is not surprising that some employers make no effort to improve their employee relations until threatened with unionization. After all, many employers did not attempt to avoid discrimination in their hiring practices until the introduction of human rights codes, and many gave inadequate attention to employees' health and safety before the passage of relevant legislation. While such techniques may be useful for improving employee job satisfaction and reducing the propensity to unionize, they are rarely effective once an organizing campaign has been set in motion.

Should management be so concerned about unionization? As we have seen, some experts feel that it may actually contribute to organizational effectiveness by reducing turnover and encouraging managerial efficiency. On the other hand, a recent survey of unionized manufacturing firms in Canada indicated that their workers' behaviour is perceived by management as its greatest problem. The authors concluded that this finding, plus an ambivalent response to the statement that the union is effective in bringing up genuine employee concerns, suggests that "unionism often does not have the positive behavioural effects which some authors maintain that it can have."[28] The variety of views on the impact of unions on organizations means that analysis of data on productivity and turnover is necessary for a full examination of the issue.

Collective Bargaining

After a trade union wins the right to represent a group of employees, union and management representatives must negotiate a collective agreement.[29] Both employers and union representatives have a legal obligation to begin collective bargaining in good faith.

Both parties value negotiating a favourable collective agreement since it defines conditions of employment and provides the structure of the labour-management relationship for one or several years. Union leaders are motivated to negotiate a favourable agreement for their members since doing so will help them win re-election. Management

[28] John H. Godard and Thomas A. Kochan, "Canadian Management under Collective Bargaining: Policies, Processes, Structure and Effectiveness," in John Anderson and Morley Gunderson, eds., *Union-Management Relations in Canada* (Don Mills, Ont.: Addison-Wesley, 1982), p. 141.

[29] For a discussion and examples of different clauses of collective agreements in Canada see: Jeffrey Sack and Ethan Poskanzer, *Contract Clauses, Collective Agreement Language in Canada*, 2nd ed. (Toronto: Lancaster House, 1985).

is motivated to negotiate an agreement that keeps labour costs to reasonable levels and preserves its right to operate the organization efficiently. Since contract negotiations are vitally important, both parties usually spend much time and effort preparing for and executing negotiations.

Before negotiations begin, both labour and management (including HRM professionals) engage in a number of preparatory activities. Representatives from the national or international union sometimes aid locals in preparing for negotiations. The union gathers information on:

1. Recent contract settlements, in the local area and industrywide.
2. Grievances under the previous contract, if one was in effect.
3. Interests and demands of union members.

HRM professionals and management also collect information on other relevant settlements. They examine grievances to determine if changes in the collective agreement could reduce grievances, and they try to forecast future economic conditions to determine how much can be offered the union.

The Bargaining Process

The actual bargaining process begins when union and management teams meet at the bargaining table. The union negotiating team generally consists of the local union's officers, its negotiating committee, and one or more specialists from the national or international union's staff. Members of the management negotiating team vary but usually include one or more production or operations managers, a labour lawyer, and a compensation specialist and/or a benefits specialist. The chief labour relations specialist usually heads the management team.

If a previous collective agreement has been in effect, the union team usually begins by presenting its proposed changes, additions, and deletions. If no contract exists, the union simply states its demands. Initially, unions frequently demand fairly large increases in wages, benefits, and other items. Both labour and management know that haggling and compromise are a traditional part of collective bargaining. After hearing the union's initial proposals, management offers a counterproposal which is usually less than it realistically expects to end up with. If many issues are to be negotiated, groups of related issues are often handled separately. For example, issues related to health and safety may be separated from hourly wages and benefits, while changes in the grievance procedure constitute yet a third area. Negotiations often begin with the least controversial issues and proceed to the more difficult ones. Separate issues may be combined or trade-offs made between various issues in order to reach an acceptable agreement. Management may, for example, agree to a higher wage and benefit package if the union agrees to a longer contract. Although this strategy would mean higher labour costs for management, its ability to maintain uninterrupted operations over a longer time would also increase.

Contract negotiations are sometimes difficult, unpleasant, and lengthy, but negotiators are legally required to bargain in good faith. This does not mean, however, that an agreement must be reached; it simply means that the negotiating parties must try their best to reach some agreement. Merely going through the motions of negotiating without taking any real steps towards reaching accord is an example of failure to bargain in good faith, which is considered an unfair labour practice.

Impasses and Resolutions

Even when both parties bargain in good faith, negotiations can become deadlocked. The result is often that labour calls a *strike*, a partial or complete withdrawal of services. Most employees have the legal right to strike, except those in certain public-sector jobs, such as fire fighting and law enforcement, deemed "essential" by particular jurisdictions. This right is limited, however, by time; in most jurisdictions, labour laws prohibit strikes: (1) before a union is certified; (2) during the term of a collective agreement; and (3) before the jurisdiction's mandatory conciliation procedures and "cooling off" period have been accomplished. A strike during one of these prohibited periods or by workers who do not have the right to strike is termed an *illegal strike* and may leave the union and/or its individual members open to fines and its leaders to prison sentences.

Management may react to an impasse with a *lockout*, a refusal to allow employees to work. This right, too, may be exercised only after the exhaustion of the conciliation process and the following "cooling off" period.

Although the strike and the lockout may be legitimate forms of bargaining, it is clear that both are disruptive.[30] In the private sector, both sides suffer an economic loss when either response is taken. In the public sector, management may or may not suffer financial loss, but authorities there are subject to public criticism when there is a loss of services, such as municipal transport or postal service. Canadian labour law, therefore, puts considerable emphasis on *mediation*, which is basically efforts by a neutral third party to establish communication between a union and management and assist them in coming to an agreement.

Mediation can be of two types: compulsory conciliation and voluntary mediation. *Compulsory conciliation* is a remnant of the "cooling off" and public information approach developed by W. L. Mackenzie King in the Industrial Disputes Investigation Act of 1907; most provinces require the intervention of a conciliation officer as a last-ditch effort to avoid a strike. The conciliation officer is appointed by a labour

[30] For a dramatization of events associated with a strike, see *Anatomy of a Strike*, a videotape prepared by the Centre for Industrial Relations and the Media Centre, University of Toronto, 1983.

relations board, and he or she reports back to it on the success or failure of the effort to reconcile the parties. When the report has been made to the board, the union is free to strike and management to lock out after a stipulated "cooling off" period (generally a week).

Voluntary mediation is an option whereby both sides request the services of a third party to assist them in negotiations. Often the conciliation officer or mediator acts as a messenger, trying to get both parties back to the bargaining table. Situations of this type are most common with parties who have little negotiation experience.

Another form of third-party intervention for impasse resolution is *interest arbitration*. In situations in which no collective agreement exists or in which a change is sought in an agreement, an arbitrator acts as a judge to decide on new terms. Interest arbitration occurs most often in the public sector.

Though some impasses do occur in contract negotiations and sometimes result in well-publicized strikes and lockouts, these drastic actions are relatively rare. In most cases, labour and management negotiate a tentative agreement, which is then approved or ratified by a vote of union members. Of course, the members have the right to reject an agreement negotiated by their representatives, but this situation does not occur often. If employees vote not to accept an agreement, labour and management return to the bargaining table.

HRM professionals often view the actual negotiation process as exciting and challenging. One reason may be that it has an atmosphere of a long poker game played for very high stakes. Bargaining may proceed at a very leisurely pace until the expiration date of the existing agreement, at which time the process begins to move rapidly, continuing for several consecutive days and nights.[31] In good bargaining relationships, labour and management may not like each other, but they respect each other.

The Grievance Procedure

Though collective agreements are written precisely and are very specific on many aspects of wages, benefits, hours, and working conditions, disputes sometimes arise regarding the interpretation of provisions. For this reason, virtually every agreement provides a grievance procedure specifying how problems of interpretation and application will be resolved. The grievance procedure is an important part of a labour agreement anywhere in the world, but it is especially important in Canada, where most jurisdictions do not permit a union to strike or management to lock out during the term of a contract. In these jurisdictions, the grievance procedure is supposed to offset the loss of the

[31] For a dramatization of the process, see *The Collective Bargaining Process*, a four-part videotape prepared by the Centre for Industrial Relations and the Media Centre, University of Toronto, 1979.

right to strike or lock out, so if such a procedure is omitted, model wording from the relevant labour relations act is deemed to be included in the collective agreement.

Given such a procedure, a *grievance* is a formal complaint by an employee (the "grievant") regarding any event, action, or practice which he or she believes violates the collective agreement. Grievances may, for example, arise from the dismissal or promotion of an employee, from the reassignment of an employee from one job to another, from the addition of duties, from the assignment of overtime to or the laying off of particular employees, from practices relating to health and safety, and so on.

Exhibit 15.7 shows the four steps in a typical grievance procedure.[32] In the first, the grievant seeks the assistance of the union steward in filing a grievance against management. If the steward agrees that the contract has been violated, a written grievance is filed and presented to the supervisor for a decision. He or she may "accept" the grievance, settling it on the spot. Or the grievance may be "denied." In that case, the grievant has two choices. He or she can accept the supervisor's denial and let the matter drop. Alternatively, the supervisor's decision may be rejected, in which case the grievance moves to the second step.

In practice, the first step of the grievance procedure can vary considerably. Some procedures do not require a written grievance, and some begin with a discussion between the grievant and the supervisor with the union steward present. Grievances may be very minor (such as a supervisor's performing the work of a subordinate) or very significant (such as a denial of a promotion, a disciplinary layoff, or a dismissal). The number of grievances filed in an organization is related to many factors, such as leadership style and consistency in the application of company policies.[33] Many employers do not encourage supervisors to settle potentially costly and significant grievances at the first step.

At the second step, the union steward usually takes the written grievance to the labour relations specialist or HRM professional. In deciding on the grievance, the HRM professional considers many factors: management's interpretation of the contract; the specific details of the grievance; previous related grievances; the potential costs and benefits of accepting or denying the grievance; and the potential relevance of the jurisdiction's human rights, occupational health and safety, and other legislation. Most routine grievances are settled at this point, with management either accepting the grievance and admitting a mistake or denying the grievance and convincing the union not to pursue it to the next step. Potentially significant and costly grievances may go to the third step. So do those in which the union refuses to accept a denial.

[32] For a dramatization of the process (using a grievance over dismissal), see *The Grievance Arbitration Process*, a videotape prepared by the Centre for Industrial Relations and the Media Centre, University of Toronto, 1975.

[33] D. Peach and E.R. Livernash, *Grievance Initiation and Resolution: A Study in Basic Steel* (Boston: Graduate School of Business, Harvard University, 1974); and E. A. Fleishman and E.F. Harris, "Patterns of Leadership Behavior Related to Employee Grievances and Turnover," *Personnel Psychology*, 1962, vol. 15, pp. 43–56.

EXHIBIT 15.7

Typical grievance procedure

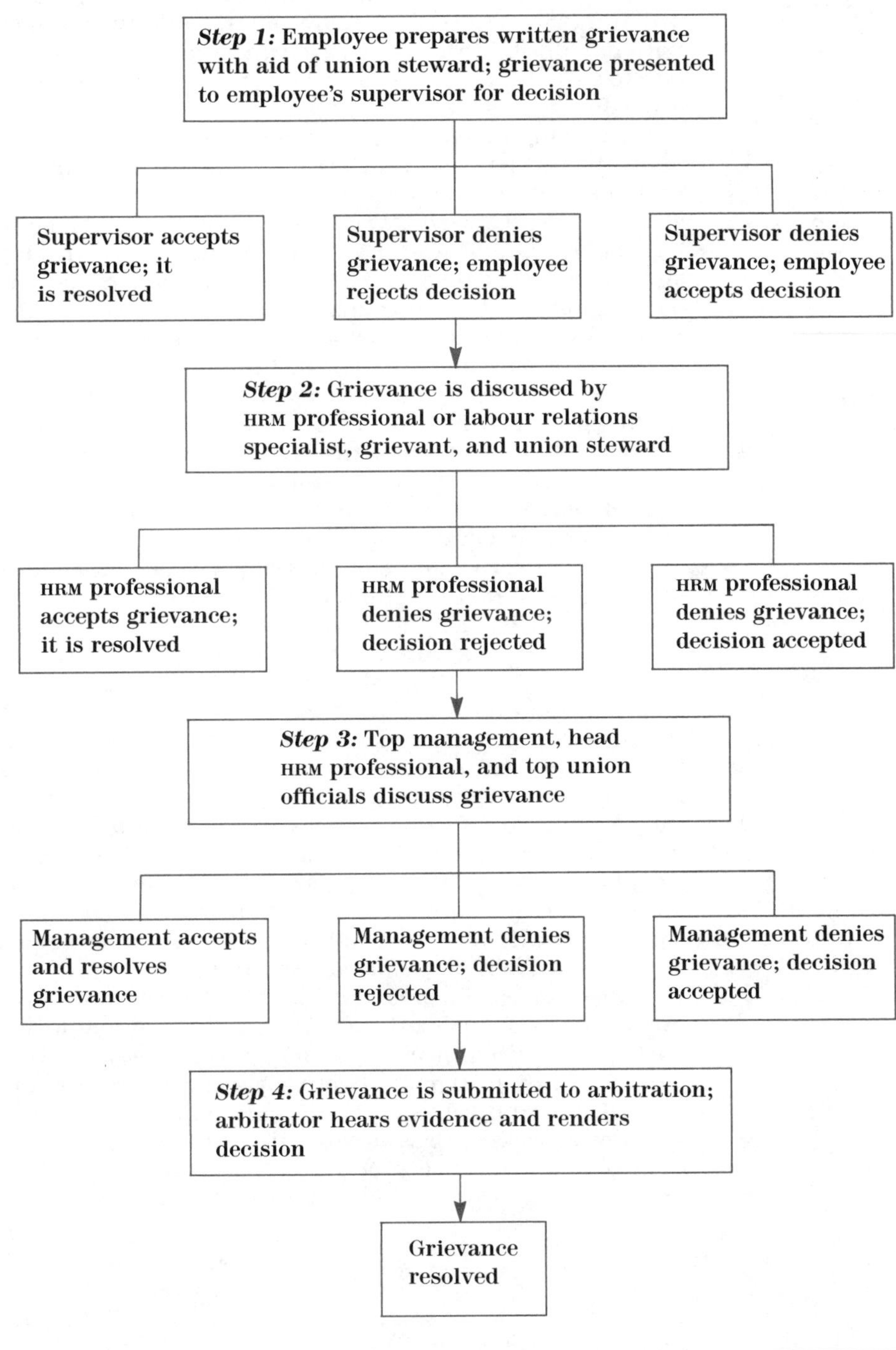

Step 1: Employee prepares written grievance with aid of union steward; grievance presented to employee's supervisor for decision
Supervisor accepts grievance; it is resolved
Supervisor denies grievance; employee rejects decision
Supervisor denies grievance; employee accepts decision
Step 2: Grievance is discussed by HRM professional or labour relations specialist, grievant, and union steward
HRM professional accepts grievance; it is resolved
HRM professional denies grievance; decision rejected
HRM professional denies grievance; decision accepted
Step 3: Top management, head HRM professional, and top union officials discuss grievance
Management accepts and resolves grievance
Management denies grievance; decision rejected
Management denies grievance; decision accepted
Step 4: Grievance is submitted to arbitration; arbitrator hears evidence and renders decision
Grievance resolved

In the third step of the grievance procedure, top management and top union officials discuss the grievance. It is common practice for an HRM professional at a plant of a multiplant location to bring in the firm's head HRM officer and often other top-level managers. The local union may be assisted by representatives from the national or international office. At this stage, grievances are often of major significance because the decision may affect the interpretation of a major contract provision.

The fourth step of the grievance procedure involves the use of a neutral third party—an arbitrator or a tripartite arbitration board—to render a decision on the grievance. This type of arbitration is properly called *rights arbitration*. Since the arbitrator or the arbitration board plays a determining role in grievances that reach this level, and since these grievances are usually important to one or both parties, both labour and management want a fair and unbiased person as arbitrator. Single arbitrators are usually selected from a list of persons agreed to by both sides. If an arbitration board is to be used, each party appoints one person and these two persons appoint a third, who serves as chairperson. If the two parties cannot agree on a chairperson within a given time limit, the labour relations board is empowered to appoint one. A majority of the arbitration board decides the issue, but if there is no majority the decision of the chair governs. Labour and management generally share arbitrators' fees.

Most collective agreements are very specific about the grievance procedure and include time deadlines for each step, exactly who is to be involved at each, and the way in which arbitrators are to be selected.

Processing grievances can be quite costly for an employer, as well as the union, even if most grievances are denied. Since an employee and the union have the right to pursue a grievance through the final step, no matter how trivial or unjust it may be, the HRM professional is under an obligation to respond. A large number of grievances often indicates dissatisfaction and problems in an organization. However, the fact that very few grievances are filed against a company does not necessarily indicate that its employees are satisfied. Some HRM professionals feel that the existence of a small number of nontrivial grievances is an indicator of a healthy labour-management relationship since some differences of interpretation of an agreement's terms are certain to arise in any normal situation.

It is also worth remembering that the grievance procedure is very important to the job satisfaction of individual employees since it provides them with a mechanism for seeking justice in the workplace. A survey of union members across the United States found that they viewed handling grievances as the most important activity of the union.[34] Employers seeking to avoid unionization are often aware of employees' desire for a grievance procedure, and sometimes attempt to provide one. Such has been the case in the U.S., where two out of three non-

[34] T.A. Kochan, *Collective Bargaining and Industrial Relations* (Homewood, Ill.: Irwin-Dorsey Ltd., 1980), p. 168.

union firms provide some kind of an internal complaint, or "Voice," system.[35] To be effective, a grievance procedure must have the support of a power independent of management. The Canada Labour Code provides such a procedure in the federal jurisdiction.

Dissatisfaction among Union Members

Up to this point, we have discussed unions as a means by which employees can influence management policies and practices. It should be remembered, however, that unions are fallible, human organizations and their members sometimes become dissatisfied with their effectiveness at the bargaining table, in the grievance process, or in other situations. There are several ways for union members to act on their dissatisfactions. One is through the democratic process and the election of new officers. Another is through an appeal procedure if one is provided in the union's constitution. A member who believes a union is not abiding by its own constitution can take it to court. Labour relations boards also offer avenues of redress. For example, in some jurisdictions, a member who requests a copy of the union's last audited financial statement and does not receive it can complain to the labour relations board, which can order that a copy be provided to both the employee and the board itself.

Another route to resolving dissatisfaction is for the employees of a bargaining group to change unions or to decide not to be represented by a union at all. Changing unions involves having a second union apply for certification. If a collective agreement is in effect, the application must be made during the "open period" provided for such applications (usually the last two months of an agreement). Other timing restrictions, which vary among jurisdictions, exist for other situations; for example, a new union may have to wait for several months if a legal strike has begun.

Employees can also apply to have their union decertified by applying to terminate its bargaining rights. This application can be filed during the "open period"; it can also be brought if the union fails to notify the employer of its desire to bargain within a stated time after certification or fails to start bargaining after giving notice (60 days is a common allotment for both periods). An application for termination must be accompanied by a petition signed by a number of the employees in the bargaining unit (45 per cent in Ontario). After conducting an enquiry to make certain the petition is a voluntary expression of employees' sentiments and that no member of management was involved in it, the labour relations board conducts a representation vote. A majority vote against the union is not uncommon in such cases.

[35] R. Berenbeim, *Nonunion Complaint Systems: A Corporate Appraisal*, Conference Board Report No. 770 (New York: Conference Board, 1980).

A union's failure, within stipulated times, to give notice of its desire to bargain after certification or to begin bargaining after giving notice can also open the way for an employer's applying to terminate its bargaining rights. On receipt of such an application, the labour relations board holds a hearing to determine whether the union has a reasonable explanation for the delay. An employer's application for termination is granted only when the union is "clearly 'sleeping' on its rights," and even then the board may hold a vote among the employees to ascertain their feelings.[36]

The details of termination and decertification vary among jurisdictions, but the various acts acknowledge two premises: (1) a union which fails to exercise its rights may lose them; and (2) a union which no longer represents the majority of employees in a bargaining unit may lose its rights—subject to the concern that a challenge must be made in a timely fashion and should not unduly impair the bargaining process.[37]

Improving Labour Relations: Preventive Mediation and QWL

The late 1970s marked the starting point for two major efforts to improve labour relations in Canada: preventive mediation and quality of working life (QWL) programs. The fact that both began in Ontario in 1978 is significant for that year marked the end of three years of the Anti-Inflation Board (AIB), which had administered a program of wage and indirect price restraint. The AIB was introduced to slow the rampant inflation of 1974 and 1975. The inflation had been accompanied by a world-leading record of time lost through strikes. While one million people observed the National Day of Protest against the AIB on October 14, 1976, the number of strikes decreased sharply thereafter as the AIB did not budge in its wage decisions.[38] With the imminent phasing out of the AIB, there were fears that a wage-price explosion would follow as it had in the post-Nixon price freeze in the United States in 1971. No wage-price explosion occurred in Canada but there was concern with the connection between wage negotiations and price increases. "There has to be a better way to manage labour-management relations," was a view often voiced in the late 1970s. It is only speculation, but perhaps the tumultuous events of the mid-1970s led to the search for "better ways."

Preventive mediation and QWL are intended to be better ways.

[36] *A Guide to the Ontario Labour Relations Act*, p. 59.

[37] This comment was provided by Rick MacDowell, a vice-chairman of the Ontario Labour Relations Board and the author of *A Guide to the Ontario Labour Relations Act*. Mr. MacDowell also provided much-appreciated help on other parts of the chapter.

[38] Frank Reid, "Wage-and-Price Controls in Canada," in Anderson and Gunderson, *op. cit.* pp. 482–502.

Preventive Mediation

Preventive mediation (PM), which was developed by the Federal Mediation Service in the United States, was introduced by the Ontario Ministry of Labour in 1978 as a way of preventing needless and futile work stoppages caused more by poor attitudes and a breakdown of communications than by a dispute over contract issues.[39]

PM has three components. The first is the establishment of joint action committees made up of small groups of management and union representatives which meet together on a regular basis, initially monthly, to discuss problems of mutual concern. The second component is the Relationships by Objectives program (RBO), where representatives of management and the union spend three days away from the workplace examining the problems which have been identified as affecting their relationships and developing specific plans for resolving them. A follow-up meeting is arranged 60 to 90 days later to ensure progress on the plans. The final component is a one-day joint training program designed to review techniques to improve attitudes and understanding of the roles of the parties.

The key to preventive mediation is a mutual desire on the part of the parties to solve their problems. A notable success story is that of Budd Canada and the United (now the Canadian) Auto Workers. They succeeded in changing a confrontational relationship of wildcat (illegal) strikes and an enormous number of grievances to an attitude of joint problem solving.[40]

Quality of Working Life

Quality of Working Life (QWL) programs are intended to increase the humanization of work through the redesign of the way tasks and jobs are organized and through employee involvement in decision-making. The various terms for QWL include quality circles, employee involvement, work redesign, and labour-management participation teams. The key to QWL is a change in managerial attitudes and practices, away from an authoritarian style toward a consultative and advisory role.[41] The rationale is that both parties benefit from QWL. By involving employees in decision-making and greater identification with the product,

[39] Ontario Ministry of Labour, "Ontario Initiatives with Respect to Preventive Mediation and Quality of Working Life," in W. Craig Riddell, Research Co-ordinator, *Labour-Management Co-operation in Canada* (Toronto: University of Toronto Press, 1986), pp. 57–71.

[40] *Ibid.*, p. 62.

[41] *Ibid.*, pp. 62–71; and pp. 73–86; Keith Newton, "Quality of Working Life in Canada"; and pp. 16–20 in Craig Riddell, *Labour-Management Co-operation in Canada: An Overview*.

See also: Don Nightingale, *Workplace Democracy: An Enquiry into Employee Participation in the Modern Organization* (Toronto: University of Toronto Press, 1981); and J.B. Cunningham and T.H. White, eds, *Quality of Working Life: Contemporary Cases* (Ottawa: Department of Labour, 1984).

it is expected there will be greater motivation and increases in productivity, as well as greater job satisfaction. While there has been considerable employee interest in the QWL process,[42] there are many skeptics among both management and unions.

For management, there are the positive prospects of improved productivity and product quality and more satisfied employees. However, a potential cost is that the role of first-line supervisors may be modified significantly through shared decision-making, compromising their flexibility to act in the pure interests of management. For unions, the opportunity for increased union and employee influence at the plant level also has a potential cost; employee involvement and identification with management may undermine the role of the union in the eyes of union members.[43]

Several government agencies in Canada have been formed to encourage QWL programs. Labour Canada has a QWL Division which supports initiatives, disseminates information through a newsletter, *Quality of Working Life: The Canadian Scene*, and sponsors conferences and studies. The Ontario Ministry of Labour's Quality of Working Life Centre under Dr. Hans van Beinum has undertaken a variety of studies and publishes a news journal called *QWL Focus*. In addition, the Canadian Council on Working Life has been established to provide a mechanism for exchanging information and to develop a network of contacts.

The most successful QWL program in Canada is the Shell chemical plant in Sarnia. The company involved the union from the beginning in planning the new plant, and the result has been a nontraditional organizational structure where employees help design their jobs and are paid on the basis of the skills they have acquired. Management and the union prepared and continually update a statement of philosophy which includes a commitment to the joint optimization of the plant's social and technical systems and to the belief that workers are responsible, trustworthy, capable of self-regulation and interested in opportunities for decision-making and growth.[44]

As in the case of preventive mediation, the most important element in the success of QWL is the commitment by both management and labour. While QWL programs have grown, the numbers are still small. As of mid-1984, the Ontario QWL Centre had identified over 30 organizations where union and management were involved in the QWL process. Not all programs lead to success, but the failure has been less well documented. Even in the Shell organization, the QWL program has not spread. Just down the road from the chemical plant, Shell operates a refinery which has the same union as the chemical plant; but this older plant does not have a QWL program. Instead, there is a traditional labour-management relationship epitomized by a 75-page collective

[42] T.A. Kochan, H.C. Katz and N. Mowes, *Worker Participation and American Unions: Threat or Opportunity?* (Kalamazoo, Mich.: The W.E. Lepjohn Institute for Employment Research, 1984).

[43] Riddell, *op. cit.*, p. 19.

[44] Norm Halpern, "Sociotechnical Systems Design: The Shell Sarnia Experience," in Cunningham and White, *op. cit.*

agreement, in contrast to the eight-page agreement (most general guidelines) for the chemical unit.

Given increased international competition on the one hand and a more highly educated work force on the other, there is no question that the interest and need for worker participation will grow.[45]

Summary

Although less than 40 per cent of the nation's labour force belongs to a union, labour relations is a major HRM function. Since the establishment of collective bargaining as the accepted mode of conflict resolution between labour and management, unionized employers have had to direct some of their resources to maintaining good labour relations, which include negotiations, administering the collective agreement, and processing and resolving grievances. Unionized employers usually have one or more labour relations specialists to deal with the many details associated with unionized employees.

Membership in labour organizations has been increasing in most geographic and industrial areas of Canada, especially in the public sector, for several decades. How organized labour will meet the challenges of the future and use its strong voice is yet to be seen. Labour relations and collective bargaining are a complex and specialized part of the HRM function.

Project Ideas

1. For several weeks, read local and/or national newspapers for reports of labour-management negotiations, strikes, or the terms of collective agreements. At least three or four examples of disputes and settlements should be found. Report for each case the employer and the union involved, the issues of the dispute or settlement, and whether the strike was legal and whether a conciliation officer, an arbitrator, or an arbitration board was involved. Also note how many cases were in the public sector and how many in the private.

2. Obtain a copy of a collective agreement between a local employer and a union. (Your instructor could assist you in this.) When you read the agreement, note each provision that may restrict management's flexibility and speed in running the organization. Also note

[45] Roy J. Adams, "Two Policy Approaches to Labour-Management Decision Making at the Level of the Enterprise," in W. Craig Riddell, *op. cit.*, pp. 87–109, and Thomas A. Kochan, Harry C. Katz and Robert B. McKersie, *The Transformation of American Industrial Relations* (New York: Basic Books, 1986), pp. 239–40.

the provisions describing employees' pay, benefits, and job security, and those that provide for safe working conditions. Consider how many of these provisions would have been included in a "psychological contract." Summarize your observations in a brief written or oral report to the class.

3. Organize a debate between two groups of students on the proposition that employees should be members of a union. The debate should be as factual as possible, rather than based upon opinions and attitudes.

4. Invite a local union officer or official to class to discuss the activities of his or her group and some collective bargaining experiences. An officer or official with several years of experience should be able to provide the class with excellent insights into labour relations.

5. Examine the labour relations act in your province and summarize the main requirements for a union's becoming certified as the exclusive bargaining agent of a group of employees. If the provincial labour relations board holds regular hearings in your city, attend a hearing on an application for certification. Note the major points at issue between union and management, such as the definition of the bargaining unit, and whether there was management interference with the attempt to organize the employees. Share your findings with the class in a brief written or oral report.

Cases

Case 15.1: Turbulence in Eastern's Skies

The 11-month dispute has been one of the most acrimonious on the Canadian labour scene. In December [of 1983] the Canada Labour Relations Board ordered Eastern Provincial Airways Ltd. to recall 40 dismissed pilots and to fire 18 nonunion pilots hired during a strike that began last January. It was the second such order in seven months, but last week [January of 1984] the company once again declared its intention to appeal. The action will force the dispute into its second year, despite the fact that the company recently had revived its fortunes.

The airline's dismissal and rehiring procedures are the major unresolved issues in the struggle between EPA's Gander-based pilots and the airline's president, Harry Steele. Since he took the airline over in 1978, Steele, a former naval officer, has transformed the 10 aircraft regional carrier from a money loser into a thriving operation with his single-minded determination to improve productivity. In fact, since last May EPA has competed successfully in the trans-Canada passenger market, operating in partnership with CP Air.

During the 134-day pilots' strike last spring, Steele enraged EPA pilots—members of the Canadian Air Line Pilots' Association—when he replied to union charges that the airline was putting productivity before safety by asking pilots to work longer hours. "Everyone talks about safety this and safety that," Steele declared. "But what is the difference between a pilot and a poor old CN bus driver?" Steele's stance prompted association claims that the company had challenged "the union's right to exist." Less than a month into the strike the airline started to hire nonunion pilots to maintain partial service. According to association spokesman Capt. Keith Lacey, at that point the striking pilots decided to make rehiring procedures crucial to any settlement.

Following an appeal by the pilots, the Canada Labour Relations Board ruled on May 27 that EPA was guilty of unfair labour practices under the Canada Labour Code for refusing to give returning pilots seniority over the nonunion pilots who had been hired to replace them. As a result, the board ordered the airline to settle the strike and to reinstate the dismissed pilots with their seniority intact. It also told Eastern Provincial to retable a proposed contract that the company had put forward during bargaining in April. Both sides had previously agreed in principal to the proposal, but disagreements over recall provisions had scuttled a resolution.

The company complied with the board order. But according to airline vice-president, Capt. Chester Walker, EPA added a covering note to the contract saying that the company considered that the proposal was retabled conditionally upon the outcome of EPA's appeal of the labour board's ruling to the Federal Court of Canada. The pilots finally accepted the proposal in early June, and, as far as they were concerned, it became a binding contract regardless of the ultimate outcome of the Federal Court action. The back-to-work agreement also complied with the board ruling that the replacement pilots be "demoted, dismissed or transferred." On June 10 the striking pilots returned to their positions and began a 45-day retraining program while the replacement pilots continued to fly the planes. Said Lacey: "Everyone thought it was over when it was over."

Then in October, after 1½ days of hearings, the Federal Court of Canada quashed the board's ruling and ordered a new hearing into EPA's dismissals and rehiring procedures. The court found that the labour board had not given the company a fair hearing. Three days after the Federal Court decision, Eastern Provincial announced that it regarded the agreement reached with the union in June as invalid in light of the new ruling. The airline placed telephone calls to 40 unionized pilots, telling them not to report for work. At the same time, EPA demoted an additional 20 senior unionized pilots to first officer status and filled senior positions with nonunion pilots.

The labour board's second decision, delivered on December 20, again ordered the airline to table the company's April contract proposal for collective bargaining—the same proposal that the union argued already was a binding agreement. The board also ordered EPA to once more recall the pilots according to their seniority by December 30 and concluded that both the union and the company had been bargaining in bad faith. The airline's latest decision to appeal the labour board's second ruling to the Federal Court means that the dispute will drag on into its second year.

Questions:

1. Based on the evidence in this case, how would you describe the relationship between EPA's management and the Pilots' Association? What is the likely effect of this relationship on the company's performance?
2. What rights is management seeking to preserve through its actions in this case? What rights and ideals are the union fighting for?
3. What specific actions of EPA or its president, Harry Steele, contributed to the intensity of the labour dispute? What is Steele's attitude toward the union as revealed through his actions?
4. What are the likely effects on the public and EPA employees of the strike, the Labour Board and Federal Court decisions, and the publicity surrounding them?

FROM: "More Turbulence in Eastern's Skies," by A. Finlayson, *Maclean's*, January 9, 1984, p. 21.

Case 15.2: A Victory Underground

Because the 150 miners at Falconbridge Copper's Lac Dufault copper and zinc mine near Rouyn, Que., were angry that their employers had refused to yield on two outstanding complaints, they adopted an unusual and dangerous pressure tactic late last month [September 1984]. Provisioned only with a few crescent rolls and coffee, 26 of them chose to remain in a lunchroom more than a half a mile below ground until the company met their demands. One issue was Falconbridge's refusal to pay full overtime wages for weekend work, but the other demand was as unconventional as the protest; the miners demanded the firing or transfer of the mine's unpopular manager, Raymond Gaetan, accusing him of treating them "in a disrespectful and arrogant fashion." The miners remained isolated below ground while the union and management conducted negotiations and the miners' wives demonstrated outside the mine's locked gates. And when the men re-emerged, haggard and hungry after four days underground, they had won a partial victory.

The miners relented only after they had secured a written agreement from Falconbridge which promised improved work schedules and premium payments for overtime. The company also agreed not to dock the wages of the 26 protesters or their fellow workers, whom the company had locked out of the mine during the protest. But the company stood firm on the issue of its controversial manager.

Said Falconbridge spokesman Ann O'Quinn, "The company has confidence in Gaetan and does not intend to let him go."

For the miners, the company's vote of confidence in Gaetan was not the only irritant that survived the settlement. They remained angry over the company's refusal to allow their union to send food down the shaft. Said Andre Gravel, representative of United Steelworkers of America Local 6610: "They tried to starve our guys out." For its part, the company questioned the workers' motives. O'Quinn called the protest a "pre-emptive act" which the union took with the knowledge that an arbitrator's verdict on the work schedule dispute was imminent. But Gravel insisted that the protest was spontaneous and added that the compromise that the men won justified their desperate gamble. Said Gravel: "It takes risks to get results."

Questions:

1. What, in your opinion, was the major objective of the miners "sit-in" strike and was the objective achieved?
2. What is your prognosis for labour relations at Falconbridge in the months ahead? What changes, if any, might result in improved labour relations at the mine?
3. In what ways is this case an example of how *not* to conduct labour relations? For example, what did labour and/or management do that they should not have done; what should they have done that they failed to do?

FROM: "A Victory Underground," *Maclean's*, October 15, 1984, p. 58.

V Issues and Challenges in Human Resource Management

16

The Future of Human Resource Management

> "Organizations are not more effective because they have better people. They have better people because they motivate to self-development through their standards, through their habits, through their climate."—Peter F. Drucker, *The Effective Executive.*[1]

This textbook focusses on the role of human resource management in maintaining and increasing organizational effectiveness. Each HRM professional must work not only within the context of a specific organization but also within the broader context of the surrounding society. In this final chapter, therefore, we examine the future of human resource management against the background of trends in Canadian society.

Four Factors Affecting Canadian Society

Four factors affecting society seem particularly pertinent to the practice of human resource management. These factors are: (1) economic conditions; (2) societal values; (3) the legal environment; and (4) technology. The four are interrelated in many ways, but each is discussed separately for the sake of clarity.

[1](New York: Harper Colophon Books, 1985), p. 170.

Economic Conditions

The country's economic condition is the most basic of the four factors influencing Canadian society and hence Canadian industry because it is so tied to all the others. Societal values, the legal environment, and the uses of new technology all affect and are affected by specific aspects of the economy as well as its overall condition.

The Canadian economy of the late 1980s seems to have stabilized after the deep recession of 1981–1983. However, the picture is mixed, with some areas experiencing greater growth than others. For example, Central Canada, particularly Ontario, has entered a period of strong growth, while growth in the West and Atlantic regions is slow, particularly in the wake of the sharp decline in world oil prices.

Our discussion of the economy and its effect on employment and the field of human resource management focusses on three key developments: (1) the increase in worldwide competition; (2) the slow decline in unemployment; and (3) the changing structure of employment.

Increase in worldwide competition. From the severe recession of the early 1980s emerged strains in the world economy that have continued into the post-recession period. Posing a major strain are a number of newly industrialized countries—Korea, Taiwan, Brazil, and Mexico—who have recently entered into competition in the field of manufactured products. Taken together with existing competition from developed countries such as Japan and West Germany, North American manufacturing has been pressured by stiff competition from imported electronics, automobiles and automotive parts, and consumer household goods including televisions and VCRS. While the Canadian manufacturing sector, especially the automobile and automotive parts industries, recovered reasonably well from the recession, the strain has been particularly apparent in the United States where the huge trade deficit has prompted imposition of import duties on products from outside the country. While Canada has enjoyed a substantial trade surplus with its neighbour, the increase in protectionist sentiment poses an immediate as well as a long-term threat to Canadian export sectors where jobs could be at risk.

A significant challenge for Canada in the next decade will be the development of export markets especially in the United States which buys almost 80 per cent of our products. The high level of productivity in export-oriented industries has a direct effect on the rest of the Canadian economy because it enables the total economy to grow in employment and standard of living. The MacDonald Commission, reporting in 1985,[2] advocated a free-trade agreement with the U.S. as a means of enhancing access to the American market and raising Canadian productivity through international specialization. The newly-elected Conservative government of Prime Minister Brian Mulroney immediately embarked on free-trade negotiations and set up a Canadian team under

[2] Royal Commission on the Economic Union and Development Prospects for Canada.

Simon Riesman. Riesman, a former federal civil servant, had negotiated the highly successful Automobile Pact of 1965 (for limited free trade in automobiles and parts). President Ronald Reagan supported the opening of negotiations, but high trade deficits in the U.S. became a political issue and may have contributed to the election in 1986 of Democratic majorities in both the Senate and House of Representatives, which favoured increased protection.

At the time of this writing, the outcome of Canada-U.S. trade negotiations is uncertain. However, with the continued existence of the Auto Pact, and barring any radical new U.S. protection measures, the Canadian economy is expected to be reasonably healthy, even in the absence of a free-trade agreement.

The slow decline in unemployment. In 1981, just at the start of the recession, the Canadian unemployment rate was 7.5 per cent, the same as in the United States. Unemployment during the peak of the recession reached almost 13 per cent and has gradually receded. However, even after three years of fairly strong growth, the rate was 9.5 per cent in 1986. In the U.S., by contrast, unemployment did not rise quite as much during the recession and by 1985 and 1986 had returned to the pre-recession level of 7.5 per cent.

Why hasn't Canada's unemployment rate returned to the level of 1981 and what are the prospects for the future? Three factors seem responsible for the slow decline in unemployment.[3] First, the recession in Canada was much deeper than in the United States, so even with roughly similar rates of growth in the recovery period it would take Canada longer to reduce unemployment. Second, the Canadian labour force has grown faster than its U.S. counterpart, primarily due to continuing rapid growth in the female labour force. Third, substantial regional imbalances have also been a factor. For example, if we take Ontario alone, the September 1986 seasonally adjusted unemployment rate of 7.1 per cent was only slightly above the 1981 figure of 6.6 per cent. The same was true in Quebec where comparable figures were 10.7 and 10.3 per cent. On the other hand, British Columbia (12.3 vs. 6.0), Alberta (9.9 vs 3.8), Nova Scotia (12.9 vs. 10.2) and Newfoundland (20.6 vs. 13.9) all had much higher unemployment rates in 1986 than in 1981.[4]

What are the prospects for the future? It is anticipated that the slow decline in Canadian unemployment rates will continue so that by the early 1990s the rate for Canada as a whole should be in the 7–8 per cent range.[5] It is also expected that regional differences in

[3] Morley Gunderson and Noah M. Meltz, "Labour Market Rigidities and Unemployment in Canada," in Morley Gunderson, Noah M. Meltz and Sylvia Ostry, *Unemployment: International Perspectives* (Toronto: University of Toronto Press, 1987).

[4] Statistics Canada, *The Labour Force*, September 1986, cat. no. T1-1001; and *Historical Labour Force Statistics—actual data, seasonal factors, seasonally adjusted data, 1985*, cat. no. 71-201 Annual.

[5] Peter Dungan and Thomas Wilson, *Alternative National Projections*, Policy Study No. 86–7, Policy and Economic Analysis Program (Toronto: Institute for Policy Analysis, University of Toronto), August 1986.

unemployment rates will narrow as oil and gas prospects and resource markets improve the economic outlook for Alberta, Saskatchewan, Nova Scotia and Newfoundland, and resource markets improve for British Columbia. While the 7–8 per cent range is still above what is referred to as the "non-accelerating inflation rate" of unemployment,[6] which is estimated to be in the 5–6 per cent range, the extent of unemployment related to a lack of demand will be much less than in the mid 1980s.

The changing structure of employment. The continuation of three major trends in the structure of employment will have significant implications for HRM professionals. These trends are growth of employment in service-producing industries; increase in female participation in employment; and growth of part-time employment. All three developments are related. We will first comment on these trends and then discuss their implications.

There has been a long-term trend away from employment in agriculture and most primary products.[7] At first, manufacturing and construction benefited from the shift of employment out of agriculture, but since the late 1950s there has been a gradual decline in the share of employment in both of these sectors. While manufacturing employment has risen slowly, its share of total employment has dropped from a post World War II high of 26.8 per cent in 1951 to only 17.3 per cent in 1986. Offsetting the declining employment has been increasing employment in the service producing sectors. For example, in 1951, the service industry sector made up 43 per cent of all employees. By 1986, the figure was 71 per cent. The largest recent growth has been in retail trade (department stores, supermarkets); finance, insurance, and real estate; personal service (especially restaurants and fast-food outlets); and education and health. Government employment grew rapidly in the 1960s and 1970s but has declined in relative terms in the 1980s.

An explanation for the shift first to manufacturing and then to services lies in the combination of standard of living and level of productivity. In a subsistence economy, most employment is in agriculture as families simply try to feed themselves. As productivity in agriculture grows, two things happen: (1) the standard of living rises enabling people to purchase commodities other than food; and (2) the rise in productivity frees individuals from farm labour so they can produce these goods. As productivity rises in manufacturing, needs and desires of individuals for a wider range of commodities can be met; for example, health and education services, entertainment, dining, and travel. In addition, many business functions, formerly provided in-house by

[6] Frank Reid, "Unemployment and Inflation: An Assessment of Canadian Macroeconomic Policy," *Canadian Public Policy* V1:2 (Spring 1980), pp. 283–99.

[7] The mining industry is an exception. Both forestry and fishing have shown decreases over time. See David Foot and Noah M. Meltz, *Canadian Occupational Projections: An Analysis of the Economics Determinants 1961–81* (Hull, Que.: Employment and Immigration Canada, 1985); Noah M. Meltz, *Changes in the Occupational Composition of the Canadian Labour Force 1931–1961* (Ottawa: Queen's Printer, 1965); and Statistics Canada, *The Labour Force*, December 1986, cat. no. 71001, Monthly (Ottawa: Minister of Supply and Services Canada, January 1987).

manufacturing organizations, can now be provided by specialists in the service sector. Examples include janitorial and cleaning services; cafeteria and protective services (guards and security personnel); and financial management services. The move to specialized services is motivated in part by advantages of economies of scale, wherein services can be provided more efficiently by specialists and at lower cost. In some cases, costs are lower than in-house, because wage rates are less than those paid in manufacturing plants.

Female participation in the labour force increased to 55 per cent of working-age women by 1985, representing 43 per cent of the total labour force. This increase was partly due to growth in employment in the service sector, which has in the past formed the bulk of jobs in which females work. Other factors behind increased female participation include: an increase in household technology; a reduction in number of children; an increase in educational level; greater expectations for a higher standard of living; and a change in attitudes toward working women.[8]

An increase in part-time work is the third major trend in the changing structure of employment. Part-time work now represents 15.5 per cent of all employment. Eighty per cent of part-time workers are women, and they are concentrated in sales and service jobs which tend to be low-paying.[9] Also, in the wake of the 1981–1983 recession, many full-time jobs were converted to part-time jobs as employers sought ways to reduce labour costs. Although considered to be employed, part-time workers tend to enjoy much less certain earning power and fewer career prospects than their full-time counterparts.

These trends have raised concern about the long-term employment picture. While the Canadian economy is expected to be reasonably healthy into the 1990s, there will still be sectors of the labour market experiencing problems.

For HRM professionals, these trends in the employment structure mean that there should be an adequate supply of candidates for recruitment into most types of work. As always, there will be some difficulty in recruiting for specialized positions, but the general labour market situation should focus on screening and retaining high quality employees. Of course, a sudden turn in the world economy, particularly the U.S. economy, could alter these prospects considerably.

[8] See: Alice Nakamura and Masao Nakamura, "A Survey of Research on the Work Behaviour of Canadian Women," in W. Craig Riddell, *Work and Pay: The Canadian Labour Market* (Toronto: University of Toronto Press, 1985), pp. 171–218; Morley Gunderson, *Labour Market Economics: Theory, Evidence and Policy in Canada* (Toronto: McGraw-Hill Ryerson, 1980), p. 57; and Sylvia Osty and Mahmood A. Zaidi, *Labour Economics in Canada,* 3rd ed. (Toronto: MacMillan of Canada, 1979), pp. 42–4.

[9] Labour Canada, *Part-time Work in Canada*, Report of the Commission of Inquiry into Part-time Work (Ottawa: Minister of Supply and Services Canada, 1983).

Societal Values

Another major factor shaping the future is societal values, the basic attitudes of the majority of the country. Throughout this text we have emphasized the significance to human resource management of federal and provincial legislation and regulatory bodies. HRM professionals must be aware of the dominant values of society, because they are at the base of the legal environment in which firms must operate.

Significant changes in those values seem unlikely in the next decade or so; the North American ethos of mixed free enterprise is well-entrenched and pervasive. It is worth noting, however, that Canada will probably continue, in general, to diverge from the United States in some interesting ways. The important one in the context of this book is that Canadians have always been far more willing than Americans to accept government participation in economic matters. From the days when public and private capital was combined to build the Canadian Pacific Railway—and with it the West—to our generation, when the CBC and CTV (both watched by the CRTC) compete to bring news across the country, few Canadians have found government partnership inherently offensive. Most also accept government in its role of attempting to reduce inequities and enhance human dignity, although they may object vehemently to particular ways in which it acts to do so.

This acceptance runs from sea to sea, even though Canada is traditionally a country of regions and even though one region or another may dispute particular restrictions. For example, although the West has an image of rugged individualism, Alberta and Saskatchewan have far-reaching human rights codes, and labour laws in Manitoba are among the country's most favourable to unions. British Columbia, on the other hand, has recently been moving to restructure its labour laws in directions which are likely to restrict union growth. No province, therefore, seems likely to pass anything resembling the "right-to-work" legislation found in a number of American states.

Thus, the cries of "too much government regulation" from various segments of the population usually translate into cries against particular regulations, although the federal government has indicated its intent to introduce some deregulation of transportation and to sell some Crown corporations. In the field of employment-related legislation, such as employment equity and pay equity, the trend is still toward more rather than less government intervention.

The Legal Environment

Perhaps the most far-reaching legislative changes in the next several years will be in the areas of pay equity and employment equity. Both attempt to remove systemic discrimination against women in the work place, the first by removing pay inequities for work of equal value and the second by removing barriers against jobs for women (and for minorities, handicapped, and native Canadians). Ontario, the federal government, Quebec, and Manitoba have taken the biggest steps in these areas, with Ontario's pay equity legislation being the most comprehensive since it applies to both the public and private sectors and sets out a comprehensive enforcement mechanism. Pay equity legislation, in particular, will require substantial input from HRM professionals on such matters as job evaluation techniques. Unions (where they represent employees) may also need to be consulted regarding pay scales and the adjustment timetable.

The interpretation and application of employment legislation in Canada is going through a period of dramatic change. Donald Carter of Queen's University recently observed, "The Canadian Charter of Rights and Freedoms has fundamentally altered the relationship between the legislature and judiciary . . . . The legitimacy of all labour legislation must be tested against the fundamental values promulgated by the Charter."[10] He goes on to note that to date, the courts have tended to favour individual rights. If this trend continues, there will be serious implications for both trade unions and employers. For trade unions, the Charter could challenge union security arrangements (in particular *Lavigne v. Ontario Public Service Employees' Union*, 1986) by raising the question of whether collective responsibility must give way to individual rights. This principle could also encroach upon the grievance arbitration process by requiring employers to wait until after the just cause issue has been arbitrated before discharging an employee. Also, will the principle of seniority still operate in the case of mandatory retirement? Recently, an Ontario Court upheld the right of universities to have mandatory retirement provisions, but there has been an appeal to the Supreme Court of Canada for a final decision. While the general trend has been toward early retirement, the abolition of mandatory retirement could affect working time of professional employees, such as teachers, where there may be preferences to continue beyond the age of 65. This is turn has implications for pension plans and for the assessment of competence on the job.

Given Canadians' general acceptance of government regulation, the legal environment seems likely to be of great importance to HRM professionals in the coming years. They already owe much of the growth of their profession to the many human rights, employment standards, and health and safety acts passed in Canada's jurisdictions since the post-war era. An increase in government regulations generally means firms must enlarge their personnel staffs and that HRM professionals must give increased attention to recruiting, record-keeping, and other administrative responsibilities. On the other hand, compliance with government mandates is often expensive, so HRM departments are likely to see concomitant emphasis on watching costs and increasing their organizational effectiveness.

[10] Donald D. Carter, "Canadian Industrial Relations and the Charter—The Emerging Issues," (Kingston, Ont.: Industrial Relations Centre, Queen's University, 1987). See also David M. Beatty, *Putting the Charter to Work, Designing a Constitutional Labour Code* (Kingston and Montreal: McGill-Queen's University Press, 1987).

As we have seen, employment standards and health and safety regulations have been in an almost constant state of flux in recent years. So have regulations concerning universal and mandated benefits. This pattern of frequent change can be expected to continue in many areas, perhaps particularly in benefits, as governments attempt to mitigate the hardships a faltering economy causes individuals, and in health and safety, as experts discover new occupational hazards, almost daily it seems.

Labour laws and regulations may also change, probably in a generally pro-union fashion. The Canadian trend has been towards requiring greater recognition from employers of employees' right to unionize. For example, several provinces, including Ontario, now require employers to deduct union dues from paycheques if the union requests this service. Five provinces (B.C., Manitoba, Newfoundland, Ontario, and Quebec) plus the federal jurisdiction, give their labour relations boards the right to impose a first collective agreement on labour and management when the two parties cannot agree.

Simply keeping track of changes in employment-related legislation will continue to be an important function of HRM professionals, especially in firms which have employees in several provinces. Responding to them so as to increase organizational effectiveness will be a major challenge of the coming years.

Technology

Technology will continue to be another major challenge to human resource management. The changes it produces exert a major influence on our work and our lives. Creating and keeping pace with new technologies are essential to maintaining a growing and prosperous economy. For example, many Canadian companies have recently invested in methods and equipment to improve product quality.

The new products and methods produced by technological innovations are related to both capital investment and the demand for labour. First, considerable capital investment is required to remain competitive in many industries. Second, capital investment in new technologies has a great impact on the demand for labour. In some industries, for example, robots are replacing people on jobs which were often heavy, routine, or unsafe. In Japan, science fiction has become a reality at the Fujitsu Fanuc Company, where robots are making robots. And the Hitachi Company is working on a "supervisor" robot which oversees other robots.[11] The trend is not restricted to blue-collar jobs. A Canadian research institute has concluded that the boom in micro-electronics will displace thousands of people in secretarial, file clerk, bank teller, keypunch operator, and similar jobs. The major

[11] "Robots Make Robots in Japan," *The Globe and Mail,* April 13, 1981; D. Lancashire, "Robots Becoming Kings of the Factory Floor," *The Globe and Mail,* March 4, 1981.

concern of this research was that such "technological unemployment" will primarily affect women since most job occupants in these positions are women.[12]

Technological advances will continue to affect organizations' needs for human resources, but they may often entail not so much a reduction in the demand for labour as a change in the kinds demanded. Drucker and many others have argued that "capital investment creates the need for more knowledge work."[13] In hospitals, for example, adding the high-technology equipment necessary for microsurgery and kidney dialysis requires additional, highly skilled employees. At the same time, however, technological advances reduce the number of employees necessary for dishwashing and other maintenance responsibilities. The result is a reduction in the number of jobs for low-skilled persons and a simultaneous increase in demand for persons with higher-level skills. This situation may grow, creating the need for redundancy planning discussed in the early chapters of this book. Employers and government must anticipate major technological changes that create unemployment in some areas and provide retraining for workers in jobs where demand is falling so that they may perform jobs in new and growing industries.

Another concern related to new technology is ensuring that high-technology machinery and methods take into account human considerations and the overall environment. A workplace such as an office with advanced electronic equipment must be examined as a total system to be sure that the technology does not result in worker fatigue, low morale, and similar problems which can reduce productivity.

Human Resource Management: What Lies Ahead

As we have seen, economic conditions, societal values, changing legislation, and technological advances will continue to affect both firms generally and the specific ways in which HRM professionals work in them. These trends' greatest overall effect on HRM staff seems likely to be an increase in the necessity of "looking at the bottom line," of planning and justifying actions on the basis of cost-benefit analysis. In other words, HRM staffers will have to be able to demonstrate their ability to contribute significantly to organizational effectiveness and profitability. Accordingly, they will have to increase their communication with staff who are outside the HRM area. This imperative may necessitate giving many HRM professionals additional training in the use of quantitative measures of evaluation.

[12] W. Peters, "Micro-Processing Seen Taking Jobs from Women," *The Globe and Mail*, March 31, 1981.

[13] Peter F. Drucker, *Managing in Turbulent Times* (New York: Harper & Row, 1986).

Moreover, the various problems facing our society, including increased world competition, an aging work force, rapid technological change, and increased government regulation, are likely to change emphases in HRM functions in the future. For example, as we have already noted, the changing structure of employment will produce a strong emphasis on retraining for new jobs and new careers. Drucker has said, "The productivity of people requires continuous learning."[14] Many leading manufacturing firms, such as IBM, AT&T, General Electric, and Xerox, already believe in investment in human resources and spend millions of dollars on training and development each year; in fact, IBM has approximately one-fifth of its employees in training at any given time. In the future, many other organizations will have to emphasize retraining.

A recent study of how HRM is viewed by CEO's of major corporations reveals some of the challenges facing the profession. CEO's want HRM staffs to concentrate on the important, people-oriented business issues such as productivity improvement and cost containment. Programs facilitating these goals include containing health care and benefit costs, redesigning compensation programs, and implementing new performance appraisal programs. HRM professionals are expected to assist with organizational changes including those related to downsizing and mergers and changes in organizational culture. The 71 CEO's interviewed felt that HRM should be more "proactive" rather than "reactive" and that too many HRM professionals lacked a "business point of view."[15]

What other changes can we predict for the years ahead? Let's look at each HRM function briefly.

Human Resource Planning and Job Analysis

Human resource planning (HRP) will be affected as employers strive to reduce the cost of implementing pay and employment equity legislation in order to maintain and enhance productivity and profits. Given a work force that will grow much more slowly than in the past, organizations will find it increasingly important to retain qualified employees. Increases, decreases, and shifts in demand for an employer's products or services will have to be anticipated and met with retraining, transfers, the use of part-time employees, and other methods appropriate to maintaining a stable work force. The increasing technological sophistication of many jobs plus shortages of skilled labour will make it less possible for organizations simply to hire new employees when demand increases and lay them off when it falls. There may not be enough skilled persons in the labour market, so organizations will need to retain present employees, perhaps retraining them for areas where labour shortages exist. Making the best possible use of human re-

[14] Ibid.

[15] James W. Walker, "Moving Closer to the Top," *The Personnel Administrator*, December 1986, vol. 31, pp. 55–57, 117.

sources requires human resource planning, and job analysis will be increasingly used for the development of career paths that can guide training and planned transfers. Only in low-skilled service jobs (such as maid, waiter, cook, and so on) will training and retention not be the major emphases of HRP.

Recruiting

For employers who require highly trained workers, especially employers in high-technology fields, recruiting will be more difficult and costly, since qualified applicants will be scarce. Recruiters will seek to attract applicants who demonstrate the ability and willingness to engage in continuous learning, as well as an interest in a long-term career with one employer. The recruiting process is likely to include closer relations with universities, colleges, and other schools that prepare students for technology-related careers. Increased numbers of apprenticeships, co-op programs, and internships will facilitate recruiting, selecting, and training people for business.

The probable shortage of experienced, high-skilled employees is likely to produce both an increase in private agencies and an upgrading and expansion of the services offered by Canada (and Quebec) Employment Centres. In both, technological advances in computers and information systems will improve the speed of and access to information about job vacancies. The shift will help applicants find jobs and help employers fill job vacancies faster.

Selection

As we already suggested, the future trend in selection will be towards screening for people with the ability and willingness to learn throughout their working lives. From a practical standpoint, developing good predictors for criteria such as learning and performing well on a series of jobs is very difficult. Both content and concurrent validation approaches are almost useless, and predictive validation requires considerable time. Some combination of predictive and construct validation is likely to prove most useful. The most potentially useful predictors may be learning-performance simulations, rather than tests of an applicant's current knowledge and skills. For example, an applicant may be given instruction in an unfamiliar task and asked to perform it. The amount of time it takes the person to master the task can be measured along with the level of task performance, and the results used to predict his or her ability to learn similar tasks. In the labour markets of the future, in which highly skilled labour is in short supply, selection may be used as much to place people into various training programs as to screen out the unqualified.

As legislation for employment equity expands and employers are more concerned about the adverse impact of discrimination, HRM professionals will have to focus on using selection to its maximum advantage for the effective utilization of human resources.

Orientation

Chapter 8 argued that orientation should help new employees adapt more rapidly to their jobs and their employer and should provide them with realistic, clear expectations of what is required of them. Developing such expectations will facilitate the retention of competent employees who are good fits in their new jobs; it may also help to eliminate those who are poor fits. Given tight labour markets and increased expenditures on training, good orientation programs will be increasingly sound investments for employers.

Training and Development

As we have seen, training and development will become essential to employers' human resource programs. With the impact of the new information technology, government, business, and educators must help workers acquire the flexibility necessary to adapt to rapid change.[16] In the future, employees may have three, four, or more different careers during their working lives. Moreover, the length of the average working life may increase because of shortages of younger employees, higher desired incomes, improved health care, and an increase in part-time employment. Training methods will make increased use of computers, video recordings, and other electronic equipment which will allow people to learn at their own pace and without being at work. Employers may develop closer relations with colleges and universities for the provision of training programs, as the costs of training increase and as educational institutions face the declining enrolments caused by the low birth rates of the past two decades.

Performance Appraisal

While it is difficult to predict specific changes in performance appraisal, it is likely to be used more frequently, primarily to identify employees' needs for training and development. It may also be used to improve productivity by monitoring employees' performance and identifying performance problems. Thus, appraisal methods are likely to become more "results-oriented," and superiors will have to become more skilled at appraising their subordinates.

Career Planning

Long-range career planning will become more difficult, especially for employees whose work is affected by technology, since innovations may

[16] Keith Newton, "Impact of New Technology on Employment," *Canadian Business Review*, Winter 1985, pp. 27–37.

cause rapid and major occupational changes. At the same time, people will have an increasing need for career planning. From the employer's point of view, it will become more closely connected to HRP and to training and development. Traditional career patterns will become less common as the length of any one career becomes shorter. Careers of the future are more likely to involve a combination of learning and work than those of the past. HRM professionals, especially those in industries most affected by technological changes, will become more involved in career planning as employers attempt to make optimal use of their available human resources.

Compensation

The compensation function has given HRM professionals their greatest challenge since the mid-1970s. At first, the challenge came from sharp increases in inflation, which combined with low productivity growth to stretch the ability of many employers to provide cost-of-living adjustments. While average employees demanded pay increases that kept up with inflation, management sought to use pay to motivate and reward above-average performers. The conflict between these two goals has eased somewhat as the rate of inflation has declined and productivity has increased. However, the introduction of pay equity legislation, whereby the rates of pay for women are to be raised to those of men in comparably valued jobs (where men are in the majority), again brings the compensation function to the fore. While the legislation in Ontario calls for a phasing-in of pay equity, the first units that will be affected are large organizations with 500 or more employees. These organizations are the ones most likely to employ HRM professionals, who will be leading players in the implementation of pay equity.

The issue of profit sharing is also one which has implications for HRM professionals. Martin Weitzman's book *The Share Economy*[17] has prompted debate over the extent to which firms should move away from fixed wages toward profit sharing. One of the major factors behind the split of the Canadian Auto Workers from the UAW was the refusal to accept in Canada the profit sharing which had been negotiated in the United States. The debate will undoubtedly continue on the issue of profit sharing and HRM professionals will be called on for advice.

Benefits

The major problem in the benefits area will be a continuation of the rapid rise in costs. Employers will undoubtedly continue to seek ways

[17] Martin L. Weitzman, *The Share Economy* (Cambridge, Mass.: Harvard University Press, 1984). See also Christopher Beckman, "Will Profit Sharing Reduce Unemployment?" *Canadian Business Review*, Summer 1986, pp. 50–2.

of reducing costs, such as requiring employees to make contributions to programs such as supplementary health care and life insurance. It is also likely that employers will make greater use of benefits as a method of retaining valuable employees. This trend may result in increased efforts to use some types of benefits as job performance incentives. Employees are likely to place increased importance on leisure time, opportunities for education and development, and supplementary health care benefits.

Health and Safety

Illnesses and accidents are costly to individuals, employers, and the economy since they often cause a productive employee to become nonproductive and dependent. This fact, plus increasing government regulation in and union attention to the area, will encourage more employers to develop health and safety programs. Moreover, since the rate for accidents that are not work-related is higher than the work-related rate, wise employers may increasingly invest in programs to maintain the health and safety of workers off as well as on the job.

Labour Relations

Chapter 15 discussed the future of union-management relations. Greater worldwide competition has increased pressure on unions from management. Unions also face pressure from their members to provide job security in declining industries, as well as cost-of-living adjustments to keep pace with inflation. Given these conditions, unions may be more willing to cooperate with management and government to improve the productivity and competitiveness of Canadian industry.

Union strength will, however, continue to grow, albeit more slowly, particularly in service industries and the public sector. If the economy weakens, unions might temper their demands on employers in return for job security. They might also increase demands for government insurance of risks, perhaps looking for government guarantees of jobs.

Summary

Human resource management will undoubtedly play a key role in meeting the challenges posed by an increasingly knowledge-based work force. International competitiveness, productivity growth, control of costs—all of these issues—require the special insights and training of HRM professionals, because, more than ever before, how the work force is managed is central to an organization's success. Lessons from Japanese management systems bear this out.

For the HRM professional, challenges come from changes in government regulations, in composition of the labour force, and in the marketplace. New legislation in pay and employment equity, along with the application of the Charter of Rights and Freedoms, require evaluation and implementation. The continued growth of the female labour force and of part-time work by both men and women requires some adaptation of staffing patterns. The move toward the use of leased employees is something to be considered by HRM professionals. Overriding all of these considerations is the state of the economy and pressures on the number of jobs which organizations will provide. With all of these considerations, HRM professionals will have a central role to play in maintaining and enhancing organizational effectiveness.

Project Ideas

1. There has been considerable discussion concerning the desirability and costs of pay equity. Organize a debate on this issue.

2. What are the particular problems of an HRM professional in an organization which sees cost advantages in increasing the proportion of its staff who work part-time, yet has little turnover and an aging work force? How might the HRM professional determine whether the perceived cost advantages of increasing the number of part-time staff would be offset by the negative impact on long-service workers? Share your thoughts with the class in a brief written oral report.

3. Given the frequent regulatory and legislative changes in employment standards and human rights legislation, these areas would seem to lend themselves to computerized record-keeping. Discuss the subject with a human resource manager of a company (try to find one that operates in more than one province) or with the head of an HRM professional association in your area.

Index

Page numbers for definitions are in boldface.
For references to specific companies, see Organizations cited.

To the Owner of This Book

We are interested in your reaction to ***Human Resource Management In Canada, Second Edition*** by Thomas H. Stone and Noah M. Meltz. Through feedback from you, we may be able to improve this book in future editions.

1. What was your reason for using this book?

    ____________________ university course

    ____________________ college course

    ____________________ continuing education

    ____________________ other (please specify)

2. Which chapters or sections, if any, were omitted from your course?

3. Do you have any suggestions for improving this text?

Fold Here

- -

Business
Reply Mail

No Postage Stamp
Necessary if Mailed
in Canada

POSTAGE WILL BE PAID BY

RICHARD KITOWSKI
Publisher
College Editorial Department
HOLT, RINEHART AND WINSTON
OF CANADA, LIMITED
55 HORNER AVENUE
TORONTO, ONTARIO
M8Z 9Z9

Tape Sh